THE EMERGENCE OF THE WELFARE STATE
IN BRITAIN AND GERMANY

The Emergence of the Welfare State in Britain and Germany

1850-1950

Edited by W.J. Mommsen
in collaboration with Wolfgang Mock

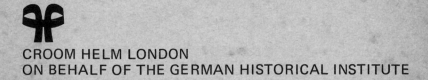

CROOM HELM LONDON
ON BEHALF OF THE GERMAN HISTORICAL INSTITUTE

©1981 German Historical Institute
Croom Helm Ltd, 2-10 St John's Road, London SW11

British Library Cataloguing in Publication Data

The emergence of the welfare state in Britain and Germany
   1. Public welfare – Great Britain – History
   2. Public welfare – Germany – History
   I. Mommsen, Wolfgang Justin
   II. Mock, Wolfgang
   361'.941   HV245

ISBN 0-7099-1710-4

Reproduced from copy supplied
printed and bound in Great Britain
by Billing and Sons Limited
Guildford, London, Oxford, Worcester

CONTENTS

TABLES

FIGURES

LIST OF ABBREVIATIONS

ADGB	Allgemeiner Deutscher Gewerkschaftsbund
AfS	*Archiv für Sozialgeschichte*
AVfK	*Archiv des Vereins für Kommunalwissenschaften*
AFSW	*Archiv für Sozialwissenschaft und Sozialpolitik*
BM	British Museum
BAK	Bundesarchiv Koblenz
CAB	Cabinet Papers
Cd	Command Papers
ZStA II	Zentralarchiv der DDR II (Merseburg)
HMSO	Her Majesty's Stationery Office
IFZ	Institut für Zeitgeschichte (München)
Jl.R.Stat. Soc.	*Journal of the Royal Statistical Society*
KStHB	*Konjunkturstatistisches Handbuch*
LSE	London School of Economics
PLC	Poor Law Commission
PP	Parliamentary Papers
PRO	Public Record Office
RABl	*Reichsarbeitsblatt*
RGBl	*Reichsgesetzblatt*
Schm. Jb.	*Schmollers Jahrbuch*
VjhZG	*Vierteljahrshefte für Zeitgeschichte*
VMB	*Verhandlungen, Mitteilungen und Berichte des Central-verbandes Deutscher Industrieller*
VSWG	*Vierteljahrshefte für Sozial- und Wirtschaftsgeschichte*
WiSta	*Wirtschaft und Statistik*
Ztsch	*Zeitschrift*

PREFACE

This volume on the history and future prospects of the modern welfare state is the outcome of an academic conference held by the German Historical Institute London and the Wissenschaftszentrum Berlin on 6-8 December 1978 in Berlin. It attempts to pave the way for an analysis of the problems of the welfare state and its historical origins, and also its likely future, that transcends the nation-state orientated historical accounts so prevalent hitherto. Nowadays social policies are no longer regarded as largely superfluous in affluent societies, as was current in many quarters in the sixties, or viewed in a marxist perspective, a mere 'Patchwork' alleviating but not overcoming the fundamental injustices of the capitalist mode of production. This collection of essays seeks to promote an interdisciplinary approach to the problems of social welfare in two industrial societies, now that social policy and welfare have become extremely important issues again. So far historians and those social scientists concerned with this field of research have tended to work in isolation from one another, without mutual exchange of knowledge and using very different methods. An attempt has been made here to give equal scope to both perspectives, although there is unquestionably still a large expanse of no-man's-land between the two disciplines. It would, of course, be in the interests of all concerned if this gap could be bridged.

The focal point of the essays is an analysis of the socio-political development of the welfare state in Great Britain and Germany. This is justified by the fact that both countries, at different times and in different ways, were pioneers in the creation of the modern welfare state. Moreover, at various stages in the development there were close contacts between Great Britain and Germany on questions of social policy which had a not inconsiderable effect on the structure of the social systems in the two countries. In many respects Great Britain served as a model for German social reformers in the nineteenth century; they attempted to emulate the advantages and to avoid the shortcomings of the British course towards industrial society. Similarly, British social reformers found the communal welfare institutions that had developed in a series of West German industrial cities after the middle of the century extremely interesting and worthy of emulation. In particular the so-called 'Elberfelder System', as Roy Hay points out in his contribution, met with great acclaim in Great Britain. On the other hand it seems that Bismarck's famous social insurance system did not play quite the key role in the development of the welfare state that has usually been attributed to it. None the less there are significant parallels between the German and British cases, for instance in so far as the entrepreneurs in both countries had shown considerable interest in a public social policy of the type implemented by Bismarck. They assumed that this would be the best way of solving the existing social problems without either interfering unduly with the free market system, weakening their competitive positions in the international arena, or imposing the resultant financial burdens exclusively on industry. Apart from that, it is well known that Lloyd George took a great interest in the German model of social insurance and indeed travelled to Germany in 1908 to get on-the-spot information about it. However, on important issues, as Hennock shows, he then adopted different, far more liberal, methods than those chosen by Bismarck and his colleagues, who were continuously faced with considerable opposition to their authoritarian approach from the Reichstag parties.

Between the two World Wars unemployment became the central concern for all social reformers. In Great Britain and particularly in the Weimar Republic it threatened to undermine the entire system of protection against poverty and deprivation, based on state-aided social insurance, that had been built up since the war. In Great Britain as well as in Germany various attempts were made to alleviate unemployment — the fundamental evil that was increasingly plunging the social insurance systems into financial crises — by means of public job creation schemes. In the last resort, however, though partly for different reasons, neither country managed to develop any effective measures in this direction. In Germany this was to have particularly disastrous consequences. Not the least of these was the fact that the crisis in German social legislation in the late 1920s contributed decisively to the fall of Müller's last parliamentary cabinet in 1928 and the collapse of the Weimar parliamentary system, which opened up the gates to authoritarian, and eventually fascist, methods of rule. The Germans, not least because of irreconcilable differences between the entrepreneurs and the workers, eventually were caught in the grips of National Socialist power politics. Admittedly the National Socialists claimed to have solved the class antagonisms and social welfare problems by the concept of the *Volksgemeinschaft*, but all they did, in fact, was to channel the existing social tensions into aggression directed abroad, the virtually unavoidable outcome being a murderous world war. Great Britain on the other hand managed to survive the 1930s with a basically intact social fabric. However, the Second World War and its impact upon the working classes sparked off the idea of creating a comprehensive system of social insurance that would include all citizens. It is William Beveridge who was the great pioneer in this field. Following his scheme, during and after the Second World War the national insurance system was gradually implemented. The British social legislation of the Attlee era served, in turn, as a pattern for the construction of a comprehensive social insurance system in post-war Germany. Despite his basically conservative attitude Konrad Adenauer, in the 1950s, borrowed from it valuable components for the German social insurance system that was to become the corner-stone of the socio-political reconstruction of West Germany.

The essays in this volume are not, however, exclusively concerned with the mutual influences and points of contact between the two countries. Rather, the objective is to give a comparative assessment of the welfare policies in both countries, taking into account the fact that widely differing initial conditions existed, as well as a different socio-political context within which to operate. However, due to practical limitations it was not possible to deal with the whole spectrum of social welfare legislation in both countries — even less so for a period covering more than a century. Instead these essays concentrate on four key problems:

(1) An analysis of the inadequacies, but also the achievements of the older forms of 'poor relief', such as had emerged within a society governed by essentially liberal principles. It becomes apparent that these systems proved to be completely inadequate under the conditions of highly developed industrial societies, but that they none the less laid important foundations for more thorough systems of welfare upon which later generations could build.

(2) The emergence of public social insurance systems as a constructive alternative to the older methods of self-help, charity, and trade union or co-operative welfare institutions.

(3) The problem of unemployment and its far-reaching social implications. Unemployment as a major factor leading to deprivation and misery was actually taken into consideration by social reformers only after the beginning of the twentieth century. However, between the wars it was to become a cardinal

issue in modern welfare policies.
(4) The emergence of comprehensive welfare systems as we have
them today.

It goes without saying that even these issues can only be dealt with
selectively, emphasising particularly important features. Other aspects,
which in themselves are very significant, such as *Arbeiterschutzgesetzge-
bung*, in other words the whole complex of social legislation concerning
the place of work, or medical care of the workers, inasmuch as this is
not an integral part of a social security system, were more or less left
aside. Also the question as to the perpetrators of public social policies
and their specific features could only be dealt with systematically in
the case of Great Britain, by R. Davidson and R. Lowe. None the less
the essays present a comprehensive picture of the emergence of the
Welfare State systems in Great Britain and Germany from the mid-
nineteenth century onwards. Above all they deal with the central
problems in research today and provide, we believe, a very good survey
of the stage present research has reached.

In the third and final section an attempt is made to look not only
at the history, but also the future prospects of the modern welfare
state, largely by means of quantifying social science. Peter Flora pre-
sents a model for a socio-metric analysis of the history of the welfare
state which allows not only a precise assessment of the various stages
in the development of welfare policies in the past, but also confident
predictions on likely future developments. His systematic approach
stands in distinct contrast to the descriptive presentations by the
historians, but may be of particular interest for this very reason. In
fact, it is likely to be extremely stimulating for historical researchers.
The contributions by Naschold and Room deal with the topical question of whether the welfare state, be it for political or economic
reasons, has now reached the limits of its development. Winding up the
whole debate on this issue, Karl W. Deutsch brilliantly argues that the
welfare state systems of the advanced industrial countries should rather
be regarded as the model for a far-reaching reorganisation of the international system as well. Thus the yawning gap in the levels of development and living standards in the industrial states on the one hand and
the Third World on the other might gradually be bridged, in the interests of the welfare of the peoples concerned, but also in order to
preserve world peace for the foreseeable future. If, within the framework of the classical nation-state, the desire to stabilise the social
order was originally the driving force behind the emergence of the

welfare state, then it is difficult to see why a similar state of affairs
cannot be reached on an international level too, so that the polarity
between extremely poor and comparatively rich nations, which today
is again a major source of international conflict, might be overcome
and a global stabilisation of the present world order thus be brought
about.

At this point thanks are due to all those who have made the publication of this volume possible, in particular to the Directors of the
Wissenschaftszentrum Berlin, Prof. Dr Karl W. Deutsch and Prof.
Dr Frieder Naschold, and to Dr H.G. Meier, who as General Secretary
of the WZB until 1979, made the conference possible. We should
also like to express our thanks to all those who have helped the editors
and staff of the GHIL by their hints, suggestions and information,
in particular Dr José Harris. Finally thanks are also due to Elke Jessett
for translating the German contributions and to Jane Williams for
attending to the editorial revision of the manuscript.

Wolfgang J. Mommsen

PART ONE

THE HISTORICAL FOUNDATIONS OF THE WELFARE
STATE

1 THE ENGLISH POOR LAW AND THE ORIGINS OF THE BRITISH WELFARE STATE

D. Fraser

This chapter will explore the complex relationship of the Poor Law and the origins of the British welfare state within three broad contexts. The three categories chosen are not discrete and mutually exclusive factors but for the purposes of analysis may be treated separately. Historiographically these three areas of explanation have figured prominently in studies of the origins of the welfare state. The chapter is structured around the theory that the welfare state originated:

(1) as a response to the harshness and inadequacies of the Poor Law both as a relief agency and as a value system;
(2) as a self-sustained bureaucratic development which evolved in a pragmatic *ad hoc* manner out of early Victorian administrative initiatives, of which the New Poor Law was the most significant;
(3) as an instrument of social control which replaced the means but not the ends of the Poor Law.

In each case the paper will test the validity of these themes both as descriptions of the Poor Law and as explanations of the development of the welfare state.

The Harsh Poor Law

The broad theory that the British welfare state grew out of a popular revulsion for and a gradual official rejection of the Poor Law satisfies two quite distinct approaches to the problem of the origins of the welfare state. First, it conforms to the predilections of the most overtly Whiggish interpretation, that which cites the growth of the welfare state as evidence of a growing enlightenment in British society and politics. On this argument, most popular in the years immediately after 1948 and perhaps most forcibly advanced by Maurice Bruce,[1] the welfare state was part of a story of progress 'onward and upward' by which a punitive and insensitive selective system was replaced by a humane and generous universal one. The welfare state was 'a good thing', *ergo* it was the product of a benevolent process. Equally, however, the harsh Poor Law fits with a second interpretation which doubts whether the growth of the welfare state was a linear progression from inhumanity to enlightenment. This argument, while acknowledging the inadequacy of the Poor Law, would characterise the growth of the welfare state as a different rather than a better provision of public services.[2] Partly through a deeper understanding of the causes of poverty, partly through the positive effects of the stigma of pauperism, partly through the growth of the franchise, governments became aware of the inadequacies of the Poor Law. Hence on largely pragmatic grounds alternative services were provided outside the Poor Law, thus freed from its morally debilitating associations. While the harsh Poor Law figures centrally in this argument, the growth of welfare is regarded not as an inexorable tide of progress sweeping the beach of destitution (the Whig view) but as an uneven cross-current which left many islands of poverty behind it and whose most advanced waves often ended up as stagnant and isolated pools when the tide ebbed. On either argument the harsh Poor Law had a profound effect on subsequent thinking, as Ramesh Mishra noticed:

> What has probably been crucial in the formation of the British ideology of welfare is the background of the extremely harsh nineteenth century Poor Law. Against the stigma of poor relief with its workhouses and means test, social provision outside the Poor Law appeared as a significant reversal and repudiation of past social policies.[3]

There is certainly much evidence to sustain the image of the harsh Poor Law, not least in the inflexible ideology which underpinned the 1834 reform. The object of the new order was not to reduce poverty but to deter pauperism and its main weapon was the punitive workhouse test. Its purpose was well characterised by the Chairman of the Sheffield Guardians in 1855:

> The great object of the poor law board is to ensure a constant unvarying and efficient discipline during the entire residence of the pauper within the workhouse. He rises to the minute; he works to the minute; he eats to the minute. He must be clean, respectful, industrious and obedient. In short the habits inculcated in the house are precisely those the possession of which would have prevented

his becoming an inmate. . . The pauper naturally enough concludes that the relief he received in the workhouse is a very inadequate return for the surrender of his liberty — the full occupation of his time — the value of his labour — the humiliation he must endure in being associated with some of the depraved and abandoned members of the community and the painful consciousness that he has lost all self reliance and self respect. Who can wonder that the honest poor should make every effort to keep out of the workhouse.[4]

The 'honest poor', thus deterred from applying for relief, would find their own salvation and the cost to the ratepayers would be correspondingly reduced. Even the widespread survival of outdoor relief, of which more will be said later, was the result of the Guardians' preference for the cheapest, rather than the most humane, form of relief. Indeed, the flowering of philanthropy, which was the almost self-justifying concomitant of the Victorian Poor Law, itself inhibited the Guardians from paying subsistence benefits. As a Marylebone Guardian explained in 1874:

The Guardians know full well that, under the present conditions of charity. . .any really deserving case is perfectly sure to be supplemented by charity, and in the interests of the ratepayers they naturally refrain from giving a larger sum when a smaller one is practically sufficient.[5]

Paupers were to be imprisoned in 'Bastilles' or sustained on meagre doles outside: it was hardly surprising that the two most persistent accusations levelled against the New Poor Law was that poverty had been made a crime and that the poor were to be starved.

There was a remarkable continuity of views across the country condemning the new system. Thomas Maberley's famous charge that the 1834 act was 'tyrannical, unconstitutional, anti-scriptural, anti-Christian, unnatural, cruel and impolitic' was but an echo of the Birmingham comment — 'a more monstrous, a more iniquitous, a more cruel, a more tyrannical measure was never brought before an English legislature.' In Bradford it was claimed that the Poor Law would 'grind the poor to the dust', in Nottingham that it would 'draw the cord tighter round the neck of the poor'.[6] And the many workhouse scandals, culminating in Andover, merely confirmed these judgements. If families were to be broken up, female paupers abused, humiliating

task work performed and starvation rations provided, it was understandable that the workhouse would be the resort of only the truly
desperate while the 'merely poor' would struggle on unaided. As a
prominent Liverpool philanthropist explained, there existed 'side
by side so much useless and needless splendour and so much unmerited
and unrelieved destitution'. Yet the Poor Law was inadequate to meet
the legitimate demands of poverty in the midst of plenty because

> the receipt of parish relief is felt so deeply to degrade the pauper
> that the best of the working class will rather starve — often do rather
> starve — than apply for it. . . .
>
> It [the workhouse] does succeed in deterring those who can
> support themselves from applying for parish support; it does
> diminish pauperism, it has effectively checked the rapid progress
> of demoralisation and ruin under the old Poor-Law of Elizabeth.
> But as a system of public charity it fails altogether. It is beyond
> the omnipotence of Parliament to meet the conflicting claims of
> justice to the community, severity to the idle and vicious and mercy
> to those stricken down into penury by the visitation of God. . .
> There is grinding want among the honest poor; there is starvation,
> squalor, misery beyond description, children lack food and mothers
> work their eyes dim and their bodies thin to emaciation in the
> vain attempt to find the bare necessities of life but the Poor Law
> authorities have no record of these struggles.[7]

The greatest cruelty in the Poor Law system was that practised upon
those who declined to apply for relief who were yet in need, those
in Lloyd George's phrase who were 'too proud to wear the badge of
pauperism'. Hence it seems reasonable to assert that the welfare state
was essentially a reaction against a harsh and unfeeling Poor Law.

On the other hand, this interpretation rests upon a condemnatory
characterisation of the Poor Law, a characterisation that derives as
much from the image as from the reality of Victorian poor relief.
Nothing fixed the image of the inhuman Poor Law more firmly in
the popular mind than the early Victorian workhouse scandals. Yet
many of these scandals were exaggerated and others were imaginary.
Those that were proved frequently derived more from incompetence
than malevolence. It was, however, politically expedient for anti-Poor
Law agitators to sustain rumours of workhouse cruelty and, for
example, in the case of the Basford scandal, which was eventually
immortalised by Engels, the whole episode derived from political

manipulation.[8] Poor Law, municipal and even parliamentary elections
could be won on an anti-workhouse vote and so popular resentment
of the new Poor Law was often fanned by a workhouse scandal. Local
political control of the Board of Guardians determined what political
colour anti-Poor Law sentiment would wear. In the early Victorian
years the anti-Poor Law vote was Tory in Salford and Nottingham but
Whig in Banbury.

The popular image of the workhouse was in fact at variance with its
actual character. Poor Law Inspectors might tell Guardians, as H.B.
Farnall did in the mid-1850s, that 'if there was one class more than
another requiring the workhouse test it was the able bodied man in
receipt of parochial relief' or that workhouses 'were intended for the
idle and for the dissolute and for those who were able to work but
would not work'.[9] In practice it was the able-bodied adult male who was
least in evidence in Victorian workhouses. The mid-Victorian radical W.E.
Forster spoke for Guardians generally when he remarked in 1850

> that it would not be supposed that the workhouse test, as generally
> understood, would be generally applied or that it was the intention
> of the Board of Guardians at any time to withhold outdoor relief
> and to substitute indoor relief. . .he would not consent for the
> honest well disposed pauper to be compelled to enter the work-
> house because he was obliged to apply to the parish for relief.[10]

During trade slumps urban industrial Guardians refused to apply
either the workhouse or the labour test because the increased demand
for relief was clearly not due to moral failing. In rural areas also the
workhouse test was rarely applied, as Sir John Walsham confirmed:

> with scarcely an exception the tendency everywhere is to sub-
> stitute outdoor for indoor relief whenever the guardians may legally
> do so. . . The *exceptions* to the Prohibitory Order. . .are almost
> invariably treated as *rules*. Outdoor relief *may* be given *ergo* out-
> door relief should be given.[11]

The workhouse might be a place of fear, but it might also be a place
of comfort. As an American scholar has remarked with reference
to the best-run union in Shropshire:

> In the case of children. . .the Union set out in the late 1830s to offer
> an education superior to any afforded by Poor Law authorities

in the Kingdom in a workhouse among the cleanest, largest, most professionally staffed in the land. Those who criticised workhouses held their tongue before the Atcham model. The inmates were generously fed and medically well watched.[12]

It was indeed the services provided within the Poor Law, and particularly within workhouses themselves, that most qualify the image of the harsh Poor Law. The debt the welfare state owes to the Poor Law may be measured in the legacy of Poor Law buildings which are now institutions of welfare and the bricks and mortar symbolise the services that were housed within. For the elderly, the sick, lunatics and children the workhouse could become a haven of improvement. Though the 1905 Royal Commission offered a blanket condemnation of Poor Law institutions, at certain times, in certain places, the workhouse might legitimately be called a welfare institution. The image of the 'pauper palace' coexists with the image of the 'pauper prison'.

Pauper education is a good example of the provision of welfare services within the Poor Law. It was a particularly sensitive issue in the light of inadequate educational opportunities for the children of the independent poor. E.C. Tufnell, an Inspector of Poor Law schools for 27 years, had no time for the argument that pauper children should be deprived of an adequate education merely because provision outside the Poor Law was lacking. Through education, he believed, pauperism would be reduced, for 'pauper parents reared pauper children. To stop this hereditary trait would be to annihilate the greater part of pauperism in this country.'[13] Tufnell's great ally in advocating district schools, where pauper children could be removed from the contamination of adult pauperism, was Assistant Commissioner Dr James Kay (later Kay-Shuttleworth). Kay drew a sharp distinction between the physical and moral condition of a pauper child. While his diet, clothes and comforts ought not to be superior to those of the labourer's child, his need for moral guidance could not be inhibited by less eligibility, since his pauperism was no fault of his own:

whenever the community encounter the responsibility of providing for the education of children who have no natural guardians it is impossible to adopt as a standard for the training of such children the average amount of care and skill now bestowed on the moral and religious culture of the children of the labouring classes generally. . .education is to be regarded as one of the most important means of eradicating the germ of pauperism from the rising generation. . . A child should not be degraded in his own estimation by being a member of a despised class. A child cannot be a pauper in the sense in which that term is commonly understood, that is he cannot be indigent as the consequence of his own want of industry, skill, frugality or forethought, and he ought not therefore to be taught to despise himself . . . it is in the interests of society that the children should neither inherit the infamy, nor the vice, nor the misfortunes of their parents.[14]

Protected from the stigma of pauperism the pauper child would be weaned away from poverty and achieve an independent adulthood.

Though only half a dozen district schools were built on the Kay-Tufnell model, many large unions, like Liverpool or Leeds, built separate industrial schools and many more developed moderately efficient workhouse schools, prompted by the five Inspectors of Poor Law schools appointed from 1847. The pauper child had a number of advantages which derived from his education within the Poor Law rather than outside it. His attendance was likely to be more continuous than the independent child whose attendance was notoriously intermittent. He obtained the priceless asset of industrial training which gave him a positive advantage in the search for employment. Though these assets were more likely to be the privilege of indoor rather than outdoor paupers, the latter's condition was benefited by Denison's Act of 1855 (18 & 19 Victoria c.34) which enabled Guardians to pay the school fees of children on outdoor relief. Some Guardians took this seriously and, for instance, in 1859 nearly two-thirds of all children on outdoor relief in Bradford were attending school, half of whom had their education financed out of poor rates. Both under that Act and the earlier 1844 legislation which allowed the creation of district schools (7 & 8 Victoria c. 101), the education of pauper children could extend from age 4 to 16. Significantly enough, it was argued at the Newcastle Commission that it was undesirable to keep the 'peasant boy' at school until he was 14 or 15 because 'it is quite possible to teach a child soundly and thoroughly in a way that he shall not forget it, all that is necessary for him to possess in the shape of intellectual attainments by the time he is 10 years old.'[15] The differences between school age within and outside the Poor Law were brought sharply in focus by the Act of 1873 (36 & 37 Victoria c.86) which repealed Denison's Act and made school attendance a condition of outdoor relief. In order to bring pauper children into line with children attending the new Board schools under the 1870 Education Act, the school age was now *reduced* to 5 to 13 years.

It was highly unlikely (though not impossible[16]) that the independent poor would take advantage of this more 'eligible' provision. Poor Law medical relief, however, posed far more problems for Guardians intent on maintaining the less eligibility principle. The story of the unplanned and, for many, unwanted growth of the Poor Law medical service is now familiar. So significant had public access to these medical facilities become that in 1885 Parliament protected medical paupers from the primitive disfranchisement which was part of the normal deterrent stigma of poor relief. Yet the effects of open access to Poor Law services logically led to increased pauperism. On these grounds one Board of Guardians opposed public vaccination: 'first because it seems it unjust that the ratepayers should be called upon to pay any portion of the medical bills of private families and, secondly, because its tendency will be to . . . pauperize the whole nation.'[17] As the Poor Law infirmaries improved, so the disequilibrium between pauper and non-pauper provision increased. Though in general the 1909 Commission concluded that Poor Law infirmaries were below the standard of voluntary hospitals, in individual unions the position could be just the reverse. In Merthyr Tydfil the only non-isolation hospital was that provided by the Poor Law and in Bradford it appeared that the treatment in the infirmary was superior even to that available to many of the middle class; this worried the Guardians greatly:

they could not shut their eyes to the fact that an amount of expenditure was going on at the Infirmary which was quite out of place in an institution supported by the ratepayers generally. The effect was to make the patients at the Infirmary better off than they were in many respectable families and much better off than workpeople with 20s, 30s or 40s per week and living in £10 or £15 houses.[18]

The very quality of the medical service offered an inducement, in the language of 1834, 'to quit the less eligible class of labourers and enter the more eligible class of paupers'.

Yet while some found this increased use of the Poor Law worrying, others welcomed it as a demonstration of the way the Poor Law could act as a welfare agency for the general good. As the health reformer Newsholme put it:

The Poor Law has become the chief organisation in the country for dealing with the bodily and mentally sick . . . [this] is no indication of a serious national condition. On the contrary the only sound inference is that the public are realising more and more the value of poor law infirmaries as hospitals for the general population and are claiming their rights as ratepayers to their use.[19]

As Michael Flinn remarked, the Poor Law medical service was eventually set 'on the road that was to lead, hesitatingly but inevitably, to Bevan's National Health Service'.[20] Nor is this mere *post hoc* justification, for elements of that NHS could be found patchily in the Victorian Poor Law and a Poor Law Medical Officer defended himself against the charge of over-generosity in language that would not have been out of place a century later:

> *the life of a sick pauper is as valuable as that of a prince, and when sick we ought to treat them both alike* . . . he needed not medical attention and medicine so much as good diet, warm clothing and comfortable rooms together with careful nursing. . . If I have erred in being too generous it is gratifying to know that my generosity has been the means of saving the life of many a man whose family would otherwise now have been receiving parish relief.[21]

An institution which could throw up a sentiment like that was not wholly divorced from the equality of access to medical facilities and the treatment of medical need without reference to means which were to be the aspirations of the NHS.

In time too, though at a meagre pace, the condtion of the aged pauper improved. By the end of the Victorian period there was widespread evidence of the elderly and their families becoming more attuned to the advantages of the workhouse as a refuge in declining years. As one observer remarked in 1895:

> When one sees knots of old men gossiping by the fire or basking in the sun: when one finds the bedridden old women carefully nursed and appropriately fed, it is difficult to help contrasting their conditions with that of some of the outdoor poor. . . It is common to hear an old inmate say that he could not bear the notion of entering 'the house' but that if he had known it was so comfortable he would have come there long ago.[22]

With the growth of workhouse visiting societies with their trips and treats, workhouse life became somewhat more varied and interesting. Again some Guardians thought too much was being done:

> too many treats were calculated to destroy the spirit of self help and self reliance of children sent from the house to gain their livelihood, by directing their thoughts back to the pleasant days spent in the Workhouse . . . there was more pleasure for people living in the house as paupers than for the working class.[23]

Some recognised too, with a form of intuitive relativism, that the poverty line moved up as the standard of living improved, 'for the standard of pauperism rises with the standard of comfort — the luxuries of one generation of paupers are the necessities of the next'.[24]

From the perspective of twentieth-century welfare standards and aspirations the Victorian Poor Law well merits its reputation for harshness and inadequacy, but from the perspective of early-nineteenth-century possibilities the Poor Law appears in a different light. In the second decade of the century under the impact of Malthusian ideas the most popular remedy for the Poor Law was its abolition. Hence the confirmation that destitution would be relieved, in effect wherever it occurred, was of some significance. As a recent writer commented:

> Imperfect the New Poor Law may have been but it did reaffirm the principle that the state had an obligation to ensure some basic standard of livelihood for its citizens. From that concern developed most of our modern programme of public welfare.[25]

Nobody saw the ambivalence of the Poor Law more clearly than Lloyd George when in his famous note of 1911 he hoped the state would acknowledge a wider responsibility for the general welfare, but added, 'it really does so now through Poor Law.' That ambivalence is neatly captured, as Ann Crowther has pointed out, in the conflicting oral testimony: some remember people queueing up to get into the workhouse, others remember the workhouse as a virulent anathema which survives the generations.[26] In such ways is the paradox displayed wherein the most hated institution of Victorian England was also the progenitor of the welfare state.

The Bureaucratic Model

Very often improvements in Poor Law services were the result of the efforts not of parsimonious Guardians or an indifferent central authority but of Poor Law officials, both local and national. It was the Medical Officers, Union clerks, Assistant Commissioners, Inspectors of Poor Law schools and visiting Commissioners in Lunacy who bullied, blackmailed and cajoled recalcitrant Guardians into local improvements. At one time it was believed that there were no nineteenth-century origins of the welfare state, but the work of MacDonagh, Roberts and Lambert established that the Victorian origins were essentially bureaucratic. The historiographical thrust thus generated established a picture of administrative growth whose prime movers were not the politicians nor the humanitarians (though they were required to sensitise opinion to 'intolerability'), but the bureaucrats. We may construct a lineage beginning with Chadwick, through Horner to Simon, to Llewellyn Smith, to Morant, Newsholme and thence to Beveridge. The bureaucratic context of welfare history has become well rooted and, as Roy Hay has pointed out, it requires a major effort to force welfare historians to consider alternative perspectives.[27]

In this area the role of the Poor Law was pivotal for two reasons. First, it was largely through the Poor Law that Victorian England became initially accustomed to bureaucratic government, for the Poor Law remit ran throughout England and Wales. The authors of the leading Edwardian text on the growth of English state activity saw Chadwick and his fellow Poor Law Inspectors as the pattern card for future administrative developments:

> Not only is the success of the great experiment due very largely to their skill and zeal; but they may also be said to have been the instruments which recommended the system of inspection to the English people so that it gradually extended to all branches of the inner administration until it has become the characteristic feature of English central government.[28]

Secondly, by a process of administrative accumulation the Poor Law attracted to itself a whole range of 'non-pauper' functions which gave it something of the character of an all-purpose welfare agency. To an extent, it had been anticipated that the Poor Law might become a skeleton on which additional services could be grafted and Commissioner George Nichols wrote, 'When the country shall have been worked into unions, each having an organized machinery . . . it can scarcely be doubted that they will be made available for other purposes as well as for the administration of the Poor Law.'[29] Poor Law expenditure grew in the nineteenth century and its distribution changed. Increased administrative functions were mirrored in the proportion of expenditure devoted to non-pauper purposes (see Table 1.1).

Table 1.1: Poor Relief Expenditure as Percentage of Total Expenditure, 1844-1900

	Total Expenditure (£m)	Percentage Expended as Poor Relief
1844	6.99	72.69
1854	7.32	72.82
1864	9.68	66.80
1874	12.85	59.64
1891	18.35	50.88
1900	26.31	43.96

What struck observers most about this burgeoning administrative machine was that it ensured uniform treatment through centralisation. As our Edwardian authorities explained:

The administration of the Poor Laws is uniform. . . The pauper must not be pampered in one union and starved in another. Every statutory or administrative rule should be rigidly carried out in every part of the kingdom. . . The local Poor Law authorities and their officers are so overdosed with orders that almost every act seems to be performed under a prescription of the Local Government Board. . . The guardians have little to do beyond carrying out the instructions contained in the General and Special Orders of the Board.[30]

Nor was this central direction limited to broad areas of policy, for local administration was constrained down to the smallest detail. Blackburn businessmen resented being 'called over the coals from time to time as they had been upon the most trivial matters even down to the thickening of the people's porridge in the workhouse', while those in Bradford complained at being 'treated as mere puppets incapable of judging whether one ought or ought not to be expend some twenty pounds out of the rates'. Disillusioned Sheffield ratepayers asked why they should elect Guardians if 'they are constantly to be controlled, thwarted, overruled, directed, ordered and coerced by the Poor Law Board in London'. Rochdale magistrates 'had no particular relish for a system which placed the body in Lancashire and the head in London'.[31]

Yet the resentful tone of these remarks gives a clue to the fact that the uniformity and centralisation of the Poor Law was more image than reality. The central authority had important negative powers of control such as the right to disallow expenditure or veto appointments. Where it did not confront a resistant local regime it could enforce its regulations, as happened in Coventry.[32] Much recent research, however, on the *practice* rather than the *theory* of poor relief indicates the ineffectiveness of central control, the variety of local administration and the perversions of the objectives of the 1834 reforms. Indeed the vigorous promotion of central initiative in the 1870s was both a reaffirmation of the principles of 1834 and a reassertion of centralisation in a relief system whose inconsistency was as marked in 1870 as it had been in 1830. 'Poplarism' was a confirmation that local autonomy not only existed but thrived within the Poor Law and that poor relief had a variegated and not a uniform character. Despite the contrary expectation and directive, the pauper was indeed pampered in one parish and punished in the next.

Table 1.2: Percentage of Paupers on Indoor Relief, Norwich, Merthyr Tydfil and Bradford

Norwich	
1841	15.32
1851	9.10
1861	10.26
Merthyr Tydfil	
1853	4.5
1863	9.3
1873	11.2
1883	11.2
1893	17.2
Bradford	
1857-71	17.2

In fact the most compelling evidence of the ineffectiveness of central direction and control lay in the mountain of statistics which the Poor Law Board itself produced.[33] The abolition of outdoor relief, so central both to the philosphy of the New Poor Law and to the propaganda of the anti-Poor Law movement, turns out to have been a myth. Taking as an example three very different towns, Norwich, Merthyr Tydfil and Bradford, evidence is provided that most paupers were relieved outside the workhouse (Table 1.2). The national figures tell the same story (Table 1.3).

Table 1.3: Percentage of Paupers on Indoor Relief, England and Wales, 1859-74

1859	14.44
1864	12.14
1869	13.86
1874	15.46

Nor was it the case that the able-bodied adult was distorting these figures, for this category was always a minority among the pauper host (Table 1.4).

Table 1.4: Percentage of All Paupers who were Able-bodied Adults

1849	21.0
1854	15.6
1859	15.7
1864	18.6
1869	16.8
1874	13.5

And the able-bodied adult male, the very object of the whole Poor Law reformation, was the least likely to see the inside of a workhouse. In Bradford, for instance, between 1857 and 1871 only 0.3 per cent of the workhouse population were able-bodied adult males and in none of the biannual returns between 1863 and 1871 was a single able-bodied adult male pauper returned as resident in the workhouse. To put it another way, only 0.6 per cent of the town's adult able-bodied male paupers were relieved within the workhouse. In the early 1870s during the Local Government Board initiative the numbers did increase, but even then nearly three-quarters of able-bodied adults were still relieved out of doors. Figures for all able-bodied paupers locally and nationally confirm the same picture (Table 1.6).

These and the many other figures which could be cited were the

Table 1.5: Percentage of Adult Male Able-bodied Paupers on Indoor Relief, England and Wales, 1859-74

1859	19.24
1864	14.77
1869	21.80
1874	28.64

Table 1.6: Percentage of Adult Able-bodied Paupers on Indoor Relief, Norfolk and England and Wales

	Norfolk	England and Wales
1850s	17.9	13.3
1860s	16.2	13.0
1870s	13.6	16.6
1880s	24.1	22.2
1890s	23.8	31.8

product of a variety of factors such as the exploitation of loopholes, false categorisations, Board compromises and downright illegality. What they add up to is an acknowledgement of the inability of the central authority to uphold its own relief principles in the face of local practice. By the end of the century the variety of *per capita* expenditure on poor relief demonstrated the total lack of uniformity in the treatment of paupers. In 1899 London spent 15s 9¾d for each of its citizens, but Northumberland only 4s 1½d. It was because of this that so many Edwardian reformers insisted that social policy could not be left to the mere whim of local predilections. If the welfare state emerged from bureaucratic initiatives the Poor Law certainly did not provide the model of uniform centralised administration. If anything, twentieth-century welfare based on common standards derived from a bureaucratic reaction against the diversity of the Poor Law.

The Poor Law as an Instrument of Social Control

Local autonomy, however, is not inconsistent with the third broad explanation, that the Poor Law (and the welfare state which succeeded it) were developed primarily as instruments of social control. There are no doubt many abstruse points to be made about the validity of social control as a psychological or sociological concept. Blissfully unaware of these, historians, in their characteristically imprecise way, have argued that the Poor Law was designed and/or used:

(1) as a means of strengthening the authority of the rulers over the ruled;
(2) in order to manipulate the labour market and particularly wage rates;
(3) as a vehicle for imposing a 'bourgeois' value system upon the working class.

In the first case the harshness of the Poor Law appears less as a device for inspiring personal initiative than as a designedly painful way of reminding paupers 'who was boss'. This was delightfully explained by one observer in 1865:

The spirit of domination strongly manifest by some of our country gentlemen was at the bottom of these extreme regulations. The independence of their positions places them beyond the pale of contradiction in their own sphere and they will not brook the violation of authority. With them, system is everything — their horses are accustomed to go so many miles, their labourers to perform so much work: and why should not these rascals of paupers be placed in solitary confinement and be shortened in their diet, for disobedience and thus bring their tempers as well as their stomachs into subjection and make them feel the power of the village squire.[34]

This social control interpretation has been vigorously put recently by Anthony Brundage who, turning the normal argument on its head, has asserted that local autonomy was not the result of resistance to centralisation but the actual object of the new regime. Allying himself with the rather doubtful case of D.C. Moore, Brundage argues that the 1832 Reform Act and the 1834 Amendment Act were both designed to sustain natural authority in 'deference communities'.[35] The merit of his approach is that he spells out the specific means by which local authority would be strengthened. These were threefold: the designation of Unions in conformity with estate boundaries, the seating of resident county magistrates as *ex officio* members of Boards of Guardians, and the multiple voting system. Reservations must be registered on all three counts.

In highlighting the drawing of boundaries in deference to the wishes of local magnates, Brundage confuses tactics with objectives. The overwhelmingly prime objective of both government and Commission in the later 1830s was to get the new system established. If the leaders of local communities could aid in that process, so much the better, and if they felt strongly that Unions should be coextensive with their estates then the Assistant Commissioners took note of that. But they never set out with the prime objective of satisfying those local demands. It was significant that Kay in East Anglia divided Coke of Holkham's estate between five Unions and drew his boundaries mainly with reference to workhouse provision. Indeed the ideal Union was said to be a mix of urban and rural, which ran quite counter to the idea of monopolistic Unions as new 'pocket boroughs'. One of the main problems in the next decades was the tension created in both rural unions with an urban heartland and in urban unions with a rural hinterland.

The *ex officio* magistrates are hardly more convincing. Again in the early years it was important to establish the status of Boards of Guardians and it certainly helped to acquire the services of the county bench, especially the peerage on the county bench. Again this was primarily tactical and one great landowner was asked to become Chairman just for the first year because 'in the meantime the machinery would be fairly set a going, which is of course a great thing in the commencement of a totally new system'.[36] In view of this it is decidedly unfortunate that Brundage's survey stops abruptly in 1839, for it seems to have been the case that even where magistrates took an *initial* interest, the boring routine of poor relief soon drove them away and in many Unions magistrates took no interest at all. It is equally unfortunate that Brundage has generalised from a rather atypical local example. Northamptonshire had an unusually high concentration of aristocratic landowners and landowning itself was concentrated in relatively few hands. In mixed counties, like Durham and Northumberland, with their plurality of interests and in the urbanised counties, like the West Riding or south Lancashire, the opportunities for unchallenged landed domination were far less.

The voting system, borrowed from Sturges Bourne, certainly did favour property owners (though it should be noted that occupiers could also become multiple voters). Yet while there was considerable criticism of the Sturges Bourne 'bricks against brains' principle where it was used before 1834 and for other elections, there was virtually no criticism of it with reference to the Poor Law itself. Parliamentary radicals kept up an attack on it and eventually in 1894 Poor Law elections were democratised. But this was largely the result of national trends in franchise reform: those who worked the system locally did not find the multiple voting system an inhibition. There were many other bones of contention which *prevented* the democratic will of the ratepayers being reflected in the composition of Boards of Guardians. As I have explained elsewhere,[37] these included an odd form of secret ballot which gave ample opportunity for the falsification of the results, disproportionate representation of individual townships or parishes on Boards of Guardians, and the utilisation of Poor Law machinery to manipulate voters' lists.

If the 'power of the squire' argument is far more complex than the simple social control model implies, we are on much firmer ground with the manipulation of the labour market. Anne Digby's work is crucial here. She shows that in East Anglia the 'squires' largely retired to their estates, which they ran with paternalism, and relieved destitution through philanthropy, and that Boards became dominated by the tenant farmers. Thus 'the board rooms of Norfolk workhouses became the focus of class struggle between farmers and labourers.'[38] It is now quite clear that various forms of labour allocation policies were utilised within the poor relief system both before and after 1834, and that the cost of labour was shared between wages and poor relief. In short there was no attempt to adopt the Ricardian free market in labour, for agricultural demand for labour was so seasonal. Wage rates and poor relief were manipulated in the interests of farmers to maintain an adequate supply of labour to meet the highest seasonal demands. In towns too the Poor Law was used to keep a fluid supply of labour near at hand. The growth of non-resident relief, the designation of five-year residents as non-settled but irremovable poor and the eventual Union Chargeability Act giving irremovability after one year's residence were all geared to the needs of an industrial system which could not afford to disperse its labour supply because of short-term fluctuations in the market.[39] The actual impact upon wage levels is less clear, but contemporaries were certainly aware of the potential of the workhouse for wage reduction:

a model prison they wanted to build in order to get the working classes under the finger and thumb of the arbitrary and avaricious manufacturers and then they would be obliged to work for what the masters chose to give or go into the model prison.[40]

It is highly problematical whether the working man thus coerced by the Poor Law abandoned his 'natural' value system and adopted an alternative set of values imposed on him by his masters. This relates to the huge area of the relationship between Victorian class consciousness, conflict, consensus and values. Since the characteristic labour demand of the twentieth century was for work or unconditional maintenance, it is perhaps reasonable to deduce that this was suppressed in the Victorian period by the forced imposition of bourgeois individualism. And that philosophy manifestly underpinned the New Poor Law. In separating the destitute from the merely poor, in dividing the deserving from the undeserving, the Poor Law explicitly extolled the virtues of self-help and individualism. As Caroline Reid has argued, 'respectability' was used by the middle class as a means of social control and nothing identified the rough from the respectable more clearly than the Poor Law.[41]

The great difficulty about this is how far this 'culture' was alien to the working class and how far it grew out of working-class experience and interests. Was that mid-Victorian consensus part of the very process of social control or an expression of shared values which served the interests of both the middle and working class? Labour attitudes to the Poor Law do give some credence to the view that the values of individualism did not have to be imposed from above, but grew naturally in the working-class milieu. If we take the whole principle of testing destitution through workhouse or labour test we find that there is little support for the notion of universal and unconditional access to relief. Nobody knew better than working men that there were proletarian drones as well as aristocratic ones. As one radical observer remarked, 'it is quite clear that no two classes of the state can be more opposed to each other than the labourer who earns his bread by the sweat of his brow and the beggar who lives upon the labour of others.'[42] Working men preferred independence to pauperism and not simply because pauperism had been stigmatised. Though many objected to the form of the labour test because it was largely unproductive, there was widespread agreement that society was entitled to use some means to establish the bona fides of any claim. The Owenite Socialist, James Hole, was convinced that a distinction had to be made between 'the industrious and the idle, the thrifty and the improvident', and so he concluded, 'a labour test should be exacted from every able bodied applicant for relief whether male or female otherwise the unthrifty have a temptation to subsist upon the earnings of the industrious and frugal.'[43] As the Chamberlain Circular noted, the normally industrious working man had a healthy distaste for pauperism and a commendable love of independence, and Keith Burgess has recently pointed out that the leadership of the Lancashire cotton operatives was adamant that improvements must derive from workers' own efforts, from individualism rather than collectivism.[44] In 1907 Ramsay MacDonald argued that 'the loafer must not be allowed to damage the claims of the deserving temporarily unemployed. So long as he is mixed up with the unemployed his little ways and escapades will be palmed off as though he were a typical example of the mass.' There is surely a continuity in labour thinking between Hole's acceptance of the labour test and the 1920s 'search for the scrounger' which, as Alan Deacon has shown, labour not only accepted but actually extended in 1924.[45]

This may of course be explained in terms of a process of cultural conditioning, part of the social control mechanism itself. Yet we should beware of that historians' arrogance which would reject contemporaries' perceptions of their own self-interest. If Victorian working men believed they were well served by thrift, respectability, industry and self-help, all values which the Poor Law sought to encourage, who are we to designate them as 'bourgeois dupes'? That working men both hated the Poor Law and at the same time shared the philosophy on which it was based only illustrates further the paradoxical role the Poor Law had in Victorian social policy.

Whether working-class assumption of the values of self-help was voluntary or not, there were many contemporaries who believed that it had been the Poor Law which had drawn the teeth from a potentially revolutionary working class. As Michael Rose explains, Rayner Stephens, the revered mob orator of the 1830s, had come to believe this in 1863:

> First of all you see they catch the lion in their toils: then they cage him within bars of iron, clip his claws, draw his teeth, tame him with soup and gruel and having severely gagged him so that he cannot give either a roar of defiance or a howl of misery, they invite the world to look at him and admire him as the very pattern of all popular lions — the contented lion, the peaceable lion, the once fierce English lion turned into the harmless Lancashire lamb.[46]

Yet by the 1880s and 1890s even those who wished to keep 'the lion in toils' were becoming aware that the Poor Law was an increasingly irrelevant instrument of social control which would have to be replaced.

The contradiction between 3 per cent pauperism and 30 per cent poverty, the paradox of designating those in receipt of poor relief as underserving *per se*, the identification of alienated social groups for whom, even the 'rulers' agreed, the Poor Law was inappropriate, all this confirmed that the Poor Law was inadequate both as a relief system and in the maintenance of social order.

The 1834 reform had begun as a contradiction: it had established a relief system whose aim was to reduce its coverage and limit its clientele. It did its work of deterrence so well that threats to order could not be contained within it nor could such improvements as it was to make gain widespread popular confidence. Though potentially a welfare organ with wide social purposes, it could never naturally develop in this way because its growth was always inhibited by its own history and traditions. The 'pauper palace' could never break out of the chains of 'the Bastille' and the contradictions between them were inherited by the welfare state itself. There are two popular but opposite stereotypes of 'welfare state man'. One is of the work-shy scrounger exploiting the social security system which has made him 'soft': the other is of the desperately needy, unwilling to apply for stigmatised benefits to which he is entitled because of his dislike of 'charity' and his preference for independence. The former derives from the image of the 'pauper palace', the latter from the image of the 'Bastille', and they show that it is values and attitudes as well as bricks and mortar which bind the welfare state and the Poor Law in uncomfortable harness together.

Notes

1. M. B. Bruce, *The Coming of the Welfare State* (London, 1968).
2. This is a recurrent, though not the only, theme in D. Fraser, *The Evolution of the British Welfare State* (London, 1973).
3. R. Mishra, 'Social Control or Social Change', unpublished paper, Glasgow conference, 1978, p. 2.
4. *Sheffield Times*, 10 Nov. 1855.
5. Col. L. Gardiner, Vice-Chairman, St Marylebone Board of Guardians, *Third Annual Report of the Local Government Board* (1873-4), Appendix, p. 134.
6. J. Maberley, *To The Poor and Their Friends* (1836), quoted by M.J. Murphy, *Poverty in Cambridgeshire* (Cambridge, 1978) p. 34; *Birmingham Journal*, 10 May 1834; *No Monopoly* (Bradford Handbill, 1837); *Nottingham Journal*, 5 Feb. 1841.
7. W. Rathbone, *Social Duties Considered* (1867), pp. 21, 48-9.
8. C.P. Griffin, 'Chartism and the Opposition to the New Poor Law in

Nottinghamshire: the Basford Union Workhouse Affair', *Midland History*, vol. II (1974), pp. 244-9.
    9. *Bradford Observer*, 30 Aug. 1855, 27 Nov. 1856.
    10. Ibid., 16 Aug. 1850.
    11. Sir J. Walsham to Poor Law Board, 7 Jan. 1856, PRO, MH 32/83.
    12. V.J. Walsh, 'Old and New Poor Laws in Shropshire 1820-1870', *Midland History*, vol. II (1974), pp. 225-43.
    13. R.J. Phillips, 'E.C. Tufnell, Inspector of Poor Law Schools 1847-1874', in *History of Education*, vol. 5 (1976), pp. 227-40.
    14. J.P. Kay, 'Report on the Training of Pauper Children', *Fourth Report of the Poor Law Commissioners* (1838), Appendix, pp. 140, 145.
    15. Report of the Newcastle Commission, PP, 21 (1861), I, p. 243.
    16. Sometimes Guardians temporarily removed children of the poor but independent family into the workhouse. The children might be educated within the Poor Law though their parents were not in receipt of poor relief. The Commission frowned on this practice as an indirect system of allowances in aid of wages.
    17. Bradford Poor Law Guardians' Minutes, 30 Apr. 1856.
    18. *Bradford Observer*, 21 Jan. 1969.
    19. A. Newsholme, *The Ministry of Health* (London, 1925), pp. 175-6.
    20. M.W. Flinn, 'Medical Services Under the New Poor Law' in D. Fraser (ed.), *The New Poor Law in the Nineteenth Century* (London, 1976), p. 66.
    21. J. Leeson to Poor Law Board, 31 Mar. 1869, PRO MH 12/14737.
    22. Twenty-fourth Report of the Local Government Board (1895), p. 29, quoted by A. Digby, *Pauper Palaces* (London, 1978).
    23. Bradford Poor Law Guardians' Minutes, 14 June 1971.
    24. J. Redlich and F.W. Hirst, *A History of Local Government in England* (London, 1903), vol. II, p. 217.
    25. J. Roach, *Social Reform in England 1780-1880* (London, 1978), p. 120.
    26. M.A. Crowther, 'The Later Years of the Workhouse 1890-1929' in P. Thane (ed.), *The Origins of British Social Policy* (London, 1978), p. 52.
    27. J.R. Hay, *The Development of the British Welfare State 1880-1975* (London, 1978), pp. 102-9.
    28. Redlich and Hirst, *A History of Local Government*, I, p. 111.
    29. *Fifth Annual Report of the Poor Law Commission* (1839), p. 25.
    30. Redlich and Hirst, *A History of Local Government*, I, pp. 204, 262.
    31. *Blackburn Standard*, 18 Jan. 1860; W. Brayshaw to PLC, 2 Aug. 1861, PRO MH12/14735; *Sheffield Times*, 18 Sept. 1858; *Manchester Guardian*, 27 Oct. 1852.
    32. P. Searby, 'The Relief of the Poor in Coventry 1830-1863', *Historical Journal*, vol. 20 (1977), pp. 345-61.
    33. The figures for England and Wales are computed from the annual reports of the central authority. Local figures derive from the work of T.D. Jones (Merthyr Tydfil), David Ashforth (Bradford) and Anne Digby (Norfolk).
    34. J. Glyde, *Suffolk in the Nineteenth Century* (London, 1865), p. 185.
    35. A. Brundage, *The Making of the New Poor Law* (London, 1978). For the theory of deference communities, see D.C. Moore, *The Politics of Deference* (Hassocks, 1977).
    36. Quoted by Digby, *Pauper Palaces*, p. 209.
    37. D. Fraser, *Urban Politics in Victorian England* (Leicester, 1976), Chapter III.
    38. Digby, *Pauper Palaces*, p. 227.
    39. For resistance of landowners to this see M. Caplan, 'Settlement Chargeability and the New Poor Law', *International Review of Social History*, vol. 23

(1978).

40. Sheffield Newspaper Cutting PRO MH12/15474.
41. C. Reid, 'Middle Class Values and Working Class Culture in Sheffield in the Nineteenth Century', unpublished Sheffield PhD thesis, 1977.
42. *Bradford Observer*, 11 Aug. 1836.
43. *Report of the Sub Committee to Enquire into the State of the Poor in Leeds* (1850).
44. K. Burgess, 'Working Class "Response" to Social Policy: the Case of the Lancashire Cotton Textile Districts 1880-1914', unpublished conference paper, Glasgow, 1978.
45. A. Deacon, *The Search for the Scrounger* (London, 1977).
46. M. Rose, 'Rochdale Man. . .' in A.P. Donajgrodzki (ed.), *Social Control in Nineteenth Century Britain* (London, 1977), p. 185.

2 ENGLISH SOCIAL POLICY AROUND THE MIDDLE OF THE NINETEENTH CENTURY AS SEEN BY GERMAN SOCIAL REFORMERS

J. Reulecke

The use of the terms 'challenge' and 'response' to characterise decisive impulses in the rise and development of the West European industrialised nations has long proved a fruitful approach. It has been modified and widened by the historical modernisation theory, which has been the subject of lively discussion in the Federal Republic too during recent years, where attention has mainly focused on the different ways and degrees in which the various states overcame their relative backlog in relation to the 'pioneer' Great Britain.[1] Karl Marx's well-known statement in the Foreword to *Das Kapital*: 'The more highly developed industrial country is only showing to the less highly developed the picture of their own future'[2] has often been the point of departure, largely because the word 'only' implies the provocative argument that the process of industrialisation moves according to inevitable laws which no country, however late its development, can evade. More recent studies have shown that Marx's statement contains only a half-truth,[3] in that not only does the developmental backlog generate its own dynamic, causing the industrialisation of the later developer to follow a course different in many respects from that of the model, but also that there are prerequisites, traditions and other factors which continue to work with varying effects and which need more consideration[4] if the modernisation process of a typical later developer, such as Germany under the influence of Prussia, is to be fully understood.

The acknowledgement of a timelag between Great Britain and Germany, which can be put at between thirty and forty years at the end of the eighteenth century and then shrank steadily up to the period of intensive industrialisation in the 1870s, is not only to be found in all modern textbooks but was also a formative element in contemporary thinking. There had been efforts since the end of the eighteenth century to cut down or eliminate the backlog in development which, particularly in the early decades of the nineteenth century, was felt to be dangerous: attempts to woo English skilled workers, industrial espionage, the propagation of new technical knowledge through state institutions, the establishment of model workshops, the promotion of visits to England to gain experience were all ways[5] in which the bourgeois and the bureaucratic elite,[6] with their belief in progress, were aiming to improve their position in the accelerating field of technical and economic development and make up some of the ground which England had gained.

Research so far, therefore, has concentrated almost entirely on the transfer and use of technical and economic knowledge, although a glance at the German literature of social criticism and reform during the 'Vormärz' (the period up to the revolution of 1848) and during the early industrialisation phase after about 1850 will show that, eagerly as the technological development was followed, at least as much attention was devoted to the social consequences of the new progress in England and that there was intense discussion of this.[7] Only Friedrich Engels' brilliantly written and certainly outstanding *Condition of the Working Class in England*[8] is generally known, and it is the only work which is always quoted in discussing the state of German knowledge of the situation of the workers in England. But Gustav Mayer has already pointed out in his biography of Engels that, in his book on England as well, Engels jumped on to a moving train that was being pulled by the 'Zeitgeist'.[9] A few years ago Hans Jürgen Teuteberg indicated areas in which the picture drawn by Engels needs modification when he compared a number of other contemporary accounts and assessments of English social conditions with Engels' work.[10] In this connection a research project, which is being funded by the Anglo-German Foundation and in which a Mannheim team is making a systematic study of comments by German travellers on the economic and social changes in England during the process of industrialisation, should yield valuable results.

Altogether, however, little has been done in this field by contemporary research, and so I should like first to limit myself to a few general arguments and then take one aspect and choose one example for our discussion of the problem of the relation between the English pattern and German social reform.

I begin with the argument that the emergence of the modern concept of a social or welfare state in Germany under Prussian influence must be seen as part of a complex process of social learning in the sense of *trial and error*, which was not only induced by the challenge of serious internal threats to society and a growing fear of revolution but received other major impulses from the recognition of the inadequacy of traditional means to eliminate social distress, and the evidence of the social consequences of industrialisation in England. Now with regard to the latter aspect, the statement that a society which was still more traditionally structured was changed by contact with a more highly developed one and received a number of major impulses from it is relatively trivial; the interesting question for the historian is how and under what concrete structural social conditions this process of learning proceeded.[11]

Social learning — and this is my second argument — whether individual or taking place in certain sectors of society, always proceeds through the interaction of communication and confrontation and, in relation to learning by the society as a whole and that of individual groups within a society, moves in more or less clearly differentiated stages:[12] Stage (a), confrontation with social problems and divergencies, is followed by Stage (b), awareness of the potential danger to society of these problems and a decision as to whether intervention is necessary and desirable. The stage of learning thus reached permits, according to Habermas, 'reflexive learning', i.e. it permits planned intervention.[13] For if the decision is positive, Stage (c) begins, the search for information on relations and possible solutions, which is followed by (d), discussion and evaluation, and perhaps experimental implementation, of certain measures before the background of a more or less explicit hierarchy of values which is partly ideologically fixed. The last stage, (e), consists of the selection and propagation of promising measures and efforts to realise these, with at the same time the development of implementation strategies. This quintessential and of course rather simplified classification should be taken as the framework for the following remarks.

The 'Vormärz', when pauperism began to assume threatening proportions in Prussian Germany and the limits of the traditional means of helping the poor became evident, marks the beginning of the first phase of the learning process. In a rather foreshortened perspective 'industry' had been identified at an early stage as the cause of all the social phenomena which were being observed with growing fear and concern but without real understanding. As Friedrich Perthes complained in 1816, industry was 'the grave of our character, our morals and our strength'.[14] Though this condemnation was largely the result of a rather conservative-romantic criticism of the fragmentation of human activities, and hence of man himself, in the factories, for instance,[15] the many reports which came from England on the living conditions of the lower classes, not only of the slums in the big cities but also the vice and depravity of the proletariat[16] during

the early decades of the nineteenth century, were often all too quickly
taken as confirmation that there was fundamentally a cause-and-effect
relation between the modern use of the machine and physical and
psychological distress. The Chartist demonstrations in 1838 and the
uprisings among the workers in the following year, especially in
Birmingham and Newport,[17] made clear to the German general public
what the foreseeable future was likely to bring if Germany followed in
England's footsteps and left social conditions largely to take care of
themselves.

However, not all observers about 1840 identified industrialisation
with the growing distress of the masses. Let us take two examples.
One of the most penetrating contemporary analyses of the more
fundamental relations is Karl Rodbertus' article 'The Claims of the
Working Class' ('Die Forderungen der arbeitenden Klassen'). Written
at the end of 1839, it raised the question of how the existing state
would have to change, especially its economic system, to prevent the
new forces, which had been released by industry and were necessary
for the future development of the world, from sliding 'into a waste-
ful regression' and history from another 'painful deviation'.[18] Rodbertus' analysis of the situation is on a highly abstract level and he is
mainly challenging the economists to evolve a new system to save
the working class from 'the blind forces at work'[19] and, by avoiding
the English mistakes, to enable them to participate in the general
progress. But another article, written at about the same time, by
the Düsseldorf councillor Karl Quentin, 'A Word at the Time of the
Workers' Coalitions' ('Ein Wort zur Zeit der Arbeiter-Koalitionen'),
under the impact of the frightening situation in England, is aimed in
a more practical direction.[20] In England as well as France the 'destructive consequences of the simple coalition of craftsmen and factory
workers for the purpose of raising their wages' were already apparent;
this had not happened yet in Germany. So much the more need, then
'to stand firm and united' and in a system of many different associations, 'waken the trust of the working class by sympathy and justice
and their intelligence by tuition and example'.[21] This would show
them the advantages of peaceful procedure. His 'serious word at this
serious time' was addressed to all 'well intentioned citizens', and
especially the factory owners.[22] It was their ignorance and their desire
for profit, together with the lack of education among the lower classes,
which had caused the general demoralisation of the workers, not
industry or freedom of trade in itself. On the contrary, the latter was
'a precious jewel' which must be treasured and kept.[23]

Although both authors see the problem in a similar way, their proposals for dealing with it are different — indeed they may be regarded as typical of extreme positions in thinking on social reform in the early phase of industrialisation in Germany. While Quentin does not mention the state but assumes that insight and the right attitude on the part of all 'right-minded men' will ultimately cure social evils and be enough to cope with the consequences of economic crises with the help of a large range of voluntary associations, Rodbertus doubts the readiness of free individuals for unity. He rather assumes, and Darwin evolved this concept at about the same time, that in such a situation one would simply have the dominance of the stronger. He speaks of a 'despotism of the rentier class'[24] and demands a system of 'state steering' instead of 'a system of freedom of occupation', this being the only way to restrict the desire for profit. There must be a new 'state economy' to ensure a just distribution of wealth, just participation of the working class in the progress of the economy and of civilisation altogether and to protect the workers from the negative consequences of the ups and downs of the general economic situation.[25] With these views on the role of the state Rodbertus also differed considerably from contemporary conservative ideas on a social monarchy or a social patriarchal state, such as those put forward by men ranging from Victor Aimé Huber to Lorenz von Stein. Rodbertus was an isolated figure during the period before 1848 — and he remained isolated all his life, despite the strong influence he was to exercise later on Ferdinand Lassalle.[26]

Karl Quentin, on the other hand, shows himself in the solution he proposes to be typical of the liberal Prussian state administrators of the time.[27] He was at best prepared to allow the state in the socioeconomic sphere the role of guarantor of individual freedom; for the rest he was convinced that the self-healing potential of a freed society would be sufficient to master the crisis without state intervention and would give optimal room for interaction to the social forces. The claim for political freedom which took first place for the liberals, especially in south-west Germany, does not appear here. The state and the social spheres are seen as distinct and separate areas,[28] between which a liberal bureaucracy could only mediate in that individual officials participated in a private capacity in the voluntary association as initiators, co-founders, leading members and partners in communication. That this standpoint was shared by many of the senior officials and that the readiness for voluntary engagement was considerable can be seen from the answers to a survey sent out by the Ministry of

Education and Cultural Affairs at the instigation of the Prussian King in the spring of 1844 on the spread and effectiveness of social associations in the Prussian provinces.[29] Certainly the optimistic belief was still widely held that social reform would be possible without simultaneous or even prior reform of political conditions.

Rodbertus' and Quentin's warnings to their contemporaries, together with the voices of a few other individual social reformers, remained isolated pioneering work until the uprising of the weavers in Silesia in the summer of 1844, which deeply shocked Prussian-German society. A daily newspaper expressed a typical reaction when a few days after the weavers had been put down it said that the unrest in Silesia had put an end to the belief that that kind of thing could only happen in France or England.[30] And when Quentin's article was reprinted a few years later the reference to the frightening example of France and England was no longer needed: the author could point to the events in his own country.[31]

The deep gap on the one hand between the misery of the workers — not only in Silesia — which had burst upon the general consciousness, and the brilliant progress of German industry on the other hand, as was demonstrated a few weeks after the weavers' uprising at the great Zollverein exhibition in Berlin,[32] gave rise to greater concern with the social question in certain circles of the liberal bourgeoisie and among senior officials.[33]

One could, therefore, regard the phase which now began as the third stage of the learning process I have just described: a socially engaged social elite engaged in communication on reform to solve the problems which constituted a basic threat to the existing social system. In the autumn of 1844 the Central Association for the Well-being of the Working Class in Prussia (Centralverein für das Wohl der arbeitenden Klassen in Preussen) was founded by members of these circles, prominent among them senior officials close to the Prussian Ministry of Finance;[34] one of the aims of the Central Association was to be — to use the modern phrase — a 'think-tank' for ideas on social reform. It was to collect information from at home and abroad and discuss attempts to ameliorate social distress, evaluate their effectiveness and pass information on to other associations which were to be founded at regional and local level. It would promote successful experiments and proven institutions and could give them financial support.[35]

It is not possible to go into the history of the Centralverein here, but I can give a brief outline: after a long and wearisome initiation phase owing to the scepticism of the authorities its active life at last began in April 1848 when the statutes were officially approved. The association existed for nearly seventy years and after 1848/9 produced a wide range of material, one of its main publications being the periodical *The Working Man's Friend* (*Der Arbeiterfreund*), which well reflects both the range and limitations of its function as a turntable for ideas. Both Quentin and Rodbertus, incidentally, were among the most active and engaged members of the Centralverein during its early phase. The association is an extremely illuminating example of the attitude of German social reformers to social conditions and sociopolitical activities in England.

In the second part of the chapter I shall give a brief outline of those English institutions and initiatives on social policy which were discussed by the Centralverein up to about 1870, including those which it apparently did not consider, and then take one example to illustrate the way in which the English experience was approached and the poles between which the discussion took place. Of course we must remember that in addition to the Centralverein other circles were concerned with social reform in Prussia during the early industrialisation phase, although they were not so important. On the conservative side, especially, there was, for instance, the 'Innere Mission' run by Wichern, and other institutions also drew in a specific way on the English development.[36] But I cannot go into these here.

In the first nine issues of the *Mitteilungen des Centralvereins* (*Information from the Central Association*), which appeared from August 1848 up to the end of 1850, social institutions in Britain play no part, apart from a brief mention of a fund to provide a marriage portion for young miners in Ayrshire,[37] while the French national workshops, the Belgian and French sickness and old age pension funds and Belgian societies for mutual assurance are discussed in detail. It seems as if up to this period England appeared to the social reformers in a negative light, they saw only the 'terrible sore of pauperism'.[38] Both the solutions evolved by Robert Owen and the statutory poor tax were globally rejected as 'Communist'.[39] When the Centralverein was founded in connection with the Zollverein exhibition of 1844 a nationalistic concept of the Fatherland played a large part in its inception, focusing on the forces and traditions inherent in the German people to heal social ills. Despite the use of the term 'association', which was then fashionable, the establishment of these social organisations was seen as a continuance of the older co-operative tradition of the Middle Ages and the early modern age. The attempt by Frederick William IV to revive the Order of the Swan, a medieval order of Mary, in 1843/4, may be seen as a particularly extreme and curious example of this.[40] The guild social institutions, journeymen's shops and so on were still well known forms of co-operative assurance and they played an important part in the craftsmen's agitation against freedom of trade. It was natural for the German social reformers to build on these structures.[41]

But in the disillusionment after the failure of the revolution of 1848, and especially under the impact of new and more detailed reports on the situation in England, the old stereotypes re-emerged. The French

> always proceed from the general and abstract truth and search — how often in vain! — for the practical and concrete, while the English ... always look only at the practical and concrete and often do not notice that they have the general truth which they hate so much caught up in it after all.[42]

And so English attempts to cope with social problems played an increasingly important role in the publications of the Centralverein after 1851. Clearly stimulus came from the fact that the Prussian Foreign Minister, von Bülow, had received from his ambassador to London, von Bunsen, a wealth of material on the English legislation of 1850 on friendly societies, which he handed on to the Minister of Trade, von der Heydt, and the Minister for Home Affairs, von Manteuffel. In February 1851 von der Heydt[43] sent all the material to the Board of the Centralverein; in his accompanying letter he describes the English legislation as 'the result of many different and detailed discussions with competent persons', which deserved careful consideration in Prussia as well. In this way the Centralverein acquired comprehensive information on the friendly societies. However, it did not see itself as fulfilling a similar function but rather compared its role with that of the statistical and scientific societies which were a particular feature of England, and 'whose patriotic activities have been partly directed to the education of the people and partly to innovative legislation and the administration of their country'.[44] Nevertheless the organisation and experience of the various friendly societies were of great interest to the Centralverein because the local organisations for the welfare of the working class which were associated with it used very similar means to improve the position of lower classes.

The English legislation of 1850 was comprehensive, having as its purpose 'to consolidate and amend the laws relating to Friendly Societies'.[45] The Prussian liberal social reformers not only gained insight into the history — which then went back fifty years — of British legislation on friendly societies, but could also recognise the characteristic differences which, with all the similarity of the various socio-political instruments, especially the diverse aid funds, still existed in this sphere between the two countries.

The differences were the result both of different traditions and of differing degrees of maturity in industrial society. As mutual assurance institutions for workers the friendly societies, although they were so numerous and followed 'many different views and interests',[46] all developed from the same idea: they were, despite the fact that persons from the upper and middle classes could be members, first and foremost self-help organisations for the workers[47] and thus as the beginning and expression of growing class consciousness were often in opposition to the employers.[48] This can be seen especially during the first two decades of the nineteenth century, when they repeatedly formed or financed cells of strike movements.[49] As external security, the friendly societies had, since 1793, a legislative framework which was continuously developed. State supervision and control of the societies had been established to protect the fee-paying members of those societies which registered.[50] The result of this principle of voluntary registration with restraint on the part of the state over all the details of internal organisation was the lack of any — or indeed any sign of — centralisation of all these individual activities. So what the Prussian social reformers saw was an extremely varied and rather confusing picture. It must also be remembered that the movement of the co-operative societies (consumer societies, building societies and loan associations) had split off from the friendly societies and that the trade unions were gaining in importance all the time. There were also the Workers' Orders, which were similar to the Freemasons' lodges. In addition to the expansion of their own system of support, they were aiming to create a particular form of comradeship among their members through social activities and education. Some of them had over a thousand independent local lodges.[51] To the Prussian social reformers the border between the purely charitable institutions and the militant workers' organisations seemed too fluid for imitation of the English development to seem desirable. Moreover — apart from their fundamental belief in the necessity for harmonious interaction between all the social forces in joint organisations — at this time they were of the opinion that the workers in Prussia were not yet ready for independent associations,[52] but needed to be brought to responsible action with regard for the general good through guidance by the middle class. All this confirmed the Central Association for the Well-being of the Working Class in its belief that its own function was not only to be the head of an ordered hierarchy of all movements to social reform but also to act as peace-maker and intermediary between the various social classes. It seemed most likely that a 'bourgeois attitude' could be created in the working class through co-operative action in associations. Here much could be learned from the English co-operative movement — and in such associations the support of bourgeois circles could best be gained, especially in the initial phases.

To make the Prussian public aware of the possibilities of such a procedure and win friends for the concept of associations, the Central-verein had to publicise the English experience and at the same time make it known what conclusions it drew from this. To this end the Verein organised public lectures and discussions in addition to its publications. There were seven of these in Berlin alone between the end of 1850 and the end of 1852, three of which were devoted to British institutions which were of importance for social policy and one to the Belgian model workshops. A major role was played by the two lectures by Victor Aimé Huber, who knew England well. His lectures opened the series and were decidedly programmatic: he first outlined the British practice of associations in general and then went into the co-operative workers' associations in great detail.[53] The third lecture on the English scene, which was given by Rudolf Gneist in September 1852, dealt with the bath and washing facilities for workers in Britain organised on a co-operative basis.[54]

From now on the subject of the British associations and the many different forms these took can be found in most of the publications by the Centralverein, particularly as Hermann Schulze-Delitzsch, a member of the association, began to put some of these ideas into practice in Germany and the Centralverein began to propagate both distributive and productive associations as the most important means of improving the condition of the working class. I cannot go into detail here, but the main focus of attention in England was on the credit and consumer goods societies (Kredit- und Konsumassoziationen) and after the mid-fifties the housing co-operatives, and finally, in the second half of the sixties, cases of 'industrial partnership' in the form of worker participation in profits and the attempts, for instance by Mundella, an entrepreneur in Nottingham, to cut down the risk of strikes through arbitration courts.[55] In this connection an important innovative idea emerged for the first time in the discussions in the Centralverein, but it was not until very much later that it was realised in wage agreements: the idea that strikes could be prevented 'if the employer succeeded in obtaining an agreement which secured the services of the workers for a longer period, which in turn would only be possible through fixed and binding agreements on wages over a longer period'.[56]

Together with these subjects reports on the effects of the British law of settlement and the Poor Laws, and of the legislation on friendly societies, played an important role. There was more detailed information on the situation of working women, the successes of some organisations like the Rochdale pioneers and developments in education, and so on. All the discussion which resulted from the comparisons between England and Germany and the insight these brought into the problems of the emerging industrial society was determined by the conviction that it was not the relations between capital and labour which was causing problems and conflicts but a distorted relationship between capitalists and workers. It was not the system which was wrong: the reason for the social distress was thought to lie in the inadequacy of those using it.[57] It was here that a comprehensive social reform must begin. The social role of the state was to guarantee personal and economic freedom, which was 'in essential and inseparable interaction with the obligation to self-help and a sense of responsibility on the part of the working class'.[58] From this point of view state intervention in England, despite the freedom of the individual there, seemed to the German liberal social reformers even after the reform of the English Poor Laws a frightening and at the same time highly instructive example:[59] out-relief for the poor had paralysed the workers; the system of giving relief to poor families on a sliding scale according to the prevailing prices of food demoralised the workers and made them 'dependents of poor relief' and this 'encouraged idleness, carelessness, vice and mass poverty'.[60] The mentality so produced was deeply rooted and determined the attitude of many workers even after the reform of the Poor Laws. Deliberately rejecting any form of state steering, state concessions or monopoly or any other form of state intervention in the 'prevailing law of free competition',[61] Wilhelm Adolf Lette, for many years Chairman of the Centralverein, spoke of a 'state co-operative', which he regarded as the ultimate goal of social development and in which the law of free competition would benefit all classes of the people equally, in so far as the complete personal and economic freedom of all its members was ensured.[62] For the same reason both

Lette and Schulze-Delitzsch rejected any form of state support, for co-operatives as well.

Although this was more or less the official line of the Centralverein, there is evidence that opinions on the social role of the state diverged widely among its members, who included such different spirits as Victor Aimé Huber and Rudolf Gneist, Karl Rodbertus and Hermann Schulze-Delitzsch, Eduard Flottwell, who was President of Brandenburg, and Friedrich Harkort, and that there was intense discussion of this, which again emphasises the element of communication and learning in the Verein. To illustrate these differences of opinion, which I think are important particularly in connection with the question of the roots of modern ideas on the social state, I shall finally consider briefly the controversy which developed at the end of 1852 between Rudolf Gneist, who was Chairman of the Centralverein after the death of Lette, from 1868 to 1895, and Karl Rodbertus, for many years the committee member of the Verein responsible for Pomerania.

At its Board meeting on 8 September 1852 the Centralverein had decided to devote more attention to the question of hygiene among the workers.[63] It took up the idea which had already been expressed by Robert Mohl in his *Police Studies* (*Polizeiwissenschaft*) in 1832[64] and by others, including doctors to the poor in England and France, that improved hygiene for the workers would not only prevent disease but that health care, including better living conditions and personal cleanliness, would also be the basis for 'spiritual well-being' and a higher degree of morality; hygiene would help to make the working class 'more satisfied, stronger and capable of greater efforts', as the English social reformers argued.[65] In response to this Rudolf Gneist gave the lecture I have already mentioned, in the autumn of 1852, in which he described the public wash and bath houses for the working class in England and produced a wealth of examples and statistical material.[66] He told his audience that at the instigation of such men as the Bishop of London and Sir Henry Dukinfield, the clergyman, an association had been formed in London in 1844 to promote and partici- pate in the building of bath and wash houses in London and other cities. Through his agitation Sir Henry finally achieved parliamentary legislation in 1846, empowering the communities, if there was a two- thirds majority, to treat the construction of these facilities as a common responsibility and finance the initial outlay by a supplement on the poor tax.[67] The running costs were to be met from the charges for use and the baths and wash houses were to have two classes: the more expensive first-class baths were to enable more prosperous persons to share some of the costs for the poorer class. In his lecture Gneist praised this as exemplary for the work of an institution which, once initiated, would be self-financing and bring great material advantages and improved hygiene for the working class.

In a sharp reply Rodbertus then accused Gneist of not clarifying the issue but confusing it.[68] In fact the public bath and wash-houses and the relevant Act of Parliament proved the opposite of Gneist's argument. With legislation giving the state a function which private enterprise appeared incapable or unwilling to fulfil, and with the establishment of two classes, the first of which was to bear some of the costs for the second, the project was the beginning of state socialism, as the state 'was enforcing through a majority decision the richer to bear the costs of amenities for the poorer'.[69] Pursuing an argument which I have already mentioned in reference to the earlier difference of opinion between Rodbertus and Quentin, Rodbertus asks whether this devious route could not be shortened: 'If the more prosperous members of society have subsequently to hand over some of their wealth to the poor, can a way not be found to give to the poor in the first place, or prevent the assets from being taken from them?'[70] He tries to make it clear to Gneist that social institutions in a liberal state, i.e. what he calls 'free state socialism', are ultimately steps on the way to state socialism, and that the case in question in England illustrates this.[71]

This highly illuminating controversy on the social role of the state between Gneist and Rodbertus, which has been largely overlooked by research so far, continued, with repeated comparisons between England and Germany, in the ensuing years.[72] Gneist criticised the beginnings of state socialism, or the 'social state', in England and France because this would result in each person being concerned only with his own occupation and pleasure and ultimately not with the state at all.[73] He advocated instead a combination of wealth and office in a community constructed on co-operative lines. This would be based on the freedom of the individual and correspond to the 'most essential part of our national character' and enable the individual to invest in it his strength, time, life and health. In this structure he envisages the upper classes as taking a special responsibility for the whole and for the lower classes in particular by taking honorary offices in the state, the local authorities and regional bodies.

After this account of two divergent views on the social role of the state in the modernisation process and the internal structure of society, in which we see the beginnings of a controversy which has lasted until the current discussion on the solution of the 'new social question',[74] let me draw a brief conclusion: at all stages of the social learning process in the early phase of industrialisation in Germany under the influence of Prussia, for which the work of the Centralverein is exemplary, the development in Britain played a major part. However, it would be wrong to speak of a simple teacher-pupil relation and indeed the relation between England and Germany should never be seen as a one-way street.[75] More comprehensive approaches to social theory, such as the work of Robert Owen and the Chartists and trade unions with their programmes and demands were at best regarded by the German social reformers of the liberal bourgeoisie as examples to be avoided at all costs;[76] but practical reform measures in England, particularly the co-operative societies, were discussed down to the minutest detail, although they were never simply copied. Altogether the German social reformers aimed to go their own way and avoid what they saw as the English mistakes.[77] The best way to characterise the German attitude to English and French socio-political developments in the period and problem areas we are concerned with is to say that it was a self-confident reception, a reception which was certainly creative and not simply imitative, but a reception which must also be seen as part of a comprehensive process of learning within the framework of the specific development of Prussian Germany on the way to the modern industrial state.[78]

Notes

1. Cf. e.g. Alexander Gerschenkron, *Economic Backwardness in Historical Perspective* (New York, 1965) (2), partially reprinted in German as 'Wirtschaftliche Rückständigkeit in historischer Perspektive' in R. Braun *et al.* (eds.) *Industrielle Revolution. Wirtschaftliche Aspekte* (Cologne/Berlin, 1972), pp. 59-78. Cf. also Hans-Ulrich Wehler, *Modernisierungstheorie und Geschichte* (Göttingen, 1975), esp. p. 49.
2. Karl Marx, *Das Kapital*, Foreword, quoted from *Marx-Engels-Werke* (East Berlin, 1972), vol. 23, p. 12.
3. Gerschenkron, *Economic Backwardness*, p. 60.
4. Cf. Reinhard Bendix, 'Modernisierung und soziale Ungleichheit' in W. Fischer (ed.), *Wirtschafts- und sozialgeschichtliche Probleme der frühen Industrialisierung* (publications by the Historische Kommission in Berlin, vol. 1) (Berlin, 1968), pp. 179-246, esp. pp. 222 ff.
5. Cf. e.g. Martin Schumacher, *Auslandsreisen deutscher Unternehmer 1750-1851 unter besonderer Berücksichtigung von Rheinland und Westfalen* (Cologne, 1968); Wolfhard Weber, 'Industriespionage als technologischer Transfer in der Frühindustrialisierung Deutschlands', *Technikgeschichte*, vol. 42 (1975), pp. 287-305.

46   *English Social Policy*

6. Bendix, 'Modernisierung', p. 224.

7. Cf. Karl Erich Born, *Sozialpolitische Probleme und Bestrebungen in Deutschland von 1848 bis zur Bismarckschen Sozialgesetzgebung*, reprinted in H.J. Varain (ed.), *Interessenverbände in Deutschland* (Cologne, 1973), pp. 72-84, esp. p. 74. For one of the earliest examinations in detail of the English situation with regard to its social aspects see the essay by Robert Mohl, *Die gesellschaftlichen Nachteile der Industrialisierung* (1835), reprinted in F. Fürstenberg, *Industriesoziologie*, 1, 2nd edn (Neuwied Berlin, 1966), pp. 273-310.

8. First appeared Leipzig, 1845.

9. Gustav Mayer, *Friedrich Engels. Eine Biographie* (reprinted Ullstein-Buch 3113/4) (Frankfurt/Main, 1975), vol. 1, p. 174.

10. Hans J. Teuteberg, 'Zeitgenössische deutsche Reflexionen über die Rolle des Faktors Arbeit in den frühen Phasen der britischen Industrialisierung (1750-1850)' in H. Kellenbenz (ed.), *Wirtschaftspolitik und Arbeitsmarkt* (Vienna, 1974), pp. 238-70, cf. esp. Teuteberg's Habilitation thesis which will soon appear in print. For early criticism of Engels' work see Bruno Hildebrand, *Die Nationalökonomie der Gegenwart und Zukunft* (Frankfurt/Main, 1948), vol. 1, and the essay mentioned in note 77 below in *Die Gegenwart*, p. 469 f.

11. Günter Wiswede and Thomas Kutsch, *Sozialer Wandel* (Darmstadt, 1978), p. 106 f.

12. Following W. Kirsch, quoted by Otto Neuloh, 'Zum Bezugsrahmen von sozialer Innovation und sozialem Konflikt' in O. Neuloh (ed.), *Soziale Innovation und sozialer Konflikt* (Göttingen, 1977), p. 24.

13. Quoted from Wiswede and Kutsch, *Sozialer Wandel*, p. 181.

14. *Friedrich Perthes Leben nach dessen schriftlichen und mündlichen Mitteilungen, aufgezeichnet von C. Th. Perthes*, 4th edn (2 vols., Gotha, 1861), p. 95.

15. Cf. Dietrich Hilger, 'Fabrik' (article) in O. Brunner *et al.* (eds.), *Geschichtliche Grundbegriffe* (Stuttgart, 1975), vol. 2, pp. 229-52.

16. Cf. Teuteberg, 'Zeitgenössische', pp. 243 and 264.

17. Cf. e.g. Michael Vester, *Die Entstehung des Proletariats als Lernprozess. Die Entstehung antikapitalistischer Theorie und Praxis in England 1792-1848* (Frankfurt/Main, 1972) (2), pp. 244 ff.

18. Quoted from Karl Rodbertus, *Die Forderungen der arbeitenden Klassen*, A. Skalweit (ed.) (Sozialökonomische Texte, vol. 5) (Frankfurt/Main, 1946), p. 9. The *Augsburger Allgemeine Zeitung* rejected the article on the grounds that the danger it drew attention to 'was not to be found in our social organisation', quoted from Carl Jantke, *Der vierte Stand* (Freiburg, 1955), p. 82.

19. Rodbertus, *Forderungen*, p. 22.

20. Karl Quentin, *Ein Wort zur Zeit der Arbeiter-Koalitionen* (Düsseldorf, 1840).

21. Ibid., pp. 22 ff.

22. Ibid., pp. 10 and 17.

23. Ibid., p. 2.

24. Rodbertus, *Forderungen*, p. 19.

25. Ibid., pp. 21ff.

26. Cf. Schlomo Na'aman, *Lassalle* (Hannover, 1970) and the correspondence between Lassalle and Rodbertus, Adolph Wagner (ed.) (Berlin, 1878).

27. Karl-Georg Faber, *Die Rheinlande zwischen Restauration und Revolution* (Wiesbaden, 1966), p. 424 f.

28. Cf. basically Reinhart Koselleck, *Preussen zwischen Reform und Revolution* (Stuttgart, 1975) (2).

29. Cf. the file ZStA I, Rep. 76, 11, Sekt. 1, Gen. 1., vol. 1, esp. the answers by Presidents Schaper of the province Rhein and Vincke from Westfalen, 41-4 and 335-8.

30. *Elberfelder Zeitung*, no. 174 of 25 June 1844.
31. In *Mitteilungen des Centralvereins für das Wohl der arbeitenden Klassen*, first issue, August 1848, pp. 80 f.
32. Cf. e.g. the diary entry by Varnhagen von Ense after visiting the exhibition on 29 August 1844; *Tagebücher von K.A. Varnhagen von Ense*, vol. 2 (Leipzig, 1861), p. 350.
33. Cf. Karl Marx, who stressed in a newspaper article of 7 Aug. 1844 that the German bourgeoisie had certainly recognised the general significance of the Silesian uprising: 'All the *liberal* German papers . . . are bubbling over with the organisation of labour, the reform of society, criticism of monopoly and competition, etc. All as a result of the labour movements.' (*Marx-Engels-Werke*, vol. 1, p. 403.)
34. In greater detail so far only by Nora Stiebel: 'Der "Zentralverein für das Wohl der arbeitenden Klassen" im vormärzlichen Preussen', typewritten thesis, Heidelberg, 1922. Cf. also the monograph I shall shortly publish on the Centralverein.
35. Cf. the programme of the Centralverein printed in vol. 1 of the *Mitteilungen* quoted in note 31.
36. The Prussian Ambassador in London, von Bunsen, had a strong influence here. Cf. Christian Karl Josias Freiherr von Bunsen, *Aus seinen Briefen und nach eigener Erinnerung geschildert von seiner Witwe*, F. Nippold (ed.) (2 vols., Leipzig, 1869).
37. Eighth issue of the *Mitteilungen* (2 vols., 1849/50), pp. 136 ff.
38. E.g. Victor Aimé Huber, *Reisebriefe aus England im Sommer 1854* (Hamburg, 1855), p. 153.
39. Ibid.
40. Heinrich von Treitschke, *Deutsche Geschichte im Neunzehnten Jahrhundert*, 5. Teil (Leipzig, 1927), pp. 241 ff; cf. also Jantke, *Der vierte Stand*, p. 67.
41. One example is socio-political activity by the Prussian 'Seehandlung' (banking-house of the Prussian state) under Christian von Rother. Cf. Hansjoachim Henning, 'Preussische Sozialpolitik im Vormärz?' *VSWG*, vol. 52 (1965), pp. 485-539.
42. Letter by Rodbertus to Gneist, 28 Oct. 1852. Original in ZStA II, Rep. 92, estate of Rudolf Gneist, MS. p. 9 f.
43. Cf. the file ZStA II, Rep. 120, D XXLL/10 No. 2.
44. *Mitteilungen*, 8th issue (2nd vol., 1849/50), p. 190 f.
45. The Consolidation Act (13 & 14 Vict., c. 115); cf. J.M. Baernreither, *Die englischen Arbeiterverbände und ihr Recht* (Tübingen, 1886), esp. p. 308.
46. Baernreither, *Arbeiterverbände*, p. 223. Baernreither states that between 1793 and 1867 altogether 38,315 friendly societies were registered (p. 222). Vester, *Entstehung*, gives about 700,000 members of these societies for the year 1816 (p. 239).
47. In Prussia during the early industrialisation phase there were similar activities only in 1848/50: the short-lived, quickly suppressed by the reaction, self-help institutions of Workers' Brotherhood (Arbeiterverbrüderung) under Stephan Born; cf. Frolinde Balser, *Sozial-Demokratie 1848-49* (2 vols, Stuttgart, 1962).
48. Baernreither, *Arbeiterverbände*, p. 123; but there were also 'patronised societies', i.e. those founded by clergymen, landowners, etc.
49. Vester, *Entstehung*, p. 239.
50. Baernreither, *Arbeiterverbände*, pp. 302 ff. Cf. also W.T.C. Blake and J.M. Moore, *Friendly Societies* (Cambridge, 1951), pp. 1-9; and Adolf M. Birke, 'Voluntary Associations — Aspekte gesellschaftlicher Selbstorganisation im frühindustriellen England', *Der Staat*, special issue no. 2: *Gesellschaftliche*

Stukturen als Verfassungsproblem (Berlin, 1978), pp. 79-91.
51. Baernreither, *Arbeiterverbände* pp. 206 ff.
52. It was only the re-emergence of the labour movement at the beginning of the 1860s which brought – at first only hesitant – recognition of the right of workers to coalition by the Centralverein. Cf. the two articles by Günter Traut-mann ('Gewerkschaften ohne Streikrech') and Ulrich Engelhardt ('Gewerkschaftliche Interessenvertretung als "Menschenrecht" ') in U. Engelhardt *et al.* (eds.), *Soziale Bewegung und politische Verfassung (Industrielle Welt*, special issue, Festschrift for W. Conze) (Stuttgart, 1976), pp. 472-537 and 538-98.
53. Victor Aimé Huber, *Über Associationen mit besonderer Beziehung zu England* (Berlin, 1851); and *Über die cooperativen Arbeiterassociationen in England* (Berlin, 1852). On Huber's conclusions from his experiences in England cf. Jantke, *Der vierte Stand*, p. 68 f.
54. Printed in *Mitteilungen*, 15th issue (3rd vol., 1851/2), pp. 4-40. According-ing to Eugen Schiffer (*Rudolf von Gneist* (Berlin, 1929), p. 52) the Centralverein had expressly requested Gneist before he went to England in the summer of 1851 to gather information on hygiene measures in England.
55. *Der Arbeiterfreund*, vol. 8 (1870), pp. 164 ff. and vol. 9 (1871), pp. 311 ff.
56. *Der Arbeiterfreund*, vol. 9 (1871), p. 310.
57. David Born, the merchant, for instance, in the third lecture held by the Centralverein, 'Über die Freiheit des Gewerbes und die Wirksamkeit des Kapitals auf die Lage der arbeitenden Klassen' (Berlin, 1851), p. 20 f.
58. (Wilhelm Adolf) Lette, 'Die Arbeiter- insbesondere die Lohnfrage in Verbindung mit der Gesetzgebung und freien Konkurrenz', *Der Arbeiterfreund*, vol. 2 (1864), p. 6.
59. Ibid., p. 5.
60. Ibid., p. 21.
61. Ibid., p. 35.
62. Ibid., p. 32.
63. *Mitteilungen*, 15th issue (vol. 3, 1851/2), pp. 1-3.
64. Robert Mohl, *Die Polizei-Wissenschaft nach den Grundsätzen des Rechts-staates* (Tübingen, 1832) vol. 1, pp. 132 ff. and 162 ff.
65. Quoted from Schiffer, *Gneist* (cf. note 54), p. 6.
66. Cf. note 54 above.
67. Sir Henry Dukinfield's Act 9 & 10 Vict. c. 74.
68. Letter from Rodbertus to Gneist of 28 Oct. 1852 (see note 42).
69. Ibid., MS., p. 6.
70. Ibid., MS., p. 10.
71. Ibid., MS., p. 12.
72. In the papers of Rodbertus and Gneist in the ZStA II there are several letters from this correspondence from 1852 to 1867. Only Erich Hahn in his thesis on Gneist makes some mention of the correspondence. Cf. Erich Hahn, 'Rudolf Gneist and the Prussian Rechtsstaat: 1862-78', *The Journal of Modern History*, vol. 49 (1977), On-Demand Supplement, D 1361-81, esp. D 1369.
73. Gneist to Rodbertus, letter of 28 Jan. 1860; ZStA II, Rep. 92, Rodbertus papers.
74. Cf. on the current discussion the two issues of the supplement to the weekly *Das Parlament – aus Politik und Zeitgeschichte*, B 10/78 of 11 Mar. 1978 and B 39/78 of 30 Sept. 1978; also Martin Pfaff and Hubert Voigtländer (eds.), *Sozialpolitik im Wandel. Von der selektiven zur integrierten Sozialpolitik* (Bonn, 1978).
75. Cf. Hans-Joachim Braun, *Technologische Beziehungen zwischen Deutschland und England von der Mitte des 17. bis zum Ausgang des 18. Jahrhunderts*

(Düsseldorf, 1974).
76. Cf. note 38 above on Huber.
77. This is especially clear from an essay entitled 'Die sociale Bewegung und der Socialismus in England' in *Die Gegenwart* (Leipzig, 1849), vol. 2, pp. 464 f. and 486 f.
78. As, for instance, Teuteberg, as one of the conclusions of the work mentioned in note 10, which is still in preparation.

3 THE CRISIS OF POOR RELIEF IN ENGLAND, 1860-1890

M.E. Rose

The Poor Law and its Historians

> If there is little pomp in this pageant, there yet may be discovered the ebb and flow of the tide of national prosperity, the waxing and waning of social and economic systems, the rise and decline of habits of social thought and methods of social control.[1]

As a young postgraduate, beginning research on the nineteenth-century Poor Law system nearly twenty years ago, I suspected that few of my colleagues in other branches of social science would have accepted H.L. Beales' claim for Poor Law studies. History to them was quaint and interesting, but scarcely social scientific. As for Poor Law history, that had surely been 'done', as the hefty volumes of Sidney and Beatrice Webb's works on the college library shelves testified.[2] The history of the English Poor Law was a familiar one. In the late eighteenth and early nineteenth centuries, the social disruption caused by rapid industrialisation and by the long-drawn-out wars with Revolutionary and Napoleonic France placed intolerable strains upon the old parochial system of poor relief. Parish officers and magistrates, disturbed by the sufferings of poor labourers and alarmed at the prospect of social unrest, granted doles of poor relief to 'make up' inadequate wages to a subsistence standard, the so-called 'Speenhamland' system of poor relief. These haphazard methods, however, brought only increased pauperism, rising poor rates and further unrest. Thus between 1832 and 1834, the Poor Law was subjected to the scrutiny of a Royal Commission of Enquiry which recommended drastic changes in the system. These were implemented by the Poor Law Amendment Act of 1834, the New Poor Law, which grouped parishes into Unions under Boards of Guardians to provide a larger local unit of administration, created a central authority, the Poor Law Commission, to control the local administrators, and put forward the idea of 'less eligibility' as the basic principle of poor relief. Under the terms of this principle, the able-bodied poor were to be offered relief only in a 'well regulated' workhouse where conditions would be less attractive than those for the independent labourer outside. This would, it was hoped, force the poor to fend for themselves rather than depend supinely on the Poor Law. Thus the nineteenth-century poor were imprisoned, like little Oliver Twist, in a grim workhouse until they were freed in the early twentieth century by the alternative provisions of the infant welfare state in the shape of old age pensions, sickness and unemployment insurance and the like. It was a pantomime in which Edwin Chadwick played the Demon King, with Lord Beveridge as the Fairy Godmother and Mr Lloyd George as Prince Charming.[3]

Since my apprentice days, of course, the script of the Poor Law pantomime has been considerably rewritten. Detailed, quantitative researches into the last years of the old Poor Law system have placed the 'Speenhamland' or 'allowance' system into its proper context in relation to the local economy. In this light, it appears to have been very far from the widespread, demoralising and ruinous influence which the inquiry of 1832-4 and many later historians believed.[4] Work on the New Poor Law of 1834 and its implementation at local level has shown that there was more continuity than discontinuity between the old system and the new, and has reduced the practical, if not the theoretical, importance of the New Poor Law in the history of English social policy.[5]

Yet, despite the importance of this work in modifying the melodramatic, simplistic version of English Poor Law history, I am still conscious of a rather static view of the nineteenth-century Poor Law as established in and after 1834. The welfare state is seen as developing from an increasing reaction to the cruelties of the Poor Law system, by the gradual establishment of alternative institutions of welfare which had no connection with the Poor Law. Alternatively, the Poor Law itself can be seen as being subject to what H.L. Beales called 'leftward deviations', setting up institutions which were to become the basis of welfare systems contradictory to the philosophy of the 1834 system. Poor Law medical relief is seen as one such. O.R. Macdonagh writes:

> In one area the New Poor Law had almost from the start turned upon its tracks and developed in a fashion alien to its origin and object alike. This was ill health. Here the rudiments of a free, non-pauperising national service gradually developed.

A notion echoed by M.W. Flinn when he argues that the Act of 1867 for establishing separate infirmaries outside the workhouses in London 'set the poor law medical service on the road that was to lead hesitatingly but inevitably to Bevan's National Health Service of the 1940s'.[6]

Whilst I am not opposed to the use of history to explain or criticise present-day institutions, this linear approach, this Whig theory of welfare, tends to develop the uncritical assumptions about the welfare state which Richard Titmuss has complained about.[7] To look for the origins of the welfare state in the nineteenth century Poor Law is to view it through the wrong end of the telescope. We must see the Poor Law in its nineteenth-century context, looking at the aims and ideals of its reformers and administrators, the reactions of its clientele, its connection with other areas of nineteenth-century life, and not as a staging post on the road to somewhere else, or as an essentially corrupt institution from which a few healthy pieces can be cut because they seem to foreshadow modern systems of welfare.

It was with these criticisms of existing writing on the nineteenth-century Poor Law and social policy in mind that I became interested in the development of the Poor Law system in the mid-nineteenth century and especially in the decades of the 1860s and the 1870s. This is a period often seen by historians of social policy as a rather flat one between the excitements of the 1830s and 1840s and the new departures of the 1880s and 1890s. I was first attracted to this period by Gareth Stedman Jones' book, *Outcast London*, which portrayed the 1860s and early 1870s as a crucial turning-point in middle-class philanthropic attitudes.[8] More recently, I was encouraged by E.P. Hennock's paper 'arguing for a rephasing of the history of social theory that emphasizes the late 1860s and the late 1890s as important periods of innovation'.[9] It is with these arguments in mind that I wish to present a tentative model which sees the 1860s as a period of crisis in English poor relief, a crisis which provided the opportunity for a radical restructuring of the system. This restructuring was a major step towards achieving the ideals of the 1834 reformers, particularly those of Edwin Chadwick. Thus, at the risk of reintroducing the flavour of melodrama I have earlier criticised, I am arguing that the New Poor Law was a creation of the 1860s and 1870s rather than of the 1830s.

The 1834 Plan and its Failure

Before discussing the crisis of the 1860s and its results, it is necessary to look briefly at the ideas of the reformers of 1834 as set out in the

Report of the Royal Commission on the Poor Laws, the work of Edwin Chadwick and Nassau Senior.[10] The *Report* put forward the idea of the well regulated workhouse as the only type of relief to be offered to the able-bodied poor. This would supply a mechanistic, self-acting test of destitution on the Benthamite pain/pleasure principle. It would force the rural labourer to be free of the low-wage-paying farmer and the paternalistic squire, and, by sending him off in search of an independent livelihood, would end the feudalism of the English countryside. Only a residuum of the incorrigibly idle would be left behind and these could be reinvigorated or scared away by workhouse discipline. The swamp of pauperism would be drained and the workhouse master, as in Harriet Martineau's tale, could lock the door of the empty workhouse and throw away the key.[11]

This was of course a grossly over-simplified solution to a complex problem — a solution arrived at by the use of highly selective evidence. It was, as R.H. Tawney described it, 'a brilliant, influential, wildly unhistorical' report.[12] Furthermore, it tended to concentrate on one problem, that of the underemployed, able-bodied farm labourer, paying less attention to the numerically greater problem of the sick, aged and orphaned poor or to the emerging problem of industrial unemployment.

Despite the obvious defects of the *Report*, however, there are indications within it of a less simplistic approach to the problem of pauperism. The recommendations that medical relief be exempt from the workhouse test, that separate institutions be provided for the aged poor and for children, that a special inquiry into apprenticeship be set on foot, and that schemes of useful employment be found for the able-bodied poor are all indicative of this.[13] It may well be, as Finer has argued, that the less sensational but more radical recommendation of the Royal Commission, that a central authority be set up to issue orders to the local authorities on the administration of poor relief, was seen by Chadwick as its most crucial one.[14] Once the political in-fighting over the Poor Law Amendment Bill was over, the new central authority could carry out more detailed investigation into difficult questions like settlement or rating, and design and supervise the implementation of collateral institutions for those to whom 'less eligibility' was irrelevant.

In fact the new central authority for poor relief established by the Act of 1834, the Poor Law Commission, was lacking in the powers which Chadwick had desired. The new local authorities, the Boards of Guardians, demanded and obtained, with or without central approval, discretionary powers over poor relief. They often continued to relieve applicants with haphazard doles of outdoor relief, baulked at the cost of building a new workhouse, or built a single institution of the 'general mixed' variety to cater for all classes of paupers. Popular resistance to the New Poor Law in the late 1830s made the government reluctant to allow the Poor Law Commission to force the pace of change, and the violent quarrels between Edwin Chadwick, as its Secretary, and the members of the Commission did little to aid the smooth functioning of the central authority.[15] The complex legal and financial problems of the Poor Law system remained unamended, or, if reform was attempted, as in the case of the laws of settlement in 1846, it was badly bungled, thus arousing further resentment and suspicion.[16] The rather ramshackle system of poor relief, which barely survived the storms of the late 1840s, bore a strong resemblance in many districts to the system in operation before 1834, and scarcely deserved the title of the New Poor Law.

The Crisis of the 1860s

Between 1860 and the early 1870s, the English poor relief system was subjected to an almost continual series of shocks which exposed its basic weaknesses and forced a searching re-examination,

London Pauperism

Trade depression together with a particularly severe winter in 1860-1 brought acute distress to large numbers of casual and seasonal workers in the trades of East London. As the number of applications for poor relief mounted, there were allegations that the Poor Law system had broken down, and private philanthropy rushed in to fill the vacuum.[17] Similar crises in the winters of 1867-8 and 1868-9 brought an even greater increase in applications for outdoor relief, and a growing fear that an unprincipled Poor Law together with indiscriminate private charity was creating pauperism on a scale akin to that in the 'Speenhamland' counties before 1834 (Figure 3.1).[18]

The Lancashire Cotton Famine

Following immediately on the heels of the first London crisis came the rising unemployment and distress caused by the cutting off of raw material supplies to the cotton industry as a result of the American Civil War. Rising applications for poor relief in the cotton districts in

Figure 3.1: Pauperism in London, 1850-1908 (paupers exclusive of insane and casual or vagrant poor per 1,000 of population)

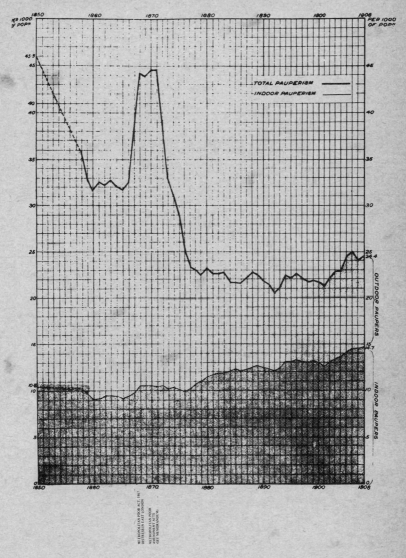

Source: Local Government Board, *Public Health and Social Conditions*, Cd. 4671 (1909), section IV, Chart 1.

Figure 3.2: Pauperism in England and Wales, Scotland and Ireland, 1850-1908 (average daily number of paupers of all classes relieved per 1,000 of population)

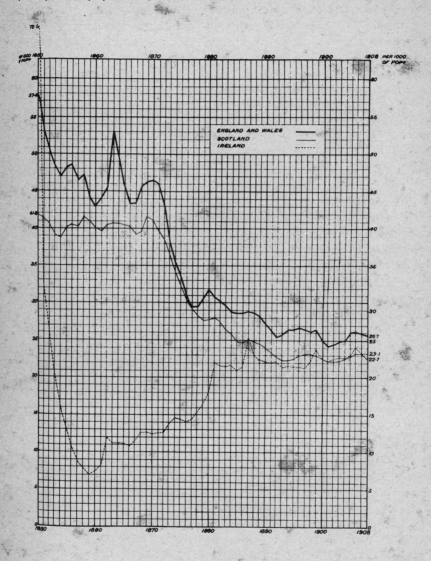

Source: Local Government Board, *Public Health and Social Conditions*, Chart 2.

1862 reached a peak of over 270,000 in December of that year (Figure 3.2). This constituted a rise of some 300 per cent in the numbers on relief as compared to a normal year, with a consequent increase in poor rates from 1s in the pound or less to more than 10s in the pound.[19] Demands of this magnitude placed a severe strain on the Poor Law system and, as in London, private charitable funds were raised to provide an alternative source of relief. From the middle of 1862, however, all charitable funds except those raised locally were channelled through a Central Relief Committee which was able to impose more stringent conditions for the granting of relief on local relief committees than the Poor Law Board, the central authority for poor relief, was able to impress upon local Boards of Guardians.[20] The Poor Law Board sent one of its inspectors, H.B. Farnall, who, as Metropolitan District Inspector, had been at the centre of the controversy over relief in East London in 1860-1, to Lancashire to act as a liaison officer between the Central Relief Committee and the Poor Law Board.[21] Not only were relief efforts more carefully organised in Lancashire than in London, but it was also recognised that the unemployed Lancashire operative was a more deserving case than the East London pauper, since his distress was obviously due to political causes beyond his control. Despite this, neither Poor Law nor private charity proved adequate to meet a crisis of this magnitude. In the face of growing fears of civil unrest and the demoralisation of the Lancashire worker through dependence on relief, the government passed the Public Works (Manufacturing Districts) Act of 1863, providing cheap loans for local authorities to encourage them to set on foot schemes of paving, draining, sewerage and the like which would provide independent employment for the unemployed.[22]

The Workhouse Infirmaries

The recurrent London crises of the 1860s and the shorter but more severe Lancashire crisis of 1862-4 focused attention on the increasing costs of, and applications for, outdoor relief. In 1865, however, public attention was drawn sharply to the unsatisfactory state of those confined in workhouses, particularly the sick. Dissatisfaction with the state of workhouse sick wards had already been voiced by disgruntled Poor Law Medical Officers, individually or through the medium of the Poor Law Medical Reform Association founded in 1856, and by philanthropists, prominent among whom was Louisa Twining, founder of the Workhouse Visiting Society in 1858.[23] Public opinion was fully roused, however, in 1864 and 1865 following newspaper reports of the deaths of two paupers in the infirmaries of the Holborn and the St Giles work-houses in London. The medical journal, *The Lancet*, feeling it to be necessary that 'public opinion should be fully enlightened and deliber-ately directed', appointed a 'Commission' of three doctors to enquire into the condition of workhouse infirmaries in London. Their reports in the summer of 1865 aroused further anxiety.[24] An Association for the Improvement of Workhouse Infirmaries was formed with the Earl of Caernarvon as its chairman, which, *The Times* remarked, would 'find something very like a fundamental change in our social institu-tions necessary to success'.[25] In face of this pressure. the president of the Poor Law Board ordered an official inquiry which was carried out by the ubiquitous Mr Farnall and Dr Edward Smith, who was appointed as a specialist Medical Inspector to the Poor Law Board in 1866.[26]

The Workhouse Child

Less dramatic than *The Lancet* revelations of the condition of the sick poor in the workhouse, but equally insistent, was the demand in the 1860s for better treatment of the workhouse child. From the 1830s, there had been strong pressure on Boards of Guardians to regard child paupers as a special case who should not be subjected to the rule of 'less eligibility'. The Poor Law Commission, urged on by Assistant Commissioners like James Kay and E.C. Tufnell, had encouraged Poor Law Unions to pool resources and establish large district schools to which children could be sent away from the demoralising atmosphere of the workhouse.[27] The debate as to the relative merits of small work-house schools and larger district schools continued in mid-century, but in the 1860s there was a growing body of opinion critical of both types of institutional treatment. On moral grounds, the critics argued that children raised in institutions were unable to cope with the pres-sures of life outside the walls once they left the institutions to seek an independent livelihood. Thus they soon returned to the workhouse, or worse still, drifted into prostitution or crime and experienced prison life. On physical grounds, it was pointed out that the large 'barrack schools' were breeding grounds for diseases like the eye com-plaint ophthalmia, which spread like wildfire through their young inmates.[28] These criticisms received powerful support in 1873 with the publication of a report to the Local Government Board by its first female Inspector, Jane Elizabeth Senior, spelling out clearly and comprehensively the defects of the 'barrack schools'.[29]

The Effects of the Crisis

Administrative Reorganisation

The first shock to the Poor Law system, the London distress of 1860-1, brought the establishment of a Parliamentary Select Committee under the chairmanship of the President of the Poor Law Board, C.P. Villiers, to 'enquire into the administration of the relief of the poor'.[30] Meeting for the first time in March 1861, the committee remained in existence for three parliamentary sessions and did not produce its final report until 1864. During the three years of its existence, it carried out a searching review of the Poor Law system, and, whilst its final report proved somewhat anodyne, its investigations provided the groundwork for a major administrative restructuring. The chief instrument of this was the Union Chargeability Act of 1865, a complex, dull and much underrated piece of poor relief legislation. The Act's main importance lay in its strengthening of the Poor Law Union at the expense of its constituent parishes. The Union, and not the parish, became the area of Poor Law finance and settlement, thus enabling it to develop into a real administrative community instead of a loose amalgamation of quarrelling member states.[31]

This strengthening of local authority was complemented two years later by legislation making the Poor Law Board a permanent department of state.[32] Previous to this, like its predecessor the Poor Law Commission, it had existed on a temporary basis with its powers renewable by Parliament at five-year intervals. The Board, in this decade, proved a far more active body than the Webbs and other administrative historians have given it credit for.[33] It identified problem areas in the poor relief system and pressed its inspectors for special reports on such topics as vagrancy, workhouse dietaries and workhouse infirmaries.[34] This activity was continued by its successor in 1871, the Local Government Board, with particular emphasis being placed upon policies regarding outdoor relief and pauper education.[35] The Local Government Board was also responsible, through the medium of the Foreign Office, for obtaining a series of reports as to the practice of poor relief in foreign countries which it published separately in 1875.[36] The Poor Law Board and Local Government Board encouraged the system of Poor Law district conferences begun by the Gloucestershire philanthropist T. Barwick Baker in the West Midlands in 1868. The Local Government Board organised a central conference in London in 1871, and by 1875 regular conferences were being held in twelve districts. These were attended by local Guardians, Poor Law officials, the inspectorate and prominent philanthropists. Papers were read and relief problems discussed, with proceedings being published after 1874.[37] The conference system provided an important medium for the exchange of ideas and for effecting closer co-operation between central and local authority, and between the statutory authorities and private philanthropy. Thus the administrative strengthening of the Poor Law system laid the basis for a more confident handling of problems and for more informed investigation and discussion of them than had been the case in the first three decades of the New Poor Law.

The Collaterals

Another result of the crises of the 1860s, particularly of those involving the sick poor and the workhouse child, was the encouragement given to the development of alternative relief institutions which could remove those for whom it was not intended from the influence of the harsh doctrine of 'less eligibility'. The inquiries into the condition of the sick poor in London workhouses led to the passing of the Metropolitan Poor Act of 1867, which provided for the establishment of infirmaries and dispensaries for the poor separate from the workhouse and financed from a common fund to which all Unions in the metropolitan area would contribute.[38] Outside London, no such statutory provision was made, but the Poor Law Board's new medical inspector, Edward Smith, carried out a series of investigations into the provision for the sick in provincial workhouses, and the Poor Law Board urged upon Boards of Guardians the importance of providing better nursing and other facilities for the sick poor in their care.[39] Whilst the response to this was cautious and limited, there is some evidence of a sympathetic attitude on the part of local authorities. In Manchester, the Chorlton Board of Guardians erected pavilion-style wards at their new workhouse, whilst in Liverpool the select vestry agreed to the introduction of trained nurses at the workhouse, a facility which was the more readily agreed to because it was privately financed.[40]

In the case of workhouse children, Boards of Guardians came under strong pressure from critics of institutional relief to adopt the Scots system of boarding out. Under this scheme, orphaned and deserted children were fostered by working-class parents in the neighbourhood, with the local authority paying for the child's upkeep and appointing visitors to maintain regular supervision of the child's care and upbringing. A National Committee for Promoting the Boarding out of Pauper Children was active in distributing propaganda pointing to the success of the system where it had been adopted both in England and in other European countries.[41] The Poor Law Board, at first reluctant to countenance the scheme, gradually gave way in face of demands from those Boards of Guardians who were enthusiasts for it. By 1876, about a third of Poor Law Unions in England and Wales were operating boarding-out systems. By the use of specialist institutions or by removal from institutional care, the sick and the child poor could have their needs met without being subjected to a system which was not designed for them.

Charity Reform

The London crisis of the 1860s not only stimulated inquiry and reform in the official Poor Law system but also caused consternation in philanthropic circles. Indiscriminate giving by private charitable agencies and individuals seemed to be more likely to create pauperism and demoralisation amongst the poor than did the inadequacies of the Boards of Guardians. Investigation of London's East End by men like Edward Denison, John Richard Green and C.B. Bosanquet alerted the professional middle classes in London to the growing gulf between rich and poor in that city, and the 'deformation of the gift' which thoughtless grants of cash, food and clothing, shorn of any personal knowledge or experience of the recipients, caused.[42] The 1860s and early 1870s witnessed a great outpouring of books and articles by the new generation of scientific philanthropists pleading for direct involvement of the charitable in the distribution of relief, with aid being given only after a careful investigation of the circumstances of each case to determine the best means of restoring the applicant to independence.[43] The foundation of the Central Relief Society in Liverpool in 1863, the revival of the District Provident Society in Manchester during the Cotton Famine and the establishment of the Society for Organising Charitable Relief and Suppressing Mendicity (the Charity Organisation Society) in London in 1868 provided the institutional machinery for co-ordinating scattered charitable organisations and infusing them with the doctrines of scientific philanthropy.[44]

The lack of co-operation between private charity and the local poor relief system in London which the inquiries of the 1861 Select Committee revealed, together with the apparently higher degree of co-ordination between the two systems achieved in Lancashire during the Cotton Famine, provided a stimulus for some closer linking of the new philanthropy and the reformed Poor Law system. In 1869 the President of the Poor Law Board, G.J. Goschen, alarmed by a further increase in pauperism and distress in East London, issued a memorandum urging Boards of Guardians in London to co-operate wherever possible with charitable organisations in the giving of relief.[45] The Charity Organisation Society responded enthusiastically to this initiative and appointed a paid secretary for the task of organising district committees of voluntary workers to organise effective co-operation between local charities and the Poor Law system.[46]

Thus, by the mid-1870s, the English Poor Law had come through its decade of crisis and had been so reconstructed as to be within sight of realising the Chadwickian ideal of 1834. The collaterals of the workhouse infirmary, the boarding-out system and even, in periods of exceptional trade depression, public works schemes could provide for those whose distress was not of their own making. Bodies like the Charity Organisation Society would act as a sifting mechanism by establishing teams of trained visitors to visit those in distress, assess the cause and nature of their need and advise as to whether they should be helped back to independence by charitable aid or scared back by the offer of the workhouse. By this means, the 'deserving poor' could be gently lifted clear of the swamp of pauperism, leaving the way clear for the pump of the workhouse test to clear the ground of incorrigibly idle, undeserving paupers. Thus in the 1870s and 1880s, the Local Government Board's inspectorate and the members of the COS launched a 'crusade against outdoor relief', urging Boards of Guardians to establish 'test workhouses' and begin more discriminating systems of relief.[47] This static analysis of the problem of urban distress, together with the optimistic assumption that it could be cured by the right application of scientific method was, as Hennock has shown, implicit in Charles Booth's surveys of East London poverty in the 1880s.[48] Booth's residual Class B, 'a deposit of those who from mental, moral and physical reasons are incapable of better work', could be dealt with by an extended Poor Law system providing labour colonies to which the denizens of Class B would be removed. This would leave more elbow room in the labour market for the group above them, Class C, the irregularly employed, who would thus obtain more regular employment and higher wages. It would also leave a clearly defined gap between Class C, 'the most proper field for charitable assistance', and the lowest category, the semi-criminal loafers of Class A. This small group would 'no longer be confounded with the unemployed', and could be 'harried out of existence'.[49]

Booth's analysis reflected the ideology of the reformed Poor Law and philanthropic systems which had emerged out of the crises of the 1860s. His advocacy of old age pensions fitted into this context. Pensions for the aged would provide yet another collateral, removing another class of the deserving above the pressures of 'less eligibility'.[50] Both the Royal Commission on the Aged Poor of 1895 and the later Select Committee on the Aged Deserving Poor, whilst unable to agree on the issue of state pensions, advocated the more generous treatment of the aged by the Poor Law system.[51]

The Testing of the Model

The model of Poor Law practice which emerged in the 1860s exercised a powerful influence over the thinking of social reformers in the second half of the nineteenth century. It remains, however, to test its practical application at local level. It is easy, as this chapter has perhaps done, to concentrate over much on the writings of advocates of the system, on the reports of the inspectorate, for example, or the account given by Thomas Mackay in the third volume of George Nicholls' *History of the English Poor Law*.[52] It is possible also to pay too much attention to London, a city on which philanthropic attention was concentrated from the 1850s onwards, and where the co-operation of Poor Law and private philanthropy was admitted to be at its closest and most successful.[53] There are, however, indications of the model's influence elsewhere. In Manchester, the Board of Guardians introduced a more stringent system of outdoor relief, 'the Manchester Rules', in 1873.[54] In Liverpool, the Central Relief Society and the energetic philanthropist, William Rathbone, worked for a more rational organisation of the systems of philanthropy and poor relief operating in the city.[55] In Oxford and in Cambridge, as Christopher Harvie has recently shown, academic Liberals and COS enthusiasts like Arnold Toynbee and Henry Sidgwick captured University seats on the Boards of Guardians and influenced the introduction of a more discriminating relief policy.[56] It remains to be seen, however, whether in the smaller manufacturing town or rural union, where the presence of the casual poor was less prominent and where guardians were not in the habit of discussing charity organisation philosophy over combination room port, the same enthusiasm for reform was present. The steep fall in outdoor relief in the 1870s, which the reformers hailed as a demonstration of the success of their system, has yet to be investigated at grass-roots level (Figures 3.2 and 3.3).

It will also be necessary to say more than space here allows about the weakening of the reform impetus and the growing criticism of the

Figure 3.3: Pauperism in England and Wales, 1850-1908 (number of paupers per 1,000 of population, distinguishing indoor and outdoor pauperism, casual and insane poor not included)

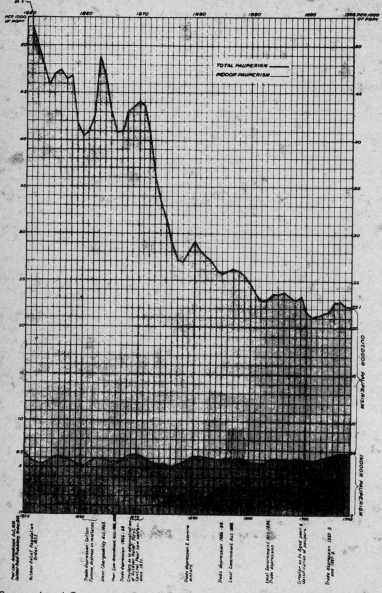

Source: Local Government Board, *Public Health and Social Conditions*, Chart 3.

Poor Law system leading to its investigation by the Royal Commission of 1905-9.[57] Here again Hennock's advocacy of the 1890s as a crucial decade seems more relevant than the conventional explanation of a shift in attitudes during the 1880s. The reform of the local government franchise in 1894 resulting in the election of working men, the 'labour Guardians', to Boards of Guardians; Rowntree's York survey of 1899 with its dynamic model showing poverty to be a far more complex phenomenon than the static picture which the scientific philanthropists had given; the growing concern about the national efficiency of the urban working classes as a whole and not of a mere residuum; the increasing dominance amongst social questions of the problem of unemployment, the Achilles' heel of the Poor Law system; all these developments served to undermine the confidence of the previous two decades in the reformed system of poor relief and philanthropy.[58]

Conclusion

What this chapter has attempted to argue is that the scheme of Poor Law reform half designed but not implemented in 1834 was remodelled under the impact of the crises of the 1860s and the fears which they aroused of increasing pauperism in an urban rather than a rural context. This scheme aimed at the elimination of pauperism and the increase of individual self-help, not through a crude system of 'less eligibility', but by means of a complex of institutions to deal with various special categories of the poor and of close co-operation with a scientific, investigative philanthropy which could sort out and allocate these categories. The extent to which this scheme was implemented at local level requires further investigation, although its advocates hoped that it would spread by example from one Poor Law Union to another. Even if these optimistic ideals were not fulfilled, the emergence of the scheme is itself significant. The crisis of the 1860s did not weaken the Poor Law and hasten its demise, thus preparing the ground for the building of the welfare state. Instead it strengthened and remodelled a system whose purpose was very different from that of the popular image of the welfare state. An understanding of this shows the Victorian Poor Law in its own right as the central strand of mid-nineteenth-century English social policy.

Appendix: the German Connection

Whilst much of the debate on poor relief and philanthropy in mid-nineteenth-century England was concentrated on national issues, reformers showed considerable interest in the systems of poor relief adopted in other European countries. In 1873, C.B. Bosanquet was instrumental in the publication of a translation of Herr A. Emminghaus' collection of essays, *Das Armenwesen und die Armengesetzgebung in Europäischen Staaten.*[59] Two years later, as has been seen, the Local Government Board officially published a series of consular reports on *Poor Laws in Foreign Countries.*[60] In all this activity, particular attention was centred on the town of Elberfeld, which had carried out a fundamental reform of its municipal poor relief system in 1852. Under the terms of this reform, the town's responsibility for the relief of its poor was vested in an *Armenverwaltung* of nine members. Subordinate to this body was a team of 18 *Armenvorsteher* (overseers) and 252 *Armenpfleger* (visitors). Service as overseer or visitor was unpaid, and was a compulsory condition of citizenship. The town was divided into sections with a visitor responsible for each section and an overseer controlling a district of 14 sections. Every application for relief was investigated by the visitor of the section from which it came, although no visitor dealt with more than four cases at one time. Applications, together with visitors' reports on them, were considered at fortnightly meetings of each overseer's district, and overseers presented a report on the state of their districts to the fortnightly meeting of the *Armenverwaltung*. Relief payments were channelled through the visitor and given at the applicant's home. Relief was given according to a strict scale, and was conditional upon there being no close relative who could be legally compelled to support the applicant, and, in the case of an able-bodied applicant, evidence being presented of genuine efforts to obtain work. No workhouse test was involved in the system, institutional relief being confined to the helpless aged, the sick and the orphaned.

The Poor Law Inspector Andrew Doyle, who visited Elberfeld in 1871 together with the Liverpool philanthropist William Rathbone, waxed enthusiastic about the system in his report to the Local Government Board.[61] Whilst the amount of relief given per case had risen under the new system, the total cost of relief and the numbers in receipt of municipal aid had fallen sharply. The success of the system had encouraged the neighbouring towns of Barmen and Crefeld to introduce it in 1863 and 1864 respectively, and all three towns were showing much lower levels of pauperism than towns like Düsseldorf

and Aachen with less carefully organised relief systems. For Doyle
and other English reformers, however, the chief attraction of the
system was the close relationship it created between the applicant
and the administrator of relief in the person of the visitor. 'The influence of this sort of intimate intercourse between the poor and those in
a much higher social position reaches far beyond the temporary result
that is immediately aimed at,' Doyle reported.[62] Indeed Elberfeld
seemed to have incorporated into its official relief system the features
which English Poor Law reformers wished to develop through the co-
operation of Poor Law and private charity.

The apparently inevitable spread of the Elberfeld system, and the
founding in Berlin in 1866 of a Society for the Prevention of Mendicity
and Pauperism to work closely with the city's *Armen-Direktion*, encouraged English reformers in the feeling that the application of scientific principles to poor relief in both England and Germany was moving
along parallel lines.[63] Indeed, the Germans might well be further advanced. *The Times* remarked in 1871:

> Even if we give it up as a bad job and confess that Prussia beats
> England in social organization, as in a few other matters, let us be
> honest and wise and admit the fair inference that the fault lies
> within ourselves.[64]

English interest in German relief systems was not, however, wholly
one-sided. One of the most authoritative studies of the English Poor
Law in the second half of the nineteenth century was that by Dr P.F.
Aschrott, *Das Englische Armen-Wesen*. This was translated into English
with an enthusiastic introduction by Henry Sidgwick in 1888.[65]
Although critical of the failure of the English workhouse system to
educate pauper inmates in habits of self-dependence, Aschrott was
generally approving of the main features of the English system which,
he felt, could 'serve as a model to other countries'.[66] There is thus
evidence of considerable mutual interest in each other's relief systems
amongst English and German social reformers in the mid-nineteenth
century, before the more publicised contacts over the Bismarckian
insurance schemes and Lloyd George's cursory instruction to Braithwaite to go to Germany and 'find out all about it'.[67] Further investigation of these mid-century contacts and of developments in contemporary relief systems in England and Germany would prove illuminating.

Notes

1. H.L. Beales, 'The New Poor Law', *History*, vol. XV (1931).
2. S. and B. Webb, *English Local Government Vols. VII-IX. English Poor Law History* (1927-9).
3. See, *inter alia*, M. Bruce, *The Coming of the Welfare State* (London 1961).
4. Mark Blaug, 'The Myth of the Old Poor Law and the Making of the New', *Jnl. of Econ. Hist.*, vol. XXIII (1963); *idem*, 'The Poor Law Report Re-examined', *Jnl. of Econ. Hist.*, vol. XXIV (1964); D.A. Baugh, 'The Cost of Poor Relief in South East England, 1790-1834', *Econ. Hist. Rev.*, vol XXVIII (1975); J.D. Marshall, *The Old Poor Law 1795-1834* (London, 1968).
5. M.E. Rose, 'The New Poor Law in an Industrial Area' in R.M. Hartwell, (ed.), *The Industrial Revolution* (London, 1970); N. McCord, 'The Implementation of the 1834 Poor Law Amendment Act on Tyneside', *Int. Rev. of Social History*, vol XIV (1969); R. Boyson, 'The Poor Law in N.E. Lancashire 1834-71', *Trans. Lancs. & Cheshire Antiquarian Society*, vol. LXX (1960); Anne Digby, *Pauper Palaces* (London, 1978).
6. O.R. Macdonagh, *Early Victorian Government 1830-1870* (London, 1977); M.W. Flinn, 'Medical Services under the New Poor Law' in D. Fraser (ed.), *The New Poor Law in the Nineteenth Century* (1976), p. 66.
7. R.M. Titmuss, *Essays on the Welfare State* (London, 1958), pp. 34-5.
8. G. Stedman Jones, *Outcast London* (Oxford, 1971).
9. E.P. Hennock, 'Poverty and Social Theory in England: the Experience of the 1880s', *Social History*, vol. I (1976), p. 91.
10. *Royal Commission on the Poor Law Report*, 1834, vol. XXVII — references here are to the edition by S.E. and E.O.A. Checkland, *The Poor Law Report of 1834* (Pelican Classics, 1974).
11. Ibid., pp. 334-97; Harriet Martineau, *Poor Laws and Paupers Illustrated* (1833-4).
12. R.H. Tawney, *Religion and the Rise of Capitalism* (Pelican edn., 1938), p. 211.
13. *Poor Law Report*, 1834, pp. 375, 430, 467, 450.
14. S.E. Finer, *The Life and Times of Sir Edwin Chadwick* (London, 1952).
15. N.C. Edsall, *The Anti Poor Law Movement 1834-44* (Manchester, 1971); M.E. Rose, 'The Anti Poor Law Movement in the North of England', *Northern History*, vol. I (1966); Finer, *Sir Edwin Chadwick*.
16. M.E. Rose, 'Settlement, Removal and the New Poor Law' in Fraser, *The New Poor Law*.
17. *Select Committee on Poor Relief. Report*, 1864 (255), vol. IX, Stedman Jones, *Outcast London*, pp. 241-61.
18. Ibid.; Helen Bosanquet, *Social Work in London 1869-1912* (London, 1914).
19. Poor Law Board, *15th Ann. Rpt.*, 1862-3, reports by H.B. Farnall; *Return Relating to the Lancashire Unions* 1863 (199), vol. LII.
20. W.O. Henderson, *The Lancashire Cotton Famine 1861-5*, 2nd ed. (Manchester, 1969), pp. 94-115; R.A. Arnold, *The History of the Cotton Famine* (London, 1864); J. Watts, *The Facts of the Cotton Famine* (London, 1866).
21. Poor Law Board, *15th Ann. Rpt.*, 1862-3, p. 14; *Letter of Instructions from the President of the Poor Law Board to H.B. Farnall, Esq.* 1862 (413), vol. XLIX, Pt. I, p. 89.
22. M.E. Rose, 'Rochdale Man and the Stalybridge Riot' in A.P. Donajgrodzki (ed.), *Social Control in Nineteenth Century Britain* (London, 1977); W.O.

Henderson, 'The Public Works Act 1863', *Economic History*, vol. II (1931).
23. Ruth Hodgkinson, *The Origins of the National Health Service: the Medical Services of the New Poor Law 1834-71* (London, 1967); J.E. O'Neill, 'Finding a Policy for the Sick Poor', *Victorian Studies*, vol. VII (1963-4); Flinn, 'Medical Services' in Fraser, *The New Poor Law*; A.F. Young and E.T. Ashton, *British Social Work in the Nineteenth Century* (London, 1956); Louisa Twining, *Recollections of Life and Work* (London, 1893).
24. *Report of the Lancet Sanitary Commission for Investigating the State of the Infirmaries of Workhouses* (1866).
25. *Association for the Improvement of the Condition of the Sick in Workhouses; Report of a Deputation to the President of the Poor Law Board* (1867) (pamphlet in Manchester Central Library, P3056/4).
26. Poor Law Board, *19th Ann. Rpt.*, 1866-7.
27. F. Duke, 'Pauper Education' in Fraser, *The New Poor Law*, pp. 67-86.
28. See, *inter alia*, Charles Dickens, 'Little Pauper Boarders', *All the Year Round*, 28 Aug. 1869.
29. Local Government Board, *3rd Ann. Rpt.*, 1873-4, Appendix 22.
30. SC *Poor Relief* 1861 (235-I) (235-II), vol. IX, 1864 (255), vol. IX.
31. 28 & 29, Vic. c. 79.
32. 30 & 31, Vic. c. 106.
33. Webbs, *English Local Government*, vol. VIII, Ch. 3. John Roach, *Social Reform in England 1780-1880* (London, 1978), pp. 156, 195.
34. Dr E. Smith, *Report of the Poor Law Board on Dietaries of Inmates of Workhouses* (1866); Poor Law Board, *Reports on Vagrancy* (1866).
35. Local Government Board, *1st-8th Ann. Rpts.*, 1871-2 – 1878-9.
36. Ibid., *Poor Laws in Foreign Countries* (1878).
37. P.F. Aschrott, *The English Poor Law System, Past and Present* (trans. H. Preston Thomas, 2nd edn (London, 1902), pp. 86-7; *Reports of the Poor Law District Conferences*.
38. 30 & 31 Vic. c. 6 (1867). Flinn, 'Medical Services' in Fraser, *The New Poor Law*; G.M. Ayers, *England's First State Hospitals 1867-1930* (1971).
39. Poor Law Board, *19th-21st Ann Rpts.* 1866-7 – 1868-9.
40. T.S. Ashton, *Economic and Social Investigation in Manchester 1833-1933* (London, 1934); M.B. Simey, *Charitable Effort in Liverpool in the Nineteenth Century* (Liverpool, 1951).
41. W. Tallack, *The Boarding Out of Pauper Children in England* (1877); C.J. Herford, 'The Boarding Out System for Orphan Pauper Children', *Trans. M/c Stat. Soc.* (1872-3); pamphlets of National Committee in British Library – B.M.8285 b.b.b. 91, 92, B.M.8288 b.b.49.
42. Sir B. Leighton, *Letters and Other Writings of Edward Denison* (London, 1872); J.R. Green, *Stray Studies*, 2nd Series (London, 1903); C.B. Bosanquet, *London: Some Account of its Growth, Charitable Agencies and Wants* (London, 1868); Stedman Jones, *Outcast London*.
43. See, *inter alia*, Sir C. Trevelyan, *Address on the Systematic Visitation of the Poor in their Own Homes* (1870); Elisha Robinson, *In What Respects May the Administration of the Poor Law be Improved* (1869); E.W. Holland, *Principles of Pauper Labour* (n.d.); J.H. Stallard, *Pauperism, Charity and Poor Laws* (1868); anon., *Confessions of an Old Almsgiver* (1871).
44. M.B. Simey, *Charitable Effort in Liverpool in the Nineteenth Century* (Liverpool, 1951); Manchester and Salford District Provident Society, *Annual Reports*; C.L. Mowat, *The Charity Organisation Society* (London, 1961).
45. Poor Law Board, *22nd Ann. Rpt.*, 1869-70, Appendix A, No. 4.
46. Bosanquet, *Social Work*.
47. T. Mackay, *A History of the English Poor Law*, vol. III, 1834-1898,

pp. 499-561; Webbs, *English Local Government* vol. VIII, pp. 435-68.

48. Hennock, 'Poverty', pp. 79-80.

49. Charles Booth, *Life and Labour of the People in London*, 1892 edn, vol. I, Chapter VI.

50. *Idem, Pauperism — a Picture, and Endowment of Old Age, an Argument* (London, 1892); *idem, Old Age Pensions and the Deserving Poor — a Proposal* (London, 1899).

51. *Royal Commission on the Aged Poor. Report*, 1895, Cd.7684. *S.C. Aged Deserving Poor*, 1899, vol. VIII.

52. Mackay, *English Poor Law.*

53. Aschrott, *English Poor Law System*, p. ix.

54. Local Government Board, *5th Ann. Rpt.*, Appendix B, No. 18.

55. Simey, *Charitable Effort*, Chapter 6.

56. C. Harvie, *The Lights of Liberalism* (London, 1976), pp. 195-6.

57. *Royal Commission on the Poor Laws and the Relief of Distress*, 1909, Cd. 4499.

58. See, *inter alia*, P. Ryan, ' "Poplarism" 1894-1930' in Pat Thane (ed.), *The Origins of British Social Policy* (London, 1978); B.S. Rowntree, *Poverty. A study of Town Life* (London, 1901); G.R. Searle, *The Quest for National Efficiency* (Oxford, 1971); J. Harris, *Unemployment and Politics. A Study in English Social Policy 1886-1914* (Oxford, 1972).

59. A. Emminghaus (ed.), *Poor Relief in Different Parts of Europe* (London, 1873).

60. Local Government Board, *Poor Laws in Foreign Countries* (1875).

61. Local Government Board, *First Ann. Rept.*, 1871-2, Appendix B, No. 35.

62. Ibid., p. 256.

63. Local Government Board, *Poor Laws in Foreign Countries* (1875), Report by L.F. Seyffardt.

64. Ibid., quoting *The Times*, 8 Dec. 1871.

65. Aschrott, *English Poor Law System.*

66. Ibid., p. xii.

67. H.N. Bunbury (ed.), *Lloyd George's Ambulance Wagon. The Memoirs of W.J. Braithwaite* (London, 1957), p. 85.

4 BISMARCK'S SOCIAL LEGISLATION: A GENUINE BREAKTHROUGH?

J. Tampke

Bismarckian social policies enjoy considerable prestige in present-day debates and publications about the origins of the welfare state. Historians both inside and outside Germany rank the social legislation of the 1880s as a decisive turning-point in modern social history. In the *Handbuch der Deutschen Geschichte* Wolfgang Treue, for example, refers to Bismarck's social legislation as 'das erste große sozialpolitische Gesamtwerk der modernen Gesellschaft'.[1] More recently Albin Gladen writes that 'das sozialpolitische Gesetzgebungswerk der achtziger Jahre hatte den entscheidenden Schritt von den tradierten Formen sozialer Fürsorge zur gesetzlichen Sozialversicherung der Arbeiter gebracht, in der Deutschland dann unter den Industrieländern für Jahrzehnte eine absolut führende Stellung einnahm.'[2] Gladen maintains the sociopolitical measures of the state gave the workers a minimal income in times of temporary or permanent hardship (*Existenzgefährdung*) which not only takes the pressure off the worker's family budget but which also gave the worker a minimum of social security (*bürgerliche Sicherheit*) which had previously been denied to him. Moreover [Auch], 'ließ sich durch ihre Auswirkungen der Gefahr einer proletarischen Verelendung der Arbeiter ein Riegel vorschieben'.[3] And a paper at the seventh International Economic History Association Congress, held in Edinburgh, August 1978, confirmed that the laurels (*der Lorbeer*) for all this has to go to Bismarck. H.J. Braun, although agreeing 'that it has rightly become old fashioned to stress the role of "great men" in historical events' nevertheless maintains that the social legislation of the 1880s 'is to a large extent due to the chancellor Bismarck'.[4] This chapter raises the question whether the evidence really supports such praise. By drawing attention to the tradition of Prussian welfare legislation the first part of this chapter will ask the question: what was new about the laws of the 1880s? The second part deals with the debate surrounding the cause of the Bills, and especially with Bismarck's role in their shaping. Finally, it will be asked, what did the legislation achieve? What was its overall impact?

The conclusion suggests that the social legislation of the 1880s has been greatly overrated, that its impact was limited and that one may well wonder whether the legislation of the 1880s was only an episode in the century-long struggle of the Prussian state and establishment to come to terms with the social impact of industrialisation.

The first factor which throws doubt on the claim that the legislation of the 1880s was a decisive breakthrough in the field of social politics was the fact that a compulsory insurance system supervised by the government and its agencies was not new. The laws introduced during the 1880s established a national insurance system to cover sick payments and accidents and also a contribution scheme to provide for invalid and old age pensions. The essence of this was not new, rather, it was in line with established Prussian tradition. T.S. Hamerow's contention that Prussia had a sound background of social responsibility[5] is shown in a number of social legislation Acts. The most impressive of these covered the coal-miners. Until 1865 coal-mining was regulated by the 1776 *revidierte Klevisch-Märkische Bergordnung*. This law, which originally had exempted the coal-miners from taxation and military duties, also restricted the work to eight hours. It guaranteed a fixed income and it assured the miners of the right to work. Although most of the mines were owned privately, the influence of the owners upon working conditions was limited. There was no female or child labour, nor Sunday shifts. Supervisory offices set up by the Prussian government ensured that the rules were upheld. Above all, the very impressive nature of these early acts of social legislation was emphasised by an advanced insurance system, the coal-miners' benefits scheme (*Knappschaftswesen*) which gave the miners free spa cures, medical treatment in case of illness or accident, sick payments during the whole period of illness and invalid payments in case of permanent disablement.[6] The social security which was provided by these laws explains the coal-miners' long-term political conservatism and the socialists' difficulties in finding a foothold in the coal region. There was no provision for old age in the *Knappschafts* funds. This is probably explained by the fact that life expectancy was still rather low for the bulk of the population in the eighteenth and early nineteenth centuries. Until the second half of the nineteenth century, most miners also had a smallholding attached to their houses, which would have provided for their food needs; moreover family ties were much stronger before full-scale industrialisation set in.

The regulation of the coal-mining industry until 1865 was one example of Prussia's social legislation before the 1880s. It was not the only one. In 1839 the Prussian government had introduced a law which placed some restrictions on the employment of child and juvenile labour and in the later 1840s it passed the *Preussische Gewerbeordnung* which entailed strong elements of social legislation by establishing a new form of guilds for artisans and craftsmen (*Innungen von Gewerbetreibenden*). These Innungen von Gewerbetreibenden, which also covered factory workers, were controlled by government supervisors and had to administer illness, invalid and old age pensions funds for members. After the 1848 Revolution the government also introduced trade or guild councils (*Gewerberäte*) for towns and cities which were made up of representatives from the trade guilds, the merchants and the industrialists. These councils were to arbitrate on a range of conflicts such as hours of work, supervision of wages and working conditions. At the same time the office of Factory Inspector was established to supervise child labour regulations.[7] Finally, and very importantly, it should be emphasised that many urban and rural communities established compulsory insurance funds against illness for citizens not covered by the guild funds.

Thus the social welfare tradition existed long before the 1880s. Admittedly these laws covered predominantly the handicrafts system, but until the middle of the century artisans and craftsmen did provide the bulk of the urban work-force. This changed when rapidly increasing industrialisation, which had set in by the second half of the nineteenth century, spelt doom for the handicraft system and when a growing number of workers found themselves employed in industries which were not covered by legislation. Moreover some of the protective laws were now withdrawn and replaced by individual contractual agreement (*freier Arbeitsvertrag*), a process which is noted especially in the coalmining industry. Thus by the 1860s/1870s there was on the one hand industrialisation at a speed unparalleled in Europe and on the other social misery and deprivation among the working population which could not remain unchecked. So in the 1880s it was not a new leaf that was turned in the history of social welfare in Germany but a return to the old principle of state interference applied to a new economic background.

Because of the deterioration in living conditions among the majority of the German work-force, there was pressure from influential sections of the community for the government to intervene again. Most active and outspoken was the enlightened academic opinion of the 'Nationalökonomen', the people around Gustav Schmoller and the Verein für Sozialpolitik. In fact the *Kathedersozialisten* right up to the war were to remain strong proponents for more effective social policies and among the firmest opponents of the socio-political *status quo*.[8] Pressure for government action came also from the ranks of some leading government administrators and from Reichstag members. Indeed Bismarck himself, after the Paris Commune, wrote to the Kaiser urging that steps should be taken to prevent conditions deteriorating to such an extent that revolution and unrest might endanger the nation. Throughout the 1870s there were demands in the Reichstag for a compulsory national insurance system; there were also protests from various leading administrators in the provinces because in many government districts an extremely precarious situation had arisen. With almost no social protection, workers who had an accident and became incapacitated for work or were temporarily unable to work had to return to their original family for survival, which normally meant that they had to return to the country. This placed a strain on the poor funds (*Armenkassen*) of Prussia's rural provinces and there was a hostile reaction from administrators in rural districts who demanded that those who left the land to work in the city should be cared for at their place of work. This in turn put such a strain on the urban poor funds that the cities' administrators soon also complained about unbearable conditions. Not surprisingly, pressure was brought upon the government to change the Employers' Liability Act and make the employers foot the bill for the accidents. It was because of this pressure that members from the heavy industries made their proposal about accident and invalid pensions.[9]

The industrialists' proposals were based on the system of *Werkwohlfahrtseinrichtungen* (employer welfare organisations), which were becoming increasingly popular in heavy industry. The most famous of these employer welfare organisations were perhaps those of the Krupp works in Essen or the Stumm-Halberg works in the Saar. These company welfare funds operated on the system of compulsory membership. Every employee had to contribute to three social funds: a medical fund, an accident fund and an old age pension scheme. The medical contribution fund, to which the employer also contributed, covered medical expenses and paid a few weeks' sick pay, although the rates for sick pay were very low, amounting to little more than a person would have received from the *Armenkassen*. The contributors' returns were thus rather meagre. The accident scheme was less impressive. Here, the Employers' Liability Act of 1871 had indeed established, as Braun puts it, 'that the employer was liable not only when it could be proved that the accident was his fault, but also, if it was the fault of the colleagues of the injured worker'.[10] But this meant in practice that the worker had to prove that he did not cause the accident, which was very difficult. At the Stumm-Halberg works, for example, 90 per cent of all accidents were held to be the fault of the workers.[11] Probably least impressive of the *Werkwohlfahrtseinrichtungen* was the old age pension system. Each employee had to pay an entrance which ranged from 2.5 to 6.33 per cent of his income. This meant an average of about 30-40 marks per annum. He was eligible for pension payments after twenty years of membership provided that two doctors had found him fully incapacitated for work. In many welfare funds a worker lost his contribution if he left the company, which in some cases would have amounted to a considerable saving. It was also not uncommon for a worker to lose entitlement if he participated in questionable political activities. To judge from the evidence, the workforce resented these employer welfare organisations,[12] yet the scheme which was suggested to the government was based on this compulsory welfare system.

In 1878 the industrialist Count von Stumm-Halberg suggested that a government-supervised scheme be introduced to provide compulsory invalid and old age insurance for the whole nation. Two years later, in 1880, the General-Director of the *Bochumer Verein*, Kommerzienrat Baare, suggested a similar scheme for accident insurance. This was primarily designed to save the employer the costs of full accident liability. It suggested the introduction of a National Insurance Fund to which employers, workers and government would each contribute one-third. These were the two key suggestions which for a number of years were widely discussed in the Reichstag and among other sections of the community. The academics basically supported the idea of compulsory insurance provided that it was part of a larger social legislation package. Briefly summarised, they suggested that the employer should pay a larger share than one-third into the accident fund, that the workers should have a considerable say in the running of sickness funds and that employers should also contribute to the old age funds. But above all, they urged the government to introduce laws regulating working conditions, providing for factory works inspection, to reconsider the working hours and to keep a closer check upon wages.[13] One important point which emerged from the academic discussion of the Bills for compulsory government insurance schemes was the actual pay-outs. The rates suggested for sick payment, accident contribution or pensions were so low that they were just above the rates of the existing Prussian poor funds. Some academics, Reichstag members and other politicians claimed that unless decent payments were made, the whole scheme would only amount to a reconstruction of the existing poor laws[14] and certainly not a measurable step towards social welfare. Some went further. Lujo Brentano, for example, argued that the scheme was bound to remain ineffective and that the government should make it possible for the workers to form and run their own sickness and old age funds.

Bismarck's chief adviser on social questions, the Under-Secretary in the Trade Ministry, Theodor Lohmann, was also sceptical about the effectiveness of some of the new compulsory funds. He suggested the creation of arbitration courts and workers' chambers to protect the interests of the employees. Lohmann saw the necessity for far-reaching factory laws and works inspections to improve working conditions and called for the employees to be given the right to establish their own independent social funds. The compulsory invalid and old age pension scheme was described by Lohmann as nonsense and he held the view that the employers should be paying for accidents which occurred in their works. Lohmann was soon on collision course with Bismarck and he left his office in 1883.[15] In future years Bismarck relied on the assistance of Gamp and Bödiker, who designed the Unfallversicherungsgesetz, and the State Secretary of the Reichsamt des Inneren, Boetticher, who drew up the Alters- und Invalidenversicherung.[16] These men's proposals were more in agreement with Bismarck and ensured that there would be as little interference in internal company matters as possible. In fact as the 1880s proceeded, Bismarck's own role in the formation of social policies became increasingly clouded as he seemed to turn his attention to other fields of importance, especially foreign policies.

The people for whom the new legislation was being prepared, the workers, were not consulted much, but they too discussed the legislation. There was only moderate interest in the old age insurance, perhaps because only a few would reach the suggested age for qualification which was set first at 70 years and later reduced to 66. They preferred compulsory government health funds to the employer welfare organisations, although their discussion also stressed the point that the planned laws were merely reconstructing the Poor Laws by shifting part of the burden upon the working population.

Although the industrialists did not have it all their own way,[17] the laws which were finally passed by the Reichstag and the Bundesrat worked largely in favour of the industrialists. The social legislation of the 1880s consisted of three Bills. The first covered accident insurance. The employers were asked to establish *Berufsgenossenschaften*, corporate organisations for the various branches of industry, statutory bodies which were funded by the employers but supervised by the newly created *Reichsversicherungsamt* (Imperial insurance office). This was different from Baare's original suggestion, which was that the government and the employees also contributed. Now the employers met the expenditure, but as the payments involved were moderate, the extra costs involved amounted to no great sums. Being the sole contributor left the industrialists in a strong position[18] and, moreover, what the employers lost on the swings they gained on the roundabouts. The medical system for sickness insurance was being two-thirds funded by the workers.[19] Sickness insurance was not nationally regulated. An employee was either a member of his company's health fund or of a local insurance institution (either the *Ortskrankenkasse* or the *Gemeindekrankenversicherung*), of a guild fund, or of a registered private fund. Finally, the third law made it compulsory for workers and employers to pay on an equal basis into an old age pension scheme. There were many exceptions to these basic laws; for example, many workers were still outside the accident insurance scheme, as only such industries and trades which were regarded as dangerous had to join it.[20] The Krankenversicherung, too, did not cover the whole work-force. Initially it included only the industrial workers, leaving domestic servants and rural workers outside the scheme. In 1892 this range was widened, but as late as 1895 barely half of the German work-force was covered by the Act.[21] As already stated, there was nothing essentially new or Bismarckian about it — the laws were in line with Prussian traditions, only set in a more industrialised surrounding. How effective were these laws? The scheme which showed at least some promise in the final years before the war was the sickness scheme, because gradually a number of union representatives came to hold influential positions on the board of the Ortskrankenkassen. This detracts little from the fact that it was run by a bewildering plethora of public and private insurance agencies, but its main shortcoming was the low rate of sick payments. On average, sick payments were made at the rate of between 50 and 60 per cent of the normal daily wage, which meant that the workers were receiving about half of their normal income when they fell ill, or marginally more than they would have received under the old Poor Law payments. After 13 weeks payment stopped, and if the recipient was still unable to work, he had to make further claims either with his industry's accident board or the pension scheme. But even if a worker was sick for only a few weeks he was likely to be in serious financial difficulties. There seems to be disagreement among economic historians whether real wages were rising or falling in the last decade and a half before the war,[22] but even if one takes the positive evaluation that there was a modest rise in real wages, this does not eradicate the fact that the average wage in Germany was only slightly above the cost of living. Thus any serious cut in income could easily lead to poverty and hardship. To lose for a number of weeks 50 per cent of normal income had serious consequences. The worker might have to borrow money or might not have been able to pay his food bill for a few weeks. Obviously these financial worries would not have helped the patient to recover. Moreover, because of the financial difficulties he or she often returned to work prematurely, immediately working overtime to pay for the accumulated debts. This complaint of low sick payments, and that consequently the insurance system was not very effective, is found throughout the 25-30 years of its operation. Hence the claim of the labour movement and of contemporary social reformers that the compulsory sickness insurance system was merely a reconstruction of the Poor Laws seems justified.

The new accident scheme brought some obvious improvements. Whereas previously a worker had to demonstrate that the employer was at fault, now compensation could be claimed for any accident regardless of who was at fault. Notwithstanding this, closer analysis does reveal that the situation seems not to have improved very much. As mentioned above, under the old scheme at the Stumm-Halberg works only 10 per cent of the workers were successful with their claim for accident payments. With the new scheme this figure improved, but only slightly. In the industries where most accidents occurred, the coal and heavy industries, the percentage of compensated accidents just reached 15 per cent per annum at the best of times.[23] It still was not easy for a worker to claim accident compensation successfully. According to the statistics of the *Berufsgenossenschaften*, by far the largest majority of all accidents were cured within 13 weeks, which meant that the illness funds were responsible for paying the injured workers. At least these were the claims of the *Berufsgenossenschaften*. The workers certainly must have had different opinions because about a quarter of all cases were taken for a revision to the industries arbitration chamber or even further to the Imperial Insurance Office. To judge from the reports of the Arbeitersekretariate, a great deal of hardship lies in this figure.[24] Not all claims to accident payments were rejected because the patient had allegedly recovered within 13 weeks. Approximately 10 per cent were turned down because the accident was not a *Betriebsunfall* (an accident at work) in the real sense of the law. The law made a distinction between accidents which were directly related to the place and nature of the work (this was a *Betriebsunfall*) and accidents of a general nature, accidents which face men at any given time and which were inherited in the danger of life. To illustrate this point with two brief examples: in one case a worker broke his leg on the path which linked the factory to the road. Here the industries arbitration board ruled that this accident could have happened to anyone under any circumstances. It was a general accident, and not a *Betriebsunfall*. This verdict, fortunately for the victim, was overruled by the Imperial Insurance Office. In another case a carrier was off-loading his cart when he was hit on the head and injured by a piece of wood which a carpenter had carelessly dropped from the second floor of the house. In this case both the industries arbitration board and the Imperial Insurance Office agreed that this was a general accident, an accident inherent in the danger of life and not a *Betriebsunfall*. Obviously the division line of this term *Betriebsunfall* was very subtle.[25] A large number of cases had to go to arbitration and as the employers were funding the scheme they were in a strong position, as the following set of statistics will illustrate. The example is taken from the annual report for the year 1900 of the brewery accident board for the state of Hessia. In 1900 there occurred about 11,000 accidents in Hessian breweries, but fortunately for the employers almost 10,000 of these accidents were cured in the first 13 weeks. Compensation had to be paid in only 1,300 cases. In the same year the breweries had to contest about 650 appeals and again the breweries were lucky because they won the revision cases at the arbitration court at the rate of 4:1. Of the two hundred cases contested at the Imperial Insurance Office again the employers won at the rate of 3:1.[26] In addition to this the Berufsgenossenschaften were keeping a constant check upon patients to ensure that there were no malingerers. Recipients of payments were constantly checked to see whether their overall condition was improving, and if the doctors considered this to be so the pension was cut by a certain percentage. To judge from the reports of the workers' secretariats this led to countless cases of hardship and human misery. For example, if a worker lost his leg but was otherwise healthy, he could barely expect to receive full benefits, especially as he was still able to work productively in such jobs as *Tütenkleben* (low-paid, unskilled outwork) to earn an income.[27] In a large number of cases recipients had their pensions reduced despite the fact that no improvement in the condition of the client had taken place. This was on the grounds of *Angewöhnung*, that the recipient was getting used to the existing state of his health.[28] Nor could the worker who stated his claim for compensation always expect much assistance from the medical profession. Three doctors in Lübeck, for example, who were working for the Berufsgenossenschaften, declared a reduction of one-third of the rent as justified because the spine of the recipient was healing. One of the Vertrauensärzte wrote:

Der Patient B. leidet an hochgradig gesteigerten Begehrlichkeits-vorstellungen und an einem gewissen Grade von Nervösitat, den er sich auf der Jagd nach unberechtigtem Vermögenserwerb erworben hat. Ich vermag mich der Anschauung derer, die in einem solchen Zustand eine entschädigungsberechtigende Unfallsfolge erblicken, nicht anzuschliessen; da eine Grenze, wo der gesunde Zustand aufhört und der kranke anfängt, überhaupt nicht zu ziehen ist. Wahrscheinlich sei die allgemeine Erwerbsfähigkeit des Mannes um einen noch viel geringeren Prozentsatz eingeschränkt.[29]

These are only a few cases to illustrate that claims which describe the accident insurance laws as impressive social legislation are not persuasive.

Least popular of the three social laws was the invalid and old age pension scheme. A worker was entitled to full old age payments if he contributed to the fund from his eighteenth year for a period of 48 years — and a year meant 300 working days. As the SPD Reichstag member Molkenbuhr commented, the poor wretch who managed to work 300 days for 48 years was hardly in a position to enjoy his old age pension.[30] Most contributors had to settle for less. In the early years of the century the average pension for both invalid and old age was about 160 marks — a fraction of the average wage-earner's income.[31] Nor were there any provisions for widows or orphans once the recipient died.

To sum up the social legislation of the 1880s: was there much to it? The most important fields of factory laws legislation for workers' protection and works inspection — laws which would have prevented accidents and illness — were not touched upon and the least one would expect from a scheme which is accredited for setting the pace in social legislation are laws regulating workers' protection. On this Bismarck shared the firm opinion of the industrialists, who regarded any such step as an interference in their own affairs and in their business efficiency.

It has been asked why Bismarck rejected all attempts to make his social policies more effective; probably the most persuasive answer

lies in the fact that since the mid-1860s Bismarck too had become a
factory owner and he fully agreed with his industrialist friends' distrust of outside interference in their own businesses.[32]

Thus by the end of the 1880s little had been achieved. There was
widespread disappointment and Bismarck himself felt that he had failed
in his domestic policies.[33] It is noteworthy that Wilhelm II not only
concentrated upon weakness in Bismarckian social policies to prepare
for the fall of the old Chancellor,[34] but also arranged for a fresh course
in German social policies. Wilhelm appointed the Government President
of Düsseldorf, von Berlepsch, as Minister for the Interior. Von Berlepsch, a most outspoken supporter of government interference in
industry, attempted to take up Theodor Lohmann's suggestions.
During the former's time of office the Reichstag had passed laws
which allowed for the formation of arbitration courts in towns with
a population of more than 20,000, shortened the working hours for
women and children and entitled workers to have their views heard
in matters of safety regulations. Moreover a number of trade inspectors
were appointed to comment on working conditions. Berlepsch also
attempted to stop the continuous deterioration of the situation in
the coal-mining industry, but this soon led to hostility from the mine-
owners and from within his own Conservative Party and to his subsequent retirement from office.[35]

There was one last attempt by a Prussian administrator to make state
social policies work in Germany. After the massive coal-miners' strike
in 1905, the Staatssekretär des Inneren von Posadowsky succeeded in
having workers' boards established in the coal-mining industry which
had a moderate say in the running of the insurance funds and the
penalty system of that industry. Members of these boards were also
to be spokesmen for complaints raised by the miners.[36] Posadowsky
managed furthermore to have the insurance scheme's sick payments
increased, but none of these steps really marked a decisive breakthrough in social policies. Still it is arguable that the elements of the
modern welfare state are more likely to be found in Berlepsch's and
Posadowsky's legislation than in the 1880s, although basically one may
doubt whether any of the pre-World War One social policies in
Germany made any measurable impact. The fact that the alleged enemy
of the state — the SPD — was receiving ever larger support throws
doubt on some of the positive evaluations referred to at the beginning
of the chapter. As has been shown recently, there was a growing sense
of disillusionment among the old Kathedersozialisten on the eve of
peace,[37] and noteworthy too was the considerable interest in countries

82 Bismarck's Social Legislation

like Australia and New Zealand,[38] which were regarded as impressive examples of advanced social policies before World War One. This shows that enlightened public opinion was still searching for effective policies, and that Germany's own social legislation was not held in high esteem. In fact the social cleavage was widening and, as Klaus Saul has shown very persuasively in his study of domestic and social policies in pre-World War One Germany, the war may well have saved the nation from violent social conflict.[39]

Notes

1. W. Treue, 'Wirtschafts und Sozialgeschichte Deutschlands im 19 Jahrhundert' in B. Gebhardt, *Handbuch der Deutschen Geschichte* (Stuttgart, 1960), vol. 3, p. 407.
2. A. Gladen, *Geschichte der Sozialpolitik in Deutschland* (Wiesbaden, 1974), pp. 78-9.
3. Ibid.
4. 'Political Economy and Social Legislation in Germany, ca. 1870-1890', p. 1.
5. *Restauration, Revolution, Reaction* (Princeton, 1970), pp. 70-3.
6. For a summary note H.G. Kirchhoff, *Die staatliche Sozialpolitik im Ruhrbergbau 1871-1914* (Köln, 1958); H. Koch, *Die Bergarbeiterbewegung im Ruhrgebiet in der Zeit Wilhelm des Zweiten* (Düsseldorf, 1954), pp. 13-14.
7. Gladen, *Geschichte*, pp. 19-27.
8. For a summary of some of their discussions: W. Vogel, *Bismarcks Arbeiterversicherung* (Braunschweig, 1951), pp. 67-92.
9. Note Hermann Molkenbuhr's speech about workers' insurance at the 1902 SPD party convention in Munich: *Protokoll über die Verhandlungen des Parteitages der Sozialdemokratischen Partei Deutschlands* (München, 1902), especially pp. 182-6.
10. Vogel, *Bismarcks Arbeiterversicherung*, p. 2.
11. Ibid., p. 24.
12. Note the reports of the *Arbeitersekretariate* frequently summarised in *Sozialistische Monatshefte* or *Neue Zeit*, e.g. Gustav Hoch, 'Sozialpolitisches aus den Berichten der Arbeitersekretariate', *Neue Zeit*, vol. 22, no. 2 (1903/4), pp. 594-9; W. Düwell, 'Aus dem Reiche der rheinisch-westfälischen Eisen und Stahlkönige', *Neue Zeit*, vol. 23, no. 1 (1904/5), pp. 69-75; and 'Werkwohlfahrtseinrichtungen', vol. 26, no. 2, pp. 833 ff.
13. For a summary of the voluminous discussion in *Schmoller's Jahrbuch*, *Soziale Praxis* or the *Archig für Sozialwissenschaft und Sozialpolitik*, see Vogel, *Bismarcks Arbeiterversicherung*, pp. 67-92; note also Stadthagen's speech to the 1906 Reichstag debate on social policies, *Stenographische Berichte* (1905/6), pp. 1196 ff.
14. Note, for example, J. Platter, 'Die geplante Alters- und Invalidenversicherung', *AFSW* (1888), vol. 1, pp. 7-41; or Molkenbuhr's speech, p. 182.
15. Vogel, *Bismarcks Arbeiterversicherung*, pp. 92-100.
16. Ibid.
17. Note Hans-Peter Ullmann's contribution, 'German Employers and Bismarck's Social Legislation' in this volume, pp. 133-49.

18. See below, pp. 136ff.
19. For details, Gladen, *Geschichte*, pp. 59-62.
20. Note, for example, Arthur Stadthagen's speech, p. 1204.
21. Molkenbuhr, *Protokoll*, p. 183.
22. For different views note G. Bry, *Wages in Germany 1871-1945* (Princeton, 1960); A.V. Desai, *Real Wages in Germany* (Oxford, 1968).
23. Note the annual statistics widely commented upon in the Kathedersozialisten and SPD periodicals.
24. E.G. Hoch's articles referred to in note 12, Stadthagen's speech to the Reichstag; A. Winter, 'Die Betriebsunfälle 1887-1897', *Neue Zeit*, vol. 18, no. 2 (1899/1900), pp. 408 ff., 441 ff., 473 ff.; E. Graf, 'Das Glück der Unfall-Berufsgenossenschaften', *Neue Zeit*, vol 1 (1883), pp. 417-28.
25. L. Fuld, 'Der Begriff des Betriebsunfalls im Sinne der Deutschen Gesetzbegung', *AFSW*, vol. 1 (1881), pp. 417-28.
26. Graf, 'Das Glück der Unfall-Berufsgenossenschaften'.
27. Ernst Lange, 'Die Weiterentwicklung der deutschen Arbeiterversicherungsgesetzgebung', *AFSW*, vol. 3 (1890), p. 389.
28. Odo, 'Der Kampf um die Rente vor dem Reichsversicherungsamt', *Neue Zeit*, vol. 25, no. 2 (1906-7), p. 776.
29. Hoch, 'Sozialpolitisches', p. 597.
30. Molkenbuhr, *Protokoll*.
31. E. Graf, 'Von unseren Invalidenversicherungsanstalten', *Neue Zeit*, vol. 22, no. 2 (1903-4), pp. 349-53.
32. Vogel, *Bismarcks Arbeiterversicherung*, pp. 136 ff.
33. Ibid.
34. W.M. Simon, *Germany in the Age of Bismarck* (London 1970) pp. 89-90, 224-7.
35. G.A. Ritter, *Die Arbeiterbewegung im Wilhelminischen Reich* (Berlin, 1959), pp. 34-6.
36. Koch, *Bergarbeiterbewegung*, pp. 86-8.
37. K. Saul, *Staat, Industrie, Arbeitergewegung im Kaiserreich* (Düsseldorf, 1974), pp. 366-9.
38. Note the author's 'Pace Setter or Quiet Backwater? – German Literature on Australia's Labour Movement and Social Policies 1890-1914', in *Labour History* (Canberra) no. 36 (May 1979), pp.3-17.
39. Saul, *Staat, Industrie*, pp. 393-4.

5 THE ORIGINS OF BRITISH NATIONAL INSURANCE AND THE GERMAN PRECEDENT 1880-1914

E.P. Hennock

Introduction

The German system of providing for specific needs by means of the compulsory insurance of the workers was introduced by Bismarck with much publicity between 1881 and 1889. Its existence was known in Britain from the first. Towards the end of the pre-war period the British National Insurance Act of 1911 applied a scheme of compulsory workers' insurance to the needs of the sick and of the unemployed. This Act was a significant departure from previous policies and was introduced by its sponsors with specific reference to the parallel German experience.

It is possible to divide British social reformers between 1880 and 1914 into those who wished to introduce state-sponsored contributory insurance systems in some form or other, and those who did not. There was a vigorous debate on this issue throughout the period. Prior to 1908 the advocates of contributory insurance were vocal but unsuccessful. After that they became the influential and effective school of reformers. One might have thought that at an early stage in the debate they would have pointed to Germany as a relevant model. Yet right up to 1905 the most passionate rejection of the idea that German practices were of any relevance to British social reform came precisely from the advocates of contributory insurance, not least from the two most prominent ones, Canon Blackley and Joseph Chamberlain. So determined were they that their position should not be confused with that of the Germans that they went out of their way to criticise and condemn the German system as totally unsuited to Britain. Only in 1905 do we find the beginnings of a different attitude, and it is not really until 1907 that this becomes a significant element in the debate between the rival points of view. Whatever may have been the case in other areas of social reform, in this particular case the interest in German models arose remarkably late and was preceded by 25 years of contempt and disapproval.

This raises three questions.

(1) What explains the long period of indifference and rejection?
(2) What accounts for the change of view, and particularly for the change of policy by the Liberal government between June and December 1908?
(3) What interest did those responsible for the making of British health insurance take in the German precedent?

In my current work I am answering each of these in turn. But within the limited scope of this chapter I propose to deal only with the third. That is bound to take a great deal for granted, and I intend to limit my introduction to what absolutely has to be said to make sense of the substance of the chapter.

Lloyd George's interest in compulsory insurance as a means of providing benefits arose from his dissatisfaction with the policy pursued by the Liberal government up to 1908, of whose consequences he became acutely aware when he succeeded Asquith as Chancellor of the Exchequer on the reconstruction of the Cabinet in April of that year. For he inherited an Old Age Pensions Bill whose features had been Asquith's responsibility, but which he was now obliged to steer through Parliament.

On taking office in 1906 the Liberal government had had no policy on old age pensions. They found themselves confronted by an extra-parliamentary pressure group, the National Committee of Organised Labour for Old Age Pensions (NCOL) which demanded universal old age pensions at 65 financed from general taxation. The cost of such a programme was beyond what any government would have been prepared to contemplate, but by 1906 the NCOL had won the support not only of the various national bodies of organised labour, but had campaigned most effectively during the general election. In March 1906 the House of Commons voted in favour of old age pensions to be financed from general taxation, and thereafter the NCOL continued to keep up the pressure on the government. In August 1906 Asquith's officials began work on an old age pensions policy, which should be close enough to the principal demands of the NCOL to take the wind out of its sails, but financially acceptable to the Treasury. The first of these requirements meant pensions separated from the administration of the Poor Law and financed from general taxation; the second meant restricting entitlement to pensions by income, by past conduct and by age so as to fit the sum of around £6 million that the Treasury was prepared to make available. The Bill that emerged in May 1908 was certainly indefensible in most of its details and the government never tried to justify it as a coherent policy. It was presented as an admittedly inadequate first step and a pledge of future benefits when more resources became available. To put it bluntly, the government had responded to political pressure by giving as little as they thought they could get away with. Some more concessions would have to be made before the Bill became law, and Lloyd George was well aware that old age pensions were unfinished business and promised indeed to be most expensive unfinished business. Yet he himself was not anxious to see more money spent on the elderly.

The immediate problem that faced him was how to deal with the pressure for a reduction of the pensions age from 70 to 65 or even 60. His Treasury advisers had kept both him and Asquith before him in ignorance of the German way of dealing with invalidity by means of contributory insurance, but he had been lectured during the debate in Parliament on the applicability of German insurance to British problems. He had heard enough to recognise that the so-called German invalidity insurance provided an alternative to massive Treasury commitments and to an indiscriminate lowering of the pensions age.

His departure for Germany in August 1908 to see German insurance at first hand was a turning point.

(1) In future, instead of reluctantly yielding to outside pressure, the Cabinet would construct its own social policy according to its own priorities.
(2) That pressure had been for the provision of benefits out of general taxation with the object of removing certain categories of the needy from dependence on the Poor Law.
(3) The cost of such demands, if yielded to, inevitably implied radical policies of taxation.
(4) The new alternative, which was reliance on compulsory insurance, would moderate the impact of social policy on taxation. But by obliging the state to rely more heavily on its powers of regulating conduct it would raise new problems both of social organisation and consent.[1]

Although Lloyd George had taken his initiative in order to deal with pressures on behalf of the aged and the infirm, the government was under the same kind of pressure on behalf of the unemployed. Here too insurance was a possible alternative, as some of the Board of Trade officials were well aware. The Chancellor's conversion to insurance cleared the way for unemployment insurance too, and from October

1908 Lloyd George and Churchill (President of the Board of Trade) were working together to convert political opinion.

New Attitudes

It was a startling new departure when one remembers the decisiveness with which compulsory insurance policies had been rejected by the government and Parliament as recently as the summer of that year. It implied a very different attitude to the German insurance schemes from that which had been dominant until then. The German experience was now relevant to the thinking of official policy-makers as it had not seemed relevant before. Not merely is this obvious now; it was an acknowledged fact at the time.

Lloyd George openly declared his conversion when he returned from his German visit in August 1908:

> I never realised before on what a gigantic scale the German pension system is conducted. Nor had I any idea how successfully it works. I had read much about it, but no amount of study at home . . . can convey to the mind a clear idea of all that state insurance means to Germany. . . It touches the great mass of German people in well-nigh every walk of life. Old-age pensions form but a comparatively small part of the system. Does the German worker fall ill? State insurance comes to his aid. Is he permanently invalided from work? Again he gets a regular grant whether he has reached the pension age or not.[2]

The consultations that Lloyd George and Churchill then undertook with trade union leaders caused these in turn to send a delegation to Germany in November, whose favourable report on the working of the German insurance system and its effect on the German labour movement was an important stage in the conversion of organised labour.[3]

Nor was Churchill slow to proclaim his own conviction. As was his way, he managed to draw what he had learnt into a single strategy. We find him urging Asquith in December towards what he called a policy of Social Organisation in emulation of what had been achieved in Germany:

> Germany with a harder climate and far less accumulated wealth

has managed to establish tolerable basic conditions for her people. She is organised not only for war, but for peace. We are organised for nothing except party politics. The Minister who will apply to this country the successful experiences of Germany in social organisation may or may not be supported at the polls, but he will at least have left a memorial which time will not deface of his administration. It is not impossible to underpin the existing voluntary agencies by a comprehensive system — necessarily at a lower level — of state action.

He argued that the government had at least another two years and sketched a six-point programme that would 'not only benefit the state but fortify the party'. 'Thrust a big slice of Bismarckianism over the whole underside of our industrial system, and await the consequences whatever they may be with a good conscience.'[4] We have no record of how Asquith took to this language. He must have been accustomed by that time to the rhetorical extravagance of his ambitious young colleague.

The government's commitment to the insurance policy was announced by Lloyd George in his budget speech of 29 April 1909. It is significant that it was linked to a refusal to lower the age limit for old age pensions. Once again, as in June 1908 when he presented the Old Age Pensions Bill, Lloyd George referred to the distress caused by premature breakdown in health, by the death of the breadwinner and by unemployment as far more deserving of government attention, but in contrast to last year he now launched into a panegyric of Bismarck's 'superb scheme' of insurance for the German workmen and their families.[5]

The crisis over the 1909 Budget and two election campaigns intervened before the promises of April 1909 could be honoured. They gave the Liberal leaders an opportunity to present German workers' insurance in a new and more favourable light. This was just as well for a very different set of attitudes was deeply entrenched.

Older Attitudes

'A system of regulation and a system of regimentation which . . . is utterly alien to the tradition of this country' — a junior Minister's phrase during the Third Reading Debate on the Old Age Pensions Bill reiterated what had become commonplace in relation to the

German insurance scheme. 'The German system could not be transplanted here,' Asquith had said, 'for one simple and sufficient reason — that it is founded on the two pillars of inquisition and compulsion.'[6]

Regimentation in this context usually referred to the compulsory nature of the scheme; *regulation* to its administrative provisions. Even Sidney Webb could use the current clichés when it suited him. In 1907 he had dismissed 'all contributory schemes of old age pensions as inherently and completely impossible, whether optional or compulsory. If compulsory they involve an impossible regimentation.' Charles Booth had regarded 'the complicated nature of the German old age pensions scheme and the practical impossibility of exercising any compulsion of this character on our people' as fatal objections. The proposals for unemployment insurance naturally also ran into the same objection that 'a compulsory scheme scarcely appeals to our English ideas'.[7]

For compulsion to be workable, a record had to be kept of everyone within the scope of the scheme. 'The workingman in this country would not submit to the system of dossiers and registration to which the German workingman submitted,' was the view of one Conservative MP. 'Sifted and regimented' was how G.N. Barnes, the Labour MP, put it when making the same point, and from the Liberal front bench Asquith had agreed. 'You cannot, even if you would, set up and work here the complicated and irritating machinery by which in Germany the necessary funds . . . are extracted from the pockets of both employers and employed.'[8]

Explanations for these impossibilities were usually given in terms of the wider political and social differences between the two countries. J.A. Spender had argued in 1892 that the idea of the state as disciplinarian and guide was in no way outlandish to those accustomed to the discipline of compulsory military service. *The Times* had said that sort of thing in 1889; there was no dearth of similar comments in 1908.[9]

W.J. Braithwaite

The construction of a national scheme of insurance against sickness and invalidity, like the creation of old age pensions in 1908, was the responsibility of the Chancellor of the Exchequer and his advisers at the Treasury. But just as the office of Chancellor was now occupied by Lloyd George instead of Asquith, so equally there appears to be little overlap in the civil servants connected with the two schemes. This was partly due to Lloyd George's unconventional choice of adviser; W.J. Braithwaite, the civil servant most closely involved in the making of what was soon to be called Health Insurance, was in fact a specialist from the Inland Revenue. As an expert on income tax, he had been sent to Germany a few months previously to investigate the German system of local income tax. English local government was badly in need of additional sources of revenue, but Braithwaite had convinced Lloyd George that the German tax system had nothing to offer. Lloyd George was impressed by him, and when he needed someone to investigate German insurance, he asked for him again.

Braithwaite was certainly no expert on Germany. He could read German only slowly and spoke it with difficulty, using another Treasury official as an interpreter. Nor had he any specialist knowledge of German institutions. For his investigation into insurance, as previously into taxation, he had to brief himself from scratch. Among the papers he received was an article on 'The Insurance of the Working Classes in Germany', commissioned in 1905 by W.T. Stead for the *Review of Reviews*, an article that had made little impact at the time.[10] But more important was the outline of a scheme that had been negotiated with the leaders of the friendly society movement by Lloyd George between December 1908 and April 1909, submitted to the government actuaries and returned with comments by them in March and August 1910.[11]

It was no longer possible to argue that, given time, the friendly societies, who already provided some protection to the most vigorous elements of the working class, would be able to embrace the working population as a whole. In a world of international competition there was no time: the protection that would maximise the human resources of the nation was needed then and there. Liberals had come to accept the view that the dynamic of voluntary mutual help had to be supplemented by means of state compulsion and subsidy. But could compulsion be applied without merely taking the place of personal initiatives and responsibility? Could the voluntary associations of mutual help remain dynamic while being shored up by the resources of compulsory taxation? What was at stake in the construction of national insurance was the relation between the organs of the state and the voluntary associations of society. That relationship lay at the heart of all Liberal political theory and practice.

The basic political necessity recognised by Lloyd George and all others of associating the friendly societies in the construction of an insurance scheme found in Braithwaite a response based on personal interest and commitment. He wanted more than the political acquiescence of the friendly society movement; he wanted a scheme that would benefit the societies and lead to the extension of the principle of mutual association and self-government. Thus he went to Germany with a set of attitudes not at all uncharacteristic of a Liberal Englishman — a belief in self-government, a distrust of bureaucracy and a feeling of unease at the possible implications of state compulsion for voluntary initiative and all the character traits associated with it.

He claimed that what had impressed him most during his first-hand investigation of German insurance, besides the usual German thoroughness, was the complexity and harshness of this 'social' legislation. 'It was amazing to find prosecutions for breaches of regulations running to many thousands in Berlin only,' he wrote. He visited the offices of a sickness fund and commented, 'It all seemed very complicated to me... I noted that 126 officials were required to manage this Society of 120,000 members.' 'German methods of officialdom and compulsion... were awful warnings to me. Something simpler and more self-working must, I thought, be found for England.'

When he reported to Lloyd George, he placed the emphasis accordingly. 'I hoped that I had not been tendentious' was his comment on his report. He also noticed that Lloyd George was discouraged by finding how much had already been done in Germany, but attracted by the idea of making employer or employed pay for extra sickness caused by either, as the Germans had done.[12]

Revulsion, Imitation and Rivalry

Here we have the three attitudes which together made up the stance of the British policy-makers towards what they had found in Germany: *revulsion*, *imitation* and *rivalry*.

(1) With Braithwaite the element of revulsion appears to have been dominant. In arguing for giving the approved societies within the British scheme maximum responsibility for their own financial solvency, in advocating the adoption of strict actuarial principles, and in many other instances, he used the German scheme, or some aspect of the three schemes, as an example of what to avoid.

(2) Lloyd George himself tended more frequently to regard the

German schemes as a quarry for devices to be copied. To
give just one example of many, he was delighted with his
discovery that the Germans paid benefits only from the fourth
day of sickness. Friendly societies had always paid from the
commencement of sickness; this device would help to spin
out the money. Braithwaite would occasionally reject a suggestion of this kind by referring to its failure in Germany, but he
found that it was sometimes prudent to accept these suggestions, even when he felt that German experience had not justified Lloyd George's hopes. Thus in their different ways both
Lloyd George and Braithwaite found the mere existence of a
working model of what they wished to create a great advantage.
Braithwaite systematically combed the German material to find
out what snags he was likely to encounter, so as to arm himself
against them.[13]

(3) As for Lloyd George, more important than the willingness to
imitate the Germans was the determination to outdo them.
This sense of rivalry was an important political factor in the
overall situation and is well caught in Lloyd George's remark
made while preparing the speech with which to introduce the
measure to the Commons. When Braithwaite commented on
the length of the speech, adding that he did not see what could
be cut except a long passage of comparison with the German
scheme, Lloyd George replied: 'I would rather get up and tell
them what the rates are to the employer and employed in
Germany, and that my scheme does not charge so much, and
does more, and then sit down without having made a speech,
than leave that out.'[14]

This sense of rivalry influenced more than just the style of presentation. It influenced the substance of the scheme, making it more
ambitious than it would otherwise have been. Less than two weeks
before the presentation of the Bill, after the actuarial calculations had
already been made and approved by the Cabinet, Lloyd George received
a paper on German contributions and benefits. He was greatly per-
turbed when he saw the large amount paid by German employers
and workers, and 'afraid that his own scheme looks small by the side
of Germany'. Pacing his room in much agitation, he decided to increase the employers' contributions by 50 per cent from 2d a week
to 3d a week. This increase made possible benefits of a kind and at a
level not previously contemplated.

I have referred already to the speech in which Lloyd George introduced the measure to the House of Commons on 4 May. It contained nine distinct references to Germany, and a further one in the subsequent section devoted to unemployment insurance. All the three attitudes that we have noticed are represented there. Four times the German scheme is cited as an example to be followed,[15] twice as a warning of what to avoid.[16] But three passages, including two of the most prominent, were clearly intended to demonstrate the superiority of the British product.

Finance

The first of these dealt with what the workers had to pay. In England that was to be 4d per week for men. In Germany the payment varied in proportion to the rate of wages, but a worker earning 24s a week, the average British wage, would be paying 9d. 'For that 9d,' said Lloyd George, 'the benefits he gets will not be equal to the benefits we shall be able to give under our Bill twenty years hence.'[17] The comparison was strained, indeed so obviously strained that one wonders that he thought the point as important as he did.

When he turned to the contribution by the state, he was able to take credit for the large amount that the Treasury already paid out by means of tax-provided old age pensions. By adding these two measures together he made the British scheme incomparably more generous than the German, and so obtained political credit for the high cost of a system whose principles he had now rejected. The £13 million, which old age pensions were costing by then, he calculated as equivalent to a weekly contribution of 5d. 'We certainly could not have offered the benefits we are offering in this measure . . . had it not been that the whole burden of pensions over seventy years of age had been taken over by the State.'[18]

This speech was merely one part of the elaborate comparisons with the German precedent that were so striking a feature of the presentation of the Bill. The Bill was accompanied by an explanatory Memorandum and by two Memoranda exclusively devoted to the German scheme. One presented a detailed comparison between the two schemes; the other a collection of testimonials by German workers, employers and Poor Law authorities.[19]

Nothing could be a more striking indication of the political importance attached to the comparison with Germany than the principal explanatory Memorandum itself. Its opening section was headed

Objects, but of its 47 lines, as many as 38 were in fact devoted to an exposition of how the Bill differed from the German scheme of sickness and invalidity insurance. Organised into four subsections, its emphasis was basically twofold. One was to commend the organisation of the British scheme as more economical, more self-governing, more convenient and less bureaucratic than the German. The other was in praise of its financial provisions, as better value than the German schemes and buttressed by a more generous state contribution. We have already seen how much this meant to Lloyd George and the special Memorandum on German insurance, published at the same time, was principally devoted to establishing point by point the financial superiority of the British Bill.

I shall not comment on it in detail. It was a somewhat slanted document. There is, however, a general point to be made about what it was attempting to do. Comparisons of the cost of contributions and benefits between the two countries were bound to be arbitrary. The British scheme operated in principle by means of uniform contributions from all members, distinguishing only between men who paid 4d per week and women who paid 3d. This provides a uniform level of benefits. The German worker by contrast contributed on a graduated scale according to the size of his earnings, and similarly received graduated benefits in accordance with the level of his contributions. This applies both to sickness insurance and to invalidity and old age insurance, but as always when it comes to details the two German schemes operated in different ways. That means of course not only that the burden of contributions fell on German workers proportionate to their ability to pay, but that benefits received by the well paid were considerably greater than those received by the lower paid.

This was the really fundamental difference between the schemes in the two countries. It is surprising how little comment it attracted at the time. The detailed Memorandum on German insurance gave no explanation. The general explanatory Memorandum mentioned it as a point of difference, but merely added that the British system of uniform contributions would reduce the inconvenience to employers. A short passage in Lloyd George's speech to the Commons on the first reading of the Bill comes much nearer to the real explanation. He drew attention to the small sums received in benefit by the lower paid in Germany and added that he had decided in favour of a uniform flat-rate scale as being the simplest means of providing benefits large enough to keep the contributors' families from want. The passage is both short and obscure and was ignored in subsequent discussion of the measure.[20] But it contains the germs of a genuine explanation. British health insurance, like British unemployment insurance, was intended to supersede the Poor Law as the protection against want caused by those factors over which the individual had no personal control. It was an aspect of the politics of poverty and was judged by what it did to protect the families of the poor from want.[21] It derived its impetus from the conjunction of two political considerations. One was a concern to protect the human resources of the nation at a time of international competition, both economic and military. The other was the need to reassure the citizen-voter that he would not be allowed, for reasons over which he had no control, to fall into the non-citizen class of paupers. It was therefore not the maintenance of comfort but the prevention of want that was at stake.

The German scheme had emerged from a very different political situation, and its subsequent modification did nothing to alter that fact. It was intended to appeal primarily to the strong, not to the weak, among the German working class. It did less to rescue the very poor from dependence on poor relief — indeed this was often used to supplement inadequate insurance benefits. It did more to provide the better paid element among the workers with benefits suited to their requirements and therefore worthy of their attention and co-operation. Of course the political problem in Britain was also how to obtain the co-operation of the comfortable working class, since it was their institutions that were to be used for the administration of the scheme. In consequence there were advantages held out to them, in particular the ability to employ their accumulated funds for purposes other than the provision of basic sickness benefits. But the difference remains. The success of the British scheme was judged by its ability to protect the weak from want. The success of the German scheme was not dependent on what it would do for the very poor, for these constituted no political menace on their own. It was dependent rather on the degree to which it appealed to the aspirations of the active and economically strongest section of the working class.

It is this contrast in the political context of the two pieces of legislation that accounts not only for the difference between graduated and uniform provision, but also for the fact that this feature of the German scheme evoked so little interest or even comment in 1911. It is rather now, in a political context far removed from the preoccupation of the Edwardians with minimum provisions, that this aspect of the German policy seems of significance in Britain.[22]

Organisation

The contrast in political context throws light also on aspects of the two schemes other than finance. It has implications for their structure and organisation. It was a characteristic of German sickness insurance that workers' representatives played an important part in its administration, i.e. that self-government by contributors was a prominent feature of the system. Through elaborate appeals procedures that relied on tribunals drawn in equal number from workmen and employers with a Civil Service chairman, workers' participation was also a prominent feature of the more bureaucratic administration of old age and invalidity insurance. This reliance on honorary service connected workers' insurance to a long and respected tradition in which such service in local administration had been the mark of citizenship. By the turn of the century this tradition was in practice under stress, and local government administration depended increasingly on the full-time salaried official.

Nowhere had the old tradition been formally repudiated, but it is obvious that around 1900, as at all times, some occupational groups were much better able to fill honorary offices of this kind than others. The heavy reliance of the insurance schemes on workers' representatives meant in practice that it was trade union officials who were being given important roles, serving alongside employers on tribunals and executive committees. What the effect of this may have been in the course of a generation or so on the attitudes of the most active and influential figures in the German labour movement is a matter of some historical interest. It is often said that in Imperial Germany the organised working class was cut off from those above them not only politically but also socially and culturally, forming as it were a world of its own with its separate institutions and values. A study of the actual working of insurance administration could throw some light on statements of this kind. It would be valuable to identify those who ran the major sickness funds or served on tribunals, as well as the issues of administration around which agreement was customary or antagonism crystallised.

How was the comparison between the administration of British and German insurance actually presented to the British public? Once again our main sources are the Memoranda that accompanied the Bill in May 1911. Although both of these devoted far more space to the details of comparative costs and benefits, they gave the greatest prominence to what they considered to be the greater merits of the British form of organisation. The general explanatory Memorandum made three points:

(1) that administration would be handed over to the friendly societies already established or hereafter to be founded;
(2) since deficits due to malingering were not to be made good by the state the members of the society would have every inducement to look after their own affairs;
(3) in Germany the system was much more bureaucratic in its management, and did not nearly to the same extent adopt the principle of self-government.[23]

In the more detailed *Memorandum on Sickness and Invalidity Insurance* the opening statement declared that the most fundamental difference between the two schemes was that of organisation. This was a reference to the fact that the British scheme combined sickness and invalidity insurance, whereas in Germany these were administered separately.[24] Apart from cheapness and simplicity, this had meant that 'the workman will from first to last be able to continue in the provident society of his choice, . . . and that at every stage of his membership his society will have a direct inducement to take an interest in his welfare.' Here, as already in the other document, the emphasis was on the way in which the friendly society movement 'will be further stimulated and strengthened by the Bill'.[25] This, too, is the stress in a subsequent section devoted to administration whose opening paragraph declared:

There is no counterpart in German insurance legislation to the unconditional autonomy which the National Insurance Bill secures to the Approved Societies of insurers to which the execution of the principal beneficiary provisions of the Bill will be entrusted. The Bill requires that the affairs of these Societies shall be subject to the absolute control of the members.[26]

The element of self-government in the German schemes was shortly described. By comparison with the absolute control proclaimed for the British approved societies it seemed small and appeared to justify the unfavourable comparison made in this respect in both Memoranda.

It is clear that what mattered to the authors of these documents was to emphasise that the scheme possessed the virtues of friendly societies. Comparison with German administration was basically made with this object in mind. This in turn points to the really fundamental fact. In so far as there was ever a model for the makers of British health insurance, it was not the German scheme but the practice of British friendly societies.

The construction of a British scheme of health insurance did not begin with a detailed study of German practices. Lloyd George's hurried tour was hardly that and it is a telling fact that the subsequent report that was produced by the Treasury in December 1908 was limited to the German invalidity and old age pensions scheme and still totally ignored the much more illuminating practices of German sickness insurance. There is some evidence that Lloyd George asked Dawson at the Board of Trade for a copy of a paper on German sickness insurance that Dawson had written, but there is no sign that he ever received it.[27] It was not among the papers given to Braithwaite in December 1910 for his briefing nor among the other working papers in connection with the Bill. Much more important were the early negotiations with the representatives of the friendly society movement in 1908-9. It was friendly society practice that was the model for the scheme from the beginning.

This fundamental fact is only reinforced by the role that Braithwaite played in the construction of the Bill from January 1911 onwards. The man with the best opportunity to study the German scheme and consider how to adapt it to British conditions had not been interested in doing anything of the kind. More even than Lloyd George's earlier advisers he was orientated towards friendly society practices and was not interested in discovering any fundamental alternatives in Germany. Had he wished to do so he would soon have come up against obstacles, but the point is that no one ever seriously tried to consider the uses of German insurance for the shaping of a British scheme except at the most trivial level of borrowing individual devices.

In this very important sense, just as unemployment insurance was undoubtedly constructed on the basis of trade union experience and practice, so health insurance took shape in relation to the experience and practice of friendly societies.

Hence no one in the Treasury team ever questioned the first of the two principles on which voluntary associations are necessarily constructed, i.e. that contributors should be free to choose their society. The other characteristic of a voluntary association was that societies should be free to refuse to admit contributors. In a sense this principle was incompatible with compulsory insurance. The combination of compulsion to join some society with freedom to be rejected by all of them was liable to produce a residue of uninsured persons whom no society wanted. In this sense it was impossible to administer a compulsory scheme through voluntary associations. Yet this was exactly what Lloyd George and his advisers wished to do. It forced them into the position where they would have to devise a different scheme for a residue of contributors whom no society wished to admit. No one knew how many of these there would be, but in March 1911 Lloyd George decided to make only minimal provision for such people and to rely on the societies to keep that residue small. This minimal provision was in fact neither insurance nor state subsidy; it was no more than a deposit account in the Post Office. It was politically acceptable only if the number of such 'deposit contributors' was in fact to be insignificant. In Braithwaite's words, 'the bill was finally a gamble. Would the Societies compete for members?'[28] Lloyd George built the Bill on the belief that they would.

Comparison with the 1870 Education Act will illustrate this point. The School Boards, just like the arrangements for 'deposit contributors', were designed to fill the gaps still remaining in the provision of a benefit made by subsidised voluntary bodies. The new administrative structures in 1870 were adequate to fill gaps of a considerable size. The 1911 policy, having subsidised the voluntary bodies, was to hope that the gaps to be filled would be small.

The decision to rely on the friendly societies was a decision to administer compulsory health insurance with a minimum of direct contact between the state and the citizen. It arose from a strong dislike of multiplying civil servants and an acute awareness of the limitations of bureaucracy. As the explanatory *Memorandum* put it:

> The greatest evil which has to be guarded against in all benefit schemes of this character comes from the danger of malingering. . . The only really effective check . . . is to be found in engaging the self-interest of the workmen themselves in opposition to it. That is why a purely State Scheme . . . would inevitably lead to unlimited shamming and deception. This Scheme is so worked that the burden of mismanagement and maladministration would fall on the workmen themselves. . . Once they realise that, then malingering will become an unpopular vice amongst them, and they will take the surest and shortest way to discourage it.[29]

It could be argued that under such circumstances friendly societies would do well to be cautious in their acceptance of new members, and leave the doubtful cases to find acceptance elsewhere. How reasonable was it to expect societies that had up to now been more noted for their caution to step out boldly into the unknown? And how likely was it that significant numbers of new approved societies would be forthcoming? In the Bill as submitted to Parliament in May such societies were intended to have all the constitutional characteristics of existing friendly societies, i.e. to be 'subject to the absolute control of the members, and with provision for the election of all committees, representatives and officers by the members'.[30]

In short, the policy on which Lloyd George had embarked was certainly a gamble. By leaving societies free to reject members on a wide range of grounds and yet creating no proper alternative organisation, he had left his scheme of compulsory insurance extremely vulnerable.

In June 1911 the powerful industrial insurance companies and collecting friendly societies, both engaged in the sale of life insurance and never before associated with sickness insurance, decided that they wished to participate in the government's scheme. This they did in defence of their lucrative life insurance business, which they feared would be absorbed by the friendly societies once these had established contact with households through the administration of health insurance. Better to administer health insurance through their own agents and use the opportunity to sell profitable life insurance as well.[31]

This decision transformed the situation. Until then the Bill had envisaged that health insurance would be administered by approved societies modelled on the normal friendly society pattern. However industrial insurance companies were very different kinds of institutions. Friendly societies consisted of self-governing local 'lodges' affiliated to national 'orders'. They ran the business of their lodges by means of honorary officers. Industrial insurance companies were centralised companies, conducting business with their customers through an army of local agents who sold policies on the doorstep and thereafter collected weekly subscriptions by calling at the house. The fact that they were paid by commission gave the agents a strong financial interest in the sale of policies. The system had been strongly criticised both then and subsequently for the high proportion of the premiums that was absorbed by commissions and other administrative costs and for the tendency to sell to ignorant people policies that were more to the agent's financial advantage than to that of the customer. In all these respects the so-called collecting friendly societies were similar to the insurance companies. The latter were limited liability companies run by directors responsible to their shareholders. The former were non-profit-making societies run by officers formally responsible to their members. But since these members had no corporate identity and no connection with the society except through its collectors, it was the collectors who in practice exercised the voting rights and controlled the society in their own interests.

There was at least one other respect in which these bodies differed from normal friendly societies. Since they had never administered sickness insurance they provided no medical treatment and had no relations with medical practitioners.

The pressure that these bodies put on the government has been described in detail by Professor Gilbert. Their army of agents, perfect door-to-door canvassers, gave them considerable political leverage. But the same active force, in contact with the very people whom the friendly societies had not been able to recruit, meant also that the companies had something to offer that the government badly needed, if the vast majority of those for whom the new insurance scheme was intended were to be enrolled in approved societies — hence their success in attacking those clauses of the Bill that had laid down that approved societies should in essentials be like friendly societies. In its final version the Bill permitted them to participate without abandoning their own specific characteristics. It dropped the insistence on local branch organisation, and separated the provision of medical treatment from the administration of insurance payments. Although the insistence on self-government remained formally written into the Bill, it had become capable of being nullified by the administrative discretion of the Insurance Commissioners, and this was what happened. The non-profit-making character of approved societies was also retained, but this presented no obstacle, since they could now be associated with profit-making bodies under what was in effect the same management. A very generously pitched margin for administrative costs was included in the actuarial calculations to cover the notoriously high administrative expenses of the collectors.

The result of this assertion of political power by commercial interests was that the British health insurance scheme was in effect less self-governing than the German one. The good intentions of May 1911 were overtaken by events. If the friendly societies properly so-called may have compared favourably with most or indeed all the German sickness funds, this was certainly not true of those approved societies connected with the commercial companies or with the so-called collecting friendly societies. The final version of the explanatory Memorandum, printed in January 1912 to accompany the Bill as passed by the

House of Commons, still proudly proclaimed that 'in Germany the system is much more bureaucratic in its management, and does not nearly to the same extent adopt the principle of self-government.'[32] Yet as far as self-government was concerned, this was now no more than a form of deception, and the administrative decisions taken in the course of the next few months served to make this clear.

The coupling of less bureaucracy with more self-government that came so easily to the British mind was in fact profoundly misleading. It had been the original determination to avoid the methods of bureaucracy and to rely on voluntary associations for the administration of the scheme that had led directly to the whittling away of the element of self-government. It had made the government vulnerable to pressure from those bodies capable of organising what the government was unwilling to organise directly through its own bureaucratic structures. At first it had seemed that this would imply no more than a working relationship in which the state lent its support to friendly societies, whose mutuality and self-government made them deserving recipients of the resources of a state organised on the principles of Liberalism.

However, the decision to leave the field open to the initiative of voluntary associations also left it open to another set of voluntary associations with very different characteristics, i.e. commercial companies. In the ensuing competition the greater resources of the commercial bodies compared with the bodies of mutual help became only too obvious, first in the political competition for the compliance of politicians, and secondly in the organisational competition for the recruitment of contributors. The pages of Braithwaite's *Memoirs* and Professor Gilbert's monograph amply demonstrate the superior political skill of the representatives of the commercial world, or rather their greater ability and willingness to hire the professional skills required. The professional advisers of the insurance companies and their allies, particularly Kingsley Wood, emerge as the really able men in this struggle. As for the friendly society leaders involved, Braithwaite called them an extraordinarily thick-headed crowd and added

> They were intensely worthy... But oh they were so difficult — often so suspicious — and always so unintelligent and unadaptable. No doubt National Insurance and the complexities of legislation were too much for men often of humble circumstances and education. But why did they not get good advice? Why did they allow themselves to be outwitted every time?[33]

The subsequent history of national health insurance shows that in the competition for contributors the commercial companies were far and away the more successful. When health insurance was investigated in 1928, it had come to be generally recognised that insurance through approved societies had failed to create a system of self-government.[34]

The reasons for this ability of commercial undertakings to act more effectively in the politics of 1911 and subsequently in society as such than voluntary mutual-help associations based on participation touch on some of the deepest changes in British society between the 1880s and the 1920s. They deserve more thought than I can give them in this chapter. But they acquire a peculiar importance in this connection because of the determination to minimise the role of the bureaucratic state. For there was in theory an alternative to the use of approved societies, namely bureaucratic structures in direct contact with the insurance contributors. They would certainly have been more expensive to the Treasury, and thereby increased the need for higher taxation with political complications which the government was anxious to avoid. (Whether they would have been more expensive for the nation than the generous administrative costs allowed to the approved societies is quite another question.) Such considerations were undoubtedly important to the Chancellor of the Exchequer. But they were not the only considerations. The preference for voluntary associations was also a positive preference, and it was only when it was too late to withdraw from the decision that its full implications became apparent.

All this raises comparative questions about the subsequent development of the German insurance system, particularly in relation to self-government within the sickness funds and to participation in appeals procedures. These are questions that I cannot answer on my present knowledge. Let me therefore sum up by returning to the sort of comparison that I have been attempting to make: relating the characteristics of the insurance schemes in the two countries to the political objectives to which they were meant to contribute. In Germany, it seems to me, the aim had been to maximise participation by the more active members of the working class in a scheme sponsored by the state and supervised by it. Hence the concessions made to them, particularly the majority representation on sickness funds, but also their role in the adjudication of invalidity claims. I make no reference to the detailed political circumstances under which the German laws were produced, but it is perhaps worth mentioning that the Sickness Insurance Law of 1883 was one in whose making Bismarck himself had taken little part, nor was he closely involved in the details of the Invalidity and Old Age Law of 1889.[35] In Britain in 1911, by contrast, the aim was specifically to maximise participation by voluntary societies, including after June the commercial companies. Commercial companies would not have been able to adopt devices for participation and self-government by contributors without submitting to fundamental structural changes. Hence the concessions made to them added up to the chance to retain the same structures as before, providing power to the directors, profit for the shareholders and good commissions for the agents.

Postscript

There was a further set of issues confronting the authors of British health insurance in which the existence of a German precedent proved of general interest. I refer to the role and remuneration of the medical profession in the scheme. This too produced Anglo-German comparisons and even a governmental paper especially devoted to the German practice.[36] It is a subject that is still to be investigated, and so cannot be dealt with in this chapter. It is not a trivial matter, touching as it does on the relation of a self-regulating profession to the organs of central as well as local government. Whether in this instance the availability of German precedents offered illumination or served to darken counsel is a matter still to be discovered.

Notes

1. I agree with the interpretation to be found in B.B. Gilbert, 'David Lloyd George, Land, the Budget and Social Reform', *American Historical Review*, vol. 81, no. 5 (1976).
2. *The Daily News*, 27 Aug. 1908.
3. Workmen's Insurance Systems in Germany. Report of the Delegation. PRO Cab. 37/96/169.
4. W.S. Churchill to H.H. Asquith, 29 Dec. 1908. The complete text is printed in Randolph S. Churchill, *Winston S. Churchill* (London, 1967) vol. II, Companion Volume Part 2, pp. 862-4.
5. 5 *Hansard* 4 (29 Apr. 1909), cols. 482-7.
6. 4 *Hansard* 192 (9 July 1908), col. 142; 190 (16 June 1908), col. 828.
7. S. Webb, Suggestions as to Old Age Pensions, 29 Sept. 1907, Asquith Papers 75 f. 137; C. Booth, 'Enumerations and Classification of Paupers and State Pensions for the Aged', *Jl.R.Stat.Soc.* vol. 54 (1891), p. 634; J. Harris, *Unemployment and Politics* (Oxford, 1972), p. 309.

8. Leverton Harris, MP for Tower Hamlets, 4 *Hansard* 190 (15 June 1908), cols. 651-2; G.N. Barnes, ibid., cols. 806-7; Asquith, ibid., col. 828. See also Alfred Mond, Liberal MP, putting a businessman's point of view, ibid., cols. 640-2.
9. J.A. Spender, *The State and Pensions in Old Age* (London, 1892), pp. 73-6; 'State Socialism in Germany', *The Times*, 19 June 1889.
10. The author was Percy Ashley, a Board of Trade official.
11. For details of these negotiations see B.B. Gilbert, *The Evolution of National Insurance in Great Britain* (London, 1966), pp. 295-303.
12. H.N. Bunbury (ed.), *Lloyd George's Ambulance Wagon. The Memoirs of W.J. Braithwaite, 1911-1912* (London, 1957), pp. 85-7.
13. Bunbury, *Braithwaite*, p. 113.
14. Ibid., pp. 152-3.
15. Collection of contributions by the use of stamps; health education by lectures and pamphlets; disability allowance conditional on the patient obeying doctor's orders. Also a long and important passage dealing with the principle of compulsory contributions from employers. This quoted the opinion of German employers to the effect that it increased the efficiency of the workers, and then showed that the employers' contribution in Germany was higher than the 3d proposed in the Bill.
16. Exclusion of casual labour; excessively generous treatment of those already over fifty at the expense of young contributors.
17. 5 *Hansard* 25 (4 May 1911), col. 615.
18. 5 *Hansard* 25 (4 May 1911), col. 619. The third passage mentioned shortly that the minimum period of contributions for a disability allowance was two years compared with five years in Germany.
19. *National Insurance Bill. Memorandum Explanatory of the Bill*, 8 May 1911, PP 1911 (HC 147) LXXIII, *Memorandum on Sickness and Invalidity Insurance in Germany*, 14 pp. (printed May 1911), 1911, Cd. 5678, LXXIII, 213. *Memorandum Containing the Opinions of Various Authorities in Germany*, 13 pp. (printed May 1911) 1911, Cd. 5679, LXXIII, 227.
20. 5 *Hansard* 25 (4 May 1911), col. 616. I have paraphrased what I take to be its meaning.
21. Hence the only form in which the principle of graduated contributions was introduced into the British scheme was to reduce the contribution for those with quite exceptionally low wages without reducing the benefits. The employer was obliged to make up the balance of the contribution and in extreme cases the state added one penny. This was graduation of a sort, but almost the opposite to what the Germans were doing.
22. When in 1957 the new German pensions law greatly increased the traditional element of graduation, it naturally emphasised this long-standing contrast between the insurance provision of the two countries. This point was brought out in the comments made on the paper during the conference.
23. *Memorandum Explanatory of the Bill*, p. 2.
24. The fact that in Germany both invalidity pensions and old age pensions were administered together, whereas in Britain they were quite separate, was of course not mentioned.
25. *Memorandum on Sickness and Invalidity Insurance in Germany*, p. 2.
26. Ibid., p. 13.
27. W.H. Clark (Treasury) to W.H. Dawson, 23 Dec. 1908, W.H. Dawson Papers 173, Birmingham University Library.
28. Bunbury, *Braithwaite*, p. 120.
29. *Explanatory Memorandum* p. 15.
30. *Memorandum on Insurance in Germany*, p. 13. For fuller details, see

Explanatory Memorandum, section 5A.

31. For this and the next three paragraphs, see the detailed exposition in Gilbert, *Evolution of National Insurance*, pp. 318-43, 358-83.

32. *Memorandum*, p. 2, PP 1911, Cd. 5995, LXXIII, 69.

33. Bunbury, *Braithwaite*, p. 92.

34. R.W. Harris, *National Health Insurance in Great Britain 1911-1946* (London 1946), Chs. 4, 5; *Royal Commission on National Health Insurance* (1928), Cd. 2596, Majority Report, Ch. 8, Minority Report, paras. 38-40.

35. Hans Rothfels, *Theodor Lohmann und die Kampfjahre der staatlichen Sozialpolitik* (Berlin, 1927), p. 55; Walter Vogel, *Bismarcks Arbeiterversicherung, Ihre Entstehung im Kraeftespiel der Zeit* (Brunswick, 1951), pp. 150-1.

36. *Medical Benefits under the German Sickness Insurance Legislation*, PP 1912-13, Cd. 6581, LXXXVIII, 749.

6 THE BRITISH BUSINESS COMMUNITY, SOCIAL INSURANCE AND THE GERMAN EXAMPLE

J.R. Hay

The other subject is labour. Whatever we ourselves individually desire, we can hardly expect that there will be no further legislation as to the conditions of employment. With increasing facilities for communication between different countries, we shall be compelled to pay serious attention, as well to what our European rivals are doing (as, for instance, in the matter of Compulsory Insurance and Old Age Pensions), as to the experiments of the great daughter countries like Australia. To deal with such questions, the legislature will want all the help it can get. Chambers of Commerce will doubtless show, in their treatment of topics like these, what some critics will regard as an employers' bias; but this will not be altogether regrettable. The ultimate line of legislation will be the resultant of a number of divergent forces; and it is in the public interest that each separate view should be presented with the utmost intelligence.[1]

The author of this passage was Professor W. J. Ashley of the Faculty of Commerce in the University of Birmingham *ex officio* member of the Birmingham Chamber of Commerce and one of the leading authorities in Britain on recent economic and social developments in Germany. His remarks are interesting both for their content and timing, coming as they did before the burst of British welfare legislation of 1906 to 1914. Addressing a business audience, he urged them to become involved in the shaping of legislation and the study of foreign practice, as he considered further state action inevitable.

Professor Hennock has dealt with the origins of national insurance and the German precedent in the previous chapter, so the focus of this chapter is at one and the same time narrower and broader than his. The narrower focus is on the reasons for some British employers' interest in German welfare, including social insurance and other measures: which groups of employers were involved and why; what was the extent of their knowledge and what use did they make of it? But it is also concerned with the implications of this study for our understanding of the relationship between social policy in one country and another. As Dr Roger Davidson recently pointed out, we lack a theory of the diffusion of social institutions corresponding to that which economists have developed to account for the diffusion of technology.[2] The widespread adoption of a variety of social welfare policies in a range of very different countries in the forty years centred on 1900 cries out for general explanation. Simultaneous but independent discovery of the advantages of social legislation is implausible, but what precise influence did foreign practice have on the receiving society? Can we use the study of British employers' reception of German practice as part of the basis for a theory of the development of the welfare state?

The interest of British employers in foreign systems of welfare was not, of course, limited to the German example, and we may be in danger of missing or underestimating important parts of the experience of both countries if we overdo our concentration on Anglo-German influences. If, as Ashley suggested, competition from abroad is the spur to social legislation, why select the German model? After all, other societies, particularly the United States of America, were developing rapidly in this period; faster than Britain and without the benefit of welfare legislation.[3] It is not enough to argue that America was a special case, that American growth was all the result of unlimited natural resources, more rapid population growth, Yankee ingenuity and the doctrine of interchangeable parts. We are now led to believe that British entrepreneurs skilfully met challenges from abroad or adopted technologies quickly according to the relative factor costs they faced. Also, they tried to give the customer what he or she wanted by skilful product differentiation.[4] Why did they not therefore take the American welfare route, i.e. limited schemes of workmen's compensation for accidents at work, no old age pensions or social insurance, and indeed very little social legislation of any kind? Why copy Germany when the traditions, culture and ideology of the United States were so much closer in many respects to those of Britain?[5] It is easier to pose this question than to answer it, but Germany did represent a greater competitive threat to Britain. It was Germany which was squeezing British trade in third markets and even in the domestic market. By 1913 Britain was importing twice as much from Germany as she was able to export to her, and imports from Germany represented about 10 per cent of Britain's total.[6]

The effects of the Boer War on the perception of military threats and domestic crises, stemming from fears of racial degeneration, have often been canvassed as reasons for the search for national efficiency

on the German model.[7] Though I have used the argument myself
in the past, I am becoming less happy with it. What I will argue is
that the German example was picked up by one group in particular
in Britain whose industrial experience was very similar in many ways
to that of parts of Germany. Birmingham was just going through
its industrial revolution in this period, unlike the textile areas of the
North of England, or London. The same appears to have happened
in Germany just a little earlier, and social legislation which seemed
to have worked for Germany could be the answer to Birmingham's
problems also.

The interest of British employers in social welfare was not something
divorced from their business concern. Rather it was an intimate part
thereof, just as much for the paternalistic employers as for those
who made a fetish of industrial efficiency, like Sir Charles Furness.[8]
Even the Cadburys and the Rowntrees and, above all, W.H. Lever,
wished to avoid the stigma of philanthropy.[9] If they characterised their
behaviour in religious or humanitarian terms it was only as part of a
consistent world-view that saw no contradiction between sound business principles and the health and welfare of their own workers — or,
by extension, of the working class generally in the society of which
they were a part.

The link between technological, commercial and profit considerations and social welfare was provided very often by technical education.
This is something which has, I believe, been neglected in the past,
perhaps because of the way in which British social policy studies have
developed out of social administrative history. Because education and
welfare are in separate administrative categories they are too seldom
studied together. Yet technical education and welfare in the nineteenth
and early twentieth centuries were very closely linked in the minds of
many British employers, and this has to be appreciated to understand
their involvement in social reform.[10]

It is also very striking how British employers made great use of their
own labourers, particularly their skilled artisans and members of trade
unions, in the study of foreign educational and welfare practice. Several
examples are discussed in this chapter and there were at least four
possible reasons for this use of artisans or trade unionists in social
inquiry abroad. There may have been an element of industrial espionage. The employers, it might be argued, did not know how to operate
the machines used in their factories and sent the men who did.[11] It
is possible that this was the case occasionally, but it is unlikely to have
been common practice. Rather, it seems that this use of artisans was to

awaken or reinforce interest in foreign competition and methods; to bring home to the leading representatives of the workers the rapidity of the development of foreign industries, particularly in the areas of traditional British pre-eminence, and the contribution which technical education or welfare made to that success.[12] Also, as a consequence thereof, employers wanted to try to moderate pressures for wage increases by giving artisans an impression of foreign wage levels, and the consequences of 'demanding more than the trade would bear'. Sometimes this tactic may have rebounded, as when one group of workers found that average wage levels were higher in their branch of the iron trade.[13] Finally, it seems that the use of artisans and trade unionists was often designed to overcome their resistance to the introduction of foreign welfare schemes. Far from being earnest advocates of German social legislation, many British workers seem to have had strong reservations about it and this could only be dispelled by experience of the schemes in practice. Trade unionists feared that state welfare would undermine their own organisations, and members of friendly societies likewise were very worried — with greater reason, as it turned out. As late as 1908 the Parliamentary Committee of the Trades Union Congress sent a delegation to Germany to study German social insurance. They returned convinced that state insurance had had no injurious effects on trade union organisation, as far as membership was concerned. They remained very cool as regards the benefits of insurance to contributors.[14] It has been argued that the leaders of the workers would support state welfare legislation only when their hold over the loyalty of the working class was secure; otherwise they would tend to oppose what they saw as state competition for that loyalty.[15] This point is further discussed below.

The transfer of information between Britain and Germany in the area covered by the social question was always a two-way process, but one gets the impression that down to the 1870s the flow of information, as distinct from cultural and literary influences, was in Germany's favour. A recent paper reported on over 150 publications by around 100 German visitors to Britain between 1815 and 1870.[16] Most of these were, no doubt, simply travellers with tales to tell. More significant were the industrial entrepreneurs who studied technical processes and social conditions, including Alfred Krupp, F.A.J. Egells, Jacob Meyer and many others.[17] In one book Pollard lists more than twenty leading businessmen who came to Britain early in the nineteenth century.[18] Many German firms set up as merchants of industrial products in the northern cities of England, particularly Manchester and Bradford.[19] The Prussian government, of course, sent civil servants like Peter Beuth to report on British industrial practice, and maintained in addition a platoon of industrial spies. Some remained at home and imbibed British ideas and social thought, like the civil servant who began each day by reading a chapter of Adam Smith's *Wealth of Nations* before breakfast.[20]

By the end of the nineteenth century, though the two-way flow continued, it appears that the balance of concern had swung the other way.[21] One sometimes gets the impression that the streets of Berlin — and other German cities — were clogged with little groups of British inquirers of one kind or another, subjecting every aspect of Germany's social institutions to more or less detailed scrutiny.[22] There were the shrill propagandists, like E.E. Williams[23] and A. Shadwell;[24] the more sober, but still publicly orientated, writers like W.H. Dawson, author of a whole series of volumes on Germany from the popular to the professional level;[25] the well heeled Germanophiles and travellers who became involved in various specific movements, such as the town planning studies, discussed by Dr Sutcliffe;[26] and there were the social investigators who sought statistical and social indicators of the level of public and private welfare provision throughout the Reich. Many of this latter group were, or became, civil servants, including W.H. Beveridge,[27] D.F. Schloss[28] and even Dawson, recruited into the Board of Trade in 1906. In addition, politicians from Joseph Chamberlain, Sir John Gorst and Sir Charles Dilke to Churchill, Haldane and Lloyd George made brief forays into Germany, while Geoffrey Drage had a rather cool look at German pensions in his book, *The Problem of the Aged Poor*.[29] Of these political visitations, perhaps the best known is that of the Liberal Chancellor of the Exchequer in August 1908. The significance of this visit was subsequently questioned by one who was very close to events at the time:

English legislation was later said to be derived from L[loyd] G[eorge]'s intense study of the German system! What is true is that he himself went to Germany for a holiday and was told something about it; that some labour members went there; that the Poor Law Report contains a short summary of it, and that a memorandum had been prepared at the Treasury; that I was given five or six days in Germany and reported on it; that Dawson later got out an official paper to show the scales of contributions and benefits in Germany. The Germans, it is true, introduced compulsion and made

insurance national. We followed them in that, but we cannot be said
to have copied their legislation. Their legislation was imposed upon
an almost clear field. Ours was superimposed on a great variety of
existing organisations.[30]

Braithwaite's account of the origins of British health insurance has
its weaknesses.[31] The German social insurance of the 1880s was not a
complete innovation imposed on a clear field.[32] Germany did not have
a single unified national system. Understandably enough, Braithwaite
underestimates Lloyd George's personal contribution, but he does highlight the curious relationship between the British and German involvement in the area of social insurance.[33] The British legislation owed
something to German practice, but it was not a carbon copy thereof,
yet the connection between the two approaches consisted of far more
than a fleeting visit by one leading British politician. In fact, the activities of the politicians, civil servants and ideologues are fairly well
known through the work of J. Harris, J. Brown, B.B. Gilbert, R. Davidson and G. Searle,[34] though an overall assessment of their influence, and
particularly their role in the transfer of German social ideas, remains
to be made.

However, the concern here is not with these figures but with an
equally numerous, though by contrast relatively unknown, group of
British employers who also sought to introduce aspects of German
social policy into Britain across the whole spectrum of policy, including
social insurance. Some British employers were interested in the assimila-
tion of British practice to that of Germany, others in the grafting of
specific aspects of German policy on to British stock and some in the
importation of new ideas into areas not covered by British policy. Yet
others studied German practice only to reject it in favour of alternative foreign models. Their motives and interests in Germany were very
varied and stemmed from quite disparate concerns and backgrounds.
Some, a few, were native Germans or had close family ties with
Germany; others had been educated in Germany; many more had begun
paying visits to Germany at impressionable ages and had maintained
business and professional contacts there throughout their lives. The
reasons for their interest were also diverse; some were interested in
broad questions of national efficiency or imbued with aspects of Social
Darwinism; some had very specific concerns which related to their
particular trades or industries; others were involved in domestic social
reform in any case and simply turned to the German example to
supplement or modify their existing commitment, and finally there

were those whose eyes were opened by German practice as they sought remedies for problems of industrial relations at home. It is no accident that the efficiency, paternalistic, bureaucratic and social control aspects of German social policy were often more attractive to employers than the ameliorative ones, but a mixture of interests was characteristic of nearly all of them. Few were single-mindedly concerned with the economic and profit implications of welfare to the exclusion of the broader social context of policy.[35] To say this is not to deny that interest in welfare was an offshoot of business concern. Few went to Germany solely to study social welfare; most, initially at least, were interested in technical or commercial matters and discovered German social policy sometimes by accident, certainly till around 1905. Thereafter, some went specifically to study social welfare within the firm and as it had been developed by the state, but most employers retained a much broader focus than social welfare as conventionally defined.

The question of German influence on British policy through employers needs to be tackled at several levels. Why were individuals concerned, why were social groups prepared to listen to and be influenced by such individuals, and what influence had these groups and their representatives on the formation of policy?

It is at the level of the individual that you would expect to find most variety of motivation and concern. Many well known figures at the national level were Germans or sons of German fathers. Alexander Siemens, born in Hanover in 1847, had served as a private in the Franco-Prussian War. He was a pupil of Sir William Siemens and served an apprenticeship with Siemens Brothers at Woolwich. He became a director of Siemens in his turn, one of the first firms, according to its historian, to institute old age pensions, a sick fund for employees and an endowment fund for widows and orphans.[36] Siemens was a member of the committee of the Free Labour Protection Association, the strike-breaking and anti-trade union organisation, but by 1911 he was appointed in a personal capacity to the Industrial Council, which was created to bring capital and labour together to try to reduce industrial action during the labour unrest immediately before the First World War.[37] Also, he was elected Chairman of the Engineering Employers Federation in 1911 and was involved in the detailed negotiations to amend the National Insurance Bill, in which the EEF claimed to have achieved most of the changes to the Bill which it sought.[38] Earlier in 1909 he had led a deputation to Winston Churchill at the Board of Trade on the subject of labour exchanges, during which he argued against these institutions, preferring instead a reserve army of skilled unemployed. Given that exchanges were to be introduced, he was concerned about their role in industrial disputes and wanted them to adopt the German practice of remaining open during a strike or lock-out and either paying no attention to the dispute or simply reporting, without comment, that a dispute was in progress.[39] The final form of legislation followed Siemens' suggestion very closely, but this happened to coincide with Churchill's own preferences. Nevertheless, Churchill had come under pressure from Labour representatives to amend his view, which in turn was based on Beveridge's assessment of the success of German practice.[40]

Other nationally known figures of German origin include Ludwig Mond, born in Cassel in 1839 and educated at Marburg and Heidelberg,[41] who formed a partnership to exploit the Solvay ammonia process with Sir John Brunner, himself the son of a Swiss pastor, a Germanophile, and Liberal MP for Northwich from 1885.[42] Brunner was a very influential back-bencher and a proponent of technical education. Mond, too, founded and endowed research laboratories. His son, Alfred, became managing director of Brunner-Mond in turn, and later chairman of the *Westminster Gazette* syndicate (one of the leading Liberal papers). He was Vice-President of the Infants' Hospital and Liberal MP for Chester. The younger Mond saw business management as a responsibility imposed on him, very much in the paternalistic German mould.[43] Yet, having studied German pensions and discussed them with German employers, he concluded that the system of contributory old age pensions was 'unnecessarily costly and cumbersome and that the same results could be achieved more cheaply through a system financed directly from taxation', i.e. the New Zealand rather than the German model.[44] This was a conclusion shared by Charles Booth and George Cadbury, among other British employers, who had studied German pensions.[45]

Karl Friedrich Bayer, of an earlier generation, arrived in Manchester and became apprentice to Richard Roberts, inventor of the self-actor mule. Later he founded the engineering firm of Bayer-Peacock with Richard Peacock. He left his considerable fortune to further science and education in Manchester, including the foundation of Owens College. Other co-founders included Thomas Ashton and Henry Enfield Roscoe, both educated in Germany.[46]

But more interest perhaps attaches to some lesser known but not less influential employers, including D.M. Stevenson, Lord Provost of Glasgow, Chairman of the Coal Export Company, who studied

German and Belgian labour colonies before becoming involved with similar schemes in the west of Scotland.[47] Alderman Joseph Jonas, Lord Mayor of Sheffield, Imperial German Consul for the city and a large steel manufacturer, tried to persuade Sheffield Chamber of Commerce to introduce the Elberfeld system of relief which he had studied. He argued that it would be a more effective way of discriminating between those genuinely seeking work and the loafers and unemployables. The Elberfeld system was already being used in Edinburgh and Bradford, according to Jonas.[48] Much of German welfare policy, therefore, had a considerable influence at the local level. Many other employers were in touch with German welfare practice over a range of issues, but citing individual cases like this does not take us very far, though it must be emphasised that, at this period, employers were not well organised in effective political groups at the national level and consequently government understanding of employer views on specific issues was often defective. Lloyd George, for example, relied heavily on contacts with individual employers rather than formal organisations, such as the Chambers of Commerce.[49] Accordingly, in this period 1900-17, the sometimes idiosyncratic views of individual employers were liable to have greater effects on government policy than was to be the case in the next generation.[50] But to gauge employer reaction to German social policy we really have to look at groups of employers or individuals who were able to carry groups with them.

One group of employers who were particularly interested in German practice, and influential in various ways in the process of reform in Britain, were the businessmen of Birmingham. In other works I have examined their role in social legislation at the national level;[51] here I shall examine the reasons for their interest in German social policy, the extent of their knowledge and some of the different uses they made of that knowledge. The main organisation involved was the Birmingham Chamber of Commerce.

The Birmingham Chamber was drastically overhauled by two of its leading members at the start of the twentieth century. Around 1900 it had only 200 members and the reputation of being the home of 'cranks and faddists'.[52] Within a decade all this had changed. The first full-time Secretary was appointed and the Chamber began to provide a wide range of services to a rapidly growing membership. By 1906 there were 950 members and the total had risen to around 1,700 on the eve of the First World War. The *Chamber of Commerce Journal* was started and a *Commercial Yearbook* for the city. When the British Association held their 83rd Annual Meeting in Birmingham in 1913, the Secretary, George Henry Wright, provided a survey of the trades of the area. The Chamber also produced several valuable reports on taxation of imperial trade and social legislation.[53]

The origins of the Chamber's interest in Germany predate this reorganisation, of course, and the focus of attention was technical education. As early as 1868 four leading members of the Chamber gave evidence to the Select Committee of the House of Commons on Scientific and Technical Instruction based on their own experience of the contribution of the educational systems of Prussia, Saxony, Belgium, France and the United States to the rapid growth of manufacturing industry in these countries.

> The rapid progress in manufactures of other countries, more especially Prussia, Saxony, Belgium, France and the United States must be without doubt ascribed, as chief cause, to the high education both general and scientific of the artisan class, as well as of the masters. Prudent practical men will note that the Government in all these countries has established schools, general or technical, that have quickly attained high excellence . . . and those who have been abroad to investigate report that it is to these Government Schools that the rapid progress of manufactures is mainly due. The safe deduction appears to be that we ought to establish similar government schools in this country.[54]

In 1873 the Chamber raised £200 by subscription to send a party of competent artisans to the Vienna Exhibition. According to the report, these members of the labour aristocracy remarked on the role of education in the exhibiting countries.

> While maintaining the excellence of English manufactures they state rates of wages paid to foreign artisans and other collateral elements, which operate in enabling the manufactures in other countries to compete, as regards lowness of cost, with those of England, chiefly arise from the superior intelligence of the artisans of the competing countries, promoted by national systems of education terminating in industrial, scientific and artistic instruction, to the furtherance and promotion of which your Committee (as on a former occasion) directs the attention of Members of your Chamber.

The reports were noticed and brought into wider public debate by various speakers.[55] Locally the members of the Chamber were urged to support a new Trade School proposed by the Midland Institute.[56] National success was, however, limited. It was not till 1890 that a national government acted on the question, and even then allocated only the proceeds of some excise duties on spirits — the so-called 'whisky-money' — to technical education. As a later Chamber of Commerce speaker remarked, rather unkindly, 'as if to distil wisdom out of whiskey [sic], genius out of gin, and business out of beer'.[57]

Meanwhile other industrialists were active in pressing for improved technical education on German lines. Sir John Brunner, Mond's partner in the alkali works, tried to persuade the Liberal Party to abandon *laissez-faire* in favour of public investment in technical education, citing German examples in support of his case.[58] His efforts were maintained throughout the 1890s and 1900s, being linked with schemes for the development of domestic transport and communications. Even a memorandum thereon, signed by eight leading Liberal businessmen in 1904, failed to produce the desired shift in the Liberals' position.[59] It was somewhat ironic, therefore, that when H.H. Asquith appeared at the centenary celebrations of the Birmingham Chamber of Commerce in 1913 he suggested that the Chamber should become more closely involved in industrial education and, in particular, should foster links with Birmingham University. Since the Council of the Chamber had been one of the prime movers in the development of the Faculty of Commerce in the University, they had a defence to this reproach, though they did not point this out to the Prime Minister.[60]

By the early twentieth century the Birmingham Chamber of Commerce had become deeply involved in the study of German social welfare. Of the 24 elected members of the Council of the Chamber in 1906 at least one-third had German experience. They had been born, educated, had travelled regularly or had business interests in that country. In addition, several *ex officio* or other leading members of the Chamber had very close German connections.[61] Perhaps the most significant was Robert Hall Best (1843-1925), one of those lesser known entrepreneurial figures who flits across the footnotes of business history thanks to the first-class biography by his son, R.D. Best, written under the guidance of the Birmingham economist, Sargant Florence. Best senior was the son of a lamp manufacturer and son-in-law of an ironmaster. He had taken over the parental firm by 1867, at which point it went bankrupt, but he took the residue and set up a business to manufacture gas light fittings, hence the title of his biography, *Brass Chandelier*. Best and Lloyds, the new firm, was a partnership until 1898, though Best himself was in sole control from 1878 onwards.[62]

Best first went to Germany to learn commercial German in 1862 and, among other things, collected funds there for the Lancashire distress fund during the United States Civil War. After his father died in 1863, he returned to visit the German agents of the firm — Haensler in Cologne and Kusel in Hamburg — and also stayed with a family in Bonn. Thereafter he made a similar expedition every year till well into middle age and noted at one point that his passport recorded 200 crossings of the German frontier.

His interest in things German had nothing to do initially with social welfare. He was impressed by the quality, craftsmanship and aesthetic appreciation of the German workmen and their ability to turn out articles in metal of a higher standard than his British workmen. Gradually he came to relate this to German trade and technical education and the discipline and skills imparted in progressive German schools.

But his first involvement in social reform based on German experience linked education with the drink problem. He was engaged with 'several respectable working men' in supporting the Nelson Street Adult Early Morning School and wanted them to set up an establishment in which mixed and moderate drinking might take place. He rejected strict teetotalism on the one hand and excessive drinking on the other. His models were the Gothenburg system and the Munich beer halls, of which he formed a somewhat optimistic impression. Despite the support of some church leaders, including the future Bishop of Carlisle, he was unable to move the Adult School Union to adopt his ideas.[63]

Nothing daunted, he decided to embark on a broader comparison of Birmingham brassworkers with their counterparts in Berlin. To assist in this he enlisted W.J. Davis, leader of the Brassworkers' Trade Union, and Charles Perks of the Hospital Saturday Fund to accompany him. The content and national impact of the report they produced are discussed further below.[64] Locally, Best put his experience to work by stressing the curative and educational aspects of the Elberfeld and Berlin poor relief systems. He wanted the Birmingham City Aid Society to co-ordinate relief through a Central Board which would strictly classify paupers and maintain a reliable intelligence service. Pauperism might be prevented by 'greater care of the children and adequate treatment of poor women in childbirth. Especial care of convalescents and repair of the temporary unfit seemed to him not only a question of charity but of good business.'[65] The Society worked fairly closely with the Poor Law Guardians and the Charity Organisation Society and was finally amalgamated with the latter body in 1914.[66]

Best then became involved in the Tariff Reform controversy, taking the protectionist side, again on the basis of German experience.[67] Finally, he returned to post-primary and technical education as a result of contacts with Dr Georg Kerschensteiner, Director of Education for Munich. Kerschensteiner's continuation schools were highly practical and vocational in character, with a strong sense of service to the community. It was these features which particularly appealed to Best, who was concerned about the number of children who took up unskilled, dead-end jobs when their education was finished. Through Kerschensteiner he was introduced to the young Cambridge scholar C.K. Ogden, who had also studied German Continuation Schools. Together the two set to work on a book which appeared as *The Problems of the Continuation School* in 1914.[68] Meanwhile, Best was able, after considerable lobbying, to gain the support of leading employers and trade unionists for day-release classes to be held at the Municipal Technical School. This scheme was due to come into operation in 1914, but was overtaken by the First World War.

Best's personal influence in Birmingham was considerable and he acted as a disseminator of knowledge of German social policy within and beyond the city. The Chamber of Commerce, partly inspired by him, was following similar lines, and other local businessmen, including John Sutton Nettlefold, were also involved in related activities.[69] The Berlin Merchants Corporation tried to establish closer and more formal connections between the two cities and the Chamber of Commerce, in return, called on the Foreign Office to extend and solidify links with Germany.[70] Other employer organisations also sent deputations to Germany to study town planning, slum clearance and public health.[71]

Why was it that Birmingham employers as a group, not just as individuals, took up German welfare so enthusiastically? In part it might appear accidental that a relatively large number of members of the Chamber of Commerce had German connections, but of course, it is not accidental for much of Birmingham's trade was done with Continental Europe (a much higher proportion than for British trade as a whole), and Germany in particular. Therefore, one might expect German merchants to be drawn to Birmingham in the way that they had been to the northern textile towns, particularly Manchester, in an earlier generation. Also, those Birmingham families who were involved in the German trade might reasonably be expected to send their sons to Germany to get to know the market, to seek out the processes of competitors, and to examine the reasons for the growth of competition. This is what happened in the case of Best, H.C. Field and several other members of the Chamber. It was only as an offshoot of this study that they became interested in German welfare.

Then, of course, there is Joseph Chamberlain's leadership in the local community. He had a long-standing interest in Germany and German welfare policy, though, as Professor Hennock pointed out, he was at pains to distinguish his own social insurance proposals from those of Bismarck. His brother, Arthur, the head of Kynoch's, the engineering and armaments firm, was the only member of the family active in the Chamber of Commerce in this period, and I cannot detect his involvement with any of the aspects of welfare discussed here. However, Joseph Chamberlain's nephew, Norman, a Liberal Unionist City Councillor, did take a very active part in the campaign to introduce labour exchanges on the German model.[72]

I think we have to look a little deeper and realise that Birmingham and its hinterland were going through an important economic change in this period; a change which one is almost tempted to call revolutionary. The typical Birmingham firm of the previous period was a small metal-working enterprise in which employers and artisans worked closely together.[73] Labour relations were characterised by close defensive collusion between masters and men, the famous Birmingham Alliances.[74] Social mobility upwards and downwards was rapid and widespread. In the late nineteenth century, however, this situation was suddenly disrupted as large-scale firms came to dominate the main metal-using industries and large-volume manufacture of components for first the bicycle and gas and then the electrical and car industries became common. Of course many small firms survived, but the balance of economic power had altered.[75] The process was intensified by the rise of American and German competition, which led employers throughout Britain to respond by speeding up work processes, introducing new machinery and beginning the dilution of engineering through the introduction of semi-skilled machine minders in place of skilled craftsmen.[76] These general trends were common to most of the engineering areas of the country, but they affected Birmingham directly and profoundly. Best's biography describes the tensions which resulted when a new-broom foreman was introduced into the firm with ideas for the rationalisation of production processes, even to rebuilding the factory on a new but adjacent site to streamline the work. This move was resisted by the workers and by Best himself; the latter because he was not prepared to go into debt to undertake the reconstruction, having vivid memories of the earlier bankruptcy when the business had been overextended.[77]

This disruption of traditional employer-employee relationships caused by the introduction of new technology and the increase in the scale of operations was not unlike that which had occurred very rapidly in Germany in the late nineteenth century.[78] There the social strains of rapid industrialisation were even more apparent and the quite explicit use of social policy to ameliorate them equally visible. Moreover, from the Birmingham employers' point of view the German schemes seemed to have worked. Social Democracy no longer appeared a revolutionary threat, the pressures generated by explosive economic development seemed to have been contained, but, more important, social insurance had apparently reduced the direct burden on the employer while providing a satisfactory level of benefits for the workers and, above all, did not appear to have reduced the competitive power of the German economy.[79] British Labour and socalist schemes, on the other hand, threatened to place the burden of cost on the employer and reduce work incentives at a time when the overseas challenge was mounting.[80] Hence the German model was one way for employers to offer a positive response to socialism yet retain, and even reinforce, the work incentives on which the prosperity of the local and national economy was based.

How deep and how accurate was the British employers' knowledge of German social legislation? Obviously, at the individual level there were enormous variations. The vast majority had little direct experience and relied on the reports of those who had made more or less profound investigations. With the partial exception of technical education, knowledge of German welfare policy was on the whole limited and very general down to around 1905. There had been several government inquiries on old age pensions, methods of dealing with the unemployed, and workmen's compensation and employers' liability, but, so far as I can detect, they made little continuing impact on any significant groups of British employers. It appears that the same is true in the case of town planning.[81] In the debate over the crisis in British industry around 1900 at least one anonymous employer wrote to *The Times* suggesting that government-sponsored welfare legislation (perhaps on the German model) could be used to break trade union leaders' hold over their members through union welfare benefits.[82] This is an interesting point since some British historians have criticised the 'new unions' of the 1890s for turning to welfare provision instead of maintaining a militant posture in face of the employers' counter-attack in that decade. It suggests that Rimlinger was correct to point to those critical periods when a struggle for the loyalty of the workers was taking place between the employers, the trade unions and the state.

The Tariff Reform controversy of 1903 contributed to an upsurge of interest in, and knowledge of, Germany among employers. Ashley's *Progress of the German Working Classes in the Last Quarter of a Century* appeared in 1904, followed by Shadwell's *Industrial Efficiency* in 1905. In April 1905 Best, Davis and Perks left for Berlin and *The Brassworkers of Berlin and Birmingham* was published later that year. The last of these was picked up by *The Times* and by politicians and social reformers throughout Britain. It certainly contributed to stirring the Birmingham Chamber of Commerce into action on social insurance and labour exchanges.[83] The next year saw the Gainsborough Reports on *Life and Labour in Germany* organised by the defeated Conservative candidate for the West Lindsey or Gainsborough Division of Lincolnshire in the general election of 1906.[84] C. Algernon Moreing had been appalled by the tactics of the British free traders, who had argued that German workers lived in poverty as the result of their system of protection, and resolved to set the record straight. His approach was the one with which we have become familiar. He got six workers from three Gainsborough firms, Marshall Sons and Co., Rose Bros., and Edlington and Co., and sent them out under J.L. Bashford. Bashford had already delivered a paper on infirmity and old age pensions in Germany to the International Congress on Home Relief held in Edinburgh in 1904, and he included a revised version thereof as an Appendix to the Gainsborough Report.

The Gainsborough and Birmingham inquiries present an interesting contrast. The former, though generally approving the infirmity and old age pensions legislation, was relatively cool and critical, pointing to the limitations of coverage and benefits, the lack of cover for widows and orphans of contributors, the continuation of discontent and antagonism between employers and employees, and the Social Democratic view that the legislation was merely payment on account. Bashford did spot that changes had occurred in the attitudes and policy of the SDP leadership, 'that there was a greater tendency amongst the responsibe socialist leaders to cooperate with the government than was formerly the case'. Moreover, the Acts had not undermined thrift or reduced wages and had contributed in large measure to the increased health and vigour of the whole nation. He also noted that employers were providing topping-up coverage of pensions and that pensions had been intended, and had probably worked, to reinforce family ties.[85]

The Birmingham study, on the other hand, was less critical and more full of wide-eyed enthusiasm for the social arrangements of Berlin. The study began with the education of the child of a brass-worker, continued with consideration of universal military service, examined housing, beer gardens, then hospitals, and concluded with a comparison of poor relief and other welfare provisions in the two cities. It was this aspect, the administration of poor relief, which even German authorities found too uncritically treated. Dr Muensterberg, then Town Councillor and head of the Berlin City Aid Society remarked, 'your conception of Berlin conditions is much too favourable.'[86] Overcrowding, recognised to be one of the chief problems in Berlin, was hardly mentioned. It was argued that the Berlin authorities had been successful in separating the honest person willing to work from the work-shy, the drunkard and the able-bodied beggar, something which was to bedevil British social insurance despite Churchill's attempt to divorce morality and mathematics. Nevertheless, the Berlin Report did strongly commend the system of labour exchanges and national insurance and, uncritical or not, the support here seems to have convinced the members of the Chamber of Commerce that both labour exchanges and national insurance should be adopted by the British government. As mentioned earlier, the influence of the Chamber on the process of reform has been discussed in another article.[87] One point made there is worth repeating. Even in the Birmingham case, the advocacy of national insurance arose out of proposals to extend British Work-mens' Compensation legislation; it was not sparked off solely by inquiries into German practice.[88]

If, as a result of these inquiries, British employers were better informed about German social provision, their knowledge remained relatively patchy rather than detailed or profound. A series of deputations from employers' organisations to Winston Churchill and Lloyd George, the British Ministers responsible for labour exchanges, unemployment and health insurance, showed that employers were still unclear about the levels of contributions and benefits in Germany, the coverage of German schemes and the attitudes of German employers to welfare legislation.[89] Partly to remedy this, but also for wider propaganda purposes, to reduce employer resistance to the National Insurance Act which built up in 1911, Lloyd George had Dawson collect the opinions of German employers on social insurance.[90] These were published as a blue book and substantial extracts were included in Dawsons's *Social Insurance in Germany, 1880-1911*, published in 1912. I have heard, though I cannot confirm it, that a degree of selection and pruning went into these reports, so that some of the more serious criticisms were omitted. The reports highlighted the general acceptance of legislation and the fact that employers were providing additional benefits on top of the state schemes. However, just as the debates on national insurance reached their peak, the British Consul in Germany, Sir Francis Oppenheimer, reported on the 1911 Reichsversicherungsordnung, which extended insurance against sickness to agricultural workers, servants, casual labourers and other categories.[91] This extension led to protests from some Chambers of Commerce, including those of Plauen, Chemnitz and Essen, at the increase of 17 per cent in the charges on industry without reference to employers. They argued that the burden on German industry was reaching unbearable limits and would now begin to tell on its competitive position in foreign markets. The costs of social insurance had doubled in cash terms in twenty years, and from around 1.89 per cent of the wages bill to 3.78 per cent. However, the criticism was somewhat undermined by the fact that progressive employers appeared to be providing at least as much again in voluntary welfare schemes over and above the compulsory element. *The Times* noted Oppenheimer's report and held it up as a warning to British employers.[92]

By mid-1911 many of the British employers, who had not been involved in the debates over social insurance which had been taking place since 1905-6, began to appreciate that insurance legislation was imminent and that they would be asked to bear part of the costs. Some employers objected to what Sir Charles Macara called Lloyd George's 'German scheme of national health insurance'. The foreign label could be used as a general term of abuse, but specific criticisms included the overall cost, the bureaucratic complexity and the unequal distribution of costs between industries.[93] Labour-intensive industries such as coal-mining would be particularly affected since wages were said to be about 70 per cent of the cost of production.[94]

The moderate criticisms of the Bill came from those bodies, particularly the Chambers of Commerce, who had been following the legislation closely.[95] Both the Birmingham and Wakefield Chambers submitted principled criticisms which suggested that workmen's compensation and national health insurance should be integrated and German practice followed. That is to say, any worker involved in an accident should first be compensated by the sickness and invalidity fund to which he contributed. Only if an injury through accident persisted should the worker come on the accident fund to which the employer alone contributed.[96]

The national body, the Association of Chambers of Commerce of the United Kingdom, put under great pressure by its backwoods members, noted that the chief argument in favour of national insurance was that the same system existed in Germany and Austria. Their response was to cite Oppenheimer's Report; to claim that the charges had been imposed in Germany before most industries had been established and to point to longer hours and lower wages in Germany and the advantages of protection in enabling employers to shift the burden on to consumers.[97]

The strongest opposition came from a new body led by Sir Charles Macara. His Employers' Parliamentary Association was founded in December 1911 specifically to fight the National Insurance Act and it drew its main strength from the textile areas of Lancashire, Yorkshire and the Midlands. It had very little effect on the outcome, but its failure in this respect heightened employers' appreciation that they lacked an effective means of pressurising government in the age of social legislation and ensuring early consultation on matters affecting industrial costs. As a consequence, the Federation of British Industries and the British Confederation of Employers' Organisations were set up in the next few years to meet these needs.

It is clear from the debates of 1905 to 1914 that there was no unified employer view on welfare in Britain, nor on the value of copying the German model. Yet there were significant and, for the time at least, influential groups of British employers who were prepared to lobby very hard for the extension of welfare legislation. Some of these derived inspiration from German pioneering in the areas of poor relief, labour exchanges, old age pensions, sickness and accident insurance, technical education and temperance reform. Much of the influence of these groups bore fruit at the local level, some at the national level, and if we are to understand why there was this concentrated burst of social legislation in Britain at this time, then that pressure and influence must be taken into account. Moreover, the type of support employers gave helped to influence the form of the legislation. Consistent employer arguments on the need to reinforce, not undermine, work incentives; to involve workers directly in the costs of reform through insurance; to strengthen elements of social discipline and training; to separate the malingerer from the honest, needy worker, all helped to ensure that these features were carried over into the Liberal reforms, which some have seen, too easily, as a complete break with the past. It is at the level of general characteristics that German influence on British social policy is perhaps strongest, though in this chapter I have not gone into the detailed comparison of specific elements of legislation in the two countries, which is necessary if a full appreciation of the German contribution is to be made.

Finally, can any general implications be derived from this single study of the transfer of social institutions and, if so, what alterations need to be made in our understanding of the development of the welfare state? Our theoretical understanding of the growth of welfare policy is very weak, despite all the high-quality writing on the subject in recent years. The strongly entrenched theories of past writers that welfare is directly related to the process of industrialisation; that welfare is the obverse of democracy or the simple response to insistent working-class pressure; that welfare is the product of growing humanitarianism on the part of society or the state as representing society; the product of bureaucratic imperatives in the establishing, quantifying and solving of social problems, have all been shown to be inadequate. So have the simpler versions of the Marxist idea that welfare is but a sham concession designed to bind the worker more firmly to capitalism, though it is at least arguable that this is the closest approximation to the reality of welfare of all those mentioned. But an adequate alternative interpretation is lacking, though it may be that a single theoretical framework is impossible to achieve.[98]

In particular, we lack any clear notion why, around the turn of the nineteenth century, a host of very different societies embarked on a wide range of social measures which appear, on the surface at least, to share common elements: old age pensions, sickness, accident and unemployment insurance, minimum wage legislation and measures for the education and protection of children. Some or all of these were introduced in countries as diverse as Germany, Denmark, Australia, New Zealand, Great Britain and Uruguay, but not to the same extent in France and the United States. Why was this, and what part did foreign models and examples play in the process? Were these measures the result of simultaneous but independent discovery and implementation, or were there forces at work which transcended nation states? Was there an international demonstration effect? Was there something in the development of international capitalism which gave rise to the welfare state?

Pat Thane has argued that the bulk of welfare legislation of this period was designed to benefit male skilled workers rather than women or the very poor, and suggests that this was because the former groups

Table 6.1: Birmingham Chamber of Commerce, Elected Members of Council, 1906 — Connections with Germany Clearly Established

	Born	Educated	Business	Travel
J.S. Taylor (Chairman)			*	
F.B. Goodman				
A.B. Mitchell		*		*
S. Allen			*	*
T.H. Ash				
H. Barrow				
E.M. Carter				
Arthur Chamberlain				
H.W. Edmunds				
H.C. Field		*	*	*
W. Harley				
O.C. Hawkes				
W.D. Hutchings				
E.H. Kannreuther				
E.C. Keay				
J.H.R. Meyer				
T.W. Petersen	*	*	*	*
W. Priest				*
D.W. Probert				
H.W.Sambidge			*	*
H. Schurhoff	*	*	*	
A. Southall				
T. Turner		*		
W. Wilkinson				
G.H. Wright (Secretary)				*
Others associated with Chamber				
R.H. Best		*	*	*
C.B. Bragg		*		*
C. Perks				*

were coming under pressure for the first time in a way that could not be catered for by their normal response of collective self-help.[99] I think there is much truth in this, but I would add that in this period employers in the countries under the most severe competitive pressures and facing the greatest actual or potential domestic unrest were prepared to risk the costs of welfare to head off more fundamental challenges to their respective systems. In order to retain control of their industries at the point of production and at the level of the national economy, they were prepared to try social welfare, along with other measures, hoping, though not necessarily confident, that productivity increases might partially offset the costs involved. Welfare might also reinforce social discipline. This was one particular attraction of the German model in Britain. The alternatives seemed to be a general round of wage increases, further challenges to managerial prerogatives in industry, and even the risk of social revolution. For both societies, these prices seemed too high. In the aftermath of the First World War, when it appeared that welfare had not yielded the productivity increases or the political peace, it was very quickly dropped as a positive strategy by those very groups of employers who had been active in support of welfare in Britain and Germany before 1914.

Notes

1. W.J. Ashley, Introduction to *Birmingham Chamber of Commerce Commercial Yearbook*, First Issue (1905), p. 19.
2. R. Davidson, Oral contribution to C. 15, 'The Comparative Study of the Development of Social and Welfare Policy', 7th International Economic History Association Congress, Edinburgh, 1978. See Report thereon in the *Australian Historical Association Bulletin*, vol. 17 (December 1978), pp. 24-33.
3. S. Mencher, *From Poor Law to Poverty Program* (New York, 1967); S. Fine, *Laissez Faire and the General Welfare State* (Ann Arbor, 1956), pp. 125-44.
4. For a summary and guide to the literature, P.L. Payne, *British Entrepreneurship in the Nineteenth Century* (London, 1974), pp. 45-56.
5. A question posed by *The Engineer*, vol. 111 (1911), p. 545.
6. B.R. Mitchell, *Abstract of British Historical Statistics* (Cambridge, 1962), pp. 284 and 322-3. For an argument that Britain and Germany were homogeneous societies and very similar, while the USA had a heterogeneous population, soil, climate and laws, see A. Shadwell, *Industrial Efficiency* (London, 1905), Chapter One.
7. G.R. Searle, *The Quest for National Efficiency* (Oxford, 1971), p. 34; J.R. Hay, *The Origins of the Liberal Welfare Reforms, 1906-14* (London, 1975), pp. 30-3.
8. Sir Charles Furness, *Industrial Peace and Efficiency* (London, 1908).
9. Lord Leverhulme, *The Six-Hour Day* (London, 1918), pp. 95 and 99-106; E. Cadbury, *Experiments in Industrial Organisation* (London, 1912); B.S. Rowntree, *The Human Factor in Business* (London, 1921).
10. The idea that education, by bringing about a change in the character of the individual, was the basic remedy for poverty, was a widely held view in the nineteenth century. The point being made here is the more limited one that employers interested in raising the level of skill and hence of the output of their workers often came to see welfare as a contribution to that process.
11. A point made forcefully to me by Prof. N.G. Butlin of the Australian National University.
12. W. Bardill, Lecture to the Birmingham Association of Mechanical Engineers, *The Engineer*, vol. 101 (1906), pp. 281-2.
13. British Iron Trades Association, *Report on the Iron and Steel Industries of Belgium and Germany* (1896), p. 23; for a discussion of the content of the report, see W.J. Ashley, *The Progress of the German Working Classes in the Last Quarter of a Century* (London, 1904), pp. 10-12. The delegation to Belgium and

Germany which compiled it consisted of 'seven employers' delegates, including several leading ironmasters and managers, and . . . seven officers of large trade unions'.

14. Public Record Office, Workmen's Insurance Systems in Germany: Report of delegation (sent by the Parliamentary Committee of the Trades Union Congress), CAB/37/96/169 (1908).

15. By Professor G.V. Rimlinger in Edinburgh, *A.H.A. Bulletin*, vol. 17 (December 1978), p. 26.

16. M. Caroli, 'Reports of German Visitors on Economic and Social Change in England in the Nineteenth Century'. I rely on the brief report by H.J. Perkin, *Social History Society Newsletter*, vol. 3, no. 2 (1978), p. 6.

17. W.O. Henderson, *Britain and Industrial Europe*, 3rd edn (London, 1972); W. Manchester, *The Arms of Krupp* (London, 1969), pp. 67-72.

18. S. Pollard, *European Economic Integration, 1815-1970* (London, 1974), pp. 86-7.

19. For discussion of the role and influence of German trading firms in Britain primarily in the first half of the nineteenth century, see S.D. Chapman, 'The International Houses: the Continental Contribution to British Commerce, 1800-1860', *Journal of European Economic History*, vol. 6 (1977), pp. 5-48.

20. C.P. Kindleberger in lectures delivered in the University of Edinburgh in 1974; W.O. Henderson, *The Industrialisation of Europe, 1780-1914* (London, 1969), pp. 72-4; the attack on monopolies in Germany did not have to wait on Smith's *magnum opus*, see H.J. Braun, 'Economic Theory and Policy in Germany, 1750-1800', *Journal of European Economic History*, vol. 4, no. 2 (1975), p. 320.

21. Ashley's book cited in note 13 is a mine of information on British inquiries into German social conditions up to 1904; see also *The Engineer*, vol. 101 (1906), p. 272.

22. The tariff reform issue was an important catalyst, though the process was well under way before 1903.

23. E.E. Williams, *Made in Germany* (1896); W.E. Minchinton, 'E.E. Williams; "Made in Germany" and after', *Vierteljahrschrift für Sozial- und Wirtschaftsgeschichte*, vol. 62 (1975), pp. 229-42.

24. A. Shadwell, *Industrial Efficiency* (London 1905).

25. W.H. Dawson, *Prince Bismarck and State Socialism* (London, 1890); *Protection in Germany* (London, 1904); *The Evolution of Modern Germany* (London, 1908); *Social Insurance in Germany, 1883-1911* (London, 1912); and many more.

26. A. Sutcliffe, 'The Rise of Urban Planning before 1914: Links between Germany and Britain', unpublished MS. I am deeply indebted to Dr Sutcliffe for allowing me to see this paper.

27. W.H. Beveridge was a regular visitor to Germany on social investigation trips throughout his life. For this period see W.H. Beveridge Papers, British Library of Political and Economic Science, III, 8, Notes and Statistics about Unemployment and Labour Exchanges in Germany; 'Public Labour Exchanges in Germany', *Economic Journal*, vol. 18 (1908), pp. 1-18.

28. D.F. Schloss, *Insurance against Unemployment* (London, 1909); *Report to the Board of Trade on Agencies and Methods for Dealing with the Unemployed in Certain Foreign Countries*, Cd. 2304 (1905).

29. G. Drage, *The Problem of the Aged Poor* (London 1895).

30. H.N. Bunbury (ed.), *Lloyd George's Ambulance Wagon, Being the Memoirs of W.J. Braithwaite, 1911-12* (London, 1957), p. 82.

31. This section was written much later, according to Professor Hennock.

32. J. Tampke, 'The Bismarckian Welfare System: a Re-evaluation', paper delivered to the Australian Historical Association Conference on the

'History of Social Welfare', Flinders University, Adelaide, September 1978; see also his chapter in this volume.

33. Braithwaite was rather shabbily treated by Lloyd George when it came to setting up the bureaucracy to implement and administer the Act which he had played a large part in drafting. Bunbury, *Braithwaite*, pp. 32-7.

34. J. Harris, *Unemployment and Politics* (Oxford, 1972); J. Brown, 'Ideas Concerning Social Policy and their Influence on Legislation in Great Britain, 1902-11', PhD thesis, University of London, 1964; R. Davidson, 'Llewellyn-Smith, the Labour Department and Government Growth' in G. Sutherland (ed.), *Studies in the Growth of Nineteenth Century Government* (London, 1972); G.R. Searle, *The Quest for National Efficiency* (Oxford, 1971); B.B. Gilbert, *The Evolution of National Insurance in Great Britain* (London, 1966).

35. See the discussion between 'A special correspondent' and Sir Benjamin Browne, 25 March and 22 April 1910, *The Engineer*, vol. 109 (1910), pp. 295, 412-13; also ibid., vol. 111 (1911), p. 493 for the importance of the control of labour. *The Engineer* generally opposed the National Insurance Bill.

36. J.D. Scott, *Siemens Brothers, 1858-1958* (London, 1958), p. 248.

37. I have discussed the composition and role of the Industrial Council in a paper on 'Employers, Labour and the State in Britain, 1890-1914', copies of which are available.

38. J.R. Hay, 'Employers' Attitudes to Social Policy and the Concept of Social Control, 1900-1920' in P.M. Thane (ed.), *The Origins of British Social Policy* (London, 1978), p. 119.

39. Deputation of Engineering and Shipbuilding Employers to the Board of Trade, 18 Aug. 1909, Public Record Office, LAB/2/211/LE500, 1909, p. 6.

40. On 22 July 1909, in the House of Commons, Churchill had stated that if labour representatives insisted he would have the regulations written so that labour exchanges would be suspended during industrial disputes. This proposal was strongly attacked by the Birmingham Chamber of Commerce which wanted the German procedure adopted. Minutes of the Council of the Birmingham Chamber of Commerce, 29 Sept. 1909, citing letter to Churchill of 30 July 1909.

41. *Who's Who* (1910), p. 1367.

42. S.E. Koss, *Sir John Brunner, Radical Plutocrat* (Cambridge, 1970).

43. H.V. Emy, *Liberals, Radicals and Social Politics, 1892-1914* (Cambridge, 1973), p. 241.

44. P.M. Thane, 'Non-contributory versus Insurance Pensions, 1878-1908' in Thane, *Origins*, p. 125.

45. T.S. and M.B. Simey, *Charles Booth* (Oxford, 1960), pp. 161-5; A.G. Gardiner, *The Life of George Cadbury* (London, 1923), p. 125.

46. D.S. Cardwell, *Science in Manchester in the Nineteenth Century* (Open University, AST 281).

47. *Glasgow Herald*, 25 July 1906.

48. Sheffield Chamber of Commerce and Manufactures, *Minutes of Proceedings*, vol. 6 (1905).

49. *Report of Deputations to the Chancellor of the Exchequer on the National Insurance Bill*, Cd. 5869 (1911), p. 41.

50. S. Buxton, President of the Board of Trade, in reply to a deputation from the Shipbuilding Employers' Federation on the National Insurance Bill, 14 June 1911. Public Record Office, LAB/2/1483/LE (1) 7150.

51. J.R. Hay, 'Employers and Social Policy in Britain: the Evolution of Welfare Legislation, 1905-1914', *Social History*, vol. 2, no. 4 (1977), pp. 435-55.

52. *Edgbastonia*, vol. 27, no. 316 (1907), p. 464.

53. I am indebted to the Librarian of the Birmingham Chamber of Commerce for considerable assistance in recent years.

54. Birmingham Chamber of Commerce, Report of Council, July 1868.
55. Ibid., February 1874; see also G.H. Wright, *Chronicles of the Birmingham Chamber of Commerce, 1813-1913* (Birmingham, 1913), pp. 249-50.
56. Reports of Council, August 1875; March 1888; March 1889; March 1890; March 1895.
57. Wright, *Chronicles*, p. 612.
58. C. Hazlehurst and J. Harris, 'Campbell-Bannerman as Prime Minister', *History*, vol. 55 (1970), p. 372.
59. Harris, *Unemployment and Politics*, p. 218.
60. Wright, *Chronicles*, pp. 652-4.
61. See Table 6.1.
62. The following discussion is based on R.D. Best, *Brass Chandelier* (London, 1940); P.W. Kingsford, 'R.H. Best, 1843-1925', *The Manager*, vol. 24 (1956), pp. 537-41; and the collection of Birmingham biographies held in the City Library.
63. Best, *Brass Chandelier*, pp. 168-74.
64. R.H. Best, W.J. Davis and C. Perks, *The Brassworkers of Berlin and Birmingham – a Comparison* (London, 1905).
65. Best, *Brass Chandelier*, p. 197.
66. R.H. Best, *The City Aid and its Future* (Birmingham, 1906).
67. Best, *Brass Chandelier*, pp. 186-93.
68. R.H. Best and C.K. Ogden, *The Problem of the Day Continuation School and its Successful Solution in Germany: a Consecutive Policy* (London, 1914).
69. Sutcliffe, 'Rise of Urban Planning', pp. 20-3.
70. *The Times*, 25 Jan. 1906.
71. *Birmingham Chamber of Commerce Journal*, vol. 4 (1906), p. 31.
72. Hay, 'Employers and Social Policy', p. 448. For Arthur Chamberlain see *Birmingham Post*, 21 Oct. 1913; 'Midlands Captains of Industry, II', *Birmingham Gazette and Express*, 12 Mar. 1907; for H.C. Field, *Edgbastonia*, vol. 27, no. 325 (1908), pp. 119-25.
73. Samuel Timmins, *The Resources, Products and Industrial History of the Birmingham and Midlands Hardware District* (London, 1866)
74. A. Fox, 'Industrial Relations in Nineteenth Century Birmingham', *Oxford Economic Papers*, vol. 7 (1955), pp. 57-70; A. Briggs, 'The Social Background' in A. Flanders and H.A. Clegg (eds.) *The System of Industrial Relations in Great Britain* (Oxford, 1954), p. 17.
75. R.A. Church and Barbara M.D. Smith, 'Competition and Monopoly in the Coffin Furniture Industry, 1870-1915', *Economic History Review*, vol. 19 (1966), pp. 621-41.
76. K. Burgess, *The Origins of British Industrial Relations* (London, 1975), especially Chapter One on Engineering.
77. Best, *Brass Chandelier*, pp. 151-7.
78. The Birmingham Alliances had collapsed by 1901 according to Church and Smith, 'Competition and Monopoly', p. 639. See also J.H. Clapham, *An Economic History of Modern Britain* (Cambridge, 1938), vol. III, p. 304.
79. Hay, 'Employers and Social Policy', p. 448; Shadwell, *Industrial Efficiency*, pp. 415-17 and 433, quoted with approval by J.S. Taylor, Chairman of the Birmingham Chamber of Commerce in proposing national insurance to the Association of Chambers of Commerce of the United Kingdom in March 1907.
80. *Birmingham Chamber of Commerce Journal*, vol. 4 (1906), pp. 173-4; ibid., vol. 5 (1907), pp. 60-3.
81. Sutcliffe, 'Rise of Urban Planning', p. 14.
82. Gilbert, *The Evolution of National Insurance*, p. 254.
83. *Birmingham Chamber of Commerce Journal*, vol. 4 (1906), pp. 3-4 and 177-8.

84. Gainsborough Commission Reports, *Life and Labour in Germany* (1907).
85. Ibid., pp. 266-86.
86. Best, *Brass Chandelier*, p. 183.
87. Hay, 'Employers and Social Policy'.
88. Ibid., pp. 448-50.
89. *Reports of Deputations to the Chancellor of the Exchequer on the National Insurance Bill*, Cd. 5869 (1911), pp. 26-9 and 36-43.
90. *Memorandum Containing the Opinions of Various Authorities in Germany*, Cd. 5679 (1911).
91. Sir Francis Oppenheimer, *Report on the Trade and Industries of Germany for the Year 1910 and the First Half of 1911*, Cd. 5465 (1911), pp. 14-16 and 105-6.
92. *The Times*, 16 Sept. 1911.
93. *Iron and Coal Trades Review*, vol. 82 (1911), pp. 100 and 106.
94. Sir Charles Macara, *Recollections* (London, 1921), p. 217.
95. *The Chamber of Commerce Journal*, vol. 30, no. 207 (1911), p. 220. This is the journal of the London Chamber of Commerce, which carried reports on the activities of Chambers of Commerce throughout the country.
96. In Germany the worker contributed two-thirds of the cost of sickness insurance, the employer one-third. Public Record Office, Treasury Papers, T/1/11284/6955. Letters to S. Buxton, President of the Board of Trade from Birmingham Chamber of Commerce, 8 Feb. 1911 and Wakefield Chamber of Commerce, 8 Mar. 1911.
97. Association of Chambers of Commerce of the United Kingdom, Circular No. 573, 30 Oct. 1911.
98. J. Carrier and I. Kendall, 'The Development of Welfare States: the Production of Plausible Accounts', *Journal of Social Policy*, vol. 6 (1977), pp. 273-84.
99. P.M. Thane, discussion of papers by G.V. Rimlinger and J. Roe, Edinburgh, 1978 (*A.H.A. Bulletin*, vol. 17 (1978), p. 26).

7 GERMAN INDUSTRY AND BISMARCK'S SOCIAL SECURITY SYSTEM[1]

H.-P. Ullmann

> In creating the workers' insurance the German *Reich*, with incomparable daring and tenacity, has achieved a work of the highest humanitarian order, which will serve as a model throughout the ages and bring it lasting glory. The edifice thus constructed is worthy of its founders, the great Emperor and his faithful counsellor, the first Imperial Chancellor... German industry has been one of the most diligent and effective supporters of this significant humanitarian achievement.[2]

These were the laudatory words bestowed on Bismarck and German industry by the Central Association of German Industrialists (*Central-verband Deutscher Industrieller*), the first and most important federation of Imperial German entrepreneurs. Yet this effusion raises three questions which I shall examine in the present chapter.

(1) What were the circumstances and the aims that led to the development of the German social security system?

(2) Did the industrialists participate in building up this system and did they indeed exercise the influence they claimed?

(3) Can it be said, finally, that the industrialists were the god-parents of the infant German welfare state?

Bismarck's Workers' Insurance

Historical research is largely unanimous in its appraisal of the social security legislation of the 1880s. This may be summarised briefly as follows: workers' insurance was primarily not a matter of social policy but of state, or rather, power politics in the interests of the newly formed Reich and the leading groups within it. This is borne out by the close links between social measures and anti-socialist laws. By repression on the one hand and limited concessions in the area of social policy on the other, the aim was to split the Social Democratic workers' movement, considered a 'danger to the state'. The 'agitators' were to be rendered politically impotent and the 'good' workers won over for the state by welfare provisions. Bismarck himself took an active and decisive part in this 'carrot and stick' policy: whether one views him as a great statesman or a manipulator of genius, workers' insurance is certainly considered to be his achievement.[3]

In the framework of this interpretation, I would suggest three changes in emphasis, which bring out aspects that have so far received less attention: the socio-political dimension of workers' insurance, its inherent 'disciplinary' elements, and, lastly, its genesis as part of a protracted process of political decisions.

While social security, in combination with the anti-socialist laws, was certainly designed to consolidate the newly formed Reich, it ought not to be reduced to an exercise in power politics alone. Insurance was also a response to prevailing social problems and to the crisis of the government's social policies hitherto. Since the 1840s these had been characterised, particularly in Prussia, by a peculiar blend of pre-industrial paternalism and liberalism. The Trade Law of 1845 and its amendments, as well as the Miners Association Law of 1854, were obviously ambivalent in their combination of individual responsibility and state compulsion. This 'liberal state' social policy, if one may call it that, ultimately left the question as to the relation between its component elements open, thus in practice blocking its own effectiveness.[4] This avoidance of a decision in Prussian social policy became, with the Trade Law of 1869, a problem for the newly established German Empire. Confronted with social unrest of hitherto unknown proportions, due to the industrial expansion of the *Gründerjahre* and economic depression, the government's 'liberal state' policies faced a serious crisis. The Employers' Liability Act of 1871 and the so-called *Hilfskassengesetze* (relief fund laws) of 1876 clearly showed that the existing framework and existing remedies no longer sufficed to solve these problems. In this situation two alternatives presented themselves: either to encourage 'self-help' insurance schemes, or to develop a state social security system.[5]

The overtones of power politics only arose in this context; they stemmed from the means employed to solve the social problems and from their close links with anti-socialist legislation. But just because of these close links state workers' insurance was not merely a positive gain, but acquired repressive aspects of its own. The question thus arises whether the ambivalence of Bismarck's social policies is not also reflected in the insurance scheme itself, and whether the combination of 'carrot and stick' was not just as much a 'stick *built into* the carrot'.[6] The Chancellor belonged to the tradition of 'liberal state' concepts, but in his workers' insurance scheme he opted for considerations of state at the expense of the liberal ones. At the same time he blocked all measures which aimed at solving the social problems through workers' protection and social reform. The reduction of social policies merely to insurance measures added a paternalist component to considerations of state: a multi-faceted social issue was thus pre-sented in the simple guise of an unsolved insurance problem that could be met by welfare measures.[7] This one-dimensional approach also affected the way social insurance was organised. According to the original drafts of 1880, this was to be based on compulsory state insurance and a government insurance institution with monopoly rights, financed through employers' contributions and state subsi-dies.[8] It is in this tightening of the rights of the state, in the concept of accident care rather than accident insurance, and in the lack of participation of those affected, that the 'disciplinary' aspects of Bis-marck's workers' insurance scheme lay.[9] It was clearly directed against non-governmental regulation of social security in the form of a 'self-help' insurance system along British lines.[10]

The Imperial Chancellor himself played a crucial part in the decision as to how the social problems were to be met, in the development of state workers' insurance and in its political enactment. Yet the role played by the supporters of his policies should not be underrated.[11] They not only provided suggestions, but also the social base and, most importantly, they were closely involved in the protracted process of decision-making. There is no doubt that Bismarck played a leading part in all this, but the sole right of decision was not his. In the political realignments of the 1870s and 1880s his position had been weakened. The expansion of government functions required a concomitant exten-sion of the government's control capabilities. This, however, posed a number of problems, among them the low level of development of the administrative machine in Prussia and the Empire as a whole, as well as resistance from inside by a civil service still largely wedded to liberal principles. To extend and redirect government functions was thus not feasible in the short term.[12] Bismarck was therefore obliged to involve industry more closely and to use its expertise as a countervailing force. The various forms of corporate organisation proposed were intended as a means of pressurising the Reichstag and had thus also an anti-parliamentary intention.[13] The Reichstag, along with the bureaucracy, was in any case the Achilles' heel of Bismarck's politics, since the split in the National Liberal Party had robbed him of a clear majority.[14] In this constellation of political forces, economic pressure groups also acquired greater weight in deciding social policy. Increased reliance on these interest groups as a means of securing political aims was, however, possible only as a manipulative, short-term device. In the longer term it produced political costs in the form of increased influence and participation. To that extent the supporters of Bismarck's social policy gradually became his fellow actors.

If these views are correct, then the process of socio-political decision-making deserves considerably greater attention than it has so far received. Its exact reconstruction would permit a more subtle answer to the debated questions as to the relations between social policies and power politics in the creation of workers' insurance; and as to the extent to which the disciplinary aspects must be attributed to the traditions of an authoritarian state, to Bismarck's paternalist-Christian attitudes, to his manipulative politics, or to the influence of particular interest groups in society; and finally, whether the social security legislation was the work of Bismarck or merely the result of a particular constellation of political forces. A thorough analysis of all these elements would be a desirable line of research that still remains to be undertaken.[15] Here I shall merely attempt to draw out one strand, i.e. the influence of German industry on the process of socio-political decision-making. It is my view that both its interest and its influence were far greater than has hitherto been assumed and that this was due to three factors: the socio-political aspects of workers' insurance, the opportunity to build disciplinary elements into it, and last but not least, the socio-political circumstances of the 1880s which led to these decisions.

Industrial Interest Groups and the Beginnings of German Social Insurance

The attitudes of German industrialists towards Bismarck's workers' insurance were sharply divided. It is possible to make a rough distinction between two groupings: opponents and supporters of state social insurance. Compulsory membership, insurance monopoly and state subsidy constituted a transition from a policy of command and prohibition to one of provision of social goods and services by the state. Thus, social insurance was not a further expansion of existing social policies but represented a qualitative leap forward and its polarising effect was correspondingly strong.

Resistance to social insurance came from those industrialists who were suspicious of state social insurance in general and of the

Chancellor's 'state-socialist' insurance schemes in particular. They were in the main adherents of liberal principles who, for the solution to social problems, looked to an industrial and cultural process, and to co-operative self-help on the part of the workers, but certainly not to the state. They regarded the insurance legislation as a 'radical departure from the existing legal system' and as an 'intrusion of socialist views'.[16] Besides these 'liberal' industrialists there existed a large group of entrepreneurs who deployed similar arguments, but for whom such liberal postulates expressed not so much basic political attitudes but rather a variety of quite diverse interests. The enemies of workers' insurance were predominantly the owners of small and medium sized companies, where working conditions were usually bad and social grievances considerable. These free-market-economy employers as a rule dispensed with social provisions at company level and showed generally little interest in social problems. Inasmuch as such enterprises were labour- rather than capital-intensive, and thus had high wage costs, the industrialists feared the burdens that flowed from the social policies of the state.[17] The production process itself also had an influence on their dislike of workers' insurance. Firms, and even entire branches of industry, with low accident rates and correspondingly low social costs, demonstrated but scant interest in social insurance. To them a redistribution of risks by the state could bring only disadvantages.[18] Finally, their dependence on exports was a further weighty counter-argument. Although the social burdens imposed by the state had little adverse effect on domestic competition, they could lead to distortions in their competitive position in world markets.[19] Based on these three variables — organisational structure, production process and market orientation — the vehemence of resistance against workers' insurance can be measured quite accurately: it increased to the degree that these factors came into play or coincided.

But apart from industrialists motivated by self-interest, the social reformers among them were equally opposed to social insurance. For them state-imposed insurance represented competition to their own benefit schemes at company level. These would have to be either restricted or continued as additional benefits with resulting higher costs. Some were already experimenting with plans for a 'constitutional factory'. They regarded workers' insurance as one-sided and inadequate, and state compulsion as a hindrance.[20]

Liberal principles, economic reasons and motives of social reform do not, however, suffice to explain the resistance to state insurance.

Beyond considerations of self-interest, the opponents were locked into larger interest groupings and wider political considerations. From the outset the Chancellor's insurance policies had not tied in with the interests of these employers but with those of big industry. Many of the small and medium-sized businesses thus saw in them the machinations of heavy industry. Resistance to social insurance in the last analysis was part of a far more deeply rooted dispute and polarisation. Social policies, along with protective tariffs, monopoly laws and nationalisation plans, were part of the whole panoply of policies for the 'protection of national labour' (*Schutz der nationalen Arbeit*), which many businessmen rejected for a variety of motives.[21]

While the opponents of workers' insurance formed a very miscellaneous grouping, the composition of the supporting faction was much more uniform. Its core was the heavy industry of the Rhineland, Westphalia, the Saar and Upper Silesia; around it were gathered a limited number of other sectors.[22] The supporters of social legislation were in the main the heads of large companies with complex organisational problems, such as recruitment of workers, the increasing difficulties of managing personnel in a large business, and the need to ensure smooth and continuous production. These requirements were met by social policies within the company which combined welfare with restrictive measures. The paternalism that had grown up in artisan manufacture and small firms in the pre-industrial and early industrial era was, however, a very different creature to the administrative paternalism of big industry. This 'secondary' paternalism replaced personal relations by a blend of pre-industrial, feudal and bureaucratic techniques of domination: welfare was now combined with social control. This was the main point of convergence with the state workers' insurance scheme. For many leaders of big industry it meant the transfer of 'proven' methods from factory to state, in order to ensure 'social peace' on a larger scale.[23] In addition, considerations of productive efficiency came into play, since heavy industry, and particularly mining, was high on the list of industrial accident rates. This also explains the interest in spreading the risk more widely through insurance. Compulsory state insurance saw to it that the burden of social expenditure would have no adverse effect on competitiveness and that the social costs of 'free' wage labour could be passed on.[24] As for marketing considerations, distortions to competitiveness did not present a problem for the supporters of social insurance in industries that did not depend heavily on exports. In any case, protective tariffs outweighed social costs.[25]

As with the opponents of social legislation, these reasons alone do not suffice to explain the attitude of its supporters. Here, too, motives must be seen in a wider context. From the point of view of self-interest, it made sense to support Bismarck's schemes as a means of further cementing their existing close relations with the Chancellor. Precisely because big industry had advocated a greater, and institutionalised, role for industrial interests, it could not now afford to reject social legislation. The political motives for its support were closely linked to this. Heavy industry was one of the main beneficiaries of the 'protection of national work' and had favoured the tariff legislation of 1879 with arguments of job preservation. Thus it could now hardly escape the obligation to do something for the workers.[26] What remained still unsolved, however, was the socio-political approach to be adopted. In this political conflict the means of power, which opponents and supporters of social legislation could each bring into play, gained crucial importance.

It is far easier to distinguish the two factions than to determine their respective political weight and the influence they were able to wield. The opponents, particularly, were a miscellaneous and numerically not easily quantifiable group. If one looks at the — from a methodological point of view unsatisfactory — reports of the Chambers of Commerce, opponents of social legislation represented a significant minority, or perhaps even a narrow majority of German industrialists.[27] Yet they possessed only limited means to articulate their views and were insufficiently organised. Even though the Chambers of Commerce provided them with a platform at regional level, they lacked the kind of established organisation on a national scale which would have secured their views a wider audience. Ever since the disputes about protective tariffs, the German Trade Congress (*Deutscher Handelstag*) had lost influence and had in any case been infiltrated by supporters of social legislation, while the German National Economic Congress (*Deutscher Volkswirtschaftlicher Kongress*), once the focal point of the 'free trade party', had also suffered a considerable decline in importance.[28]

The active supporters of social security legislation, by comparison, were numerically a much smaller group. In terms of numbers employed, they represented less than one-third of all companies, and in terms of the total number of firms with insurance obligations, only 2 per cent.[29] But they were a more homogeneous and articulate, and as such a more powerful, group. Heavy industry had organised itself in the Association of German Iron and Steel Industries (*Verein Deutscher Eisen- und Stahlindustrieller*) and in the *Langnam-Verein* (Association for the Protection of Common Economic Interests in the Rhineland and Westphalia), while the advocates of protective tariffs had joined together in the Central Association of German Industrialists (*Central-verband Deutscher Industrieller*). This latter provided the operational centre for the supporters of workers' insurance, where even then the interests of heavy industry clearly predominated in all questions of social policy. Because of its connections with the mining associations, these interests could be incorporated smoothly into the policies of the Central Association. In addition to this organisational monopoly position, there existed informal contacts with the administration that had been developed during the protective tariff negotiations. Above all, though, there were the well established tactics of 'approaching the Chancellor directly whenever possible', as the industrialist Servaes had put it. The opponents of social legislation had nothing comparable to set against this close co-operation with Bismarck.[30]

It is not possible to examine the industrial influences in detail here, since this would require a comprehensive description of all workers' insurance legislation. The concern here is to outline only three decision-making areas, in order to see by what channels, with which means and with what success the supporters of social legislation were able to carry the day and also to note where the opposing forces were most effective.

The influence of heavy industry was greatest in the *initial phase of the state insurance scheme*. First, it was responsible for the fact that the social consequences of inadequate accident liability were not solved merely by amending the Liability Act of 1871, but by a state accident insurance scheme. The associations of heavy industry provided Bismarck with the necessary arguments for his decision and they also supported him against opposition from inside the civil service and elsewhere. Secondly, it was the industrial leaders in favour of state social legislation who drew up the draft for the first Accident Insurance Act. It was their proposals, and not those of the bureaucracy, which provided the basis for further discussion.[31]

In this area of decision Bismarck and heavy industry depended on each other. The Chancellor lacked the technical knowledge and the necessary support to bring his concepts of social legislation to bear in the face of resistance from the bureaucracy, while the industrialists were keen to co-operate, as they sought a solution to social problems that was favourable to their own interests and hoped that state insurance would head off more far-reaching demands for reform.[32] In addition, both sides had a 'fundamental outlook' in common. Bismarck and the leaders of heavy industry were agreed that repressive policies towards the Social Democratic workers' movement should be followed by positive measures. But neither 'free' contracts of employment nor the authority of the employer within his firm, nor the existing right of coalition and the authority of the state were to form part of these. Thus only a state insurance scheme which provided a paternalist blend of welfare and disciplinary elements could be envisaged. 'Social insurance', as one critic put it, 'is definitely not workers' protection; it seeks to help the worker without hurting the employer.'[33]

The first draft of the Accident Insurance Law of 1880 reflected this, albeit informal, working agreement. It showed to what extent 'governmental' and 'company' paternalism went hand in hand and where it diverged. There was unanimity on virtually all major points; the only fundamental difference arose on the question of premium payments. This, however, was significant: by not requiring contributions from workers, the Chancellor had intended the socially integrative effects of the scheme to benefit the state exclusively, while the industrialists desired some of the benefits to accrue also to their companies, through workers' contributions and a share in the administration of the scheme that went with it.[34]

Both the Chancellor and the leaders of heavy industry watched the further development of accident insurance legislation with growing displeasure. Both saw it as a departure from the satisfactory beginnings of 1880. Industry's supporters of social insurance could hardly influence the changes in the Act once it was before the Reichstag, as they had been able to when the laws were still being planned. In so far as they were able to score further successes, as for instance the elimination of the controversial workers' committees, they owed these to the help of the Chancellor and the Civil Service. The opponents of social insurance had equally little direct influence on the Reichstag, but through their connections with political parties they played a considerable role in the revision of government drafts. Many of the changes which the majority, consisting of the Conservative, Centre and National Liberal parties, was able to effect conformed to the interests of the opponents.[35]

Compared to this, the second major area of decision, the Health Insurance Act of 1883, was surrounded by far less political controversy. The Chancellor himself took little part in the drafting, since he considered the whole scheme to be a 'changeling'. Lohmann's draft could therefore from the outset incorporate major criticisms by opponents and follow a less controversial course.[36] In addition, both factions within industry attached less importance to the reform of health legislation as such. For heavy industry this law was nevertheless of interest as an adjunct to accident insurance. If all accident cases involving only temporary disability could be made the responsibility of health insurance agencies, the number of compensation cases could be reduced by 90 to 95 per cent, and costs by over 10 per cent. Furthermore, workers paid two-thirds of health insurance contributions, while accident insurance was borne by the employer alone.[37] Of equal importance to employers were the factory health schemes (*Betriebskrankenkassen*). The employers in the Central Association demanded compulsory factory health insurance in order to gain a legal handle to combat the trade unions' independent health insurance schemes.[38] Finally, the supporters of insurance saw these two demands as a way of putting their influence to the test. The employers in heavy industry were displeased by the changes in the original draft of the Accident Insurance Bill that had come about through co-operation between the government and political parties. Health insurance was therefore to be a test case from which they would be able to draw their conclusions.

This produced largely negative results. The Chancellor's scant interest and disagreements with the administration led, even at the preparatory stage, to a draft which favoured the opponents of state insurance and disappointed the hopes of heavy industry. At the next stage, too, during the deliberations in the Reichstag, this group of industrialists was unable to help their interests along to the desired extent. It proved impossible to push through a closer linking of accident and health insurance or indeed special privileges for factory health insurance schemes.[39]

At the General Assembly of the Central Association of German Industrialists in September 1883, the leaders of heavy industry indicated for the first time that they would have to reconsider their co-operation in the area of social insurance legislation. Even at this stage — and not only with the introduction of the *Neue Kurs* in the 1890s — industry became increasingly critical of state social legislation.[40]

In the third major area of decision-making, therefore, defensive and interest-group policies predominated. Industrialists gave reluctant support to *old age and disability insurance*, with the main objective of preventing these being organised on the basis of trade associations (*Berufsgenossenschaften*). In 1887 the trade associations of accident insurance organisations had joined together to form the Federation of German Trade Associations (*Verband der Deutschen Berufsgenossen-*

schaften). This new federation soon began to expand its activities, demanding recognition as the overall representative of German industry and justifying this demand by claiming that as the central organisation of compulsory state insurance associations, it represented a much larger number of employers than the independent associations. This posed a direct and·massive threat to the position of the Central Association of German Industrialists and its claim to represent all German employers, and to the latter's organisational monopoly as the main industrial association. Viewed in the light of these interests, it is understandable why heavy industry so sharply attacked any expansion of the role of the trade associations into the field of old age and disability insurance.[41]

It appears that for these reasons the by now rather half-hearted supporters of Bismarck's social insurance policies once more decided in favour of co-operating with the Chancellor. Adhering to the old adage 'influence through co-operation', heavy industry again succeeded in achieving its objectives during the preparatory stages of the Bill: the final draft no longer envisaged control over this insurance by the trade associations.[42]

German Industry and the Founding of the Welfare State

In conclusion I would put forward the following points by way of a summary.

(1) The contributions made by German industrialists in founding the welfare state remain in many ways ambivalent. A significant minority — perhaps even a majority — completely rejected the creation of a state social security system for a variety of reasons. The scheme only received support from a small number of active and well organised members of big industry.

(2) These industrialists were interested in a solution which would deal with the growing social problems in conformity with their own concepts, i.e. primarily as a solution to the question of accident liability. What they had in mind was a transfer to the state of 'proven' methods of industrial paternalism, which blended welfare and disciplinary elements. State social security measures were to them acceptable only in the shape of social insurance. This 'fundamental outlook' they shared with Bismarck. The choice between the alternatives of a 'self-help'

scheme or state workers' insurance was thus, through their co-operation, decided in favour of a state system. The initially strong position of heavy industry in this socio-political decision-making process, as well as the close alignment of its interests with Bismarck's, gradually lost importance and thus carried less weight during the second stage of legislation, the parliamentary debates.

(3) For this reason, the German social security system no longer matched the initial concepts of its supporters in industry. Most of their original objectives disappeared in the nearly ten-year process of changes made by government and Reichstag. During this transformation the emphases on power politics and discipline diminished and stress was laid on the social advantages of the insurance system. This shift illustrated at the same time the main flaw in heavy industry's concept of social policy: 'company' paternalism was not susceptible to being carried over directly to state level, for once arrived there it took on other qualities.

(4) The German welfare state thus began with the support, and at the same time against the wishes, of industry. This ambivalence is well illustrated by the arguments employed by heavy industry after the fall of Bismarck: 'German industry', it declared time and again, 'has been one of the most diligent and effective supporters of this significant humanitarian achievement.'[43] This retrospective view, however, was not aimed at creating continuity but merely intended to disguise the resistance to state social policies in the post-Bismarck era.

Notes

1. The brief lecture format has been only slightly altered for publication and a few notes have been added.

2. Henry Axel Bueck, *Der Centralverband Deutscher Industrieller 1876-1901* (3 vols., Berlin, 1902-5), here vol. 2, pp. 791 ff.

3. On this consensus in research cf. also Gustav Schmoller, *Vier Briefe über Bismarcks sozialpolitische und volkswirtschaftliche Bedeutung* (Leipzig, 1899), pp. 29 ff.; Hans Rothfels, 'Prinzipienfragen der Bismarckschen Sozialpolitik' in *idem, Bismarck. Vorträge und Abhandlungen* (Stuttgart, 1970), pp. 166-81; Friedrich Lütge, 'Die Grundprinzipien der Bismarckschen Sozialpolitik', *Jb.f. Nationalökonomie u. Statistik*, vol. 134 (1931), pp. 580-96; Karl Erich Born, *Staat und Sozialpolitik seit Bismarcks Sturz. Ein Beitrag zur Geschichte der innenpolitischen Entwicklung des Deutschen Reiches 1890-1914* (Wiesbaden, 1957), pp. 20 ff.; *idem,* 'Die Motive der Bismarckschen Sozialgesetzgebung',

Die Arbeiterversorgung, vol. 62 (1960), pp. 33-9; *idem*, 'Staat und Sozialpolitik im Deutschen Kaiserreich' in *Geschichte der Gegenwart*, Festschrift f. Kurt Kluxen, Ernst Heim and Julius Schoeps (eds.) (Paderborn, 1972), pp. 179-97. Research on Bismarck in recent years has refined this interpretation but not substantially altered it. See also Hans Rosenberg, *Grosse Depression und Bismarckzeit. Wirtschaftsablauf, Gesellschaft und Politik in Mitteleuropa* (Berlin, 1967), pp. 192 ff.; Michael Stürmer, 'Konservativismus und Revolution in Bismarcks Politik' in *idem* (ed.), *Das Kaiserliche Deutschland. Politik und Gesellschaft 1870-1918* (Düsseldorf, 1970), pp. 143-67; Hans-Ulrich Wehler, *Bismarck und der Imperialismus* (Cologne, 1969), esp. pp. 459 ff.

4. On Prussian social policy cf. Friedrich Syrup and Otto Neuloh, *Hundert Jahre Staatliche Sozialpolitik 1839-1939* (Stuttgart, 1957), pp. 49 ff.; Karl Erich Born, 'Sozialpolitische Probleme und Bestrebungen in Deutschland von 1848 bis zur Bismarckschen Sozialgesetzgebung' in *VSWG.*, vol. 46 (1959), pp. 29-44; Wolfgang Köllmann, 'Die Anfänge staatlicher Sozialpolitik in Preussen bis 1869', *VSWG*, vol. 53 (1966), pp. 28-52; Heinrich Volkmann, *Die Arbeiterfrage im preussischen Abgeordnetenhaus 1848-1869* (Berlin, 1968); on mining legislation cf. Wolfram Fischer, 'Die Stellung der preussischen Bergrechtsreform von 1851-1865 in der Wirtschafts- und Sozialverfassung des 19. Jahrhunderts' in *idem*, *Wirtschaft und Gesellschaft im Zeitalter der Industrialisierung* (Göttingen, 1972), pp. 148-60, and Klaus Tenfelde, *Sozialgeschichte der Bergarbeiter an der Ruhr im 19. Jahrhundert* (Bonn, 1977), pp. 163 ff.

5. On the crisis of 'liberal state' social policy cf. Adolf Lehr, *Aus der Praxis der früheren Haftpflicht-Gesetzgebung und der sich an dieselbe anschliessenden Unfallversicherung* (Leipzig, 1888); Louis Baare, 'Gesetz-Entwurf betreffend die Errichtung einer Arbeiter-Unfall-Versicherungs-Kasse nebst Motiven', *Annalen des Deutschen Reiches* (1881), pp. 69-90; also, 'Begründung zum Entwurf eines Gesetzes, betr. die Versicherung der in Bergwerken, Fabriken und anderen Betrieben beschäftigten Arbeiter gegen die Folgen der beim Betriebe sich ereignenden Unfälle', *Sten. Ber. des Reichstages*, IV Leg. Per., 4. Sess., (1881), vol. 3, no. 41. The Liability Act of 1871 extended employers' liability in the event of an accident, but left the onus to prove negligence on the employee. This, as a rule, led to lengthy court proceedings, resulting in compensation in less than 20 per cent of cases. The *Hilfskassengesetze* (relief fund laws) were similarly ineffectual, since they linked the advantages of establishing norms to the right of the state to intervene, thus removing any interest on the part of insurance organisations to submit to the new legislation. It was not even possible to achieve a stratification of the indeterminable number of insurance schemes. In addition, the repressive nature of the anti-socialist laws further reduced the number of independent insurance schemes. For details see Friedrich Kleeis, *Die Geschichte der sozialen Versicherung in Deutschland* (Berlin, 1928), pp. 60 ff. and 104 ff.; G. Honigmann, 'Art. Arbeiterversicherung', *Handwörterbuch der Staatswissenschaft*, vol. 1 (Jena, 1890), pp. 519-30; Gerhard A. Ritter and Klaus Tenfelde, 'Der Durchbruch der Freien Gewerkschaften Deutschlands zur Massenbewegung im letzten Viertel des 19. Jahrhunderts', in *idem*, *Arbeiterbewegung, Parteien und Parlamentarismus. Aufsätze zur deutschen Sozial- und Verfassungsgeschichte des 19. und 10. Jahrhunderts* (Göttingen, 1976), pp. 55-104. The crisis of social policy had repercussions on communal poor relief as a consequence of the *Unterstützungswohnsitz-Gesetz* (subsidised housing law).

6. It is essential here to refer to the original drafts of the early 1880s rather than to the modified laws passed by the Reichstag. Bismarck's intentions are most clearly reflected in the first draft of the accident insurance Bill. Cf. note 8.

7. Cf. Hans Rothfels, *Theodor Lohmann und die Kampfjahre der staatlichen Sozialpolitik (1871-1905)* (Berlin, 1927), pp. 48 ff.; Volker Hentschel, 'Das

System der sozialen Sicherheit in historischer Sicht 1880-1975', *AfS*, vol. 18 (1978), pp. 307-52. The social sciences have in recent years examined the question of social security in great detail for reasons of topicality. From the wealth of existing literature I would just mention Christian von Ferber, *Sozialpolitik in der Wohlstandsgesellschaft* (Hamburg, 1967); Axel Murswieck (ed.), *Staatliche Politik im Sozialsektor* (Munich, 1976); Christian von Ferber and Franz-Xaver Kaufmann (eds.), *Soziologie und Sozialpolitik* (Opladen, 1977); Tim Guldimann, *Sozialpolitik als soziale Kontrolle* (Frankfurt, 1978).

8. 'Entwurf eines Gesetzes, betr. die Versicherung', see note 5 above.

9. The Chancellor retained the principle of 'state paternalism' in all drafts of the accident insurance legislation and used it also as a basis for old age and disability schemes. Cf. Walter Vogel, *Bismarcks Arbeiterversicherung. Ihre Entstehung im Kräftespiel der Zeit* (Brunswick, 1951); Ernst Hunkel, 'Fürst Bismarck und die Arbeiter-Versicherung', diss., Erlangen, 1909; Rudolf Pense, 'Bismarcks Sozialversicherungspolitik. Versuch einer Darstellung seiner Pläne und deren Verwirklichung', diss., Greifswald, 1934. An exception to this was the health insurance, in the creation of which Bismarck played only a small part. Public subsidy and government organisation were lacking even at the drafting stage. The disciplinary aspects were therefore less pronounced from the outset.

10. The official responsible in the Prussian Ministry of Trade, Theodor Lohmann, clearly appreciated this thrust in the direction of compulsory state insurance. In drafting his proposals for a health insurance Bill, he therefore argued in favour of retaining independent health insurance schemes (Rothfels, *Lohmann*, pp. 55 ff.). In the 1880s these independent health schemes *(freie Kassen)* became an important stepping-stone in the revival of the trade union movement (Ritter and Tenfelde, 'Durchbruck', pp. 80 ff.). But in health insurance, too, the impact produced by a state-organised insurance scheme became evident in the action later taken against the independent schemes. For details see Florian Tennstedt, 'Sozialgeschichte der Sozialversicherung' in *Handbuch der Sozialmedizin* (Stuttgart 1976), vol. 3, pp. 385 ff.

11. Cf. Wolfgang J. Mommsen, 'Das Deutsche Kaiserreich als System umgangener Entscheidungen' in *Vom Staat des Ancien Régime zum modernen Parteienstaat*, Festschrift für Theodor Schieder, Helmuth Berding *et al.* (eds.) (Munich, 1978), pp. 239-65.

12. On resistance from the civil service cf. Rothfels, *Lohmann*, pp. 26 ff.; Karl Thieme, 'Bismarcks Sozialpolitik', *Archiv für Politik und Geschichte*, vol. 9 (1927), pp. 382-407. On the structure and reorientation of the administration see Eckart Kehr, 'Das soziale System der Reaktion in Preussen unter dem Ministerium Puttkamer' in *idem, Der Primat der Innenpolitik. Gesammelte Aufsätze zur preussisch-deutschen Sozialgeschichte im 19. und 20. Jahrhundert*, Hans-Ulrich Wehler (ed.) (Berlin, 1970), pp. 64-86, and Rudolf Morsey, *Die oberste Reichsverwaltung unter Bismarck, 1867-1890* (Münster, 1967).

13. Cf. Julius Curtius, *Bismarcks Plan eines Deutschen Volkswirtschaftrates* (Heidelberg, 1919); Kurt Marzisch, 'Die Vertretung der Berufsstände als Problem der Bismarckschen Politik', diss., Marburg, 1934; Heinrich August Winkler, *Pluralismus oder Protektionismus? Verfassungsgeschichtliche Probleme des Verbandswesens im Deutschen Kaiserreich* (Wiesbaden, 1972).

14. Michael Stürmer, *Regierung und Reichstag im Bismarckstaat 1871-1880* (Düsseldorf, 1974), pp. 265 ff.; Heinrich Heffter, *Die Kreuzzeitungspartei und Bismarcks Kartellpolitik* (Leipzig, 1927).

15. Some pointers on the description of socio-political decision-making processes are to be found in Hans Peter Widmaier, *Sozialpolitik im Wohlfahrtsstaat. Zur Theorie politischer Güter* (Reinbek, 1976), esp. pp. 56 ff.; *idem* (ed.), *Politische Ökonomie des Wohlfahrtsstaates* (Frankfurt, 1974).

16. Cf. Hans Gehring, *Die sozialpolitischen Anschauungen der deutschen Freihandelsschule* (Jena, 1909); *Verhandlungen, Mitteilungen und Berichte des Centralverbandes Deutscher Industrieller* (hereafter *VMB*), no. 15 (Berlin, 1881), pp. 28 ff. and 59 ff. (quotation pp. 30 and 29). The views put forward by the industrialist Klewitz are typical for the arguments of 'liberal' employers. Within the Centralverband they remained bitterly opposed outsiders.

17. On working conditions in small and medium-sized firms cf. Jürgen Kuczynski, *Darstellung der Lage der Arbeiter in Deutschland von 1871 bis 1900* (Berlin, 1962), pp. 343 ff.; Vogel, *Bismarcks Sozialversicherungspolitik*, p. 35. In greater detail on business management and social policies within firms, see Jürgen Kocka, 'Management und Angestellte im Unternehmen der Industriellen Revolution' in Rudolf Braun *et al.* (eds.), *Gesellschaft in der industriellen Revolution* (Cologne, 1973), pp. 162-201, esp. pp. 172 ff.; Ludwig Puppke, *Sozialpolitik und soziale Anschauungen frühindustrieller Unternehmer in Rheinland-Westfalen* (Cologne, 1966).

18. For example, see classification of risks of the Leipzig 'Accident Bank' (reprinted in Lehr, *Praxis*, pp. 82 ff.) and information in *VMB*, no. 17 (Berlin, 1882), pp. 34 ff. Consumer goods industries had, in the main, low accident rates.

19. 'Die Arbeiterversicherung des Deutschen Reiches', *Sächsische Industrie* of 16 Jan. 1907, pp. 34 ff.

20. Cf. Hans Jürgen Teuteberg, *Geschichte der industriellen Mitbestimmung in Deutschland* (Tübingen, 1961), pp. 254 ff.

21. This mistrust of social security became particularly obvious in the disputes about organising old age and disability insurance on the basis of trade associations. Cf. Carl Alexander Martius, *Materialien zur Beurteilung der Frage der Interessenvertretung von Industrie und Handwerk* (Berlin, 1895), pp. 12 ff.

22. The supporters of workers' insurance gathered around the interest groups representing heavy industry and protective tariffs. On their membership structure cf. Helga Nussbaum, 'Zentralverband Deutscher Industrieller (ZDI) 1876-1919' in Dieter Fricke *et al.* (eds.), *Die Bürgerlichen Parteien in Deutschland. Handbuch der Geschichte der bürgerlichen Parteien und anderer bürgerlicher Interessenorganisationen vom Vormärz bis zum Jahre 1945*, vol. 2 (Leipzig, 1970), pp. 204-15; Dirk Stegmann, 'Art. Unternehmerverbände' in *Handwörterbuch der Wirtschaftswissenschaft*, vol. 8 (Stuttgart, 1978), pp. 155-71; *VMB*, no. 21 (Berlin, 1883), pp. 109 ff.

23. Cf. Kocka, 'Management', pp. 172 ff.; *idem, Unternehmer in der deutschen Industrialisierung* (Göttingen, 1975), pp. 73 ff.; Puppke, pp. 143 ff.; Friedrich Zunkel, *Der Rheinisch-Westfälische Unternehmer 1834-1879. Ein Beitrag zur Geschichte des deutschen Bürgertums im 19. Jahrhundert* (Cologne, 1962), pp. 237 ff.; Herbert Büren, 'Arbeitgeber und Sozialpolitik. Untersuchungen über die grundsätzliche Haltung des deutschen Unternehmertums gegenüber der Sozialpolitik in der Vorkriegs-, Kriegs- und Nachkriegszeit', 2 vols., diss., Cologne, 1934, esp. vol. 1, pp. 52 ff.; Gaston V. Rimlinger, 'Sozialpolitik und wirtschaftliche Entwicklung: Ein historischer Vergleich' in Braun, *Gesellschaft*, pp. 113-26. In addition, heavy industry possessed many years' experience of social policies, both on national and company level. Through working with the mining associations (*Knappschaften*) they had experienced state compulsory insurance and its effects, worker participation in its financial administration and the costs associated with such schemes. They were thus in a position to make a fair assessment of the advantages and disadvantages of social security.

24. *VMB*, no. 17 (Berlin, 1882), pp. 10 ff.

25. Cf. Karl W. Hardach, *Die Bedeutung wirtschaftlicher Faktoren bei der Wiedereinführung der Eisen- und Getreidezölle in Deutschland 1879* (Berlin,

1967, pp. 16 ff.

26. For details see Helmut Böhme, *Deutschlands Weg zur Grossmacht. Studien zum Verhältnis von Wirtschaft und Staat während der Reichsgründungszeit 1848-1881*, 2nd edn (Cologne, 1972), pp. 357 ff.; Walter Lotz, *Die Ideen der deutschen Handelspolitik von 1860 bis 1891* (Leipzig, 1892), pp. 122 ff. On the employment policy arguments put forward by supporters of protective tariffs cf. Karl W. Hardach, 'Beschäftigungspolitische Aspekte in der deutschen Aussenhandelspolitik ausgangs der 1870er Jahre', *Schm. Jb.*, vol. 86 (1966). The close connection between protective tariffs and social policy was made particularly obvious at the General Assembly of the *Centralverband Deutscher Industrieller* in 1879. Cf. Bueck, *Centralverband*, vol. 2, pp. 1 ff. and 74 ff.; *VMB* no. 15 (Berlin, 1881), pp. 53 ff.

27. Cf. the survey by L. Francke, 'Die Stimmen der deutschen Handels- und Gewerbekammern über das Haftpflichtgesetz vom 7. Juni 1871 und der Reichs-Unfallversicherung-Gesetzentwurf vom 8. März 1881', *Zs. des Kgl. Preussischen Statistischen Bureaus*, vol. 21 (1881), pp. 397-416.

28. To avoid a split, the German Trade Congress virtually excluded the insurance issue altogether. Cf. Julius Gensel, *Der Deutsche Handelstag in seiner Entwicklung und Tätigkeit 1861-1901* (Berlin, 1902), pp. 105 ff.; *Der Deutsche Handelstag 1861-1911*, vol. 1 (Berlin, 1911); *Verhandlungen des Neunten-Sechszehnten Deutschen Handelstages zu Berlin* (1880-1889). On the Economic Congress cf. Volker Hentschel, *Die deutschen Freihändler und der volkswirtschaftliche Kongress 1858 bis 1885* (Stuttgart, 1975).

29. Statistics from Bueck, *Centralverband*, vol. 2, pp. 259 ff. The estimate is methodologically inaccurate since it includes double counts and assumes too small a number of compulsorily insured. The Accident Insurance Act affected 3.5 million people in 270,000 firms (Tennstedt, 'Sozialgeschichte', p. 432). If one takes the overestimated figure of 1 million workers as a base, the supporters, in terms of employees involved, were able to marshal less than a third. If one assumes an average company size of 200 employees, no more than 5,000 firms (i.e. 2 per cent of insurable units of production) can have been involved.

30. On the organisations of heavy industry cf. Böhme, *Deutschlands Weg*, pp. 359 ff.; Ivo Nikolai Lambi, *Free Trade and Protection in Germany 1868-1879* (Wiesbaden, 1963), pp. 113 ff.; Clemens Klein, *Aus der Geschichte des Vereins Deutscher Eisen- und Stahlindustrieller* (Düsseldorf, 1924); Josef Winschuh, *Der Verein mit dem langen Namen. Geschichte eines Wirtschaftsverbandes* (Berlin, 1932); Nussbaum, 'Zentralverband'; Stegmann, 'Art. Unternwehmerverbände'; Bueck, *Centralverband*; Hartmut Kaelble, *Industrielle Interessenpolitik in der Wilhelminischen Gesellschaft. Centralverband Deutscher Industrieller 1895-1914* (Berlin, 1967). On co-operation with Bismarck cf. *VMB*, no. 15 (Berlin, 1881), pp. 56 ff. Servaes quotation from Böhme, *Deutschlands Weg* p. 388.

31. Cf. Rothfels, *Lohmann*, pp. 48 ff.; Vogel, *Bismarcks Sozialversicherungspolitik*, pp. 92 ff. Bismarck based himself on the work of Louis Baare (see note 5). See also W. Bacmeister, *Louis Baare. Ein Westfälischer Wirtschaftsführer aus der Bismarckzeit* (Essen, 1937), pp. 225 ff. and Th. Baare, 'Die Anfänge der deutschen Sozialgesetzgebung. Ein archivalischer Beitrag zu den Beziehungen Bismarcks zu L. Baare', *Gelbe Hefte*, vol. 9 (1934), pp. 549-61. Baare's memorandum formed the basis of the draft legislation. It had been agreed with the leaders of Rhineland-Westphalia's major industries. Cf. Bueck, *Centralverband*, vol. 2, pp. 79 ff.

32. Cf. Vogel, *Bismarcks Sozialversicherungspolitik*, p. 40; *VMB*, no. 15 (Berlin, 1881), pp. 60 ff.

33. Eduard Heimann, *Soziale Theorie des Kapitalismus. Theorie der Socialpolitik* (Tübingen, 1929), p. 175.

34. In detail *VMB*, no. 15 (Berlin, 1881), pp. 5 ff.; Bueck, *Centralverband*,

vol. 2, pp. 99 ff. In all these drafts of the legislation, heavy industry had insisted that workers should pay a part of the contributions. Cf. *VMB*, nos. 15-28 (Berlin, 1881-4); Vogel, *Bismarcks Sozialversicherungspolitik*, pp. 4 ff.; Tennstedt, 'Sozialgeschichte', pp. 424 ff.

35. A detailed study of the interconnection between political parties and economic interests and its effects on social legislation still remains to be done. On the deliberations in the *Reichstag* cf. Otto Quandt, *Die Anfänge der Bismarckschen Sozialgesetzgebung und die Haltung der Parteien (Das Unfall-Versicherungsgesetz 1881-1884)* (Berlin, 1938) (reprinted Vaduz, 1965); Erich Stock, *Wirtschafts- und sozialpolitische Bestrebungen der deutschkonservativen Partei unter Bismarck 1876-1890* (Breslau, 1928), pp. 94 ff.; Karl Heidemann, 'Bismarcks Sozialpolitik und die Zentrumspartei, 1881-1884', diss., Göttingen, 1930; R. Müller, 'Die Stellung der liberalen Parteien im Deutschen Reichstag zu den Fragen der Arbeiterversicherung und des Arbeitschutzes bis zum Ausgang des 19. Jahrhunderts', diss., Jena, 1952; Hertha Wolf, 'Die Stellung der Sozialdemokratie zur deutschen Arbeiterversicherungsgesetzgebung von ihrer Entstehung bis zur Reichsversicherungsordnung', diss., Freiburg, 1933.

36. In detail, Rothfels, *Lohmann*, pp. 54 ff. (quotation p. 55); Kleeis, *Geschichte*, pp. 104 ff.; Tennstedt, 'Sozialgeschichte', pp. 385 ff.

37. Cf. *VMB*, no. 16 (Berlin, 1882), pp. 25 ff.; no. 17 (Berlin, 1882), pp. 8 ff.; no. 18 (Berlin, 1882), pp. 4 ff.; no. 19 (Berlin, 1883), pp. 5 ff.

38. Bueck, *Centralverband*, vol. 2, pp. 197 ff.; *VMB*, no. 25 (Berlin, 1884), pp. 6 ff.

39. Cf. K. Görres, *Handbuch der gesamten Arbeitergesetzgebung des deutschen Reiches* (Freiburg, 1893), pp. 4 ff. and references in note 36 above.

40. Shorthand record of the delegate conference at Stuttgart, *VMB*, no. 25 (Berlin, 1884), pp. 6 ff.

41. On old age and disability insurance cf. Kleeis, *Geschichte*, pp. 139 ff.; Pense, 'Bismarcks Sozialversicherungspolitik', pp. 30 ff.; Hunkel, *Fürst Bismarck*, pp. 95 ff.; Tennstedt, 'Sozialgeschichte', pp. 448 ff.; Lütge, 'Grundprinzipien', pp. 592 ff. Old age and disability insurance was first presented in 'outline'. Trade associations were envisaged as organisers. Cf. *VMB*, no. 38 (Berlin, 1888), pp. 3-34. For details on the Federation of Trade Associations (Berufsgenossenschaftsverband) and the arguments with the Centralverband see Fritz Tänzler, *50 Jahre Unfallversicherung. Eine Denkschrift den deutschen Berufsgenossenschaften gewidmet vom Verband den deutschen gewerblichen Berufsgenossenschaften* (Berlin, 1935). 'Mitteilungen über die Stellung des Centralverbandes Deutscher Industrieller zu den Bestrebungen des Verbandes der Deutschen Berufsgenossenschaften für die Unfallversicherung der Arbeiter', *VMB*, no. 39 (Berlin, 1888), pp. 3 ff. This thrust became particularly dangerous when the Berufsgenossenschaften began to make common cause with the enemies of heavy industry both within the Centralverband and outside. Cf. C. Ungewitter, *Ausgewählte Kapitel aus der chemisch-industriellen Wirtschaftspolitik 1877-1927* (Berlin, 1927), pp. 376 ff.

42. Bueck, *Centralverband*, vol. 2, pp. 431 ff.; *VMB*, nos. 41-6 (Berlin, 1888-9).

43. Bueck, *Centralverband*, vol. 2, p. 792.

8 STATE AND UNEMPLOYMENT IN GERMANY 1890-1918 (LABOUR EXCHANGES, JOB CREATION AND UNEMPLOYMENT INSURANCE)

A. Faust

On 27 January 1907, the Kaiser's birthday, the political economist Walter Troeltsch took the opportunity to address an audience at Marburg University on 'The Unemployment Problem'. In doing so he certainly did not choose an obscure topic for the Kaiser's birthday lecture, for as he rightly claimed, of all the spectres haunting modern economic development none preoccupied the public as much as unemployment.[1] A few years later his Leipzig colleague Gerhard Kessler made the remarkable observation that while there were statistics available about the Berlin cattle market which could give daily information to anyone interested in the number, quality, turnover and price of pigs and cattle for sale in Berlin, statistics about the German labour market had not got beyond inadequate and incomplete monthly reports, which appeared late.[2] Contradictory as Troeltsch and Kessler's statements seem, they are symptomatic of the situation relating to unemployment in the last years of peace in the German Empire.

For a long time it was not only the workers' movement and the social reformers who were conscious of the socio-political relevance of unemployment. The view was widespread that 'of all the tasks piling up, none looms larger than the need to do something about the plight of the unemployed.'[3] There was no shortage of programmes and initiatives, but translating them into action and institutions was a slow and tedious process. Heinrich Herkner put into words the disquiet of social reformers when he referred to unemployment insurance as the 'still incomplete wing of the impressive, towering edifice of our social insurance'.[4] Much more progress had been made in other socio-political areas.[5] I have already indicated the problems that will be discussed in this chapter. The questions are:

(1) Why did the complex unemployment issue only come to the fore towards the end of the nineteenth century, emerging relatively late as a concern of a socio-politically aware public and responsible politicians?

(2) Why did it then take such a relatively long time for this to become the subject of state intervention?

In general terms, the answer can be found in a range of socio-economic, political and theoretical factors, linked closely to contemporary awareness of the need for and feasibility of an unemployment policy and its socio-political implications. In analytical terms it makes sense to separate acceptance of the need for a policy from political and technical practicability, because this distinction plays a not unimportant part in the history of unemployment policy.

There was already a fairly wide consensus of opinion in the 1880s that protecting employees collectively against the risks of sickness, accident and old age was not only sensible but also realisable, but the same attitude to the risk of unemployment did not develop until later.

As long as liberal dogma made the economic fate of each individual dependent on his own ability, and as long as public opinion, influenced by traditional political economists and the dynamics of the Industrial Revolution, believed that everyone who wanted to find a job could do so, the unemployed must appear work-shy and unemployment self-inflicted. The unemployed could be best helped, or rather punished, by traditional poor relief. The realisation that the causes of unemployment could be rooted in the economic system would have diametrically opposed middle-class liberal progressive optimism. As late as 1870, any suggestion of a link between poverty and unemployment could be countered by pointing out the freedom of trade in a liberal state.[6]

Several things changed this situation: first, the onslaught of industrialisation, which increased the number of dependent employment contracts and consequently the number of people potentially affected by open unemployment; secondly, the 'Promotion crisis' of 1873/9 and the 'Great Depression'; and, thirdly, the critical writings on social reform and the loss of authority of liberal economic principles. It thus became clear to a wider public that unemployment was in no way an individual's fault but a social phenomenon rooted in the economic system; consequently, it was the responsibility of the whole of society to combat and alleviate it.

Attitudes are quite different now from thirty years ago, a Berlin councillor wrote in 1911:

The causes of greater unemployment lie in far-reaching economic crises, inherent in the nature of major industrial concerns, industrialists' organisations and company cartels, quite apart from any natural influences. They are also linked to state economic policies, which are geared to the interests of the public in general, rather than the individual. The resulting ebb and flow in employment opportunities is something that the individual worker or employee has no influence over. Therefore in the interests of justice, the general public which endorses the existing economic order should also come to the defence of those who are damaged by it.[7]

So, gradually, an acceptance of the need for a public state unemployment policy grew.

As a result of linking unemployment theoretically with the capitalist industrial system, with its analysable crisis-ridden structural changes and market fluctuations, it thereby lost much of its imponderability and inscrutability and an unemployment policy became technically possible. What contributed to this were the unemployment figures in the 1890s which — despite Kessler's criticism — gave information about the structure of unemployment as well as the actual extent of it and thus corrected exaggerated suppositions.

The 'significant and lasting contribution' of the first major, methodologically inadequate, unemployment survey of 1895 organised by the Imperial Statistical Office was in 'correcting and determining the lasting features of public attitudes to the scope of unemployment. Above all it indicated that unemployment up to that point had been considerably overestimated'.[8] The gradually increasing awareness of the social nature of unemployment created (and still creates) a specific problem for any unemployment policy. Each successive refinement of employment statistics (like observations of the economy) could not change the fact that the risk of unemployment still retained unpredictable features, and has escaped exact prognosis even to the present day.[9] The resulting problems in drawing up figures were a further delaying factor in introducing unemployment insurance as opposed to other types of insurance where the risk of illness, old age and inability to earn one's living was mathematically under control.

The longer this went on, the greater the inclination became to push these considerations into the background. As one Cologne City Councillor put it: 'We should not only talk about . . . achieving an ideal situation. We should concentrate first of all on what can be done. The poorest of the workers mustn't be made to wait so long that help comes too late. We must help them as far as we can with present means.'[10]

It is also ultimately due to the intensification of the social conflicts, which, after the collapse of the Socialist Law of 1890, determined the

internal political climate of the Empire, with its rapid strengthening
of the workers' movement and self-organisation of the employers,
that what was developed and perceived in the final years of the nineteenth century became concrete in the form of programmed declara-
tions, decrees and the first socio-political measures. For the use of the
unemployment question as a political instrument, which went hand in
hand with this, added a new socio-political field of conflict to those
already existing, and one which was somewhat explosive because of
its consequences for socio-political power groupings.

One the one hand, a clearly defined unemployment policy was
supposed to have a defusing effect on conflict, taking the wind out of
the labour movements' sails. On the other hand of course, every intervention in the labour market balance had to have far-reaching consequences. It restricted the scope of employers both inside and outside
the factories and made the large landowners fearful of a continuation of the migration of country people into the towns, and thus fearful for their social position. It was also as the very result of the unemployment policy, which improved welfare and stabilised business,
that the labour movement expected to further its political aims.

The fact that in the struggle for power in the Empire the parties
were quick to pursue their own interests with regard to an unemployment policy influenced to a large extent the speed at which it took
shape and the specific way it was organised. In this context, the problem of political implementation took on a particular significance.

This is made clear if one looks at the development of the three
related means of combating unemployment directly and of alleviating
its consequences, on which the socio-political programme and practice
concentrated from an early stage: the labour exchanges, which by
making available all possible jobs sought to avoid or at any rate reduce
unemployment; job creation, which provided employment and income
temporarily for those who could not find work; and finally, unemployment insurance, in case, for any reason, there was still a lack of
employment opportunities. All three measures were not unknown
in Germany at the start of the 1890s, but now, for those reasons
already mentioned, the problem of unemployment was tackled with
a breadth and an intensity hitherto unknown.

Labour exchanges spread most rapidly. In Prussia in 1894 just
200,000 posts were filled as a result of non-commercial employment
offices, while by 1904 1.1 million had been filled in the whole German
Reich and in 1912 3.6 million (with a total labour force of 18.3 million
manual and clerical workers and civil servants in 1907).[11]

What stood the labour exchanges in good stead was that from the very start their necessity was undisputed, since, in addition to reducing unemployment, they had a further equally important task to fulfil.

With the growth of towns and industrial conglomerates, with increasing regional mobility, with job specialisation and the separation of job and trade, with increasing inability of individual employers and would-be employees to oversee the labour market, there arose the need for institutions which were in a position to restore the clear picture which had been lost through industrialisation.

'The great value in social and economic terms is surely beyond doubt. An unlimited amount of good is done by it; unemployment, need and misery are kept at a distance from employees, and employers who need them can be sent workers.'[12] At an early stage unemployment and labour market policies came together in a demand for some 'institution which would put employers and potential employees in touch with each other simply, fast and cheaply'.[13] Thus discussion centred very little on the purpose of a labour exchange but dealt more with how it could be most suitably organised. And this was an eminently political issue, something those with vested interests were very aware of from the beginning. Whoever controlled the employment centres 'controls the labour market and dominates industry',[14] because organised job allocation has an indirect effect on employment through the market overview it creates. In addition it can have a direct influence on working conditions, such as wage rates and working hours, shifting the political balance of power in the labour market by following appropriate guidelines in the continuing process of job allocation, and through tactical action in a labour dispute. The notorious employers' blacklists served this purpose in exactly the same way as the trade union payroll limitations.

It was therefore not so much a natural characteristic of an early stage of development as above all a consequence of the way they functioned within the socio-political struggle to promote self-interest that labour exchanges quickly split up in an extraordinary way into employment offices serving employers, employees and agricultural organisations as well as the modernised guilds and municipalities. In 1916, for example, there were 61 different non-commercial labour exchanges in Frankfurt a.M. and 45 in Halle.[15] And the state neither could do nor wanted to do very much to oppose this trend.

But the towns initiated considerable activities in well understood self-interest. They covered Germany with a network of local agencies 'because they take care of the unemployed, removing the burden from poor relief; they increase the tax capability of employer and employee and give the city authorities a clear view of the employment situation and the poor'.[16] 'Above all, however, through possible job creation, they take the edge off the threat which gatherings of large numbers of unemployed present for any community.'[17]

But these municipal exchanges, particularly those jointly administered with the help of employer and employee representatives, found it difficult to win the support of suspicious industrial and agricultural employers, because they were favoured by employee organisations. 'Jointly administered labour exchanges serving the trade unions' was the cheap but effective battle-cry of the employers.[18] In southern Germany, which was relatively liberally governed and less affected by social conflicts, they received a certain amount of state help, but this was largely denied them by the Prussian government as well as by the Imperial authorities.

Although it was soon blatantly apparent that labour exchanges were urgently in need of unification, state decree and depoliticisation, the Reich refrained from interference which would be bound to evoke opposition from one side or the other. Although they had no wish to 'dismiss jointly administered schemes out of hand', the view in 1909 was still that 'the time is not yet right to make such provision compulsory, and we will probably have to wait a long time before there is any possibility of compulsory provision.'[19]

Characteristically, a law was passed before 1914 in the one area where all contracting parties were in agreement — in that of those commercial labour exchanges, whose excesses were generally condemned and which were therefore placed under stricter control in 1910.[20]

Although it was the municipal employment office which was at pains to be politically neutral, and which became dominant, albeit closely followed by the employers' offices, and although at the same time the one-sided employment officials moderated their militant stance, this was not due so much to state and civic pressures as to employers' fear of state intervention backed by legislation and the view, growing first among the trade unions and later among the employers, that an employment office was hardly a suitable tool for political conflict and that success in cases of labour strife depended more on the strength of the organisation, the discipline of the members and their tactics.

The trade unions admitted very early on that they could only establish their own agencies in a few limited employment sectors, but their opponents also had to recognise that even domineering, rigidly controlled employment offices were no serious hindrance to the workers' organisations. In the period preceding World War One labour exchanges started to become public institutions concentrating on specific matters relating to the labour market and it was the municipal authorities who made the most significant contribution to this.

The second measure was job creation. Intended to prevent the harmful consequences of the sloth of unemployment, it was natural that the public authorities were considered solely responsible for it, so from the outset it lacked a good deal of socio-political dynamite. But while again both the Reich and the federal authorities did not go beyond cautious approval, it was once more the towns, whose costs of poor relief were directly affected by economic fluctuations, which seized the initiative in ever increasing numbers by offering relief work, particularly in the winter months of high unemployment: in 1894/5 there were only 14 towns involved, in 1902/3 there were 30 and in 1908/9, 58.[21] As the number of people employed in this way was 11,500 in 1909/10, it was of course, nothing more than a beginning, which can only be considered worthy of attention when judged by the difficulties put in its path. These obstacles were both practical and theoretical.[22]

First, the municipal authorities, by virtue of their range of responsibility, were seldom in a position to offer any work of a demanding nature but had to limit the work to stone-breaking, digging, sweeping away the snow, etc., activities which were only possible for certain categories of workers.

Moreover, the towns sought anxiously to prevent relief work from becoming a permanent institution, so as not to have it claimed as recognition of the 'right to work', for behind this they suspected 'the Medusa head of social anarchy'.[23] Although it had long since been reduced to a 'dead formula',[24] the 'right to work' threatened middle-class self-awareness like a magical incantation,[25] meaning to them nothing less than the 'obligations on the state and municipal authorities at all times to provide appropriate employment and reward for the unemployed'[26] — which would incidentally have considerably overstretched local financial resources.

As it was, the financing of this measure represented a further hurdle. Job creation around the turn of the century had little in common with modern employment policies. There was no understanding of the stimulating effects on the economy of a public expenditure policy linked with market demand and possibly in deficit.[27] According to the prevailing practice the domestic budget was strictly geared to 'productivity', i.e. to the immediately recognisable benefit of job creation for the general public, and this limited the scope of the municipal authorities even more, especially in years of crisis, since they collected less tax. It took long-term experience with continuous mass unemployment, as occurred in the 1920s, to overcome these reservations.[28]

Unemployment insurance came long after labour exchanges and even job creation.[29] But discussions continued all the more heatedly; the consequences of unemployment insurance for the social balance of power were too obvious for an easy consensus of opinion to have been found.

The views concerning unemployment insurance could easily be inferred from the policy of the trade unions. From early on they had begun to develop a system of support which in 1913 protected some 3.2 million members from complete destitution as a result of unemployment.[30] They were by no means simply motivated by charity, but first and foremost by their aim of heightening the attraction and thereby the impact of their organisations and of freeing labour conflicts from the pressure of the 'industrial reserve army'. With the help of unemployment benefit the 'trade union struggle' could be carried on 'more successfully and more incisively'.[31]

If the trade unions, with their financial potential in mind, soon joined in the cry from social reformers and Social Democrats for a universal national unemployment insurance system, even though such a system would have difficulty in carrying out the functions normally fulfilled by labour organisations, there were nevertheless fundamental conflicts over insurance, compounded by organisational and technical problems. And in view of the unanimous and massive resistance from industry and agriculture to this 'monstrous project'[32] which was in direct opposition to their fundamental convictions and economic interests, the national authorities took refuge in the view that the time was 'not yet ripe'[33] for a national system. They used the undeniable organisational problems as an excuse to reject any political responsibility.

As in all internal politics in Germany in the years immediately before the war, so too with the complicated issues discussed here. The internal political immobility resulting from opposing forces drifting into deadlock had a restricting effect, against which the Imperial authorities knew no other means than carefully to steer a middle path. In addition to this they had also set themselves other socio-political priorities. More important for them and also more easily enforced than unemployment protection was the reform of social insurance and the introduction of insurance for office workers in 1911. The 'definite conclusion' to social legislation subsequently announced expressly included unemployment insurance.[34]

As federal governments saw no point in isolated action by individual states, it was the municipal authorities who yet again did not avoid what was urgently required. But the inadequacies and financial risks of municipal insurance were indeed considerable and for this reason by 1914 only 16 municipal authorities had ventured this step.

It was no coincidence that they all served a variety of industries and trades, without the politically and socially problematic predominance of one or just a few trades and large concerns. None of the towns lay in the heavily industrialised areas of central and west Germany.

And it was not a coincidence either that with one exception all the municipal authorities followed the example of the Belgian town of Gent and relied heavily on the support of the trade unions to help organise unemployment benefit — and so, strictly speaking, it was not a question of municipal insurance but of municipal benefit funds which in 1913 were responsible for approximately 20,000-30,000 people. This minimised the administrative costs, made it easier to curtail an undertaking in a shorter period of time, but politically offered little scope for the future.

Nevertheless, these towns did demonstrate that unemployment insurance was a practicable proposition in the same way as they played a leading role in general in many fields of economic and social policy by involving themselves directly, something which was later aptly termed 'municipal socialism'.[35]

Most civil servants and politicians at federal and national level refused to take over this role as far as unemployment policy was concerned because in essence it was a question of the predictable and intended expansion of the new measure to include socio-economic and therefore political power bases, of control of the labour market and the power balance between the various agencies involved in this market; of the social and economic freedom of action open to private industry; and of positions taken in the distribution of the national product, and finally also, the role of the state in this process. These were all areas of conflict that did not fundamentally challenge an industrial capitalist system like that of the German Reich, but they did put to the test its capacity for reform and integration. Admittedly, national and federal authorities avoided the risks by preferring to adopt a delaying rather than an initiating role, watching developments set in motion by the groups concerned. So in their unemployment policy they followed a 'diagonal' approach too,[36] which characterised the domestic policy of the Wilhelmine Reich and which in turn influenced the format of the socio-political *status quo*.

So, to return to the questions raised at the start of this chapter, it was mainly the political dimension inherent in the unemployment problem which delayed state intervention, even though the measures needed were tried and tested. And as any comparison of job allocation, job creation and unemployment benefit policies shows, theoretical and organisational factors also had a delaying effect. But once they had achieved agreement in principle from interested parties to the need for better protection against the risk of unemployment, they retreated behind the differing chances of political consensus in the three areas.

In this respect little changed even during the First World War, for the heralded 'internal truce' quickly proved to be illusory. Nevertheless the war meant a big step towards a unified national policy on labour exchanges and unemployment insurance, whereby job creation temporarily took a back seat.[37]

The considerable increase in unemployment which occurred in the first months of the war made the inadequacy of the measures against unemployment only too apparent. It is true that fairly soon the labour market suffered a general shortage of labour, but the question of unemployment was still relevant in view of the unavoidable transition difficulties after peace had been concluded, while at the same time increased demands were made on the labour exchanges because of the necessary redistribution of scarce labour resources due to a wartime economy. But just as the militarisation of the labour market, which culminated in the Auxiliary Service Bill of 1916, took place only half-heartedly and with compromises on all sides,[38] so the federal states and the Imperial and military authorities set about standardising the employment offices with caution and with particular regard to sparing the feelings of the employers. Even if public labour exchanges continued to gain ground, the decisive legislative steps were not taken.

Neither did they participate in unemployment insurance. But protection against the consequences of unemployment was to some extent boosted when in the very first weeks of the war the municipal authorities introduced wartime unemployment benefits on a broad basis within the framework of a wartime welfare scheme and a little later this was supported by Reich funds.

Thus for the time being and until the Weimar Republic, unemployment protection was relegated to the level of welfare — this, however, did not carry the stigma of poor relief. Yet what is decisive in the long term about this is that even in such circles, which had hitherto acted with reserve, it was accepted that unemployment insurance was the responsibility of the whole of society, and especially of the Reich itself. Thus an important change took place which paved the way for national unemployment insurance.

Without doubt war conditions provided a certain impetus for state intervention in social matters, even in the question of unemployment. But at the same time this means they did not instigate any new developments but forced pre-existent discussions and tendencies into the open. Nor did they resolve or bring the matter to a conclusion — that was left to a new political system.

Notes

1. Walter Troeltsch, *Das Problem der Arbeitslosigkeit* (Kaisergeburtstagsrede, Marburg, 1907), p. 5.
2. Gerhard Kessler, *Die Arbeitsnachweise der Arbeitgeberverbände* (Leipzig, 1911), p. 1.
3. Alexander Kossmann, 'Die Arbeitslosigkeit und ein neuer Vorschlag zu ihrer Bekämpfung', *Berichte des Freien Deutschen Hochstifts zu Frankfurt am Main*, vol. 11 (1895), pp. 366-84, here p. 368.
4. Dritte Verbandsversammlung und Arbeitsnachweiskonferenz on 9, 10 and 11 October 1902 in Berlin, Berlin 1903 (*Schriften des Verbandes Deutscher Arbeitsnachweise No. 4*), p. 119.
5. We can only touch here on the fact that this delay is an international rather than a specifically German problem. Cf. Gaston V. Rimlinger, *Welfare Policy and Industrialization in Europe, America and Russia* (New York, 1971); Peter Flora, Jens Alber, Jürgen Kohl, 'Zur Entwicklung der europäischen Wohlfahrtsstaaten', *Politische Vierteljahresschrift*, 18 (1977), pp. 707-72.
6. A. Emminghaus, *Das Armenwesen und die Armengesetzgebung in europäischen Staaten* (Berlin, 1870), p. 24: 'The poor law of a state which no longer recognises any settlement or commercial limitations does not have to concern itself with poor people capable of work. Some will be dealt with by police penalties, the others have to be left to voluntary care.'
7. Herman Leidig, *Die Arbeitslosenunterstützung der Stadt Schöneberg* (Berlin, 1911), p. 17. Similarly, B. Jastrow, W. Badke, *Kommunale Arbeitslosenversicherung, Denkschrift und Materialsammlung, vorgelegt dem Magistrat Charlottenburg* (Berlin, 1910); *Denkschrift über die Arbeitslosenversicherung* (Ed. Grossherzoglich Badischen Ministerium des Innern, Karlsruhe, 1909); Karl Kumpmann, *Die Reichsarbeitslosenversicherung* (Tübingen, 1913). On the wider connections in the interpretation of poverty and unemployment: Emil Münsterberg, *Die deutsche Armengesetzgebung und das Material zu ihrer Reform* (Leipzig, 1887); Dieter Schäfer, *Die Rolle der Fürsorge im System der sozialen Sicherung* (Cologne, Berlin, 1966); Heinz Strang, *Erscheinungsformen der Sozialhilfebedürftigkeit* (Stuttgart, 1970); Frank Niess, *Geschichte der Arbeitslosigkeit*.

Ökonomische Ursachen und politische Kämpfe: ein Kapitel deutscher Sozial-geschichte (Cologne, 1979).

8. Kumpmann, *Reichsarbeitslosenversicherung*, p. 30; similarly Georg Schanz, *Neue Beiträge zur Frage der Arbeitslosen-Versicherung* (Berlin, 1897), p. 163. Of course the interpretation of statistical evidence varied according to vested interest. Whilst employers readily played down unemployment, the labour movement saw a long-term growth in the 'industrial reserve army'. Social democrats used information on the structure of unemployment, as well as the overall figures, to support their arguments in favour of socio-political demands, e.g. *Correspondenzblatt der Generalkommission der Gewerkschaften Deutschlands*, vol. 12 (1902), pp. 289-92; *Die Neue Zeit*, 20 Jan. 1901/2, pp. 533-7. For the employers' view see *Der Arbeitgeber* (1911), p. 249; Vereinigung der Deutschen Arbeitgeberverbände (ed.), *Bericht über die Arbeitsnachweiskonferenz in Hannover am 7. November 1913*.

9. Ludwig Preller, *Praxis und Probleme der Sozialpolitik* (Tübingen, Zürich, 1970), pp. 70, 311: 'The close connection between all unemployment and economic policy and the fact that in modern industrial states this economic policy is "manipulated" to a large degree, casts doubts on whether unemployment can be regarded as "accidental" and establishes that it cannot be assessed, i.e. cannot be calculated in terms of insurance mathematics.' Cf. also Stephan Leibfried, 'Die Institutionalisierung der Arbeitslosenversicherung in Deutschland', *Kritische Justiz*, vol. 10 (1977), pp. 291-301.

10. Dritte Verbandsversammlung, 1902, p. 185.

11. Georg Evert, 'Die Arbeitsvermittlung in Preussen während des Jahres 1894', *Ztsch. d. Kgl. Preussischen Statistischen Bureaus*, vol. 36 (1896), pp. 1-87; die bestehenden Einrichtungen zur Versicherung gegen die Folgen der Arbeitslosigkeit im Ausland und im Deutschen Reich. Bearbeitet im Kaiserlichen Statistischen Amt, Abt. für Arbeiterstatistik (Berlin, 1906), Part II; Erhebung über Arbeitsnachweise im Deutschen Reich nach dem Stande von Ende 1912. Bearbeitet im Kaiserlichen Statistischen Amte, Abt. für Arbeiterstatistik (Berlin, 1913) (=Sonderbeilage zum Reichs-Arbeitsblatte No. 6). On the history of employment allocation, Paul Francke, 'Zur Geschichte des öffentlichen Arbeitsnachweises in Deutschland', diss., Halle, 1913; Otto Uhlig, *Arbeit – amtlich angeboten. Der Mensch auf seinem Markt* (Stuttgart, Berlin, Cologne, Mainz, 1970); Niess, *Geschichte der Arbeitslosigkeit*.

12. Verhandlungen der ersten Verbandsversammlung und Arbeitsnachweiskonferenz am 27 September 1898 in München, Berlin, 1899 (=*Schriften des Verbandes Deutscher Arbeitsnachweise, No. 1*), p. 4. Cf. also Adolf Weber, 'In view of such complexity of the labour market there can no longer be any doubt that organisation of the labour market is an urgent requirement of our time.' Zweite gemeinsame Arbeitsnachweiskonferenz der Hauptstelle Deutscher Arbeitgeberverbände und des Vereins Deutscher Arbeitgeberverbände am 20 Oktober 1911 in Wiesbaden. Shorthand record of the proceedings, Berlin, 1911, p. 8.

13. 'Die Arbeitsvermittlung in Bayern (Nach dem Stande am Schlusse des Jahres 1894)', *Ztschr. des Kgl. Bayerischen Statistischen Bureau*, vol. 28 (1896), pp. 126-205, here p. 126.

14. Hans Delbrück, 'Die Arbeitslosigkeit und das Recht auf Arbeit', *Preussische Jahrbücher*, vol. 85 (1896), pp. 80-96, here p. 86.

15. Verzeichnis der Arbeitsnachweise im Deutschen Reich nach dem Stande vom 1. Mai 1916. Bearbeitet im Kaiserlichen Statistischen Amt, Abt. für Arbeiterstatistik (Berlin, 1916).

16. Karl Möller, 'Die Centralisierung des gewerblichen Arbeitsnachweises im Deutschen Reich', *Jahrbuch für Gesetzgebung, Verwaltung und Volkswirtschaft im Deutschen Reich*, vol. 18, no. 2 (1894), pp. 341-82, here p. 358.

17. Carl Conrad, *Die Organisation des Arbeitsnachweises in Deutschland* (Leipzig, 1904), p. 182.

18. This is the title of a brochure published in Berlin in 1910 by L. Thielkow, Secretary of the Iron Industries Association, Hamburg.

19. Staatssekratär des Innern Delbrück, 14 Dec. 1909. Shorthand note of the parliamentary debates, vol. 258, p. 357.

20. *Soziale Praxis XIX* (1909/10), cols. 550-2, 853-5; *Kommunales Jahrbuch*, vol. 3 (1910), pp. 409 ff.

21. Kaiserlich Statistisches Amt, Abt. für Arbeiterstatistik. Die Regelung der Notstandsarbeiten in Deutschen Städten (Berlin, 1905) (=*Beiträge zur Arbeiterstatistik, No. 2*); Ernst Bernhard, 'Die Vergebung der öffentlichen Arbeiten in Deutschland im Kampf gegen die Arbeitslosigkeit' (Berlin, 1913) (=*Schriften der Deutschen Gesellschaft zur Bekämpfung der Arbeitslosigkeit, No. 1*); Harald Winkel, 'Zur historischen Entwicklung der Arbeitsbeschaffungsmassnahmen', *Hamburger Jahrbuch für Wirtschafts- und Gesellschaftspolitik*, vol. 21 (1976), pp. 317-32.

22. *Statistisches Jahrbuch Deutscher Städte*, vol. 5 (1896) ff., *Kommunales Jahrbuch*, vol. 2 (1909) ff.

23. Georg Adler, *Über die Aufgaben des Staates angesichts der Arbeitslosigkeit* (Tübingen, 1894), p. 43.

24. Martin Martiny, 'Das Recht auf Arbeit in historischer Sicht' in Ulrich Borsdorf, Hans O. Hemmer, Gerhard Leminsky, Heinz Markmann (eds.), *Gewerkschaftliche Politik. Reform aus Solidarität*, Zum 60. Geburtstag von Heinz O. Vetter (Cologne, 1977), pp. 449-66, here p. 465.

25. August Baab, *Zur Frage der Arbeitslosenversicherung, der Arbeitsvermittlung und der Arbeitsbeschaffung* (Leipzig, 1911), p. 317.

26. Ibid.

27. Walter Adolf Jöhr, 'Konjunktur (II) Politik' in *Handwörterbuch der Sozialwissenschaften*, vol. 6, pp. 114-32; Theodor Pütz, 'Geschichtliche Wandlungen der Konjunkturschwankunken und Konjunkturpolitik' in Franz Greiss and Fritz W. Meyer (eds.), *Wirtschaft, Gesellschaft und Konjunktur*, Festgabe für Alfred Müller-Armack (Berlin, 1961), pp. 167-87.

28. Die Einrichtung von Notstandsarbeiten und ihre Erfolge. Gutachten von Beigeordnetem Dr. Paul Hartmann (Barmen) und Beigeordnetem Dr. Rudolf Schwander (Strassbourg Alsace) (Leipzig, 1902) (=*Schriften des Deutschen Vereins für Armenpflege und Wohltätigkeit*, No. 58), p. 59.

29. Der gegenwärtige Stand der Arbeitslosenfürsorge und -Versicherung in Deutschland (Berlin, 1913) (=*Schriften der Deutschen Gesellschaft zur Bekämpfung der Arbeitslosigkeit*, no. 2); Michael T. Wermel, Roswitha Urban, *Arbeitslosenfürsorge und Arbeitslosenversicherung*, 3 vols. (Munich, 1949) (=Neue Soziale Praxis, No. 6/I-III); Hansjoachim Henning, 'Arbeitslosenversicherung vor 1914: Das Genter System und seine Übernahme in Deutschland' in Hermann Kellenbenz (ed.), *Wirtschaftspolitik und Arbeitsmarkt* (Munich, 1974), pp. 271-87; Niess, *Geschichte der Arbeitslosigkeit*.

30. Die Verbände der Arbeitgeber, Angestellten und Arbeiter im Jahre 1911 (ff.), Berlin 1913 (ff.) (=*Sonderhefte zum Reichs-Arbeitsblatte*); Gustav Brüggerhoff, *Das Unterstützungswesen bei den deutschen 'freien' Gewerkschaften* (Jena, 1908).

31. *Die Neue Zeit*, 16 Feb. 1897/8, pp. 356-63, here p. 356.

32. H.A. Bueck in a committee meeting of the Central Association of German Industrialists, 11 June 1892; *Verhandlungen, Mitteilungen und Berichte des CDI*, no. 58 (Berlin, 1892), pp. 28 f.

33. Staatssekretär des Innern v. Bethmann Hollweg, 13 Nov. 1908. Shorthand record of Parliament, vol. 233, p. 5489.

34. Staatssekretär des Innern Delbrück, 20 Jan. 1914. Shorthand record of parliament, vol. 292, p. 6637.
35. Heinrich Heffter, *Die deutsche Selbstverwaltung im 19. Jahrhundert. Geschichte der Ideen und Institutionen* (Stuttgart, 1950), p. 610.
36. Hans-Ulrich Wehler, *Das Deutsche Kaiserreich 1871-1918* (Göttingen, 1973), pp. 100 ff.; Gerhard A. Ritter, *Gesellschaft und Politik im Kaiserreich 1871-1914. Arbeiterbewegung, Parteien und Parlamentarismus* (Göttingen, 1976), pp. 10-20; Gustav Schmidt, 'Innenpolitische Blockbildungen in Deutschland am Vorabend des Ersten Weltkrieges', *Aus Politik und Zeitgeschichte. Beilage zur Wochenzeitung Das Parlament*, B 20/72, 13 May 1972, pp. 3-32.
37. See the references in notes 11, 21, 29 above and also: Bureau für Sozialpolitik, Behördliche Massnahmen zur Arbeitsvermittlung im Kriege (Berlin, 1918); Julia Dünner, *Der deutsche Arbeitsnachweis im Kriege bis zum Erlass des Hilfsdienstgesetzes* (Regensburg, Berlin, Wien, 1918); Gerda Simons, *Die Erwerbslosenfürsorge während des Krieges* (Berlin, 1919) (=*Schriften der Deutschen Gesellschaft zur Bekämpfung der Arbeitslosigkeit, No. 5*).
38. Gerald D. Feldman, *Army, Industry, and Labour in Germany 1914-1918* (Princeton, 1966), particularly pp. 197 ff.

PART TWO

UNEMPLOYMENT AND THE CRISIS OF THE WELFARE POLICIES IN THE INTERWAR PERIOD

9 KEYNES AND THE TREASURY VIEW: THE CASE FOR AND AGAINST AN ACTIVE UNEMPLOYMENT POLICY 1920-1939

R. Skidelsky

I

The Treasury View which Keynes confronted between the wars was first developed as a defence of the nineteenth-century tradition of British government finance against the 'abnormal' expedients of war finance and the clamour for state intervention that came out of the First World War. There was no specific 'Treasury View' in the nineteenth century, because there was no dissent from the great orthodoxies of public economic policy: free trade, the gold standard and minimal public spending. The Treasury View, like Conservatism, became identifiable as such only when it started to be contested.

The main aim of Victorian budgetary policy was to balance the annual accounts of the central government at the lowest possible figure.[1] This principle, with its corollary that money was best left to 'fructify in the pockets of the people', had been suspended in two crucial respects between 1914 and 1918. First, government spending had greatly increased, both absolutely and as a proportion of the national income, to finance war production. (It rose from one-twelfth to over half the national income between 1913 and 1918.) Secondly, the larger part of this increased expenditure was met not by taxation, but by printing new money. (The quantity of money rose from £1,588 million in December 1913 to £3,151 million in December 1919.) War finance, in other words, was primitive deficit finance, without any understanding of how to transfer resources to the war effort. At any rate, its crudities and social injustices, leading to massive inflation, helped prevent it from being viewed by either the 'sensible' right or left as a possible model for public finance in peacetime, despite the fact that it had produced full employment.

Also suspended during the war was the gold standard. The effect of a doubling of the price level on the exchange was masked by the prohibition of gold exports, pegging the exchange artificially to the dollar, and financing external purchases by selling off assets or borrowing from the United States and Empire countries. In 1919 the pound was 'unpegged' and allowed to float down to its true level. Wage increases without any immediate reduction in government spending pushed prices higher and the pound lower. Thus, during the war the exchange was 'managed', and managed largely by Keynes who had entered the Treasury as a temporary civil servant in 1915. He drew on this experience in his suggestions for a 'managed' currency in 1922-5. But the association of currency management with inflation and all the other dislocations and inconveniences of war was too sharp and too recent for sound men to place any faith in it as a permanent system.

On the other hand, the war had also brought about a considerable change in social attitudes and class relations, which worked against any easy return to pre-war conditions. It had weakened the hold of Puritanism in all classes, and of deference in the working class. (The middle and upper classes found it more and more difficult to get servants after the war.) It had greatly strengthened the position of the trade unions in industry, and of the labour movement in politics. Capitalism and bourgeois rule were both felt to be under threat. Finally the war, precisely because it had produced an active state, greatly strengthened the disposition to look to the state to improve economic conditions, especially on the part of the left. The Treasury View was thus designed as a defence not just against 'abnormal' wartime expedients, but against new and disturbing pressures arising from the social system. But in this last function lay a great difficulty. War might be merely an unpleasant interlude, but democracy and powerful trade unions could not be got rid of so easily. 'Normalcy' now included features which had not existed, or existed to the same degree, in 1913.

The two primary aims of immediate post-war British economic policy were to restore the 'automatic' gold standard and balance the budget. The relationship between the two was reciprocal. Restoring a stable currency required the elimination of inflationary government spending; the restored gold standard in turn would automatically *prevent* inflationary government spending. These were not just British but international aims, endorsed by the Genoa Conference of 1922. The re-establishment of the gold standard was deemed the 'essential prerequisite' of economic reconstruction, after the currency disorders of the immediate post-war period. The 'first and essential steps' in achieving this common purpose were 'to balance national budgets by contraction of expenses rather than by increase in taxation, to stop inflation by ceasing to cover budget deficits by recourse to paper money, and to cease borrowing for unproductive purposes'.[2]

The rationale for restoring the gold standard was stated by the famous Cunliffe Report of 1918. The great merit of the pre-war gold standard, according to Cunliffe, was that under the Bank Charter Act of 1844 there was no means whereby legal-tender currency could be increased except by the importation of gold from abroad to form the basis of an increase in the note issue of the Bank of England. There was thus an automatic check to any inflationary increase of the money supply. At the same time the gold standard provided an automatic corrective to any balance of payments deficit. Export of gold led to a raising of discount rate. The steps taken to make it effective in the market necessarily led to a general rise of interest rates and a restriction of credit. New enterprises were postponed and demand reduced. The result was a decline in prices in the home market which by checking imports and stimulating exports corrected the adverse balance.[3] The pre-war gold standard thus provided an automatic guarantee against both public and private vices. It made impossible public profligacy; and it punished, by the scourge of unemployment, private extravagance.

Another aspect of the doctrine is worth noting. The Cunliffe Report did not specifically advocate restoration of the pre-war parity. But this was inherent in its view of the political function of the gold standard, and was generally accepted as the objective of public policy. For the notion of the gold standard as the guardian of economic morality 'above politics' rested on the immutability of the sterling-gold ratio established on the advice of Sir Isaac Newton in 1719. It was its very longevity, as part of the 'natural order of things', which protected it from political interference. Stabilisation at a reduced parity would be an act of political management; and currency depreciation would thereafter always be open to a government as an alternative to balancing its accounts. Currency depreciation, in other words, was the royal road back to mercantilism, to government control over the economy in the interests of its clients. One cannot understand the mental atmosphere of the time unless one realises that the 'rules of sound finance' were seen as a defence not just against economic catastrophe but against state socialism. They were the price of freedom; the Bank and Treasury saw themselves as guardians of that freedom.*

Balancing the budget in the circumstances of 1918-22 automatically meant deflating the economy. Bank Rate was put up to 6 per cent in November 1919 and 7 per cent the following April. Currency in

---

* As the Cunliffe Report noted (paragraph 6), under the gold standard 'banking could be safely permitted a freedom from State interference which would not have been possible under a less rigid currency system.'

circulation was reduced by 10 per cent between September 1920 and September 1921. The budget was balanced in 1920-1 through a combination of increased taxation and reduced expenditure: government spending came down from 61.7 per cent of the GNP in 1918 to 27.7 per cent in 1922, the most spectacular cuts being associated with the Geddes Axe which fell in that year. Unemployment rose from 700,000 (6 per cent of insured workers) in December 1920 to 2,200,000 (18 per cent) in June 1921, and remained at a million and a half or more until the beginning of 1923. Taking 1913 as 100, wholesale prices came down from 300 at the end of 1919 to 160 by the end of 1922; wages from 220 to 170. Deflation thus led to a rise in real wages for those who remained in employment. This subsequently became the basis of the Treasury argument that unemployment persisted at a high level because wage costs remained too high.

As unemployment mounted towards 2 million in 1921, in cruel mockery of the politicians' promise to build a 'land fit for heroes', pressure mounted on the Lloyd George coalition to 'do' something about the problem. A number of schemes were started: export credits were made available; a Trade Facilities Act in 1921 empowered the Treasury to guarantee loans for approved capital developments designed to relieve unemployment; an Unemployment Insurance Act had brought virtually the whole working population within the ambit of insurance and in addition granted benefits without contributions to demobilised soldiers and civilians switching from war to peace production. But the amounts made available by the central government were very small: the UGC, for example, could only spend a maximum of £3 million a year. In 1921 therefore, Lloyd George set up a Cabinet Committee on Unemployment under Sir Hilton Young to see what more could be done.* Special interests (the railway lobby, municipal authorities, etc.) immediately started pressing their claims for assistance. It was against the various proposals for expanding government spending to relieve unemployment submitted to the Committee that the Treasury View defined itself. Its various

---

* Undoubtedly an important motive was fear of political and industrial unrest: 'There is no doubt that the situation in regard to unemployment is grave, especially in view of the activities of the Communist Party. . . When the Cabinet Committee last considered the matter they were concerned to take steps to prevent the Communists from exploiting the hungry man' (Treasury Minute, 1921, T.172/1208).

elements, as revealed in Otto Niemeyer's* drafts for the Chancellor of the Exchequer, can be listed.

(1) Costs of production were too high:

> The root cause of unemployment at the present time is that the costs of production are so high that purchasers either from abroad or in this country cannot afford to buy. The main item in the cost of production is the cost of wages. Any step which maintains prices means an ultimate increase in unemployment.

The Treasury had done its bit in balancing the budget and paying off £260 million of debt. This had led to a substantial drop in wholesale prices and 'the turning of practically all the foreign exchanges in our favour'. The trouble was that 'retail prices and with them wages have not fallen to anything like the same extent and until they have fallen the full benefit of the check to inflation could not be reached'. Continuing unemployment was the direct consequence of this failure of wage costs to adjust to the fall in prices.

> Experience has shown that the earnings of British industry are not sufficient to pay the present scale of wages all round. Consequently if present wages are to be maintained a certain fraction of the population must go without wages. The practical manifestation of which is unemployment.

(2) Government spending cannot permanently increase employment. If the spending were properly funded, i.e. covered by taxation or by genuine borrowing, it would merely diminish private spending and thus decrease employment elsewhere. It

* Sir Otto Niemeyer was Controller of Finance at the Treasury from 1922 to 1927 and the principal architect of the 'Treasury View'. His father was a German immigrant, from a north German professional family, who came to Britain in 1870, marrying Ethel Rayner, daughter of a Liverpool West African merchant. He had clashed with Keynes once before the 1920s − in the Civil Service Examination in 1908, when he came first and Keynes came second. Keynes entered the India Office, from which he soon resigned to take up a lectureship in economics at Cambridge, while Niemeyer went to the Treasury where he stayed. One wonders what would have happened to twentieth-century economic thought had Keynes gone to the Treasury.

was, therefore, a device for subsidising some groups at the expense of others. In any case, as a practical matter, it was not possible. 'It is . . . obvious that we are very near the limit of taxation. It is less generally realised that the Exchequer is also rapidly approaching the time when it cannot borrow more money.' This left only inflation. Inflation as a device for reducing real wages would only work if 'prices, and particularly export prices, can . . . be kept in advance of wages'. But

> now that Labour's collective bargaining is so effective . . , it is by no means certain that the indirect taxation which is the true effect of inflation would fall upon the wage earners in a depressed standard of living. It seems not improbable that they would succeed in passing the burden on to . . . the possessor of capital by obtaining proportionately increased wages.

The process of inflation would thus be cumulative 'and at that point the exchange runs off the card. The only advantage of relief works 'lies in their psychological effect as an indication that the authorities are anxious to do something for the unemployed and also because they help keep the unemployed out of mischief'. But if carried beyond a very limited point, they were bound to conflict with the overall strategy of bringing down costs.

(3) If government attempted to solve economic problems, that would remove all incentive for those directly concerned to shoulder their responsibilities. For example, if local authority loans were to be guaranteed by the government, 'we should never get them to move again on any subject without a guarantee. Witness our difficulties in weaning banks from Treasury guarantees against ordinary business risks which it is their function to do.' Niemeyer commented on a proposal to lend the railway companies money. 'The Companies could easily get the money themselves at a price. They don't do so, because the work is not remunerative at present prices. It will not become so, merely because the loan is a government loan.' And Montagu Norman, on a proposal to expand export credits: 'The banks already finance all the sound risks. The Government will be left with all the bad ones.' If the state became

'lender of the last resort' it would soon find itself saddled with all industry's bad debts.[4]

II

Interestingly enough, Keynes did not at first oppose the policy of high interest rates to break the boom. On 8 July 1920 he wrote, 'I am still a dear money man.' And looking back on the episode in 1942, he commented that

> with all the methods of control, then so unorthodox, excluded, I feel myself that I should give exactly the same advice that I gave then, namely, a swift and severe dose of dear money, sufficient to break the market, and quick enough to prevent at least some of the disastrous consequences which would otherwise ensue.[5]

Nor is there any evidence that Keynes at first opposed the Cunliffe policy of returning to gold convertibility at the old parity. It was only when the policy of deflation failed to restore prosperity that he started to question it, and the object to which it was directed — restoring the gold standard at the old parity.

In his *Tract on Monetary Reform* (1923), Keynes provided a monetarist explanation of unemployment. If prices are falling through the contraction of money, businessmen cannot recoup their money outgoings at a later date, and therefore curtail their operations, hence unemployment.[6] The Treasury would not have disagreed. Deflation, after all, was intended to lower the price of labour, partly through the lever of unemployment. But lower prices, the Treasury would have argued, would make possible increased sales abroad, thus not only re-employing temporarily idle men in the export trades, but enabling an expansion of employment in these trades. Increased sales abroad would cause gold to flow back, permitting credit expansion, enlarged investment, increased employment, higher productivity, higher real wages, and so on. Keynes's earliest break with orthodox opinion was to deny that the process would work in this smooth way. A stickiness had entered into the adjustment process; or more precisely two — one external, the other internal.

The external stickiness had to do with American policy. The Cunliffe Report had assumed that gold movements occasioned by payments imbalances *automatically* set in motion corrective forces. Thus any influx of gold into the United States would lead to a rise in US prices. US goods would become less competitive; British goods more competitive. Gold would flow from the United States to Britain, restoring the original position. But Keynes pointed out that the American Federal Reserve Board had 'demonetised' gold by refusing to allow gold inflows to augment the money supply and thus produce the internal price rises which would have caused gold to return to Europe. America's mercantilist posture doomed Britain's deflationary strategy. The Treasury and the Bank of England hoped that reductions in domestic wage costs would enable Britain to improve its external balance sufficiently to go back to gold at the old parity. But Britain could not secure the required increase in its exports in face of America's dear money, high-tariff policy. Britain must manage its currency in its own national interest, as America was already doing. That interest, Keynes made clear, lay in stable prices, to which everything else, including exchange, should be adjusted. This implied either a 'managed' currency, or a stabilisation at a lower parity — one which did not involve any further deflation.[7]

If external adjustment was sticky, even more so was internal adjustment. The Cunliffe Report, the Treasury and the Bank of England all assumed that domestic prices (including the price of labour) would readily adjust to whatever the required level of exchange was. Keynes became increasingly doubtful about whether this was so. Already in the *Economic Consequences of the Peace* (1919) he had foreseen the end of the nineteenth-century system under which the working class 'accepted from ignorance or powerlessness, or were compelled, persuaded, or cajoled . . . into accepting, a situation in which they could call their own very little of the cake that they and nature and the capitalists were co-operating to produce'.[8] In the *Tract*, he noted that 'the organisation of certain classes of labour — railwaymen, miners, dockers, and others', allied to the 'windfalls of the profiteer' had enabled the working classes to improve their relative position, and in many cases their absolute position, in the post-war period of rapid inflation.[9]

The view that such organisation made money wages highly resistant to downward adjustment was given brilliant and mordant expression in *The Economic Consequences of Mr. Churchill*, written immediately after Churchill, as Chancellor of the Exchequer, had returned Britain to the pre-war gold standard in April 1925. Churchill's policy, based on the 'vague and jejune meditations' of his Treasury advisers, had increased the price of British exports by 10 per cent at a time when there was already heavy unemployment in the export trades. This meant that Britain would have to reduce its sterling prices by 10 per cent to restore even the previous position, unsatisfactory though that was. This logically entailed reducing everyone's wages by 2s in the pound, since America would manifestly not increase its prices by 10 per cent to restore British competitiveness. The Treasury, Keynes went on, still lived in a dream world in which costs were 'automatically' adjusted to a given exchange rate. But there was no way of reducing wages except by a 'struggle with each separate group in turn', using the instruments of mass unemployment and lock-out and, in view of the 'disappearance of an effective mobility of labour and of a competitive wage level between different industries', facing each group of workers with the choice between 'starvation and submission'. The only alternative to this was living off American credit, to change 'from being a lending country to a borrowing country'; in other words, to put Britain in pawn to other countries in order to maintain an over-valued currency.

Keynes's forecast was prescient. After the disastrous episode of the General Strike and the miners' lockout, the government shrank from the logical consequences of its own policy. Unwilling to break up what economists called the rigidities of the British system for fear of social costs, it adopted a compromise policy. It retained the new gold parity, did nothing to force wage-price adjustments, and by banking policy made an effort to hold foreign funds in the London market. As J.R. Hicks remarked later, 'No democratic government dares to be associated with wage-reductions; and thus the influence of the State was nearly always directed against those adjustments which it made necessary by its own policy.'[10] In other words, the restored gold standard was managed by attracting short-term funds to London, enabling the City to make loans out of them at great profit to Germany and Austria. This was the system which collapsed in 1931.

The force of Keynes's attack, and its rapid justification by events, was the first great shock to the lofty confidence of the Treasury. Churchill, who had always had misgivings about the policy of going back to gold, soon came to regard it as the greatest mistake of his life. In the months and years following 1925, refuting and ridiculing Keynes became almost an obsession in the Treasury. His articles were carefully scrutinised and rebutted; one memorandum starts condescendingly, 'I am sorry to see that Keynes is renewing the Press propaganda which has done him little credit as a politician and considerable harm as an economist.'[11]

The big guns were immediately called in to answer Keynes's attack on the Chancellor. The following are excerpts from Niemeyer's minute of 4 August 1925:

> By fixing our exchange rate we have brought before ourselves the realities of our position in a predominantly gold market world. These realities could be obscured by a varying exchange: but they could not be *changed*. Realities are often not pleasant . . . but they have to be faced.
>
> Mr. Keynes says that with the exchange at 4.32 last June everything was all right. If this means anything it means that we should have fixed the pound at that rate. But no one seriously suggests that sterling should have been thus devalued. Indeed, how could such a course benefit a nation which is after all on balance a creditor for sterling?
>
> Three months is too short a period for a real judgment. . . Wages . . . have not yet dropped. In fact, as the cost of living has dropped and *money* wages have not, *real* wages have increased. But as the process continues, money wages will drop . . . and the temporary export handicap will have disappeared.
>
> Mr. Keynes has always argued that currency should be regulated not by gold or any other fixed point, but by internal prices, letting external exchange go hang. . . It has never been tried in practice; and so far as I know, has received no support from practical men either in banking or trade. . . . We should all like to see price stability: but surely it must be *world price stability*. This country is above all things a world trading country, importing, exporting, financing all over the world. Least of any can it be content with a desert island stability unrelated to what is happening in the rest of the world. In order to get real stability we must first get a stable measuring rod to measure our prices with prices in other currencies. This is what we get from our fixed standard.

Sir John Bradbury, former Joint Permanent Secretary to the Treasury, admitted on the same day that 'appreciation has no doubt been an element though not in my belief the most important element in diminishing the power of British coal to compete,' but argued that to have devalued the pound would have been to 'write down our assets permanently by 30 or 10 per cent according to the moment chosen, without any compensating reduction in our liabilities' and to have disappointed all those who had 'anticipated' the restoration of the pre-war parity.

(A charming reference to speculators!) Since Keynes rejected the only feasible policy-wage reductions — he was left with no policy. 'The late Mr. Micawber, I believe, followed the practice of drawing bills for his housekeeping expenses secured on the hope of something turning up. Mr. Keynes would deal with the dollar exchange on similar lines.'

A year later, Niemeyer had abandoned argument for assertion:

I do not suggest that all our monetary problems are solved. But I believe the step taken last year was right and has rebounded to the credit of this country and enhanced the reputation of London as a financial centre. I believe it was well timed and . . . carried out with the maximum of technical skill. . . At any rate, we have descended from the clouds on to terra firma. . . It is true that the full benefit of the policy cannot be seen so long as other countries in Europe allow their exchanges to rocket: but those countries are learning, by bitter experience, the damage that currency depreciation ultimately inflicts on their economy and I believe that there is now none that is not desperately anxious to follow us to a safe anchorage.

By December 1927, Frederick Leith Ross was taking comfort from the stabilisation of the lira (like the pound, over-valued). There remained the problem of France, but

there is little doubt that . . . the franc too will be stabilised. . . In retrospect, the action of the British Government in going back to the gold standard in 1925 marks the turning point. We led the way. . . It is a slow process, but it may be hoped that it will be an enduring achievement.

By 1928 a different reality could no longer be evaded. Niemeyer minuted:

It is true, of course, quite true that the reduction of money wages to correspond with the reduction of prices has been the outstanding difficulty since our return to the gold standard and that the Chamberlain-Bradbury Committee* seriously under-estimated this difficulty. Political influences have not only operated to mitigate

* To whose 'vague and jejune meditations' Keynes had referred in his article.

the hardships of industrial depression, but have been engaged to a large extent in a deliberate attempt to counteract economic forces by means of subsidies.

As always, it was the fault of the politicians.[12]

III

At the heart of the policy of deflation was the belief that British exports (and employment) could be increased by cutting wage costs. Keynes rejected this on two grounds: other countries would protect themselves against any large increase in British exports; and the attempt to reduce wage costs carried unacceptable social costs. Britain had returned to the gold standard in 1925 with the unsuccessful legacy of the previous four years' deflation in the shape of a million and a half unemployed. Further attempts to reduce money wages were ruled out after the experience of the General Strike. The alternative of exchange depreciation, which Keynes had also advocated, was barred by the return to the gold standard. Moreover, defence of the new parity in a situation of inflexible money wages required a rate of interest higher than the domestic employment situation warranted. Thus all 'orthodox' policy instruments for increasing employment – devaluation, cutting wages, bringing down the rate of interest – were ruled out. Britain had arrived at an underemployment equilibrium. This was the starting-point of Keynes's post-1925 thinking. The problem was no longer to analyse the processes, and consequences, of deflation, but to find some way of talking about the new situation, and some method of escape from it.

The language Keynes developed was the language of savings and investment. Unemployment was due to over-saving in relation to existing investment opportunities. Keynes set out to explain how such over-saving could occur, which the classical theory denied. He gave two basic reasons. The first was the existence of a 'transfer problem'. Keynes developed this argument in connection with both the attempt to transfer English savings abroad and the attempt to pay German reparations. Suppose the English save £50 million with the idea of investing it abroad. The money can be transferred across the exchanges only by means of a trade surplus of that amount. Classical theory – derived in this respect from David Hume – held that the balance of trade adjusted automatically to the amount of foreign liabilities through adjustments in relative prices brought about by gold movements. Keynes argued that the process was not automatic; if something happened to prevent the required surplus from developing, the savings would run to waste in the form of business losses and unemployment. And this was precisely what was happening. Effective transfer was prevented, Keynes argued, for two reasons. First, other countries were determined to prevent the British from enlarging their export surplus, by use of restrictive trade, or monetary policies. Secondly, the stickiness of British money wages prevented British industries from increasing their competitiveness in world markets: wages were too high to create a sufficient trade surplus to finance foreign lending on the scale desired at the existing exchange rate. The first explanation, then, for 'over-saving' was the state of the foreign balance. But it was equally difficult to find employment for these savings at home, because of the high interest rates dictated by the need to defend the over-valued pound. The situation from which Britain suffered could thus be characterised as an excess of voluntary savings over what could be invested abroad with the given state of the foreign balance, or invested at home at the prevailing rate of interest. It was out of this analysis (which was to be formally elaborated in the *Treatise on Money* (1930)) that Keynes developed his argument for government spending on public works to use up the surplus savings.[13]

In 1925, Lloyd George, an instinctive advocate of public spending, had offered to finance a committee of experts to draw up a new economic programme for the Liberal Party. Keynes was one of its members and wrote key sections of its two major publications, *Britain's Industrial Future* (1928) and *We Can Conquer Unemployment* (1929).

Lloyd George wanted to finance his public works programme by means of a big National Development Loan on the principle of the War Loans: like Roosevelt a few years later, he saw the fight against unemployment in military terms. But where was the 'new' money to come from if it was to avoid the deadly charge of inflation? Keynes supplied an answer: it was to come from 'idle' savings, savings for which there was no business use at a rate of interest determined by the need to defend an over-valued currency. Although there was much to be done in Britain, it could not, in the depressed condition of trade, yield a profit at a borrowing rate of 5 per cent. It was for the government itself to borrow the money at 5 per cent and do the work at 3 per cent, the difference to be made up by savings on unemployment insurance and the increased revenue that would come to the Exchequer from revived industrial activity.

Keynes first publicly revealed this new line in an article for the *Evening Standard* on 31 July 1928, entitled 'How to Organise a Wave of Prosperity'. It provoked the usual counterblast from his old adversary, Niemeyer, now transferred to the Bank of England. Keynes wrote, 'The fundamental blunder of the Treasury and of the Bank has been due to their belief that if they looked after their deflation of prices, the deflation of costs would look after itself.' In his reply, Niemeyer dramatically shifted the line of defence. The problem was no longer wage costs, he argued, but obsolete machinery and industrial organisation. It was this that held costs above world prices. In other words, the new slogan was not wage reductions, but 'rationalisation'. But he was forced to admit that the process of 'cleaning up' would take a long time:

> I am convinced, however, that it is only by far-sighted schemes of reorganisation that we can hope to re-establish our economic supremacy while maintaining our present standard of living and that there is no magic remedy for the present discomforts.

Keynes went on to expound his 'magic remedy':

> Every public Department and every local authority should be encouraged and helped to go forward with all good projects for capital expansion which they have ready or can prepare — roads, bridges, ports, buildings, slum clearances, electrification, telephones, etc., etc. When we have unemployed men and unemployed plant and *more savings than we are using at home* it is utterly imbecile to say that we cannot afford these things.

Niemeyer commented:

> Now it seems to me definitely untrue to say that we have 'more savings than we are using at home.' On the contrary, we have, during the past three years, lived to a great extent on borrowings from abroad. . . Moreover, what we invest in foreign loans must, sooner or later, be exported; and insofar as it is sunk in development schemes for the Empire, it is probably exported almost at once in the form of capital goods. In these circumstances, it is really absurd of Mr. Keynes to suggest that we have savings which are available and are not being used.

(Notice here the 'sooner or later' and 'probably' — all too characteristic of the Treasury style.)

Niemeyer went on:

> In fact, the contrary is, of course, the case. The result of our high labour costs and social services is to encourage consumption and reduce savings so that the margin of capital available for production and development schemes tends to be inadequate. All that Mr. Keynes's policy would achieve would be [to divert] our inadequate capital resources from economic to uneconomic schemes of development... The result will soon be seen in adverse exchanges and gold exports: and eventually you will find that you must either reverse your policy and restrict credit — thus throwing your plant and men idle again — or draw more and more on the capital of the country to feed the population until the day comes when you are faced with national bankruptcy. It is the same principle as the Soviet Government is trying, in circumstances infinitely more favourable than ours for the operation of such a system.
>
> ... Though the situation still looks gloomy, we may be nearer the end of troubles than appears on the surface. There is no doubt that, during the past seven years, we have always had to meet unfair competition from one or other of the European countries which was passing through an exchange crisis. First of all it was Germany, then it was France, then Italy and Belgium, then France again... As conditions settle down in these countries (and especially if Mr. Keynes could induce them to inflate a little) our manufacturers should have a much better chance of recovering the markets they have lost and keeping them in the future.[14]

IV

The final evolution of the Treasury View takes us into the years of world depression which opened in 1929. Keynes himself made no significant theoretical additions to his policy until he started making use of Kahn's multiplier in 1933. For its part, the Treasury, in a reply to Lloyd George's proposals for a big public works programme to be financed by loan, tightened up its reply to the 'over-saving' thesis:

> When business is slack there is a tendency for money to hang in the banks, particularly on time deposit. A great part is cash of

manufacturers, awaiting use and kept liquid. A further part is foreign balances. Something may be due to growth of time deposits of small tradesmen, etc. These funds do represent a slackening in the circulation of money and employment. But they are not idle. They may be used in commercial advances or credits and in taking up bills of accpetance for traders as well as in loans in the short money market. It is a far cry from this to the assumption that the issue of further Government securities would suffice to attract this money into long term investment... The prospect therefore is a marked rise in the rate of interest on these loans ... with a serious reaction on the rate for local authorities and industries and consequent disturbance of trade and employment. In these circumstances, a very large proportion of additional Government borrowings would divert money which would otherwise be taken soon by home industry. If it were possible to divert funds going abroad it would stimulate imports and injure the export trades ... Keynes says that investment abroad has but slight relation to the export of British goods. But it is for him to prove.

Costs of production lie at the root of the problem... The loan programme would do nothing to reduce and it might increase, costs; at most it is a palliative and temporary... Finally, *on a long view*, if the programmes were successful for a time, it would tend to make industry struggle on as it is instead of rationalising itself.[15]

With unemployment mounting towards 3 million, the contention that all savings would be 'taken up soon' became increasingly implausible. In these circumstances, the Treasury fell back on two practical arguments. The first involved the question of confidence:

It is a matter for serious reflection whether, if a great Government loan had to be raised in such circumstances ... many investors would not come to the view that this country was a bad country in which to invest; there might arise something in the nature of a flight from the pound with all its serious reactions upon the exchange, upon short-term money rates in this country and upon the prospects of a trade revival.[16]

This would be especially so if the loan policy was connected with a public works programme requiring 'the assumption of bureaucratic powers far wider and more far reaching than would be tolerated by the public except in time of war'.[17]*

The second practical argument, which held sway for much of the 1930s, arose out of the experience of trying to organise an admittedly small-scale public works programme in the period 1929-31. Sir Richard Hopkins, Otto Niemeyer's successor as Controller, and probably the most influential of the Treasury Knights, minuted on 19 October 1932:

> My own belief is that the answer to this [controversy on over-saving or under-saving] is purely empiric but quite conclusive. We have tried this policy [of public works] pretty vigorously [!] for a period of ten years or more. We have at all times found it hedged round with practical limitations. Schemes that can be put in hand at once are small and unprofitable. The difficulties of moving labour to the proper point and housing it there are extremely great. With an immense expenditure both of money and of labour, and never at the speed which was intrinsically desired, we have now managed to do pretty nearly everything that was worth doing, and in the process we have never succeeded in touching more than the fringe of the problem of unemployment then existing. Rightly or wrongly, the borrowing of large sums for public work has come to depress the community as being a wasteful process. It has never done any visible or calculable good, and it certainly could not at the present time make any but the most negligible impression upon the figures of unemployment with which we are contending.[18]

Britain's abandonment of the gold standard on 21 September 1931, by freeing monetary policy from its previous external constraint, made possible the adoption of the most orthodox part of Keynes's remedy — cheap money. This led to the housing boom. Protection for the manufacturing industry, under the Import Duties Act of 1932, also had some employment-creating effects. The start of recovery at the end of 1932 lessened the pressure to experiment with more unorthodox remedies.

In March 1933, Keynes, in a series of articles for *The Times* later

* There is a letter addressed to Sir Frederick Phillips of the Treasury from the economist Henry Clay at the Bank of England dated 1 February 1935 which says, 'The American example suggests the real difficulty about any public expenditure to stimulate employment; you can never be sure that the Government expenditure will not discourage public enterprise by as much as it increases private enterprise — not by diverting resources but by undermining confidence in the future.'

reprinted as a pamphlet entitled *The Means of Prosperity*, made public use, for the first time, of Kahn's employment multiplier to buttress his arguments for state spending to relieve unemployment. The multiplier showed how a given expenditure of money would set off successive rounds of spending and thus produce a cumulative increase in employment. Its importance, in the argument between Keynes and the Treasury, was to demonstrate that a given expenditure had calculable 'ripple' effects resulting in a total of employment many times greater than the initial employment given by the expenditure. This hit directly at Hopkins's argument that 'immense expenditure' on public works could only be expected to touch the 'fringe of the problem'.

Keynes's articles as usual received close scrutiny by the Treasury and the Bank. The new generation of senior officials — particularly Sir Richard Hopkins and Sir Frederick Phillips — were much more sympathetic to Keynes's position than Sir Otto Niemeyer had been in the past, but still felt bound to reject his suggestions. 'The one gilt-edged argument', Phillips minuted, 'is *delay*. Keynes's whole point is the urgency of immediate action, whereas we know perfectly well that public works don't get started in a year and don't get in full working order for three years.'[19] Phillips also reiterated the earlier theoretical objection: Keynes's argument was right only 'if there are large unused savings and if they can be attracted into investment by issuing gilt-edged stock without raising the long-term rate of interest'.[20] The continued refusal of the government to embark on large schemes of deficit finance to deal with unemployment led Keynes to wonder in 1939 whether it could ever be politically possible for 'a capitalistic democracy to organise expenditure on the scale necessary to make the grand experiment to prove my case — except in war conditions'.[21]

In their recent book, *The Economic Advisory Council 1930-39*, Susan Howson and Donald Winch argue that Keynes's comment understates the extent of conversion to his ideas which had in fact taken place. They argue that Keynes, through his membership of the Economic Advisory Council, and its successor, the Committee on Economic Information, exerted a growing influence on Treasury thinking, particularly on that of Sir Frederick Phillips, Treasury Under-Secretary from 1932-9, and a member of the Committee on Economic Information, and Sir Richard Hopkins, the Second Secretary.* Most of the Com-

---

* The Economic Advisory Council was set up by the Prime Minister, Ramsay MacDonald, in January 1930 as a kind of 'economic general staff' of economists, statisticians and 'practical men' to advise the government on economic policy.

mittee's 27 reports to the Government 'bore the impress of Keynes'.[22] The Committee not only forecast the 1937 recession, but suggested Keynesian responses: maintaining low interest rates and counter-cyclical public works policies.[23] The Treasury was slowly converted. By 1934 it was prepared to admit that 'the connection between increased foreign lending and increased exports was not close',[24] implying the dropping of the full employment assumption that had characterised Treasury thinking in the 1920s. By 1935, Hopkins and Phillips had come to believe that 'the stage now reached in the general recovery is one at which the expansion of public borrowing would be useful for keeping up the impetus'.[25] Howson and Winch conclude that by 1937 'the macroeconomic position which we associate with Keynes's *General Theory* had altered the thinking of the most important policy-making civil servants in the Treasury'. This conversion 'also provides an explanation for the apparent rapidity with which Britain moved over to being a highly managed economy on Keynesian lines after 1939'.[26]

These are important conclusions, supported by a thorough investigation of the relevant reports, minutes and memoranda. However, it does not follow from this that there was a comparable political willingness to adopt Keynesian measures. For this there are two main reasons. First, once recovery had started there was no real pressure on politicians to do so. Britain, it must be remembered, was growing at about 4 per cent per annum between 1932 and 1937, a growth rate exceeded only by Germany's in that period. Secondly, the link between Keynesianism and public works was regarded as a definite political liability, implying large expenditures with little immediate result, and vexatious bureaucratic controls, or even 'dictatorship'. 'Fiscal Keynesianism' — the kind that could work by varying tax rates or government spending on existing services — required a public sector *already* enlarged for other reasons; and this it took another world war to achieve.

Although Treasury officials were starting to talk a Keynesian language

---

It was succeeded in 1932 by the Committee on Economic Information, described by Sir Arthur Salter as 'a small and secretly reporting body of economists which ... continued to advise the Government — in vain — till the eve of the Second World War in 1939' (*Slave of the Lamp*, p. 87). Its Chairman was Sir Josiah Stamp; other members were Salter, Keynes, G.D.H. Cole, Hubert Henderson and Denis Robertson, as well as the two Treasury officials, Sir Frederick Phillips (from 1935) and Sir Frederick Leith-Ross. The Committee on Economic Information became the Economic Section of the War Cabinet in 1940, and was absorbed into the Treasury in 1947.

by the mid-1930s, their actual expenditure recommendations were extremely modest. For example, in 1935 Hopkins and Phillips thought the government should 'encourage and help the local authorities to raise loans and undertake public works, up to a total of about £60m'.[27] This was about half the total sanctioned by the Labour government between June 1929 and June 1930. Certainly no one in the Treasury or government was prepared to raise, for employment purposes, anything like the £400 million Defence Loan of 1937, doubled two years later, which in fact was what lifted Britain out of recession in 1937-8 and abolished unemployment by 1940. For these reasons, Keynes was quite right to wonder in 1939 whether, without a war, his remedies would be adopted 'on the scale' necessary to prove his case.

It is easy to see that, in the period under review, Keynes was right and the Treasury wrong. But this was far from clear at the time. Undoubtedly, Britain should have stabilised (if at all) at a lower parity in 1925; and many of the problems of the 1920s (particularly the high interest rates) stem from the pursuit, and later defence, of an over-valued currency. But the Treasury was right, taking a longer view, to warn of the risks of inflation in currency 'management', while one may feel that the Treasury and Keynes alike were remarkably blind to the structural problems of the British economy.

In the debate over the 'transfer problem' in the late 1920s, it is not clear that Keynes got the better of the argument. He is generally felt now to have ignored the price and, more important, the disposable income, effects of transferring money across the exchanges.

It has become conventional to say that British governments should have started great public works schemes between the wars. But the kind of programmes advocated by Lloyd George and Oswald Mosley (both with Keynes's support and advice) ran up against strong administrative and political obstacles which would have been very difficult to overcome in peacetime. Direct subsidies to employers of the kind briefly made by Baldwin to the coal-owners in 1925 would have been simpler, but ran counter to the whole British administrative tradition, rooted in the absolute separation of public and private functions. (This has now virtually disappeared.) Quite apart from the theoretical problem, there was a distinct lack of administrative flair in tackling the unemployment problem, of the kind Beveridge was able to bring to the organisation of the social services.

Even though Keynes's arguments were beginning to make headway on the theoretical plane by the 1930s, the administrative and confidence objections to loan-financed government spending remained; and, in any case, with recovery, there was little political pressure for it. So despite the conversion of the Treasury Knights, government finance remained strictly orthodox, and unemployment was finally swept away by rearmament programmes undertaken for other reasons.

Notes

1. A.J. Taylor, *Laissez-Faire and State Intervention in Nineteenth Century Britain* (London, 1972), p. 60.
2. W.A. Brown, *The International Gold Standard Reinterpreted 1914-1934*, Summary of the Financial Resolution of the Genoa Conference, vol. 1, p. 343.
3. *First Interim Report of the Committee on Currency and Foreign Exchanges After the War*, Cmd. 9182, paras. 2-4.
4. PRO: Prem 11/30; T. 172/1208.
5. J.M. Keynes, *Collected Writings*, vol. XVII, pp. 184, 185, 186.
6. Ibid., vol. IV, pp. 36-7.
7. Ibid., vol. IV, pp. 167-9, 198-9, 201.
8. *Idem, Economic Consequences of the Peace*, p. 12.
9. *Idem, Tract*, pp. 27-30.
10. J.R. Hicks, *The Theory of Wages* (London, 1932), p. 177.
11. PRO: T. 175/26.
12. PRO: T. 176/16.
13. For a good discussion see Susan Howson and Donald Winch, *The Economic Advisory Council 1930-1939: a Study in Economic Advice during Depression and Recovery* (Cambridge, 1977), pp. 51-3.
14. PRO: T. 176/16.
15. PRO: T. 175/26.
16. 'National Debt and State Borrowing: a Note Prepared by the Treasury, July, 1930' in R. Skidelsky, *Politicians and the Slump* (London, 1967).
17. PRO: T. 175/42. Memorandum by Sir Richard Hopkins, 16 June 1930.
18. PRO: T. 175/70. Pt. 1.
19. Ibid.
20. PRO: T. 175/17. 14 Mar. 1933.
21. Q. Donald Winch, *Economics and Policy* (London, 1969), p. 266.
22. Sir Arthur Salter, *Slave of the Lamp* (London, 1967), p. 87.
23. Howson and Winch, *Economic Advisory Council*, p. 108.
24. PRO: T. 175/84, q. ibid., p. 108.
25. Ibid., p. 130.
26. Ibid., p. 109.
27. Ibid., p. 130.

10 THE CRISIS OF GERMAN UNEMPLOYMENT INSURANCE IN 1928/1929 AND ITS POLITICAL REPERCUSSIONS

B. Weisbrod

On 27 March 1930 the last parliamentary government of the Weimar Republic came down over a question that was seemingly of secondary importance. The battle to raise unemployment insurance contributions by 0.5 per cent was ultimately also decisive for a Hindenburg Cabinet, which was at last to bring order to the Reich and Prussia, not only, if necessary, against the opposition of the Reichstag but above all without the Social Democrats. As it was the Social Democrats who, by the way they voted, had brought down the Müller government they quickly incurred the criticism from their own ranks as well that they had caused their own downfall. It is still said that the party permitted 'social policy (unemployment benefits) to be placed before state policy (salvaging the jeopardised parliamentary system) and had, as a result, to accept its elimination'.[1]

This argument, which is, by the way, a valuable example of historical legitimation for the current discussion on the limits of the welfare state, needs criticism and historical explanation in two respects. First, it presupposes that 'social policy' can lead a separate and merely subsidiary existence and so distorts the question whether one of the functions of 'state policy' should not have been to support the threatened parliamentary system materially and with legitimation by strengthening the social aspects of the constitution. Secondly, the argument implies a methodological problem: it would be hard to prove that further concessions by the Social Democrats over the question of unemployment insurance would have contributed to the internal stabilisation of the political system, particularly if their opponents were prepared to force them from power at almost any price.

In this chapter both of these objections will be illustrated by discussing the 'reform of unemployment insurance', which made the material crisis in unemployment provision of 1928/9 a crucial element in the general debate on the Weimar economic and social constitution which marked the beginning of the decline of parliamentary democracy.

The Act on Labour Exchanges and Unemployment Insurance

(AVAVG) of 16 July 1927[2] did indeed seem to be a breakthrough in consolidating the social policy of the Weimar state: in Article 163 of the Weimar constitution not only 'the right to work' had been guaranteed, but also provision for 'the necessary subsistence' during unemployment. With proper pride the Reich Minister of Labour pointed out that with about 17.25 million workers and employees Germany now had statutory unemployment insurance for a larger number than any other country.[3] However, it could not be denied that the pioneer role which Germany had played in social insurance had been taken over by England in 1911 and 1920 when admittedly a smaller number of workers and employees were insured against unemployment.[4]

There were, first, structural reasons for this relatively late development of unemployment insurance in Germany, as indeed in other countries — for example the lack of homogeneity of the national labour market and the incalculability of the specific risk. Above all, however, the 're-definition of unemployment as a social risk' constituted a break with the 'paternalist tradition of social care which had been particularly long and effective in Germany' which did permit insurance against the secondary risks to the individual resulting from his employee status, for example sickness, accident, old age, but not insurance against 'this actual risk-status itself'.[5] Moreover the problem of the labour market did not emerge in post-war Germany until the stabilisation of 1923/4 due to the demobilisation decrees and the inflationary full employment boom. It was only when the German economy really began to recover in the business year 1927 that the conditions finally seemed ripe for the establishment of the insurance principle in unemployment benefits.[6]

In fact, however, a binding social consensus on unemployment as a social risk had not been achieved with the Unemployment Act (AVAVG), nor did the intended settlement of the unemployment question in self-administration automatically ensure agreement between the parties on the labour market. The view that the AVAVG constitutes a decisive date in German post-war social policy therefore needs some modification on two accounts: the battle over principles between the supporters of social care and the supporters of insurance (a confrontation in which characteristically the parties on the labour market changed sides after inflation[7]) concealed the fact that the two forms were mixed in the reality of unemployment benefits. After the decrees on unemployment payments of 1923/4[8] had introduced compulsory contributions it was hardly possible to deny to the contributors their right to benefit. Conversely, the gradual infringement of the insurance

principle during the 'reform of unemployment insurance' opened the
door for the change to insurance with the character of care or provision, a development which was finally sealed by the reintroduction of
the means test by the Papen government.[9] A further modification
of the view of the AVAVG as a paradigm for social policy seems
justified if one compares the unanimity of the parties in the Reichstag
over this question[10] (they actually only simulated agreement on the
functions of self-administration) with the very close vote on the Emergency Working Time Law of 8 April 1927: the DVP was practically
split, every tenth SPD member abstained.[11] This vote, and not that
on the AVAVG, was the pattern for the parliamentary settlement of
conflict issues concerning social policy during the following Grand
Coalition government.

Like the change in the decree on working hours, which did not restore the eight-hour day but simply made work beyond this more
expensive and enabled heavy industry in particular to continue with
two shifts in continuous operation,[12] the establishment of the insurance principle in unemployment benefits should be seen less in the
context of the beginnings of economic recovery than against the
background of the severe economic crisis of 1925/6. That is true
not only with regard to the very long and wearisome process of legislation which cannot be discussed in detail here, but also generally to the
experience of mass unemployment which was something completely
new. After the drastic fall in employment in the winter of 1923/4,
when the number of registered unemployed reached nearly 2 million
in January 1924, and the percentage of union members unemployed
reached 27.8 per cent and short time rose to 20.8 per cent,[13] a number
of the objections to the implementation of unemployment insurance
were refuted: 'The question of checking the will to work and the question of "acceptable work" were hardly relevant any more; nor was the
notorious "blame" issue still regarded as a serious obstacle.'[14] Nor, in
view of the extent of the crisis in 1925/6 could it still be argued that unemployment of these proportions was only due to personal misconduct or
cyclical fluctuations. Clearly there were structural causes as well and
questions of working morale were hardly appropriate to solve them.[15]
Between December 1925 and February 1927 the number of union
members unemployed never dropped below 15 per cent and the winter
months brought peaks of up to 23.7 per cent (January 1926). Between
November 1925 and August 1926 there were moreover never less than
15 per cent of union members on short time, and in January 1926
every fourth member was affected.[16]

The importance of structural causes for the labour market crisis was generally recognised, as can be seen from the current phrase 'rationalisation crisis', but there was no agreement on the reasons for and the extent of structural unemployment.[17] The argument of the 'population theorists', who regarded the relative increase in the population due to the war as of decisive importance for Germany's difficult economic situation, was politically particularly explosive.[18] In fact the population of the German Reich measured over the same territory had by 1925 risen by 8 per cent over 1910; in 1925 1.1 million Germans were counted who had formerly resided outside the post-war frontiers.[19] However, the absorption of more than 1.7 million into the work-force between February 1926 and October 1927 proved that there was no need to wait for the entry of the low-birth-rate years for the work-force to be spared a 'chronic labour crisis'. More reliable indicators, such as the relative stagnation tendency and the social redistribution of unemployment, however, suggested that the danger of a long-term structural unemployment was by no means over in spite of the boom of 1927: characteristically the labour market recovery followed the upswing in production of the spring of 1926 only very slowly and even in 1927 the annual average for union members unemployed hardly dropped below 10 per cent.[20] It was also noted that the white-collar workers, who regarded themselves as differing from the blue-collar workers largely in having greater job security, were increasingly suffering from the same fate as the blue-collar workers.[21] In July 1926, for the first time in history, the unemployment ratio for white-collar workers rose above that of 'ordinary wage-rate workers'.[22] This development, which produced a heated controversy over protection measures for older employees, ultimately removed any doubts that the rationalisation wave had quantitatively and qualitatively produced a new kind of unemployment. However, it was not until the world economic crisis that the euphoric belief in the economic possibilities of rationalisation, which the unions had also shared to some extent, was destroyed.[23]

The extent to which the parties on the labour market still relied on the efficiency of a rationalised industry can be seen from the relatively low unemployment rate on which the system of unemployment insurance was constructed in 1927.[24] The envisaged contribution of 3 per cent to be borne in equal parts by employers and employees allowed for continuous payments to about 800,000 unemployed. After that the need fund of the Reich Office for Unemployment Benefits and Unemployment Insurance (para. 159 AVAVG) constituted a reserve, from which another 600,000 unemployed could receive benefits for three months before the Reich loan obligation (para. 183 AVAVG) came into force.[25] The Minister of Labour, Brauns, had already pointed out during the discussions in the Reichstag in February 1927 that this insurance was only enough to cope with cyclical unemployment. Longer-term unemployment due to persistent labour market crises would have to fall under crisis provision, first established in November 1926, 'paid for exclusively out of public funds and therefore administered according to the principles of public charity'.[26] Those who were involuntarily unemployed, were able-bodied and willing to work finally received crisis aid after they had proved their need, from public funds according to paras. 101 and 167 of the AVAVG (4/5 Reich, 1/5 local authorities), if they did not yet qualify under the 26 weeks' waiting period for unemployment insurance or had already exhausted the 26 weeks' payments given under the insurance.[27] Together with the Reich loan obligation this arrangement was already a breach with the pure insurance principle, but it seemed to be a flexible solution to help the local authorities, who otherwise would have had to carry the full burden of aid to the long-term unemployed.

However, the Reich Unemployment Office came up against its financial limits in its very first year: the number of the recipients of the full insurance benefits was on average 890,051 every month in 1928.[28] From January onwards Reich loans had to be used. The Reich had made an initial sum of RM 50 million available for 1927 and an additional sum of RM 100 million was provided in 1928;[29] the budget of 1929 already accounted for a loan of RM 250 million. One of the reasons for this development was the deterioration in the economic situation, which was noticeable in the consumer area after the spring of 1928.[30] Another was the extraordinary increase in seasonal unemployment in the winter of 1928/9. According to figures from the free trade unions the number of their members unemployed in the 'seasonal group' rose to 68.1 per cent in February 1929 as compared with 30.1 per cent in February 1928. But unemployment in the 'cyclical group' as well almost doubled, from 6.2 to 11.4 per cent over the same period.[31] The Reich Office issued a special regulation on seasonal workers in an attempt to prevent the massive unemployment in the building industry and agriculture from eroding the financial basis for the insurance: after a prolongation of the statutory waiting period in the winter of 1927/8 had made little difference, the Reich Office used the powers granted by the AVAVG (paras. 99 and 110) to limit the period for receipt of benefits for 'unemployment common to the occupation' for certain jobs and for a specific period in the year to six weeks. The decree, dated 18 December 1928, provided that those who would cease to be eligible under this decree were to be given 'special aid', made available in an Act with limited applicability of 24 December 1928. In the structure of its rates and the needs test to be used this special aid was similar to the existing crisis aid.[32] This was the first major break with the insurance principle[33] and it pointed the way for the vehement 'reform' debate which now began, especially as the financial situation of the Reich Office deteriorated further in the spring of 1929.

A few months after the employers on the Ruhr had effectively underlined their demand for 'reform of arbitration' by locking out about 230,000 workers,[34] the Federation of German Employers' Associations joined the offensive with a claim for 'reform of unemployment insurance'. On 1 May 1929 it issued a public memorandum demanding financial reform of the Reich Office solely by reduction in benefits of between RM 400 million and 500 million per year: not only were the rates for benefits to be lowered by widening the base for assessment and orienting benefits to the locally prevailing wage rates, but seasonally unemployed and those whose other sources of income, including the incomes of members of their families living with them, were sufficient to live on, were to be taken out of the insurance.[35] The unions opposed the transfer of the risk to the individual unemployed and the break with the insurance principle by this *de facto* reintroduction of the needs tests, and demanded instead an increase in the contributions payable of 1 per cent from 1 June 1929,[36] which should supply about RM 275 million per year. Right at the beginning of the ominous conflict over insurance reform it was clear that behind the immediate issue, 'Fewer benefits or higher contributions?', it was the social consensus on the nature of unemployment as a social risk that was being debated.

The lengthy process of the formation of political opinion became particularly critical, first through the fact that the unions and employers could carry their points of view through the wing parties in the Grand Coalition right into the cabinet: Curtius, the Reich Minister for Economic Affairs of the German People's Party (DVP), met the proposals of the Reich Minister of Labour, Wissell (SPD), to increase the insurance contributions immediately not only in the Cabinet but in the Reichstag as well with a categorical refusal.[37] Secondly, the financial reform of the Reich Office became increasingly part of the question of the consolidation of Reich finances generally, which was growing more and more urgent through the deterioration in the economic situation and the obligation which had been entered into during the negotiations on reparation payments to ease the tax burden on industry.[38] As agreement was not reached between the government parties on the first draft of an amendment to the AVAVG in May, a special commission was appointed by the Reich Minister of Labour in July 1929 to try and reach a compromise. With an estimated unemployment rate of 1.1 million, the expected annual deficit would be RM 279 million. The commission proposed that RM 165 million should be saved by various changes, especially by grading benefits according to the length of time contributions had been paid. Admittedly most members of the commission had rejected the radical proposal of the DVP representative, who wanted the full claim for benefit to be considered only after 52 weeks, and a claim for half the amount after 39 weeks of contribution. But the modified recommendation of the commission, to reduce the benefits, if contributions of 26 – 52 weeks were paid, to 70 per cent for lower wage-earners and to 50 per cent for higher wage-earners, seemed an elegant solution to the problem of seasonal unemployment. On the other hand, however, there was a majority on the commission in favour of the trade union proposal that the rest of the deficit be cleared by a 0.5 per cent increase in contributions for a limited period.[39]

Although the government was successful in obtaining agreement with the Prussian government in the Reichsrat, which widened the political base for its draft, which was now divided into a main section on the general saving measures and a subsidiary section with the financial measures that were limited in time, the conflict over the issue during the debates in the Reichstag in September 1929 was as bitter as ever. During the first reading the DVP insisted 'due to basic considerations on social policy' on a rejection of the higher contributions, relying on a deterioration in the financial situation to enforce the ruling it desired when the drafts were rejected.[40] The SPD stated that a compromise would only be possible if there was no doubt that the Reich would provide additional support: the consolidation of Reich finances and the reduction of the tax load should not be paid for by cut-backs in social policy.[41]

The amendment to the AVAVG, which was finally passed by the Reichstag on 3 October 1929, with 238 votes for and 155 against with 40 abstentions by the DVP, did not correspond to the compromise solution put forward by the commission on the important point of the increase in contributions.[42] The Reich Minister of Labour had to delete this part of the draft to ensure savings of at least RM 100 million for the Reich Office. It is true that the new version of the Act did not contain general cuts in benefits either; it also excluded the graded benefits and the needs test which the employers had demanded, but the aim of 'removing bad practices and misuse' concealed some real deterioration.[43] A redefinition of unemployment prevented claims from temporary work, which meant that especially traders and farmers or members of their families and married women could be made dependent on the traditional support from their families. A purge on the 'fringe of the labour market' also freed homeworkers and employees with 'insignificant occupations' from compulsory insurance. It is characteristic of the direction the policy on unemployment was taking, which got under way here and led to a violent debate on second incomes during the world economic crisis,[44] that both these measures particularly affected women, even though the risk, from an insurance point of view, of an unmarried female contributor was considerably less, and that of a married female contributor often the same as that of the male contributors.[45] The Act also envisaged that instead of the grading principle, the waiting period before the first insurance claim should be extended to 52 weeks as a sort of 'entry fee', as it were, within a period of two years. Finally, in cases of 'unemployment usual in an occupation', benefits during the first six weeks in the higher pay grades were only to be given according to the lower rates of crisis aid, although no needs test would be applied.[46] This simply postponed the need for fundamental reform of the insurance. In addition to the annual deficit of RM 181 million, which still remained and which could have been eliminated to a large extent by the proposed increase in the contributions, there was now a further deficit of RM 200 million to 250 million for the winter months to be met.

Even this modest result was politically uncertain right to the last minute. The compromise was jeopardised by the DVP just a day before the final vote, although the financial arrangements clearly revealed the unequal tactical positions of the wing parties: the Social Democrats had to accept lower benefits, even if the cut was less severe than had originally been proposed, while the DVP was able to prevent contributions being raised.[47] The right wing of the party, which was close to the heavy industry on the Ruhr and had already caused difficulties for Stresemann in the spring of 1929 over the coalition question, had gone on the offensive: the vote over the Young Plan, the tax relief for industry, the consolidation of the Reich budget and the reform of unemployment insurance formed a critical constellation of material for parliament for the winter of 1929/30 and the way at last seemed open to fix the DVP as an 'interested party', force the SPD out of the government and prepare for a right-wing coalition.[48] Even on 2 October the parliamentary group of the DVP had unanimously rejected the special Act with limited applicability and the main amendment to the AVAVG with a clear majority. It was only Stresemann's selfless devotion which brought the party finally to abstain.[49] He was able to prevent the coalition from breaking up, but his death, which occurred on the same night, was already casting shadows.

This completed the scenario for the end of the Grand Coalition. The DVP was now mainly concerned to get the SPD to share responsibility for the tax relief proposals before the Young Plan was passed and to tie the Centre Party to it over finance reform. So during the negotiations on the AVAVG amendment the party had let it be known that 'circumstances could arise in two months which would enable the DVP to raise contributions by ½%.'[50] And in fact, in December 1929, the finance programme which Stresemann had requested the SPD Finance Minister Hilferding to put back in September brought the long-contested increase in contributions of 0.5 per cent.[51] But the measure came far too late to help the Reich Office. As the unemployment ratio had again reached the peak of 20 per cent registered in the crisis winter of 1925/6 it was also hardly likely to induce the DVP to abandon its old claim to lower benefits and no loan obligation on the part of the Reich.[52] In this key reform issue, for which the refusal to raise the contributions had always only a functional role, the DVP was no longer interested in a compromise with the Social Democrats. Even against the recommendation of its own Finance Minister, Moldenhauer, and the Reich President, it finally rejected the 'sacrifice by those on fixed incomes' in March 1930, which the SPD had introduced as the last possibility of compensation to meet the general responsibility towards the 'social risk' of unemployment and ease the burden on the budget.[53] With its absolute refusal to admit any reform of unemployment insurance that did not correspond to its own views, the DVP held a trump card until the passing of the Young Plan, and with its help the party could bring down the Grand Coalition and blame the SPD, despite tactical concessions. The SPD reached the limits of what it could take when in the famous Brüning compromise over the cover draft of March 1930 the increase in the insurance contributions to 4 per cent as originally envisaged was again dropped and the Reich obligation to lend was practically suspended for the foreseeable future. Under these circumstances the SPD, and especially the trade union wing, was no longer prepared to 'share responsibility for tax reform to relieve industry and at the same time to reduce the range of social policy'.[54]

The battle over principles against the increase in the contributions had fulfilled its political purpose for the DVP. It may be that the unions and the SPD were blinded by the 'principal, ideological and tactical emphasis on employment insurance as a symbol for social policy as a whole'.[55] Certainly with its motto 'The party and the government are two things, the party and the unions are one' the left wing of the SPD was under a dangerous illusion as to the possibilities of the SPD as an opposition party.[56] But ultimately the question of unemployment insurance reform, even in 1929, was not whether contributions should be raised by 0.5 per cent or even 0.25 per cent: 'the issue was rather the whole system of combating unemployment itself.'[57]

The system of self-administration in unemployment insurance was for the employers rather a means of restraining public expenditure policy than the expression of a common obligation to lessen the 'social risk' of unemployment. As far as the trade unions were concerned, this 'social risk', on the contrary, also meant recourse to public funds if necessary. For the employers, however, the demand for financial consolidation of the Reich Office was at the same time a means 'for the protection of *justified* benefit claims, as well as the maintenance of a satisified German work-force, preventing the *unjustified* use of the benefit services which is equally damaging both financially and as regards the morale of the workers'.[58] Ultimately this attack on the 'bad practices and misuse' in unemployment insurance was orientated to the idea of individual blame and individual responsibility, even in the case of unemployment long since no longer only due to cyclical causes. The workers' morale argument played an important role here, even though the foreseeable financial effect of the needs test would have been comparatively modest: after the reintroduction of the needs test in cases of special aid, only 5 per cent of the seasonally unemployed could be excluded from benefits.[59] In addition, successfully relieving the burden on the Reich budget could only lead to a burdening of public funds, which still had to support an increasingly large proportion of the unemployed, despite the speculation that the needs test would be a psychological deterrent within the sphere of public aid.[60]

The refusal to increase contributions was bound up with another consideration which was of fundamental importance for the employers' economic policy: in their view the only way to stimulate economic activity and thus create more jobs was greater capital formation in industry through a lower tax and social burden.[61] To them, therefore, higher costs to industry in the form of higher contributions, although half of this would have come from the workers, was as inadmissible as the unlimited obligation on the part of the Reich to lend, which would limit the room for tax cuts. There was another decisive reason why the employers were not prepared to accept that benefits could not be changed: the amount of benefits, like the number of unemployed, was one of the decisive factors for the wage level. This argument was hardly used in public but it was clear from the current employers' demands for 'reform of arbitration' that insurance protection for the unemployed with a state guarantee was as great an obstacle to their aim to lower wages as the system of collective workers' rights under state guaranteed wage agreements. Even industrial leaders who were willing to compromise complained privately that the AVAVG had 'destroyed the supply and demand relationships on the market' and made it impossible 'as long as the law remains in force, to regulate wages according to cyclical conditions'.[62]

The wage policy function of unemployment insurance was also clear to the unions. The implementation of the DVP proposals of 1929 would have made 60 per cent of those unemployed dependent on a rate of benefits which was below the old public aid level.[63] The unions regarded the employers' demands for 'arbitration reform' and 'reform of unemployment insurance' as an 'attack on those achievements in post-war policy which will safeguard the wages level'.[64] Moreover, the free trade unions were also not prepared on principle to accept a cut in benefits through grades based on length of membership (as opposed to wage classes as the Act envisaged). This proposal, which the Christian unions had supported on the commission of 1929, was to them the adoption of the principles of private insurance and hence irreconcilable with joint liability for statutory state insurance.[65] They therefore also insisted that the state must continue to be obliged to lend if the 'joint risk partnership in industry' found itself facing a crisis. If the insurance contributions were only to be regarded as a kind of special tax 'raised within industry to meet the costs of the fund of reserve labour',[66] then there should be political decision over this tax as over the others which were intended to relieve the labour market.

This reveals a dilemma for the free trade unions, who, even in the defensive phase of social policy after 1928, had entertained the illusory hope that the 'new quality of social policy' would be bound to bring the parliamentary state which they had helped to form on to their side. In particular they expected from unemployment insurance 'the inclusion of a social counter-principle in the capitalist-run economy', a 'pointer away from capitalist to social production'.[67] But there was no guarantee that the individual worker would have a 'definite share' in the social product through a new distributive order, for instance within the framework of the AVAVG, nor did the alliance with the 'representatives of political authorities' within the scope of social self-administration constitute a realistic perspective for the achievement of this end.[68] Experience over 'reform of unemployment insurance' was disillusioning as far as this concept of 'economic democracy' was concerned. If the co-operation of the workers in the state was to be made dependent on the sacrifice of one of their most important views on social policy, as the *Gewerkschaftszeitung* wrote on the occasion of the amendment to the AVAVG, the workers would 'naturally have to defend their social policy even against the state if it tried to sneak out of its responsibilities'.[69] As shown by the collapse of the Grand Coalition, such a withdrawal inevitably had not only disastrous political consequences, but it was also hardly likely to bring success for the trade unions, whose very reliance on the state had been an expression of a specific weakness in the wage debates during the stabilisation phase of the Weimar Republic.

That the dilemma of the workers' movement can by no means only be explained by a specifically German illusion of the state, based on authoritarian ideas, or by a tactical error, becomes clear from a mere cursory glance at the course of the crisis of unemployment insurance in England which is quite comparable. During the argument about the reform of unemployment insurance the German employers and trade unions had tried to take individual aspects of the English insurance system as models: whereas the trade unions laid great stress on state participation in the increased contributions,[70] the employers preferred the grading of benefits according to the length of time a worker had contributed and a special regulation for seasonal unemployment.[71] In fact the contradictory short-term objectives of the parties on the German labour market seemed to be partially realised in the English unemployment insurance. However, the fall of the MacDonald government in August 1931, which was admittedly caused by the trade unions' attitude on the question of unemployment insurance, but which became inevitable because of the agreement of the Conservatives to the political conditions of credit of the banking world, shows that in this case too a decision was being made not only on the 'general subordination of social policy to budgetary orthodoxy',[72] but also on long-term political objectives.[73]

During the crisis of the Weimar Republic the demands of the employers for 'working morale' and the illusions of the free trade unions as regards 'economic democracy' were locked in an insoluble conflict, which was only covered insufficiently by social self-administration in unemployment insurance. The unions finally lost the battle over the economic and social constitution of the Weimar Republic, because the 'concept of collective responsibility in social self-administration could be countered by the economic power of private industry'.[74] As long as the battle was primarily over the form of unemployment insurance and not the causes of unemployment and hence means of reducing it, Weimar social policy was limited to combating symptoms. It is this distance, despite the hesitant beginnings in the economic crisis of 1925/6 and the later turn to work creation policy during the world economic crisis, which separates that policy from the modern concept of the welfare state, specially characterised by the aim of full employment since the Second World War.

Notes

1. Werner Conze, 'Die politischen Entscheidungen in Deutschland 1929-1933' in W. Conze und H. Raupach (eds.), *Die Staats- und Wirtschaftskrise des Deutschen Reichs 1929/33* (Stuttgart, 1967), p. 207.
2. *RGBl* I 187.
3. Cf. *Deutsche Sozialpolitik 1918-1928. Erinnerungsschrift des Reichsarbeitsministeriums* (Berlin, 1929, p. 168).
4. Cf. the account in Bentley B. Gilbert, *British Social Policy 1914-1939* (London, 1970), pp. 51 ff.
5. On the 'structural difficulties' cf. Stephan Leibfried, 'Die Institutionalisierung der Arbeitslosenversicherung in Deutschland', *Kritische Justiz*, vol. 10 (1977), pp. 289-301, quotations on pp. 297 and 291.
6. The account of the passing of the unemployment legislation (AVAVG) is in Ludwig Preller, *Sozialpolitik in der Weimarer Republik* (Stuttgart, 1949), pp. 363 ff., in Bernhard Weller, *Arbeitslosigkeit und Arbeitsrecht, Untersuchungen der Möglichkeiten zur Bekämpfung der Arbeitslosigkeit unter Einbeziehung der Geschichte des Arbeits- und Sozialrechts* (Stuttgart, 1969), pp. 43 ff, and particularly in Michael T. Wermel and Roswitha Urban, *Arbeitslosenfürsorge und Arbeitslosenversicherung in Deutschland* (Munich, 1949) (Neue Soziale Praxis, vol. 6/II), pp. 24 ff.
7. While the unions, in order to develop the Gent system further, held to the view that the state was responsible for aid and after stabilisation supported the insurance principle (however with state guarantees), the employers who had at

first supported the insurance principle for financial reasons later supported the retention of the means test according to the aid principle, but without demanding state guarantees.

8. The decree on the provision of funds for unemployment aid of 15 October 1923 (*RGBl* 1 984) on the basis of the Enabling Act of 13 October introduced compulsory contributions; the decree on unemployment aid of 16 February 1924 (*RGBl* 1 127) introduced claims.

9. The various decrees on the basis of the emergency decree on measures to maintain aid to the unemployed and social insurance and to relieve the burden of aid on the local authorities of 14 June 1932 (*RGBl* 1 273) also brought *inter alia* a cut in the rates for aid by one-quarter and one-half compared with 1927 (Wermel and Urban, *Arbeitslosenfürsorge*, p. 65).

10. Of 420 members 355 voted for the AVAVG on 7 July 1927. Cf. the list of names in *Verhandlungen des Reichstags*, vol. 393, pp. 11380 ff.

11. Cf. loc. cit., pp. 10659 ff. The voting here was 196 for and 184 against.

12. Cf. in more detail Bernd Weisbrod, *Schwerindustrie in der Weimarer Republik. Interessenpolitik zwischen Stabilisierung und Krise* (Wuppertal, 1978), pp. 319 ff.

13. The figures are based on estimates by the Institut für Konjunkturforschung, *Konjunkturstatistisches Handbuch* (1933), pp. 15, 24 and 29.

14. Wermel and Urban, *Arbeitslosenfürsorge*, p. 41 f.

15. On the 'minor' crisis of 1925/6 cf. more recently Fritz Blaich, *Die Wirtschaftskrise 1925/26 und die Reichsregierung. Von der Erwerbslosenfürsorge zur Konjunkturpolitik* (Kallmünz, 1977). On structural unemployment cf. pp. 15 ff.

16. *KStHB* (1933), pp. 24 and 29.

17. Cf. Otto von Zwiedineck-Südenhorst, 'Beiträge zur erklärung der strukturellen Arbeitslosigkeit', *Vierteljahreshefte zur Konjunkturforschung*, vol. 2 (1927), Ergänzungsheft 1, p. 15/77. Cf. also Julius Hirsch, 'Rationalisierung und Arbeitslosigkeit' in *Die Bedeutung der Rationalisierung für das Deutsche Wirtschaftsleben*, ed. by the Industrie- und Handelskammer in Berlin (Berlin, 1928), pp. 53-76.

18. Blaich, *Wirtschaftskrise*, p. 17 f.

19. Cf. Wolfgang Köllmann, 'Bevölkerungsentwicklung in der Weimarer Republik', in Hans Mommsen, Dietmar Petzina and Bernd Weisbrod (eds.), *Industrielles System und politische Entwicklung in der Weimarer Republik* (Düsseldorf, 1974), pp. 77 and 81.

20. Blaich, *Wirtschaftskrise*, p. 16 *KstHB* (1933), p. 24.

21. Preller, *Sozialpolitik*, pp. 166 ff.

22. Ulf Kadritzke, *Angestellte – Die geduldigen Arbeiter. Zur Sociologie und sozialen Bewegung der Angestellten* (Frankfurt, 1975), p. 192.

23. There are still no more recent detailed studies on the 'new type of unemployment'. Cf. also Eva Cornelia Schöck, *Arbeitslosigkeit und Rationalisierung, Die Lage der Arbeiter und die kommunistische Gewerkschaftspolitik, 1920-28* (Frankfurt, New York, 1977), pp. 165 ff. There is extensive material in the study of 'long-term' unemployment and analysis of unemployment in selected industries in Manuel Saitzew (ed.), *Die Arbeitslosigkeit der Gegenwart* (Munich and Leipzig, 1932) (Schriften des Vereins für Sozialpolitik 185/I and II).

24. Cf. the account in Wermel and Urban, *Arbeitslosenfürsorge*, esp. pp. 63 ff.

25. In the government drafts of September 1925 and December 1926 the emergency stock was only enough to provide benefits for 200,000 and 400,000 unemployed res. for three months.

26. Cf. *Verhandlungen des Reichstags*, vol. 392, pp. 8896 ff.

27. By the decree on crisis aid for unemployed of 28 September 1927 the period for aid was also restricted to 26 weeks. *RGBl* I 315.

28. There were also 139,643 receivers of support in crisis aid. Cf. the first report from the Reich Labour Office for the period from 1 October 1927 to 31 December 1928 in *RABl* 1929/II, Supplement to no. 6, p. 86 f. Comprehensive statistics for 1927 and 1928 can also be found in Erwin Rawicz, *Die deutsche Sozialpolitik im Spiegel der Statistik* (M. Gladbach, 1929), pp. 127-221.

29. Cf. Wermel and Urban, *Arbeitslosenfürsorge*, pp. 6 ff.

30. From May 1928 onwards the index of consumer goods production dropped and remained below the index base of 1928 = 100, while the index of producer goods production rose to 104 in 1929. *KStHB* (1933), p. 41 f.

31. Cf. *Jahrbuch 1929* of the ADGB (Berlin, 1930), p. 336. The seasonal group included gardeners, masons, heavy ceramics among chemical workers and the building industry unions.

32. The Reich took over 4/5 of the costs and the Reich Labour Office 1/5. Cf. Bernhard Lehfeldt, 'Arbeitslosenunterstützung bei berufsüblicher Arbeitslosigkeit', *RABl* 1929/II, pp. 1-4. In crisis aid as well, the persistently high unemployment rate in the winter brought a special arrangement; cf. Min. Rat. Beisiegel, 'Die Neuregelung der Krisenfürsorge', *RABl* 1929/II, pp. 263-5.

33. Wermel and Urban, *Arbeitslosenfürsorge*, p. 7.

34. Cf. Weisbrod, *Schwerindustrie*, pp. 395 ff.

35. Cf. *Reformvorschläge der Vereinigung der Deutschen Arbeitgeberverbände zum Gesetz über Arbeitsvermittlung und Arbeitslosenversicherung* (April 1929). Cf. also 'Geschäftsbericht 1927/1929' (*VDA Berichte* Hft. 24), pp. 189 ff. and G. Erdmann, 'Die Arbeitslosenversicherungsreform', *Der Arbeitgeber*, vol. 19 (1929), pp. 265 ff.

36. Cf. the statement against the 'long-planned blow' from the VDA in *Gewerkschaftszeitung*, vol. 39, no. 19 (1929), of 11 May 1929, pp. 289 ff.

37. In the Cabinet on 6 May 1929 (*Akten der Reichskanzlei, Weimarer Republik: Das Kabinett Müller, II*, bearbeitet von Martin Vogt, vol. 1 (Boppard, 1970), p. 641), in the Reichstag on 5 June 1929 (*Verhandlungen des Reichstags*, vol. 425, p. 2089).

38. Cf. on the relation between reparation payments and finance policy: Ilse Maurer, *Reichsfinanzen und grosse Koalition. Zur Geschichte des Reichskabinetts Müller (1928-1930)* (Bern and Frankfurt, 1973), esp. pp. 68 ff.

39. Cf. *Die Verhandlungen der Sachverständigenkommission für Fragen der Arbeitslosenversicherung, July 1929* (Berlin, 1929), pp. 13 ff.

40. Cf. the remarks by the DVP-MdR Pfeffer on 30 September 1929, *Verhandlungen des Reichstags*, vol. 426, p. 3151.

41. Loc. cit., p. 3127.

42. Gesetz zur Änderung des Gesetzes über Arbeitsvermittlung und Arbeitslosenversicherung vom 12. Okt. 1929, RGBl I, p. 153. The list of names is in *Verhandlungen des Reichstags*, vol. 426, pp. 3245 ff.

43. For the following cf. Bernhard Lehfeldt, 'Die Reform der Arbeitslosenversicherung durch das Gesetz vom 12. Okt. 1929', *RABl* 1929/II, pp. 435-42.

44. Cf. *Gutachten zur Arbeitslosenfrage. Erstattet von der Gutachterkommission zur Arbeitslosenfrage* (Brauns-Kommission), Part One (Berlin, 1931), pp. 11 ff.

45. From April 1928 to March 1929 women comprised one-third of the contributors, but only one-fifth of those receiving primary benefits. In every 100 male contributors, 9.3 received primary benefits, whereas for the same number of women it was only 4.26, and in the case of married women 9.4 (*Verhandlungen der Sachverständigenkommission*, pp. 157 and 160).

46. Moreover the benefit payments were oriented to a longer assessment

period and the local wage rates, in accordance with the demands of the employers; in addition pensions, retirement pay and half-pay were offset. However, the greatest saving came from the reduction in contributions to sickness benefits for the unemployed.

47. Cf. the statement from the SPD at the party leaders' meeting on 1 Oct. 1929 in *Das Kabinett Müller II*, vol. 2, p. 987.

48. Cf. in more detail Weisbrod, *Schwerindustrie*, pp. 467 ff. and Maurer, *Reichsfinanzen*, pp. 80 ff.

49. Maurer, *Reichsfinanzen*, p. 85. Cf. also *Gustav Stresemann, Vermächtnis. Der Nachlass in drei Bänden*, Henry Bernhard (ed.) (Berlin, 1933), vol. 3, p. 583.

50. Cf. *Das Kabinett Müller II*, vol. 2, p. 989.

51. According to the law on a limited increase in the contributions to unemployment insurance of 27 December 1929 (*RGBl* I, p. 244) the new rate, which was uniform throughout the Reich, only applied from 1 January to 30 June 1930. On the position of the DVP, which had made its agreement to the increase dependent on 'binding guarantees' for the tax relief programme, see Maurer, *Reichsfinanzen*, pp. 99 ff.

52. With an unemployment rate of 22.4% in January 1930 (*KStHB* 1933, p. 24), the number of recipients of full benefits from the insurance was 2.2 million and those receiving crisis aid numbered 250,000; 281,000 were receiving charity from the cities, who were having to bear the increasing burden of long-term unemployment (*WiSta*, vol. 10 (1930), p. 379). Moreover in January 1930 about 1.7 million were on short time. Even if the increase in the contributions had remained effective beyond 30 June and the number of unemployed had been kept down to 1.1 million on average for the year, a loan of RM 226 million would have been needed; every additional 100,000 unemployed needed RM 100 million; cf. Wermel and Urban, *Arbeitslosenfürsorge*, p. 23.

53. On the importance of the battle over the 'sacrifice' for the finance policy of the Brüning government as well, see Hans Mommsen, 'Staat und Bürokratie in der Ära Brüning in Gotthard Jasper (ed.), *Tradition und Reform in der deutschen Politik*, Gedenkschrift für Waldemar Besson (Berlin, 1976), pp. 94 f.

54. Cf. in more detail Maurer, *Reichsfinanzen*, pp. 129 ff. Quotation on p. 139.

55. Helga Timm, *Die deutsche Sozialpolitik und der Bruch der Grossen Koalition im März 1930* (Düsseldorf, 1952) (Beiträge zur Geschichte des Parlamentarismus und der politischen Parteien, vol. 1), p. 204.

56. Cf. Stampfer's comments on the SPD congress in Magdeburg, Minutes, p. 174.

57. Preller, *Sozialpolitik*, p. 428.

58. *Reformvorschläge der VDA*, p. 4.

59. Since possession of land and cattle could be taken into account relatively often in the case of the seasonally unemployed, even less could have been expected from a general needs test. Cf. *Verhandlungen der Sachverständigenkommission*, pp. 92 and 161 ff.

60. The proportion of unemployed receiving public aid in the overall number of supported unemployed, which was about 15% in 1927, rose in 1928/9 to 20-25%. Cf. F. Memelsdorf, 'Die gemeindliche Erwerblosenfürsorge in den deutschen Grossstädten in den Jahren 1927-1929', *Städte und Statistik*, Supplement to *Der Städtetag*, no. 5 (1930), pp. 17-22.

61. The demands from the industrialists are in the *Denkschrift des Reichsverbandes der Deutschen Industrie, Aufstieg oder Niedergang? Die deutsche Wirtschafts- und Finanzreform 1929* (Berlin, 1929) (Veröffentlichungen des RDI, vol. 49).

62. Cf. the comments by the RDI-Geschäftsführer Kastl at the RDI board

204   *The Crisis of German Unemployment Insurance*

meeting on 16 January 1930. Minutes p. 31, Bayer-Archiv, 62/10/4.

63. Cf. *Soziale Praxis*, vol. 38 (1929), p. 964.

64. Cf. S. Aufhäuser, 'Der politische Kampf um die Arbeitslosenversicherung und ihre sozialpolitische Bedeutung', *Die Gesellschaft*, vol. 7 (1930), p. 401.

65. Cf. Bruno Broecker, 'Die Sozialpolitik am Scheidewege', *Die Arbeit*, vol. 6 (1929), p. 484.

66. Loc. cit., p. 488.

67. Aufhäuser, *Kampf*, pp. 395 ff.

68. Cf. *Wirtschaftsdemokratie. Ihr Wesen, Weg und Ziel*, ed. for the ADGB by Fritz Naphtali (Berlin, 1928), pp. 135 and 150.

69. *Gewerkschaftszeitung*, vol. 37, no. 37 (1929) of 14 Sept. 1929, p. 579.

70. Cf. Erwin Rawicz, 'Die finanzielle Organisation der deutschen Arbeitslosenversicherung', *Die Gesellschaft*, vol. 7 (1930), pp. 404-29.

71. Cf. *Reformvorschläge der Vereinigung der Deutschen Arbeitgeberverbände*, pp. 8 and 11.

72. Ross McKibbin, 'The Economic Policy of the Second Labour Government 1929 – 1931', *Past and Present*, vol. 68 (August 1975), p. 113.

73. Since the formation of the National Government satisfied the banks as security for lending, even without the demanded programme, and the threatened far-reaching inroads into unemployment insurance were avoided, the suggestion seems to be justified 'that reductions in insurance had been a political weapon rather than a party principle' (Gilbert, *Social Policy*, p. 174). Cf. also for details Robert Skidelsky, *Politicians and the Slump. The Labour Government of 1929 – 1931* (London, 1967), pp. 334 ff.

74. Preller, *Sozialpolitik*, p. 429.

11 CREATION OF EMPLOYMENT AS A WELFARE POLICY. THE FINAL PHASE OF THE WEIMAR REPUBLIC[1]

M. Wolffsohn

Semantically speaking, the expression 'welfare state' can have two meanings: on the one hand it can mean that people in the state concerned 'fare well', that they feel content, or should do. In other words, it can be a description of an existing or a desired state of affairs. On the other hand, the concept can also imply that the state is doing well. The question to ask would then be 'who is the state?', but we are not concerned here with a treatise on the philosophy of the state. If, however, we took 'the welfare state' to refer to the people in the state, we could also take it as referring to those who rule the state. The term has a variety of overtones.

During the final phase of the Weimar Republic, there can be no question of a 'welfare state' in the strict semantic sense of the term, either with reference to those who ruled or those who were ruled. And it can certainly not be used as a description of a state of affairs at that time. It is possible that the measures to create employment were intended as a move towards a 'welfare state' in one sense or another, so we should, therefore, consider the motivation of the politicians in supporting or rejecting such measures.

However, let us first of all define the concept 'creation of employment'. Plans for the creation of employment should be taken to include all economic, political, social and financial measures, including fiscal and credit policies, designed to counter unemployment. Each of these, in as far as their objective is the combating of unemployment, can be seen as creating employment.

It is usual 'to distinguish between direct and indirect creation of employment.[2] Transport Minister Treviranus differentiated between job creation from an economic and from a socio-political basis.[3] I see this as more appropriate because it makes the main emphasis of each approach clearer. Direct, or socio-politically based, provision of employment can be taken to include all measures whose primary objective is the re-employment or first-time employment of those who are without work, by means of public contracts. These measures are expected to produce three secondary effects:

(1) newly created income increases purchasing power, stimulates in-company investment, thereby generating new opportunities to increase the work-force, which in turn boosts purchasing power, setting in motion an economic cycle;

(2) additional turnover and income mean increased public revenue, primarily through taxes, and lessen the burden on public funds through a decrease in unemployment benefit payments;

(3) increased income makes saving feasible, or is used for the repayment of debts.

Indirect provision of employment or that based on economic policy aims to encourage re-employment or first-time employment of those who are out of work by stimulating company initiatives. This can be achieved by easing taxation, or providing substantial investment grants, or by the creation of the appropriate political climate, which could be termed psychological investment aid. Provision of employment as a means of overcoming an unemployment and an economic crisis uses both a direct and an indirect approach. This is why it is usual to find combined measures adopted so that it is only possible to talk about different emphases in creating employment.

The question of underlying motives for a state policy of direct and indirect job creation was first examined using the records of the Chancellery and the Finance Ministry. It would be wrong to consider only the UK and West Germany when looking at possible links between welfare policies and measures designed to stimulate employment. Similar techniques were being used at about the same time or a little earlier in Sweden[4] or Palestine in 1927,[5] and one should certainly include President Roosevelt's 'New Deal' in the United States.

A cursory glance makes it clear that public economic activity at that time coincided with the suspension of 'normal Parliamentary processes'. In other words, the Opposition, or former Opposition, became part of the government. It was the time of 'Grand Coalitions', the 'Governments of National Unity'. From 1930 onwards parliament was largely excluded from the political decision-making process in Germany by the introduction of the presidial Cabinet system. This is also true of England and the Jewish self-governing institutions in Palestine, and to a certain extent applies to the Weimar Republic, although in this instance parliamentary procedure was suspended by means of Article 48, despite united opposition from left and right in the Reichstag. Nevertheless, with the exception of Sweden, it is appropriate to speak of an 'elite cartel' of 'pro-system Parties'.[6]

It would be interesting to pursue the question of whether at least the introduction of welfare state measures can only succeed politically when such elite cartels exist. Can we detect a structural prerequisite for such measures, or is it only an 'industrial accident'? Is it necessary to go through a teething phase in setting up a welfare state that can only be successfully overcome with the help of the combined forces supporting the state?

All the political entities so far mentioned were at that time a long way from being welfare states. They were much more concerned with ameliorating or correcting an acute emergency situation. If the country was to survive, it was essential to create work for the unemployed. There was no thought then of setting up a welfare state.

Structural Pre-conditions

Unemployment increased steadily from 1930 onwards.[7] The rise in unemployment figures and the increase in voting support for radical groups opposed to the system, the NSDAP and KPD (National Socialists and the Communists) ran almost parallel. This is not to equate the 'red' with the 'brown'. Adding their votes together is based on the assumption that the NSDAP and the KPD represented the most radical alternatives to the system at the time. Combining the NSDAP and the KDP votes seems sensible in that it makes clear the increasing power of those opposed to the Government.[8]

Many political decision-makers, even in the Brüning era, including the Chancellor, were in no sense supporters of the Republic, but were also worlds away from the objectives and methods of the National Socialists, although Brüning is depicted in some West German and DDR studies as the forerunner of Adolf Hitler.[9] This interpretation either confuses Brüning's subjective intentions with his objective function, or lays one-sided emphasis on the objective function.

Combining the NSDAP and KPD votes assumes that the political decision-makers in Brüning, Papen and Schleicher's presidial Cabinets were not aiming towards a National Socialist solution. Even less were they considering a Communist solution. This does not need to be emphasised. Accordingly, the impressive NSDAP and KPD election successes must have been seen as a threat by both the German Nationalist and Social Democrat politicians in charge at the time.

Reactions

The problems of non-radical policies were clearly heightened by the rising unemployment figures. Did the non-radical politicians draw the appropriate conclusions, in other words the planning or implementation of measures designed to provide work?

Before we examine the motives of politicians in supporting or opposing job creation programmes, we must first establish the priority accorded to such measures, for example, in the Cabinet. Only then can we make a reasoned assessment of motives. The charts which follow give some indication of the importance the Cabinet attached to measures designed to create work as a means of overcoming the crisis between 1930 and 1934.[10] (See Figure 11.1)

If we compare the movement of the line depicting unemployment totals with the line indicating the number of Cabinet sessions concerned with work creation, we can establish three things.

(1) Conquering unemployment was by no means first on the Brüning government's list of priorities. If we consider the extent of unemployment even during this Chancellor's period in office, the politicians' reticence seems, to say the least, surprising. There was only a change of course shortly before Brüning's resignation. And this came too late.

(2) Under Papen the Cabinet turned its attention to the question of job creation relatively frequently. It is possible that the government anticipated political as well as economic advantages from a policy of increased employment provision.

(3) Contrary to all expectations, the subject was rarely discussed in Schleicher's Cabinet. Did the government not attach as much importance to it as is variously asserted?[11]

Although we are not going to consider the National Socialist phase further, it is still useful to bear in mind that those in power were clearly aware, particularly in the early stages of their regime, of the propaganda value of measures designed to create employment. It must, however, be added that other general political priorities dominated, particularly in the first six months of 1933, although these did not exclude more intensive dealing with the unemployment problem. Quite the opposite: the National Socialist regime grappled with the problem more frequently than each of its three predecessors.

The 'pressure from the streets' on politicians, measurable and

Figure 11.1: Unemployment and the Government's Reaction Expressed in the Number of Cabinet Sittings

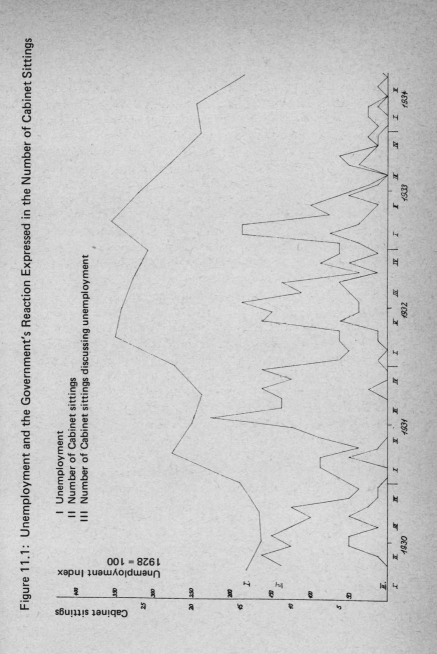

I   Unemployment
II Number of Cabinet sittings
III Number of Cabinet sittings discussing unemployment

Figure 11.2: Unemployment and Submissions to the Ministry of Finance

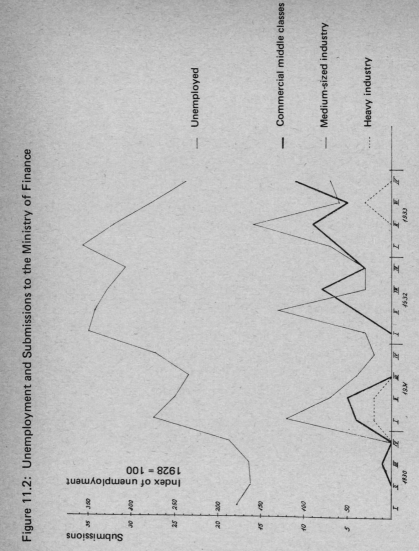

Submissions

Index of unemployment
1928 = 100

— Unemployed

— Commercial middle classes

— Medium-sized industry

...... Heavy industry

visible in the election results, has already been mentioned as a structural factor. To what extent was pressure also exerted on the government by economic pressure groups, wanting the introduction of work-creating measures? The ADGB (German Trades Union Confederation) was asking for job creation programmes considerably earlier than their 'parent party'.[12] Apart from the employees, were employers also interested in direct or indirect measures designed to combat unemployment?[13] Was there any correlation between the developments in unemployment and the suggestions and demands being put forward by major industries, medium-sized companies and skilled crafts guilds?

We can take as indicators the unemployment index and the list of petitions submitted to the Finance Ministry.[14] Because of the form in which they are available, submissions to the Chancellery are unsuitable as a measuring device as they have only been collated for the period November 1923–July 1933.[15] On the other hand, all petitions handed in to the Finance Ministry between August 1930 and the end of 1934 are available. Submissions from agricultural interest groups are used as a basis for comparison, as agriculture was after all directly affected by improvement measures that counted as 'job creations'. The group of 'individuals' mainly includes the professional and self-employed, and it is therefore possible that some of those in this category should be grouped under the heading of middle-class tradesmen or small businessmen. It was not possible to obtain more detailed information about these people in the relevant reference books. We can, however, proceed on the certain assumption that none of this 'hidden minority' belongs in the major industrialist category.

Figure 11.2 shows that medium-sized industry, middle-class professionals and skilled craftsmen were much more actively involved in advocating measures designed to increase employment than were major industrial concerns. As, however, the files of the Finance Ministry, like those of the Chancellery, are almost exclusively concerned with submissions relating to direct provision of employment (in the terms of our definition) and employers' organisations or industrialists mainly supported indirect measures, we should not place too much emphasis on these findings.[16]

In using this approach, however, we need to consider the methodological question of whether submissions from individual employers or employer organisations are a useful indicator of the extent of interest or disinterest in a particular policy. As regards the structural framework we can make a summary.

(1) Since there was a correlation between the increase in unemployment and the growth of political radicalism, which made the implementation of work-creating measures a matter of urgent necessity for those responsibly in government, it can be assumed that at the time optimal propaganda use was made of job creation programmes.

(2) The movements of the lines on the graph shows that politicians in a position of responsibility in the Brüning, Papen and Schleicher governments were only too aware of the economic and political need for measures to combat unemployment. (Not all of them acted accordingly.) It is, however, true that data relating to the Brüning and Schleicher administrations are ambiguous.

(3) Medium-sized industry and the self-employed middle classes supported measures designed to decrease unemployment with growing intensity as unemployment rose, showing a preference for direct intervention.

(4) Major industrial enterprises decided in favour of indirect creation of employment.

(5) There is no close correlation between the timing of major industries' demands for direct job creation and developments in the unemployment situation.

(6) Those in medium-sized industries and skilled craftsmen tried (in the absence of other possibilities?!) to influence the authorities far more than the major industrialists or ADGB representatives did through written submissions, which suggests that the latter had more effective means at their disposal.

The Brüning Government

As early as May 1930 Industry Minister Dietrich, with the agreement of Labour Minister Stegerwald, asked to be allowed to lay before the Cabinet the question of seasonal adjustment in the economy through public works programmes.[17] In his paper Dietrich particularly supported restoration work on public buildings to be carried out in the winter. Because of the acute shortage of finance, he suggested that future budget allocations could be transferred and advances on future reserves made possible. He regretted not being able to set in motion an upsurge in the economy through public contracts, but at the same time was opposed to any increase in the money supply, and called therefore for a 'sensible distribution' of available resources. Admittedly in doing this Dietrich nullified the stimulating effect of any public contracts from the outset, because the monetary cycle was not expanded, and economic activity was not stimulated, but merely transferred to another sector.

Only a few days later, Minister of Posts Schätzel was widely circulating proposals for a railway development programme costing 400,000,000 Reichsmark, because the previous year's expenditure of 510,000,000 Reichsmark had shown such 'far-reaching effects'.[18]

Brüning was energetically in favour of work creation through the national post and rail services, because he considered it 'indispensable', otherwise 'the other parties in the Reichstag* would seize this opportunity'.[19] Apart from an unconcealed distancing of himself from parliament and Social Democracy which is clear from his memoirs, this statement by Brüning makes it obvious that he was well aware of the propaganda value of work creation measures. He must, therefore, have had powerful reasons for not introducing a comprehensive job creation programme and being satisfied with only limited steps.

In so far as it is possible to talk about a 'welfare policy' in this instance, it can only imply the 'welfare' of the ruling politicians. The 'welfare' of the electorate was only a means to a political end.[20]

On 19 May the Cabinet agreed the following proposals[21] to combat unemployment: major contracts for the post and rail services; encouragement of a house-building programme, particularly for small units of accommodation; negotiations concerning local authority debts, as the extent of these debts was holding back the allocation of building contracts. In addition to this, the Cabinet decided to increase the road-building programme and the Finance Minister was commissioned to implement all contracts as soon as possible.

A policy to provide employment in this context can clearly be seen as 'survival politics' by the government, a perfectly legitimate undertaking that has very little to do with 'welfare policies'.

Brüning's economic policies were extremely inconsistent. In the summer of 1930, the government was planning at one and the same time powerful deflationary measures, such as increases in taxation and a reduction in public expenditure, whilst also expecting a programme of job creation to be successfully implemented that Trendelenburg, then Secretary of State for Industry, costed at 1,300,000,000 RM.[22]

Detailed proposals for the financing of these measures were not

---

* Brüning was referring mainly to the SPD. — MW.

available, and the resistance of the President of the National Bank was well known. He was afraid of an inflationary policy brought about by credit financing. The Chancellor apparently wanted to overrule the President's reservations. He intended to inform the public about all the proposals relating to work creation and asked for a compilation of each Department's contracts to help him in this. He did not, however, seem completely certain of his policy, because it was only *after* the 14 September general election that he proposed to the Cabinet the 'implementation and expansion of measures designed to promote employment'.[23] The emphasis was intended to be on agricultural improvement and road-building. It was hoped to raise the necessary finance through foreign loans.

It is remarkable that Brüning only turned his attention to the implementation of work creation programmes *after* the elections, although he was well aware of the favourable propaganda value of such measures. Possibly he was afraid of inducing public fear about inflation by introducing employment measures that were supposed to be credit-financed. No clear justification is obvious. We can, however, assume with certainty that conquering unemployment was not first on the government's list of priorities for 'survival politics'. Otherwise a different political line would have been pursued.

The work creation programme adopted in September, like its July precursor, was already being nullified in its effects at the planning stage by other government economic policies; the government wanted to increase various taxes and limit expenditure. The price of coal was reduced by 6 per cent on 15 October. These measures had as little to do with an effective work creation programme as the 1 December emergency decree. All this did was to accelerate the deflationary spiral.

This creation of employment, initially conceived to counter the SPD, was linked with political attempts to impress employers. In granting various public contracts, which in any case were not that numerous or far-reaching, the government had no intention of making a gift to individual firms or subsidising them. They were following clearly defined economic and socio-political objectives, which certainly did not increase the attractiveness of the contracts in the eyes of participating industrialists.

Minister of Posts Schätzel drew up guidelines for the awarding of Post Office contracts[24] that were designed to reduce the prices of those companies taking part by 10 per cent.[25] The Industry Minister of the day, Trendelenburg, had also already begun to establish such guidelines.[26] A broadly based employers' front was formed to protest vigorously against the measures. It did not do any good. Employment Minister Stegerwald wanted to go even further than his colleagues: companies which received supplementary contracts should meet certain conditions. Contracts were to be based on long-term delivery dates, to make overtime unnecessary. Local materials were to be used in the work as far as possible. Trade inspectors were supposed to supervise the implementation of the contracts and report any infringements to the department concerned with job creation, which would then pass on the information to the Ministry of Labour. Stegerwald went even further in his proposals.[27] The department responsible for public contracts should not award any to companies with 'openly expressed anti-social attitudes', failure to observe local or collectively agreed conditions of employment and dismissal threats designed to achieve rates of pay below the minimum wage agreement. Stegerwald accused the companies of the 'Berlin Metal Industries' of this,[28] and was not afraid to point out to the Prussian Minister for Trade and Industry the overtime being worked at Siemens, AEG, Borsig and Stock & Bergmann, hoping in so doing to undermine the practice.[29] The Cabinet, who had Stegerwald's proposals before them, merely took note of them without any further actions.[30]

Even Stegerwald's suggestion that compulsory schooling should be increased from eight to nine years was due more to the politics of survival than to any social policies. Increasing compulsory schooling could, according to the Labour Minister, contribute to the 'reassurance of the working masses'.[31]

It is right to describe Brüning's policies as 'deflationary'. It should not, however, be overlooked that in 1931 in particular the supply of paper money in circulation was considerably expanded. [32] This took place principally in order to guarantee the 'Russian trade deals', consignments from German companies to the Soviet Union.[33] The 'Russian trade deals' were seen by the government as a contribution towards increased employment and were supposed to boost German exports. In view of the 20 per cent devaluation of the pound sterling in September 1931, as well as the various barriers to foreign trade erected by other countries, such contracts seemed an unavoidable necessity to the government. To guarantee the transactions the government assumed liability for 35 per cent of the contract and the federal states 25 per cent in the event of cancellation. The remaining 40 per cent was provided by credit from banking consortia.[34]

The Russian trade deals, which can be seen as indirect creation of employment, were based on foreign relations policy (Stegerwald's 'orientation towards the East') as well as on employment market policies (also Stegerwald's), although there were certainly voices raised in the Cabinet, such as Secretary of State Schäffer's and Trendelenburg's, who would have preferred to spend the anticipated 300,000,000 Reichsmark on domestic contracts. They were thinking of the railway contracts that AEG, Poensgen and Klöckner had already entered into negotiations over.[35] In the autumn of 1931, the Reichsverband der deutschen Industrie (RDI — National Confederation of German Industry) turned to the National Bank and asked for re-discounted credit, because the machine industry in particular had adapted to the Russian trade due to the slump in domestic orders.[36] In the Cabinet session of 2 March 1932 Industry Minister Warmbold asked the assembled Ministers to agree to new government aid totalling 120,000,000 Reichsmarks to underwrite the contracts that had already been signed with the Soviet Union.[37] If finance broke down the Industry Minister anticipated 'serious consequences' for the employment market.[38] Finally he also pointed out that guaranteeing previously agreed work was in the best interests of the iron, carriage and machine tool industries. Labour Minister Stegerwald who only a year previously had been amongst the strongest proponents of the Russian trade agreements, only gave his agreement initially for top-level discussions concerning further finance, and instead demanded with some force 'clarification of other state-financed projects'. Above all else, proposals for settlements and other projects which interested employers 'should be considered for once'.[39] Finally, Stegerwald also pointed out that the free trade unions were starting their discussions on measures to combat unemployment on 23 March 1932 and the government ought to anticipate 'any such action'. In the end, the Cabinet agreed to Stegerwald's proposed top-level discussions over the future of the Russian trade agreements and one month later the agreements were ratified.[40]

The motivation for such policies of indirect job creation was clearly employer-orientated. There were, however, other equally employee-orientated viewpoints, such as Stegerwald's. One can look in vain in both instances for a coherent economic concept underpinning these policies.

Projects to build suburban housing estates were energetically demanded by Finance Minister Dietrich in 1931 because in his opinion the housing development policy pursued up to that point was not capable of 'absorbing the considerable numbers of unemployed'.[41] Poerschke, the senior adviser in the Finance Ministry, saw the unemployed who were in receipt of unemployment benefits as a 'reserve army' which he considered a 'political, economic, and social danger' and was therefore in favour of a reduction in their numbers as a 'powerful necessity'.[42] The housing projects could not be regarded as work creation measures in the sense of the definition used so far. They also had little in common with welfare policies. Like so many of this government's actions they were in every respect survival policies without vision. They cannot even be ascribed to any clear special interests.

The Final Phase of Brüning's Government

It would be inappropriate here to test the findings of Henning Köhler and Wolfgang J. Heilbich. It would also be superfluous to point out that in spite of the reparation payments, there was from an economic point of view no necessity for deflationary policies. Horst Sanmann has already proved this.[43]

As any outline of the political and economic priorities in state employment creation policies would, however, be incomplete without some consideration of the problem of the reparation payments, we have included a brief comment on certain aspects, without wishing to revive old controversy.

(1) A not inconsiderable section of leading representatives of German industry urged the primacy of the reparation question.[44] The employers' representatives on the provisional economic council believed, for example, that an improvement in the German economy, and the solution to the unemployment problem that went with it, could only be achieved after the removal of 'external obstacles'. As long as this external burden remained, capital could not be attracted on to the market for lack of confidence.[45]

(2) The government's policy of 'wait and see', with regard to work creation, was particularly approved by the Foreign Office, as well as by Dietrich, Treviranus and even Warmbold.[46] And here we must bear in mind that Warmbold was invited into Brüning's second Cabinet as 'the man from IG Farben'[47] and Treviranus enjoyed a high reputation amongst broad sections of industry.[48] According to a number of sources,[49] Secretary of State Trendelenburg was particularly trusted by industry but seems on the other hand, like Stegerwald, to have con-

sidered creation of employment more important. Trendelenburg, for example, voted in favour of the adoption of the
Lautenbach plan.[50]

Source material suggests that the government bureaucracy had to fit
in with policies that gave priority to reparation. The Secretary of
State for the Treasury, Hans Schäffer, wrote, for example, to Wagemann saying that his plan contained much 'of practical value', but
'given the state of affairs in the foreseeable future, in particular before
a new stage in the reparation issue has been reached', it could not be
put into effect.[51] In April 1932 Cabinet council members Ronde and
Reichert, who were leading civil servants in the Industry Ministry,
did not expect any decision about a possible extension of credit for
a comprehensive work creation programme until the problem of reparation payments had been solved.[52] Accordingly, external relations were
given priority over economic and welfare policies.

Another former civil servant in the Industry Ministry, Hans Joachim
Rüstow, still believes today that Brüning did not want to introduce
any employment programme until the question of reparation had been
resolved. Quite apart from this, the Chancellor lacked any understanding of the latest concepts in economic policy.[53]

However one may judge the question of the relative primacy of work
creation or reparation settlement, it is indisputable that in early 1932
Brüning's government undertook new measures to prepare the way for
a work creation programme. The level of administrative preparation
at national as well as local level was, however, totally inadequate.[54]

Creation of Employment as a Political Tool?

Within the industry council of the day the employers' side and the
employees represented two different concepts which Transport Minister Treviranus described as 'economic' and 'political/socio-political'
respectively.[55] The employers' representatives, in whose name Georg
Solmssen of the Deutsche Bank spoke, believed firmly in the principle
that the 'cure' for the economy should be administered 'without
any consideration of the resulting unemployment figures'. They also
rejected public works programmes and a related expansion of credit,
supporting indirect creation of employment.

The employee representatives, on the other hand, believed that
'something should be done as soon as possible', as the unemployment

situation could provoke political unrest.[56] They therefore spoke out strongly in favour of more visibly effective direct measures to create jobs.

Which of the two approaches did the Brüning government decide to favour? Henning Köhler puts forward the view that in its work creation programme the government was following a socio-political approach.[57] Brüning and Treviranus supported a 'political/socio-political approach' and spoke in favour of falling back on 'hand and spade work' in carrying out projects.[58] Otherwise the government tried to steer a middle course between the various interests in this matter also. In accordance with his priorities in economic policy the Chancellor wanted to reduce social security payments on 20 February, but he also bore in mind the socio-political problems associated with any such measure. He thought that it was too much to expect of the working people and apart from this held the view that it could not be carried politically.[59] In this, Brüning adopted arguments put forward by the employers' and by the employees' sides. The interests of the professional and skilled middle classes were not taken into consideration, a political stance that shows an astonishing discrepancy with the significance of this group and which considerably contributed to the rise of National Socialism.

In March 1932, the government increased its efforts to set up a work creation programme. But whether these efforts should be viewed in conjunction with the cut-backs in unemployment benefit as 'spiritual distraction', as Stegerwald is said to have called it, seems doubtful in view of the standpoint adopted by this Minister otherwise.[60] In the controversy over the reduction in working hours, for example, he completely changed his views in line with trade union arguments. Whereas during the autumn of 1930 he, like the German Employers' Federation, was of the opinion that a legally enforced reduction in the working week would raise production costs, and must, therefore, be rejected, in April 1932 he spoke energetically in favour of the introduction of the 40-hour week. This attitude isolated him inside the Cabinet, because Brüning preferred voluntary agreement to legal enforcement.[61] Secretary of State Trendelenburg was particularly vehemently opposed to the idea of a statutory reduction in working hours.[62] He gave as his reason for rejection that 'compulsory measures' would 'rouse employers strongly against the government'. In addition, he thought it was an 'unreasonable demand on employers'.

Members of the government do not seem to have been sure of the effect of their socio-political approach to work creation in political voting terms. But it is precisely in this instance that one could talk of a 'welfare policy', if this is taken to mean a fair balance of perception of different interests. Treviranus expected that this type of work creation programme would have a particularly favourable psychological effect on those sections of the community with 'leanings towards right-wing radicalism'.[63] His analysis was accurate: in the first instance, unemployment strengthened right-wing radicalism, in other words the National Socialist Party, and later measures to promote the provision of employment had a real influence, even a multiplier effect, on NSDAP voters.

In the face of pressure from the trade unions Stegerwald urged the implementation of job creation schemes and advised that a 'definite positive statement on the question of work creation' should be made before the emergency session of the Trades Union Congress. The public should not be given the impression that 'the national government's activity is all negative'.[64] Finance Minister Dietrich was of the opinion that for political and economic reasons 'something extraordinary' needed to happen to be able to survive the winter somehow.[65]

Brüning was far more sceptical and cautious. He did not want to make 'this sort of decision' before the local and presidential elections. In contrast to several of his Ministers who evidently saw public work creation programmes as their last hope, Brüning seemed to think that introducing such projects before the election was close to political suicide. Brüning got his own way. The Cabinet agreed a resolution not to talk in public about a work creation 'programme'.[66]

Notes on Priorities in National Work Creation Policies under Brüning

(1) In general the Brüning government seems to have aimed for a middle or middling course between the demands of employers and employees in the social and political question of employment provision. No consideration was given to the interests of skilled craftsmen or the professional middle classes.

(2) During Brüning's period as Chancellor the central issue in employment debates at national level was optimum economic efficiency. The fact that the results of the policy looked very different does not alter this, since we are looking at intentions rather than effects.

(3) In purely economic terms, the few real employment creating

measures that the Brüning government introduced, such as the Russian trade agreements and the national rail contracts, only balanced out the damage caused by the four 'emergency decrees to guarantee industry and finance' and the reductions in social security payments. Brüning's attitude to work creation, like his economic policy, can therefore be described as contradictory.[67]

(4) Brüning's government generally believed that provision of employment was more a part of socio-political rather than economic policy. If this distinction is not made, misunderstandings can arise in any judgement of Brüning's work creation measures. Since welfare policies ought to have a long-term basis, the short-term psychologically directed work creation measures introduced by the Brüning government cannot be described as steps towards a welfare state.

(5) There can be no clear answer to the question of whether Brüning would have rejected an active economic policy on principle, even after the reparation payments problem had been solved.

(6) In political terms the Brüning government thought that a solution to the reparation problem was more important than measures to generate employment. Many members of the government recognised the political voting significance of work creation, but even they gave precedence to a solution of the reparation question, particularly Treviranus and Dietrich.

(7) Plans for measures to generate employment can be traced back to the beginning of Brüning's period as Chancellor. It would be wrong to attribute them to spring 1932.

(8) Definite beginnings of an indirect expansion in the money supply can be seen in the 'Inflation des Finanzwechselgelds' (inflation in paper bills), particularly the credit measures for the Russian trade agreements. In the spring of 1932 members of the Cabinet were prepared to increase the money supply and to make advances against taxation. This willingness was not followed by action.

(9) In the spring of 1932 administrative preparations at the lower levels, particularly in the towns, were inadequate for any major public works contracts.

(10) Some measures, in particular the estate-building programmes and emergency work, had nothing more in common with work creation than the name. They were more an expression

of total uncertainty in economic policy.

(11) At the same time tendencies towards more direct economic state influence through work provision can be detected, such as directions relating to working hours, a central office of work creation, and guidelines for the allocation of contracts, moves which to some extent were contested within the Cabinet.

(12) Foreign trade figures show that the Soviet Union boosted the capitalist economy through work-providing contracts. In this way they made it harder for their own 'brothers' to come to power. Non-radical forces missed their chance and the National Socialists took advantage.

The Papen Government

We must dispense here with a comprehensive outline of the job creation measures initiated by Papen's government,[68] but particular attention deserves to be paid to the introduction of tax credits. As this was matter of indirect provision of employment, it might be assumed that major industrial interests lay behind this policy.

What is known about Warmbold, who was brought into the Cabinet in October 1931 on the prompting of IG Farben,[69] is that he was one of the exponents of an active economic policy, linked to an expansion in the money supply. The definitive draft of the tax credit scheme went back to a discussion between Warmbold and Hans Schäffer, according to Luther's information.[70] Towards the end of 1931 and the beginning of 1932 Warmbold is said to have already put forward the idea of tax credit certificates to Brüning in a comprehensive memorandum.[71] Schwerin-Krosigk also points out that Warmbold indicated that measures to generate money and credit were indispensable in a ministerial discussion in December 1931.[72] The Chancellor for his part ignored these suggestions, which in the opinion of the 'German letters from the Führer' led Warmbold to his later resignation. The head of the Defence Ministry also confirms that Warmbold was not able to carry through his suggestions for stimulating the economy and thereby promoting increased employment during Brüning's government.[73]

Schwerin-Krosigk writes that Warmbold was influenced to promote a policy of credit expansion by Wagemann.[74] Treviranus[75] and the 'German letters from the Führer'[76] also point out how close in content Warmbold's and Wagemann's views were. An item in the *Berliner*

Tageblatt, 17 June 1932, gives further clues to the intellectual origins of Papen's work creation measures.[77] As there were no traces of a denial of the statement in either the newspaper or Cabinet records, it must correspond to the truth. According to this item, Warmbold was only prepared to join Papen's Cabinet as Industry Minister if he was allowed to form a presidial economic advisory council. This council should be the 'ultimate arbitrator' in the event of differences on economic matters between Warmbold and a majority [sic] of the Cabinet. The formation of this conclave was approved, and its members comprised: Schmitz (Director of IG Farben), Wagemann (Warmbold's brother-in-law and President of the National Statistical Bureau as well as head of the Institute for Monetary Research) and Popitz, who, according to the *Berliner Tageblatt*, was a friend of Warmbold's. It was also known that Popitz was, in currency matters, *novarum rerum cupidus*.[78]

Calling into being this type of conclave of men that Warmbold could trust to carry his economic policy ideas against a Cabinet majority must undoubtedly have given him a very powerful position. The suspicion must arise that IG Farben was behind the new course in currency, credit and economic policy. Schäffer's records confirm that there was also agreement between Wagemann's and Max Ilgner's concepts of currency policy.[79] And Ilgner was a Director of IG Farben.

Opposing Interests in Import Quotas for Agricultural Produce

Some indications suggest that the various work promotion measures of the Papen government were in no way intended in the first instance to revive industrial production. This seems to have been a much more incidental, admittedly not unwelcome, side-effect of the pursuit of the ultimate objective, aid for agriculture: 'Welfare policies' for the landowners.

Leading representatives of agricultural interests had always urged a reduction in agricultural imports into Germany. President Hindenburg always had a sympathetic ear for this interest group and Heinrich Brüning, not least of all, felt the effects of this. No politician who wanted to be sure of Hindenburg's support could settle on a policy that was likely to provoke a veto from landed interests. On the other hand, limitations on German imports must affect large sections of export-orientated industries, who could expect foreign counter-measures. The effects of this threatened serious consequences for the already bleak employment market. An economic policy which could be carried out under existing conditions had to take account of this conflict of interests, although in terms of economic efficiency it would be indecisive.

Papen's government had accordingly to steer a middle course between the interests of industry and agriculture. This is reflected in the emergency decrees of 4 and 5 September 1932, in which political compromise was achieved at a cost of internal inconsistency, and the economic policy measures appear self-cancelling.[80] Hans Schäffer's diary gives some insights into the context and background to the controversies between the various politicians involved.[81] President Hindenburg exerted more and more pressure for immediate aid for agriculture. Together with a few Ministers who were not attending the Lausanne Conference, he even wanted to use the absence of the Ministers who were in Lausanne to urge an immediate change of direction in trade policy. Through Secretary of State Meissner Hindenburg explained to the government that 'self-sufficiency had to be introduced' and the agricultural economy must 'at long last be helped by customs policy'. In future, trade agreements should only be signed with countries with which Germany had a positive balance of payments. In doing this, Hindenburg used as his reference point Schleicher, who was supposed to have also spoken out against 'most favoured national preferences and the export fixation'.[82]

But Schleicher was by no means isolated in the Cabinet in this view. As late as July a majority of Cabinet members felt the same way.[83] The government worked on the assumption that world trade was in any case shrinking and it was, therefore, senseless to take any account of exports. Instead of this, agriculture should be helped by higher prices. This price rise was expected to produce a recovery in agricultural production and increased agricultural purchasing power would in turn benefit industry, leading to greater industrial employment. The protagonists of this course of action did, however, admit that the decline in exports would create a gap in industry, which would have to be bridged until such time as the newly strengthened agricultural purchasing power could fulfil the same function. The means of bridging this gap was supposed to be an employment creation programme.

As Secretary of State Planck put it, these plans were in line with 'the personal wishes of the old man, who insisted most strongly on them'. Hindenburg really does seem to have exercised strong pressure, because the import quota measures were carried in a Cabinet session in September, despite a Cabinet vote of 6:4 against restrictions.[84]

In the case of these measures by the Papen government there can be no question of either a recognition of major industrialists' interests or an 'alliance' between agriculture and industry. The Reichslandbund (National Agricultural Alliance) complained that Industry Minister Warmbold (if one suspects for a moment that he did not represent particular industrial interests) opposed the introduction of quotas regulating agricultural imports.[85]

If the theory is valid that Papen's government wanted to resolve the conflict between industrial and agricultural interests at the cost of a weaker third party, namely the working classes, by allowing statutory wage reductions as a compensation for concessions in trade policy,[86] then the following premises must be empirically verifiable:

(1) industry would have had to agree to the wage policy clauses in the emergency decree of 5 September 1932;

(2) the government would actually have had to have wanted to resolve the conflict at the expense of the work-force.

It remains to be seen whether these two premises were fulfilled.

The Dispute within the Papen Government

The urgent need for immediate creation of employment became increasingly obvious, not just in Germany. Papen, the new Chancellor, wanted to give the population a 'spiritual uplift' in his government policy speech.[87] As an intention, this generally had a favourable effect on the investment climate. The first steps towards provision of employment taken by the new government remained well within the framework of the previous economic policy. References to self-sufficiency tendencies, mentioned in connection with agricultural import quotas, first came in a comment by the Home Secretary, von Gayl, on 14 June: in the government's declaration concerning the emergency regulations which was to take place the same day, the idea of a 'strengthening of the domestic market' must be made clear, von Gayl explained.[88] Gayl clearly wanted to link self-sufficiency with work creation. In the Cabinet session of 3 June he had already stressed the need for the government's policy speech to emphasise employment provision.[89] The Home Secretary, who was very closely in touch with agricultural interests, soon received covering support from the Food and Agriculture Minister, von Braun. Von Braun recommended to the

Chancellor that he put creation of jobs 'publicly in the front line of all his economic policies',[90] and spread the suggestion that a Commissioner for Employment should be appointed[91] to operate as a central office for the provision of employment. This suggestion, based on the idea of more state intervention in the economy, was certainly in line with the general view of agricultural interest groups, who, unlike broad sections of industry, saw the increase in state responsibilities as a welcome protection.

The suggestions put forward by Industry Minister Warmbold on the other hand were directed more towards an encouragement of private enterprise. Warmbold and Braun represented two totally opposing concepts of the role of the state in the economy. It is not surprising that there were frequent disputes between the two over this basic question and over the agricultural import quotas controversy.[92] It is clear from his statement in the Cabinet on 11 July setting out his view that the general situation could hardly be kept in check economically, and asking whether one 'ought perhaps now to come out with a work creation programme'[93] that Braun was not thinking only of agricultural aid when he talked about employment provision. This comment was made in connection with a Cabinet declaration concerning the 'Preussenschlag' of 20 July.

It cannot, however, be proved that other members of the government were equally anxious to introduce work creation schemes as a tactical weapon. Even the similar sounding statement by Employment Minister Schäffer, quoted by Petzina, cannot be traced either in the Cabinet records, or their related files, or in the file Petzina refers to.[94]

These direct job creation measures were largely based on orthodox concepts of economic policy. In the disputed issue of the reduction in the working week the government encouraged the introduction of short-time working committees in the regional employment offices instead of statutory provision. Voluntary agreements to limit working hours were supposed to be reached. Without doubt that was a yielding to the wishes of numerous industrialists who resisted strongly any statutory reduction in hours. The German Trades Union Confederation, the SPD and the Communist Party, on the other hand, urged a statutory reduction in the working week.[95]

For 'political and objective reasons', the continuing suburban estate building programme was considered 'absolutely essential'.[96] To put a stop to this seemed to the Employment Minister 'politically unfeasible'.[97]

It was only in July that indications of a change in previously accepted economic policy and related employment provision began to mount up. But the government's attitude was still contradictory. Finance Minister Schwerin-Krosigk made it clear to the other Ministers that public work creation measures only make sense as an encouragement for a healthy economy, and not as a cure for a stagnating one.[98]

Creating employment by direct intervention was just a case of a shift in purchasing power. Instead of this, Schwerin-Krosigk recommended administrative reforms to simplify social legislation and an easing of credit policies. Labour Minister Hans Schäffer had other solutions in mind. He emphasised the connection between the state of the employment market and a 'more sympathetic credit policy on the part of the banks' as well as 'correct' foreign exchange and trade policies.

This idea of the Labour Minister's, linked as it was to an unrestricted trade policy, directly contradicted the objectives of the Minister for Food and Agriculture.

The latter, therefore, immediately repeated his suggestion for the appointment of a Commissioner for Employment during the same Cabinet session, justifying his view with the explanation that if the Labour Minister was to be in charge of measures to create employment, then the commission would ensure their smooth implementation, so that there was no chance of any 'bureaucratic obstacles' arising. In other words, Schäffer's powers were to be curtailed directly.

The 'Government's Draft Economic Programme' of 28 July, which already contained significant aspects of Papen's 28 August Münster programme speech, is the actual turning-point in the Papen Cabinet's economic policies. The government explained that it stood for private industry and private property. It wanted to keep state intervention to regulate the economy in narrow limits and private industry should be freed from the 'limitations and restrictions' which hindered a full working-out of the effects of productive power. It was not the state's role to 'take over the risks inherent in the private sector' and state resources should only be used when they were urgently required 'in the public interest'.[99] This draft proposal did not refer to direct provision of employment, but the government had still not completely given up the idea. Bracht, who took over responsibility for the Prussian Ministry of the Interior on 20 July, spoke in favour of a job creation programme to employ as many people as possible, for its psychological effect. In carrying out this work, it would be necessary to dispense with the use of machines 'as far as possible', even if this approach was 'uneconomic'.[100] The Chancellor was strongly in agreement with this idea and many members of the government still saw employment provision in terms of uneconomic emergency work, financed from the normal domestic budget. Luther, the President of the National Bank, lessened his opposition to financing job-creating measures by bills of exchange and agreed in future to treat work creation bills like trading bills, though insisting that the sum appropriated should be limited to 200,000,000 Reichsmark.[101]

Records suggest that the idea of an unorthodox course in economic policy, above all a credit policy, was gaining ground in the government even before the débâcle of the 31 July elections.[102] The election victories of the NSDAP seem to have hastened the breakthrough in economic policy.

On 10 August Schäffer, the Minister of Labour, left no one in any doubt that the survival of Papen's government depended on economic progress, and the Finance Minister added that the fate of 'any government depended crucially on whether or not it succeeded in taking 2,000,000 unemployed off the streets'.[103]

Once the Cabinet had reached fundamental agreement, responsibility for working out the details of the new economic plan was shared between Warmbold, Schwerin-Krosigk, the President of the National Bank, Luther, and his Deputy, Dreyse. Von Braun, the Minister for Food and Agriculture, was also called in.[104]

On 26 August Warmbold recommended to the Cabinet that they find alternatives to 'artificial work creation programmes' that would 'ease employers' deficit financing, leading them to take on more employees'. More specifically, Warmbold envisaged:[105]

(1) tax relief in the form of tax credits for the following 12 months, totalling 1,800,000 Reichsmark. Warmbold expressly rejected compulsory loans;

(2) the deficit in the national budget should be met by a single tax surcharge on high incomes and capital;[106]

(3) an easing of tariff levels, although the Labour Minister only wanted to agree to this if it was conditional on an increase in the work-force;

(4) to prevent an accumulation of tax credit notes, which were also intended to serve as a credit record, Warmbold, with Luther's agreement, wanted to exclude small businesses from the scheme as far as possible. Papen agreed and suggested that the lower limit for tax certificates should be 50 RM.[107]

But it would be wrong to deduce from this that there was any intention of putting small companies at a disadvantage because this form of credit was intended to finance repair contracts that small craft-based companies in particular had shown an interest in. Warmbold justified this preference for repair work with the argument that new investment was unnecessary in view of existing unused productive capacity. It was primarily small to medium-sized companies that were to be considered when the repair contracts were allocated and the National Bank should influence the commercial banks so that 'local branches could be prevailed on to take an interest in protecting and preserving those medium and small companies that were still capable of surviving'.

The representatives of leading trade organisations, particularly the professional middle classes, did, however, consider it desirable that the 'technical provisions of tax credit certificates should be better adapted to the requirements of companies with low tax liability', and also wanted house rental tax included in the accreditation system.[108]

Finance Minister Schwerin-Krosigk did not expect large national companies to make use of the subsidies to promote employment, and the associated possibility of reducing basic wage levels, and in fact as he said, he had no objection to excluding firms with more than 10,000 employees from the scheme. In spite of this, he did not want to put it forward as a proposal, for reasons he did not give. His main fear was that the measures could adversely affect employers who for social reasons had introduced short-time working in their factories to avoid more lay-offs and 'inconsiderate employers' would benefit by this.[109]

A declaration of intent by Papen testifies to the balance between various interests inherent in the government plans. In the Cabinet's programme discussions he pointed out that the plans considerably eased the burden on industry and that, therefore, 'another measure must be introduced to counterbalance this socially.'

In the discussions between Hindenburg, Papen and Schleicher in Neudeck on 30 August[110] the President gave his approval to the government's plans, though asking that 'sacrifices should be evenly distributed between the various occupational levels', and Schleicher emphasised the necessity to 'preserve the social character' of the measures 'under all circumstances'.

That the government saw 'work provision' in a social category is implied by the normally well informed 'A-Letter' of 19 August,[111] which states that there were negotiations between the Papen government, the German Trades Union Confederation, the Christian trade unions and the National Socialist Party to 'work out a major job

creation programme as a basis for agreement'. A movement towards
the coming co-operation between the various political groups could
already be detected in Gregor Strasser's 10 May speech to Parliament.
The President of the German Regional Government Council, Günter
Gerecke, seems to have been active 'most gratefully'.[112] During a
Cabinet session on 31 August, Papen pointed out that Gerecke had
succeeded in 'creating an organisation in which nearly all political
persuasions, from National Socialist to free trade union were represented', and even Schleicher found Gerecke's organisation 'interesting'.[113]

In the Chancellery files,[114] there are references to an *Arbeitsaus-
schuss für ein Arbeitsbeschaffungsprogramm* (Working Committee
for Employment-creating Programmes), whose members, listed in the
order in which they are given in the records, included representatives
of the following organisations: National Socialist Party; the Steel
Helmets (*Stahlhelm*); the National Agricultural Alliance (*Reichslandbund*); the National Banner (*Reichsbanner*); the free trade unions;
the Werewolves (*Werwolf*); the Schleswig-Holstein Agricultural and
Farmers Alliance (*Schleswig-Holsteinischer Land- und Bauernbund*);
and the General Association for Work Provision and Aid for the Unemployed.

The Working Party used as its basis the guiding principles of the
German *Landgemeindetag* (Provincial Government Council) which
were otherwise described as inflationary (for example by Luther in
the Cabinet session of 30 August), because of the planned increase in
the non-cash money supply.[115]

The common ground between the government and the various
groups must have been very slight indeed. The NSDAP representatives
put a draft resolution to the Work Creation Committee of the German
Provincial Government Council pointing out that no action had
followed Papen's announcements about job creation. 'Representatives
of various political persuasions willing to build up a society . . . have
set aside their individual political efforts . . . waiting for the measures
that were announced to be carried out.' The National Socialists held
Industry Minister Warmbold, Labour Minister Schäffer and the 'hesitant
and vacillating stance of the Chancellor' responsible for the delays in
implementation and the attitude of the President of the National Bank,
described as 'rigid, exhausting itself in negative criticism', was particularly blamed.[116]

It is not possible to determine exactly how far the non-partisan
approach was carried in Gerecke's organisation. In his memoirs, which

are heavily influenced by a glorification of the GDR,[117] Gerecke claims that he was speaking out in favour of a 'popular front tactic' as early as 1931, but the German Trades Union Confederation rejected all forms of co-operation with the Communist Party.[118]

Gerecke also writes that he refused Papen's offer of a Cabinet appointment as 'Co-ordinator for Work Creation' because he 'did not want to work under any circumstances with a man of political views like Papen's'.[119] Gerecke seems to have magnanimously set aside these reservations when he became Commissioner for Work Creation in Hitler's government.[120] In any case, negotiations with Gerecke broke down at the end of September, because he would not deviate from a policy that involved boosting the non-cash money supply.

There can be no doubt that the Papen government wanted to support 'free enterprise'.[121] The assumption was that this would be lost if the government's plan to revive the economy failed.[122] As Papen's own statements underline, the government's work creation measures were intended to have a socially balancing effect and to deprive the political left in particular of the objective basis for their arguments. The work that was available should be distributed amongst as many people as possible.[123] 'Unless I am much mistaken', Papen commented in presenting a Government Bill, 'that has been the Alpha and the Omega of every work creation programme advanced by those on the left of this noble House.'[124] It was precisely this intended political neutralisation of the left and the 'psychological error in dealing with the workers', as Frieda Wunderlich put it in the magazine *Soziale Praxis*,[125] that provoked resistance from the workers' parties and organisations and drew them closer together. The German Trades Union Confederation and the SPD, who had previously held very different views about work creation, aimed at a compromise.[126] The unity in the employers' camp must have been particularly strengthened by Papen's constitutional plans for the 'New State' whose implementation would have meant the end of any effective representation of employers' interests. Perhaps Papen needed a 'social peg' like employment provision to effect his plans and to take the heat out of any confrontation with organised labour?

But in many matters relating to work provision, organised labour did not represent the wishes of the total work-force, and the government's socio-political intentions did not go entirely unnoticed. This is particularly well illustrated by the arguments over a statutory reduction in working hours. There seems to have been an identity of interests between the wishes of employers and those employees who were in work. *Soziale Praxis* reported that groups of employees were against the unions' demands for a reduction in the working week, because this would prevent an increase (*sic*) in income.[127] Schleicher was afraid that growth in short-time working would 'lead to increased radicalism amongst the workers' and, therefore, expressed considerable reservations about the reduced working week in factories 'contracted to the Army'.[128] The Minister for Agriculture and Food shared Schleicher's concern over the radicalisation of those who were in work, but also believed that this had to be accepted as a risk because finding work for the unemployed was of 'such importance in domestic policy terms'.[129]

Material available gives no indication of a planned social or economic suppression or division of the work force by Papen's government, and in view of organised labour's understandable objections to the government's intention to emasculate them politically, the Papen government's work creation measures cannot be termed 'socially reactionary' or 'class struggle from the top',[130] but as Bracher put it in another context referring to Brüning,[131] Papen's proposals were 'unpolitical politics' (*unpolitische Politik*). They were certainly not 'welfare politics'.

There was an apparent misunderstanding between the government and their opponents over the government's economic intentions and their opponents' willingness to recognise them, caused partly by the government's tactical and psychological objectives.

Initially, the Chancellor's reform plans made labour organisations justifiably wary. For understandable and legitimate political reasons, the trade unions opposed Papen's economically necessary work creation measures, although *unorganised* labour was favourably disposed towards them. This created a double danger for the unions. First, the government plans for the 'New State' proposed to neutralise them politically; secondly, a policy of job creation removed part of the social justification for employee organisations. It was also possible to foresee that the political power that led Germany out of the misery of unemployment would have 'the whole nation behind them regardless of political party'.[132]

Schleicher's work creation policy represents an attempt to strike a balance between public and private measures. Given political conditions at the time, this could only be a precarious balance. But this was not something that began with Schleicher's period of office. It could already be detected in Papen's time. Braun, the Minister for Agriculture and Food, and Warmbold, the Industry Minister, personified this balance in Papen's Cabinet, and both were also members of the Schleicher Cabinet. In this sense it is possible to talk of a simultaneous discontinuity of policy and continuity of politicians. During Papen's government Braun had already suggested a *Zentralstelle für Arbeitsbeschaffung* (Central Office for Work Provision), an idea that met with little enthusiasm inside the Cabinet.[133] Warmbold, on the other hand, wanted to stimulate production through a revival of private enterprise initiatives.[134] Schleicher's appointment of a Commissioner for Work Creation must, therefore, have fitted in with Braun's agriculturally orientated ideas. Schwerin-Krosigk also points out that there is no other possible explanation for his comment that in deciding in favour of the steady introduction of public work creation programmes, Schleicher was particularly under the influence of the 'landowner' Gerecke. But in the controversy over import quotas, the Schleicher government overruled the wishes of agricultural interest groups. The delicate balance was restored. Warmbold and Braun had to reach an agreement because Schleicher insisted on it in Cabinet.[135] If they could not agree, he was not prepared to have them in the Cabinet.[136] The Provincial Government Council was particularly displeased by the fact that Warmbold could then prevent the import restrictions demanded by landed interests.[137]

To maintain the balance, Warmbold had to accept increased public involvement in direct work creation measures. Schleicher himself endangered this precarious parallelogram of power by his attitude to agricultural aid, which he considered unpromising,[138] and by his sympathetic attitude to the trade unions.[139]

The delicate balance between the various concepts of work creation inside Schleicher's Cabinet is perhaps most clearly illustrated by Günter Gerecke,[140] the Commissioner for Work Creation. The broad political spectrum of his organisation had already roused the interests of the Papen government. But by November 1932 his suggestions for job provision no longer seemed to have commanded widespread support. In his briefing report to Schleicher in November 1932, Bredow wrote that after talking to many of Gerecke's 'support groups', he could no longer claim the existence of a 'really strong' front 'ranging from National Socialists to the SPD'.[141] Gerecke's colleague, Kordemann, who tried to establish contact with the Trades Union Confederation in August 1932 as Gregor Strasser's link man,[142] provoked tension with Hitler. The latter demanded that Kordemann, a National Socialist Party member, should give up his work with Gerecke. Kordemann refused, resigned his party offices, but remained a party member.[143]

The common ground between Strasser and the trade unions cannot have been very large, as both, according to a comment by Strasser, were hoping to win the support of the same social groups by work creation programmes. In front of the leader of the Free Trade Union of Bank Employees, Marx, Gregor Strasser explained to Tarnow, his opposite number from the German Trades Union Confederation in discussions, that the National Socialist Party 'ought now to attract the support of the working people'.[144] Tarnow disputed this. The policy would not win support for the NS Party from the 'class-conscious workers' and would only lose them the backing of the lower middle classes. But Gregor Strasser believed that the middle classes were 'so stupid that you could tell them anything'.[145]

Gerecke, the Commissioner for Work Creation, tried to gain the support of the employers' representatives, who according to his own reports[146] combined with the Provincial Government Council to make polemic attacks on his plans (the exceptions being Otto Wolff and Tilo von Wilmowsky). He protested that there was no conflict between his work creation programmes and the interests of private enterprise.[147]

Schleicher's announcement in his first Cabinet session[148] that the socio-political measures under the 5 September emergency decree were to be revoked was certainly in line with the wishes of the German Trades Union Confederation.[149] As early as 29 November, Liepart urged Schleicher to end the supplementary employment premiums, on the grounds that they had had 'no noticeable effect'.[150]

According to Gerecke, the employment bonuses were also opposed by 'large sections of industry and agriculture'.[151] The delicate balance in work creation policies was in no way disturbed by the suspension of the pay policy measures of 5 September.

The 'Principles for a Work Creation Programme' that Gerecke submitted to the Ministerial Committee for Work Creation on 19 December 1932 were more socio-politically motivated.[152] They foresaw public sources as the exclusive providers of employment with first priority in the allocation of contracts being given to districts with a high proportion of unemployed. Work should not be awarded to 'general contractors', i.e. to one single large firm, but to smaller and medium-sized concerns.[153] Tax credits for the resulting increase in employment were to be taken into account in assessing quotes made and were supposed to lead to lower tenders from companies. In fulfilling the contracts companies were to revert as far as possible to manual labour.

The reactions of specific interest groups to the Schleicher government's work provision policy are made clear in a discussion between Industry Minister Warmbold and representatives of the leading industrial organisations on 19 December 1932.[154] The representatives of the German Employers' Federation and the German Council for Trade and Industry raised the question of import quotas, strengthening their rejection of import restrictions and appealing at the same time for an unrestricted trade policy. The representatives of wholesale and export trades, the leading association of private traders, and, surprisingly the craft unions spoke out against subsidies,[155] and also pointed out the favourable effect on employment provision of a suspension of house rental tax. The representatives of the craft unions also asked for supplementary funds for house renovation programmes, in addition to the 100,000,000 Reichsmark security already agreed by the government[156] and were in favour of leaving authorisation for these programmes in the hands of the Labour Minister rather than transferring it to Gerecke. They evidently did not expect Gerecke to appreciate their needs fully. Their distant attitude to him is hardly surprising when one considers that available sources make no reference to the involvement of craft unions in the formulation of the German Provincial Government Council's work creation programme. They could not conceal a certain disappointment about Gerecke's specific work creation policy, which had 'aroused general hopes' and asked what, apart from announcements, was actually happening. The push from the craftsmen's representatives does not seem to have been entirely without success and it turned out that Labour Minister Syrup was the right man as far as the craftsmen's demands relating to renovation work were concerned. On 23 December, in a memorandum to the Finance Minister,[157] he put the case for continuing renovation work, dividing up flats in old buildings, creating settlements on the edge of town, plus government loans for private house-building. An order from the Minister of Labour followed on 24 January 1933 envisaging 50,000,000 Reichsmarks as a guarantee for lost renovation and partition subsidies and as a contribution towards the cost of converting other premises into flats.[158] Tiburtius, a member of the Hauptgemeinschaft, specifically backed the craftsmen's proposals concerning work creation. In addition, he recommended the continuation of settlements on the land, which was very significant for the employment market, but was critical of the *Osthilfe*, a view that the spokesmen of the German Council of Commerce and Industry endorsed.

Apart from the craft unions, representatives of leading industrial organisations showed no particular signs of discontent with Schleicher's work creation policies and the government in any case soon made a goodwill gesture to the craftsmen. The suggestions and wishes of economists related far more to problems that were rooted in Papen's period in office.

But representatives of the German Central Association of Banks and Bankers made a crucial distinction: they wanted to know from the Industry Minister whether the Schleicher government was aiming towards a free or a centrally planned economy. This question, even though it was put in an extreme form, touches on the central problem in Schleicher's work creation programme. Preserving the delicate balance between various interests led to uncertainty as to the government's chosen course in organisational and economic policy. This impression must have been strengthened by the fact that in disputes over matters relating to work creation policy, first the protagonists of one point of view, then those of another gained the upper hand. In the controversies inside the Cabinet over the role of public works programmes and limitations on agricultural imports, the opposing viewpoints were clearly personified by Ministers Warmbold and Braun.

This conflict was another heritage from Papen's period in office, when the demands of agriculturalists for increased state intervention in the economy could be weakened by import quota policies. This was the price that those supporting the reactivation of private industry had to pay at the time. But what was already a delicate balance in a disputed area during Papen's government became even more precarious under Schleicher, following the removal of import restrictions on agricultural produce. This was another result of Schleicher's general policy concepts. In contrast to Papen, he worked on the arithmetically clear, but internally inconsistent, principle that he could not govern successfully without the consent of employer organisations and sections of the NSDAP.[159] And this shook the delicate but still surviving balance from Papen's day, in favour of a different balance that was aimed at but never achieved.

However favourable Schleicher's political objectives seemed to a successful implementation of work creation programmes without resorting to authoritarian or totalitarian methods, and however promising they might have been, and promised to be, in economic and sociopolitical terms (even in 'welfare policy' terms for the ordinary citizen) they were nevertheless unrealistic under the circumstances at the time. Neither the supporters of an economic order geared to the needs of private industry nor the representatives of the trade unions or of agriculture, who admittedly were in favour of increased public intervention for very different reasons, were fully satisfied.

In the end, Schleicher fell between all the stools. Uncertainty over the government's line in economic policy remained and led inevitably in such uneasy times to new insecurity. The policy did not generate confidence, because it lacked a clear standpoint, which is what was needed at the time. But without confidence in the continuity of general and organisational policy, no increase in private industry's propensity to invest could be expected.

Schleicher was aiming at too heterogeneous a political spectrum, which stood as little chance of survival as the former 'work creation coalition' in the German Provincial Government Council, led by the Commissioner for Work Creation. The unemployment problem and the crisis in the economy could not be resolved without a secure political regime, and the interested parties showed no signs of being willing to reach a workable political compromise which would have allowed the crisis to be solved without the use of terror tactics.

Summary

The work creation policies of the Brüning government were characterised by crisis management, lacking in true perspective, and made more difficult by external political circumstances. Brüning's successor Papen pursued economic policy concepts which could have led to a 'welfare state' as an incidental by-product. (The term was first used by Papen in his inaugural speech on 2 June 1932 in a dismissive sense.) The welfare of the 'subjects' or citizens would have been stabilised by the 'New State'. The objective was, however, the reconstruction of the state, and the provision of help for landowners.

Schleicher set welfare state priorities for the citizens, but was too indecisive. The various groups and parties had too different interpretations of what constituted 'welfare'. Even — or perhaps particularly — a welfare state requires compromise as a basic political principle, i.e. the willingness to relinquish some interests. This is indispensable in resolving an acute emergency situation.

Notes

1. I have dealt with this topic extensively in M. Wolffsohn, *Industrie und Handwerk im Konflikt mit staatlicher Wirtschaftspolitik? Studien zur Politik der*

Arbeitsbeschaffung in Deutschland 1930-1934 (Berlin, 1977). The central issue in these studies is whether or not interest-determined priorities can be detected in work creation policies during those years. The following groups were taken into account in the research: major industrialists from various industries; medium-sized companies; central and local craftsmen's organisations.

2. 'Arbeitsmarkt/Arbeitslosenhilfe', *Soziale Praxis*, no. 49, 7 Dec. 1933, pp. 1428 ff. Also Leo Grebler, 'Work Creation Policy in Germany 1932-1935', *International Labour Review*, vol. 35 (1937), p. 336.

3. Memorandum from the Transport Minister (Treviranus) to the Secretary of State for the Chancellery concerning work creation, 19 Mar. 1932, BAK R 2/18646.

4. Cf. H. Clark, *Swedish Unemployment Policy 1914-1940* (Washington, DC, 1941); A. Montgomery, *How Sweden Overcame the Depression 1930-1933* (Stockholm, 1938).

5. Cf. Yonathan Shapiro, *The Formative Years of the Israeli Labour Party 1919-1930* (London/Beverly Hills, 1976); also Y. Shapiro, *Democracy in Israel* (Hebrew) (Ramat-Gan, 1977), p. 71.

6. Cf. on the concept of pro- and anti-system parties Giovanni Sartori, *Parties and Party Systems* (Cambridge, 1976).

7. Statistics in Wolffsohn, *Industrie und Handwerk*, Ch. 1.

8. Ibid.

9. Eg. Emil Carlebach, *Von Brüning zu Hitler. Das Geheimnis der faschistischen Machtergreifung* (Frankfurt am Main, 1971). Wolfgang Ruge, 'Heinrich Brünings posthume Selbstentlarvung', *Zeitschrift für Geschichtswissenschaft* (1971), pp. 1261-73.

10. Compiled and calculated from BAK R 43 I/1142 − 1170. Unemployment figures are taken from Willi Hemmer, *Die unsichtbaren Arbeitslosen. Statistische Methoden − soziale Tatsachen* (Zeulenroda, 1935), pp. 184 ff. Where more than one Cabinet session took place on a given day, each one is reckoned separately. Other figures can be deduced: Wolffsohn, *Industrie und Handwerk*.

11. Eg. Eberhard Czichon, *Wer verhalf Hitler zur Macht?* (Cologne, 1967).

12. Cf. for more detail Michael Schneider, *Das Arbeitsbeschaffungsprogramm des ADGB* (Bonn/Bad Godesberg, 1975).

13. A detailed answer cannot be made within the framework of this chapter. I must therefore refer to the second part of my work already quoted.

14. BAK R 2/18815 − 18829 (vol. 18821 is not available).

15. BAK R 43 I/2047 and R 43/538.

16. Compiled from *Der Arbeitgeber*, years 1930-3.

17. Industry Minister Dietrich to the Secretary of State for the Chancellery, 14 May 1930; BAK R 43 I/2037 (Pünder).

18. Minister of Posts Schätzel to the Secretary of State for the Chancellery, 14 May 1930, BAK R 43 I/2037.

19. Extract from the minutes of the Ministerial discussions of 19 May 1930, loc. cit.

20. W.J. Helbich, *Die Reparationen in der Ära Brüning. Zur Bedeutung des Young-Planes für die deutsche Politik 1930-1932* (Berlin, 1962) and Henning Köhler, 'Arbeitsbeschaffung, Siedlung und Reparationen in der Schlussphase der Regierung Brüning', *Vierteljahreshefte für Zeitgeschichte*, vol. 17 (1969), pp. 276-307 deal comprehensively but conflictingly with this question. For the purpose of our debate, this controversy is completely uninteresting in so far as the borderline between historical science and detective work has become fluid.

21. Extract from the minutes of the Ministerial discussions of 19 May 1930, BAK R 43/2037.

22. Minutes of the Ministry session, 30 July 1930, BAK R 43 I/2038.

23. Minutes of the Ministry session, 24 July 1930, BAK R 43 I/1446,

24. Schätzel to the Chancellor, 23 June 1930, BAK R 43 I/2938.
25. Minutes of the Ministerial discussion of 21 July 1930, BAK R 43 I/2038.
26. Ibid.
27. Minister of Labour to the Secretary of State for the Chancellery, 15 July 1930, BAK R 2/18813.
28. Labour Minister to Transport Minister and Minister of Posts, 1 Aug. 1930, loc. cit.
29. Labour Minister to the Prussian Minister for Trade and Skilled Crafts, 1 Aug. 1930, loc. cit.
30. Minutes of the Ministerial session, 30 July 1930, BAK R 43 I/2038.
31. Minutes of the Cabinet session of 11 Nov. 1930, BAK R 43 I/1147.
32. W. Grotkopp also refers to this in *Die grosse Krise. Lehren aus der Überwindung der Wirtschaftskrise 1929/32* (Düsseldorf, 1956), p. 174; Köhler, 'Arbeitsbeschaffung', has completely overlooked this.
33. Cf. for further detail Wolffsohn, *Industrie und Handwerk*.
34. Submission by the Industry Minister, 11 Apr. 1932, BAK R 43 I/1455.
35. Minutes of the Ministerial discussions, 20 Mar. 1931, BAK R 43 I/1449.
36. Cabinet paper, 1 Feb. 1932, BAK R 43 I/1455.
37. Minutes of the Ministry session, 2 Mar. 1932, loc. cit.
38. Cabinet paper, 1 Feb. 1932, loc. cit.
39. Ministry session, 2 Mar. 1932, loc. cit.
40. Submission by the Finance Minister on work provision, 11 Apr. 1932, BAK R 43 I/2045.
41. Finance Minister Dietrich to Chancellor Brüning, 3 Sept. 1931. BAK R 43 I/1452 and BAK Dietrich Papers, 307.
42. Submission of Ministerialrat Poerschke: 'Programm zur Minderung der Arbeitslosigkeit durch Schaffung von Kleinsiedlerstellen', 5 Aug. 1931, BAK R 2/1921.
43. Horst Sanmann, 'Daten und Alternativen der deutschen Wirtschafts- und Finanzpolitik in der Ära Brüning', *Hamburger Jahrbuch für Wirschafts- und Gesellschaftspolitik*, no. 10 (1965), pp. 109-39.
44. Cf. for the years leading up to 1932 Jörg-Otto Spiller, 'Reformismus nach rechts. Zur Politik des Reichsverbandes der Deutschen Industrie in den Jahren 1927-1930 am Beispiel der Reparationspolitik' in Hans Mommsen, Dietmar Petzina and Bernd Weisbrod (eds.), *Industrielles System und politische Entwicklung in der Weimarer Republik* (Düsseldorf, 1974), pp. 593 ff. Also Wolffsohn, *Industrie und Handwerk*, Part Two.
45. Memorandum from the Transport Minister concerning the deliberations of the National Economic Council on 23 Feb. 1932. Sent to the Secretary of State for the Chancellery, 19 Mar. 1932, BAK R 2/18646.
46. Note concerning the agenda for the Cabinet session of 28 Apr. 1932, BAK R 43 I/1455.
47. Hans Schäffer's diary, 30 June 1932. Conversation between Brüning and Schäffer, Institute für Zeitgeschichte, ED 93/21. As proof, Schäffer showed Brüning on 14 July 1932 the minutes of the meeting with the union which took place in October 1931 at the Hotel Adlon, loc cit., 14 July 1932.
48. Cf. the chapter on heavy industry in Wolffsohn, *Industrie und Handwerk*.
49. Schäffer's diary, 28 July 1932, IFZ ED 93/21; cf. also conversation between Schäffer and Otto Wolff, 13 Aug. 1932, loc. cit. In this conversation Wolff explained that 'industrial confidence' in Trendelenburg was high. Gerecke writes in his memoirs that Trendelenburg introduced Brüning to 'a small circle of industrialists and bankers': G. Gerecke, *Ich war königlich-preussischer Landrat* (Berlin (DDR), 1970), p. 163. Cf. also Schwerin-Krosigk records, IFZ ZS/A 20, vol. 4.

50. Exchange of views on the Lautenbach plan. Confidential departmental discussion in the Industry Ministry, 12 Feb. 1932, BAK R 43 I/2045.

51. Schäffer to Wagemann, 28 Jan. 1932. Schäffer's diary, IFZ ED 93/32.

52. File entry concerning the discussion in the Ministry of Labour on 1 Apr. 1932 about work creation, BAK R 43 I/2045 and an entry about the discussion in the Industry Ministry, 5 Apr. 1932, loc. cit.

53. From 1926 until shortly before Brüning's dismissal Rüstow was an official constitutional adviser in the Industry Ministry and worked closely with Lautenbach and Trendelenburg. I learnt this in a talk with Professor Hans-Joachim Rüstow on 26 October 1973 at his home in Allmanshausen on the Starnberger See.

54. Cf. for further detail Wolffsohn, *Industrie und Handwerk*, pp. 68 ff.

55. Memoir from the Transport Minister to the Secretary of State for the Chancellery about the deliberations of the national economic council on 23 Feb. 1932. Dated 19 Mar. 1932, BAK R 43 2/18646.

56. Loc. cit.

57. Köhler, 'Arbeitsbeschaffung', p. 279.

58. Departmental Heads discussion, 25 Jan. 1932, BAK R 43 I/2042.

59. Departmental Heads discussion, 20 Jan. 1932, loc. cit.

60. Köhler claims this in Henning Köhler, 'Sozialpolitik von Brüning bis Schleicher', *Vierteljahreshefte für Zeitgeschichte*, vol. 21 (1973), p. 148. Does this not indicate a contradiction between this statement by Köhler and his hypothesis that the Brüning government was taking a socio-political line in its approach to work creation matters? According to Köhler, the remark was made by Stegerwald in a Cabinet session on 4 Mar. 1932. Checking this out in Hans Schäffer's diary showed that it must have taken place on 14 March. (Köhler based his statement on this source.)

61. Although the 'Deutschen Führerbriefe' (DF), which had close links with heavy industry (confirmed in Wolffsohn, *Industrie und Handwerk*), believed that Warmbold was also in favour of this 'crazy' plan (DF 3 May 1932).

62. Minutes of the Ministerial meeting, 25 May 1932, BAK R 43 I/2043.

63. Departmental Heads discussion, 25 Jan. 1932, BAK R 43 I/2042.

64. Extract from the minutes of the Ministerial session of 12 Apr. 1932, BAK R 43 I/2042.

65. BAK Luther's posthumous papers, vol. 368. Entry by Luther dated 6 May 1932.

66. Comment by the Secretary of State for the Chancellery, 2 Mar. 1932, BAK R 43 I/2045. Also file entry concerning a Ministerial discussion, 1 Apr. 1932, loc. cit., and Departmental Heads discussion of 11 Apr. 1932, AVfK DGT B/3030. Note for the attention of the President of the German Provincial Government Council.

67. D. Petzina, 'Élemente der Wirtschaftspolitik in der Spätphase der Weimarer Republik', *VjhZG*, vol. 21 (1973), p. 129, shows the ambiguity of Brüning's economic policy on the basis of the conflict between a 'bureaucratic-interventionist' economic policy and one based on liberalism arising out of the experience of the immediate pre-war period. Petzina believes (pp. 132 ff.) that a change in economic policy was impossible at the time, because the Brüning government lacked the 'stabilising base of popular support'. If this is the case, however, it is legitimate to ask whether Papen, who pursued a changed economic policy, had this 'stabilising base of popular support'.

68. Cf. Wolffsohn, *Industrie und Handwerk*, pp. 78 ff.

69. See previous chapter.

70. Luther's posthumous papers. Entries on 25 Aug. 1932 and 27 Aug. 1932, BAK Luther's posthumous papers 369.

71. 'Deutsche Führerbriefe', 2 Sept. 1932, IFZ.

72. Schwerin-Krosigk, IFZ ZS/A-20, vol. 4. Cf. also the reference from Finance Minister Dietrich in the previous chapter (partial extract, Fazit 1931).

73. Parliamentary Under-Secretary in the Ministry of Defence to Bredow, June 1932 (no exact date), Army Military Archive, Bredow's posthumous papers, N 67/1.

74. Schwerin-Krosigk ZS/A-20, vol. 4.

75. Treviranus to Regedanz 22 June 1932, Army Military Archive. Schleicher's posthumous papers, N42/22.

76. 'Deutsche Führerbriefe', 22 Jan 1932.

77. Taken from BAK R 43 I/1166; also *Frankfurter Zeitung*, 18 June 1932.

78. Schwerin-Krosigk IFZ ZS/A-20, vol. 4.

79. Schäffer Papers, ED 93/46. Grotkopp, *Die grosse Krise*, p. 173, writes that Ilgner was involved in the development of the Wagemann Plan.

80. For example the reaction of Frieda Wunderlich, 'Jahreswende-Krisenwende?', *Soziale Praxis*, 5 Jan. 1933, p. 5.

81. See particularly the Schäffer entries for 2 July 1932 and 6 July 1932, IFZ ED 93/21, which form the basis for this account.

82. This information comes from an extract from the Schäffer entry for 2 July 1932. Schäffer learnt about it in a telephone conversation with the Press Officer at the Industry Ministry.

83. Record of the conversation with Secretary of State, Planck. Entry dated 6 July 1932, loc. cit.

84. In the end only Papen, Schleicher, Home Secretary Gayl and Braun, the Minister for Food and Agriculture, voted for import quotas. Secret file entry, concerning a discussion between Ministry Director Posse, Dr Spitta (wholesale and foreign trade) and von Brakel (Confederation of German Industry), Krupp Archive, undated, FAH IV E 180.

85. Letter from the 'Reichslandbund' (National Agricultural Alliance), signed by Kalckreuth, to W.J. Reichert of the German Iron and Steel Industries Council, 21 Dec. 1932, HA/GHH (Historical Archive of the Gutehoffnungshütte AV Oberhausen), Reusch Papers, 40010124/3a.

86. D. Petzina, 'Elemente', pp. 127 ff.

87. Minutes of the Ministerial discussions, 2 June 1932, loc cit.

88. Minutes of the Ministerial discussions, 14 June 1932, loc. cit.

89. Minutes of the Ministerial discussions, 3 June 1932, loc. cit.

90. Minister for Food and Agriculture (von Braun) to Chancellor Papen, 22 June 1932, BAK R 43 I/2045.

91. He had already made this suggestion to the Cabinet on the previous day. Minutes of the Ministerial discussions, 21 June 1932, BAK R 43 I/456.

92. Cf. Schwerin-Krosigk IFZ ZS/A – 20 vols., I and IV. Also S. von Kanitz to Schleicher, 29 Nov. 1932; Army Military Archive, Schleicher's posthumous papers N 42/31 and the letter from the National Agricultural Alliance signed by Kalckreuth to W.J. Reichert, 21 Dec. 1932, HA/GHH Reutsch Papers, 40010124/3a.

93. Minutes of the Ministerial discussions, 11 July 1932, BAK R 43 I/1457.

94. D. Petzina, 'Hauptprobleme der deutschen Wirtschaftspolitik 1932/3', *VjhZG*, vol. 15 (1967), p. 20. Filed under IFZ MA 151/16.

95. Schneider, *Arbeitsbeschaffung, passim*.

96. Note on a discussion concerning suburban settlements held on 22 June 1932 between the Minister of Labour, the Secretary of State for the Chancellery, the Secretary of State for the Treasury and the Commissioner for Suburban Settlements, Sassen, BAK R 2/19123.

97. Minister of Labour Schäffer to Finance Minister Schwerin-Krosigk,

18 Aug. 1932, BAK R 2/18647.
98. Here, as in the following, minutes of the Ministerial discussions of 21 July 1932, BAK R 43 I/1457.
99. Draft Economic Plan for the Papen government. Discussion paper laid before the Ministerial discussion group, 28 July 1932, BAK R 43 I/1457.
100. Minutes of the Ministerial discussions, 28 July 1932, loc. cit.
101. Ibid.
102. Petzina, 'Hauptprobleme der deutschen Wirtschaftspolitik', p. 21, puts the emphasis for the breakthrough in economic policy more firmly on the election victories of the National Socialist Party.
103. Minutes of the Ministerial discussions of 10 Aug. 1932, BAK R 43 I/1457.
104. Ibid.
105. Minutes of the Ministerial discussions of 26 Aug. 1932, BAK R 43 I/1457.
106. The SPD were also pursuing similar plans, as well as the KPD. See Schneider, *Arbeitsbeschaffung*, pp. 155 ff. and Czichon, *Wer verhalf Hitler zur Macht?*, p. 135, note 108.
107. Minutes of the Ministerial discussions, 27 Aug. 1932, BAK R 43 I/1457. The 'draft directives for the increase and maintenance of job opportunities' envisaged a minimum contribution of 10.00 RM; cf. Minutes of the Ministerial discussions, 27 Aug. 1932, loc. cit. The other figures are also taken from the Ministerial discussions, 26 Aug. 1932, loc. cit.
108. Weekly action report of the German Confederation of Industry, no. 19 (1932), 8 Sept. 1932, Krupp Archive FAH IV E 180, discussion in the Industry Ministry. Present were the Ministers for Industry, Labour and Finance, Luther, Kraemer and Kastl of the RDI, Brauweiler from the VDA, Bernstein and Solmssen from the Central Association of Banks and Bank Employees, Ravené and Keinath (German wholesale and foreign trade), Hamm and Demuth (German Chamber of Commerce and Industry), Grünfeld and Tiburtius (Hauptgemeinschaft) and Kuntze (Craftsmen). Cf. also the German Chamber of Commerce and Industry (DIHT) circular dated 7 Sept. 1932, BAK Silverberg Papers, 250. Grünfeld and Kuntze put forward these views.
109. During the Ministerial discussion of 3 Sept. 1932, BAK R 43 I/1457.
110. Deposition by Secretary of State Meissner on the discussions in Neudeck on 30 Aug. 1932, Army Military Archive Schleicher's posthumous papers, N 42/22.
111. *A-Letter* (*A-Brief*), no. 266, dated 19 Aug. 1932.
112. *Berliner Tageblatt*, 18 Oct. 1932. Also AVfK DGT B/2054 I.
113. Minutes of the Ministerial discussions of 31 Aug. 1932, BAK R 43 I/1457.
114. BAK R 43 I/2046.
115. Ibid.
116. Gerecke to the Secretary of State for the Chancellery on 27 Sept. 32, BAK R 43 I/2046.
117. Gerecke, p. 7. describes himself as 'one who recognises the humanistic [sic] policies that the GDR Government has pursued energetically and constructively from the outset'.
118. Ibid., p. 171; on scientific advice, Eberhard Czichon, Schwerin-Krosigk (IFZ ZS/A – 20, vol. 8) points out in detail various of Gerecke's errors. Above all, he describes as 'crazy' the assertion made by Gerecke that Schleicher in urging the Cabinet to adopt a public works job creation policy was trying to 'dynamite' the Papen Cabinet. Schwerin-Krosigk emphasises that the Cabinet in any case already pursued a policy of work creation and credit generation.

The point at issue was simply whether or not local government should be more directly involved in financing the projects, as Gerecke wanted.

119. Gerecke, p. 191.

120. Gerecke writes that he yielded to 'Hindenburg's pressure'; ibid., p. 233.

121. Minutes of the Ministerial meeting, 29 Sept. 1932, BAK R 43 I/1457.

122. Minutes of the Ministerial meeting, 12 Sept. 1932, BAK R 43 I/1457.

123. Minutes of the Ministerial meeting, 3 Sept. 1932, BAK R 43 I/1457.

124. Draft government policy statement for parliament, 3 Sept. 1932, loc. cit.

125. Frieda Wunderlich and Wilhelm Polligkeit, 'Jahreswende – Krisenwende', *Soziale Praxis*, Zentralblatt für Sozialpolitik und Wohlfahrtspflege, 5 Jan. 1932, p. 2.

126. See Schneider, *Arbeitsbeschaffung*, section III. The differences between the ADGB and the SPD cannot be discussed in detail here, and Schneider in any case deals with them comprehensively.

127. Wunderlich and Polligkeit, 'Jahreswende', p. 8.

128. Schleicher to the Minister of Labour, 17 Dec. 1932, loc. cit.

129. Minister for Food & Agriculture to Minister of Labour, loc. cit, 27 Dec. 1932.

130. Schneider, *Arbeitsbeschaffung*, p. 192, quote from Leipart.

131. Karl-Dietrich Bracher, 'Brünings unpolitische Politik und die Auflösung der Weimarer Republik', *VjhZG*, vol. 19 (1971), pp. 113-23.

132. 'Die Möglichkeiten des Generals von Schleicher', unsigned paper 'according to the American point of view', 29 June 1932, BA Military Archive, Schleicher Papers, N42/22.

133. Czichon, *Wer Verhalf Hitler zur Macht?*, p. 45.

134. Schwerin-Krosigk IFZ ZS/A – 20, vol. 1; also Industry Minister Warmbold to Finance Minister Schwerin-Krosigk, 7 Dec. 1932, BAK R 2/18659. Warmbold's letter covers 'general questions of work creation' including the Gerecke Programme.

135. Schwerin-Krosigk IFZ ZS/A – 20, vol. I.

136. Ibid., vol. IV.

137. Letter from the National Agricultural Alliance (signed Kalckreuth) to W.J. Reichert from VDESI, 21 Dec. 1932, HA/GHH Reusch Papers 40010124/3a.

138. Schleicher to Major A.T. von Müldner, 20 Sept. 1930, BA Military Archive, Schleicher Papers, N42/52.

139. According to Hans Schäffer, the trade unions approved of Schleicher because they 'had something military about them' (Hans Schäffer's diary, 1 Aug. 1932, IFZ ED 93/22). According to Woytinski, Schleicher considered the union members 'good honest German men' (Wladimir Woytinski, *A Stormy Passage. A Personal History through two Russian Revolutions to Democracy and Freedom: 1905-1960* (New York, 1961), p. 473).

140. Schwerin-Krosigk IFZ ZS/A – 20, vol. I.

141. Information report by Bredow to Schleicher, 25 Nov. 1932, BA Military Archive, Bredow's posthumous papers, 97/2.

142. See Schneider, *Arbeitsbeschaffung*, pp. 153 ff.

143. Information report by Bredow to Schleicher, 10 Jan. 1933, BA Military Archive, Bredow's posthumous papers, 97/3.

144. Hans Schäffer's diary, 10 Oct. 1932, IFZ ED 93/23. Marx told Schäffer about this conversation. Schneider, *Arbeitsbeschaffung*, p. 154, did not believe that it had been 'definitively proven' whether or not there was any contact between the ADGB and Gregor Strasser.

145. Ibid.

146. Gerecke, p. 201. But Gerecke himself seems to have had reservations as early as October 1932 about his own plan. Cf. Colonel Bredow to Schleicher, 25 Oct. 1932, BA Military Archive, Schleicher Papers N42/22.

147. Foreword by Gerecke to Nimetz/Grünewald, *Das Sofortprogramm des Reichskommissars für Arbeitsbeschaffung* (Berlin, 1933), p. 4.

148. Minutes of the Ministerial discussions, 3 Dec. 1932, BAK R 43I/1458.

149. Cf. the memorandum from Leipart Schleicher, 29 Nov. 1932, AVfK DGT B/2054 II.

150. Ibid., also in what follows.

151. Entry concerning the session of the Ministerial Working Party on Work Creation, 19 Dec. 1932, BAK R 43 II/540c.

152. 'Basis for a Work Creation Programme', 19 Dec. 1932, BAK R 43 II/540.

153. The conditions for implementing the National Socialist work programme contained similar provisions.

154. Record of a discussion between the Industry Minister and the leading industrial organisations, 19 Dec. 1932, Krupp Archive, FAH IV E 185. As government representatives, the following took part in the discussions alongside the Industry Minister: Secretary of State Schwartzkopf, the Ministerial Heads Reinhardt, Posse and Heintze, the Ministerial advisers Hoppe and Ronde, as well as 'a few government advisers'. The Confederation of German Industry was represented by von Simson, Kraemer, Kastl, Herle and Heinecke. Grund (the President), Huber and Demuth spoke for the German Chamber of Commerce and Industry. Derlien and Herrmann came from the National Association of Skilled Trades Craftsmen, and Engel and Keinath from the National Alliance for Wholesale and Overseas Trade. The interests of the German Retailers' Association were represented by Tiburtius, and Solmssen and Bernstein were present on behalf of the Central Association of Banks and Banking.

155. The rejection of subsidies by the National Association of Skilled Trades Craftsmen is surprising because Heinrich August Winkler's study of the middle classes gives numerous instances of support for subsidies amongst craftsmen. There was clearly a considerable difference between the programme and the behaviour of these organisations. There was no wish to see others receive subsidies.

156. Minutes of the Ministerial discussions of 14 Dec. 1932, BAK R 43 I/1458.

157. Minister of Labour Syrup to Finance Minister Schwerin-Krosigk, 23 Dec. 1932, BAK R 43 I/2046.

158. Deutsche Bau- und Bodenbank AG – Deutsche Gesellschaft für öffentliche Arbeiten, 'Die Entwicklung der deutschen Bauwirtschaft und die Arbeitsbeschaffung in Jahre 1933', p. 65.

159. Cf. Karl-Dietrich Bracher, Wolfgang Sauer, Gerhard Schulz, *Die nationalsozialistische Machtergreifung* (Cologne/Opladen, 1962), p. 41, on Schleicher's objectives.

PART THREE

THE BREAKTHROUGH OF THE WELFARE STATE
AFTER THE SECOND WORLD WAR

12 SOME ASPECTS OF SOCIAL POLICY IN BRITAIN DURING THE SECOND WORLD WAR

J. Harris

Until very recently the history of British social policy during the Second World War has been dominated by the shadow of Richard Titmuss, whose book *Problems of Social Policy* was widely recognised as one of the most impressive contributions to the Civil Series of the Official War Histories. Titmuss's book in no sense attempted to be a comprehensive history of all aspects of social policy throughout the war period. On the contrary, it concentrated almost exclusively on areas of social policy designed to meet the war emergency — namely, provision for evacuation, the Emergency Hospital Service, and help for the victims of air attack. The book said little about wartime developments in the non-emergency areas of social policy or about the planning of post-war reconstruction; and it ignored all the crucial areas in which wartime discussion of social policy closely overlapped with economic and fiscal policies such as control of unemployment, social services budgeting, the outline of a post-war housing programme and proposals for public control of the development and use of land. Nevertheless, on the basis of his research into war emergency services Titmuss attempted to formulate a general interpretation of wartime social policy, which has often been cited by historians and sociologists — such as Marwick, Pelling, Abrams and Andreski — as part of the much wider debate on the interrelationship of war and social change.[1] Titmuss saw the war as affecting the history of welfare on three different levels — popular attitudes, information about social problems, and governmental response. He argued that the circumstances of the Second World War created an unprecedented sense of social solidarity among the British people, which made them willing to accept a great increase of egalitarian policies and collectivist state intervention. He claimed that the impact of bombing and evacuation had dramatically exposed certain chronic social evils that had hitherto lain concealed from the public eye — problems like child poverty, malnutrition and the gross geographical imbalance of health and medical services that prevailed at the start of the war. And he thought that the war for the first time made central government fully aware, not merely of the moral desirability but of the sheer strategic necessity for having a civilian population that was contented, efficient, well nourished and physically fit. All these pressures, Titmuss concluded, came to the fore at the time of the retreat from Dunkirk: they meant that

> for five years of war the pressures for a higher standard of welfare and a deeper comprehension of social justice steadily gained in strength . . . the mood of the people changed and, in sympathetic response, values changed as well. . . Dunkirk, and all that the name evokes, was an important event in the wartime history of the social services. It summoned forth a note of self-criticism, of national introspection, and it set in motion ideas and talk of principles and plans.[2]

These plans, moreover, were more than merely a crisis response to a temporary situation; they were to provide a practical and ethical framework for the long-term reconstruction of British society when the war came to an end.

Titmuss's analysis was a bold attempt to impose a coherent pattern on the vast mass of wartime social policy documentation; and few who have read *Problems of Social Policy* can have failed to be impressed by the skill and imagination with which he mastered prosaic technical questions and made the dry bones of administrative history spring to life. It is not, however, surprising that, as wartime documents have been opened up to non-official historians, Titmuss's interpretation of wartime social policy seems increasingly to need some kind of refinement and modification. Of recent works only P.J.H.J. Gosden's quasi-official study of the wartime education services seems fully to support the Titmuss thesis – concluding that the war acted as a crucible within which public opinion was 'revitalised' and official education policies were galvanised to life.[3] By contrast, the conclusions of other recent historians have been considerably more ambivalent and more cautious. Paul Addison's study *The Road to 1945* endorsed the view that the war helped to forge a new political consensus, but suggested at the same time that the atmosphere of optimistic social solidarity was by no means as universal as Titmuss seemed to suppose. Addison argued, moreover, that the consensus 'represented a dilution of Conservative rather than Labour politics' and that it was important mainly in the upper reaches of the political system, among 'the upper middle-class of socially-concerned professional people, of whom Beveridge and Keynes were the patron saints'.[4] More specifically, the work of Land

and MacNicol on the history of family allowances found little evidence
of a new governmental concern with the problem of family poverty or
with promoting physical efficiency. Instead they suggested that family
allowances were introduced partly to curb wage demands and to
palliate wartime taxation, and partly to maintain an individualised
version of the old Poor Law principle of 'less eligibility'.[5] My own
research on Beveridge suggested that, far from seizing upon social
reconstruction as a morale-boosting exercise for winning the war,
the initial reaction of most politicians and civil servants was to regard
it as an inconvenient luxury that could not be seriously considered
until after the return of peace.[6] All these studies lead one to pose the
question of how far the Titmuss thesis, extracted mainly from the
wartime emergency services, can be legitimately applied to wartime
social policy as a whole — to those developments in thinking about full
employment, income maintenance, social security and the setting up
of a national health service that we loosely associate with the coming
of the welfare state.

In this chapter I shall not attempt to formulate any alternative
hypothesis to that of Titmuss — in fact I think it would be premature
to do so until more extensive research into wartime and post-war
domestic politics has been carried out. I shall, however, try to draw
out certain interesting features of wartime social policy formation —
features that seem at least partly to explain both the relative speed
with which wartime reforms were adopted and the ultimate failure
of such reforms to meet the political and economic requirements
of the post-war period. To draw out these themes, I shall look mainly
at the areas of reform associated with the influence of Beveridge; that
is, primarily the reconstruction of social security and to a lesser extent
the promotion of full employment. To do this I shall look not only at
the Beveridge Report, but at the work of the cluster of official and
quasi-official committees that produced or criticised the Beveridge
Report and worked on its practical implementation. I shall examine
the light that they throw upon the political assumptions behind wartime social policy formation and upon both popular and official expectations of the post-war welfare system. I shall consider also just how
far they substantiate Titmuss's perception of the relationship between
war and the British 'welfare state'.

First, then, the Beveridge Report on Social Insurance and Allied
Services and the committee that produced it. The committee was
appointed in June 1941, partly to take over the work of the defunct
Royal Commission on Workmen's Compensation, partly to tie up some

loose ends in the pre-war system of national health insurance, and partly to enable the Treasury to ward off the demands of the family allowances lobby that had become increasingly vociferous since the outbreak of war.[7] The Treasury did its best to keep the work of the committee secret and hoped that Beveridge would not report until the end of the war.[8] Beveridge himself, however, rapidly transformed the writing of his Report into a panoramic review of all existing social services and into a blueprint for post-war reconstruction. After only one meeting with the Civil Service members of his committee and before witnesses had even been invited to give evidence, he had mapped out what were to become the major landmarks of his final Report — namely, subsistence level family allowances, a comprehensive national health service, maintenance of full employment, and a universal system of contributory insurance to cover predictable social needs from the cradle to the grave.[9] Over the next year and a half Beveridge's Civil Service advisers were allowed to make virtually no substantive contributions to his policy proposals; and indeed most of them seem to have been bewildered and embarrassed by what they saw as Beveridge's attempt to stampede the government into a premature public commitment to post-war social reform. Their main contribution to the work of the committee was in trying to iron out some difficult and sometimes insoluble technical problems — such as how to fit unmarried mothers and deserted wives into a context of contributory insurance, and how to reach a national definition of subsistence that could be applied uniformly to widely different socio-economic regions, ranging from the Highlands of Scotland to London and the south-east.[10]

Beveridge's Report was therefore very much a one-man production, but it was not for that reason necessarily untypical of attitudes in the country at large. When Beveridge actually got round to inviting members of the public to give evidence, it was very striking just how many of the witnesses — drawn from trade unions, employers, co-operative societies, friendly societies, insurance companies, research institutes, local authorities and professional groups — supported or demanded the kind of policies that Beveridge himself already had in mind. Again and again witnesses pressed spontaneously and independently for measures which subsequently became the main policy proposals of the Beveridge Report — namely, family allowances, full employment, a national health service, comprehensive insurance, subsistence-level benefits, abolition of the Poor Law and virtual abolition of all alternative forms of means-tested public assistance. In so far as witnesses seriously disagreed with Beveridge, it was frequently in defence of fairly obvious vested interests; the trade unions, for example, supported Beveridge on nearly every major issue – with the exception that they wanted workmen's compensation to continue to be paid for solely by employers.[11] Opposition to universal insurance within the trade union movement came almost exclusively from bodies with a very low liability to unemployment or with specially favourable arrangements under the existing insurance system, like the National Union of Railwaymen.[12] Even the big insurance companies claimed to favour a great expansion of statutory insurance services – provided that they could retain the privilege of acting as government agents for door-to-door collection.[13] Moreover, even witnesses who put forward serious practical alternatives to Beveridge's proposals did so within a framework of general agreement with his overall ideas. For instance, the research institute, PEP, and the economist James Meade proposed that insurance might be financed through a surcharge on the income tax; and representatives of the ILO and of the Association of Approved Societies proposed various models of progressively graduate insurance of the kind prevailing in many Continental countries.[14] No witnesses, however, seriously challenged Beveridge's central emphasis on insurance as the first line of defence against poverty, and few of them questioned his belief that such a system should be directed and standardised by a central government authority. No witnesses raised the fundamental question of how far contributory insurance could meet the need of distressed persons who were permanently outside the labour market; and no single witness before the committee clearly expressed the free market objections to state welfare that had so often been put forward (not least by Beveridge himself) in the years between the wars. Among members of the business community who gave evidence or gave private advice to Beveridge, there was some anxiety about the costs of his scheme and considerable doubt about whether anything could be done in wartime; but there was virtually no criticism at all of the *principle* of state insurance, and some businessmen clearly welcomed Beveridge's proposals as a logical complement to the movement for rationalisation of industrial management.[15] At the opposite end of the spectrum, none of the witnesses expressed anything remotely approaching the 'servile state' theory of welfare that had found support in certain sections of the labour movement during the First World War. Trade union and labour evidence was indeed remarkable for its virtually unanimous support for contributory insurance and bureaucratic collectivism – and perhaps even more remarkable for its hearty condemnation of shirkers, scroungers and other undesirables who failed to pay contributions and battened on the state.[16]

Beveridge's discussions both with people who gave evidence and with the Civil Service members of his committee were conspicuously lacking in any kind of detailed analysis of the underlying principles of the new society that was to emerge in Britain after the war, though many were agreed that it was to be a radically different society from that of the 1930s.[17] In the final draft of his Report, however, Beveridge claimed that his proposals were merely an iceberg tip of what was really needed for social reconstruction, and that much more far-reaching policies would be required to fight what he described as the war against the Five Giants of Idleness, Ignorance, Squalor, Disease and Want.[18] The vague and rhetorical tone of this statement has led most historians not to take it seriously and to assume that what Beveridge was really engaged in was a patching operation which, in conjunction with Keynesian employment policies, would leave the economic bases of capitalism substantially intact. There is, however, some substantial evidence to suggest that this was not in fact the case, and that Beveridge did seriously see his social insurance proposals as part of a far-reaching social revolution. The underlying political principles of Beveridge's Report and the supplementary policies that he believed to be necessary were spelt out much more clearly at this time in discussions with another committee of the Ministry of Reconstruction — the Advisory Panel on Home Affairs convened by Sir William Jowitt in the spring of 1942. The Advisory Panel on Home Affairs was a group of businessmen, social scientists and professional experts (together with one Labour and one Conservative MP), called together by Jowitt to advise him on the range of scientific and expert opinion that was being canvassed on issues of post-war social reform. Apart from Beveridge himself, the most prominent members of the panel were Seebohm Rowntree, G.D.H. Cole, Lord Horder (the King's physician), Samuel Courtauld, Sir Samuel Beale and representatives of Guinness's, Marks and Spencer, British Copper, the Austin and Morris engineering works, and various other heavy industrial firms.

The records of this panel reveal much more clearly than the records of the Social Insurance Committee some of the basic political and economic assumptions that subsequently underlay the Beveridge Report. In particular Beveridge's contributions to the panel revealed just how far he had deviated from what may be thought of as mainstream liberalism; and they reveal also some significant differences between his conception of 'full employment' and post-war planning and that being put forward by the disciples of Keynes. In these dis-

prevailing in other advanced economies, including the construction of an official Cost of Living Index. For the task, it recruited the two leading wage and price statisticians of the day, A.L. Bowley and G.H. Wood. The Board also implemented the first Census of Production, designed not only to provide data for the fiscal controversy, but also to determine the amount of disposable national income, the level of industrial productivity, and in conjunction with the wages census, the ratio of labour costs to total costs of production. The welfare implications of the Census were profound and its direction was accordingly entrusted to two 'progressive' economists — H.W. Macrosty, a Fabian and recognised expert on industrial organisation, and A.W. Flux, a protégé (like Llewellyn Smith) of Alfred Marshall and former professor of political economy at Owens College, Manchester and McGill University.

Meanwhile, as the demand for a national unemployment policy moved to the centre of political debate, W.H. Dawson, the leading specialist on German social legislation, was engaged to make exhaustive inquiries into the German system of labour exchanges; to be joined in 1907 by W.H. Beveridge, a prominent member of the Central (Unemployed) Body for London, and an expert on the problems of under- and unemployment and on the structure and viability of foreign schemes of unemployment insurance. The Board of Trade responded to impending minimum wage legislation in similar fashion, recruiting as statistical investigators G.T. Reid, a specialist in the economics of sweated labour at the LSE and activist for the Anti-Sweating League, and Ernest Aves, an expert on the casual labour market and Home Office adviser on Australian and New Zealand wage boards.

This continued recourse to fresh expertise had equally invigorating effects upon the Board of Trade's administration of industrial relations. In the late 1890s, Labour Department officials either mediated or arbitrated in the majority of disputes settled under the Conciliation Act, but as they assumed a greater variety of duties, increasing reliance was placed upon a small pool of fee-paid umpires and conciliators. Familiarity with the technical and cost structures of trades involved in strikes and lock-outs was a major consideration in their selection. The role of occupational groups with least industrial experience such as lawyers, national politicians and ecclesiastics was significantly less in state arbitration than in private dispute procedures. Equally marked was the very much higher representation of industrial professions such as architects and surveyors, and the extensive use made of the scientific and industrial expertise of the Mines and Mercantile Marine Inspector-

cussions Beveridge expounded in much greater detail than in his Social Insurance Report the strategy that he thought would be necessary to conquer the Five Giants. In a series of papers between June and October 1942 he suggested that this strategy would involve permanent statutory control of both prices and wages, abolition of free collective bargaining, public ownership of land and housing, and an immense expansion of secondary and adult education. Full employment was to be maintained not by Keynesian-style regulation of consumer demand, but by state control of the allocation of manpower, massive industrial training schemes, public control of investment and by the phasing out of private ownership of the means of production. This would involve, wrote Beveridge in June 1942, 'making up our minds to becoming a community in which undertakers' profit as the guide to production disappears permanently over a large part of the whole field of economic activity'.[19] And, a month later, he argued that 'ownership of the Means of Production is not one of the essential British liberties and cannot be allowed to stand in the way of social reconstruction after the war.'[20]

Beveridge's views were not necessarily representative of the other members of the Advisory Panel, but nevertheless the discussions of the panel suggest that they were by no means regarded as extraordinary or unique. Moreover, one of the most striking points that emerges from these discussions is that they seem to have been largely acceptable to the business and labour representatives, and it was mainly the small group of civil servants that sat in on the panel's meetings who reacted to Beveridge's proposals with apprehension and alarm. When Beveridge's proposals on full employment were discussed by the panel on 15 July the senior civil servant present, Sir Alfred Hurst of the Offices of the War Cabinet, objected that 'before making revolutionary changes in our pre-war economic system it was desirable to examine the possibilities of improvement'.[21] Hurst was supported by the panel's Conservative Party representative, Henry Willinck, and by the liberal social scientist Seebohm Rowntree, who complained that 'once it was begun there was no stopping place before a complete system on Russian lines had been achieved and with it total sacrifice of freedom.' Beveridge's proposals were, however, strongly supported by the Labour representative, John Wilmot, who seemed totally unabashed by the proposed statutory controls on trade unions and argued that 'state planning does not in the least imply the Russian system and loss of liberty... The things we dislike in Russia are mainly concerned with political and not economic organisation.' Wilmot, it should be noted, was in no way representative of Labour's far left; he was the chairman of a bank, an authority on fiscal questions, and subsequently one of Attlee's few trusted confidants on the manufacture of nuclear weapons. Even more striking was the support that Beveridge's views received from the panel's businessmen, who, in some cases reluctantly, but in some cases with surprising enthusiasm, declared their support for 'community planning', state investment in social and community services, 'State ownership of development rights' and control of large sectors of industry either by public utility corporations or by the appointment of state directors to the boards of private firms.[22] Whatever may have been their private opinions, not one of the representatives of several of the largest private firms in the country expressed dismay at the prospect of becoming merely executive or managerial cogs in a post-war corporate state.

Beveridge's Report on Social Insurance was virtually complete by September 1942, but publication was delayed until December — reputedly because some of the Cabinet objected to it as 'too revolutionary'.[23] The highly favourable popular response to the Report appears to confirm the view that Beveridge was in some sense giving utterance to a deep-rooted popular consensus. Once again, one of the most striking things about public discussion of the Report was the surprisingly narrow range of opinion that it covered — in the sense that both ends seem to have been lopped off the normal peacetime political spectrum. A columnist from the *Daily Telegraph* made much of the fact that she had trapped the unwitting Beveridge into describing his report as 'half-way to Moscow',[24] but no major paper on the right seriously suggested that services such as pensions and health care should any longer be left to provision through the private market. At the opposite extreme the Socialist Party of Great Britain, representing all of 200 members, complained that the Report was mere middle-class moralism, diverting attention from the real issues of economic revolution; but this view was not shared, for instance, by the British Communist Party, which for a time adopted Beveridge as a proletarian hero and continually portrayed him in the *Daily Worker* as the popular victim of bureaucratic Whitehall inertia.[25] Within the Labour Party there were a few complaints from constituency organisations about the regressive aspects of flat-rate contributions; but Labour generally gave enthusiastic support to Beveridge, and his Report was warmly praised by left-wing intellectuals like Cole, Tawney and Laski[26] — all of whom in earlier years had denounced Beveridge as the prototype of bureaucratic tyranny. Representatives of *Tribune* regarded the Report as 'not . . . the last word in social wisdom', but nevertheless

Tribune MPs like Aneurin Bevan were much more concerned with using the Report as a stick to beat the Tories with than with formulating any alternative proposals.[27] Once again, what was conspicuously absent from Labour discussions was any echo of that fear of centralised welfare bureaucracy that had been so prominent during the First World War; and in the shipyards of Clydeside, traditionally the heartland of grass-roots industrial syndicalism, meetings of workers passed overwhelming resolutions of support.[28] It is clear from other sources that Labour supporters during the war *were* seriously divided about how far simply fighting the war should be given priority, and how far it should be deliberately used as a forcing-ground for social revolution; but little hint of this debate entered into the party's discussion of Beveridge in 1942-3.

Among civil servants and Ministers the response to Beveridge's proposals was much less enthusiastic and uncritical than among the public at large. As is well known, Churchill himself thought that planning for reconstruction should mainly be left until after the war, and claimed that he could not commit himself to Beveridge's proposals without a general election to test popular support.[29] The Chancellor of the Exchequer, Kingsley Wood, was doubtful whether resources would be available in the post-war economic climate; and he was sceptical about whether the public would be willing to put up with the necessary degree of taxation once released from the constraints of war.[30] Lord Cherwell, Churchill's personal adviser, thought that the *Beveridge Plan* would ultimately prove self-financing and 'worth its cost'; but he was afraid that increased social services expenditure would create a bad impression in America and deter American willingness to shoulder the cost of the war.[31] Brendan Bracken, the Minister of Information, had initially welcomed the Report as a powerful piece of propaganda for boosting wartime morale; but he was highly embarrassed by the reaction of his colleagues and rapidly withdrew the popular version of the *Beveridge Plan* that had been circulated among the troops for 'compulsory discussion'. Among Labour Ministers Ernest Bevin declared that many parts of the Report were unacceptable to the unions,[32] even though it had in fact been warmly welcomed by many unions and had been drafted after close consultation with the TUC. Bevin's anger at the pressure of Labour back-benchers, who demanded immediate action on Beveridge, led to his virtual withdrawal from all contact with the Parliamentary Labour Party from the spring of 1943 to the middle of 1944.[33] Attlee and Dalton welcomed the plan, but were lukewarm in pressing for its implementation –

Dalton in particular fearing that over-zealous demand for reform would drive Churchill to act on his threat of calling a general election.[34] Among Labour Ministers, the only ones who gave whole-hearted support to Beveridge were Herbert Morrison and Sir William Jowitt — and Jowitt took care to reassure his colleagues that the Report was 'thoroughly consistent with the reforming traditions of parties of all complexions' and had 'nothing to do with the framing of Utopias'.[35] There was a similar dragging of feet at official level. In the Treasury the first wind of Beveridge's draft proposals had created something of a panic in July 1942; and in October an anonymous Treasury memorandum expressed the view that the plan would entail an excessively high level of peacetime taxation, divert funds away from savings and investment, and sabotage post-war economic expansion.[36] This was the nearest that anyone in government circles came to condemning Beveridge in terms of orthodox economics, and suggested that the famous pre-war Treasury point of view was by no means dead. Two months later criticism of a rather different kind was put forward by an interdepartmental committee of civil servants under the chairmanship of Sir Thomas Phillips, which was set up to scrutinise the Beveridge Report in December 1942. This committee accepted the broad outline of Beveridge's proposals but whittled them down in a number of significant ways. They rejected the principle of subsistence-level benefits; they questioned the need for family allowances and proposed that, if given at all, they should be given in kind rather than in cash; and they suggested that there was an irreducible class of hopeless, feckless persons for whom it would always be necessary to retain a large residual system of deterrent and disciplinary means-tested poor relief.[37] This whittling down of Beveridge's basic proposals was continued by the reconstruction committee under Thomas Sheepshanks, which was set up to consider the practical implementation of Beveridge, and produced the Government's Social Security White Paper of 1944.[38]

All these responses suggest that Ministerial and official reaction to Beveridge was considerably less than enthusiastic, and they certainly do not accord with Titmuss's vision of a government suddenly awakened to social reform as a tool of national efficiency. Again, however, one thing that is striking about both Ministerial and official comment on the Beveridge Report is the very narrow range of views and criticism expressed. With one exception Ministers were not unfavourable to the Report's primary emphasis on universal contributory insurance; their view was not that such reforms were undesirable, but that they could not be introduced so rapidly or so cheaply as Beveridge supposed.[39] The exception was Ernest Bevin, who thought (as indeed in private did Beveridge himself) that social insurance should be merely a part of a much wider programme of social reconstruction, involving full employment, large-scale measures of industry-based welfare and reform of the system of wage-bargaining. Like Churchill however (and in this respect totally *unlike* Beveridge), Bevin thought that the introduction of such a programme would have to be postponed until after the end of the war.[40] Other serious alternatives to the Beveridge Report similarly failed to make political headway. At the official level the most notable of such alternatives came from Hubert Henderson, the Oxford economist and wartime Treasury adviser, who criticised universal insurance for wasting resources on people not in need. He suggested instead a form of what would nowadays be called negative income tax, that is to say means-tested benefits financed out of direct taxation, and based on the same coding as each person's annual assessment for income tax.[41] But this approach to welfare was firmly squashed by Keynes, who was an enthusiastic pro-Beveridgite and who was convinced that insurance was the cheapest method available of protecting people against poverty. Keynes argued, in terms that have been used by revenue departments ever since, that negative income tax could only be introduced after total reconstruction of the whole taxation system, and that contributory insurance was an invaluable safeguard against popular myths of the Exchequer's bottomless purse.[42] Outside official circles the most challenging criticism of the Beveridge Report came not from the right or left, but from the secretary of the Women's Liberal Federation, Lady Juliet Evangeline Rhys Williams, who published her alternative strategy for poverty in 1942-3. In this she proposed that every citizen should receive from the state a basic minimum income benefit regardless of whether they were employed or unemployed, married or single, old or young, rich or poor. This universal minimum income would be financed out of a single flat-rate Social Security Tax payable on all earned or unearned income at a rate which in peacetime would be fixed at around 8s or 9s in the pound. Such a scheme, Lady Rhys Williams claimed, would have the merit of extreme administrative simplicity, in that it would abolish at a stroke the duplication between collection of taxes and collection of insurance. It would provide for groups who got left out of contributory insurance, such as the chronic sick, deserted wives and the self-employed. Unlike insurance or public assistance it would abolish marginal disincentives to work, since workers would not lose the benefit when they became employed. It would, she claimed, abolish social antagonism between tax-payers and recipients of welfare, since everyone would automatically be a member of both groups. It would help to maintain full employment, because the level of the Social Security Tax could be used as a form of economic regulator; but at the same time it would promote savings and investment by reducing marginal tax rates for those with very high incomes.[43] However, like most schemes for abolishing bureaucrats, Lady Juliet's proposals met with an official wall of silence. Beveridge himself refused to read them, and her proposals were never taken seriously by the Reconstruction Secretariat — possibly because she was better known as a fashionable society hostess, the author of several successful Hollywood film scripts and the daughter of Elinor Glyn.

Returning to my original question about the applicability of the Titmuss thesis to wider issues of wartime social policy, clearly the little tract of wartime policy formation that I have examined is by no means necessarily representative of wartime policy as a whole. If one looked at policy-making in the areas of health and education, or at Treasury and Cabinet Office thinking about taxation and full employment, very different patterns might emerge. Nevertheless, from the debate that surrounded and followed the Beveridge Report I think it is possible to make certain tentative generalisations.

In criticism of Titmuss's thesis there appears to be little evidence that the war in itself induced heightened government awareness of social welfare either as a tool of national efficiency or as a means of enhancing social solidarity. On the contrary, most Ministers were fearful that an over-hasty commitment to social reform would hamper the prosecution of the war and retard post-war economic revival. In support of Titmuss's thesis I think there *is* considerable evidence of some kind of social policy consensus, both among reformers and among the public at large. It seems, however, to have been a consensus of a rather peculiar kind. It was a consensus based not upon a reconciliation or compromise between conflicting ideas, but rather upon the falling away of certain interests and opinions that were powerful features of the normal peacetime spectrum of opinion in British political life. At one end of the spectrum, as I have shown, left-wing criticism of the bureaucratic or coercive nature of state welfare was virtually non-existent; the majority of socialists and the bulk of the trade union movement enthusiastically supported the Beveridge Report — even though Beveridge himself envisaged that his Report would need to be backed up by labour and manpower policies that would severely curtail trade union liberties. At the opposite end of the spectrum the free market view of welfare seems only to have been put forward — and then remarkably feebly — from within the Treasury itself. Even within the centre, however, attitudes to welfare were by no means typical of moderate attitudes to welfare that had prevailed before the war — on the contrary, there appears to have been a marked shift in favour of state planning and centralised bureaucratic control. The removal of normal political opposition to collectivist social programmes meant that (at least after February 1943 when a back-bench revolt in Parliament compelled the government to commit itself to Beveridge) the planning of post-war reconstruction was able to forge ahead with relative speed. But it meant also that the kind of welfare state policies designed in the 1940s were ill-equipped to meet the criticisms, either of free marketeers or of theoretical socialists or simply of moderate people who disliked paying taxes or who disliked excessive official-dom, when all these groups began gradually to resurface in the years after the war. My criticism of the Titmuss thesis is not therefore that the wartime consensus did not exist; it is rather that the thesis did not fully explore the nature of that consensus, and that it perhaps exaggerated the extent to which the artificial circumstances of war could provide a permanent stable basis for the post-war welfare state.

Convincing explanations for the peculiarly narrow spectrum of opinion that dominated social policy in the early 1940s, and for its bias towards centralised control, are not hard to find, but they are difficult to pin-point with any great precision. One obvious factor is the sense of artificial unanimity created by the menace of Hitler which tended to muffle ideological conflict. But while this explanation is plausible for the actual fighting of the war, there seems to be no particular reason why anti-totalitarian sentiment should have silenced debate on questions of social policy. Another explanation, suggested by Professor Margaret Gowing, is that the immense network of war-time controls was imposed without any serious infringement of liberal democracy and that this tended to quieten fears about the tyranny of 'planning' and made people more willing to accept state intervention.[44] But this seems to beg the further questions of *why* manpower controls were imposed so easily in the first place and *why* they were so strongly resisted when the war came to an end. A more generalised explanation is to ascribe the lack of controversy to the peculiar circumstances of all war situations, in automatically silencing anyone who is inclined to rock the boat. But this explanation will not do if we compare social policy in the Second World War with social policy in the First World War. The First World War had, if anything, intensified conflict over questions of social welfare, and reactions both of labour and of business interests in the two wars could scarcely have been more different. In 1916 a government measure to introduce universal unemployment insurance as a defence against post-war depression had been almost totally wrecked by the opposition of both workers and employers.[45] Throughout the First World War a substantial section of the labour movement had seen government social welfare as a thinly disguised form of coercion by a repressive state. Like the Second World War, the First World War had brought about extensive government control of industry and the absorption of businessmen into public administration; but most businessmen-administrators of 1914-18 — men like Sir John Beale and Eric and Auckland Geddes — had been almost uniformly hostile to extension of social welfare and had had no doubt whatsoever that commercial enterprise should return to private management as soon as peace was restored. Just why it was that the business community during the Second World War appears to have been considerably more sympathetic both to the expansion of welfare and to expansion of state control seems to require further investigation and research. One factor that may have been important was that during the 1920s and 1930s the structure of certain large-scale businesses had become increasingly indistinguishable from that of public utilities; and as L.P. Carpenter has shown, there was during the 1930s a significant growth of support within the business community for policies of national planning and some form of 'corporate state'.[46] The discussions of Jowitt's Advisory Panel on welfare, unemployment, planning and post-war control of industry suggest that during the early 1940s this may possibly have become a dominant view, though it is by no means clear whether Jowitt's business advisers were representative or whether he simply chose individuals known to be favourably inclined to state intervention. My general conclusion is that we need to look more closely at the influence of such groups, and at the much wider relationship between social welfare and the British war economy, before the nature of the consensus is fully understood and before the wider aspects of the Titmuss thesis can be either rejected or sustained.

Notes

1. Richard Titmuss, 'War and Social Policy' in *Essays on 'The Welfare State'* (London, 1963), pp. 75-87.
2. Richard M. Titmuss, *Problems of Social Policy* (London, 1950), p. 508.

3. P.J.H.J. Gosden, *Education in the Second World War: a Study in Policy and Administration* (London, 1976), pp. 431-3.
4. Paul Addison, *The Road to 1945* (London, 1975), pp. 271, 277.
5. Hilary Land, 'The Introduction of Family Allowances, an Act of Historic Justice? in Phoebe Hall *et al.*, *Change, Choice and Conflict in Social Policy* (London, 1975), pp. 157-230; John MacNicol, 'Family Allowances and Less Eligibility' in Pat Thane (ed.), *The Origins of British Social Policy* (London, 1978), pp. 173-202.
6. José Harris, *William Beveridge: a Biography* (Oxford, 1977), pp. 422-6.
7. Ibid., pp. 382-3.
8. PRO PIN8/85, Sir George Chrystal to Sir John Maude, 2 July 1941.
9. Beveridge Papers, IXa, 37(2), 'Social Insurance – General Considerations', July 1941.
10. Harris, *Beveridge*, pp. 385-6.
11. PRO CAB 87/88, Minutes of Social Insurance Committee, QQ. 505-9; CAB 87/79, 'Trades Union Congress, Replies to Questions submitted by Sir William Beveridge', 3 Apr. 1942.
12. PRO CAB 87/77, Minutes of Social Insurance Committee, 25 Mar. 1942.
13. Ibid., QQ. 1693, 1871, 1877.
14. Beveridge Papers, VIII, 27, J.E. Meade to D.N. Chester, 28 Aug. 1941; *Social Insurance and Allied Services. Memoranda from the Organisations*, Papers 7 and 19; PRO, CAB 87/77, Minutes of Social Insurance Committee, QQ. 2464-71.
15. *Social Insurance and Allied Services Memoranda from the Organisations*, Papers 2 and 5.
16. PRO CAB 87/88, Minutes of Social Insurance Committee, QQ. 325, 350, 438, 2362, 2374-5.
17. PRO CAB 87/88, Minutes of Social Insurance Committee; 17 and 25 Aug. 1942.
18. *Social Insurance and Allied Services*, p. 6.
19. Beveridge Papers, VIII, 45, 'Reconstruction Problems: Five Giants on the Road', revised drafts, 25 June 1942.
20. Beveridge Papers, VIII, 45, MS. notes by Beveridge, *circa* July 1942.
21. Beveridge Papers, VIII, 45, Advisory Panel on Home Affairs, Minutes, 9 July 1942. In my *William Beveridge: a Biography* (p. 433) I wrongly ascribed this statement to one of the Panel's business representatives.
22. Beveridge Papers, VIII, 45, Advisory Panel on Home Affairs, minutes, 5 Aug. and 26 Oct. 1942; 'A Note on Community Planning', by H. Morris, 23 July 1942; 'Government Influence in Industry', *circa* Dec. 1942.
23. Passfield Papers, Beatrice Webb's diary, 26 Oct. 1942 (based on information from Stafford Cripps).
24. *Daily Telegraph*, 2 Dec. 1942. Beveridge's secretary, Miss E. Chambers, recalls that the phrase was casually suggested to Beveridge by the interviewer herself: Beveridge was extremely annoyed when it was made the central theme of the *Daily Telegraph* report.
25. *Daily Worker*, 5 Nov. 1943.
26. Harris, *Beveridge*, p. 424.
27. Michael Foot, *Aneurin Bevan* (London, 1975, Paladin edition), vol. 1, pp. 407-9.
28. Beveridge Papers, IXa, 37(i), 'Clydeside Workers and the Beveridge Plan', 18 Mar. 1945.
29. PRO CAB 66/34. Note on 'Beveridge Report' by the Prime Minister, 15 Feb. 1943.
30. Cherwell Papers, Off. 45.6, 'The Financial Aspects of the Social Security

Plan', n.d.; Addison, *Road to 1945*, p. 220.

31. Cherwell Papers, Off. 42.1, memorandum on 'Economic Effects of the Beveridge Plan', 22 Jan. 1943; Off. 32-B, Cherwell to Churchill, 25 Nov. 1942 and 11 Feb. 1943.

32. Dalton Papers, Hugh Dalton's diary, 18 Feb. 1943.

33. Bullock, *Ernest Bevin* (London, 1960), vol. II, pp. 232-3.

34. Dalton Papers, Hugh Dalton's diary, 16, 18 and 24 Feb. 1943.

35. PRO CAB 66/30, 'Outline of Statement on Reconstruction Problems', by the Paymaster-General, 14 Nov. 1942.

36. Henderson Papers, 'The Social Security Plan.' Memorandum prepared in the Treasury, n.d. [Oct-Nov. 1942].

37. PRO PIN 8/85, Report of the Official Committee on the Beveridge Report, early 1943.

38. *Social Insurance* (Cmd. 6550, 1944).

39. Francis Williams, *A Prime Minister Remembers*, (London, 1964), p. 56.

40. Bullock, *Ernest Bevin*, p. 229.

41. Henderson Papers, 'The Principles of the Beveridge Plan', 4 Aug. 1942; and 'Draft Memorandum on the Social Security Plan', 22 Dec. 1942.

42. Henderson Papers, 'The Beveridge Proposals' by J.M. Keynes to B. Webb, 3 Mar. 1943.

43. Lady Juliet Rhys Williams, *Some Suggestions for a new Social Contract: an Alternative to the Beveridge Report proposals* (1942), *Something to Look forward to* (1943).

44. Margaret Gowing, 'The Organisation of Manpower in Britain during the Second World War', *J. Cont. Hist.* vol. VII, nos. 1-2 (1973), pp. 147-67.

45. Harris, *Beveridge*, pp. 255-6.

46. L.P. Carpenter, 'Corporatism in Britain 1930-45', *Journal of Contemporary History*, vol. II, no. 1 (1976), pp. 3-25.

13 BUREAUCRACY AND INNOVATION IN BRITISH WELFARE POLICY 1870-1945

R. Davidson and R. Lowe

Over the last twenty-five years, the role which historians have attributed to bureaucracy in the evolution of the British welfare state has varied greatly.[1] Many administrative historians, adhering to the pattern of self-generating government growth advanced by MacDonagh in the 1950s, have argued that civil servants and 'bureaucratic imperatives' rather than politicians, pressure groups or external social forces provided the key determinants of the extent and character of welfare initiatives. This thesis has, however, been progressively undermined by the shift in British welfare history from a narrow institutional approach to one in which the process of policy-making is analysed from a broader societal perspective. When viewed in relation to their social, political and intellectual environment, administrators no longer possess a monopoly of initiative. Welfare innovation is revealed as a complex process of interaction between a range of political, industrial and professional groups of which the bureaucracy forms but one, and by no means a homogeneous, element. A similar reappraisal of the role of bureaucracy has emerged from the increasing stress of welfare historians upon the importance of the 'locality' in social policy-making and the consequent shift of research away from traditional sources such as departmental archives which had inevitably inflated the significance of civil servants.

The focus of research has principally been on the period from 1870 to 1916, and it is these years which the first half of the chapter examines with particular reference to the contrasting response of different groups of civil servants to the problems of social policy. The period between the First World War and the foundation of the welfare state has received comparatively little attention, despite the pioneering work of the two civilian war histories and the availability, since the mid-1960s, of most relevant government records.[2] This neglect is both curious and dangerous. It is curious because the inter-war years saw increasing public concern about the political influence of the Civil Service, a constant stream of inquiries into its organisation and the rise to respectability of public administration as an academic discipline.[3] It is dangerous because it masks a subtle change in the nature of British government, which renders comparisons over time of the innovatory role of the Civil Service very difficult. Largely as a result of the Liberal welfare reforms and the First World War, Britain was rapidly losing her decentralised form of government and drawing closer to the experience of Continental Europe. As Elie Halévy noted, 'Britain was becoming bureaucratic.'[4] This meant not so much that high officials were taking more policy decisions, although ministers were being faced — especially in social policy — with decisions of increasing technical complexity. Rather, it meant that the scope of government activity was expanding and with it the power of a larger number of officials, be they drafting regulations to implement the decisions of Parliament or exercising their discretion in the treatment of individual clients. Delegated legislation and administrative discretion added an extra dimension to bureaucracy, and it is through this extra dimension that the second half of the chapter reviews the innovatory record of the inter-war Civil Service.

Bureaucracy and Innovation 1870-1916

Recent studies of specific areas of policy-making have generated increasing support for the view that after 1870, civil servants ceased altogether to fulfil an innovative role in the development of welfare concepts and measures; that 'the general picture is of a bureaucracy gently ossifying' with welfare initiatives originating outside the Civil Service, 'from zealots and from political pressures, programmes and contingencies'.[5] These studies have also served to stress that 'innovation' and 'policy-making' are not synonymous, that it is possible to make policy by developing and consolidating an existing trend, or simply by impeding alternative courses of action, and that while, therefore, civil servants might have ceased to fulfil a creative function, they remained influential and a powerful force for conservatism.

Thus, it is evident that, 'with the possible exception of the Medical Department, the whole administration' of the Local Government Board in the period 1870-1914 'was shot through with a reactionary strain' and that its conservatism seriously inhibited the efforts of political chiefs, including John Burns, to introduce welfare provisions.[6] The bulk of the late Victorian and Edwardian Home Office establishment is held to have displayed a similarly negative attitude to social reform. In none of the main areas of legislation, such as penal reform, the amendment of trade union law or the introduction of workmen's compensation did permanent officials play a genuinely innovative role.[7] Likewise, it has been convincingly demonstrated that the notion of self-generating bureaucratic growth cannot provide the core of any explanation of educational policy-making after 1870, the contribution of most pre-war administrators being 'essentially conservative and defensive'.[8]

This view of bureaucratic negativism cannot be reconciled with the response of the Board of Trade to a range of social and industrial problems in the period 1886-1916. An analysis of unemployment policy clearly demonstrates that 'the ideas and perspectives' of dynamic civil servants could still be 'of crucial importance' in initiating policy, 'even within the much more formal structure of government that evolved in Whitehall after 1870'.[9] Labour officials played a highly innovative role in shaping the principles and structure of labour exchanges, unemployment insurance and the Development Commission.[10] They were also largely responsible for the positive strategy adopted by the late Victorian and Edwardian state towards industrial unrest. By creative administration, they secured the viability of government conciliation and arbitration machinery and moderated the incidence and effects not only of rank and file militancy, but also of the more provocative tactics adopted by industrialists and the judiciary towards trade unionism.[11] The provision of minimum wage machinery under the Trade Boards Act of 1909 was similarly motivated by the economic and social ideology of the labour establishment of the Board of Trade. Finally, while its social objectives have remained the subject of debate, historians are generally agreed that it was 'the *administrative* elite of New Liberalism' that improvised a manpower policy in the early years of the First World War.[12] Why was it, therefore, that the labour administration of the Board of Trade was so much more innovative than that of other departments of social administration?

Variations in recruitment procedures provide one major explanation for the dynamism of the Board of Trade.[13] Before 1914, the senior labour establishment of the Board of Trade was not appointed by open competitive examination but selected for their 'peculiar qualifications not ordinarily to be acquired in the public service'. As Table 13.1 demonstrates, prior to their appointment (at an average age of about 42 years), they had acquired an impressive range of experience and expertise. Of the thirteen officials, seven were recognised social statisticians, seven were specialists in industrial relations and the procedures of collective bargaining, six in the problems of unemployment and underemployment, while as many as eight possessed specialist knowledge of 'sweated' labour and minimum wage legislation. The majority had already participated as witnesses, investigators or commissioners in governmental inquiries into social problems relating to the labour market, and many had also played an active role in some form of radical politics as specialist advisers.[14]

The origins of such expertise were varied. Five of the officials had been associated with the 'New Oxford Movement' of the 1880s with its concern to mitigate the social costs of industrialisation, five had participated in the University Settlement Movement and four in the celebrated Booth inquiry into *The Life and Labour of the People of London*. Seven were active members of the Royal Statistical and/or Economics Society, while the same number possessed experience of trade union organisation, ranging from the most exclusive craft unionism to the 'New Unionism' of the transport workers. Nine had previously undertaken social work either for the Charity Organisation Society or a distress committee.

This pattern of specialist recruitment was in marked contrast to that of other departments of social administration. Apart from the Assistant Secretary of the Poor Law Division, the senior establishment of the Local Government Board was appointed by open competition. Officials were not expected to have any practical experience of workhouse administration, housing, unemployment, medical care, or of any of the range of environmental problems for which the Board was responsible. Even the Poor Law Inspectorate, whose average age on appointment was around 40, possessed little previous expertise. They were appointed as 'laymen' for their 'tact and savoir faire' and their *general* capacity to guide and influence local authorities'.[15]

The Home Office displayed a similar adherence to 'generalist' recruitment. The most senior posts continued to be reserved for experienced lawyers but by 1912, of the 42 posts in the upper establishment, 39 were staffed by former university graduates recruited by open competition. A few had acquired legal qualifications subsequent to their appointment, but the majority possessed no specialist knowledge of the social problems, such as factory and workshop conditions, alien immigration, truck and inebriacy, with which the Home Office was empowered to deal.[16] As one Assistant Under-Secretary observed, the Home Office

increasingly consisted of an Oxford group of young men, quite inexperienced and who will never have experience. . . It is as though you sought to govern the Church exclusively from London by an

Table 13.1: Board of Trade: Senior Labour Establishment[a] 1886-1914 Curricula Vitae

	(1) H.L. Smith	(2) A.W. Fox	(3) G.R. Askwith	(4) E. Aves	(5) I. Mitchell	(6) D.C. Cummings	(7) W.B. Yates	(8) F. Schloss	(9) J. Burnett	(10) C.E. Collet	(11) C.J. Drummond	(12) J.J. Dent	(13) W.H. Beveridge
Age on appointment	'79	34	46	50	40	47	52	49	50	32	44	37	30
Degree	•	•	•	•				•					•
Barrister			•										
Areas of Particular Expertise													
Social statistics	•	•		•			•	•		•			•
Industrial relations	•		•		•	•			•		•		
Unemployment	•			•				•					•
Sweating	•		•					•	•				
Areas of Previous Involvement													
'New Oxford Movement'	•												•
University Settlement	•	•		•									
Booth inquiry	•			•					•	•			
Royal Statistical/Economic Society	•							•		•	•		•
COS/Distress Committee	•									•	•		
Trade unionism	•			•	•	•	•		•		•	•	
Government inquiry	•	•	•	•		•		•	•	•	•	•	•

Note: a. Only the heads of the Labour Exchange, Unemployment Insurance and Trade Board establishment are included.

Civil Service Career Development

(1) 1893-7 Labour Commissioner; 1897-1903 Deputy Clomptroller-G(eneral); 1903-7 C-G; 1907- Permanent Secretary

(2) 1895-7 Agricultural Labour Correspondent; 1897-1903 Assistant Labour Commissioner; 1903-7 Labour Commissioner and Deputy C-G; 1907-9 C-G

(3) 1898-1909 Umpire and Conciliator under the Conciliation Act; 1909-11 C-G; 1911- Chief Industrial Commissioner

(4) 1908-12 Personal Staff C-G; 1912- Chairman of Trade Boards

(5) 1907-11 Labour Correspondent; 1911- Assistant Industrial Commissioner

(6) 1908-11 Labour Correspondent; 1911- Assistant Industrial Commissioner

(7) 1903-9 Umpire under Conciliation Act; 1909-11 Chairman of Trade Boards; 1911- Unemployment Insurance Umpire

(8) 1893-9 Personal Staff C-G; 1899-1902 Investigator; 1902-7 Senior Investigator; 1907-8 Director, Census of Production

(9) 1886-93 Labour Correspondent; 1893-1907 Chief Labour Correspondent

(10) 1893-1903 Labour Correspondent; 1903- Senior Investigator for Women's Industries

(11) 1893-1907 Labour Correspondent; 1907- Chief Labour Correspondent

(12) 1893- Labour Correspondent

(13) 1908-9 Personal Staff C-G; 1901-11 Director of Labour Exchanges; 1911- Director of Labour Exchanges and Unemployment Insurance Branch

office composed of men taken straight from the clerical training colleges.[17]

Furthermore, recruits to the Factory Inspectorate were not required to demonstrate practical experience of factory work or a conversance with factory or sanitation law, merely 'broad culture' and the ability to 'deal with manufacturers on equal terms'.[18]

Ostensibly, the Education Department subscribed to a recruitment policy more akin to that of the Board of Trade, examiners and inspectors being appointed as 'experts' without recourse to open competition. In reality, the department's definition of expertise was essentially synonymous with the concept of the professional civil servant formulated by Northcote and Trevelyan. The bulk of the establishment was selected for academic distinction and ability to 'associate on terms of equality with the managers of schools and the clergy of different denominations'. They were both socially and ideologically divorced from the realities of elementary education. There was no consistent recruitment of administrators with a genuine and varied experience of the education system and when specialists *were* appointed, it was merely 'a series of placatory gestures, owing much to particular commitments of individual politicians and officials' such as Acland and Morant. Moreover, recruitment procedures were only marginally affected by the reorganisation of secondary education in 1902, despite the insistence of the Bryce Commission on the need for 'an educational authority in the highest sense' which fully comprehended the social repercussions and practical implications of its administration.[19]

Variations in recruitment patterns were clearly reflected in the contrasting attitudes of social administrators to welfare policy. Indeed, the correlation between innovation and recruitment patterns in late Victorian and Edwardian social administration closely conforms to that posited by organisational theorists.[20] At the Board of Trade, labour officials were receptive to new functions and the formulation of fresh policy initiatives rather than a passive adherence to precedent. They were problem-orientated rather than career-orientated. The fact that the Labour Department was less socially and educationally exclusive than other welfare departments also engendered a more innovative response to social and industrial problems.[21] In contrast, permanent officials at the Home Office, Local Government Board and Education Department displayed a negative attitude to social administration, viewing it primarily as a source of income and status. As 'professional' bureaucrats, they conceived of their role as the performance of prescribed duties rather than the creation of new ones, with the emphasis on the efficient application of rules or a 'code' according to precedent.[22]

The senior officials of the Local Government Board were notoriously unreceptive to new areas of responsibility. This was, in part, an effect of institutional constraints such as Treasury control, but primarily a function of their social and administrative ideology. Such was their inertia and disinvolvement from questions of reform that major areas of housing, medical and environmental need were neglected.[23] Similar inertia characterised the Home Office. Many clerks viewed their bureaucratic role as a means of securing professional status, a gentlemanly life-style and an entrée to the London season.[24] Within the Office, there emerged a generalist elite identifying with the social, educational and professional views of peer groups in other areas of Whitehall rather than with specific departmental objectives. Much legislation, such as the Criminal Law Amendment Act of 1885, was initiated by external pressure groups in the face of Home Office apathy, and even after extensive internal reforms in the 1890s most officials remained unresponsive to mounting public concern over social issues such as sweating, inebriacy and penal reform that fell within their remit.[25] The observation of the Permanent Under-Secretary in 1906 that 'No news is always good news at the Home Office'[26] was indicative of the negative attitude prevailing in the establishment.

Meanwhile, at the Education Department, the examiners 'resembled an arrogant intellectual coterie whose major considerations were financial security and the opportunity to pursue literary interests in a congenial atmosphere'. They displayed little inclination to influence policy and were content merely to observe the Education Code. The inspectorate possessed greater potential for innovation. They were in constant contact with the schools and were subject to fewer institutional constraints. However, in practice they shared the social and administrative conservatism of the examiners, their disinclination to be more than passive commentators, and their lack of interest in the quality and long-term objectives of the educational system.[27]

The extent to which administrators seek to influence policy is not solely determined by their social origins and mode of recruitment. It is equally dependent upon their degree of access to policymaking. Officials remain innovative 'only if their responsibilities are important enough to them to have a significant effect on major policies in their areas of specialization'.[28] In this respect, the staff of the Labour

Department of the Board of Trade enjoyed a particularly favourable administrative environment.

First, the administration of the labour market, as distinct from pauperism, factory conditions and education, was a comparatively new area of government growth as yet unconstrained by a vast body of Statute Law needing uniform treatment. Secondly, in deference to the campaign for a Ministry of Labour, the Labour Department was accorded semi-autonomous status within the Commercial, Labour and Statistical Branch of the Board, thus avoiding much of the formalised routine that had overtaken other areas of the Board's activities.[29] Thirdly, not only did the Labour Commissioner have direct access to the permanent and political chiefs of the Board of Trade, but file procedure within the Labour Department was also designed to incorporate as many specialists as possible within the policy-making process.[30]

Moreover, as the career development appendix to Table 13.1 indicates, labour administrators enjoyed unusually favourable promotion prospects. There was, after 1880, an increasing demand in industrial and political debate for a co-ordinated treatment of labour and commercial issues. There was a growing concern with the need, on the one hand, to assess the social costs of industrialisation and the social repercussions of commercial measures such as Tariff Reform, and on the other, to evaluate and mitigate the effects of industrial unrest, unemployment and social deprivation on productivity, cost competitiveness and 'national efficiency'.[31] Board of Trade labour officials were ideally equipped to undertake such tasks. Although specialists, they were not 'zealots' dedicated to specific labour reforms. Their philosophy of state intervention was essentially an operational one based on a general commitment to positive welfare administration in which both social and commercial priorities had to be balanced. As Llewellyn Smith observed in 1904:

> the best guarantee for wise dealing with matters relating either to labour or commerce is to deal with each in the light of the other; i.e. to keep questions of the 'conditions of the people' in mind when dealing with a commercial question, and to remember the effects on commerce and foreign competition when dealing with such matters as the regulation of labour.[32]

Labour officials were not only ideologically suited to more senior posts within the Board of Trade. They also possessed the necessary expertise.

Many were skilled statisticians and familiar with the cost, market, employment and managerial structures of British industry. In addition, several were trained economists, and in a period when no substantial body of professional economists existed, their advice was considered vital to the determination of commercial and industrial policy.[33] The promotion prospects of Labour Department officials were further reinforced by the propensity of Permanent Secretaries such as Sir Courtenay Boyle and Sir Francis Hopwood to delegate authority, to incorporate experts into the policy-making process and to capitalise upon their administrative potential.[34]

In contrast, specialists had minimal access to policy-making in other areas of British social administration. The accumulation of legal and administrative precedent and the presence of a second or third generation of Oxbridge-educated, classically trained civil servants recruited by open competition placed a premium on the application of formal rules and consultation procedures to domestic policy. As a result, after 1880, many specialists such as lawyers, doctors and engineers merely became another part of the bureaucratic system defending group or professional interests.[35]

At the Home Office, the rationalisation of office procedure after 1880 merely reinforced the status of 'generalist' first-division clerks in the central secretariat. Modification of the promotion structure in the 1890s was designed to secure a reasonable professional career for the graduate entrant rather than to capitalise on the administrative potential of specialists in the sub-departments. As a result, the innovative role of expertise that characterised Home Office legislation in the 1870s was markedly absent from the process of subsequent penal and industrial policy-making.[36] The views of the Prison Inspectorate were as effectively 'sterilised' by Ruggles Brise, the Prison Commissioner, as they had been under the autocratic regime of Du Cane, while the response of the Industrial Department to expert advice was aptly compared to the reaction of a 'Jesuit establishment to heresy'.[37]

The role of expertise suffered from similar erosion at the Local Government Board with the increasing subordination of the medical staff to the lay secretariat. In the 1880s, medical officers played an active part in formulating policy relating to environmental health, but thereafter were unable to exert more than 'sporadic influence'. The views of medical experts were rarely sought even on issues such as disease control and scientific research; and as late as 1910, the Chief Medical Officer had no regular share in advising the Board's President on health matters.[38] Meanwhile, at the Education Department, the mid-Victorian practice of insulating the establishment from any direct contact with educational practitioners was perpetuated. The majority of policy decisions continued to be made without recourse to specialist advice. Indeed, the need for the lay secretariat to defer to an educational expert was expressly rejected by the Cross Commission, and although the establishment of a Department of Special Enquiries in 1894 aimed to secure the full participation of specialists in educational policy-making, with the exception of Robert Morant, their innovative role proved short-lived.[39]

The question remains as to how the labour administration of the Board of Trade evaded the enervative effects of longevity to which bureaucratic structures are commonly subject. Why, as it assumed more complex tasks and acquired increasing 'sunk costs' in established procedures, was its innovative response to social and economic problems not displaced by a commitment to precedent and the mechanics of administration?[40] The most convincing explanation lies in the recruitment of fresh expertise as specialists such as Llewellyn Smith were promoted or new areas of administration contemplated, and the insistence that:

> key posts should not be filled by open competition but be retained for exceptional men attracted by a definite prospect of congenial work of sufficient scope, but not attracted by so nebulous a thing as the Civil Service as a whole.[41]

The continued recruitment of specialists was vital to the maintenance of the Labour Department as an effective research and intelligence unit.[42] In response to mounting concern at the economic and social effects of industrial unrest, D.F. Schloss, an expert on wage determination, was employed in the 1890s to investigate alternative forms of industrial remuneration such as profit-sharing. Similarly, A. Wilson Fox, a specialist on the rural labour market, was enlisted to assess the viability of land reform and agricultural labour colonies as methods of reducing unemployment and contemporary fears of 'urban degeneration'. After 1900, the concern with 'national efficiency', tariff reform and a more 'scientific' treatment of poverty shifted the focus of investigation upon working-class purchasing power and consumption patterns and the cost structure of British industry. The Board of Trade therefore undertook a series of inquiries into working-class wage rates, earnings and standards of living in the United Kingdom as compared with those

ates. Even lawyers were often selected as much for their specialised knowledge of particular trades as for their professional status.[43]

However, the overall deployment and guidance of umpires remained the responsibility of permanent officials such as Llewellyn Smith and Wilson Fox. As, after 1905, they became increasingly preoccupied with a massive programme of commercial and welfare legislation, the administration of the Conciliation Act became more formalised and the strategy of the Board of Trade towards labour unrest increasingly determined by 'generalists' who lacked both the temperament and specialist skills necessary for successful industrial diplomacy. To counter this tendency, G.R. Askwith, the Board's most experienced industrial negotiator, was appointed Comptroller-General in 1909 and in 1911 elevated to the rank of Chief Industrial Commissioner with a separate department devoted exclusively to industrial unrest and staffed by full-time negotiators. These included Isaac Mitchell, former Secretary of the General Federation of Trade Unions, and D.C. Cummings, former General Secretary of the United Society of Boilermakers and Chairman of the Parliamentary Committee of the TUC. This injected fresh expertise at a critical juncture. Askwith and his Assistant Commissioners were more conversant with recent shifts in the ideology and tactics of management and labour, and therefore better equipped to advise the government as to the most effective strategy to adopt in a period of mounting industrial strife.[44]

Askwith's appointment as Comptroller-General was not merely a function of his success as an industrial negotiator. He was also a leading expert on minimum wage legislation. As a member of the Anti-Sweating League, he had collaborated with Charles Dilke in his campaign for a system of wage boards and his evidence had proved decisive in convincing the 1907 Select Committee on Homework as to their viability.[45] Askwith was, therefore, ideally equipped to frame the Trade Boards Act of 1909 and to oversee its inception. Furthermore, he was insistent that its central administration should not be staffed by 'protégés or desk officials' and that the chairmanship of Trade Boards, a key post co-ordinating their wage-fixing functions with the enforcement and control procedures of the Board of Trade, should be reserved for a man of 'calibre and expertise'.[46] Hence, W.B. Yates, a barrister with extensive experience of industrial litigation and collective bargaining, was appointed as the first Chairman of 1909, to be succeeded in 1911 by Ernest Aves.

Meanwhile, the staffing of the newly established Labour Exchange System provided the final example of the conscious use of selective recruitment to ensure creative administration. This was especially vital in the appointment of labour exchange managers, for it was they, as with the Poor Law Guardians, who articulated social policy in the localities and could influence the extent to which local needs and community structures might modify, frustrate or even generate central welfare initiatives. As it was impossible for any automatic test of 'employability' to be devised centrally, exchange managers possessed a considerable amount of discretionary power. Furthermore, they stood at the interface of the welfare system and the unemployed and hence constituted a focus for a whole range of frictions shown to characterise the interaction of social administrators and their clients.[47] Ideally, they required experience of the labour market, familiarity with industrial and commercial employment structures, and an aptitude for personnel management and social work.

A breakdown of the occupational backgrounds of labour exchange managers appointed between 1909 and 1912 demonstrates the success of the Board of Trade's recruitment procedures in meeting these requirements.[48] Some 19 per cent had been employed by labour bureaux or distress committees. A further 10 per cent had been social workers or investigators. Six per cent were from industrial professions such as engineering, architecture and accountancy, while 29 per cent had experience of industry and commerce in either a managerial, supervisory or secretarial capacity. Eighteen per cent possessed first-hand knowledge of the labour market as craftsmen or unskilled workers, of whom one-half were trade union officials. Only 6 per cent were recruited from the Civil Service, and of those, the majority were from the inspectorate. Similarly, the bulk of the 4 per cent recruited straight from university and further education were mature students from institutions such as the London School of Economics and Ruskin College with a previous record of industrial employment.

While the selection, consultation and promotion procedures of the Board of Trade were highly conducive to innovation, certain features of the social, political and institutional environment in the period 1880-1914 were equally favourable. First, the structure of labour policy-making was such as to devolve responsibility upon departmental ministers and permanent officials. Social problems such as unemployment and industrial unrest were rarely discussed systematically at Cabinet level and the lack of political consensus as to the correct strategy to adopt ensured that initiative remained in Whitehall.[49] Moreover, in part because of its low status and high turnover of political chiefs, the Board of Trade's policy had traditionally been heavily influenced by the economic and social views of its senior officials.[50]

Secondly, recent research would suggest that, after 1870, the constraints of Treasury control upon policy-orientated expenditure were by no means as rigorous and uniform as was once supposed.[51] The welfare initiatives of the Board of Trade were especially immune to Treasury control. Many such initiatives were highly cost-effective. The investigative and statistical functions of the Board accounted for less than 2 per cent of its total expenditure in the period 1886-1914, while the cost of operating the Conciliation Act never exceeded £8,000 per annum before 1914.[52] Furthermore, these provisions were capable of generating a degree of public, parliamentary and Cabinet support for additional welfare expenditure, such as the establishment of minimum wage machinery, against which Treasury control was unlikely to prevail.[53] It has also to be remembered that, although the economic determinants of labour problems were increasingly recognised, the pre-war labour policy of the Board of Trade primarily involved the reform of social administration rather than the introduction of economic or fiscal controls. Confrontation with organised financial interests or with a conscious and articulate Treasury point of view was, therefore, largely avoided. In addition, the shift of Liberal financial ideology towards interpreting social expenditure as productive expenditure, and the growing conviction within the business community that selective social investment was not incompatible with social control and economic efficiency seriously compromised the Treasury's ability to contain the extensive programme of social and industrial legislation initiated by the Board of Trade after 1905.[54]

Thirdly, the innovative role of its officials was facilitated by the relationship between bureaucracy and labour before 1914. The spirit in which the Board of Trade administered labour problems was one of 'enlightened paternalism'. Despite its pretensions to be an impartial arbiter reconciling the conflicting interests of managerial and labouring groups within society, the process of labour policy-making was not a genuinely pluralist one.[55] The pattern of the Board's pre-war welfare initiatives, as for example its efforts to rationalise the labour market and to eradicate sweating, was to impose welfare schemes in a unilateral fashion.[56] Trade union leaders were consulted primarily to gain their co-operation in containing rank and file hostility to state controls rather than to democratise the process of economic and social policy-making. In initiating social provisions, civil servants were, therefore, relatively uninhibited by the need to consult and to compromise with the welfare perspectives of the working classes.

Clearly, such factors were conducive to innovative bureaucracy in *all* areas of social policy. However, it was at the Board of Trade that the type of welfare administrator who could and would take full advantage of delegated authority predominated. While the professional elite at the Home Office, Local Government Board and Education Department became increasingly receptive to the Treasury's objectives of a rationalised career structure with uniform administrative procedures,[57] the labour establishment of the Board of Trade had the commitment and capability to resist Treasury control and to preserve their autonomy in policy-making.[58] Similarly, they possessed the motivation and specialist knowledge to exploit both the growing consensus among the managerial and political elite in favour of state intervention in the labour market, and the inability of the work-force to mobilise effective resistance.

Bureaucracy and Innovation 1916-45

The First World War changed, or at least accelerated a change, in the basic organisation, management and responsibilities of the Civil Service. New ministries, such as the Ministries of Labour, Health and Pensions, were created in response to the advance in political democracy which had culminated with the 1918 Reform Bill in the trebling of the electorate; and a new range of social services was provided which increased expenditure on social policy from 4.2 per cent of GNP in 1910 to 11.3 per cent by 1938. In order to prevent a recurrence of the administrative duplication and waste spawned by the war, the Permanent Secretary to the Treasury in 1919 was recognised formally as Head of the Civil Service, with an appropriate increase in the power and influence over the service which he had been slowly accreting since the 1870s. These developments, promising central co-ordination of greatly expanded social services provided by specialist Ministries, encouraged the hope (especially during the euphoria of post-war reconstruction) that bureaucracy had a creative role to play in the evolution of welfare policy.

By the 1940s, however, this hope had seemingly been dashed. The perceived failures of economic and social policy (combined with similar failures in foreign policy and the initial conduct of the war) made the public highly critical of both the power of the Civil Service and the use of that power. The storm which had been gathering throughout the 1930s broke during Sir Horace Wilson's tenure of the permanent secretaryship of the Treasury (1939-42). Especially to those politicians and experts who had desired fundamental policy changes in the 1930s, Wilson personified all the evils of overbearing Civil Service influence. The Secretary of the leading Civil Service union (who has provided the most telling portrait of Wilson) likened him to a 'typical priest-politician of an earlier age' and concluded that he was 'in a more powerful position in Britain than almost anybody since Cardinal Wolsey'.[59] The Labour Party joined with radical Conservatives to demand his dismissal in a campaign of personal animosity unparalleled in the history of the reformed Civil Service.[60] The full extent of the damage which Wilson and his Treasury colleagues were held to have wreaked in progressive policy was well summarised by Keynes in 1939:

> The civil service is ruled today by the Treasury school, trained by tradition and experience and native skill to every form of intelligent obstruction... We have experienced in the twenty years since the war two occasions of terrific retrenchment and axing of constructive schemes [1922 and 1931]. This has not only been a crushing discouragement for all who are capable of constructive projects, but it has inevitably led to the survival of those to whom negative measures are natural and sympathetic.[61]

Historians, including the historians of social policy, have tended to endorse these partial, contemporary observations. On the political power of the Civil Service, Max Beloff has written that the inter-war period was 'one in which the higher civil service in Britain probably reached the height of its corporate influence'.[62] In social policy, B.B. Gilbert has agreed that 'critical decisions, although frequently highly political in interest, were made by administrators.'[63]

The alleged negativism of the Civil Service was confirmed by Skidelsky in his analysis of the failure of the second Labour government. He concluded: 'the pioneering civil service tradition of Chadwick, Kay-Shuttleworth, Simon and Morant was quite extinct: a different attitude reigned, sceptical and ultimately pessimistic.'[64] This conclusion has generally been accepted by the authors of case studies in inter-war social policy. Abrams has attributed the failure of reconstruction between 1918 and 1920 in part to 'obstacles of administration'.[65] John MacNicol, in his study of the rejection of family allowances, has concluded: 'predominantly upper middle-class with public school/Oxbridge educations, senior civil servants undoubtedly displayed strong class loyalties that made them hostile or indifferent to a campaign aimed at assisting working-class mothers and children.'[66] Alan Booth has found in regional policy that the bold attempts by 'irregular' public servants to resolve the fundamental economic causes of regional poverty were hampered by their permanent staff 'taken from the branches of those departments which had so conspicuously failed to find new methods of dealing with unemployment in the previous fourteen years'.[67] Anne Crowther has recorded that in Poor Law policy during the 1920s 'the Ministry of Health was even less willing than its predecessor to sanction expenditure', and that its policy towards vagrants 'was devised by a body of officials who believed in the principles of deterrence set up in 1882. They made little attempt to consider the problem of vagrancy in the context of the economic difficulties of the post-war years.'[68] Finally, José Harris has repeated Beveridge's denunciation of 'Laodicean permanent secretaries and ministers' and his demand in 1940 for a return to the pre-1914 'dynamic administrative tradition of Morant and Llewellyn-Smith'. Her own study of the official reception of the Beveridge Report echoes with the familiar sound of 'bewildered and embarrassed' civil servants 'dragging their feet' around Whitehall.[69]

The concurrence of so many historians with the inter-war criticism of bureaucracy is remarkable, the more so as it does not fully accord with their own descriptions of the development of social policy. John MacNicol, for example, admits both 'the remarkable way in which Ministry of Labour officials had predicted the problems' of unemployment relief in the 1930s by the early 1920s and that 'by the late 1930s . . . Government bodies dealing with the able-bodied unemployed had come round to a virtual recommendation of family allowances.'[70] Alan Booth has stressed the 'revolution in the idea of Government's relationship with private industry' sustained by regional policy after 1936 and that 'by 1939, most of the policies which have subsequently been reintroduced since 1945 had been introduced under the Special Areas legislation'.[71] José Harris has noted that by 1940 there was already within the Civil Service pressure for an inquiry such as the Beveridge Committee and that several departments, including the Home Office and the Ministry of Health, had prepared well researched demands for 'far-reaching' social reforms; she has also noted the essential artificiality of wartime consensus and the extremity of Beveridge's economic views on the Advisory Panel on Home Affairs, which civil servants alone (mindful of their future responsibility to implement and maintain the new services in peacetime) sought to question.[72] R.A. Butler has admitted that the 1944 Education Act, for which he gained such political credit, was largely the creation of civil servants before his entry into office; and, if Howson and Winch are to be believed, there was even a Keynesian revolution erupting in the Treasury before 1940, which would have fundamentally altered the economic climate in which social policy was formulated.[73] All these examples of the Civil Service's ability to anticipate problems, to prepare remedies, to develop new policies as the result of the practical problems of administration and to inject an air of administrative reality into the formulation of high policy, suggest that bureaucracy played a constructive role in inter-war social policy which historians to date have tended either to ignore or to underplay.

A major reason for historians' neglect has been identified by Max Beloff. He has written: 'the anonymity of the civil service may or may not be a valuable convention of the constitution: it is one which the historian of modern Britain accepts at his peril.'[74] It has, nevertheless, been accepted. The continuing influence of no single official or department on the development of social policy has been rigorously studied. No biographical study exists of the two men, Sir Warren Fisher and Sir Horace Wilson, who were successive Heads of the Civil Service between 1919 and 1942, let alone of any social administrator. Departments have not been treated as organic entities which might combine a variety of opinions.[75] The phrase 'official policy' has been used loosely, even within the same study, to mean the pronouncements of Ministers, the Treasury View, or the opinions of departmental civil servants expressed either collectively or individually — the choice depending, it would seem, on whichever portrays the government machine in the most unfavourable light. Such inadequacies of approach have obscured the dynamics of public administration, especially the existence of policy battles within and between departments, and have prevented historians from drawing comprehensive conclusions about the influence of bureaucracy on inter-war social policy.

The alleged negativism of the inter-war Civil Service has traditionally been ascribed to two factors: the social and educational exclusiveness of its elite and the pernicious influence of Treasury control. There can be little question of the exclusiveness of the higher Civil Service, be it defined broadly as all administrative-class officials (who numbered about 1,500 by 1939) or more narrowly as those who were in regular contact with Ministers (who numbered about 500). Socially, 80 per cent of senior officials were children of parents in classes I and II of the Registrar-General's 1911 social classification, whereas only 18 per cent of the total population fell into these classes; educationally, the nine top 'Clarendon' public schools accounted for one-fifth of successful entrants into the administrative class by 1939 (a drop from one-quarter in 1914) whereas Oxford and Cambridge accounted for 89 per cent of entrants (a rise from 80 per cent in 1909-14).[76] Two inter-war innovations had in fact encouraged greater exclusiveness. First, the regrading of all civil servants into four classes (the administrative, executive, clerical and writing assistant classes) in 1919-20 had identified each class with a particular stage in the educational system and hence with the general educational attainment of different social classes. A greater social mix might have been attained by increased promotion from the executive class (recruited largely from secondary-school-leavers) to the administrative class (recruited from graduates) but, despite much talk, such promotion remained 'a theoretical rather than a practical possibility'. Secondly, by an administrative rather than a political decision, an interview was introduced into the qualifying examination for the administrative class and this undoubtedly prejudiced, at the margin, the chances of those candidates who 'would most probably have provided a social leaven'. Thus, despite the social revolution of the war, the improvements in secondary and provincial university education, and the change in both the extent and the nature of governmental responsibilities, the Civil Service retained its pre-war exclusiveness. It had indeed become easier for the child of a manual worker to become a Minister than a top civil servant.

Treasury control over all areas of policy was also intensified during the inter-war period. To make the Civil Service more homogeneous, the Treasury insisted that all Ministries should appoint finance and establishment officers to standardise financial and recruitment practices; appointment to these posts, and to the top two positions in each Ministry (the Permanent and Deputy Secretaries) should be made not by the departmental Minister but by the Prime Minister acting on Treasury advice; and all policy initiatives requiring increased public expenditure should be submitted to the Treasury before being sent to Cabinet. These reforms, allied to the Treasury's traditional authority as the finance Ministry, gave it immense power and influence over both the personnel of the Civil Service and the nature of policy. Since Treasury officials had no direct contact with the public and were trained to criticise rather than to execute policy, they had little immediate sympathy for the staffing needs of the new social service Ministries; and since they held rigidly to classic economic orthodoxy, they opposed major increases in public expenditure which the proper development of the new Ministries required. The Treasury's potential for opposing innovation in social policy was therefore great and can be well illustrated from the experience of the Ministry of Labour, which was closely involved in major developments in inter-war economic and social policy and was, moreover, the direct legatee of the dynamic administrative tradition of the labour departments of the pre-war Board of Trade.[77]

In personnel management, the Treasury could control the staffing levels of all Ministries as well as influence the recruitment, training and promotion of all officials. Severe restrictions on the number of their staff meant that the social services Ministries could not maintain their statistical departments (which had been one of the mainsprings of pre-war reform), develop research departments for the planning of long-term policy (as recommended by the 1918 Haldane Committee) or improve their services to the public. In the specific case of the Ministry of Labour, the demands of routine administration (especially unemployment insurance) soon curtailed the work of its statistical department and forced the closure of its publicity, intelligence and exchange policy departments. The government was thus left in a state of 'statistical nakedness'[78] which handicapped its proper examination of policy options, and the Ministry was unable to explain its policy fully to the public, inform the Cabinet adequately of current opinions on social policy, or gain an overview of unemployment policy which might have obviated the need for the constant redrafting of insurance legislation between 1920 and 1934. In 1919, the Treasury also expressly forbade the use of section 4 of the 1859 Superannuation Act, by which the pre-war Board of Trade had recruited its mature social reformers; vetoed the training of local staff (who might have lessened public antipathy to bureaucracy) except in their spare time; and discouraged specialisation within the administrative class. By the 1930s, it had become a principle of promotion that when either of the top posts in a Ministry fell vacant it should be filled from outside that Ministry, for senior civil servants were seen essentially not as policy specialists but as experts in the working of the governmental machine who could save their Ministers from parliamentary embarrassment.[79] As G.K. Fry has argued, this development ran exactly counter to the needs of the social service Ministries:

> When administrative work had been relatively simple and homogeneous [in the nineteenth century] it had been treated as if it needed departmental specialisation: whereas, now it had become more complex and might well have needed more specialisation, it was thought of as being homogeneous.[80]

In the formulation and execution of policy, the Treasury could use to great effect its administrative powers and influence over promotion as well as the political muscle of the Chancellor of the Exchequer in Cabinet. Restrictions on staff and finance could emasculate departmental policy and the Treasury did use its administrative power to frustrate policy even, on occasion, in defiance of declared government objectives. This was true, for example, in minimum wage legislation between 1921-4, regional policy, especially in 1938, and (most probably) in unemployment relief between 1934 and 1935.[81] The Treasury also used establishments and finance officers as Trojan horses within each Ministry to ensure that, even in the formulation of policy, economy was always given highest priority: the unemployment insurance staff of the Ministry of Labour realised that constant consideration of finance was 'eminently safe as regards limitation of current expenditure, but it prevent[ed] any rapid progress or development' of policy; and they sought to return to the pre-war Board of Trade practice whereby the finance officer simply checked the proper expenditure of money. Their case, however, was rejected.[82] It would also not have escaped the notice of ambitious officials that the road to promotion did not lie through opposition to the Treasury. Treasury officials were often arrogantly dismissive of anyone seeking fundamental change. Keynes, when supporting Lloyd George's expansionary employment programme in 1929, was described as living in

a little economic world of his own up at Cambridge and he is pleased to consider the group of theorists up there as representing the sole exponents of 'modern economic thought'. In fact, the rest of the universe treats their theories with much scepticism and their general acceptance is in reverse ratio to the dogmatism with which they are expressed;

and the first regional commissioner for England and Wales, a successful businessman who did much to revolutionise regional policy, was dismissed equally contemptuously.[83] This attitude could easily corrupt ambitious young officials such as Sir Wilfred Eady, one of the Ministry of Labour's most talented officers in the 1920s. In 1927, while acknowledging that 'the support of Mr Keynes is nowadays officially a dubious reference,' he used such support to strengthen the conclusion of his own statistical research that orthodox analyses of unemployment were inadequate and that greater state intervention was needed if the economy was to be restructured and poverty reduced. By 1936, how-

ever, as Secretary of the Unemployment Assistance Board, he had
succumbed to the anti-statistical bias of the Treasury, claiming that
in calculating the amount of relief for the unemployed there were
'no scientific standards... The matter was one of social convention
and expediency.'[84] He duly rose to the second secretaryship of the
Treasury.

Social and educational exclusiveness and an increase of Treasury
control, however, cannot by themselves explain (let alone prove)
negativism throughout the whole inter-war Civil Service. On the one
hand, an increasing intake of Oxford and Cambridge graduates might
be seen as conducive to good government at a time when the two
universities still attracted the ablest students (as far as the deficiencies
of the state education system would permit). The increasing complexity
of administration also necessitated greater informal contact between
officials and hence the desirability of their sharing some common background. Moreover, alternative methods of recruitment variously recommended by administrative reformers guaranteed no antidote for the
'unconscious' upper-middle-class bias which senior officials were in
danger of acquiring after appointment.[85] Sir Horace Wilson himself
had been promoted from the ranks and as the son of a furniture dealer,
educated at the LSE, enjoyed none of the traditional exclusiveness of
a Treasury mandarin; specialists rose to high administrative posts
within the Ministries of Health and Transport with little noticeable
effect; even the mature experts recruited by the pre-war Board of
Trade either became divorced from social policy after its period of
heroic expansion (such as Beveridge and Llewellyn Smith) or remained
in office as increasingly conservative influences (such as Mitchell and
Reid).[86] As at the pre-war Board of Trade, it was the personality of
leading officials and subsequent departmental morale, as much as
their social class and the method of recruitment, which fashioned
official attitudes.

On the other hand, increased Treasury control should be seen essentially as the consequence not of administrative initiative but of political
and public will. It was not imposed unilaterally, but had been requested
by Parliament and the 1918 Haldane committee: and, as was argued
in 1943:

> Treasury control is really Government control exercised through the
> Chancellor of the Exchequer and his department: and a decision
> by the Treasury, at whatever level it may be taken, is in substance
> a decision by the Government to which any other Department

immediately affected is a consenting party: for if it does not consent, it is always within its power, in the last resort, to ask that the decision should be reviewed by the Government as a whole.[87]

Between the wars, the Treasury was indeed successfully challenged on both establishment and policy matters. For example, the early attempt to downgrade all social service Ministries by staffing them with executive rather than administrative class officials was defeated; and unemployment insurance policy provided a succession of defeats for the Treasury, culminating in 1934 in a rejection of its original proposals for a national unemployment authority — a rejection which has persuaded one historian of the existence of 'genuinely independent departments and permanent civil servants'.[88] When the Treasury did use its administrative powers successfully to block a government's publicly declared policy, its action always had the ultimate sanction of a Minister.[89]

Any observed increase in the power and negativism of the Civil Service, therefore, has to be explained in terms of the individual personalities of senior officials and the political environment and conventions within which they worked. In 1941, Dale argued persuasively that there were 'more and more "yes-men" ' in the administrative class. As the Civil Service was opened to merit, the number of officials with independent means (and views) declined, to be replaced by recruits of a slightly lower social status whose need to pass examinations throughout their formative years had narrowed their horizons and exhausted their 'animal spirits'. Consequently, while politics became more professional (in the sense that Ministers were more conscientious if not more expert), officials became less self-confident and assertive. This meant that if there were any increase in official power, it was in unsupervised detailed administration, not in the formulation of high policy: 'There are now many more officials and they do many more things than 40 or 50 years ago: but in reality they do no more without the authority of Parliament and Ministers. Bureaux have grown, but not bureaucracy.'[90] The *apparent* increase in official power can be explained by political vacillation and duplicity. The new pressures of democratic politics forced Ministers to grant, in principle, increasingly generous social services, the full financial implications of which they then tried to modify by stricter administration. In the 1920s, for instance, politicians declined to repeal legislation but directed a 'tightening-up' campaign in the administration of unemployment insurance, the Poor Law and the Unemployment Grants Committee. In the 1930s officials again bore the brunt of popular disfavour when the National government tried to 'accomplish politically unpopular ends without suffering from the political consequences thereof';[91] the favoured device then was the semi-autonomous administrative board, such as the Unemployment Assistance Board and the Special Areas Commission. In all these instances, although retrenchment appeared to be at the discretion of officials, it was in fact directed by politicians. This was true even when the 1924 Labour government restricted the payment of unemployment insurance. As Alan Deacon has argued, these restrictions cannot 'be explained in terms of civil service pressure. It is certainly true that . . . officials were apprehensive of the effects of paying extended benefit for unlimited periods, but [there is] no evidence to suggest their intervention was decisive.'[92] It is anticipated that other case studies will confirm that for too long, civil servants have been used as convenient scapegoats, especially for those governments who failed to realise the promises of reform.

Despite Dale's testimony, the observed negativism of senior officials should also be related not so much to personal shortcomings as to the environment in which they worked: the indecision of Ministers, the demands of Parliament and, above all, the lack of consensus concerning social reform. These major issues can only be covered briefly in a short chapter. First, it is becoming clear from detailed research that the majority of Ministries contained groups of progressive civil servants; but Ministers and Cabinets (inevitably) did not always accept their advice.[93] Secondly, the constant need for Ministers to defend in Parliament every detail of social administration played a major part in encouraging centralisation and 'timidity'; indeed, in the 1930s, it was coming to be widely questioned whether Ministerial responsibility was compatible with administrative efficiency.[94] To take but one example, resort to precedent became a distinctly attractive practice in the real administrative and political world where millions of citizens had to be treated equally and any MP could question Ministers about any supposed injustice suffered by any one of his constituents. Thirdly, lack of consensus about the direction of future social reform greatly discouraged innovation.[95] Before 1914, public opinion at least had not discouraged reform; as a direct result of the war, however, there was (even within the Civil Service) a general revulsion against centralised bureaucracy and consequently against any policy — such as a large-scale public works programme — which threatened to increase it. For every reformer urging greater administrative initiative there were hundreds of taxpayers urging less. Furthermore, it should be remembered that the prejudices of officials largely reflected those of the public they served: dislike of scroungers, for instance, and the belief that the social wage should not exceed the industrial wage were not (then as now) unique to unemployment insurance officials. Indeed, those who now suggest that inter-war officials should have emulated the bureaucratic innovators of the nineteenth century should ponder the wider, constitutional implications of their suggestion. When the poor were unenfranchised there was perhaps some justification for officials to develop social policy independently of Ministers; after the 1918 Reform Bill, however, when the majority of adults either individually or collectively could exercise a degree of political power, independent bureaucratic action could be portrayed as a gross infringement of parliamentary democracy.

In the formulation of high policy, therefore, the power of inter-war bureaucracy would seem to have been unduly exaggerated; and any negative bias in official advice should be seen largely as an accurate reflection of the mood of the electorate and of Ministers whom the Civil Service was constitutionally bound to serve. The steady (if unspectacular) expansion of the social services, however, did give civil servants a new opportunity to demonstrate their powers of innovation, albeit at a relatively low administrative or even regional level; and the improvement in the range and quality of those services (together with the efficient execution of most administration and planning during the Second World War) suggest that, at this level in particular, bureaucratic innovation was far from dead. Further detailed research is again needed to establish fully this argument: and it is to be feared that, owing to the informal nature of much administration and the idiosyncratic preservation policies of social service Ministries, government records may be far from complete.[96] One of the ironies of inter-war social policy, indeed, is that the only series of records well preserved are those of the Treasury: thus there is a historiographical temptation to assume (as one suspects the Treasury has always assumed) that Treasury opinion and policy are synonymous with the thoughts and actions of the whole Civil Service.

The innovatory record of inter-war bureaucracy can be upheld on two general counts. First, the British Civil Service never permanently blocked, for political or other motives, policy innovation in the way that bureaucracy in the USA resisted the implementation of the New Deal. Secondly, when political leadership was forthcoming, officials responded. Bevin, for instance, as a trade union leader, was highly sceptical of the creative qualities of his officials when he became

Minister of Labour in 1940 but was soon impressed by their ability; and his Ministerial record is a prime example of constructive partnership between outstanding political drive and determination and broadminded administrative realism.[97] However, it is the record of the local services of government, particularly in the 1930s, which demonstrates the true versatility and originality of centralised bureaucracy. Although the Unemployment Assistance Board and the Special Areas Commission had initially been created to outflank public calls for greater public expenditure, they developed as humane and efficient services which to the unemployed man at least (if not to the administrative historian) meant far more than extravagant gestures in Parliament. Millett has commended the way in which the UAB produced the 'machinery, and more importantly an atmosphere, whereby local discretion could be exercised under central influence and guidance' and Booth has been forced to concede that the 'experimental, controversial' bureaucracy of the Special Areas Commission worked.[98] Their achievement was matched by a longer-established agency, the employment exchanges, which before the First World War had been a focus for trade union hostility but which, by the 1930s, was receiving the approbation of commentators as diverse as PEP and Quentin Crisp.[99]

The success of these local services both revealed the existence of policy initiative within Whitehall and encouraged its further development. On the one hand it revealed (within the Ministry of Labour at least) an increasingly enlightened establishments policy which encouraged decentralisation and deepened the understanding of administrative-class officials by providing them with a sustained 'field-training' programme in its regional offices. This policy was the creation of one of many underrated inter-war officials, Humbert Wolfe, who 'believed that people who showed talent and originality, in any direction, could apply that ability to the work and development of the Ministry. He wanted to humanise the relationship between the Ministry and the public.'[100] His recruitment policy did not perhaps match the pre-war Board of Trade's concentrated recruitment of social reformers, but for the implementation of policy, if not for its formulation, it had a beneficial effect. On the other hand, the daily immersion of local agencies in the practical problems of social administration enabled them to modify existing policy, through the exercise of administrative discretion, and, by adding to the groundswell of informed opinion, to become another 'stick' to beat the government into the acceptance of further reform.[101] Consequently, a new breed of progressive administrator, steeped in practical experience, started to supersede those

pioneering social planners who had been demoralised by the retrenchment of the 1920s. The Ministry of Labour may, of course, have been
an exception among government departments, like the pre-war Board of
Trade, but in the light of the growing homogeneity of the Civil Service
this would seem unlikely. By the late 1930s, after all, even the Treasury
itself was showing a greater appreciation of social policy. Its non-
specialist recruitment policy had required all its own aspiring officials
to serve an apprenticeship in a spending department. Just as social
administrators, therefore, were trained to take greater account of
budgetary policy, so Treasury officials were slowly being made aware
of the need to balance narrow financial interests against wider
economic and social considerations.[102]

Conclusion

Individual case studies of the role of the Civil Service in British welfare
policy between 1870 and 1945 demonstrate, like most empirical
research, the dangers of too-ready generalisation. The record of bureaucratic innovation varied greatly over time, between departments and
even between groups of departmental officials. The social, political
and intellectual environment in which the Civil Service worked was
also constantly evolving, as were the duties which civil servants were
constitutionally called upon to discharge. In brief, as state intervention expanded after 1870, so too did bureaucracy and the nature of its
responsibilities. Politics became increasingly professional and pluralistic
and thus the 'independent' role which an exceptional civil servant could
play in the formulation of policy was restricted; implementation
of policy, on the other hand, assumed far greater importance. The increasing size and complexity of administration necessarily required
a greater standardisation of recruitment and bureaucratic procedures
and this tended to discourage initiative. Open competition, owing to
the nature of the education system, confirmed rather than weakened
the social exclusiveness of officials; and procedural developments
(such as the requirement that departmental policy after 1919 could
be represented to the Treasury only by establishment and finance
officers and the convention that Cabinet discussed reports such as
the Beveridge Report only after mastication by inter-departmental
committees) could and did militate against the swift acceptance of
new ideas. However, where popular will was sufficiently articulate and
politicians amenable, where the social services were expanding and

where the administrators remained in close contact and sympathy with their clients, there was still scope for bureaucratic initiative. The innovatory record of the British Civil Service had long rested on the achievements of the exceptional official and, as the history of the pre-war Board of Trade and the post-war Ministry of Labour shows, there remained at all levels within the service administrators of exceptional ability.

The main theoretical considerations of bureaucracy have concerned its technical efficiency and its political power. Between 1870 and 1945, two contrasting attempts were made to adapt the organisation of the British Civil Service to the perceived requirements of its new economic and social responsibilities. The attempt by the Fabians, at its strongest during the pre-1914 Liberal government and reaching its climax in the 1918 Haldane Report, faded during the retrenchment of the 1920s; the attempt by the Treasury, which gathered momentum in the 1870s and was greatly strengthened by the post-1918 reforms, also had its limitations exposed by the real political and administrative pressures of the 1920s and 1930s. The Civil Service largely resisted attempts at rational organisation and in its variety and contradictions reflected the nature of the parliamentary democracy it served. With regard to its political power, commentators have described an increasingly conservative influence exerted on policy by the vested interests of the Civil Service machine: the only policy decisions, it is held, to be swiftly executed (especially during the inter-war period) were those involving cuts in public expenditure. The case has yet to be proved, however, that the Civil Service failed in either of its prime constitutional duties: to present a full and balanced account of policy options to democratically elected Ministers, be they Conservative or Labour, and to implement faithfully all political decisions. Officials had an increasingly important responsibility in advising politicians on the practical administrative aspects of implementing policy, but in the actual formulation of policy (given the changing political climate and, after 1918, the dislike — shared by officials themselves — of centralised bureaucracy) their influence seemingly waned. It is again tempting to conclude that in its political attitudes, and especially in its inter-war conservatism, the Civil Service merely reflected contemporary political assumptions.

Within Britain, the practical experience of and philosophical attitude towards bureaucracy had long differed from that of Continental Europe and the pragmatic development of the Civil Service between 1870 and 1945 largely continued this tradition. The danger is that international comparisons of the role of bureaucracy in the simultaneous development of welfare states in Western industrialised nations will employ theoretical frameworks which will obscure the variety and flexibility of British bureaucracy which, at all levels, was its essential characteristic.

Notes

1. For the following survey, see especially V. Cromwell, 'Interpretations of Nineteenth-century Administration: an Analysis', *Victorian Studies*, vol. IX (1966), pp. 245-55; G. Sutherland, 'Recent Trends in Administrative History', ibid., vol. XIII (1970), pp. 408-11; P. Thane (ed.), *The Origins of British Social Policy* (London, 1978), pp. 11-19; J.R. Hay, *The Development of the British Welfare State 1880-1975* (London, 1978), pp. 1-12, 102-8.

2. *The Carnegie Endowment's Economic and Social History of the World War; The History of the Second World War: UK Civil Series.*

3. For a summary of the public inquiries, see *(Fulton) Royal Commission on the Civil Service* (HMSO, 1966-8), vol. 3 (2), memorandum 10. The most notable contemporary commentary on the Civil Service is H.E. Dale, *The Higher Civil Service* (1941); a full bibliography may be found in G.K. Fry, *Statesmen in Disguise* (London, 1969)

4. E. Halévy, *A History of the English People in the Nineteenth Century*, vol. VI: *The Rule of Democracy, 1905-14*, rev. edn (1961), p. 262.

5. G. Sutherland (ed.), *Studies in the Growth of Nineteenth-Century Government* (London, 1972), p. 8.

6. K.D. Brown, 'John Burns at the Local Government Board: a Reassessment', *Journal of Social Policy*, vol. 6 (1977), pp. 157-70; M.E. Craig, 'Bureaucracy and Negativism: the Local Government Board 1886-1909', unpublished MA thesis, University of Edinburgh, 1975.

7. J.H. Pellew, 'Administrative Change in the Home Office: 1870-1896', unpublished PhD thesis, University of London, 1976; A. Williamson, 'Some Retarding Factors on Penal Reform 1895-1914', unpublished MA thesis, University of Edinburgh, 1976.

8. G. Sutherland, *Policy-making in Elementary Education 1870-1895* (Oxford, 1973), p. 343; Sutherland, *Studies*, Ch. 10.

9. J. Harris, *William Beveridge: a Biography* (Oxford, 1977), p. 3.

10. J. Harris, *Unemployment and Politics: a Study in English Social Policy 1886-1914* (Oxford, 1972), p. 351.

11. R. Davidson, 'The Board of Trade and Industrial Relations', *Historical Journal*, vol. XXI (1978), pp. 571-91.

12. J. Hinton, *The First Shop Stewards Movement* (London, 1973), pp. 30-1, 46; R. Davidson, 'War-Time Labour Policy 1914-1916: a Reappraisal', *Scottish Labour History Journal*, vol. 8 (1974), pp. 3-20.

13. For a full description of the origins and nature of such procedures, see *Majority Report of the Royal Commission on the Civil Service* P(arliamentary) P(apers) 1914 (Cd. 7338) XVI, Chs. 1-2.

14. For example, during the 1892 general election, Llewellyn Smith helped formulate the labour policy of the Liberal Progressives, while Wilson Fox fulfilled a similar function for the 'Tory Democrats'.

15. *Royal Commission on the Civil Service, Mins. of Ev.*, PP 1912-13 (Cd. 6210) XV, pp. 179-90.

16. Ibid., pp. 112-33; Pellew, 'Administrative Change', Chs. 1, 4.
17. C.H. Dudley Ward and C.B. Spencer, *The Unconventional Civil Servant, Sir Henry J. Cunynghame* (1958), p. 241.
18. PP 1912-13 (Cd. 6210) XV, q. 5253.
19. Sutherland, *Studies*, Ch. 10; Sutherland, *Policy-making in Elementary Education*, Chs. 2-3; A.S. Bishop, *The Rise of a Central Authority for English Education* (Cambridge, 1971), p. 254.
20. See, for example, A. Downs, *Inside Bureaucracy* (Boston, 1966), pp. 228-30.
21. On the relationship of social homogeneity to innovation, see Sutherland, *Studies*, pp. 9-10; R.K. Kelsall, *Higher Civil Servants in Britain* (London, 1955), p. 34.
22. Sutherland, *Studies*, pp. 130-1.
23. Brown, 'John Burns', pp. 158-63; R.M. MacLeod, *Treasury Control and Social Administration: a Study of Establishment Growth at the Local Government Board 1871-1905* (1968).
24. Pellew, 'Administrative Change', pp. 326-7.
25. Ibid., Chs. 4, 6; Williamson, 'Some Retarding Factors', Chs. 4, 6; R.M. MacLeod, 'Social Policy and Chronic Alcoholism 1870-1900', *Journal of the History of Medicine and Allied Sciences*, vol. 22 (1967), pp. 227, 239, 243.
26. Williamson, 'Some Retarding Factors', p. 46.
27. Sutherland, *Policy-making in Elementary Education*, pp. 341-2.
28. Downs, *Inside Bureaucracy*, p. 108.
29. R.M. MacLeod, 'Specialist Policy in Government Growth: Aspects of State Activity 1860-1900', unpublished PhD thesis, Cambridge University, 1967, pp. 147-9.
30. See, for example, the range of officials consulted on the reform of trade union law; Davidson, 'The Board of Trade', pp. 582-3.
31. See G.R. Searle, *The Quest for National Efficiency* (Oxford, 1971).
32. PRO Lab 2/213/L156/1904.
33. A.W. Coats, 'Political Economy and the Tariff Reform Campaign of 1903', *Journal of Law and Economics*, vol. II (1968), p. 185.
34. See, for example, C. Boyle, *Hints on the Conduct of Business: Public and Private* (London, 1900), p. 124.
35. R.M. MacLeod, 'Statesmen Undisguised', *American Historical Review*, vol. 78 (1973), p. 1403.
36. Pellew, 'Administrative Change', pp. 137, 141, 198-9, 255-302.
37. Williamson, 'Some Retarding Factors', p. 21; BM Add MS. 45989 fos. 172-3, H. Cunynghame to H.H. Asquith, 19 Dec. 1907.
38. Brown, 'John Burns', p. 163; J.L. Brand, *Doctors and the State* (Baltimore, 1965), pp. 34-6, 81-4.
39. Bishop, *Central Authority*, pp. 120-1; Sutherland, *Studies*, p. 281.
40. R.K. Merton, 'Bureaucratic Structure and Personality' in R.K. Merton et al., *Reader in Bureaucracy* (New York, 1967), pp. 365-6.
41. *Royal Commission on the Civil Service*, PP 1912-13 (Cd. 6535) XV, q. 13110, evidence of Sir H. Llewellyn Smith.
42. For the importance of this function to welfare developments, see Davidson in Sutherland, *Studies*, pp. 251-61.
43. R. Davidson, 'Social Conflict and Social Administration: the Conciliation Act in British Industrial Relations' in T.C. Smout (ed.), *The Search for Wealth and Stability* (London, 1979), pp. 185-6.
44. Ibid., p. 193.
45. Dilke Papers, BM Add MS. 43920, fos. 47-8, Askwith to Dilke, 7 Mar. 1908; *Report of the Select Committee on Homework*, PP 1908 (246) VIII, p. 14.

46. PRO BT 13/134, Askwith to Smith, nd 1909.
47. See Merton, *Reader in Bureaucracy*, pp. 368-70.
48. This analysis is based on *Return of Public Service Appointments*, PP 1912-13 (455), LVI.
49. Harris, *Unemployment and Politics*, p. 351; Davidson, 'Board of Trade', p. 571.
50. J.A.M. Caldwell, 'The Genesis of the Ministry of Labour', *Public Administration*, vol. 37 (1959), p. 370; P. Smith, *Disraelian Conservatism and Social Reform* (London, 1967), p. 242.
51. M. Wright, 'Treasury Control 1854-1914' in Sutherland, *Studies*, Ch. 8.
52. Calculations based upon PP *Annual Appropriation Accounts*.
53. Wright, 'Treasury Control', p. 218.
54. H.V. Emy, 'The Impact of Financial Policy on English Party Politics before 1914', *Historical Journal*, vol. XV (1972), p. 117; J.R. Hay, 'Employers and Social Policy in Britain: the Evolution of Welfare Legislation, 1905-14', *Social History*, vol. IV (1977), pp. 435-55.
55. Davidson, 'Board of Trade', pp. 581-2.
56. N. Whiteside, 'Welfare Insurance and Casual Labour: a Study of Administrative Intervention in Industrial Employment, 1906-1926', *Economic History Review*, vol. XXXII (1979), pp. 507-522.
57. Wright, 'Treasury Control', p. 225.
58. See, for example, Harris, *Unemployment and Politics*, p. 328.
59. W.J. Brown, *So Far* (London, 1943), pp. 220-1.
60. P. Addison, *The Road to 1945* (London, 1975), pp. 60, 66, 110.
61. *New Statesman*, 28 Jan. 1939.
62. M. Beloff, 'The Whitehall Factor: the Role of the Higher Civil Service 1919-39' in G. Peele and C. Cook (eds.), *The Politics of Reappraisal* (London, 1975), p. 210.
63. B.B. Gilbert, *British Social Policy, 1919-39* (London, 1970), p. 308.
64. R. Skidelsky, *Politicians and the Slump* (London, 1970 edn), p. 430.
65. P. Abrams, 'The Failure of Social Reform 1918-20', *Past and Present*, vol. XXIV (1963), p. 47.
66. J.S. Macnicol, 'The Movement for Family Allowances in Britain, 1918-45', unpublished PhD thesis, University of Edinburgh, 1978, p. 495.
67. A.E. Booth, 'An Administrative Experiment in Unemployment Policy in the Thirties', *Public Administration*, vol. LVI (1978), p. 148.
68. M.A. Crowther, 'The Later Years in the Workhouse', in Thane, *Origins*, pp. 51-2, and 'Vagrants and the Poor Law 1882-1929' (unpublished), p. 13.
69. Harris, *William Beveridge*, pp. 365, 369 and 'Some Aspects of Social Policy in Britain during the Second World War', this volume, pp. 247-62.
70. J.S. Macnicol, 'Family Allowances and Less Eligibility' in Thane, *Origins*, pp. 177, 191-2.
71. Booth, 'An Administrative Experiment', p. 151, and 'The Timing and Content of Government Policies to Assist the Depressed Areas, 1920-39', unpublished PhD thesis, University of Kent, 1975, p. 374.
72. Harris, *William Beveridge*, pp. 382, 386, 389; see also this volume, pp. 250ff.
73. Lord Butler, *The Art of the Possible* (London, 1971), pp. 93-4; S. Howson and D. Winch, *The Economic Advisory Council 1930-39* (Cambridge 1977), pp. 157-8.
74. Beloff, 'The Whitehall Factor', p. 227.
75. This was attempted in R. Lowe, 'The Erosion of State Intervention in Britain 1917-24', *Economic History Review*, vol. XXXI (1978), pp. 270-86.
76. Much of this paragraph, which refers only to the home Civil Service, is

based on Kelsall, *Higher Civil Servants*. The quotations are from pp. 52 and 75.

77. For an elaboration of subsequent references to the Ministry of Labour, see R. Lowe, 'The Ministry of Labour, 1916-1924: a Graveyard of Social Reform', *Public Administration*, vol. LII (1974), pp. 415-38, and 'The Demand for a Ministry of Labour, its Creation and Initial Role, 1916-24', unpublished PhD thesis, London University, 1975, esp. pp. 210-34.

78. D.N. Chester, *Lessons of the British War Economy* (1951), p. 43.

79. There is a spirited defence of this philosophy in Dale, *Higher Civil Service*, Appendix C.

80. Fry, *Statesmen in Disguise*, p. 58.

81. See Lowe, 'Erosion of State Intervention', pp. 278-81; R.H. Campbell, 'The Scottish Office and the Special Areas in the 1930s', *Historical Journal*, vol. XXII (1979), p. 180; J.D. Millett, *The Unemployment Assistance Board* (London, 1940), pp. 122-3.

82. PRO Lab 2/1907/CEB 649/1922.

83. PRO T161/303/S40504/04; T172/1828. The latter recorded that 'we think that if Mr Stewart is carefully handled it should not be difficult to keep him both contented and reasonably straight. It seems desirable that you the Chancellor of the Exchequer should see him and tell him in confidence of the general budget situation so that he may see (what probably has not dawned on him) that there are not countless millions available.'

84 PRO Lab 2/1215/ED 48401/1926; sixth meeting of the UAB, Violet Markham papers (box 27), quoted in Macnicol (thesis).

85. Dale, *Higher Civil Service*, pp. 46-54.

86. The fate of pre-war bureaucratic innovators was mixed. Some died (like Morant and Aves); some were pushed into backwaters by Lloyd George (like Braithwaite and Llewellyn Smith); some resigned out of frustration with their political masters (like Beveridge, Keynes and Askwith); others were attracted away from social policy to other, especially international, challenges (like H.B. Butler and Lord Salter).

87. PRO Prem 4/8/6.

88. F.M. Miller, 'National Assistance or Unemployment Assistance? The British Cabinet and Relief Policy', *Journal of Contemporary History*, vol. 9 (1974), p. 165.

89. References as in note 81.

90. Dale, *Higher Civil Service*, pp. 133, 139.

91. Millett, *The Unemployment Assistance Board*, p. 220.

92. A. Deacon, *In Search of the Scrounger* (London, 1976), p. 37.

93. See, for example, Lowe, 'Erosion of State Intervention', pp. 276-82.

94. The contemporary debate is summarised in Millett, *The Unemployment Assistance Board*, Ch. 3.

95. See, for example, the evidence in Whiteside, 'Welfare Insurance'.

96. See Dale, *Higher Civil Service*, pp. 40, 163. Oral history can, perhaps, repair some of the damage.

97. A. Bullock, *The Life and Times of Ernest Bevin* (London, 1977), vol. 2, pp. 119-22.

98. Millett, *The Unemployment Assistance Board*, pp. 207-14; Booth, 'An Administrative Experiment', pp. 151-2.

99. PEP, *Report on the British Social Services* (1937), p. 98; Q. Crisp, *The Naked Civil Servant* (London, 1977), p. 57. Crisp was a homosexual of extravagant (to say the least) manner. He found 'a truly enlightened' man in an employment exchange manager: 'When I turned . . . to thank him he said "If it all gets too much for you, come and see me again: I will see what I can do". As he uttered these words, he placed his hand on my shoulder, a gesture which,

in the circumstances, amounted to a daring vote of confidence.'

100. R. Church, *The Voyage Home* (London, 1964), p. 107.

101. Macnicol, in Thane, *Origins*, pp. 191-2: Booth, 'An Administrative Experiment', p. 153.

102. This was the specific intention of Treasury policy. It was Sir Warren Fisher who rejected recruitment direct from university for 'if you do that, they then get to work and take their little pens in their infant hands and they write away little criticisms of every sort and kind, very clever ones no doubt, but there is no training for constructive work.' Quoted in H. Roseveare, *The Treasury* (London, 1969), p. 253.

14 THE SOCIAL POLICY OF THE ATTLEE GOVERNMENT*

J. Heß

The creation of the welfare state was one of the main achievements of the Attlee government. But though there have been many advances in the various fields of social policy after 1945, the welfare state has not succeeded in its principal aim of the abolition of poverty. A vast literature exists to illustrate this and many other less vital inadequacies of the present system.[1] There are also a number of general historical studies on the evolution of the British welfare state.[2] But there is no thorough and detailed study of the various problems of Attlee's social policy, just as there does not yet exist a critical overall assessment of the Attlee period.[3] It would be futile to attempt to close this gap by a short essay. So what this chapter will try to do is to outline some general features of Attlee's welfare state and to examine more particularly certain aspects of the social security system. Finally, it will raise the question as to how the Labour Party reacted to its own achievements at the end of the Attlee period.

In this context there is no real need to find a perfect definition of what social policy is.[4] It may suffice to use Arthur Marwick's definition of the welfare state, 'as one in which full community responsibility is assumed for four major sectors of social well-being: social security, which means provision against interruption of earnings through sickness, injury, old age, or unemployment; health; housing; and education'. He also mentions the state's 'responsibility to maintain reasonable standards of living and to look after the cultural health of society.'[5]

In 1945 the Labour Party gained most of its political impetus by its determination to avoid the economic and social failures of the interwar period by far-reaching reform measures. It was mainly because of the war that a more general approach to reform had become possible. The reconstruction planning of the Coalition government was pushed ahead and stimulated by the ideas and demands of individuals, parties and interest groups. Though there was a consensus that Britain after

---

* In preparing this paper I have been greatly helped by the comments of G.R. Carr and D. Fraser.

1945 would not and must not resemble the Britain between the wars, the overwhelming Labour victory in 1945 showed that after the radicalising influences of the war it was Labour rather than the Conservatives that was believed to be able to fulfil the widespread hopes for a new Britain of economic efficiency and social security. Even if the influence of the wartime experiences was vital, it ought not to be forgotten that to a great extent 'the agreement on the need for social reform, a planned economy and full employment' derived already from the pre-war decade.[6] The long tradition of reform thinking in the Labour movement, reaching much further back, must also be mentioned here.[7]

Moreover it must be emphasised that the Labour Party in May 1942 — at a moment when William Beveridge together with his committee was busy putting together his famous Beveridge Report on the Social Services — at its annual conference not only welcomed the establishment of the inter-departmental committee led by Beveridge, but also clearly stated that

in the view of the Labour Party there should be: a) One comprehensive system of social security. b) Adequate cash payments to provide security whatever the contingency. c) The provision of cash payments from national funds for all children through a scheme of Family Allowances. d) The right of all forms of medical attention and treatment through a National Health Service.[8]

The positive reaction to Beveridge's proposals and the demand for their immediate realisation after the end of the fighting, as expressed at the 1943 annual conference of the Labour Party,[9] were just as logical in the social reform tradition of the Labour movement as the pro-Beveridge activities by Labour in Parliament and in the Cabinet.[10] The government reconstruction planning in 1943 and 1944 which resulted in the important White Papers on the National Health Service, on employment policy and on the social services was apparently also strongly influenced by the Labour Ministers, who held key posts in the Reconstruction Committee of the Cabinet.[11] Though we have to be careful not to exaggerate the role of these Labour politicians in formulating the details of the reform proposals during the war, it is evident that they were strongly committed to social reform policies.

The 1945 Labour aspirations for the reform of the social services were part of a closely interwoven general reform package, aiming at full employment, the establishment of effective economic controls, public ownership of vital parts of industry and social welfare.[12] The motives behind the ideas for social policy reform were partly humanitarian, partly political and partly economic. To end the social miseries of the past, to avoid a recurrence of the human waste of the pre-war period, and to achieve a higher degree of social equity and social unity, these aims were strongly influenced by humanitarian impulses. At the same time they were an expression of the basic political values of the Labour movement, especially of its fundamental objective of achieving more equality. Keynesian ideas found expression in the objective of maintaining a high level of purchasing power. The redistributive function of the social services was clearly seen. But after 1945 it was soon recognised that it was the lower-income groups that 'financed the social security schemes through their direct and indirect tax payments, and that in the redistribution of incomes that took place the transfer from rich to poor was much smaller in size than the transfer of income inside the lower income groups themselves'.[13] Still, the maintenance of the food subsidies after 1945, the immediate post-war adjustments in the taxation system under Dalton, by which the lowest income groups were considerably relieved,[14] and the establishment of the welfare state were all interconnected means of bringing about a fairer distribution of income within the class-ridden British society. This, however, did not amount to social revolution. But building on a long history of pragmatic reform thinking, and strongly entrenched in its democratic and parliamentary tradition, Labour had already made it quite clear in its 1945 election manifesto that its post-war reform programme was not implying a 'weekend revolution'.[15] It was a moderate policy of gradual change, put into practice by a rather aged team of Labour politicians.[16]

Turning now to the particular sectors of the welfare state, there is little need to write at length about education. First, because of its concentration on the implementation of the Butler 1944 Education Act, Labour's innovatory action in this field after 1945 was minimal.[17] Second, education as a particular field of social policy does not belong to the subject-matter of any of the other contributions to this book. Its importance as a social service would indeed require a book of its own.

Under the immediate post-war conditions housing represented 'the most pressing post-war social need'.[18] This was clearly recognised by the Labour government. As early as August 1945 Attlee stated in a Cabinet Note that no delay could be afforded in pushing on with the housing programme and that 'the utmost drive and vigour' had to be put 'into the campaign for houses'.[19] The Attlee government, however, did not fulfil its promise to create a Ministry of Housing and Planning. The main responsibility for housing remained with the Ministry of Health. Aneurin Bevan's record as regards house-building was poorer than that of his Conservative successor after 1951 and has therefore been criticised, but it must not be forgotten that he had to face grave financial and material shortages.[20] Thus a recent commentator has concluded that 'in the circumstances Labour's achievement was rather better than it is normally painted,' stressing especially and with great justification that Bevan displayed 'a laudable, if not always attainable ambition' to improve the standard of housing.[21]

The introduction of the National Health Service — recently described as 'perhaps the most beneficial reform ever enacted in England'[22] — clearly has pre-war and wartime roots.[23] But it was Aneurin Bevan as the Minister of Health in the Attlee government who strongly influenced particular aspects of the structure of the service and played an important personal role in the struggle for its institution. The campaign which the British Medical Association led against the implementation of the National Health Service Act[24] made this reform measure one of the most hard-fought issues facing the post-war Labour government.[25] Bevan, in order to break the doctors' still very strong opposition, was forced in 1948 to state that it was not his intention to introduce a state-salaried medical service. Whether this was a real concession can indeed be doubted, as Bevan did not seem to have believed in the possibility of introducing this old aim, especially of the Labour left, within a short time. In the Cabinet meeting of 20 December 1945 he had stated, for instance, that the proposed remuneration system for the doctors should 'lead eventually to a full-time salaried service'.[26]

Against the opposition of local authority interests — which were expressed in the Cabinet by Herbert Morrison, the Lord President of the Council, as a defender of the strong local government traditions of the Labour Party — Bevan succeeded in convincing the Cabinet of the necessity of a clear-cut nationalisation of all hospitals whether they had been local authority or voluntary hospitals, and of the need to introduce a new regional organisation for the administration of the hospital system.[27] The general practitioners were also brought under a new administrative structure. The main purpose of the whole measure was to overcome the existing patchwork of very unequally distributed medical services and to provide the whole population with a really comprehensive service irrespective of means. Thus the new

National Health Service was not based on the insurance principle, but was financed out of taxation for most of its costs. Because of the previous lack of medical provision, but also the unexpected expansion of medical costs, finance soon became a continual problem.[28] The introduction of charges on spectacles and dentures in 1951 broke with the principle of a completely free health service. The overall financial requirements for government spending under Cold War conditions clearly restricted the financial scope of the new service. One of the results was that initially it obtained few new resources. Hospital buildings were only improved or renewed in the sixties, and few local health centres were built. Still, it seems fair to characterise the Labour government's measure as 'a noble start'.[29]

After this very brief and by no means comprehensive survey of the other socio-political activities, the social security system introduced by the Attlee government will be treated in more detail. The key question in this context is whether the Labour government did indeed do nothing more than 'put the Beveridge plan into action'.[30] It should be remembered here first that any government established at the end of the Second World War would have had to implement the greater part of the Beveridge Report, as G.D.H. Cole pointed out in 1949.[31] In one of its pre-election pamphlets Labour stated quite openly in 1945 that there was 'no very wide margin of difference between the declared policies of parties on this question'.[32] This remarkable agreement as part of the wartime consensus lasted basically, though not in all details, well into the fifties.[33] Therefore it would be wrong to say that the postwar social security system was the result of Labour's aspirations only. There is an element of doubt, however, whether the Conservatives would have given the same priority as Labour to this field of reform. Furthermore the general content of their reform package would certainly have looked different. It has been underlined by Arthur Marwick that the Conservatives would not have stuck to the truly revolutionary principle of universality.[34] So, irrespective of the co-operative attitude of the Conservatives in the parliamentary discussions of much of the social services reform legislation,[35] the actual introduction of the welfare state owed a great deal to the reforming zeal of the Labour Party.[36]

According to Beveridge, there existed three basic assumptions on which his plan would have to be based: first, the maintenance of full employment after the war (the Labour government did its best in this field, only to discover soon that it was not faced with the problems of a slump and unemployment, but with inflationary pressure and a severe shortage of labour); second, a National Health Service; third, the payment of family allowances. The last was introduced by the Family Allowances Act of 1945, which was passed just before the 1945 election by both sides of Parliament and which was the first measure the Labour government put into practice in the social security field. Immediately after its return to power, Labour turned with great speed to the realisation of its reform programme. In the 1945/6 session three major social policy Acts were passed (among a lot of other legislation): the National Health Service Act, already mentioned above, the National Insurance Act and the National Insurance (Industrial Injuries) Act. the last placed workmen's compensation — the reform of which had long been discussed — on a completely new footing, making the state and no longer the employer responsible for the payment of benefit in case of industrial injury. Industrial injury benefits and disablement pensions became part of the social insurance system and as such they were to be based on compulsory weekly contributions. Still, they differed in one very important aspect from other forms of benefit: benefit in case of industrial injury was to be still considerably higher than in case of sickness or unemployment. This difference had been enforced under strong union pressure; the unions had threatened that they would have their men in Parliament vote against the Bill unless an even higher sum of benefit was accepted, but eventually they proved willing to compromise at 45 shillings per week for an individual benefit recipient[37] (instead of 26 shillings as in all other cases). This was 73 per cent higher than sickness or unemployment benefit, a difference which, though not challenged in principle, was reduced to 63 per cent in the late 1960s.[38] This difference in benefit as well as its inclusion in the social security system had already been recommended by Beveridge. The measure differed from his proposals by making the payment of the higher rate independent of the workman's contribution record, from the time of his injury, without any intermediate period of incapacity such as the 13 weeks Beveridge had suggested.[39]

The example of the National Insurance (Industrial Injuries) Act is the first that shows how much the social security legislation of the post-war Labour Government was founded on the ideas and proposals of Beveridge. There were differences, though, sometimes in details, but also on more substantive issues. Before these are dealt with it should first be stated that the Beveridge Report was a continuous point of reference in the discourses of the Cabinet and the Social Services Committee, i.e. the Cabinet Committee for the supervision of social policy reform, which was chaired by A. Greenwood, the Lord Privy

Seal and functioned from 1945 to 1947. Moreover, Attlee in his speech on the National Insurance Bill explicitly acknowledged that it was based on the Beveridge Report.[40]

As the main deviations from Beveridge's proposals José Harris has named 'the rejection of the subsistence principle, the exclusion of friendly societies from administration of benefits, the whittling down of his conception of a "housewives' policy" and the failure to national- ise industrial insurance'.[41] There was also an important positive differ- ence: retirement pensions were to be paid at their full level in 1946, whereas Beveridge had wanted a gradual levelling up in stages over twenty years before the full pensions would be paid. This deviation from the insurance principle was obviously influenced to a great extent by the expectations and demands from within the Labour movement. The Attlee government was confronted with even higher demands at the 1946 annual conference of the Labour Party (actually demanding the same higher benefit level for old age pensioners and other benefit recipients as in the case of industrial injury), but refused to accept these.[42] The insurance principle involved clear financial limitations, for higher benefits would also have made higher contributions neces- sary, and these were considered to be already 'on a very high level indeed', as James Griffiths, the Minister of National Insurance, con- ceded.[43] It was on the immediate introduction of full level retire- ment pensions that Griffiths based his claim at the 1947 annual confer- ence of the Labour Party that they had legislated for a scheme 'infi- nitely better than the scheme contemplated in the Beveridge Report',[44] a claim that certainly contained a lot of justified pride, but hardly the whole truth.

As regards the negative deviations mentioned by Harris, no more will be said here about the more restricted provisions for housewives. The other three issues, however, deserve some comment. None of them actually formed a real point of discussion in the meeting of the Cabinet or the Social Services Committee. More research will be necessary to clear up what happened before these stages were reached, i.e. on the level of administrators and experts within the Ministry of National Insurance.

Labour Party papers and spokesmen explicitly stressed in 1949 that the failure to nationalise industrial insurance had been the 'great exception' in realising the main proposals of the Beveridge Report.[45] After long and difficult internal discussions this aim got a central place in the election programme for 1950.[46] The outcome of the 1950 election and new doubts on nationalisation as a means of socialist policy in general, however, made all practical steps in this direction impossible.

Beveridge and with him the Liberals had considered the inclusion of the friendly societies in the administration of the social security system a vital point in order to provide for the possibility of voluntary action and thereby the personalisation and humanisation of national insurance.[47] The Labour government nevertheless decided in favour of the introduction of a direct central administration by the state, as only a state administration seemed to fit a comprehensive state scheme. Yet the administration of the social security services remained to some extent patchwork, since the Ministry of National Insurance held responsibility for only part of a field, in which the Ministry of Health, the Ministry of Pensions and the National Assistance Board were also to be active. In order to establish at least some kind of link between the government departments and the public, several advisory committees both at the central and at the local level were instituted, such as the National Insurance Advisory Committee, the Industrial Injuries Advisory Council or the National Insurance Local Advisory Committees. Advice about the operation of the law and the scrutiny of any new regulations made by the Minister were their main tasks. Both central committees were small, with less than ten members who were appointed by the Minister after consultation with the employers, the trade unions and others.[48] This hardly gave the public a real voice.

There is no doubt that from a 1946 standpoint the National Insurance Bill, in consolidating the existing schemes of insurance against sickness, unemployment and old age was 'the culmination of half a century's development of our British Social Services', as was claimed by James Griffiths in his opening speech on the second reading of the Bill.[49] This implied a high degree of continuity which mainly found expression in the deliberate adherence to the insurance principle. But how did the leading Labour politicians consider it possible to combine the insurance principle with a sufficient standard of benefit, or to put the question in another way, how could an insurance system with flat-rate contributions and flat-rate benefits and the aim of universality provide the 'National Minimum Standard', which Griffiths expected to be established at the time?[50] Especially if on the one hand actuarial rectitude was accepted as a basic pre-condition of the whole scheme, i.e. a clear relation between the benefit level and the contribution level, and if on the other hand there was an absolute limit to the contribution level with regard to the general workman's financial capacity.

Contrary to the assertions of José Harris and contrary to what actually happened to the spending power of national insurance benefits after 1948, Labour Ministers seem to have believed in 1946 that they were going to provide something like a subsistence basis. How was this possible? Without going into too much detail, it is necessary to mention here that the National Insurance Act provided the following standard benefit rate: 26 shillings per week for a single recipient and 42 shillings for a couple. The standardisation of this rate for sickness benefit, unemployment benefit and retirement pensions was certainly an achievement of the Labour government, especially as this standardisation in some cases implied considerable increases above the pre-1946 level. More important in our context, however, is the question of how these basic figures were arrived at.

In his memorandum of 9 November 1945[51] James Griffiths stated that he in fact did not intend to fix the rates of benefit and pensions on an absolute subsistence basis. Beveridge had actually come to the conclusion in 1942, too, that because of the enormous variations in working-class rents all over the country it was not feasible to introduce real subsistence benefits. Therefore he had allowed himself 'to be stuck with the paradoxical proposition that benefits should be based on subsistence needs and yet should be uniform for all parts of the country', a proposition which provided the Official Committee on the Beveridge Report with an easy excuse for rejecting the principle of subsistence in early 1943.[52] James Griffiths in his argument did not go as far back as that, but approvingly quoted the 1944 Coalition White Paper on Social Insurance in which it had been stated that

> the conception of relating individual payments precisely to individual needs is not really capable of realisation in an insurance scheme and that the right objective is a rate of benefit which provides a reasonable insurance against want and at the same time takes account of the maximum contribution which the great body of contributors can properly be asked to bear.

So Griffiths concluded that it was 'in fact impracticable to make the rates vary at any time according to the precise needs of different individuals' or 'to vary them at short intervals of time according to variations in the general cost of living'. In order to nevertheless give the scheme a sound base from the outset, in his view two essential requirements had to be satisifed:

a) The leading rates must be fixed initially at figures which can be justified broadly in relation to the present level of the cost of living; and b) definite arrangements should be made for a review of the rates from this point of view at periodic intervals.[53]

While the first principle was sound, the second was not.

Unless private evidence to the contrary can be found, there is little denying the fact that the Minister of National Insurance seemed to believe in 1946 what he said when he asserted in his introductory speech on the National Insurance Bill in Parliament that he had 'endeavoured to give a broad subsistence basis to the leading rates'.[54] That J. Griffiths was serious in aiming at the introduction of a system which provided 'a broad subsistence basis' can also be confirmed by the stress on this aim in his speech on social security already at the 1944 annual conference of the Labour Party: 'We affirm the principle that these benefits ought to aim at providing what is sometimes called subsistence standard, though I prefer the term we have used, a national minimum standard of life below which no one shall fall.'[55] As to the figure of 42 shillings for a couple − only this figure will be explained here, as all other figures were more or less all derived from it − it had been arrived at by taking up Beveridge's so-called subsistence figure and adapting it to the 1946 money value. Beveridge had first estimated the 1938 cost of living and then in 1942 added 25 per cent to it in view of wartime price increases. The Labour government proposed in 1946 to raise the basic figure by 31 per cent above the pre-war level and expressed the ill-founded confidence, which proved to be nothing more than a 'pious wish',[56] that it would be able to hold the cost of living at this new level of 31 per cent above pre-war prices.[57] While Beveridge had, in this way, proposed 40 shillings, Griffiths' calculation resulted in the 42 shillings mentioned above. Apart from the over-optimistic idea of being able to stabilise the cost of living under inflationary post-war conditions over long periods of time − an idea which obviously reflected both the inter-war conditions of little economic growth and a marked over-confidence in the steering capacities of the state in economic developments − the orientation on Beveridge's basic figure was doubtful; for it has to be questioned what basic standard was really provided by his figure. Yet the Labour spokesman felt justified, as he could refer to the fact that in 1942 Beveridge's calculations had been accepted 'in all quarters of the House and, indeed, outside the House'.[58] Though Attlee admitted in his speech on the following day that the proposed benefit level represented no more than a 'very modest standard of life',[59] no one in the Cabinet or before in the Social Services Committee had questioned the validity of the calculations and principles of the Minister of National Insurance. On the contrary in both bodies Griffiths enjoyed 'general support'.[60] Hugh Dalton, then Chancellor of the Exchequer, was proud that the pension rate of 42 shillings was more than twice as high as the 20 shillings paid to a retired couple at that time.[61] To mention a last witness who certainly cannot be suspected of wanting to flatter the Labour government: the Conservative R.A. Butler stated in his speech on the National Insurance Bill too that 'there is, clearly, a subsistence basis for all pensioners, whether they are in dire need or not.'[62]

But, indeed, what seemed to be a subsistence basis in 1946, at least in a broad sense, ceased to be so later. The retail price index — I am not sure whether Beveridge had used this source, but it is certainly a good indicator of the general price trend — was in 1948 72 per cent higher than in 1938.[63] It goes without saying that there must have been a considerable loss of value in the standard benefit rate of 42 shillings even before the whole system started on 5 July 1948, the appointed day. According to Heclo, the flat-rate benefit level in Britain in 1948 corresponded to only 19 per cent of the average industrial wage.[64] Evidently this could no longer be called a subsistence basis.[65] Nor was there an adequate provision for further price increases. Only in the mid-fifties did the increases in National Insurance benefits catch up with the rise in the retail price index.[66] The review of the rates only after intervals of five years and the denial of an automatic cost of living adjustment which Griffiths had strongly defended in 1946, and which became part of the National Insurance Act,[67] were at the heart of this problem. Here was the main reason why a great number of recipients of benefit could not make ends meet with their National Insurance benefit and had to apply for supplementary assistance, which again implied a means test.[68] This dependency of many recipients of National Insurance benefits on needs-tested assistance — even if these needs tests cannot be compared with the notorious household means tests — constituted a major inroad into the principle of universality and of benefit paid of right as a consequence of the insurance principle.

Compared to the major problem of the purchasing value of the intended National Insurance benefits and pensions, the problems really discussed in the Cabinet were of relatively less importance. The first concerned the payment of continuous unemployment benefit without time limit,[69] the second the amount that should be paid to single old age pensioners (21 or 26 shillings per week) and the third the general retirement procedure. All these points had been raised by the Chancellor of the Exchequer in an attempt to reduce the financial burden.[70] While there is little need to deal in detail with these points of discussion here, it should certainly be emphasised that the Labour government indeed was prepared to put a heavy financial load on the shoulders of the state by establishing the welfare state. It was estimated in 1945 that for National Insurance and National Assistance together the Treasury in 1948 would provide £179 million (this was expected to rise to £278 million in 1958 and to £380 million in 1968), while £331 million in each of these years would come from the contributions of insured persons and employers and £21 million from the interest of existing funds.[71] In reality these figures did not materialise, first of all because of the continuity of full employment, with a rate of unemployment much lower than the 8 per cent that had been reckoned with in 1945, and secondly because of the introduction of earnings-related contributions in the sixties.[72] The National Insurance system was steadily financed for 73 to 90 per cent of its expenditure by contributions. Still, it was quite clear that only the future of the British economy would decide whether it would be possible to fulfil the hopes and promises of the social security measures in the period 1946 to 1948.

If the 1948 National Assistance Bill is only mentioned in passing, it must not be forgotten that it was to become of much more far-reaching importance than its progenitors had thought. When Aneurin Bevan introduced the National Assistance Bill in the House of Commons in November 1947, he stressed its role by calling it 'the coping stone on the structure of the Social Services in Great Britain'.[73] National Assistance was considered as a help in residual cases, for all those who were not at all or not sufficiently covered by the National Insurance benefits, because for instance their previous contributions did not come up to the required level. As has already been said, the low level of National Insurance benefits made it necessary for many of its recipients to apply for National Assistance. Most of it was paid in supplementation of retirement pensions, for example in 1949 48.2 per cent of total National Assistance expenditure.[74] As was clearly recognised within a few years, in this manner National Assistance was underpinning the whole scheme of National Insurance.[75]

Aneurin Bevan remarked in the same speech that the introduction of the National Assistance Bill marked the end of a whole period of

the social history of Great Britain.[76] This air of finality was typical of
Labour's approach to the social security questions in the last years of
the Attlee government. In the proud feeling of having abolished the inhuman Poor Law, which had existed since Elizabethan times, and of
having put in its place 'the most comprehensive system of social
security ever created', expanding the social services 'to the highest
level ever reached',[77] Labour looked to a past which no longer seemed
to threaten the present. This explains such claims as that in 1950:
'Destitution has been abolished.'[78] In the fifties and sixties it became
obvious that there was little reason for so much self-congratulation and
confidence. Without looking too far into the subsequent years, it is
obvious that the orientation on the past blinded the leading Labour
politicians to the forthcoming problems. There was also little understanding of the problems of deprivation and maladjustment, the importance of which seemed less prominent in the post-war attempt to
provide for rather basic needs.[79]

Most important, however, was that in the immediate post-war
years Labour had spent most of its innovatory energy, so that hardly
anything of it was left at the end of its term of office. R.H.S. Crossman rightly wrote in 1952:

> after scarcely four years in office, the Government had fulfilled its
> historic mission. The nationalisation of half a dozen major indus-
> tries, the construction of an all-in system of social security and
> a free health service, and the tentative application of planning to
> the national economy — the achievement of these reforms seemed
> to have exhausted the content of British socialism.[80]

This 'loss of momentum', another phrase used by Crossman in the same
essay, certainly manifested itself in the field of social security (it was
also true in other fields, but that need not concern us here). So it was
frankly stated in the 1950 election programme 'that new commitments
for further expansion of our social services can only be accepted as
production goes up; indeed, more production will be necessary to
underpin the immense changes on which we have already embarked'.
The generally accepted conclusion at the time was that 'what is needed
now is not so much new legislation as the full development, through
efficient and economical administration, of all the services provided by
the Acts passed in Labour's first term of office.'[81] Under the pressing
economic needs of these years[82] Labour did not dare to look ahead.[83]
The stress was put on consolidation, on the completion of what had

been begun, but this could not conceal the vacuum as far as constructive policies were concerned.

It would be wrong, however, not to mention that some inadequacies were already realised at this stage. The group of Labour parliamentarians who published the pamphlet *Keeping Left* in 1950 distinctly emphasised that the minimum set by the scales of National Assistance ought to be raised immediately, because it was no longer sufficient to maintain health and to prevent malnutrition.[84] While this comment still remained within the bounds of the old flat-rate universalist system and showed little more perspicacity in realising social needs than the official party statements, a really new idea was first expressed in the circles of the British Labour Party in 1950.

One problem of the flat-rate contributions and flat-rate benefit system was its regressive character. Because even at the outset it hit the low wage-earners quite hard already, there was no possibility of raising standards by raising contributions, as the low income-earner would not have been able to cope with such an increase. The logical consequence was to graduate the scheme. A very first step in this direction had already been taken in the National Insurance Act itself, as exceptionally low-paid workers had to pay smaller contributions.[85] But this was an exception just in order to make sure that the flat-rate system would work at all. The first real sign of thinking further ahead can be found in a speech by J. Griffiths at the 1946 annual conference of the Labour Party. Looking towards the future, he reflected on the possibility of devising at a later stage 'some method of financing our Social Insurance schemes which does equate more fairly the contribution made by everyone to his or her ability to pay that contribution'.[86] From this reference to progressive contributions there was still a long way to go to a system combining earnings-related contributions with earnings-related benefits. It was at the special top-level conference of the Labour Party at Dorking in May 1950 that it was proposed to provide 'additional superannuation to those who were prepared to pay higher weekly contributions'.[87] Instead of offering universal protection against poverty on a very basic level indeed, the new aim became the maintenance of real income, the provision of a safeguard against the loss of an acquired standard of living.[88] For a long time to come the Labour Party could not make up its mind about this vital change of principle, as the flat-rate structure of national insurance seemed to symbolise equality and so was too deeply engrained in its thinking. Earnings-related benefits after all preserve in time of sickness, unemployment and old age those inequalities of income which are present during a working life, and so are inconsistent with the basic principle expressed in the fundamental Labour aim of 'work or maintenance'.[89] However, the growth of private superannuation schemes in the fifties which resulted in new inequalities, as the larger part of the working population was not covered by such schemes, led to a new approach.[90] With Labour out of power, the Conservatives had the chance to start their own superannuation scheme in 1959/61.[91] Only in 1966 did Labour introduce earnings-related unemployment and sickness benefits. In this way, a two-tier system of flat-rate plus earnings-related benefits replaced the uniform Beveridge system of the forties.

Let us ask finally whether the Attlee government missed a chance in the field of social policy. It certainly did not achieve a 'social revolution' as was so easily assumed in the late 1940s.[92] Instead it confined itself to an extension and modification of the existing social services. But whether this was indeed 'little more than an administrative tidying up of social security provisions'[93] still remains to be discussed when all sources are open and it is possible to assess the achievements of the Labour government in the full knowledge of the internal and external difficulties under which it had to work. Even then there will be no common view. It is evidently very much a question of perspective whether the easing of the stresses of a continuing capitalist society is regarded as a success or whether it appears as unimportant compared with a real change in the fundamental structures of society.[94] From this angle the creation of the welfare state can have the appearance, to a considerable degree, of a substitute for the transformation of society.[95] From a more pragmatic point of view the answer may very well be that it was remarkable under the immediate post-war circumstances that the Attlee government achieved as much as it did.[96] 'Perfect' solutions could not be expected, especially not at the end of the Second World War, which had such a devastating effect upon Britain's material resources. It should also not be overlooked — quite apart from the particular circumstances of those years — that generally each so-called solution in the development of social policy tends to lead to a host of new problems overlooked and/or created by that 'solution'.[97] Bearing all this in mind, there is much reason to accept that Labour in 1951 had accomplished much or most of its rather limited pre-war and wartime mission.[98] The aims of the Labour movement, or rather the majority of it, did not imply sweeping structural changes. The modesty of its reform programme allowed for nothing more than modest reforms, directed at overcoming the worst excesses of the pre-war capitalist system in Britain. It was such an attitude which informed the 1950 Dorking conference statement that 'we can no longer base our appeal on the need to sweep away oppressive social evils. Many of them have already been removed. To this extent our own success in the past is making things difficult for us now.'[99] In the same vein Anthony Crosland stressed in 1952 that 'the easy and spectacular things have all been done.'[100] At the end of a long journey Labour had to shed some traditional views and find new bearings under the conditions of welfare capitalism. Then unanticipated factors began to show the insufficiency of the universalist insurance-based and minimum-oriented approach and new social needs beyond those of the mere abolition of want came more and more to the foreground.

Notes

1. Cf. Eric Butterworth and Robert Holman (eds.), *Social Welfare in Modern Britain* (Glasgow, 1975); L.J. Macfarlane, *Issues in British Politics since 1945*, 2nd edn (London, 1978), pp. 54-82.

2. Cf. R.C. Birch, *The Shaping of the Welfare State* (London, 1974); Maurice Bruce (ed.), *The Rise of the Welfare State. English Social Policy 1601-1971* (London, 1973); Derek Fraser, *The Evolution of the British Welfare State* (London, 1973); J.R. Hay, *The Development of the British Welfare State 1880-1975* (London, 1978).

3. Michael Sissons and Philip French (eds.), *Age of Austerity* (London, 1963) cannot be regarded as such. For the best recent survey cf. C.J. Bartlett, *A History of Postwar Britain 1945-74* (London, 1977), pp. 1-93.

4. Cf. David G. Gill, *Unravelling Social Policy. Theory, Analysis, and Political Action towards Social Equality* (Cambridge, Mass., 1973), p. 24.

5. Arthur Marwick, 'The Labour Party and the Welfare State in Britain, 1900-1948' in Henry R. Winkler (ed.), *Twentieth Century Britain. National Power and Social Welfare* (New York, 1976), p. 172.

6. John Stevenson and Chris Cook, *The Slump. Society and Politics during the Depression* (London, 1977), p. 281.

7. Cf. Marwick, 'The Labour Party'.

8. *The Labour Party 41st Annual Conference Report 1942*, p. 132.

9. *The Labour Party 42nd Annual Conference Report 1943*, pp. 136-42.

10. Cf. Paul Addison, *The Road to 1945. British Politics and the Second World War* (London, 1975), pp. 222-5; Alan Bullock, *The Life and Times of Ernest Bevin*, vol. 2, *Minister of Labour, 1940-1945* (London, 1967), pp. 225-32; Bernard Donoughue and G.W. Jones, *Herbert Morrison. Portrait of a Politician* (London, 1973), pp. 314-16; Michael Foot, *Aneurin Bevan 1897-1945* (St Albans, 1975), pp. 407-10.

11. Cf. Addison, *The Road to 1945*, pp. 239-47.

12. Cf. *Let us Face the Future* (London, 1945); *The Labour Party 44th Annual Conference Report 1945*, pp. 89-104.

13. James Callaghan, 'The Approach to Social Equality' in Donald Munro (ed.), *Socialism. The British Way* (London, 1948), p. 140; Roy Jenkins, 'Equality' in *New Fabian Essays* (London, 1952, 3rd edn 1970), p. 70.

14. Cf. Hugh Dalton, *High Tide and After. Memoirs 1945-1960* (London, 1962), pp. 24-31, 109-20; Callaghan, 'Approach', pp. 131-7.

15. *Let us Face the Future*, p. 6.

16. Cf. David Howell, *British Social Democracy. A Study in Development and Decay* (London, 1976), pp. 135-77.

17. Cf. A. Marwick, *Britain in the Century of Total War. War, Peace and Social Change 1900-1967* (Harmondsworth, 1970), pp. 358-9; Margaret Cole, 'Education and Social Democracy' in *New Fabian Essays*, pp. 91-120.

18. Bartlett, *Postwar Britain*, p. 60.

19. PRO: CP(45) 118 (CAB 129/1), Ministerial Responsibilities for Housing. Note by the Prime Minister, 16 Aug. 1945, p. 2. (Transcripts of Crown copyright records in the Public Record Office appear by permission of the Controller of Her Majesty's Stationery Office.)

20. Cf. M. Foot, *Aneurin Bevan 1945-1960* (St Albans, 1975), pp. 57-87.

21. Bartlett, *Postwar Britain*, p. 60.

22. Peter Calvocoressi, *The British Experience 1945-75* (London, 1978), pp. 35-6.

23. Cf. Brian Watkin, *The National Health Service. The First Phase. 1948-1974 and After* (London, 1978), pp. 1-17.

24. Cf. Foot, *Bevan 1945-1960*, pp. 138-210.

25. Macfarlane, *Issues*, p. 2.

26. PRO: CM 65 (45) (CAB 128/2), p. 339.

27. PRO: CM 43 (45) 18 Oct. 1945 (CAB 128/1), pp. 178-80.

28. Cf. Watkin, *NHS*, pp. 28-34.

29. Bartlett, *Postwar Britain*, p. 64.

30. Kathleen Woodroofe, 'The Making of the Welfare State in England. A Summary of its Origin and Development', in Winkler, *Twentieth Century Britain*, p. 164.

31. G. D.H. Cole, 'The Dream and the Business', *The Political Quarterly*, vol. 20 (1949), p. 201.

32. *Straight Left!* (London, 1945), p. 14.

33. Cf. V.N. George, *Social Security. Beveridge and After* (London, 1968), p. 239.

34. Marwick, *Britain in the Century of Total War*, pp. 344-5.

35. Cf. J.D. Hoffman, *The Conservative Party in Opposition 1945-51* (London, 1964), p. 235.

36. Pauline Gregg, *The Welfare State. A Social and Economic History of Britain from 1945 to the Present* (London, 1967), p. 81.

37. Cf. PRO: 3rd and 4th meeting of the Social Security Committee on 1 and 8 Oct. 1945 (CAB 134/697) and CM 39 (45) 9 Oct. 1945 (CAB 128/1), pp. 145-6.

38. Cf. George, *Social Security*, p. 178.

39. Cf. Gregg, *Welfare State*, p. 43.

40. *H.C. Debates* 418, col. 1896.

41. José Harris, *William Beveridge. A Biography* (Oxford, 1977), p. 460.

42. *The Labour Party 45th Annual Conference Report 1946*, pp. 116-19.

43. Ibid., p. 117.

44. *The Labour Party 46th Annual Conference Report 1947*, pp. 206-7.

45. Labour Party Archive: RD 312/Sept. 1949, Industrial Assurance as a Public Service, p. 1.

46. *Labour Believes in Britain* (London, 1949), pp. 19-20; cf. *The Labour Party 48th Annual Conference Report 1949*, pp. 200-8.

47. Cf. Harris, *Beveridge*, p. 458; Clement Davies, *H.C. Debates* 418, cols. 1785-6.

48. Cf. George, *Social Security*, pp. 92-5.
49. *H.C. Debates* 418, col. 1734.
50. Ibid., col. 1742.
51. PRO: SS (450 18 (CAB 134/697), National Insurance Bill. Benefit and Pension Rates. Memorandum by the Minister of National Insurance.
52. Cf. Harris, *Beveridge*, pp. 399, 422.
53. As note 51.
54. *H.C. Debates* 418, col. 1742.
55. *The Labour Party 43rd Annual Conference Report 1944*, p. 151.
56. Marwick, 'The Labour Party and the Welfare State', p. 189.
57. Cf. Dalton, *High Tide*, p. 111.
58. *H.C. Debates* 418, col. 1741; cf. PRO: CP (45) 315, 1 Dec. 1945 (CAB 129/5), Report by the Social Services Committee on the National Insurance Scheme. Memorandum by the Lord Privy Seal, p. 1.
59. *H.C. Debates* 418, col. 1900.
60. PRO: SS (45) 7th meeting, 12 Oct. 1945 (CAB 134/697); CM 60 (45) 6 Dec. 1945 (CAB 128/2).
61. Dalton, *High Tide*, p. 65.
62. *H.C. Debates* 418, col. 1771.
63. Macfarlane, *Issues*, p. 30.
64. Hugh Heclo, *Modern Social Politics in Britain and Sweden. From Relief to Income Maintenance* (New Haven, 1974), p. 258.
65. Cf. Barbara Wootton's commentary already in 1949: 'the world in which we all pay our insurance contributions, secure in the knowledge that these do really provide enough to fall back on in sickness, unemployment, or old age, seems as far away as ever. I do not suggest that it would have been feasible in present circumstances to have provided more generous benefits: but it is depressing to have to run so fast in order so nearly to stay in the same place' ('Record of the Labour Government in the Social Services', *The Political Quarterly*, vol. 20 (1949), p. 103).
66. Cf. George, *Social Security*, p. 211.
67. *H.C. Debates* 418, col. 1741. It must not be forgotten, though, that there was no such provision for a regular adjustment at five-yearly intervals in the 1944 White Paper. Cf. G.D.H. Cole, *The Intelligent Man's Guide to the Post-War World* (London, 1947), p. 567.
68. William A. Robson gives the following rising figures of benefit recipients who claimed national assistance/supplementary benefit in 1951 and 1972: 16 per cent of those receiving unemployment benefit (1972: 24 per cent) and 22 per cent of the retirement pensioners (1972: 28 per cent) (*Welfare State and Welfare Society. Illusion and Reality* (London, 1976), p. 146).
69. This was the most important of these points. After long discussions in which the left wing of the Parliamentary Labour Party got strongly involved a compromise was found which did not introduce unlimited payment of unemployment benefit, but, with an eye on the exceptional post-war situation, introduced a generous procedure of lengthening the payment period by regular six-monthly intervals after appearing before a local tribunal. Cf. Marwick, *Britain in the Century of Total War*, pp. 347-8; Heclo, *Modern Social Politics*, p. 148.
70. PRO: CP (45) 323, 5 Dec. 1945 (CAB 129/5), National Insurance Scheme. Memorandum by the Chancellor of the Exchequer; CM 60 (45), 6 Dec. 1945 (CAB 128/2).
71. SS (45) 30, 27 Nov. 1945 (CAB 134/697), National Insurance Scheme. Note by the Lord Privy Seal, p. 13.
72. Cf. George, *Social Security*, p. 62.
73. *H.C. Debates* 444, col. 1603.

74. George, *Social Security*, p. 228.

75. *The Welfare State*, Labour Discussion Pamphlet no. 4 (London, 1952), p. 14.

76. *H.C. Debates* 444, col. 1603.

77. *Labour Believes in Britain*, p. 4.

78. *Labour and the New Society* (London, 1950), p. 5.

79. Cf. Vic George and Paul Wilding, *Ideology and Social Welfare* (London, 1976), p. 81.

80. R.H.S. Crossman, 'Towards a Philosophy of Socialism' in *New Fabian Essays*, p. 1.

81. *Labour Believes in Britain*, pp. 18-19.

82. Cf. J.E. Meade, 'Next Steps in Domestic Economic Policy' (Labour Party Archive: RD 201/November, 1948).

83. Cf. Margaret Cole, 'Social Services and Personal Life' in Munro, *Socialism*, pp. 88-126.

84. *Keeping Left. By a Group of Members of Parliament* (London, 1950), p. 3.

85. In such a case the workman would pay only 2s 8d per week, instead of 4s 7d, while his employer would have to pay the difference, paying 5s 9d instead of 3s 10d normally. There would be no change in the state part of the contribution which was 2s 1d for each male employee. This relief only applied to adult workers earning less than 30 shillings per week.

86. *The Labour Party 45th Annual Conference Report 1946*, p. 117.

87. Labour Party Archive: R 3/ June 1950, Summary of Discussions at the Conference held at Beatrice Webb House, Dorking, 19-21 May 1950, p. 16.

88. Cf. George, *Social Security*, p. 10.

89. *The Welfare State*. Labour Discussion pamphlet no. 4 (London, 1952), pp. 13-17.

90. Cf. Heclo, *Modern Social Politics*, pp. 259-70.

91. Ibid., pp. 270-3.

92. Cf. Ralph Miliband, *Parliamentary Socialism. A Study in the Politics of Labour*, 2nd edn (London, 1972), p. 307.

93. R.M. Titmuss, *Income Distribution and Social Change* (London, 1965), p. 188. Cited in George and Wilding, *Ideology and Social Welfare*, p. 81.

94. For such a critical socialist approach cf. J. Saville, 'The Welfare State: an Historical Approach', in Butterworth and Holman, *Social Welfare in Modern Britain*, pp. 57-69.

95. Birch, *The Shaping of the Welfare State*, p. 64.

96. Bartlett, *Postwar Britain*, p. 44.

97. Heclo, *Modern Social Politics*, p. 287.

98. Cf. Howell, *British Social Democracy*, p. 176.

99. As note 87, p. 2.

100. C.A.R. Crosland, 'The Transition from Capitalism', in *New Fabian Essays*, p. 68.

GERMAN POST-WAR SOCIAL POLICIES AGAINST THE BACKGROUND OF THE BEVERIDGE PLAN. SOME OBSERVATIONS PREPARATORY TO A COMPARATIVE ANALYSIS

H.G. Hockerts

Control Commission for Germany (British Element): Export of the *Beveridge Plan* into Occupied Germany?

While the British social security system was fundamentally reformed between 1945 and 1948 on the basis of the *Beveridge Plan*,[1] the German social security system was equally on the verge of a break in continuity and of a new beginning. In 1946/7 the Manpower Directorate of the Allied Control Commission, the highest authority of the quadripartite administration, worked out a draft for a 'compulsory social insurance law for Germany' which deviated to a considerable degree from the traditional principles of the German social insurance system.[2] Whereas the guiding principle in Germany had hitherto been to cover only the economically weak groups in need of special protection — which as a matter of principle excluded more highly paid employees and the self-employed — the intention now was to extend the insurance to all citizens (with the exception of employers with more than five employees). The Allied draft, just as the *Beveridge Plan*, thus aimed at a social insurance model that would encompass the entire nation. And while German social insurance hitherto had been organised according to specific groups and classes of the population, the idea was now, again as with the *Beveridge Plan*, to introduce a uniform organisation structured along regional lines, rather than on the former multitude of insurance categories[3] tailored to cover specific population sectors, each with different contributions and benefits.

Certain parallels to the simultaneous reforms in Britian are thus evident. This might lead to the assumption that it was the intention of the Manpower Division of the British Control Commission — CCG (BE) — to introduce the *Beveridge Plan* in Germany.[4] This Manpower Division — in the judgement of one expert — was 'easily the best group of civil servants in the CCG and this was the direct result of Ernest Bevin's interest in its formation when he was at the Ministry of Labour'.[5] The main criterion for recruitment was that the person should already be an established civil servant in the Ministry of Labour. As this Ministry had a large departmental (i.e. executive grade mostly outside London) staff, it was possible to recruit able and reliable people who knew that their work in Germany, if good, would stand to their credit on their return to the United Kingdom.[6]

The first issue of the 'Arbeitsblatt für die Britische Zone' — which was controlled by the Manpower Division — opened with a report on the *Beveridge Plan*.[7] In a later issue, the Director of the Division's Social Insurance Branch gave an account of the British reform Acts.[8] In 1946 Lord Beveridge himself toured the British sector of occupied Germany and delivered lectures on the British reform programme in several German cities.[9]

Does this indicate that there existed some sort of missionary zeal with regard to social policy on the part of the British occupation forces? Indeed not. The British Manpower Division came to Germany with the directive to preserve as far as possible the traditional German social security system.[10] The driving force behind the reform planning in the quadripartite Manpower Directorate was not the British, but the Russians and Americans, who both had German advisers steeped in the tradition of socialist and trade union demands for reform. The draft for a reform Bill, on the other hand, which the British submitted for deliberation by the Manpower Directorate, was a verbatim translation of a paper written by a former civil servant in the German Ministry of Labour.

Although exaggerating a little, one could say that the British Manpower Division always thought in financial terms at first: it wanted to cut costs and save money. That thrift was the aim can be illustrated by a number of examples, for example the fact that social insurance benefits in the British-occupied sectors were scaled down much more than in, say, the American one. During the deliberations on the Allied draft for reform, the British argued successfully in favour of lowering the established German benefit levels. In this way they intended to ensure that social insurance could be financed entirely without state funds. While the *Beveridge Plan* envisaged large public subsidies for social insurance, the British occupation forces in Germany (who were not alone in this, however) strove for total absence of subsidies from public funds and the Allied draft reform law accordingly envisaged a social insurance system financed exclusively out of contributions.[11] The consideration of economy was equally overriding for the British assent to the streamlined organisational structure and the extension of insurance to wider sections of the population, which the Allied draft legislation envisaged. The one seemed a suitable method of cutting costs, the other would bring in more contributions and was thus desirable in order to compensate in some measure for the absence of state subsidies. This British policy of economy must be seen against the background of a worsening economic situation at home: to lower the costs of German social insurance would help towards making occupied Germany self-sufficient and thus relieve the British taxpayer of the responsibility of subsidising vital German imports.

German Opposition

The Allied draft legislation conflicted with the manifold interests of wide sections of the middle class, who particularly protested against the proposed extension of compulsory insurance and the streamlining of the organisation. This opposition movement was led by the private insurance companies, the medical profession, artisan and agricultural organisations, industrialists, white-collar workers and traditional insurance funds, whose existence was threatened by this reform. Sections within the German trade union movement also rejected the draft, albeit for different reasons, and most emphatic among them was the Federation of Trade Unions in the British sector.[12] Its protest was directed against the inadequacy of the proposed benefits and the envisaged abolition of all fixed subsidies from public funds.

The German opposition to the draft received ideological reinforcement from anti-Nazi arguments. The National Socialist 'Deutsche Arbeitsfront' had also endeavoured to include *all* citizens in a uniformly organised system of social security, although, because of the war, no serious attempt to put this into practice had ever been made.[13] But the existence of such plans had been public knowledge and one may imagine with horror how their realisation would have transformed the institutions of social security into instruments of political subjugation. In a counter-move, some members of the German opposition to Hitler had demanded the retention of the traditional German social security system.[14] Now, after 1945, this passionate rejection of Nazi tendencies towards centralisation and collectivism was transferred, partly out of conviction, partly for tactical reasons, to the Allied reform programme.[15] A comparison of the German and British development thus shows up one important difference: in Britain the war experience had engendered a sense of national solidarity and confidence in state intervention and had thus prepared the ground for the Beveridge reforms; in Germany, by contrast, the experience of Nazi misuse of power had provoked opposition to any form of government-imposed centralisation or collectivism.

In another respect, too, the points of departure in Germany and Britain were quite different: in Britain the reform of the social security system was seen as a national task, while in Germany it threatened to take on the guise of an imposition by the occupation forces. This, from the outset, provoked opposition, especially because of a widespread consciousness that Germany, ever since Bismarck, had been the leading nation in matters of social policy. That reform should now be dictated by the occupying forces was therefore resented all the more keenly. These sensitivities were further exacerbated by the circumstance that the tradition of social policy was virtually the only one with which Germany, defeated in war and deformed by National Socialism, could still identify, which it could refer to and be 'proud' of. It was no accident that Adenauer, in a mass rally of the Christian Democrat Union in August 1946, said emphatically:

> We must hold on to this social insurance. We are proud of it. And as for the proposals Beveridge has recently made in Hamburg, I can only say that we Germans have already had such things these past thirty years.[16]

The Social Democrat camp was no less emphatic in its opinion 'that social insurance, which was created seventy years ago through German initiative, ought to be reformed now too by German authorities'.[17] In addition there existed, particularly in the minds of leading trade unionists in the British sector, a tactical consideration: it was not inconceivable that the new system of social insurance, which the Allied Control Commission intended to implement, would, in view of Germany's ruined economy, soon run into serious financial difficulties, and they feared that this might bring sound principles of reform into lasting disrepute and thus offer a dangerous handle for nationalist agitation.[18]

The Failure of Allied Reform Plans

In January 1947 the Allied draft Bill was ratified (in a modified form) in the Russian sector. The three Western Allies, however, did not take the parallel step. In July 1947 the Allied Manpower Directorate had reached agreement on virtually all points of the draft (the only question to remain a matter of controversy was whether civil servants should be included or not); yet early in 1948 the draft legislation failed to pass the Allied Control Council. The American and British military governors, Lucius D. Clay and Brian H. Robertson, declined to give their assent. An examination of the reasons for this failure leads to three conclusions which, from the angle of a particular field of research, supplement and modify historiographical attempts to formulate a paradigm of Anglo-American policies during the period of occupation.

(1) As far as the reform of the social insurance system was con-concerned, the frequently employed historical paradigm that 'the British were prevented by the Americans from introducing reforms' does not apply.[19] The British withdrawal from the Allied reform project was due to growing doubts within the British military government. A letter which the Social Insurance Branch of the British Manpower Division wrote to the Finance Division in February 1948 may be regarded as symptomatic:

'In short, it has to be admitted that we have unfortunately been manoeuvred into a false position on agreeing to the reform of social insurance in the quadripartite machine and shall be grateful for anything you can do to frustrate or delay the course of this highly controversial measure in the Finance Directorate'.[20]

(2) The Cold War changed the framework of the reform project: to the degree that the East-West conflict escalated and the creation of a West German state thus assumed political priority, it became more important for the Western powers to come to an understanding with the prevailing West German views than to reach an accord with the Soviet Union, which could only be achieved on the basis of the quadripartite draft law.

(3) The historical paradigm of a 'prevented new order', according to which the American occupation forces and the German bourgeoisie, in a tacit coalition of capitalist interests, prevented progressive reforms,[21] does not apply to the social insurance policies. In this area, the German opposition gained in effectiveness and strength precisely because it had the support of important sections of the trade unions.

The Frankfurt Economic Council: the Postponement of Decisions on Principle (1948/9)

In the context of the currency reform, the British and American military governments in June 1949 transferred the matter of social insurance reform into German hands. This brought the bipartite Economic Council, i.e. the German legislative body in the American and British sectors of occupation, into play. The Economic Council's *Sozialversicherungs-Anpassungsgesetz* (SVAG) raised the benefits considerably beyond the level envisaged in the Allied draft law, but dispensed with a structural reform of social insurance, since such fundamental decisions were to be reserved to the parliament of the new West German state which was about to come into being. An increase in benefits was indeed a priority, since those sections of the population who depended on such payments, especially the pensioners, had sunk into deep poverty: if one takes the cost of living index of 1938 as 100, this had gone up by 73 points by the end of 1948, while the average old age pension for workers had only risen by 35 points.[22]

German resentment was thus all the greater when in December 1948 the bipartite Control Office of the Anglo-American military governments prevented the SVAG from taking effect. For a further year the pensioners had to suffer the effects of the surge in inflation which followed the currency reform and the liberalisation of the economy, without receiving any compensatory allowances.

The First Bundestag (1949-53): Specific Post-war Problems and the Reconstruction of the Traditional Social Insurance System

The Social Democrat Party (SPD), which inclined towards the model of the British welfare state, was in opposition for the duration of the first Bundestag (and until 1966). The Christian Democrat Union (CDU), the leading party in government – in coalition with the liberal Free Democrats (FDP) and the conservative German Party (DP) – had nailed the defence of the traditional German social insurance system to its mast. It was of course not social insurance on which the social policies of the first German Bundestag were focused, but on the management of the specific problems brought about by the war. The *Lastenausgleichsgesetz* (Equalisation of Burdens Act) of 1952 set in motion a programme of massive redistribution that was to benefit more than 10 million refugees and people who had been bombed out.

Several Acts were passed to look after the 4 million people who had been invalided, widowed or orphaned by the war. As about a third of the necessary housing was lacking, a building programme with massive subsidies from public funds was initiated, the efficiency of which, incidentally, greatly impressed Lord Beveridge.[23] As far as social insurance was concerned, the traditional structures were – almost – completely reinstated. While the German Trade Union Federation and the SPD aimed at a standardised insurance structure as a matter of principle, the parliamentary majority re-established the traditional diversity of insurance funds. It should be noted in this connection that leading officials of these institutions held important positions in all three governing coalition parties. Yet even the SPD agreed to splitting superannuation insurance into two, one for workers, the other for white-collar employees, and shortly before the parliamentary elections of 1953, the Bundestag voted *unanimously* for the reintroduction of a special *Bundesversicherungsanstalt für Angestellte* (a federal institution for the insurance of white-collar employees). The only explanation for the SPD's consent must be the fact that a few months earlier, during elections to the self-governing bodies of the social insurance system, an overwhelming majority of employees had voted for electoral lists advocating a separate insurance for white-collar workers. This result so clearly demonstrated the wishes of sought-after voters that in a parliamentary election year no party dared to vote against hiving off once more the insurance for white-collar employees. Despite the existence of the two separate institutions, in 1957 uniform norms of contributions and benefits for both insurance branches were established.

The Position in 1953: a Need for Comprehensive Reform?

At the end of the first legislative period in 1953, the rate of social expenditure in the Federal Republic (defined as the share in the net national product at factor costs) stood at 19.4 per cent and was thus higher than in all other comparable countries. In the same year the figure for Britain was 12.5 per cent and for Sweden 13.5 per cent.[24] The high German rate reflects the ratio between a large number of beneficiaries – due to the war – and a comparatively low national product and was thus not the result of a particularly high level of social benefits; on the contrary: no one denied that many of the benefits were inadequate and that considerable lacunae also existed.

So it had been hoped in vain that the first Bundestag would introduce a system of family allowances. No one denied, moreover, that the system of social security was very fragmented, badly co-ordinated and to most people quite incomprehensible. With a certain time-lag attempts were therefore made in 1952/3 to institute comprehensive reforms and in this the example of the *Beveridge Plan* exercised — positively and negatively — considerable influence. This will be illustrated in the next three sections.

British Impulses for Academic Discussion in Germany

The *Beveridge Plan* and the British reforms based on it received very careful attention in Germany. In this connection a study visit to London by 19 German experts in January 1953 was indicative. Some of them were scholars (Prof. Hans Achinger, Prof. Gerhard Mackenroth), others worked in the field (the chairmen both of the social policy committee of the SPD, Prof. Ludwig Preller, and of the CDU, Heinrich Lünendonk). For two weeks they conferred with leading British experts (such as Christine Cockburn, Richard M. Titmuss and Alan T. Peacock)[25] and while they did not hesitate to criticise the British system,[26] most of them seem to have been 'impressed by its uniformity, clarity and its basic conception'.[27]

Some of the British concepts had an immediate effect on German scientific discussion. This was particularly true of the willingness to work towards a systematically and comprehensively conceived plan for reform, and to regard economic, financial and social policies as one conceptual entity. It is thus no accident that the first German 'models for a social plan' came from authors who had observed the British development with particular involvement.[28] Alan T. Peacock's analysis of redistribution[29] provided the direct impulse for Hartmut Hensen's pioneer work in Germany, *Die Finanzen der sozialen Sicherung im Kreislauf der Wirtschaft* (*The Finances of Social Security in the Economic Cycle*).[30] Significant, too, was how readily during the 1950s English terms such as 'prevention' and 'rehabilitation' were received into the German vocabulary. Preventive health care and measures for the reintegration of the physically handicapped into the work process had not been unknown to the German social security tradition but the fact that this aspect was stressed in German discussions after the war much more than before has largely been due to the British model.

Out of a great number of possible examples of the close links between British and German discussions, I just want to mention one more: under the influence of Beveridge and Keynes the German dogma that the long-term funding of superannuation insurance requires large capital reserves was severely shaken. Beveridge, on the contrary, had emphasised that 'a state with the power to compel successive generations of subjects to insure themselves, and to levy taxes, is freed from the obligation to accumulate reserves for statistical purposes.'[31] Gerhard Mackenroth, in his now famous lecture of 1952, took up this thought,[32] and it was against this background that in 1955 Wilfrid Schreiber formulated the concept of the 'contract between generations': in order to fund the payment of social provisions, the generation in work at any given moment cedes certain of its rights to consumption to those not yet or no longer working; whereas the accumulation of large capital reserves to cover such entitlements made no sense in terms of the national economy: if one were to run down such reserves in times of crisis, this would merely have an aggravating, procyclical effect. In a crisis, Schreiber went on with Keynesian arguments, help could only come from the state's responsibility 'to provide subsidies through an autonomous creation of purchasing power, in order to compensate for the crisis-induced decrease in contributions.'[33] The turn away from the principle of funding pensions out of capital reserves, and towards the idea of covering them by transfer payments instead, was an important pre-condition for the great Pensions Reform Act of 1957, which I shall return to below.

SPD: Reform Planning in Approximation to the *Beveridge Plan*

The SPD was considerably influenced by the *Beveridge Plan* and this was in no small measure due to the great efforts by Walter Auerbach. A Social Democrat emigrant, Auerbach had worked from 1939 to 1946 in the London Secretariat of the International Transport Federation and had taken an indirect part in the preparation of the *Beveridge Plan*.[34] From 1946 to 1948 he was Vice-President of the *Zentralamt für Arbeit* (Central Labour Office) in the British-occupied sector and has since been one of the leading influences in the social policy committee of the SPD party executive.

On his initiative the SPD in 1952 put forward a motion in the Bundestag — without success — to appoint a 'kind of German Beveridge Committee', in order to prepare a comprehensive programme of social reform.[35] He also had an important hand in preparing a plan for reform within the party. The first interim result of this work was published by the SPD party executive under the title *Basic Principles for an Overall Social Plan of the SPD*.[36] It was a very brief document which merely outlined certain ground rules, but it contained certain significant parallels to the *Beveridge Plan*. Some of the tendencies common to both will be briefly sketched. It must be noted, though, that the Social Democrat plans for reform were not influenced by the British model alone. The Swedish example as well as the general stage of discussion within the International Labour Organisation played an important part too. Of particular significance were the results arrived at during the International Labour Conference of 1944 in Philadelphia, which in turn had largely been based on the recommendations contained in the Beveridge Report.

The functions which the *Beveridge Plan* envisaged for social insurance — i.e. the abolition of poverty by ensuring an income in case of unemployment, illness, accident, old age or the death of the breadwinner — was by no means a novelty in German eyes. What was new, at least in this systematic and theoretically well conceived form, was the recognition that social insurance can only successfully fulfil its function of alleviating poverty if three pre-conditions are met: (1) avoidance of mass unemployment through economic policies aimed at full employment; (2) comprehensive health care and a service for work rehabilitation; (3) family allowances.

The SPD plan recognised these three pre-conditions. (1) Just as the Beveridge Report had done, the Social Democrat authors of this plan also emphasised that social security cannot be divorced from a policy of full employment and that, conversely, full employment would only be possible with an effective social security system. Here the authors were thinking particularly of the productive effect of safeguarding health and the capacity to work, and of the stabilising effects certain monetary benefits would have on the economic cycle. (2) Just as with Beveridge, the Social Democrat authors also envisaged the establishment of a kind of 'National Health Service' which would integrate all health care services and benefits and be financed largely out of taxes.[37] Yet in contrast to the British plan, and following the German tradition, they laid great stress on the principle of a decentralised, participative administration. (3) Just like Beveridge, the SPD also demanded child allowances for each second and subsequent child, payable out of public funds.

As far as the cash benefits of social insurance were concerned, the SPD favoured a uniform, non-contributory, tax-financed basic pension for every citizen either permanently disabled or of pensionable age. This corresponded to Beveridge's concept of a 'flat-rate national minimum' for every disabled or pensionable citizen. But unlike Beveridge, the SPD further envisaged additional earnings-related pensions, financed through contributions from wages. This more markedly individualistic principle was deeply rooted in the German social insurance tradition, whereas in Britain the basic National Insurance Act of 1912 had already followed the principle of flat rates for both pensions and contributions.

The SPD plan deviated from the traditional German social security system in that it aimed at including *all* citizens, and at shifting the emphasis on finance through taxes instead of contributions. Coupled with a demand for a reform of the tax system (less indirect and more direct progressive taxation) this shift — just as in Britain — was to achieve greater vertical redistribution. The SPD, again like Beveridge, nevertheless respected the principle of encouraging achievement and individual initiative. 'In establishing a national *minimum*, it should leave room and encouragement for voluntary action by each individual to provide more than that minimum for himself and his family,' Beveridge had written.[38] Similar views came from the SPD: the citizen was to receive only 'certain basic rates more or less as of right', since in this way 'the interest of the individual to look after his own security and his active participation would be aroused and encouraged.'[39]

The Federal Government: Reform Planning Independent of the *Beveridge Plan*

If one leaves out of account certain not unimportant internal differences, the position of the leading government party after 1949 can be summed up as follows: the CDU, much more than the SPD, stressed the need for private initiative, for incentives and the individual's responsibility for his own security,[40] and therefore sought to limit more narrowly the extent of government intervention. In its first party programmes it rejected the idea of extending compulsory insurance to the self-employed and employees in higher wage brackets. It emphasised the importance of financing social insurance as far as possible through contributions for specific purposes (insurance principle) and less through taxes (state maintenance principle). This aimed at correlating as closely as possible personal (earnings-related) contributions to (equally earnings-related) insurance benefits and thus at bringing the distributive mechanisms of the market to bear on the benefit structure of social insurance. Seen in this light, social benefits are not purely and simply an attribute of citizenship, but the equivalent of individual contributions made. The guarantee of a minimum income for all, in this conception, is only envisaged in the form of means-tested public assistance, with the possible associated stigma of personal failure. The fact that Christian Democrats in the fifties treated the term 'welfare state' either with scepticism, or rejected it altogether, is a consequence of this bias in their programme.

It must be said, though, that between 1953 and 1955 the Federal government — to whom the CDU largely ceded the initiative in this matter — made serious attempts to work out a comprehensive plan for the reform of the social security system. Chancellor Adenauer in particular was for a time greatly interested in such a plan, which would 'not superimpose the thousandth or elevenhundredth amendment to Bismarck's laws', but represent 'a thorough overhaul of social legislation to meet modern needs'.[41] In order to achieve this, he wanted to see the appointment of a government commission, under the chairmanship of an independent academic or an elder statesman; to justify this — for Germany — unusual step he referred to the British practice of appointing Royal Commissions.[42] After two years of internal government wrangles, with endless inter-departmental rivalries and conflicts as to aims, the project got stuck and no commission was ever set up. In his search for an alternative, Adenauer took the initiative himself and asked four social scientists whom he trusted to work out 'a comprehensive concept for a reorganisation of the social security system'. The result of this endeavour was published in 1955 and has since become known as the 'Rothenfels Memorandum' (*Rothenfelser Denkschrift*).[43]

This memorandum is particularly interesting in that it illustrates the evolution of socio-political thinking in Germany. It took for granted that companies, in a capitalist economic system, generate more costs than they contribute, as they do not have to pay for large portions of the 'social costs'. While the welfare state may be said to nationalise these externalised costs, the Rothenfels Memorandum now argued that those who create them should also pay for them, i.e. the companies themselves. Organised into federations, the employers were to compensate the loss of income in case of accident, illness, rehabilitation and seasonal unemployment. In some ways this meant the resuscitation of certain elements of pre-industrial workers' legislation (which placed the onus for the care of workers on employers). Not only were the employers to be responsible for direct labour costs, but for most of the reproduction costs of labour as well.

The memorandum sought to inject a whole hierarchy of social agencies (family, firm, insurance funds) between state and individual and to allocate many of the social security functions to the lower levels, in order to ensure a correspondingly strict limitation of costs payable by the state. The liberal principle of limiting state intervention and Catholic sociology's 'subsidiary principle' ('Subsidiaritätsprinzip') — according to which the larger social units, especially the state, ought to take over only those functions which lesser social units cannot perform equally well — formed the background for this concept.

The memorandum did, however, argue that it was the state's responsibility to create the *pre-conditions* which would allow the individual and the smaller social units to develop their resources effectively and fully. It was, for instance, to be the state's role to ensure 'a normal degree of chances of development' for all young people, to compensate for differences between town and country, and to ensure for all those able to work also 'the right to work', through appropriate economic and employment policies. It was also recognised that social benefits cannot be considered merely as a burden on the economy, but must be seen as a 'pre-condition for the productive employment of resources'. It is thus not possible to define the memorandum as being 'for' or 'against' the welfare state, since it links a number of heterogeneous conceptual elements.

Although the concrete proposals for reform contained in the Rothenfels Memorandum were by and large not put into practice, the attempt to design an alternative to the British welfare state model was quite characteristic of the prevailing thinking within the CDU. This is most clearly illustrated by the example of the Child Allowance Law of 1954, the first step in German post-war child allowance legislation. These allowances — even in international comparison — represented the latest form of benefits within the social security system. Internationally its take-off point must be dated as late as the Second World War or immediately after. It did not have its roots in the traditional 'workers' problem', for it is not concerned with a particular section of society, but with questions that touch all of modern society; yet their nature is such that the traditional German 'insurance principle', for technical reasons, if for no others, hardly provides an adequate instrument.

It thus seemed reasonable to place the responsibility for this provision on the state and to finance it out of general taxes. (SPD and

Beveridge both made the same demand.) But it was precisely this which the CDU rejected. It transferred this responsibility to the employers who, in order to finance it (the employers' contribution was fixed at a certain percentage of the total payroll), had to create special insurance funds (*Ausgleichskassen*); each professional branch, meanwhile, was to pay for the cost of child allowances for its members out of its own funds. The CDU pushed this arrangement through, against the opposition of both SPD and its own coalition partners, and against many sceptical voices from among employers. All that has come to light so far indicates that the CDU did not arrive at this decision under pressure from interest groups, but for reasons of principle, especially because of its adherence to the 'subsidiary principle'.[44]

Dynamische Rente (1957) v. Flat-rate Subsistence Pension: was the *Beveridge Plan* Overtaken?

While a comprehensively conceived reform of social insurance did not get off the ground during the Adenauer era, certain important partial reforms did come about. The most important of these was the structural reform of the compulsory superannuation system in 1957. In this reform three separate aspects must be distinguished.

(1) The levels of the then paid pensions were raised by about 60 per cent.[45] For the pensioners at the time, who had until then lived in the shadow of economic revival, this meant an instance of overdue justice: a belated compensation, facilitated by the boom, for their enforced renunciation of consumption, whereby they had contributed to the national economy's creation of capital after 1948/9.

(2) More important in the long term was the attempt to find a fundamental solution to the traditional problem of the discrepancy between the benefits provided by a statically conceived social insurance — based on the premiss of wages and prices remaining stable over a long period — on the one hand, and a rapid rise in production, wages and prices on the other. This was resolved by introducing 'dynamic' pensions. This represented an innovation in two respects: the initial pension rate was now arrived at by not only taking into account all contributions paid throughout a working life, which may have been overtaken by movements in prices and wages since, but

by computing them at current gross wage levels; and secondly, the stipulation of an annual adjustment of pensions payable, without clearly defining the points of reference by law, but which in practice so far (until 1978) has meant their being related to gross wages. In other words the guiding principle was to be that the earnings of workers still engaged in the production process and the pensions of those who have retired from it should develop on parallel lines, and that workers should participate in economic growth not only during their working life (by way of wages), but in retirement (by way of pensions) as well.

(3) In addition, the fundamental decision was taken to establish a relation between workers' pensions and former earnings: the pension was to be of a level which would ensure that the standard of living earned by work should be maintained in old age. Retirement from work was no longer to lead to a sudden reduction in living standards; on the contrary, the 'wages replacement function' of pensions was designed to ensure that in retirement the individual's position within the social structure corresponds to that of his former working life.[46] To give a quantitative example: a person who has been insured for forty years and has always earned the average wage of all insured receives a (net) pension of 60 per cent of the current (gross) average wages of those working and insured.[47]

This reform must thus be seen as an attempt once and for all to achieve a break with the traditional cycle of old age and poverty. Opinion polls at the time showed that the response was overwhelming. The Allensbach Institut für Demoskopie summed it up as follows: 'To our knowledge there has been no other case where a measure, an institution or even the constitution and symbols of state have evoked as positive an echo as this pension reform.'[48] The reform not only had a material and socio-psychological effect on recipients of superannuation, disability and widows' pensions, but also on the attitudes and expectations of those still working, since it promised to prolong the benefits of economic growth into the retirement period and to provide more equitable norms for the distribution of the national product between generations. The pension reform of 1957 thus had a strengthening and consolidating effect on the young Federal Republic that cannot be overestimated.

It must be stressed, though, that while the new pension system did effect a marked horizontal redistribution (the working generation, by way of high contributions, ceding a relatively large portion of its claim to consumption to the generation in retirement), it had little effect on vertical redistribution.[49] Pension insurance was now even more strictly oriented on the principle of a direct correlation between individual earnings-related contributions and the size of the pension. It thus projected the differentiation of earnings, and with it the distributive effects of market mechanisms, into pensions as well. It was consequently a non-levelling system, but one which put a premium on achievement and maintained individual status.

The situation of pensioners in Britain at the same time was highly unsatisfactory. Roughly 25 per cent of pensioners depended on (means-tested) supplementary benefits.[50] (Even *before* the pension reform only 2-3 per cent in Germany had depended on supplementary public assistance.[51]) The flat rate barely covered the minimum subsistence level. In addition it created − for all its egalitarian appearance − great inequalities of income: (a) between recipients of low pensions and those still at work, and (b) between that third of the British work-force employed by companies which provided private occupational pension schemes (three-quarters of such benefits not being financed by the companies, but through tax concessions, in other words by the tax-payers at large[52]) and those less fortunate who depended solely on a small state pension.[53]

The low level of the flat rate was no accident, for a system of a uniform pension for all citizens can 'for financial reasons, but also for reasons of work ethics, only envisage relatively small benefits, which will just maintain a bare subsistence level, but not a well-earned standard of living'.[54] To that extent the − apparently − egalitarian flat rate left a lot of room for − differentiating − private insurance business, and it is interesting in this connection that in 1956/7 the private insurance companies in Germany argued in favour of introducing a minimum flat-rate state pension for all citizens,[55] while the SPD had meanwhile abandoned this demand. At the back of it there must certainly have been the thought that 'dynamic pensions', with the function of replacing wages, would leave much less scope for private insurance business than a flat-rate system; the latter would greatly enhance an interest in securing additional private benefits and thus, despite its roots in British and Swedish welfare-state concepts, be far less of a welfare-state measure than the reform prepared by the Bundestag.

'The Flat-Rate Subsistence Pension − a Fading Hope' was how

the Labour Party summed it up in 1957.[56] Indeed, the central concept of the *Beveridge Plan* – the abolition of poverty through a guaranteed minimum income for all – had been overtaken by history, through the concepts of the new German pension system, i.e. the preservation of the relative social status. The former had fitted an impoverished war and post-war economy, but the new scheme was commensurate with a prospering industrial society.[57] It appears almost symbolic that in the general Bundestag elections of 1957, the German pensioners helped to secure the triumphal return of the governing party, while in the same year British pensioners mounted a protest march through the streets of London.[58] Whereas in 1953 German experts had visited London to study the British system, it could be reported in 1957 that 'the English are studying the German pension reform.'[59]

Taking some cues from the German system – although it would be erroneous to assume a simple and direct causal connection – the British National Insurance Act of 1959 amended the concept of a minimum flat rate: it introduced a supplementary, earnings-related pension system, which took effect in 1961. Conversely, the 'dynamic pension' concept in Germany was amended in 1972 by the introduction of a sort of 'minimum ceiling': since then the pension has been calculated as if the recipient throughout his working life had always received at least 75 per cent of the average earnings of all the insured. Thus, in the longer term, one can observe a certain convergence of the two, initially extremely different, superannuation systems: the British now includes elements of earnings-related differentiation, while in the German scheme the links with individual earnings have been loosened, in order to guarantee adequate minimum security for all insured persons.

The Federal Republic in the Adenauer Era: an Unwilling Welfare State?

When the Labour Party took office in 1945 it was with the declared aim of turning Britain into a welfare state (and when the Conservatives returned to power they did at least not reverse the reforms of 1945/8). The leading government party in the Adenauer era (1949-63), by contrast, had an *a priori* sceptical attitude towards any increase in state intervention in order to promote a welfare state. 'In spite of its neo-liberal leanings', as Gaston V. Rimlinger so accurately put it, the Federal Republic at the end of the Adenauer era 'was in reality an advanced welfare state'. For corroboration, Rimlinger refers to 'the nearly universal coverage of employed persons and the relatively high levels of contributions and pensions'.[60] The fact particularly worth mentioning in this context is that all German workers, in case of illness, have been entitled to 90 per cent since 1957, and 100 per cent since 1961, of their net earnings for the first six weeks. (The *Beveridge Plan* and the National Insurance Act of 1946 also envisaged a flat rate for sick pay, which was supplemented in 1966 by a system of earnings-related additions.) In 1963 public social expenditure stood at 17.1 per cent of GNP in Germany, 13.8 per cent in Sweden and 11.8 per cent in Britain.[61] In Germany, at the end of the 1950s, between 12 and 13 per cent of average earnings were deducted for social security; in Britain that figure was 4 per cent; even including tax payments, the contributions made by the average British worker were considerably lower than those of his West German colleague.[62]

Given the 'neo-liberal leanings' of the ruling political forces, how can this development towards a welfare state in Germany be explained? Out of a welter of political and structural factors I shall here list only the nine probably most significant: (1) the growing quota of employed persons[63] automatically raised the number of insured and thus (2) increased the political weight of voters with an interest in state social benefits, which (3), given a parliamentary democracy, competing political parties and periodic general elections, gained a relatively strong influence. (Major reforms were, in the main, passed just prior to general elections.) (4) The demographic development (an increase in the ratio of old people) automatically raised the costs of the social security system.[64] (5) Specific post-war problems necessitated increased state intervention. (6) Continuing economic growth left more scope for distribution, so that an increase in social demands could be met out of current revenues. (7) Against the background of crises and catastrophes in German history, groups within the governing party considered active social policies a pre-condition for the internal stabilisation of the new liberal-democratic state. (8) In view of the division of Germany, this motive of stabilisation gained an added dimension through a sense of threat from the Communists: West Germany's social policy aimed in no small measure at making the population 'socially resistant' and thereby 'to engender greater immunity against Communist influence and infiltration'.[65] Conversely, the Adenauer governments were intent on creating a social order in West Germany which would be attractive also to the East Germans, in order to counteract the solidification of the German partition. (9) A further factor was that one wing of the leading government party belonged to the open-minded social traditions of the Christian social movement, while the decidedly neo-liberal wing was being reconciled by the non-levelling structure of the German social security system.

Some Unresolved Problems at the End of the Adenauer Era

Probably the greatest success in the field of social policy of the Adenauer era was to secure the economic status of those who either temporarily (through sickness) or permanently (through old age) have ceased to be wage-earners. Measured against the awareness of problems and the catalogue of demands contained in the Beveridge Report, a number of important questions remained unresolved. Here I can cite only a few.

(1) Expansion and effective co-ordination of benefits in kind, i.e. especially of social services. This task — which the *Beveridge Plan* had particularly emphasised — gained urgency to the degree that in the area of (monetary) security of income, social insurance was attaining its major objectives. Yet in the early 1970s it could still be said that 'the economic-monetary bias of West German social policy contrasts with a general reluctance to provide services.'[66]

(2) The development of a comprehensive social budget, oriented in the medium term on the extent, structure and probable development of social expenditure, and a clarification of its position within the overall framework of national accounts. The first attempt to arrive at this type of social budget was presented by the Federal government in 1969.[67]

(3) The codificaton of social legislation, gathering all social security provisions in a lucid, non-contradictory and complete code of law. The first part of a — still unfinished — code of social law came into force in 1976.

(4) The question of pensions for non-earning housewives is at present at the centre of social policy debates in Germany. Virtually all participants are in favour of giving housewives independent security, instead of the current system which grants them only an indirect share in pension provisions, with less rights than their husbands.[68] A concept has thus become topical once more which Beveridge had expressed in his demand

to treat women 'not as persons dependent on their husbands, but as partners' and to grant 'housewives independent insurance status'.[69]

For the instances cited here, the *Beveridge Plan* had provided some important initial ground work. Even if some of the proposals no longer seem to provide entirely convincing solutions, hindsight nevertheless shows how momentous the new ideas generated by his plan have proved to be, for 'in the context of economic policy and an integrated theory of social needs, he showed a comprehensiveness that at the time had not been achieved in any other country'.[70]

Notes

1. *The Beveridge Plan. Social Insurance and Related Benefits*, Report by Sir William Beveridge presented to the British Parliament in November 1942 (Zürich/New York, 1943).
2. Regarding the following, cf. generally: Hans Günter Hockerts, *Sozialpolitische Entscheidungen im Nachkriegsdeutschland, Alliierte und deutsche Sozialversicherungspolitik 1945 bis 1957* (Stuttgart, 1980).
3. Re pension insurance example: separate pension schemes for workers, miners and white-collar employees; for health insurance: independent company, regional, craft guild and employee insurance funds, etc.
4. Cf. Horst Peters, *Die Geschichte der sozialen Versicherung*, 2nd edn (Bonn/Bad Godesberg, 1973), p. 130.
5. Austen Albu, *Memories*, Ch. III, p. 13 (as yet unpublished).
6. Alun M. Morgan in a letter to the author of 8 Aug. 1978.
7. *Arbeitsblatt für die Britische Zone*, vol. 1 (1947), pp. 28-30. The first article in the editorial section of the first issue.
8. T.J. Beatty, 'Soziale Sicherheit in Grossbritannien', *Arbeitsblatt für die Britische Zone*, vol. 2 (1948), pp. 338-40, 419-22. Cf. also C.W. Cole, 'Staatliche Fürsorge in Grossbritannien', ibid, pp. 293-5.
9. Text of a lecture: William H. Beveridge, *Soziale Sicherheit und Vollbeschäftigung* (Hamburg, 1946).
10. Cf. George Foggon, 'Alliierte Sozialpolitik in Berlin', in Reinhard Bartholomäi *et al.* (eds.), *Sozialpolitik nach 1945. Geschichte und Analysen* (Bonn/Bad Godesberg, 1977), pp. 33-6. The British military government's social insurance directive no. 1 of 18 August 1945, reprinted in *Arbeitsblatt für die Britische Zone*, vol. 1 (1947), p. 10 f., was thus correspondingly 'conservative'.
11. A German trade unionist in a discussion with the deputy military governor argued therefore quite skilfully that 'state subsidies were an absolute necessity': 'that this is true can be deduced from the fact that according to the Beveridge Plan approximately 50% of the cost of pensions will be borne by the state.' Cf. Minutes of a meeting of the *Zonenbeirat* of the British sector 14/15 August 1946, reprinted in Walter Vogel and Christoph Weisz (eds.), *Akten zur Vorgeschichte der Bundesrepublik Deutschland 1945-1949* (Munich/Vienna, 1967), vol. 1, p. 673.
12. Cf. Die Gewerkschaftsbewegung in der britischen Besatzungszone,

Geschäftsbericht des Deutschen Gewerkschaftsbundes (Britische Zone) 1947-1949 (Cologne, 1949), p. 320f.: it had been 'due to the energetic representations made by the German Trade Union Federation that both the British and American military governments decided not to implement the completed draft law in their areas of occupation'.

13. Karl Teppe, 'Zur Sozialpolitik des Dritten Reiches am Beispiel der Sozialversicherung', *Archiv für Sozialgeschichte*, vol. 17 (1977), pp. 195-250; Florian Tennstedt, *Geschichte der Selbstverwaltung in der Krankenversicherung von der Mitte des 19. Jahrhunderts bis zur Gründung der Bundesrepublik Deutschland* (Bonn, 1977), pp. 219-25. The Reichsarbeitsministerium (Ministry of Labour), incidentally, had the Beveridge Report translated 'for departmental use only' immediately after its publication.

14. Cf. Wilhelm Ritter von Schramm (ed.), *Beck und Goerdeler*, Gemeinschaftsdokumente für den Frieden 1941-4 (Munich, 1965), p. 127f.

15. Cf. for instance a statement on the reform of social insurance by the Ärztekammern (Associations of the Medical Profession) in the three Western sectors of occupation, of 3 November 1946: 'The medical profession is against the idea of a uniform insurance and a uniform administration, since this might imply the threat of political mis-use.' They found it 'hard to understand that a dangerous political aim, which the Nazis, after 1933, had tried to achieve, should now, after their elimination, be put into practice' (documents in private hands).

16. Speech in Essen on 24 August 1946 (Archiv der Stiftung Bundeskanzler-Adenauer-Haus, Rhöndorf). Adenauer referred to a speech (cf. note 9) which Beveridge had made in Hamburg and elsewhere during a visit to Germany.

17. Declaration by the SPD parliamentary advisory council at the Stuttgart *Länderrat* Meeting, 7 October 1947 (Protokoll der 25. Tagung des Länderrats; Parlamentsarchiv des Deutschen Bundestags, Bonn).

18. Walter Auerbach's verbal communications to the author.

19. Thus, for instance, Lutz Niethammer, 'Zum Verhältnis von Reform und Rekonstruktion in der US-Zone am Beispiel der Neuordnung des öffentlichen Dienstes', *VjhZG*, vol. 21 (1973), pp. 177-88; quotation p. 177.

20. Social Insurance Branch to Finance Division, 10 Feb. 1948 (Bundesarchiv, Koblenz, Z40/27).

21. Cf., for instance, Eberhard Schmidt, *Die verhinderte Neuordnung 1945-1952. Zur Auseinandersetzung um die Demokratisierung der Wirtschaft in den westlichen Besatzungszonen und in der Bundesrepublik Deutschland* (Frankfurt, 1970).

22. Cf. Georg Tietz, 'Die Entwicklung der Durchschnittsrenten in der Invalidenversicherung und der Angestelltenversicherung seit 1938', *Bundesarbeitsblatt*, vol. 6 (1955), p. 1087.

23. Cf. José Harris, *William Beveridge, a Biography* (Oxford, 1977), p. 465.

24. *The Cost of Social Security 1949-1957* (International Labour Office, Geneva, 1961). A tabulated summary in Detlev Zöllner, *Öffentliche Sozialleistungen und wirtschaftliche Entwicklung. Ein zeitlicher und internationaler Vergleich* (Berlin, 1963), p. 29.

25. A selection of conference reports by some participants: Walter Auerbach, 'Beveridge-Plan – 10 Jahre danach. Erfahrungen und Lehren', *Soziale Sicherheit*, vol. 2 (1953), pp. 134-73; Heinrich Lünendonk, 'Soziale Sicherung in England', *Sozialer Fortschritt*, vol. 2 (1953), pp. 59-63, 85-8; correspondence between Ludwig Preller and Heinrich Lünendonk, reprinted in *Sozialer Fortschritt*, vol. 2 (1953), pp. 102-6; Karl Osterkamp, 'Soziale Sicherung in England', *Gewerkschaftliche Monatshefte*, vol. 4 (1953), pp. 179-82.

26. Preller, for instance, saw the following *disadvantages* in the British system: (1) the low level of social benefits (such as sick pay and old age pensions); (2)

the absence of a special disability pension (which the Beveridge Plan had proposed, but which had not been introduced; until 1971 disabled persons in Britain received only sick pay); (3) financial contributions of employees to accident insurance (which in Germany was paid by the employer alone); (4) the fact that medical specialists worked almost exclusively within hospitals; (5) the absence of self-administration. What Preller considered *problematical* was, amongst other things, the principle of a flat rate pension, since it did not allow a relation between benefits and earnings. The overcrowding of hospitals and consulting rooms in Britain was, in his view, due to 'the still inadequately solved problem of providing a free service'.

27. Cf. Ludwig Preller (as note 25), p. 103f. Preller stressed, amongst others, the following *advantages* of the British system: (1) the simple and comprehensible structure of its organisation, contributions and benefits; (2) the principle of universality; (3) the conceptual linking of a social benefits system with a policy of full employment; (4) the emphasis on social services, e.g. preventive health care and rehabilitation, which in its systematic 'linking of curative, re-training and labour-market services, was a particularly valuable fruit of the recognition that health care is a public responsibility'.

28. Walter Auerbach, 'Modell eines Sozialplans', *Die Krankenversicherung* (1952), reprinted in idem, *Beiträge zur Sozialpolitik* (Neuwied-Berlin, 1971), pp. 23-32; Gerhard Mackenroth, *Die Reform der Sozialpolitik durch einen deutschen Sozialplan* (Schriften des Vereins für Socialpolitik NF, vol. 4) (Berlin, 1952).

29. Alan T. Peacock (ed.), *Income Redistribution and Social Policy. A Set of Studies* (London, 1954). Peacock endeavoured to include a report on the Federal Republic in this omnibus edition; but he stated that the German statistical material available had been insufficient. The pioneer character of Peacock's studies was duly appreciated in Hans Achinger, 'Wer bezahlt die soziale Sicherung?', *Deutsche Zeitung und Wirtschaftszeitung*, 4 Aug. 1954.

30. Hartmut Hensen, *Die Finanzen der Sozialen Sicherung in Kreislauf der Wirtschaft. Versuch einer ökonomischen Analyse* (Kiel, 1955). This was a dissertation written under Mackenroth. Later Elisabeth Liefmann-Keil, during the preparation of her standard work, *Ökonomische Theorie der Sozialpolitik* (Berlin/Göttingen/Heidelberg, 1961) had conversations with Peacock, Titmuss and others.

31. *Beveridge Plan*, para. 24.

32. Cf. note 28.

33. Wilfrid Schreiber, *Existenzsicherheit in der industriellen Gesellschaft* (Cologne, 1955); quotation from an (unpublished) memorandum by Schreiber to the German Federal government, dated 31 Dec. 1955.

34. Cf. Gerd Muhr's obituary of Walter Auerbach in *Soziale Sicherheit*, vol. 24 (1975), p. 131.

35. Cf. Protokoll der Tagung des sozialpolitischen Ausschusses beim Parteivorstand der SPD of 17/18 Nov. 1951 (unpublished).

36. The text published in 1952 was reprinted with an explanatory contribution by Ludwig Preller in the brochure *Die Grundlagen des sozialen Gesamtplans der SPD. Unsere Forderung auf soziale Sicherung* (Bonn, 1953). More comprehensive and detailed was the 'social plan for Germany' which the SPD party executive published in 1957. However, this plan (partly because the traditional social insurance structure had been consolidated in the meantime) no longer referred back to all ideas contained in the preliminary plan of 1952. For instance, the demand for a flat basic rate for every citizen had been dropped.

37. On the question of organisation and finance the published plan did not go into definite proposals, but merely spoke of an 'effective amalgamation'.

In the SPD party executive's social policy committee the view that the health service should be financed out of public funds existed side by side with another which was in favour of raising part of the money from insurance contributions (Preller suggested 20 per cent). Moreover, within the SPD, Preller advocated the adoption of the British model of a family doctor (and of periodically entering all citizens on general practitioners' lists; GPs receiving a *per capita* fee for this responsibility; encouraging the system of one doctor being responsible for the entire family). A proposal on these lines was incorporated into the 'social plan for Germany', but was never put into practice in the Federal Republic.

38. *Beveridge Plan*, para. 9.
39. Ludwig Preller (as note 36), p. 27 f.
40. A comparison of attitudes on social policies on the part of CDU and SPD has been outlined by Gaston V. Rimlinger, *Welfare Policy and Industrialization in Europe, America, and Russia* (New York/London/Sydney/Toronto, 1976), pp. 466-87.
41. Quotation from an (unprinted) Adenauer speech on 3 February 1956; for details cf. Hans Günter Hockerts, 'Adenauer als Sozialpolitiker', in Dieter Blumenwitz *et al.* (eds.), *Konrad Adenauer und seine Zeit. Politik und Persönlichkeit des ersten Bundeskanzlers* (Stuttgart 1976), vol. 2, pp. 466-87.
42. In the Federal Cabinet on 6 April 1954 (unpublished minutes) the Federal Minister of the Interior also argued in favour of 'creating a government commission on the lines of the English Royal Commission'; cf. an (unpublished) letter from this Minister to the Chancellor's Office, dated 16 Dec. 1953.
43. *Neuordnung der Sozialen Leistungen. Denkschrift auf Anregung des Herrn Bundeskanzlers erstattet von den Professoren Hans Achinger, Joseph Höffner, Hans Muthesius, Ludwig Neundörfer* (Cologne, 1955). Adenauer circulated this memorandum among cabinet colleagues in June 1955, with the remark 'that in line with the English example, he had asked an independent commission to investigate the question of social reform' (unpublished records).
44. Not least at the insistence of middle-class employers, the financing of child allowances was taken over by the Federal government in 1964.
45. For a more detailed statistical breakdown cf. Sozialbericht 1958 (Deutscher Bundestag, 3. Wahlperiode, Drucksache 568), p. 23.
46. Quotations from the explanatory part of Regierungsentwurf des Rentenreformgesetzes, 23 May 1956 (Deutscher Bundestag, 2, Wahlperiode, Drucksache 2314), pp. 57, 61.
47. The explanation of the pension formula in Gaston V. Rimlinger (as note 40), p. 179, does not take account of the net-gross difference.
48. Cf. a report on the observation of trends by the Institut für Demoskopie Allensbach in *Bundesarbeitsblatt*, vol. 11 (1960), p. 66. Also Gerhard Schmidtchen, *Die befragte Nation* (Freiburg, 1959), p. 167.
49. Quite rightly, Gaston V. Rimlinger also emphasises this (as note 40), pp. 180, 191.
50. Cf. Brian Abel-Smith, 'Lohngebundene oder Einheitsrenten in Grossbritannien? Zur gegenwärtigen Auseinandersetzung um die Reform des Beveridge-Systems', *Sozialer Fortschritt*, vol. 5 (1956), pp. 226-8.
51. Cf. *Die öffentliche Fürsorge* (Federal Ministry of the Interior, Cologne, 1956), p. 28.
52. Richard M. Titmuss, who informed the Anglo-German conference about this in January 1953, was highly critical; cf. the conference reports by Walter Auerbach (as note 25), p. 170 and Ludwig Preller (as note 25), p. 103.
53. Brian Abel-Smith, who belonged to those members of the Fabian Society who worked for a reform of the Beveridge system, in 1956 commented on this as follows: 'the early post-war vision millions of people had of a classless retire-

ment, assured by uniform Beveridge pensions, has faded. If nothing is done, we can certainly expect to have "two nations" of the old: one nation with two pensions (state and occupational) and another with just one pension (state).' The introduction of earnings-related pensions would 'bring about greater equality for old people than subsistence rates, where supplementing these through occupational pension schemes depends on luck'. Abel-Smith therefore pleaded 'for the creation of some inequality in order to avoid even greater inequalities' (as note 50).

54. Wolfram Fischer, 'Der Wandel der sozialen Frage in den fortgeschrittenen Industriegesellschaft', *Soziale Probleme der modernen Industriegesellschaft* (Schriften des Vereins für Sozialpolitik NF, vol. 92) (Berlin 1977), vol. 1, pp. 35-68, quotation p. 47.

55. Cf. a memorandum circulated in May 1956 by the Association of Life Insurance Companies: 'Die elastische Staatsbürgergrundrente als Grundlage einer echten sozialen Reform'. Partly reprinted in Max Richter (ed.), *Die Sozialreform. Dokumente und Stellungnahmen* (Bad Godesberg, n.d.) (loose leaf collection). Cf. also unsigned article, 'Die Privatversicherung nimmt das Wort', *Sozialer Fortschritt*, vol. 5 (1956), p. 113 f.

56. *National Superannuation. Labour's Policy for Security in Old Age* (London, 1957). This programmatic declaration was based on studies in which Titmuss and Abel-Smith had also participated. The programme envisaged the introduction of a wage-related superannuation scheme, as well as automatic adjustment of pensions to the cost of living index (this aimed at safeguarding the value of pensions in real terms, but not – as in Germany – at the pensioners participating in economic growth). Lord Beveridge fought against the principle of wage-related pensions and rejected particularly the idea of an automatic adjustment of pensions. Cf. José Harris (as note 23), p. 463 f.

57. That in the 'course of economic growth the crux of the "security" problem is shifted from maintaining the "subsistence level" to maintaining "relative social status" ' is emphasised also by Peter Flora, Jens Alber and Jürgen Kohl, 'Zur Entwicklung der westeuropäischen Wohlfahrtsstaaten', *Politische Vierteljahresschrift*, vol. 18 (1977), pp. 707-72, quotation p. 722.

58. Cf. a photo on title page of *Welt der Arbeit*, Wochenzeitung des Deutschen Gewerkschaftsbundes, 8 Mar. 1957.

59. Thus the heading of a report in *Welt der Arbeit*, 22 Feb. 1957. 'Rarely', it went on, 'have the newspapers read by English working people followed a foreign social policy measure with as much interest as they do now in the case of the German pension reform.' The head of the social insurance department of the Federal Ministry of Labour recognised with some pride certain details in the Labour Party's National Superannuation Scheme as regulations contained in the German reform legislation: Kurt Jantz, 'Zum System der Sozialen Sicherheit in England', *Bundesarbeitsblatt*, vol. 8 (1957), pp. 480-7.

60. Gaston V. Rimlinger (as note 40), p. 184.

61. *The Cost of Social Security, 1961-1963*. A statistical summary in Ludwig Preller, *Praxis und Probleme der Sozialpolitik*, vol. 2 (Tübingen/Zurich, 1970), p. 554.

62. Cf. Andrew Shonfield, *Geplanter Kapitalismus. Wirtschaftspolitik in Westeuropa und USA* (Cologne/Berlin, 1968), p. 106.

63. Detlev Zöllner (as note 24) sees the quota of (non-agricultural) workers as the prime determining factor for the rate of social benefits.

64. Correlation analyses carried out by H.C. Wilensky regarding the size and growth of social benefits have shown that, compared internationally, 'the closest correlation' existed between 'the rate of social benefits per capita of population and the ratio of over-65s to the population as a whole'. Quoted according to

Wolfram Fischer (as note 54), p. 54.

65. From the preface by Chancellor Adenauer in *Deutschland im Wieder-aufbau. Tätigkeitsbericht der Bundesregierung für das Jahr 1955* (no place, n.d.), p. IV.

66. Hans F. Zacher, 'Faktoren und Bahnen der aktuellen sozialpolitischen Diskussion', *Archiv für Wissenschaft und Praxis der sozialen Arbeit*, vol. 3 (1972), pp. 241-66, quotation p. 241.

67. Hermann Berié, 'Das Sozialbudget als Instrument der staatlichen Sozialpolitik' in *Soziale Probleme der modernen Industriegesellschaft* (Schriften des Vereins für Socialpolitik NF, vol. 92/II), Berlin, 1977, pp. 830-68.

68. As long as the husband is alive the non-earning housewife has no direct legal claim to a pension of her own. As a widow she has an indirect claim to 60 per cent of her husband's pension. Yet if the wife dies, the husband continues to receive 100 per cent of 'his' pension.

69. *Beveridge Plan*, paras. 106 and 117.

70. Hans Achinger, *Sozialpolitik als Gesellschaftspolitik. Von der Arbeiterfrage zum Wohlfahrtsstaat*, 2nd edn (Frankfurt, 1971), p. 102f.

PART FOUR

PAST AND FUTURE OF THE WELFARE STATE IN
SOCIAL-SCIENTIFIC PERSPECTIVE

16 SOLUTION OR SOURCE OF CRISES? THE WELFARE STATE IN HISTORICAL PERSPECTIVE[1]

P. Flora

The modern welfare state had its beginnings in Europe about a century ago, and it has since been a central element in the profound changes which European societies have undergone — and will have to master in future. The basic aim of the welfare state was a 'defensive policy of integration and stabilisation'. In the sense of preserving existing structures, welfare state policy long remained defensive and to a large extent still does. But the answers to the questions of who was to be integrated and what had to be stabilised have changed.

Initially, the policy of integration was directed exclusively at the working class, whose militancy against the system was to be restrained and channelled, and it was the capitalist economic system and the prevailing political order that was to be stabilised. Today, the welfare state has grown far beyond the working class and lost its purely defensive character, but integration and stabilisation still remain central functions.

Since its inception the idea of the welfare state has rarely been a truly inspiring ideal; its success as a mobilising force can hardly be compared with that of nationalism or socialism. Only once, in the troubled England of the Second World War, inspired by Beveridge's pen, did it generate an enthusiasm that found a considerable echo in the Anglo-Saxon world. From the beginning, the welfare state obviously had its enemies as well as its sceptics. Some thought it did too little, others too much; some saw it as the beginning of revolutionary change, others feared it might paralyse revolutionary impetus. Neither Marxists nor the followers of Durkheim were able to accept the welfare state as an adequate solution to the problems posed by the crisis of European societies, of which their diagnoses diverged widely. Beyond that, there had always existed the fear that the welfare state might undermine the will to work, hinder economic productivity and the capacity for innovation, and place too large a burden on the public purse. The question of limits has accompanied the welfare state ever since its modest beginnings.

Aside from pressing distributive conflicts and ideological controversy, however, a rather positive assessment of the welfare state's stabilising role and its successes as an integrative force has generally predominated. In principle, the need to establish the agencies of the welfare state was only rarely disputed and controversies usually centred around their extent and the form they should take. Thus virtually all political forces in Europe played a part in building up the welfare state. Bismarck, the authoritarian conservative, laid one of the most important foundation stones; Lloyd George and Beveridge, the Liberals, revolutionised the British welfare state; the Scandinavian welfare states were largely the creation of Social Democrats, while on the Continent the Christian Democrats made considerable contributions.

As the work of many, the welfare state represents a relatively broadly based common denominator and is thus an important element of political consensus. Yet for the same reason it lacks clear contours, and this is detrimental to a more emphatically ideological political integration. It may nevertheless be said that the undeniable integrative successes are not merely based on material achievements, important as these may be — they are also due to their being shaped by certain fundamental values, however weak and diffuse, which our societies generally accept: social security, relative equality of opportunity, the notion that everybody has a right to a guaranteed minimum chance in life and that certain forms of inequality are not legitimate.

In recent years — and even before the so-called oil crisis — sceptical and indeed pessimistic voices have become more clamorous. That this should happen after the welfare state had passed through the phase of its greatest growth in history may contain an element of irony, but there may also be a causal connection. One is reminded of Schumpeter's prediction that capitalism is most likely to perish through its successes. The increasingly critical and anxious voices, however, have not led to a diagnosis of the 'crisis of the welfare state' which is even remotely unanimous. Indeed it remains a matter of dispute whether such a crisis exists at all. Only one thing seems certain: if there does exist a more deep-seated 'crisis of the welfare state', this would be a serious matter, since the system of social security, education and health services has become central to the institutional order of our societies.

I should therefore like to examine the somewhat rhetorical question as to whether the welfare state, instead of overcoming crises, now generates them. In order to do this, I must first clarify my understanding of the meaning of the word 'crisis' and then sketch the historical macro-constellation in which the welfare state developed as a solution to crises. Thirdly, there follows a brief description and analysis of the growth of the welfare state. The fourth, and most extensive, section will examine the question of whether today's welfare state, within a new macro-constellation, now threatens to become a source of new crises.

What is a Crisis?

Three basic elements serve here to define the concept of crisis. They emphasise different aspects: 'crisis symptoms', 'macro-constellation' and 'institutional change'. I begin by defining observable crisis symptoms. This is intended to prevent frivolous invention of crisis. We must differentiate between crisis symptoms at two levels of analysis (see Figure 16.1): at the 'national-political' level, an imbalance in the national budget and instabilities of political institutions; at the 'social-structural' level, an increase in social conflict and growing symptoms of social disintegration.

Figure 16.1: Historical Macro-constellation

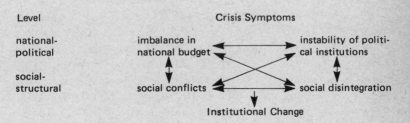

Our second task is an attempt to define the extent to which these crisis symptoms have a 'structural origin'. I do this in order to counter the current habit of blowing up even comparatively small problems into full-scale 'crises'. In this perspective we have to ask ourselves to what extent different crisis symptoms are interrelated, and whether they indicate only a passing problem or must be seen as symptoms of more fundamental problems. To this much more vexed question of structural roots I would apply the concept of 'historical macro-constellation'.

The third element of crisis is the most speculative. It is the notion that an empirically observable and structurally based 'crisis' can only be 'solved' by institutional change. This brings us to the

link between 'crises', their problems and causes, and the practical
tasks of designing possible solutions and realising them politically.

Crisis Symptoms at the National-political Level

Imbalance in the National Budget. In his *Politics and the Stages of
Growth*, Walt W. Rostow develops a concept of equilibrium which is
related to national budgets. According to Rostow, societies are in
political equilibrium if mobilised resources more or less equal expenditure, if the amount and distribution of expenditure solve the problems
arising from the political process, at least to the degree that ever present
dissatisfactions can be contained within the existing institutional
order. He defines three central problem areas which in principle are
common to any government or political leadership:

(1) 'security' (protection of territorial integrity and national inter-
    ests);
(2) 'welfare and growth' (care for the common good and, as far
    as is relevant, promotion of growth);
(3) 'constitutional order' (protection of the constitution, resolu-
    tion of conflicts through jurisdiction, maintenance of law and
    order).[2]

With minor changes to Rostow's categories, I predicate what follows
on four areas of government responsibility: *external security — internal order — growth — welfare*. Between, as well as within, these categories a number of conflicts are conceivable and the basic problem
of a budget's 'political arithmetic' does not just consist of a sufficient
mobilisation of limited resources, but in their politically 'correct'
allocation. The welfare state competes for these resources and the question thus arises as to whether and in what way it contributes to a
potential imbalance between revenue and expenditure, or to an imbalance between the structure of expenditure and the relative importance of the various policy areas of government.

Instability of Political Institutions. The problems of continuing budgetary imbalances have an important bearing on the stability of political
institutions. In our mass democracies this depends on the extent to
which political decisions and compromises can be arrived at in the
context of party structures, parliamentary majorities and various forms
of government. Of course, stability should not be confused with rigid-
ity; it must also mean flexibility, that is to say, the problems that

arise must be decided and dealt with in a manner so as not to induce large sections of the community to search for other means to reach their objectives or to withdraw from the political process altogether. This opens up an entire spectrum of crisis symptoms, ranging from 'illegitimate' political behaviour, or non-participation, via changes in party structures to unstable parliamentary majorities and governments. Such manifestations of political instability can, of course, be traced to a variety of causes. But is the welfare state perhaps one of them? The answer, at least at first glance, is by no means an easy one.

Crisis Symptoms at the Social-structural Level

Distributive Conflicts. A wide range of conflicts can arise from imbalances in the national budget and from instability of political institutions, both as a cause and a consequence. Distributive conflicts are in the forefront. We may conceive of the welfare state as the attempt to influence such conflicts, either directly (redistribution by the state), or indirectly (protection against loss of earnings regulating conditions of employment). The welfare state, on the other hand, may itself become the cause of new conflicts of distribution (e.g. working population *v.* pensioners).

For the historical macro-analysis of distributive conflicts recent political sociology offers us two concepts: 'crisis of distribution' and 'cleavage structure'. The Princeton 'Studies in Political Development' attempted to analyse a country's political development as a sequence and overlapping of various crises of 'identity', 'legitimacy', 'participation', 'penetration' and 'distribution'.[3] In this scheme, the European welfare states represent a 'solution' to the 'crisis of distribution' in those countries.

The concept of relatively clearly identifiable 'crises' and 'solutions' has, however, proved less useful than that of 'cleavage structure'. Stein Rokkan employs this term in his model of the development of European political parties and distinguishes five main cleavages in European history (subject *v.* dominant culture; church(es) *v.* government; primary *v.* secondary economy; workers *v.* employers, owners; Communists *v.* socialists, social democrats).[4] One would have to ask whether the welfare state has decisively influenced these cleavages (the end of class politics?), or whether it has created new divisions ('welfare backlash' of the middle class?).

Social Disintegration. Social conflicts certainly provide a gauge with which to measure the degree of integration or disintegration of a society. But I would make a distinction between this and the crisis symptoms of social disintegration in the narrower sense, i.e. signs of increasing instability of smaller social groupings and an increase of 'deviant' and self-destructive behaviour. In Durkheim's sense, these would have to be seen as the result of a weakening of 'moral integration' and its 'disciplining' and 'motivating' components.[5] This touches especially on the integrative force of family and school, although almost all other institutions possess such functions to some degree as well. In recent years, a number of questions have arisen as to the connection between welfare state and social disintegration. For instance: does the welfare state encourage an inflation of expectations and thus create dissatisfaction and anomie? Has it contributed to an imbalance between the individual's rights and responsibilities *vis-à-vis* the community? Has it, by combining bureaucratic regulations with more individualised provisions, further weakened intermediary structures, notably the family?

Historical Macro-constellation

Has the welfare state, instead of being a 'solver' of crises turned into a 'generator' of them? In order to examine this question, it does not suffice to define observable crisis symptoms and to make assumptions about possible and empirically investigable connections with the welfare state. Rather it is necessary to place these symptoms and connections in a larger historical and structural context that permits us to comprehend the genesis and development, the structure and functions of the European welfare state as part of a more general process of evolution and transformation. To this end it may be useful to look first at macro-sociological theories of development, which define *stages* of development, and perhaps refine them by distinguishing between various *types* of society.

I prefer to speak in terms of macro-*constellations* which, while connected with the ideas of stages of development and different types of society, cannot be reduced to these alone. A brilliant example for the analysis of a macro-constellation is offered by Max Weber's 'Die sozialen Gründe des Untergangs der antiken Kultur' ('The Social Causes of the Decline of Classical Civilisation'); his approach also appears promising for the question examined here.[6]

The concept of macro-constellation avoids exaggerated notions concerning the inherent 'systemness' of various types of society and an orderly sequence of evolutionary stages, as well as a disregard for external influences. It is based on the assumption that we can distinguish several central, but historically limited, *structural elements*, which possess a relatively high degree of autonomy and thus quite independent developments. These developments, *processes of growth and contraction*, combine to form various constellations which are historically rather unique in character.

Therefore, if clear signs of permanent budgetary imbalance, persistent instability of political institutions, or a marked increase in social conflicts and symptoms of social disintegration combine with a specific historical macro-constellation, we may indeed speak of a crisis. Since the macro-constellation — almost by definition and certainly in its tendency — is hardly susceptible to being shaped politically, the 'solution' to such a crisis would lie in adaptation and reform of social institutions which appear more amenable to such influence.

Institution-building and Reform

Conditions of stability, degree of integration and potential for conflict within a society are decisively influenced by its institutional order. Social development can be understood essentially as a process of institution-building, institutional differentiation and fusion. This process produces new units of action with specific interests, normative orientations and criteria of rationality.

Rainer M. Lepsius has distinguished four aspects of institution-building and reform: allocation of competence, which governs the freedom of action and the responsibilities of these new units; allocation of resources, which determines the means put at their disposal for the execution of their tasks; allocation of legitimacy, which determines the criteria for justifying the exercise of their competence; and finally the allocation of control, regulating the settlement of inter-institutional conflicts.[7]

From this perspective, the emergence of the modern European welfare state may be seen as the creation of new institutions, aimed at modifying the conditions of stability, the degree of social integration and the potential for conflict. It may be defined as the emergence of more differentiated units (for example trade unions, social security agencies, service bureaucracies) with new interests, a new normative orientation and new criteria of rationality (for example, principle of social security *v.* profitability). Thus, if it is true that the welfare state has changed from a 'solver' to a 'generator' of crises, it would be necessary to analyse the possibilities for institutional solutions, by reordering the allocations of competence, resources, legitimacy and control between old or new units of action.

The Macro-constellation during the Initial Phase of European Welfare States

I shall attempt first to give a — necessarily brief and thus over-simplified — sketch of the historical macro-constellation towards the end of the last century, when the modern welfare state came into being. In this I follow Max Weber's fundamental perspective: his understanding of the dynamic of European societies as deriving from specific processes of differentiation.

The basic distinction here is between the evolution of a capitalist 'world' economy on the one hand and a system of modern states on the other. It is a central characteristic of this constellation that no single state is capable of controlling the development of the economic system, but that conversely the development of states and the state system shows a remarkable inherent dynamic. The two elements of this constellation have two corresponding balancing factors: the balance of power and the balance between the demand for essential raw materials, sources of energy and foodstuffs and their supply. As a rough indication of the time scale, it may be said that this constellation had its origins in the sixteenth century and had been stabilised by the second half of the seventeenth century.[8]

The first public welfare institutions came into being at that time. Their origins, functions and their strongly repressive character must be seen as clearly linked to the first two elements of this constellation. In part they were a reaction to the problems created by the monetarisation of agriculture and by a new and expanding labour market, but they were also the consequence of the secularisation of church property. Their most important function consisted not only in the maintenance of public order, but also in the support of a capitalist labour market.[9] But even then a third element in the constellation began to be apparent: population growth, which narrowed the margin of food supply and increased rural unemployment.

The further development of older welfare institutions can be traced well into the nineteenth century without any decisive changes taking place. Change became possible and necessary only after two new elements in the constellation had begun to emerge: industrialisation and the development of mass democracy. In the context of the formative period of absolutist states, we have become accustomed to speaking of 'penetration', but this in reality did not go very deep. The same is probably true of capitalism's 'penetration' of self-sufficient local units. To a certain degree state and market were 'surface phenomena'.

This changed profoundly with industrialisation, for only then did capitalism become the dominant economic system. The expansion of the exchange of goods on a world-wide scale reduced the possibilities of self-sufficiency further and further and created new, uncontrollable dependencies. Profound changes were also brought about by the development of mass democracy, which not only imposed new responsibilities on the state but also legitimised the immense expansion of state resources, which had been made possible by industrialisation.

To this point, we have discussed five elements in this early constellation: capitalist economy and industrial society, nation state and mass democracy, and population development. However, I would not wish this last element to be understood as a purely 'demographic' one, limited to population growth and age structure. A further essential component is the changing structure and function of the family: the pattern of division of labour between the sexes; the kind of responsibility the family shoulders for its growing and dying generations; the degree of material security, emotional protection and moral integration it is capable of offering. A sixth element is required to

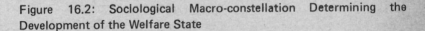

Figure 16.2: Sociological Macro-constellation Determining the Development of the Welfare State

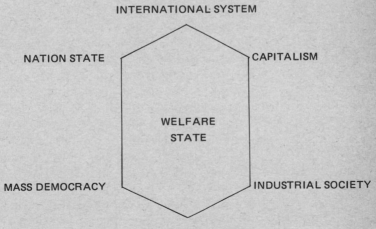

INTERNATIONAL SYSTEM

NATION STATE

CAPITALISM

WELFARE
STATE

MASS DEMOCRACY

INDUSTRIAL SOCIETY

FAMILY/POPULATION

define this constellation: the development of the international system. Here two aspects should be distinguished: Europe's expanding and subsequent loss of control over the world and its consequences for the global distribution of wealth and for world production; secondly, the degree of international tensions, the frequency and violence of wars, and thus the destruction of riches and the squandering of production which could have been put to other purposes.

How then did the macro-constellation appear in the initial phase of the modern welfare state? This is the period extending roughly from the 1870s to the beginning of the First World War. In the early 1870s a new political order had been established in Central Europe, industrialisation increased apace and the development of mass democracy had already received its first impulses.

This period saw the high point of the European nation states and European domination of the world, although there were already signs of impending change. With the unification of Italy and Germany, the principle of nationally defined frontiers had triumphed, resisted only, and increasingly feebly, by the old Habsburg Empire. The reciprocal connection between internal unity and national strength played a central role, and may serve to explain why the newly established German Reich, as the parvenu amongst the great European powers, became a pioneer in the development of the modern welfare state.

This period saw the general breakthrough of industrial societies. In Rostow's terminology, Britain's 'take off' had been accomplished long before, as had that of France, Belgium and Germany, and by 1900 the Scandinavian countries, Italy and Austria-Hungary had followed suit.[10] In some countries the national product quadrupled between 1870 and 1913, while in most others it at least tripled.[11] This, however, does not mean that the European societies had already reached Rostow's stage of 'general mass consumption'. For the initial level of wealth had been too low, investment requirements too great and the distribution of income too unequal. Furthermore, the population grew too rapidly, more rapidly than ever before or since. It represents the climax in the European populations' 'demographic transition'. The rate of natural population growth was on average clearly above 1 per cent.[12]

Population growth and industrialisation led to a massive shift of population from country to towns, which in turn grew more quickly than before or since. While around 1870 only one in six Europeans (not counting Eastern Europe) lived in a town with 20,000 inhabitants or more, by about 1910 one in three did so. The number of people living in cities with 100,000 inhabitants or more rose from 16 million around 1870 to 48 million around 1910, and its relative share from 10 to 20 per cent. Industrialisation and urbanisation of such dimensions and speed inevitably created immense social problems. These were not only shaped and exacerbated by the capitalist economic structure, but partly even caused by it. Although cyclical trends were a much older phenomenon and, according to Rostow, the relative amplitude of the shift of employment did not increase at the time, an ever greater proportion of the population was now affected by these cyclical economic movements.[13]

It is thus easy to see that this was also a period of intensified class struggle and distributive conflict, and that it was a decisive phase in the mobilisation of the working class and the organisation of workers' movements, with their twin pillars — trade unions and labour parties. The development of trade unions was facilitated by the fact that the freedom to organise into groups had, in the majority of European countries, been legally established even before 1870.

Germany and England led the way in 1868 with the formation of central trade union federations, and by the end of the century all other countries had followed. The trade unions learned to use the strike weapon. In some countries the relative number of strikes rose tenfold during the period, and the relative number of strikers involved rose twenty times (see Tables 16.1-16.3).[14] The workers' parties, the other pillar of the workers' movement, became the prototype of modern mass parties. These, too, were established in all European countries at that time, beginning with Germany even before 1870 and with the British Labour Party coming last shortly after 1900. By the turn of the century, labour's representatives were to be found in virtually every European parliament.

This also serves as an indication that this was the decisive period for the development of mass democracy. The franchise, however, was not an invention of that era, and the growth of mass democracies, with universal suffrage and governments responsible to parliament, was not completed until after the First World War. This early period nevertheless saw the greatest extension of the franchise and even before the First World War voting turn-outs reached high levels; and there was no real reduction of voting rights, not to speak of abolition. Parliamentary control was also everywhere established during that time, with the exception of Germany and Austria.

The development towards mass democracy inevitably brought new tasks for governments, but it equally strengthened the legitimacy of their demands for resources. Buoyed by economic growth, the absolute revenues of the European states rose remarkably, and they slowly took for themselves a greater share of the national product. A relatively

Table 16.1: Relative Number of Strikers[a]

Years	IT	FR	UK	IR	FI	BE	AU	DE	GE	SW	NO	NE	SZ	Years
1871-5		83												1871-5
1876-80	116	288												1876-80
1881-5	172	278								107				1881-5
1886-90	211	404								107				1886-90
1891-5	462	497	2 703*							99				1891-5
1896-1900	1 558	611	1 317							455				1896-1900
1901-5	2 127	882	879		848	1 322		275	760	808				1901-5
1906-10	1 842	1 175	1 647		537	1 317		406	965	3 557	228*	706		1906-10
1911-15	4 832	851	4 297			1 412*		767	930	519	707	599	218	1911-15
1916-20	2 263*	2 743	7 097		4 323	8 104*	6 056	1 383	3 438	2 733	1 734	1 123	1 149	1916-20
1921-5		1 511	3 894		382	3 272	850	2 974	5 098	2 951	2 629	1 687	333	1921-5
1926-30		1 393	2 176	243	612	1 823	144	147	1 111	1 185	4 737	1 471	221	1926-30
1931-5		404	1 449	564	106	1 854		262		1 054	1 609	470	165	1931-5
1936-40		6 699*	1 851	965	203	1 421		1 127		474	1 380	575	113	1936-40
1941-5			2 492	404*				257		1 006	1 658	171	75	1941-5
1946-50		14 977	2 107		3 290	6 147	419	688		445	465	940	263	1946-50
1951-5	11 617	6 829	2 855	746*	977	3 969	1 243	208	875	355	408	342	68	1951-5
1956-60	8 320	7 085	3 263	611	5 590	3 591	1 006	982	252	37	1 061	612	12	1956-60
1961-5	14 843	10 613	6 245	1 996	1 855	691	2 718	1 784	563	53	500	358	11	1961-5
1966-70	20 886	10 753*	5 872	3 609	3 835	1 061	235	1 232	353	388	87	347	3	1966-70
1971-5	29 572	10 559	5 405	3 022	5 422	1 996	643	4 410	766	614	3 368	487	59	1971-5

a Number of strikers per 100,000 persons of the economically active population; 5-year averages of annual rates.

☐ 2,000 and more strikers per 100,000 persons of the economically active population.

Table 16.2: Relative Number of Strikes [a]

Years	IT	FR	UK	IR	FI	BE	AU	DE	GE	SW	NO	NE	SZ	Years
1871-5	0.5												0.9	1871-5
1876-80	0.7	0.6											0.2	1876-80
1881-5	0.8	1.4											0.4	1881-5
1886-90	1.7	2.3	6.5*				1.1			1.2			1.3	1886-90
1891-5	5.9	3.0	5.2				2.1			1.7			2.0	1891-5
1896-1900	9.6	3.7	4.8				2.8			1.5			2.6	1896-1900
1901-5	5.8	6.1	2.6			2.9	5.8	6.0	6.6	4.3		6.4		1901-5
1906-10	5.9	4.3	2.7		8.5	4.6	3.0	7.6	9.3	8.2		7.2		1906-10
1911-15	3.5*	5.0	5.2		4.0	5.2*	—	4.5	6.7	10.3	4.8	12.1		1911-15
1916-20		4.0	5.6		11.6	13.8*	12.3	18.9	6.5	4.6		16.5	9.3	1916-20
1921-5		4.7	3.4		3.2	5.4	6.4	4.5	10.2	25.0	5.8	9.9	3.3	1921-5
1926-30		1.6	1.7		2.5	4.3	0.9	1.6	1.8	10.8	7.7	7.0	1.8	1926-30
1931-5			2.3	4.6	0.8	2.5		1.3		7.3	7.5	5.6	1.4	1931-5
1936-40		34.1*	4.7	6.3	1.3	3.5		0.9		4.9	3.5	2.6	1.1	1936-40
1941-5			8.4	8.7		4.5		0.3	—	2.0			1.0	1941-5
1946-50	8.2	9.1	7.2	5.6*	4.8	6.5		1.4		4.4	3.2	4.8	1.2	1946-50
1951-5	9.8	9.8	8.4	6.9*	3.2	3.7		0.5		2.1	2.5	1.7	0.3	1951-5
1956-60		9.0	11.1	4.7	2.8	2.4		2.2	2.1*	0.9	1.3	1.7	0.2	1956-60
1961-5	18.3	10.3	10.0	7.2	2.6	1.2		1.4	0.8	0.6	0.6	1.3	0.1	1961-5
1966-70	16.9	11.7	11.0	10.4	6.3	2.5		1.6	1.0	1.3	0.5	0.7	0.1	1966-70
1971-5	23.5	17.1	10.4	15.4	17.0	4.8		4.5		1.6	0.8	2.6	0.2	1971-5

Note: [a] Number of strikes per 100,000 persons of the economically active population; 5-year averages of annual rates.

[boxed] 8 and more strikes per 100,000 persons of the economically active population.

Table 16.3: Relative Number of Working Days Lost [a]

Years	IT	FR	UK	IR	FI	NE'	AU	DE	GE	SW	NO	NE	SZ	Years
1871-5														1871-5
1876-80														1876-80
1881-5														1881-5
1886-90										20				1886-90
1891-5			942							41				1891-5
1896-1900	150		442							97				1896-1900
1901-5	147		165		303			132	259	375	76*			1901-5
1906-10	205		314		360			88	341	1345	253	100		1906-10
1911-15			786		451			188	260	162	492	147		1911-15
1916-20			788		102			432	372	1109	669	344		1916-20
1921-5			1363		303		579	603	784	1192	1874	535		1921-5
1926-30			1604	58	18	378	139	44	231	571	770	154	65	1926-30
1931-5			91	154	60	255	8	61		733	1477	217	36	1931-5
1936-40			105	361		96		338		190	558	23	18	1936-40
1941-5			89	64*				19		789			8	1941-5
1946-50			104	106*	672	499	55	185	–	24	52	76	38	1946-50
1951-5	242		189	81	90	189	23	4	52	88	59	16	9	1951-5
1956-60	276		131	326	770	362	22	111	29	7	157	36	1	1956-60
1961-6	637	141	227		148	63	59	244	19	4	105	8	6	1961-6
1966-70	941	131*		591	106	88	9	19	7	37	13	13	0	1966-70
1971-5	999	175	518	272	4196	183	8	345	43	63	69	34	1	1971-5

Note: [a] Number of working days lost per 100,000 persons of the economically active population; 5-year averages of annual rates.
□ 500 and more working days lost per 100,000 persons of the economically active population.

large part of it was spent on developing the economic infrastructure, while expenditure on external security, despite the tensions which resulted from imperialist competition, remained relatively low, since the period was for Europe one of comparative peace and small wars. Thus, according to Rostow's terminology, there remained a margin for other tasks: internal order and welfare. And in view of the social upheavals of that era, increased spending on these two categories seemed urgently required.

To summarise briefly: the structural problems of the emerging, capitalistically organised industrial societies produced, apart from other crisis symptoms, a rapid increase of social conflicts and efforts to mobilise forces hostile to the prevailing system. These forces, however, were mediated by means of evolving parliamentary institutions and with the aid of the increased resources which states could devote to domestic problems, since there was no threat of large-scale wars or preparation for them. This was the take-off point for the modern welfare state which, after having achieved this breakthrough, entered an astounding dynamic of expansion.

Essential Characteristics and Expansion of the Welfare State

The aims and institutional emphases of the emerging welfare state are in various ways related to the kind of crisis existing at the time and to the characteristics of the constellation within which it developed. Thus it is not surprising that it was initially directed almost exclusively at the working class, seeking to win it over to the capitalist system and the prevailing political order by means of some increase in *security* and a somewhat greater degree of *equality*. But in a much more general way, too, we find certain characteristics of the constellation and its constituent elements in the institutions of the welfare state itself. Hans Achinger, long ago, pointed a critical finger at three general characteristics: *monetarisation, bureaucratisation and excessive legislation*,[15] which are closely linked to the elements 'capitalism', 'nation state' and 'mass democracy'.

Beyond that, a fourth general characteristic of the welfare state results from its combination with the structural element 'industrial society'. Not only does it increase and reinforce the innumerable processes of *differentiation*, so typical of industrial societies, but to some extent it even creates these itself. Thus it has contributed to the demise of many intermediate forms, partial solutions and overlapping of functions which gave pre-industrial societies their specific flexibility. And it has furthermore grown at the expense of intermediate structures.

If one looks for a concrete definition of the term welfare state, one rarely meets with consensus, and some would rather abandon the term altogether.[16] I believe, however, that we need this concept without defining it too closely. If we assume that we are dealing with a relatively closely linked complex of governmental measures and institutions, the exact boundaries become less important; much more significant seems to be the definition of institutional emphases which, historically, shift more slowly than the boundaries.

Structural phenomena such as the welfare state rarely have an exact hour of birth. The advent of the modern welfare state is nevertheless frequently dated back to Bismarck's social legislation, i.e. workers' accident, sickness and old age insurance. With these measures a new institution of income protection was created, differing in a variety of ways from the older poor relief, especially in its greater functional specialisation and bureaucratic standardisation, and through the establishment of a legal right as a consequence of collecting contributions.

But, to my mind, the most important difference lies in the inherent dynamic force of social security. Poor relief, both with regard to the extent of its provisions and the sectors of the population it covered, was, as a matter of principle, strictly limited in scope. Social security, on the other hand, is an institution aimed at covering the entire population, and its growth is perhaps comparable to the extension of the franchise. Yet while the right to vote was extended downwards from the privileged classes to the less privileged ones, social security expanded upwards on the social ladder. With this expansion its aims were shifted from protecting the basic income of a relatively homogeneous social class to protecting the relative incomes of very diverse social strata. Here lies a second element of expansion through which social security provisions are dragged into disputes about distribution and status, so that simple growth appears as the simplest solution.

The emphasis on social insurance being an institutional innovation thus appears to be historically justified. It is nevertheless only one important institution among others that partly pre-date it (protective legislation), are distinct from it (public assistance), were begun at roughly the same time (tax reforms), or followed some time later (national housing and employment policies). Special attention must be given to public health and education, which, next to social security, are today institutional corner-stones of the welfare state, with a comparable expansive dynamism of their own.

I cannot here go into a detailed description of how the tasks of the welfare state have grown to link this growth to changes in the macro-constellation during the inter-war years and the two decades after the last war. But before turning to the question as to whether we are today seeing the emergence of a new macro-constellation and what the consequences of this might be for the expanding welfare state, I should like to indicate the latter's general development under three simple headings: *modest beginnings, continuous growth, acceleration in recent years.*

How modest the beginnings were, at least in hindsight, can be measured if we examine how the social security provisions for accident, ill health, old age and unemployment have since been extended. As the graph on the following page shows, these four systems together had by 1910 reached an average in Europe of only a tenth of what they are today.[17] And it should be noted that the differences between individual countries were considerable. Germany, in the vanguard with the most advanced social insurance, public education and health systems, spent a total of 2.6 per cent of GNP on social insurance and poor relief, 2.7 per cent on education and 0.7 per cent on health in 1913. Its total 'social expenditure ratio' amounted to approximately 6.1 per cent.[18] Compared to this 'peak value' before the First World War, social expenditure in 1975 in Europe varied between just under 20 per cent and over 28 per cent of GNP.[19]

The expanding social security system also demonstrates how continuous the growth was on a European average. Not even in the period between the Depression and the end of the Second World War was there stagnation or indeed a reduction. This obviously was true only of Europe as a whole, and it does not necessarily reflect an accurate picture of the benefits. Moreover, Jens Alber has demonstrated that this general pattern conceals important variations. Until 1900, it was largely the authoritarian states in Europe that promoted expansion; between 1900 and 1914 it was predominantly the parliamentary democracies with liberal governments, and in the inter-war years growth appears to be linked to increases in socialist votes and socialist partici-pation in government. After 1945 these differences become blurred and converge in general expansion.[20]

The most recent acceleration of this expansive trend can more easily be demonstrated by showing the development of public expendi-ture, since the growth in social security coverage has meanwhile reached its 'natural' limits. The development of transfer payments can be followed on Table 16.4. It shows that in 22 of the 25 years between

Table 16.4: Growth of National Product and Transfer Payments: European Averages

Years	Annual Growth Rates of Transfer Payments at Current Prices		Annual Growth Rates of GNP at Current Prices		Difference in Growth Rates	Transfer Payments in Per Cent of GNP		Years
	Average	Standard Deviation	Average	Standard Deviation	Standard Deviation	Average	Standard Deviation	
1975	23.7	5.0	12.5	7.1	11.2	16.1	5.1	1975
1974	20.9	6.2	14.1	5.3	6.8	14.4	4.4	1974
1973	17.0	10.1	14.7	3.5	2.3	13.7	4.1	1973
1972	16.0	3.3	12.3	2.8	3.7	13.5	4.2	1972
1971	15.1	3.9	11.0	2.0	4.1	13.0	4.0	1971
1970	12.0	4.8	11.5	2.0	0.5	12.5	3.8	1970
1969	13.8	6.8	11.2	2.8	2.6	12.0	3.5	1969
1968	13.2	4.8	8.7	2.3	4.5	11.8	3.7	1968
1967	13.2	3.7	7.6	2.5	5.6	11.3	3.3	1967
1966	11.9	3.1	7.9	1.2	4.0	10.8	3.3	1966
1965	17.4	7.5	9.4	1.8	8.0	10.4	3.3	1965
1964	12.7	7.2	11.7	2.6	1.0	9.7	3.1	1964
1963	13.7	5.3	8.6	2.4	5.1	9.7	3.2	1963
1962	13.5	3.8	8.6	2.5	4.9	9.3	3.0	1962
1961	11.1	4.5	9.1	2.0	2.0	8.8	2.8	1961
1960	7.1	11.6	12.4	5.8	-5.3	8.7	2.8	1960
1959	8.5	5.6	6.7	2.2	1.8	9.3	2.6	1959
1958	11.1	5.4	4.4	4.1	6.7	9.2	2.7	1958
1957	14.6	8.5	7.3	2.4	7.3	8.9	2.6	1957
1956	10.2	3.9	8.2	2.7	2.0	8.4	2.5	1956
1955	10.5	6.3	8.6	3.7	1.9	8.3	2.5	1955
1954	5.7	4.6	6.7	3.2	-1.0	8.1	2.7	1954
1953	9.9	3.4	5.8	3.0	4.1	8.1	2.7	1953
1952	19.0	9.7	10.7	4.4	8.3	7.7	2.7	1952
1951	17.3	12.7	17.9	8.5	-0.6	7.2	2.7	1951

Source of data for the various countries: OECD.

Figure 16.3: The Growth of Social Insurance Coverage in Western Europe

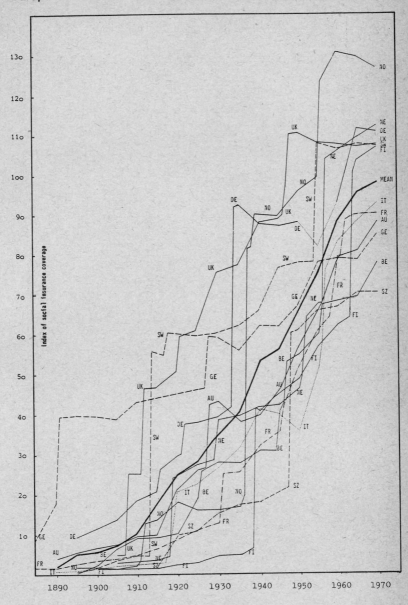

1951 and 1975, the European average of transfer payments grew more rapidly than GNP and that since 1961 this has happened consistently every year. In the first half of this period the average share of transfer payments of GNP rose by 2.5 percentage points from 7.2 to 9.7 per cent, and in the second half by 6.4 percentage points to 16.1 per cent. Accelerated growth of transfers occurred even if one disregards the recession years 1974 and 1975, and the trend can also be demonstrated similarly for social expenditure as a whole.

Table 16.5: Economic Growth and Transfer Payments

	r	lag		r	lag		r	lag
1951	0.66		1960	0.36	-0.05			
1952	0.65	0.25	1961	0.70	-0.10	1969	0.08	0.21
1953	-0.22	0.29	1962	0.56	0.50	1970	-0.17	0.19
1954	0.67	-0.71	1963	0.62	0.21	1971	-0.27	0.22
1955	0.16	0.28	1964	0.13	0.13	1972	0.14	0.02
1956	0.47	0.52	1965	0.16	0.11	1973	-0.17	0.27
1957	0.28	0.19	1966	0.39	0.58			
1958	0.12	0.32	1967	0.38	0.62	1974	0.51	0.31
1959	-0.22	-0.03	1968	0.31	0.73	1975	0.50	0.33

The first column shows the correlation coefficients (r) between growth rates of GNP and growth rates of transfer payments (at current prices) for an average of 11 European countries in the respective year. The second column shows the lag correlation coefficients (lag) between the growth rates of transfer payments in each year and the growth rates of GNP of the previous year.

Source: J. Kohl, 'Trends and Problems in Post-war Public Expenditure Development in Western Europe and North America' in P. Flora and A.J. Heidenheimer (eds.), *The Development of Welfare States in Europe and North America* (New Brunswick, NJ, 1979).

These increases would have been inconceivable without the economic growth since the 1950s. This does not mean, however, that one can discern a systematic correlation, at least not at first glance. As Table 16.5 shows, the correlation coefficients between the European growth rates of transfer payments and GNP were over 0.5 in only 8 of the 25 years and below 0.3 in 12 years; the period between 1969 and 1973 is particularly remarkable, since there appears to be no visible correlation.

We know very little about the forces that were and still are at the base of this expansion. Too little, since more comprehensive knowledge would be the pre-condition for a better grasp of the problems which might result from an enforced end to the expansion of the welfare state. But we also know far too little about the effects the welfare state has had, about its integrative successes and failures. What has been its real contribution to the stabilisation of democracy, the weakening political radicalism? What influence did it have on the development of the European workers' movements and why was it not capable of preventing Fascism? To what extent has it contributed to a defusing of social conflicts, and what were its effects on the general integrative forces within European societies and on their capacity for innovation? And on the other hand, have the disintegrative, destabilising, conflict-generating effects of the welfare state increased in the past decade, or can this be expected in the future? An answer to this latter question presupposes a better understanding — both theoretical and empirical — of the expansive forces and integrative effects to date. We tend to lack systematic empirical research into this question rather than more general diagnoses of 'the crisis of the welfare state'.

The main arguments put forward in this context tend to be relatively old and in their general tendency belong to three traditions: the Marxist school, Durkheim's theoretical approach, and the tradition of liberal-conservative political sociology. For the Marxists and the followers of Durkheim, matters are relatively clear-cut. For the former, the welfare state cannot be an adequate solution, since it leaves the institution of private property untouched. But in this institution they see specific instabilities, conflicts of distribution and problems of development, which leave the welfare state relatively helpless.

For the Durkheimians, the welfare state cannot be an adequate solution since it does not ensure the necessary moral and social integration, but on the contrary weakens the integrative functions of intermediate structures; by inflating expectations, it promotes anomic tendencies, and by individualising benefits it encourages 'selfish' tendencies in our societies.[21]

The third tradition is concerned in the main with the relation between citizen and welfare state. The threat to individual freedom through increased bureaucratic powers — and indirectly also through a lack of self-restraint — is one side of the argument, to which Tocqueville still seems highly relevant. A possible imbalance between government performance and citizen demands as indicated by the current slogan of 'government overload' represents the other side of the argument, and has an equally worthy ancestry. As early as 1918, Schumpeter, in his book *Krise des Steuerstaates* (*The Crisis of the Tax State*) pointed out that it was in principle possible for the state to be defeated by its social expenditure.[22]

This outlines the basic perspectives which we (re-)discover in current diagnoses of the crisis. I shall take up some of the questions raised and the arguments employed in the following section and attempt to link them a little more closely to observable developments and crisis symptoms.

Crisis of the Welfare State in a New Macro-constellation?

Has a new macro-constellation emerged, or is it about to do so, in which persistent imbalances in the national budget and instability of political institutions combine both with an increase in social conflict and in social disintegration to produce a 'crisis'? Has the welfare state in this context turned from being a 'solver of crises' into their generator? If our societies in the next ten or twenty years were indeed to be exposed to greater stresses, both internally and externally, what would the welfare state and other institutions have to look like in order to ensure a degree of freedom and consensus within these societies, while at the same time supporting their willingness to change and their capacity to innovate, and thus to safeguard Europe's role and independence in a changing world?

These are of course highly speculative questions which cannot be answered in this form. But it is not a matter of answers in any case. Here I would merely attempt to sketch a line of possible research by formulating the questions more precisely and by making certain assumptions about possible — and perhaps not entirely implausible — developments and problems.

A New Macro-constellation?

Many see the so-called oil crisis of 1973 as a turning-point in the development of European societies and of Western industrial countries generally. It was, without doubt, an event of far-reaching implications, considering not only its economic repercussions and the consequent price revolution but also the uncertainties about the future which resulted from the abruptness of the change. The event in itself does not create a new macro-constellation, but is perhaps a symptom of a development which may combine with other trends that are largely unconnected with it to form a new constellation (see Figure 16.4).

My intention here is to indicate briefly the potentially crisis-producing trends contained in the six basic elements of the constellation. On the *international level*, the inherent political instability of the world system might be exacerbated by the continuing divergence of

Figure 16.4: Possible Changes in the Macro-constellation

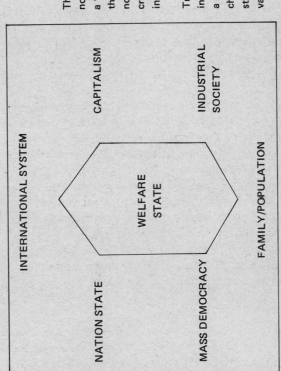

Changes in Europe's (or the West's) economic and military position and increase in international tensions?

INTERNATIONAL SYSTEM

CAPITALISM

The state's growing economic responsibility within a 'mixed economy' — in the face of worsening economic conditions and increases in the power of interest groups?

Transition to a 'post-industrial society' through a revolution in education, changes in the employment structure and changes in values?

INDUSTRIAL SOCIETY

NATION STATE

WELFARE STATE

MASS DEMOCRACY

FAMILY/POPULATION

Weakening of the integrative power of the nation state through growing international interdependence and attempts at integration?

Weakening of parliamentary institutions through increased power of interest groups, inflexibility of the party systems and demands for more direct participation?

Continuing 'demographic transition', a new division of labour between sexes, weakening of marriage and family?

the distribution of life chances and the flow of information; while the instability of the world economy, the imbalance between world-wide demand for and supply of basic raw materials, energy and foodstuffs would, in view of the expected population growth and probable further industrialisation, at least continue. Thus a sharpening of international conflicts would not appear improbable. In combination with a shift, even if only a relative one, in military power, and against a background of European dependence on raw materials, this could lend greater weight to international demands for a redistribution of wealth.

On the *level of individual states*, the continuing growth of the role and responsibility of governments in the economic field might, in the face of the increasingly difficult problems of unemployment, inflation and persistent balance of payment problems result in a weakening of the integrative power of the nation state and its parliamentary institutions. A weakening of the nation state could also result from growing international interdependence and movements towards integration, while parliamentary institutions might be weakened through the gradual increase in the power exercised by interest groups and through the inflexibility of party structures.

On the *level of social structure*, such developments might make the solution of potentially sharper conflicts of distribution more difficult; it might also create or exacerbate new conflicts about political demarcations, institutional arrangements or national aims. A more lasting weakening of social integration is equally conceivable, especially as a result of a revolution in education and of an emerging new division of labour between the sexes. This might mean greater instability of the institutions of marriage and family, and would make a continuing long-term reduction in the birth rate and the ageing of the population probable. All these developments are obviously mere possibilities, and their probability cannot be defined with any accuracy. But in the context of observable crisis symptoms on the 'national-political' and 'social-structural' levels, they should certainly be discussed in greater detail.

Crisis Symptoms on the National-political Level

In accordance with the reflections contained in the last section, we shall first examine the problems of the national budget and the signs of instability in political institutions. Thus the first question concerns possible 'structural' imbalance between revenue and expenditure.

New Tax Revolts? On two occasions in the past century Europe experienced an extremely high rise in the tax burden: during the

First World War and since the mid-1960s. Before the First World War the ratio of taxes to national product in practically all European countries was less than 10 per cent.[23] During the First World War revenue increased extraordinarily and did not return to its original level once the war had ended – the much-cited 'displacement effect'.[24] From the middle of the 1920s until the mid-1930s the average European tax ratio rose from approximately 15.5 per cent to just over 17 per cent. The Second World War produced another, although smaller, 'displacement effect' and since the 1950s the average tax ratio rose as follows: 1955 22.9 per cent, 1960 23.4 per cent, 1965 25.4 per cent, 1970 29.6 per cent and 1975 31.3 per cent. This shows a marked acceleration in the increase of the tax burden. This development is even more remarkable if we consider not the ratio of total taxes to GNP, but the corresponding ratio of income tax and social security contributions. The percentages for these two items combined were as follows: 1955 13.7 per cent, 1960 15.2 per cent, 1965 18.0 per cent, 1970 21.1 per cent and 1975 27.4 per cent (see Table 16.6). Thus they doubled within a period of twenty years, with almost half the increase occurring in the last five years.

This indicates the limits of further relative increases in the state's revenue, even without the expectation of declining growth rates. These limits are almost impossible to determine empirically, but can be quite easily defined in principle: they lie where the tax state, in the long term, undermines its economic foundations, and where parliamentary democracy loses its political support. Harold L. Wilensky had indicated clear symptoms of a tax protest or even of a 'tax-welfare backlash'.[25] With the exception of Denmark (and the US) these protests should, in my view, not be taken as too dramatic. None the less, they are symptomatic if viewed against the background of the history of tax revolts. According to Gabriel Arden, a French fiscal sociologist and historian, tax revolts were a frequent phenomenon during the formative stages of absolutist states; they have practically disappeared since the first half of the nineteenth century and have, with few exceptions, remained in abeyance ever since.[26]

The disappearance of tax revolts was due to two developments: the increase of available resources and the ease of their extraction resulting from industrialisation. Simultaneously, the extension of the franchise and the growth of parliamentary institutions increased the legitimacy of expanding state revenues. The problem of 'penetration' was thus partially solved by institutionalising 'participation'.

In the face of the not unrealistic expectation of declining growth

Table 16.6: Income Tax and Social Security Contributions in Per Cent of Net National Produce at Market Prices

Years	AU IT	AU SC	BE IT	BE SC	DE IT	DE SC	FI IT	FI SC	FR IT	FR SC	GE IT	GE SC	IT IT	IT SC	NE IT	NE SC	NO IT	NO SC	SW IT	SW SC	SZ IT	SZ SC	UK IT	UK SC
1975	6.7	10.3	14.5	13.7	24.5	0.8	17.3	6.6	4.4	17.2	11.7	15.6	9.7	25.3	14.0	20.5	16.2	15.9	26.1	9.0	15.1	9.0	17.1	7.4
1974	7.2	9.6	12.4	12.5	27.1	0.9	18.4	5.7	4.6	15.7	12.2	14.8	6.9	19.4	13.5	19.5	16.6	15.6	22.9	8.6	13.6	8.2	12.4	6.7
1973	6.8	9.6	11.3	12.4	23.2	2.3	17.8	5.8	3.9	14.8	11.6	14.3	4.6	15.9	13.1	17.0	15.7	16.1	21.8	8.5	12.9	7.8	11.0	5.9
1972	6.2	9.3	10.7	12.1	24.4	2.3	17.1	5.3	4.2	14.6	10.1	13.5	4.3	13.9	13.1	17.0		14.9	21.5	8.7	11.9	6.1	11.6	5.8
1971	5.9	9.3	10.0	11.8	24.9	2.1	16.3	5.3	3.8	14.5	10.5	12.8	3.7	13.1	12.5	16.8	14.5	13.7	21.7	8.3	11.5	6.2	12.4	5.4
1970	5.7	9.0	9.5	11.3	23.2	2.0	15.8	4.9	4.0	14.3	9.4	12.4	3.3	11.7	11.8	15.9	13.3	11.4	21.0	7.6	11.6	6.1	12.7	5.7
1969	5.5	9.1	9.0	10.5	17.2	2.0	15.1	4.6	4.3		8.9	11.9	3.4		11.7	15.4	16.8	11.3	21.5	7.8	11.4	6.1	12.1	5.3
1968	5.5	9.0	8.8	10.5	18.4	2.1	13.7	4.7	4.0	16.3	8.7	11.5	3.2		11.4	14.9	16.4	10.9	20.2	7.6	11.0	5.4	11.4	5.4
1967	6.0	8.9	8.3	10.4	16.5	2.1	13.4	4.8	4.9	15.7	8.8	11.3	3.1		12.2	13.9	15.7	10.0	19.5	6.6	10.3	5.3	11.0	5.2
1966	6.0	8.6	7.8	10.4	16.1	2.1	12.5	4.1	5.0	15.5	8.8	11.2	3.0		11.7	13.3	14.7	8.4	19.3	5.7	10.3	5.2	9.9	5.1
1965	5.5	8.4	7.2	10.1	14.5	2.1	11.7	4.0	5.1	15.4	8.4	10.7	3.0		10.7	12.4	15.2	7.8	18.4	5.4	9.5	5.1	11.2	5.1
1964	5.3	7.8		8.8	13.4	1.9	11.6	3.6		15.0	8.8	10.5	2.7	8.7	10.9	11.2	15.2	7.6	17.7	5.3	9.8	5.3	10.3	4.7
1963	5.1	7.6		8.1	13.3	1.5	10.3	3.2	4.8	14.7	8.8	10.8	2.6	7.8	10.4	11.0	15.0	7.6	17.0	5.1	9.2	5.0	12.0	4.6
1962	4.9	7.6	6.9	7.6	12.9	1.5	8.5	3.1	4.6	14.0	8.5	10.6	2.3	6.5	10.7	9.2	15.2	7.5	17.6	4.3	9.7	5.0	12.4	4.5
1961	4.6	7.1	6.1	7.2	11.7	1.6	9.2	2.8	4.7	13.5	8.0	10.4	2.1	5.7	10.5	9.0	14.9	6.7	17.3	3.6	8.3	5.0	11.4	4.3
1960	4.1	6.7	6.1	7.0	11.4	1.6	9.8	2.9	4.4	12.5	7.1	10.3	2.0	5.6	9.9	9.0		6.4	17.9	3.5	8.7	5.0	11.3	3.9
1959	4.2	6.9	5.9	6.7	11.7	1.6	13.2	0.0	5.0	12.7	7.2	10.3	1.9	5.3	9.7	8.8	14.7	6.2	16.6	2.9	8.1	4.6	14.5	4.7
1958	4.3	7.1	5.8	7.0	11.9	1.6	12.8	0.0	4.6	12.0	6.7	10.5	1.9	5.0	9.9	8.9	17.0	4.1	17.0	2.3	8.6	4.5	14.6	4.8
1957	4.5	6.6	5.9	6.5	11.8	1.6	11.6	0.0	4.3	11.9	6.9	9.9	1.8	4.7	9.2	8.7	16.9	3.7	18.1	2.4	7.5	4.5	14.3	3.8
1956	4.0	6.7		6.1	11.6	1.4	10.7	0.0	4.2	12.0	7.7	8.9	1.8	4.6	9.2	5.2		3.2	16.7	2.1	8.3	4.5	14.0	3.9
1955	4.0	6.4		6.0	10.5	1.5	9.5	0.0	3.9	11.9	7.5	8.8	1.6	4.0	8.9	5.0	16.1	3.1	17.0	2.0	7.6	4.5	14.8	3.9
1954		6.0	5.3	5.8	9.9	1.5	9.1	0.0	4.1	11.7	8.2	8.7	1.5	3.9	8.6	5.1	15.4	3.0	16.9	1.1	8.7	4.5	14.9	3.7
1953		6.1	5.5	5.6	9.9	1.5	10.5	0.0	4.3	11.5	8.5	8.6	1.4	3.4	9.3	5.2	16.0	2.9	16.6	0.8	7.8	4.7	16.1	3.9
1952		6.0			9.7	1.5	9.5	0.0	3.5	11.2	8.3	8.3	1.2	3.0	10.6	5.0	16.6	2.5	14.3	0.8	8.5	4.5	17.1	3.8
1951		6.1			9.3	1.5	9.2	0.0			7.1	7.9	3.3	5.8	10.9	4.6	14.6	2.2	15.0	0.8	7.7	4.5	15.6	3.9
1950		6.6				1.5	12.1	0.0			4.5	8.2			9.5	4.7	16.6		13.5	0.8			17.8	4.2

IT = Income tax in per cent of net national product at market prices.
SC = Social security contributions in per cent of net national product at market prices.
Source: OECD.

rates (at least in real income) and the possibility of growing demands on expenditure, tax protests — until now somewhat of a curiosity — could easily become more serious. If one considers developments since the Second World War as a second historical phase of 'penetration', the strategic safeguards for the state's necessary revenues would have to be found in new and extended forms of 'participation'. On the other hand, attempts to 'hide' 'visible taxes' by increasing indirect taxation and by relieving the middle-income groups most affected by progressive taxation from some of its burden would in principle only result in shifting a potential tax protest to other income groups, while an increase in the public debt would merely shift the burden on to future generations. This would mean a return to the budgets of the nineteenth century, when the payment of debts swallowed a much larger share of public expenditure, the only difference being that then it was a case of paying off war debts.

If one assumes that political limitations to further relative increases in revenue are foreseeable, or at any rate conceivable, the role of public expenditure, and the potentially growing demands made on it, acquires crucial importance. I have attempted to summarise these possibilities in the outline in Figure 16.5.

External Security, Internal Order, Economic Growth. Favoured by relatively peaceful conditions and an economic growth rate unique in history, the expenditure of European countries on external security has, since the Korean War, seen an overall decline as a proportion of GNP (see Table 16.7). This has precluded large-scale conflicts over trade-offs between defence and social expenditure.[27] It has, however, also meant that cuts in defence spending, which in any case could only be achieved as a long-term process, cannot be expected to produce any real easing of the domestic burden of expenditure. On the contrary, a greater demand for expenditure is easily conceivable. A relative increase might simply result from continued low economic growth, or be enforced by a redistribution to Europe of the defence burden within NATO, which must be expected in the medium term. But the crucial question will be what happens to the world economy and to the world political system.

In another chapter of this volume, Karl W. Deutsch analyses the political instability of the world system and proposes the development of an 'international welfare state' as a long-term solution. Instability results from continuing tensions between the capitalist and

Figure 16.5: Potential Sources of Expenditure Growth

EXTERNAL SECURITY	INTERNAL ORDER	GROWTH	WELFARE
(1) Relatively certain: Relative growth in the power of developing countries lends greater weight to demands for redistribution, higher international transfer payments and/or higher defence spending.	(1) Possible: Weakening of the integrative power of the nation state and of parliamentary institutions, resulting in increased costs for the maintenance of law and order.	(1) Relatively certain: Scarcity of raw material and energy, and worsening terms of trade, necessitating higher research spending, technical innovation and adaptation of capital stock.	(1) Possible: Continuing relatively high rates of unemployment resulting in higher spending on unemployment benefits and a policy for the protection of jobs.
(2) Possible: Increase of international tensions through competition for scarce raw material and energy resources, as well as balance of payments problems.	(2) Possible: Weakening of social integration resulting in increasing costs for control of 'deviant' behaviour.	(2) Possible: Continuing relatively low growth rates necessitating targeted support of labour-creating schemes, promotion of investments, for fiscal reasons as well as for political and employment policy reasons.	(2) Possible: Continuing relatively high inflation resulting in increased costs for public housing and in subsidies for other goods.
(3) Probable: Through relative increase in Europe's importance, redistribution of NATO defence costs, placing greater share on Europe.		(2) Probable: Increased expenditure on measures for the protection of the environment.	(3) Certain: Changes in the age structure of the population resulting in higher costs for old age pensions.
(4) Possible: Continuing relatively low economic growth might increase defence costs, even if all other conditions remain more or less stable.			(4) Possible: Higher transfer payments to families and other expenditure to increase birth rates and to strengthen the integrative capacity of family.
			(5) Possible: Increasing costs of self-destructive behaviour resulting from social disintegration.
			(6) Probable: Serious problems in curtailing increases in spending on health and education (a) because of specific problems regarding increases in productivity and (b) because status groups are involved in the distributive process; changes in the age structure resulting in a lighter burden on education, but a heavier health bill.

Table 16.7: Defence Expenditure in Per Cent of National Product

Years	AU	FI	SW	SZ	BE	DE	FR	GE	IT	NE	NO	UK	US	Years
1976	1.1	1.4	3.3	2.1		2.4	(3.9)	(3.4)	(2.6)	3.4	3.1	5.1	(5.4)	1976
1975	1.2	1.5	3.4	2.0	3.1	2.6	3.9	3.6	2.8	3.5	3.2	5.0	6.0	1975
1974	1.0	1.4	3.5	2.0	2.8	2.4	3.7	3.6	2.9	3.3	3.1	5.1	6.1	1974
1973	1.0	1.4	3.6	2.0	2.8	2.1	3.8	3.4	2.9	3.3	3.1	4.9	6.0	1973
1972	1.0	1.5	3.7	2.1	2.8	2.3	3.9	3.4	3.1	3.4	3.3	5.2	6.6	1972
1971	1.0	1.5	3.7	2.2	2.8	2.5	4.0	3.3	2.9	3.4	3.4	5.0	7.1	1971
1970	1.1	1.4	3.6	2.2	2.9	2.4	4.2	3.3	2.7	3.5	3.5	4.8	7.9	1970
1969	1.2	1.4	3.6	2.3	2.9	2.5	4.2	3.6	2.7	3.6	3.6	5.0	8.7	1969
1968	1.2	1.7	3.7	2.4	3.1	2.8	4.8	3.6	3.0	3.7	3.6	5.4	9.3	1968
1967	1.3	1.6	3.8	2.6	3.1	2.7	5.0	4.3	3.1	3.9	3.5	5.7	9.4	1967
1966	1.3	1.6	4.1	2.7	3.1	2.7	5.0	4.1	3.4	3.7	3.5	5.7	8.4	1966
1965	1.2	1.7	4.1	2.7	3.2	2.8	5.2	4.3	3.3	3.9	3.7	5.9	7.5	1965
1964	1.5	1.8	4.1	2.8	3.4	2.8	5.3	4.6	3.3	4.3	3.4	6.0	8.0	1964
1963	1.3	1.9	4.2	2.7	3.4	3.0	5.6	5.2	3.3	4.4	3.5	6.2	8.7	1963
1962	1.1	2.4	4.1	2.8	3.5	3.0	6.0	4.8	3.2	4.5	3.6	6.4	9.2	1962
1961	1.0	1.8	4.0	2.7	3.4	2.6	6.2	4.0	3.1	4.5	3.3	6.3	9.0	1961
1960	1.2	1.7	4.0	2.5	3.6	2.7	6.4	4.0	3.3	4.1	3.2	6.5	8.9	1960
1959	1.4	1.7	4.6	2.9	3.7	2.6	6.6	4.4	3.3	4.0	3.6	6.7	9.4	1959
1958	1.5	1.6	4.7	3.2	3.7	2.9	6.8	3.0	3.4	4.7	3.5	7.0	10.0	1958
1957	1.3	1.5	4.6	3.0	3.8	3.1	7.3	4.1	3.5	5.2	3.6	7.2	9.9	1957
1956	0.9	1.6	4.1	2.3	3.5	3.0	7.8	3.6	3.6	5.7	3.6	7.7		1956
1955	0.2	1.6	4.3	2.8	3.7	3.2	6.5	4.1	3.7	5.6	4.0	8.1		1955
1954	0.1	1.4	4.3	2.7	4.6	3.2	7.4	4.0	4.0	5.9	5.1	8.7		1954
1953	0.5	1.5	4.2	3.2	4.8	3.4	9.2	4.2	3.7	5.5	5.1	9.6		1953
1952	0.6	1.4	4.0	3.8		2.8	8.7	5.8	4.5	5.5	4.0	9.8		1952
1951	0.9	2.0	3.5	3.0		2.1	7.2	5.9	4.3	4.9	3.1	7.8		1951
1950	0.7	1.3	3.4	2.5		1.7	5.6	3.6	4.0	4.8	2.4	6.4		1950
1963-76	1.2	1.6	3.7	2.3	3.0	2.6	4.5	3.8	3.0	3.7	3.4	5.3	7.5	1963-76
1953-62	0.9	1.7	4.1	2.8	3.8	3.0	7.0	4.0	3.5	4.9	3.9	7.4	(9.4)	1953-62

1950-6: GNP; 1957-76: GDP.

Source: SIPRI and OECD.

Communist systems of alliances. More fundamental still is the discrepancy between the absolute poverty of the majority of the world's inhabitants and the ever increasing proliferation of both information and sophisticated weapons. A potential increase of international tensions would inevitably lead to greater defence spending and/or international transfer payments. According to Deutsch, a very real, if problematic, opportunity to decrease the world's political instability in the long term would consist in switching defence expenditure to transfer payments. This might help to start the development of an 'international welfare state', with aims similar to those of national welfare states: increase of security and lessening of inequalities by stabilising the income of poorer countries and by supranational safeguards to ensure a world-wide minimum standard of nourishment, health care and educational opportunity. Thus, if defence expenditure and transfer payments are added together, future increases in spending on external safeguards do not appear improbable.

In the sphere of internal order, however, we are on much less certain ground. Signs of a weakening of public order in Europe since the 1960s are fairly clear, but we possess an insufficient empirical base to judge what these trends might be in the longer term. Increasing demands for expenditure (for the maintenance of law and order, for the control of 'illegitimate' forms of conflict and 'deviant' behaviour) are, however, conceivable. An increase in these types of conflict could not merely be the result of lower economic growth rates, but also the product of a long-term weakening of the nation state's integrative power and of its parliamentary institutions. An increase in 'deviant' behaviour, as a consequence of the weakening of the integrative powers of family and educational establishments, is equally conceivable.

While a large shadow of doubt lies over the future development of expenditure on internal order and external security, forecasts as to the promotion of economic growth seem more feasible. In his latest work, *The World Economy, History and Prospects*, Rostow interprets the price revolution of 1972-6 as the result of a world economic imbalance which has increased since the 1960s (world-wide industrialisation/increase of easily accessible energy sources; growth of world population/increase in world food production). The consequences of this were further exacerbated by the inflation of the post-war years and the weakening of the world monetary system. In his comparatively optimistic prognosis for the future he sees the problem of natural resources primarily as one of price; its solution does, however, depend on industrial societies adopting the correct policies of investment and technology and on regulating competition for scarce raw materials through international agreements.

Even if this can be achieved, he does expect that high prices for energy and many raw materials — and for air and water — will make equivalent increases in prosperity unlikely, in comparison with the period 1951-72. Beyond that, he expects relatively high rates of unemployment, since past high levels of employment were mainly based on the expansion of energy-intensive sectors and the public services, where further growth, at least to a comparable extent, is equally unlikely. New areas of employment must be opened. From such potential new areas (research, alternative energy sources, energy conservation measures in house construction and mass transport, protection of the environment and urban renewal), as well as from the state's responsibility for full employment and the political need to decrease external economic dependence, Rostow deduces the necessity of further growth in state intervention and penetration. Growing expenditure on the promotion of general investment for fiscal and political reasons, as well as for reasons of employment policy, deliberately aimed spending on research, technological innovation and the adaptation of capital stock appear highly probable.

In the face of a potential decrease in political manoeuvrability as regards the relative growth in revenues and the potentially increasing demands on the public purse for external security, internal order and economic growth, the question arises as to the future of the welfare state. Is it, too, likely to expand further? And what would the effects of more severe restrictions be on its integrative functions?

Expenditure on 'Welfare'. If one examines the relative growth in public spending in Europe between 1950 and 1975, one finds that this can be largely traced back to an increase in social expenditure, which in 1975 as a proportion of GNP varied between just under 20 and just over 28 per cent.[28] The first half of the 1970s saw a clear acceleration of this development. It is as yet difficult to ascertain whether it has been possible to curb this acceleration. But it is possible to conceive of developments which would make a further increase in the demands on the public purse probable.

One such possibility results from continuing relatively high rates of unemployment and inflation. In his study of the 'Crisis of the British Welfare State', Rudolf Klein has pointed to categories of spending which usually do not come under the heading of social expenditure, but which, because of their function, nevertheless belong in this

374 *The Welfare State in Historical Perspective*

category: spending on the protection of employment for reasons of social policy and the subsidy of essential consumer goods. Given continuing low economic growth, this might well indicate a more general and longer-term development.[29]

If this can be regarded as only a possibility, another aspect must be seen as more or less certain: an increase in expenditure on pensions, because of the probability of continuing low birth rates. Without institutional reform, increases in contributions would be the inevitable consequence of the shift in proportion between contributors and recipients. This might lead to a tendency to counter this development in the long term by measures to encourage larger families. Greater social expenditure on the family may also result from the attempt to curb self-destructive behaviour and thus to decrease the social costs resulting from it, by strengthening the integrative capacity of the family.

Finally, in the sphere of health care and education it may prove difficult to prevent further increases in spending — not only because of the specific problems regarding productivity increases in these personnel-intensive areas. More important is the fact that in both spheres status groups are largely in control of their internal administration and are also able to exercise considerable external influence. In the long term, a further expansion of education also appears probable, but shifts in the age structure may bring some relief. For the health sector, on the other hand, an ageing population would represent an additional burden.

If we draw up a balance sheet of the various possibilities, probabilities and imponderables regarding the future development of public revenue and expenditure, the expectation of increasing budgetary imbalances is not implausible. If one is inclined to the belief that parliamentary governments tend to choose the path of least resistance, they would tend, if faced with budget imbalances, to increase their debts rather than levy higher taxes or cut expenditure. Yet if such measures were inevitable, governments would send the tax collector, or use their red pencils, where they would expect the least protests. The question whether our governments do in fact tend to behave in this way has not yet been researched systematically enough to allow such a general answer. One thing, however, seems certain, and appears to contradict this prevailing view: in the period between 1950 and 1975 West European governments tended *not* to cut investment in favour of public spending and transfer payments, even during the 1970s. This has been shown by Jürgen Kohl in his analysis of the development of expenditure in the post-war years.[30] But he has also demonstrated that the countries' national debt has not only increased in recent years, but over a rather longer period of time. This points to a 'structural' imbalance of national budgets which, if further increased, might lead to a sharpening of social conflicts. In such circumstances the stability of political institutions — and of course political leadership — would become even more important.

Instability of Political Institutions. Morris Janowitz, in his *Social Control of the Welfare State*, has examined the possible links between political instability and the expansion of the welfare state and developed, as a result, a — perhaps exaggeratedly — pessimistic perspective. His argument runs roughly as follows: The system of social stratification has become an ever more complex product of two factors: the capitalist economic system and the welfare state. Achieving an income through exchange of services, based on job differentiation and ownership of capital, is entangled increasingly with achieving an income through transfer payments and other public benefits, based on equal treatment and a universally applied standard. An already complicated social structure is thus rendered even more complex and ambivalent. As a result, the citizen encounters greater and greater problems in defining his political interests. This leads to increased volatility in political preferences and a loosening of the links between social groupings and political parties. Clear political majorities occur less and less frequently. This in turn diminishes parliament's capacity for decision-making and also the stability of governments; political institutions suffer a loss of legitimacy: 'welfare benefits change the pattern of social stratification and economic inequality, which in turn condition political participation and party orientation and help to explain the emergence of weak political regimes.'[31]

Theories that simplify complex matters to this degree are of course appealing, but we should not be seduced. At the present state of research this theory merely represents an — albeit interesting — linking of largely unproven hypotheses. But before searching further for the causes of a growing instability of political institutions, one should first ascertain whether this trend does indeed exist, since the period following the last war has been for Western Europe one of extraordinary institutional stability. I outlined in the first section an entire spectrum of possible symptoms of institutional instability. Insufficient data prevent me from analysing the pattern of 'illegitimate' political behaviour (particularly political terrorism) and the development of party structures, and I shall thus confine myself to two aspects.

Table 16.8: Voter Turn-out (voters in per cent of enfranchised population)

Years	AU	BE	DE	FI	FR	GE	IR	IT	NE	NO	SW	SZ	UK	Average	Without SZ	All countries	Without SZ
1977		95.1	88.7				76.3		88.0	82.9							
1974-6	92.8	90.4	88.2	73.9		90.7		93.2			91.7	52.4	78.8/72.8	82.5	85.8	83.3	86.1
1971-3	92.4	91.5	87.2/88.7	81.4	80.9	91.1	76.6	93.1	79.1/83.5	80.2	90.8	56.8		83.4	85.8	83.1	85.3
1968-70	91.8	90.0	89.3	82.2	80.0	86.7	76.9	92.8		83.8	89.3/88.3		72.0	85.0	85.0	82.4	84.5
1964-7	93.8	91.6	85.5/88.6	84.9	80.9	86.8	75.1		94.9	85.4	83.9	63.8	77.1/75.8	83.6	85.3	84.3	85.8
1960-3	93.8	92.3	85.8	85.1	68.8	87.7	70.6	92.9	95.1	79.1	85.9	64.5		83.5	85.2	83.0	84.1
1957-9	94.2	93.6	83.7	75.0	77.1	87.8	71.3	93.7	95.6	78.3	77.4	68.5	78.7	82.7	83.9	82.7	83.9
1954-6	96.0	93.2		79.9	82.2		76.4		95.5		79.6	68.7	76.8	83.1	85.0	84.0	85.3
1951-3	95.8		80.8/80.6	74.6	80.2	85.8	75.3	93.9	95.0	79.3	79.1	69.8	81.9	82.6	83.8	83.4	84.6
1948-50	96.8	94.4/92.6	81.9	78.6		78.5	74.2	92.2	93.7	82.0			83.6	85.3	85.3	83.7	84.9
1945-7	94.3	90.3	86.3/85.8	74.9	79.8/81.9			89.1	93.1	76.4	82.7	71.7	72.6	82.9	84.1	81.8	82.7
1945-76	94.2	92.0	85.6	80.2	79.0	86.3	74.6	92.5	91.7	80.6	84.1	64.5	77.0	83.4			
1940											70.3						
1937-9		93.3	79.2	66.6		88.8	76.2/76.7		94.4	76.4/84.0		51.9		77.7		75.4	
1933-6		94.7	80.7	66.2/62.9	84.4	82.0/84.1	81.3		94.5	77.6	74.5	78.3	67.0	79.2		80.6	
1930-2	90.2	94.3	81.5	65.9	83.4	75.6	76.5				67.6	78.8	72.5	78.6		81.2	
1927-9	89.2	94.0	79.7	55.8/55.6	83.7	77.4/78.8	68.1/69.0		92.7	68.1	67.4	77.1	75.4	75.6		77.2	
1923-6	87.0	92.8	78.6/77.0	57.4	83.0		61.2	63.8	91.4	69.9	53.0	75.1	65.6/73.2	73.8		73.8	
1921-2		91.1		58.5			45.5	58.4	93.0	67.9	54.2	76.4	66.2	68.1		73.0	
1919-20	84.4/80.3	88.5	80.6/74.9	67.1	71.0	81.7/79.2		56.6			55.3	79.2		73.5		71.7	
1918			75.5						93.0	60.5			49.0				
1919-39	86.2	92.7	78.8	61.3	81.1	80.9	72.7	59.6	93.2	74.0	62.0	77.5	70.0	81.4			

Source: J. Kohl, HIWED Report No. 6 (see note 1).

Table 16.9: Government Parties' Share of Parliamentary Seats

Years	AU	BE	DE	FI	GE	IT	NE	NO	SW	UK	Average	Years
1949	100.0/87.3	79.7/63.2	38.5	27.0	51.7	53.1	76.0	50.7/56.7	48.7	61.4	58.7	1949
1950	87.3	63.2/50.9	38.5/39.6	27.0/28.0	51.7	53.1/58.0	76.0	56.7	48.7	61.4/50.4	56.9	1950
1951	87.3	50.9	39.6	28.0/55.0/59.5	51.7	58.0/60.4	76.0	56.7	48.7/61.7	50.4/51.4	57.4	1951
1952	87.3	50.9	39.6	59.5	51.7	60.4	76.0/81.0	56.7	61.7/59.1	51.4	59.5	1952
1953	87.3/89.0	50.9	39.6/42.3	59.5/33.0/—	51.7/68.4	60.4/44.6	81.0	56.7/51.3	59.1	51.4	59.8	1953
1954	89.0	50.9/52.4	42.3	—/53.5	68.4	44.6/50.0	81.0	51.3	59.1	51.4	59.1	1954
1955	89.0	52.4	42.3	53.5	68.4	50.0	81.0	51.3	59.1	51.4/54.8	59.8	1955
1956	89.0/94.5	52.4	42.3	53.5/66.5	68.4	50.0/44.6	81.0/84.7	51.3	59.1/54.1	54.8	60.2	1956
1957	94.5	52.4	42.3/53.0	66.5/39.5/—	68.4/65.9	44.6/49.5	84.7	51.3/52.0	54.1/45.9	54.8	61.9	1957
1958	94.5	52.4/49.1/59.0	53.1	—/73.5	65.9	49.5/45.8	84.7/51.4	52.0	45.9/48.1	54.8	62.1	1958
1959	94.5/95.2	59.0	53.1	73.5/24.0	65.9	45.8	51.4/62.7	52.0	48.1	54.8/57.9	55.2	1959
1960	95.2	59.0	53.1/49.7	24.0	65.9	45.8	62.7	52.0	48.1/49.1	57.9	56.4	1960
1961	95.2/96.3	59.0/84.9	49.7	24.0	65.9/61.9	45.8/50.5	62.7	52.0/49.3	49.1	57.9	56.1	1961
1962	95.2/96.3	84.9	49.7/43.4	24.0/56.0	61.9	50.5/—/56.1	62.7	49.3	49.1	57.9	58.0	1962
1963	96.3	84.9	43.4	56.0/—	61.9	56.1	62.7/61.4	49.3/50.6	49.1	47.9	61.2	1963
1964	96.3	84.9	43.4	—/49.5	61.9	56.1	61.4	50.6	49.1/48.5	57.9/50.3	61.1	1964
1965	96.3	84.9/66.8	43.4	49.5	61.9/59.3	56.1	61.4/70.7	50.6/53.4	48.5	50.3	60.3	1965
1966	96.3/51.5	66.8/59.2	43.4	49.5/76.0	59.3/90.1	56.1/42.2/58.0	70.7/42.0	53.4	48.5	50.3/57.8	59.4	1966
1967	51.5	59.2	43.4/50.8	76.0	90.1	58.0/42.2	42.0/57.3	53.4	48.5	57.8	57.8	1967
1968	51.5	59.2/60.3	50.8/55.9	76.0/78.5	90.1	42.2/58.0	57.3	53.4	48.5/53.6	57.8	60.1	1968
1969	51.5	60.3	55.9	78.5	90.1/51.2	58.0	57.3	53.4/50.7	53.6	57.8	61.6	1969
1970	51.5/49.1	60.3	55.9	78.5/—/72.0	51.2	58.0/42.2/50.3	57.3	50.7	53.6/46.6	57.8/52.4	55.9	1970
1971	49.1/50.8	60.4	55.9/40.0	72.0/—	51.2	58.0/42.2/50.3	57.3/54.7	50.7/49.3	46.6	52.4	55.4	1971
1972	50.8	60.4	40.0	—/27.5/53.5	51.2/54.7	50.3/58.9	54.7/49.3	49.3/31.3	46.6	52.4	49.1	1972
1973	50.8	60.4/76.4	40.0/12.5	53.5	54.7	58.9/56.7/44.6	49.3/64.7	41.3/40.0	46.6/50.0	52.4	48.9	1973
1974	50.8	76.4/48.1	12.5	53.5	54.7	44.6	64.7	40.0	50.0	52.4/47.4/50.2	51.4	1974
1975	50.8	48.1	12.5/30.1	53.5/76.0	54.7	44.6	64.7	40.0	50.0	50.2	48.7	1975
1976	50.8	48.1	30.1	76.0	54.7/51.0	44.6/42.4/41.7	64.7	40.0	50.0/51.5	50.2	50.9	1976

— = Caretaker Cabinet.

Sources: v.Beyme, Mackie/Rose, Keesing's Archiv der Gegenwart.

According to Janowitz, there ought to be an increase in political alienation and thus a decrease of political participation, as well as a reduction in the strength of political majorities. These claims can be examined on the basis of voting turn-outs and parliamentary majorities in Europe since the Second World War, for which the figures in Tables 16.8 and 16.9 have been assembled.[32]

The pattern of voting turn-outs is clear: with one exception, there appears to be no great change on average. The one exception is perhaps rather baffling: given its considerable and continuing decline in voting turn-out, Switzerland appears to be undergoing some major change in its political system. In contrast to voting turn-outs, a more general and dramatic change can be observed in the pattern of parliamentary majorities. In the ten countries selected here (Belgium, Germany, Italy, Netherlands, Austria, Scandinavia, United Kingdom), the government majorities (i.e. the governing parties' share of parliamentary seats) in the period between 1949 and 1972 stood at just under 59 per cent; there was no year when they fell below 55 per cent. In the five years from 1972 until 1976, on the other hand, it is no longer possible even to speak of majorities, since even the average share of seats in parliament fell below the 50 per cent mark, if only just to 49.8 per cent. It is impossible to be certain whether this represents a lasting change, and it is of course entirely open to question whether this has anything to do with the welfare state in the first place. Independent of the exact causes, however, this pattern, in view of the existing, and in future possibly increasing, political stresses within European societies, represents a phenomenon that gives rise to some concern.

Crisis Symptoms on the Social-structural Level

In this area, too, I must confine myself, because of insufficient data, to certain aspects of distributive conflicts and signs of disintegration. I shall first examine the development of labour disputes and then briefly discuss the question as to whether the growth of the welfare state has resulted, or may possibly result, in a new 'cleavage structure'. In the concluding section on social disintegration I shall concentrate, apart from some general reflections, on two 'crisis symptoms': suicide and divorce rates.

Labour disputes. Labour disputes are among the few phenomena which in post-war Western Europe have shown a divergent pattern. In contrast to the inter-war years, a clear distinction is possible between 'strike-prone countries' and 'low-strike countries'. Among the strike-prone countries are of course Italy, France and the United Kingdom (for this purpose called 'top countries') but also Ireland, Finland and Belgium. All others belong to the low-strike countries. If we take the period 1946-70 as a whole, the strike-prone countries had six times as many strikes as the low-strike ones, ten times the number of workers took part in strikes, and six times as many working days were lost. In the 'top countries' these rates were even higher: eight times more strikes and sixteen times the number of participants.

But beyond these significant differences, a clear divergence is also observable: an increase of labour disputes in strike-prone countries and a decrease in the low-strike countries. Thus all three indicators in the first group (number of strikes, strikers and working days lost) were in the second half of the 1960s above the average for the entire period, and in other countries below the average.

Irrespective of whether one takes the entire period 1946-70, or only the second half of the 1960s as a yardstick, the first half of the seventies saw a general increase of labour disputes everywhere — across the whole of Europe and in every respect. It would certainly be an exaggeration to speak in terms of a conflagration, but the increase is nevertheless an obvious one. On a European average, the number of strikes compared with the second half of the 1960s rose by more than 50 per cent and the number of strikers involved by just under 40 per cent, while the number of working days lost was trebled. What is more, no European country escaped this wave.

Whether this means that the increase has led to a greater convergence is difficult to answer. If we take the entire period 1946-70 as a yardstick, the difference between the two types of country in the years 1971-5 is even greater than the average for the entire period. If we compare it, however, with the second half of the 1960s, the differences in the first half of the 1970s are again lessened. It is well not to lose sight of what this signifies: strike-prone countries still have eight times as many strikes, six times as many strikers and thirteen times more working days are lost.

Another apparent trend, however, may become even more important than these intensifying distributive conflicts: the fact that governments are increasingly drawn into such conflicts. One reason for this is the growth of the welfare state which, through taxes, transfer payments, services and benefits increasingly determines the actual living standards. Wage bargaining between employers and trade unions thus tends to spill over into bargaining about social benefits between unions and government. This could mean that the relative institutional isolation of labour disputes, and the consequent relief of the political system, may thus gradually be lost.

The Welfare State – a Source of 'Cleavage'. As the welfare state distributes and redistributes, it is not only drawn into conflicts, but can itself, through its institutional provisions, create specific antagonisms or conflicts of interest. Is it conceivable that divergent attitudes towards the welfare state may generate political 'cleavages' which become firmly entrenched in the social structure as differences of interest, and in party programmes as political alternatives, and thus determine political attitudes over a longer period of time? For Harold W. Wilensky such a development is easily conceivable. He suggests that an increasing differentiation between opponents and advocates of the welfare state – even among wage-earners – will become more probable as the upper strata of the working class become more middle-class through greater mobility in jobs and education, and as a consequence adopt a middle-class anti-egalitarian ideology; the greater their social distance from the underprivileged and socially visible group of welfare recipients becomes; and the weaker the political organisation of the working class which might otherwise counter such a development.[33] However, according to Franz Urban Pappi, there are so far in Western European countries – as distinct from the US – no signs of a development of this kind, which in his opinion would be conceivable in Germany only as the result of a consistently egalitarian social policy.[34]

Next to factors such as 'changes in social stratification', 'strength of the labour movement' and 'radically egalitarian policy', the extent and form of welfare state institutions will be of central importance. The danger of 'cleavage' decreases as the coverage of potential and actual beneficiaries increases, and depends on the political balance between 'redistributive' and 'earnings-related' benefits. On the other hand, it would be greatest where limited coverage combines with marked and visible redistribution (for instance in greater emphasis on social assistance in relation to social insurance).

A Crisis of Social Integration? In the first section, I distinguished between the 'crisis barometer' of social conflicts and symptoms of social disintegration in the narrower sense: instability of social groups, self-destructive and 'deviant' behaviour. Both phenomena may have the same roots, however: rapid social change, which frequently creates an imbalance between expectations and the possibility of their realisation, casts doubt on prevailing values, loosens social bonds and unsettles social groups. In comparison, Durkheim's notion of social integration implies relatively stable 'moral integration' through comparatively intense and permanent 'social interaction'. He considers both aspects important and hardly distinguishable. Thus social disintegration also has two sides: anomie and egoism, that is to say normative insecurity and weakness of social bonds.

In order to ascertain long-term tendencies in societies' capacity for social integration, one would have to examine a broad spectrum of indicators. Unfortunately we face unusual difficulties here: the value of crime statistics is disputed, information about self-destructive behaviour, such as drug use, is notoriously unreliable and the instability of social bonds and groups becomes known only as a matter of institutional concern. Thus I must base my analysis on two indicators only: suicide and divorce rates.

Ever since Durkheim's great study, increasing suicide rates have time and again been regarded as symptoms of social disintegration. Although we today regard suicide statistics with justifiably greater scepticism, I none the less think that a comparison of medium-term trends is possible. Table 16.10 shows that in Europe in the 1930s there was a general and marked increase in suicides compared with the figure for the 1920s. The post-war period, compared to the inter-war years, shows no such general and uniform pattern. Although on average fewer people took their lives, developments in individual countries differ: while in the affluent areas of Central and Northern Europe (Germany, Benelux countries, Scandinavia) the suicide rate since the end of the 1960s has increased, England and Italy (but also Switzerland) experienced a decrease. The irregularity of these patterns, however, does not mean that other forms of self-destructive behaviour have not generally increased; there are indeed some indications that this is the case.

Compared to suicides, the pattern of divorce rates is staggering in its clarity, generality and uniformity (see Table 16.11). From the beginning of the 1950s until the mid-1960s, there was almost complete stability. The average European divorce rate (divorces per 1,000 inhabitants) stood at 0.82. In the second half of the 1960s the rate went up everywhere inexorably; in 1970 it stood at 1.16 and reached 1.7 in 1975. This means that the rate doubled in the course of a decade. I believe that the growing instability of the institution of marriage is only one symptom among others of a broader and more profound disturbance of social integration. In the absence of any other empirical

Table 16.10: Suicides per 100,000 Inhabitants (averages of annual rates)

Years	AU	BE	DE	FI	FR	GE	IT	NE	NO	SW	SZ	EW	European Average	Years
1974-6	23.5	(15.9)	21.7	(25.0)	(15.4)	21.2	4.2	10.0	9.4	19.5	(19.5)	7.7	16.1	1974-6
1971-3	22.7	15.3	24.1	23.1	15.7	20.5	4.6	9.3	8.6	20.5	19.0	7.9	15.9	1971-3
1968-70	22.8	15.7	20.9	22.3	15.5	21.0	4.9	8.0	8.2	21.9	17.5	8.8	15.6	1968-70
1964-7	22.8	14.6	18.9	19.9	15.2	20.5	5.1	7.4	7.3	20.1	17.6	10.7	15.0	1964-7
1960-3	22.3	14.2	18.8	20.6	15.6	19.2	5.3	7.1	7.2	17.8	18.2	11.7	14.8	1960-3
1957-9	24.1	14.3	21.6	21.1	16.6	19.3	6.1	7.3	7.5	18.4	20.6	11.7	15.7	1957-9
1954-6	23.1	14.0	23.1	19.6	16.5	19.6	6.3	6.7	7.4	18.3	21.9	11.5	15.7	1954-6
1951-3	22.9	13.6	23.5	17.0	15.4	18.8	6.5	6.7	7.0	17.2	21.5	10.3	15.0	1951-3
1948-50	23.6	13.9	24.8	16.2	14.9	(20.9)	6.4	6.6	6.9	15.2	23.2	10.9	15.3	1948-50
1948-76	23.0	14.6	22.0	20.3	15.6	20.0	5.4	7.6	7.7	18.7	19.8	9.9	15.4	1948-76
1936-8	40.7	17.2	19.7	18.7	—	28.6	7.6	8.2	6.7	16.0	25.4	12.8	(18.3)	1936-8
1933-5	39.3	17.7	18.4	18.1	20.5	28.3	8.4	8.2	6.5	16.4	26.7	13.5	18.5	1933-5
1930-2	41.5	17.4	17.9	21.6	19.5	28.6	9.7	8.6	6.9	16.7	26.9	13.3	19.1	1930-2
1927-9	35.6	15.6	16.9	17.5	18.8	25.5	9.7	6.9	6.2	14.8	24.9	12.5	17.1	1927-9
1923-6	32.5	(14.0)	(14.6)	13.8	19.1	23.8	9.3	6.3	6.2	14.1	23.8	10.5	(15.7)	1923-6
1919-22	(22.7)	(13.6)	13.9	9.9	21.3	20.6	7.6	6.8	5.8	14.5	22.5	9.6	(14.1)	1919-22
1919-38	(34.4)	(15.7)	16.6	15.2	(20.4)	25.5	8.7	7.4	6.3	15.4	24.8	11.8	16.9	1919-38

Table 16.11: Divorces per 1,000 Inhabitants

Years	AU	BE	DE	FI	FR	GE	NE	NO	SW	SZ	EW	SO	Years
1975	1.43	1.12	2.62		1.27	1.73	1.47	1.39		1.39	2.45	1.50	1975
1974	1.41	1.04	2.60	2.14	0.96	1.59	1.42	1.29		1.27	2.31	1.29	1974
1973	1.33	0.86	2.52	1.89	0.96	1.45	1.33	1.18	2.09	1.25	2.16	1.28	1973
1972	1.33	0.81	2.63	1.78	0.94	1.40	1.12	1.02	2.22	1.20	2.43	0.99	1972
1971	1.34	0.73	2.70	1.56	0.93	1.31	0.88	0.96	2.06	1.11	1.52	0.86	1971
1970	1.39	0.66	1.93	1.31	0.79	1.26	0.79	0.88	1.91	1.02	1.20	0.82	1970
1969	1.35	0.67	1.83	1.27	0.75	1.20	0.71	0.82	1.80	0.96	1.06	0.75	1969
1968	1.32	0.63	1.56	1.17	0.72	1.10	0.64	0.80	1.72	0.91	0.95	0.85	1968
1967	1.21	0.63	1.43	1.13	0.75	1.06	0.59		1.55	0.86	0.90	0.53	1967
1966	1.19	0.61	1.40	1.06	0.74	0.99	0.55		1.56	0.82	0.82	0.63	1966
1965	1.16	0.58	1.37	1.01	0.72	1.00	0.50		1.41	0.84	0.79	0.52	1965
1964	1.16	0.58	1.37	0.98	0.69	0.96	0.51	0.67	1.38		0.74	0.47	1964
1963	1.14	0.56	1.38	0.93	0.63	0.88	0.49	0.67	1.27	0.82	0.68	0.43	1963
1962	1.12	0.51	1.38	0.89	0.65	0.87	0.48	0.68	1.25	0.83	0.62	0.39	1962
1961	1.14	0.50	1.43	0.88	0.71	0.88	0.49	0.68	1.21	0.86	0.55	0.35	1961
1960	1.14	0.56	1.46	0.83	0.66	0.88	0.49	0.66	1.23	0.87	0.52	0.35	1960
1959	1.20	0.48	1.42	0.84	0.66	0.89	0.49	0.62	1.30	0.89	0.54	0.33	1959
1958	1.17	0.47	1.46	0.84	0.70	0.88	0.47	0.59	1.25	0.85	0.50	0.35	1958
1957	1.17	0.50	1.43	0.81	0.69	0.86	0.48	0.58	1.23	0.89	0.53	0.34	1957
1956	1.22	0.48	1.46	0.86	0.71	0.86	0.51	0.60	1.26	0.85	0.59	0.37	1956
1955	1.29	0.50	1.53	0.85	0.72	0.91	0.51	0.58	1.29	0.89	0.60	0.41	1955
1954	1.32	0.45	1.52	0.83	0.72	0.96	0.52	0.62	1.27	0.90	0.63	0.43	1954
1953	1.35	0.47	1.49	0.83	0.73	1.03	0.52	0.62	1.26	0.90	0.69	0.46	1953
1952	1.42	0.48	1.55	0.85	0.78	1.12	0.56	0.64	1.21	0.87	0.77	0.53	1952
1951	1.48	0.50	1.55	0.89	0.79	1.25	0.59	0.65	1.23	0.90	0.66	0.38	1951
1950	1.52	0.59	1.61	0.92	0.83	1.67	0.64	0.71	1.21	0.90	0.70	0.42	1950
Average of Annual Rates 1950-75	1.28	0.61	(1.09)	0.78	1.12	0.68	(0.78)	(1.47)	(0.95)	1.00	0.62		

Marriages per 100 Inhabitants

Years	AU	BE	DE	FI	FR	GE	NE	NO	SW	SZ	EW	SO
1975									22.6			
1970/71	22.8	25.5	24.0	21.8	23.5	25.1	24.0	23.7	23.9	24.1	25.6	23.7
1966/68		25.7	23.6		23.3	24.5		23.2	23.8		25.7	23.6
1960/62	22.7	25.0	23.1	20.3	23.3	23.2	20.8	21.9	23.1	22.7	25.4	22.3
1947/54	22.2			19.8						21.6		

indicators, however, I must rely much more on speculation in what follows.

One may cite a variety of reasons for the growing social disintegration, but one factor in particular may have been of crucial importance: the expansion of education since the beginning of the 1960s, which in historical comparison would certainly merit the term 'revolution'. Rapid social change is a key to the understanding of social disintegration. This development may not only have been crucial because of its speed, but also because of its direct effect on integrative institutions, such as family and public education. Educational expansion has probably influenced the relation between the sexes and the generations – and thus marriage and family. Education is certainly an important factor in the emergence of a new division of labour between the sexes and the anomic phenomena that go with this. The opening up of higher education to social groups which had previously less access to it has probably resulted in a greater alienation between generations. The educational establishments themselves have probably also lost some of their integrative power, through their growth and changes in structure and function, and have thus contributed to greater anomy in the relationships of social origin/education/professional status. Individual imbalances between increased and more diffused expectations (for social mobility) and the possibilities of realising these combine with structural imbalances between the educational system and the labour market.

For critics in a Durkheimian tradition, this educational expansion, with its emphasis on opportunities for individual development and the concomitant increase in expectations, is only a symptom of a more general trait of the welfare state, which can be described by the following catch phrases: weakening of 'intermediary structures' and strengthening of 'egoistic' and 'anomic' tendencies through promotion of individual goals, claims and rights, without a corresponding development of social responsibilities and without a strengthening of social loyalties. 'The welfare state is a strategy for making use of collective symbols and practices to achieve goals that are cast in an individualistic mold.'[35]

Possible Directions of Institutional Change

For the purpose of pointing to fruitful areas for future research some conclusions may perhaps be drawn from the above.

(1) There indeed exist several symptoms which indicate increasing

instability within European societies; but it appears urgently necessary to achieve greater empirical certainty about such trends, to widen and to differentiate the spectrum of indicators, and to search systematically for causes and interconnections; this would be the first task for additional research.

(2) At a minimum, it is not improbable that these symptoms may indicate 'structural problems', i.e. they may be related to a changed macro-constellation; a second task for research would thus consist in deepening the theoretical analysis of the elements of such a constellation and to promote empirical analysis of their disruptive effects.

(3) The argument that the welfare state, through its growth, has become a 'crisis-generating' structural element does not appear implausible. At the same time, its stabilising effects must not be overlooked, and after all we have not established a direct link between it and all the crisis symptoms; a third task would therefore consist in systematic analysis of its expansive trends and its disintegrative effects.

(4) The term 'crisis' should not be taken to mean a specific event at the end of a steady increase of instability, disintegration and conflict, but rather as a whole period in which such phenomena, while generally on the increase, may vary in their timing. Although it cannot be determined whether we are in fact living in such a period at present, we can nevertheless say that our interpretation should not take the so-called oil crisis or the world recession of 1974/5 as their point of departure. The 'post-war era' had come to an end before that point in time, and the trends vary not only in their causes, but also in the timing of their origins.

To reflect on the possibility of institutional solutions, even before one possesses a more precise grasp of the problems and their causes, seems hardly appropriate. But we can ask questions as to the possible direction of institutional change, although the analysis must of necessity be of a highly speculative nature. At the forefront are relationships between the welfare state and elements of the macro-constellation. In this context, the relationships between the elements *'international system'* and *'family/population'* present themselves mainly as problems of institutional adaptation to changes in the world economy and the population structure.

The relationships of the welfare state to *'mass democracy'* and

386 The Welfare State in Historical Perspective

'*capitalism*' go far beyond such problems. They are constituent parts of the Western type of welfare state, which is their product and yet also an attempt to stabilise them. The welfare state is at the same time based on democratic consensus and capitalist productivity, and can endanger both through excessive bureaucratisation. A growing weakening of the Western welfare states' liberal-democratic and market economy roots would certainly also alter its basic character. Yet its character can in the long run only be maintained by institutional change: a strengthening of political participation through decentralisation and a linking of the — frequently contradictory — forms of parliamentary, corporatist and direct democracy; a 'democratisation' of the economy, through decentralised property policy and industrial democracy. Such changes, however, would not leave untouched the institutions of the welfare state but would require a redrawing of its boundaries *vis-à-vis* 'economy' and 'society'.

Relations with the elements '*nation state*' and '*industrial society*', finally, make the welfare state a crucial structural phenomenon of all modern societies, and potentially profound changes in the welfare state would thus have to be analysed in the context of changes in the former. If the state establishes a comparatively greater degree of security and equality of its citizens, this must mean more bureaucracy and greater individualisation. This double aspect of the nation state's welfare policies could undergo a change in trend, if, in the process of increased international redistribution and integration, the security and equality of states and regions become relatively more important. Beyond that, a weakening of national integration might make a greater shift of authority and resources to sub-national collective groups possible (particularly firm and family), as the concomitant inequalities would thus be rendered somewhat more acceptable. Through this a more unified concept of social security might be developed, where legal claims against state or firm become merged with a security based on a wider spread of property and education and strengthened family solidarity.

A development of this kind might combine with changes in the industrial society, with which the welfare state has entered into a symbiosis, by strengthening and supporting its differentiation processes. Behind the aseptic concept of differentiation lies hidden the fragmentation of our lives into a 'period of education', 'working life' and 'retirement', a division between family and working life; compartmentalisation of 'work' and 'leisure', a neat distinction between 'health' and 'sickness', etc. A partial decrease in differentiation through the development of intermediate forms of employment could not only strengthen the family, by facilitating a new division of labour between the sexes, it could also help to prevent the emergence of many problems (such as imbalances between education and the labour market) and relieve the welfare state of some of its burdens (for example by solving the pension problem caused by changes in the age structure). Such a process of lessening differentiations might be made possible through the expansion of education and technological progress, and be supported by changes in values. With a loosening of the rigid organisation of work, there would be profound changes both in the industrial society and the welfare state.

According to Weber, de-differentiation could lead to less dynamism. Perhaps this is just what is required. This, however, takes our speculations much too far. Empirical observation and analysis of 'crisis symptoms' — and not speculation — must be our first and most important step.

Notes

1. This chapter was produced as part of the HIWED Project, which is being carried out, with the generous support of the Volkswagen Foundation, at the Research Institute for Sociology of the University of Cologne. I should like to thank all my colleagues most warmly for their support: Jens Alber, Richard Eichenberg, Joachim Heinlein, Karl-Heinz Korn, Franz Kraus, Winfried Pfenning and Kurt Seebohm.

2. Walt W. Rostow, *Politics and the Stages of Growth* (Cambridge, 1971).

3. See in particular the following: Leonard Binder *et al.*, *Crises and Sequences in Political Development* (Princeton, 1971); Raymond Grew (ed.), *Crises of Political Development in Europe and the United States* (Princeton, 1978).

4. Stein Rokkan, *Citizens, Elections, Parties* (Oslo, 1970).

5. See particularly Emile Durkheim, *Le Suicide* (Paris, 1960) and *idem*, *L'Education Morale* (Paris, 1974).

6. It is the analysis of a macro-constellation of central *structural elements* (the institution of slavery at the intersection of economic, administrative and military order), as well as *processes of growth and decline* (the shift from coasts to the interior and the resulting weakening of transport; the end of imperial expansion and the resulting drying up of the supply of slaves). See Max Weber, 'Die sozialen Gründe des Untergangs der antiken Kultur' in Max Weber, *Soziologie — Weltgeschichtliche Analysen — Politik* (Stuttgart, 1964).

7. Rainer M. Lepsius, 'Modernisierung als Institutionenbildung. Kriterien institutioneller Differenzierung' in Wolfgang Zapf (ed.), *Probleme der Modernisierungspolitik* (Mannheim, 1976).

8. See Immanuel Wallerstein, *The Modern World System* (New York, 1974).

9. See Frances F. Piven and Richard A. Cloward, *Regulating the Poor. The Function of Public Welfare* (New York, 1971).

10. See Walt W. Rostow, *The World Economy, History and Prospects* (London, 1978).

388   *The Welfare State in Historical Perspective*

11. See Angus Maddison, *Economic Growth in the West* (New York, 1964).
12. See Peter Flora, 'Quantitative Historical Sociology', *Current Sociology*, vol. 23, no. 2 (1975).
13. See Rostow, *The World Economy*.
14. These data come from Winfried Pfenning, who is preparing a comparative study on the development of trade unions and strikes in Western Europe for the HIWED project.
15. Hans Achinger, *Sozialpolitik als Gesellschaftspolitik* (Hamburg, 1958).
16. For a discussion of the term 'welfare state' see the first chapter in Peter Flora and Arnold J. Heidenheimer (eds.), *The Development of Welfare States in Europe and North America* (New Brunswick, NJ, 1979).
17. The index is designed to facilitate a comparison of the growth of social security systems in the various European countries. It consists of a weighted average of the population covered (in per cent of the economically active population) in all four systems. The four percentages were weighted as follows: old age insurance 1.5, health and unemployment insurance 1.0, accident insurance 0.5. In the case of subsidised voluntary insurance, the corresponding percentages were halved. The bold line represents the 'European average', i.e. the average of the index values of all European countries.
    For a more extensive analysis of the index see Peter Flora, Jens Alber and Jürgen Kohl, 'Zur Entwicklung der westeuropäischen Wohfahrtsstaaten', *Politische Vierteljahresschrift*, vol. 18, no. 4 (1977).
18. See S. Andic and J. Veverka, 'The Growth of Government Expenditure in Germany since the Unification', *Finanzarchiv*, n.s., vol. 23 (1963/4), pp. 169-278.
19. See Jürgen Kohl, 'Trends and Problems in Post-war Public Expenditure Development in Western Europe and North America' in Flora and Heidenheimer, *Development of Welfare States*. See also Jürgen Kohl, 'Staatsausgaben in Westeuropa. Ansätze zur empirischen Analyse der langfristigen Entwicklung der öffentlichen Ausgaben seit Ende des 19. Jahrhunderts, dissertation, Mannheim, 1979.
20. Jens Alber, 'Modernisierung und die Entwicklung der Sozialversicherung in Westeuropa', dissertation, Mannheim, 1979.
21. Both traditions have been taken up again in recent years, particularly in America. Here I shall only name O'Connor on the one hand, and Daniel Bell or Morris Janowitz on the other: James O'Connor, *The Fiscal Crisis of the State* (New York, 1973); Morris Janowitz, *The Social Control of the Welfare State* (New York, 1976); Daniel Bell, *The Cultural Contradiction of Capitalism* (New York, 1976).
22. Joseph Schumpeter, 'Die Krise des Steuerstaates' in Rudolf Goldscheid and Josef Schumpeter, *Die Finanzkrise des Steuerstaates. Beiträge zur politischen Ökonomie der Staatsfinanzen*, Rudolf Hickel (ed.) (Frankfurt, 1976).
23. These data come from Kurt Seebohm, who is preparing a comparative analysis of the development of Western European tax systems for the HIWED Project. They give the average tax ratio of approximately ten countries. The tax ratio is defined as the share of total taxes in the net national product at market prices.
24. This concept was first developed by Alan T. Peacock and Jack Wiseman, *The Growth of Public Expenditure in the United Kingdom* (Princeton, 1961).
25. Harold L. Wilensky, *The 'New Corporatism', Centralization and the Welfare State* (New York, 1976).
26. Gabriel Arden, *Histoire de l'Impot* (2 vols., Paris, 1971 and 1972).
27. I would like to thank Richard Eichenberg for providing a summary of the present state of discussion in the literature in this field. Eichenberg is preparing

a comparative analysis of the development of welfare and defence expenditure in the post-war period for the HIWED Project, entitled 'Defense/Welfare Trade-offs in the Expenditure Patterns of Advanced Industrial States'.

For an analysis of France as an exception to the general rule, see Edward L. Morse, *Foreign Policy and Interdependence in Gaullist France* (Princeton, 1973), Ch. 4.

28. Kohl, 'Trends and Problems'; *idem*, *Staatsausgaben in Westeuropa*.

29. See Rudolf Klein, 'The International Crisis of the Welfare State: the Case of Britain', manuscript, 1976 University of Bath.

30. Kohl, 'Trends and Problems'; *idem*, *Staatsausgaben in Westeuropa*.

31. Janowitz, *Social Control*, p. 86.

32. In preparing this table the following sources were used: Klaus von Beyme, *Die parlamentarischen Regierungssysteme in Europa* (Munich, 1973) and Thomas T. Mackie and Richard Rose, *The International Almanac of Electoral Statistics* (London, 1974). For the period after 1972 *Keesings Contemporary Archives* were used. In calculating European averages the first figure was always used in principle, if the government stayed in office for more than one month. Work on the first two sources revealed some inaccuracies. Since we have not yet finished examining all the data, Table 16.9 may still contain some mistakes.

33. Harold L. Wilensky, *The Welfare State and Equality. Structural and Ideological Roots of Public Expenditures* (Berkeley, 1975).

34. Franz Urban Pappi, 'Einstellungen zum Wohlfahrtsstaat' in Zapf, *Probleme*, pp. 213-18.

35. Janowitz, *Social Control*, p. 105.

17 COMMENTS ON PROFESSOR PETER FLORA'S ANALYTICAL PERSPECTIVE OF THE WELFARE STATE

G.V. Rimlinger

The central question raised by Professor Flora in his chapter is whether the welfare state has developed from an instrument to manage social 'crises' to a causal factor of such 'crises'. To raise this kind of question indicates that there is at least some presumption that the modern welfare state has indeed become a destabilising force. Flora is well aware that historians may find an old-fashioned ring to the idea that social welfare measures may lead to social and economic disaster. The ideological conflicts which accompanied the rise of the welfare state produced many predictions of dire economic and social consequences. But these conflicts over social principles, economic redistribution and political power have long since given way to a broad consensus. In modern societies the welfare state has been endorsed practically across the whole political spectrum. And yet, it is precisely in this mature setting that a growing number of social scientists — economists, sociologists, political scientists — have begun to question the future of the welfare state.

Questioning by social scientists of the inherent limitations and possible internal contradictions of the welfare state is not entirely new. Some thirty years ago the sociologist T.H. Marshall raised fundamental questions about the practical limits of social measures aiming at greater equality and about their possible contradiction with prevailing economic and social structures.[1] Nevertheless, the number of critical voices among social scientists questioning not the legitimacy but the impact of the welfare state has sharply increased over the last decade. The motivation behind this questioning may be related to the rapid increase over the same period of welfare state expenditures in all advanced industrial societies. There is a general realisation that in a number of countries recent rates of increase are not sustainable, for both economic and social reasons. Yet, further substantial increases are very difficult to control in a context of rising expectations about basic equality and minimum levels of comfort. This is the kind of setting that inevitably invites thoughts of crises and disasters.

Much of the literature on the problems of the modern welfare state, especially the economic literature, is concerned with the growth of the economic burden imposed upon the active labour force by increasing cohorts of old age pensioners and by ever rising costs of education and medical care. To some extent this is a technical concern, which calls for technical solutions, but the underlying ramifications are very wide. They affect not only income distribution, but also capital accumulation and labour productivity, and hence the material base of the welfare state. In the United States there are strong voices, led by the Harvard economist Martin Feldstein, urgently calling for a curtailment of social security programmes for the sake of restoring the country's economic vitality. Flora recognises the importance of these trends, but his own analysis is at a quite different level. He recognises that the demands for welfare programmes are part of a broad range of problems facing the modern state, and the resolution of these problems involves a lot more than economic considerations.

Flora's conceptualisation of the problems of the welfare state involves a macro-sociological approach in a comparative historical framework. It is an approach which is of interest to the social and economic historian for two reasons. First, it relies in part on the historian for its sources of data and historical perspective. Second, and perhaps more important, it can provide hypotheses and questions to guide the historian's inquiries and shape his interpretations. Flora approaches the welfare state as a structural/functional adaptation to the broad economic, social and political transformation represented by the rise of the modern state and by industrialisation. He sees this adaptation as being fundamentally defensive in nature; it has always served to preserve the existing order against socially destructive forces. It is not clear to what extent this view is compatible with the concept of the welfare state as an intended instrument of social change. On the other hand, a 'welfare state crisis' seems to occur when the institutions and structures associated with the welfare state become a source of unintended change, or rather a cause of disruption in what Flora calls the historically prevailing 'macro-constellation'. A stable macro-constellation, if I interpret him correctly, represents a system of mutually adapted structural elements which has developed historically and is in some kind of dynamic equilibrium. A crisis situation must be thought of not as a specific event but as a series of developments over a prolonged period of time during which disruptions cause the functional impairment of various elements of the macro-constellation. Such disruptions are presumably severe enough to be beyond self-correction. Their effects would be cumulative and would eventually lead to a re-adaptation of structural elements in a new macro-constellation. Disequilibrating forces which may emanate from the modern welfare state include persistent public deficits, prolonged political instability, substantial increases in social conflicts and widespread indication of various forms of social disintegration. The causal links between these forces and the welfare state are an important part of the analysis.

Flora applies these concepts to a schematic review of the development of the welfare state in Western Europe. He notes the inherent tendency of the welfare state to expand and in particular its growth acceleration in recent times. The most notable conclusion he reaches from this overview is rather sobering. Although he does not discuss the various attempts to explain the historical development of the welfare state, Flora insists that we know very little about the forces behind its steady growth over the last hundred years. He maintains also that we know far too little about the impact which the welfare state has had on social relations. No doubt what Flora has in mind in making these sweeping statements are explanations which have general theoretical validity. One can argue of course that such statements apply not only to the development of the welfare state but to the whole process of economic and social development. After several decades of study by economists and other social scientists, we have not greatly advanced our general theoretical understanding of development.

In the second half of the chapter Flora again returns to his opening query of whether the welfare state has indeed become a destabilising factor in the current macro-constellation. This question can now be considered in terms of the theoretical concepts developed earlier. Somewhat disarmingly, he informs us that at the macro-sociological level at which he poses the question it is in fact not answerable. I take this statement to mean that in the present state of our knowledge it is not possible to make scientifically valid predictions about the outcome of the highly complex interactions of the elements of a macro-constellation. Indeed, one may wonder if it is possible even to specify in rigorous terms any stable pattern of interaction. The social historian and the historical sociologist may discover in retrospect how structures subjected to disequilibrating forces have become altered and realigned, but it would be something quite different for the sociologist to predict such changes in any detail. The objective of Flora's chapter is consequently not to give a direct answer to the title query. It aims rather to provide research guidelines on the long-term evolution of the welfare state.

The framework for this research is provided by what Flora considers the major elements of the present macro-constellation of the Western world, namely the international system, the national state, capitalism, mass democracy, industrial society and family/demographic trends. Each of these broad and complex elements is subject to pressure points which may eventually alter the macro-constellation. Flora reviews the various crisis symptoms at the governmental/political and at the social/ structural levels. He puts considerable emphasis on sources of increased pressures for public spending. He realises no doubt that the ability of governments to cope with all the welfare and other demands depends fundamentally on the prospects for continued economic growth, although he does not dwell very much on this subject. He does not seem to be overly concerned about the Malthusian ghost of world population outstripping resources in an environment which is being rapidly degraded. The future of the welfare state would indeed be precarious if the now somewhat discredited predictions of the Club of Rome were to be realised. Flora prefers to align himself, and many would agree with him, with the more optimistic scenario of world economic potential presented in a recent book by W.W. Rostow, entitled *The World Economy: History and Prospects* (1978). In the end Flora concludes that although there are pervasive pressures for increased public spending and mounting resistance to taxation, and while there is evidence of growing social instability and reasons to be concerned about the availability of resources, it remains an open question whether these forces will bring about fundamental changes in the welfare state. We simply have to know more and have to have a better understanding of the interplay of the forces involved.

The first research task will therefore have to be a more profound study of the empirical evidence on the various forces affecting the welfare state. Flora seems to have in mind here particularly quantitative indicators of social change which allow cross-national comparisons. The explanatory power of empirical evidence, however, depends on its theoretical relevance. Without an adequate theory, we really don't know what kind of evidence we should collect. This may be the reason why Flora lists as his second research task the improvement of our theoretical understanding of how shifts in macro-constellations take place and how they may be related to social crises. Finally, he notes also the need for more research on the causes of growth and the consequences of the welfare state, especially with regard to social integration and stability.

One finds it hard to disagree with someone who reveals the complexity of a phenomenon and makes a good case for the need for more research. In this regard Professor Flora's chapter certainly renders a useful service. The main problem historians and perhaps other social scientists will have with his approach is the high level of theoretical abstraction it involves. It is not easy to translate highly abstract socio-logical concepts into relevant empirical research questions. That may simply be a reflection of the complexity of the problem and of the state of our knowledge. As Flora himself makes quite clear, some of the central questions he raises are of a highly speculative nature. There is a need for a more sharply focused research agenda, but I do believe that the comparative historical/sociological approach practised by Flora and others is the most promising road to follow.

Note

1. T.H. Marshall, 'Citizenship and Social Class' (Marshall Lectures, Cambridge, 1949), reprinted in *Class, Citizenship and Social Development* (New York, 1965).

18 THE FUTURE OF THE WELFARE STATE

F. Naschold

The attempt to arrive at certain conclusions about the future of the welfare state, if it is to have some claim to being well founded, requires as an initial step some prior consideration as to method. The scientific base for the usual sociological prognostications is, as a rule, provided by an extrapolation of trends in their manifold forms and varying degrees of complexity.[1] This is based on the assumption that social developments which have been observable in the past will continue in a similar — or predictably modified — form in future. A typical example of this is the flow of statistical calculations emanating from the German Ministry of Employment about the development of old age pension insurance in the Federal Republic, or by the highly complex and comprehensive analyses of social trends in the development of the welfare state by Peter Flora.[2] This kind of analysis usually implies two assumptions: first, that the structural pattern of the social pre-conditions which determine, for instance, revenue and expenditure trends in old age insurance will remain more or less constant, and, second, that the values society places on such trends and patterns remain unchanged. In a great number of social areas such assumptions are probably quite realistic in the shorter term. Viewed over a longer period, however, they may prove highly misleading, because accuracy of prediction may turn out to occur less frequently than forecasting errors. The longer the period covered by the forecast and the more complex and 'turbulent' the social area which is being analysed, the more likely is it that breaks in the social structure and far-reaching value changes occur which are no longer susceptible to being deduced from an analysis of past developments. In this case mere extrapolation of the past would lead to a congealing of future development potential.

In order to avoid this 'extrapolative error' in the analysis of the future course of the welfare state, it is necessary to go beyond the mere registration and extrapolation of the superficial indicators of social developments and to make at least an attempt to understand the essential structure of social developments in the area of social policy. This might then provide a first step towards statements about the future course of the welfare state.

In the following necessarily sketchy examinations, I shall first look at the controversy in the appraisal of the welfare state as it is now, arising out of the criticism levelled at it by the 'new radical conservatism'. I shall then attempt to show that hidden behind these positions lie two historically alternative 'social configurations' and 'social ideas' — to employ the central concepts of the leading theoretician of social policy in the Weimar Republic, Eduard Heimann[3] — which determine the basic structure of the welfare state's dynamic. Against this perspective I shall, in conclusion, examine the static and dynamic elements in the system of social forces which determine both the history of the welfare state and its future.

Crisis of the Welfare State? The Present Controversy about its Future

According to the prevailing view within liberal-parliamentary, capitalist industrial countries and their prevailing scientific paradigm — the liberal theory of modernisation[4] — the creation and extension of the welfare state is seen as the consequence of the political development of various fundamental elements of modernisation: equality of economic, social and political rights of the citizen, combined with a greater degree of political mobilisation and participation and an increase in the state's ability to exercise control, based on, and as a consequence of, economic and social developments since industrialisation. According to this theory, general modernisation led to a universal development syndrome, containing three main elements: structural social differentiation, an increase in the state's ability to exercise political control, and equality of citizens. The inherent tensions, particularly between the modernising principle of equality on the one hand and differentiation and the state's control functions on the other, threaten to impair the political system's three universal functions — the legitimising, the executive and, above all, the service function. Out of all these interacting frictions arise the 'development crises' of society which, in the social area, appear in the form of modernisation crises of 'redistribution', in conjunction with crises of 'penetration, political participation and integration'. In the development of the welfare state, the processes of political development, combined with tendencies towards economic and social modernisation, lead, via historical and specifically national methods for the resolution of crises, to different patterns and levels of solution in each case. Thus, when dealing with a crisis of redistribution by a political strategy of modernisation, the fundamental structure of the welfare state is seen as having a twofold aim:

(1) state-guaranteed minimum standards of income, nourishment, health, accommodation and education as a civic right and not a charity; (2) redistribution of income between social classes and strata. The usual inventory of political development theories also contains the — rarely explicit and more usually implicit — assumption, derived from the general theory of modernisation, that while the political process of modernisation does not offer unilinear and definitive solutions, it does provide modernised twentieth-century societies, each in their different way, with satisfactory solutions of a level and quality adequate to their social systems, not only able to meet development crises as they arise, but sufficiently adaptable to cope with potential new demands. Thus, in the view of numerous observers, the central aims of state welfare policies in the modernised countries are being realised to a considerable degree and are of satisfactory quality, even though they may require gradual reform.

In the wake of the rapid expansion of the welfare state in the post-war era, this development has, since the early sixties, met with criticism, directed mainly against mounting costs, the ineffectiveness of welfare state institutions and over-regimentation.[5] Certainly since the early seventies these have come together in a more fundamental position — the 'new radical conservatism' which diagnoses a profound 'crisis of the welfare state'. This refers in particular to four areas within it: its specific package of measures and the social repercussions thereof, the political economy and the political control structure of the welfare state, as well as the problems this welfare development has posed for the social structure. In the following I shall briefly sketch these critical views of the welfare state as held by their most prominent proponents.

Criticism of the various packages of welfare measures and the benefits in cash, kind and services which the state provides in the field of education, social services, old age, subsidised housing, etc., is directed against their redistributive effects, since these are divorced from events in the market-place — a subject of controversy of many years' standing in Anglo-Saxon and Scandinavian countries, the details of which will not be gone into here. But the criticism is also directed, especially in Germany, against the form in which these services are rendered.[6] It is claimed that the control and handling of welfare services are characterised by excessive economic thinking, legalism, bureaucracy and professionalism in dealing with the wide variety of individual and collective human problems. The term 'economisation of social policies' is intended to highlight the problem that social policies are largely subjected to the demands of the economic process, that social measures serve as instruments of aid and repair in capital-oriented production and that there is a tendency to ignore needs that cannot be satisfied by cash payments.

'Excessive legalism in social policy' means, in historical perspective, that there is less and less elbow-room for decentralised action on the part of independent local administrations because of centrally imposed norms. This in turn creates more isolated cases of need, while social problems are defined as individual insurance cases. There is a tendency also to ignore the small supportive social units, and their biographical and social cohesion, which provide the framework for the individual's capacity to act.

These tendencies to think in legalistic and purely economic terms have brought a corresponding increase in bureaucratism in the administration of welfare measures. Typical of this is the prevailing strategy of 'passive provision of services' and the schematic and abstract supply of services, as well as the usual forms of a formally bureaucratic administrative apparatus, with such consequences as functional fragmentation and duplication, lack of continuity, incoherence and reduction of individual choice.

The degree of bureaucracy in the provision of social services goes largely hand in hand with an excess of professionalism. The prominent position of the professions, particularly in the area of health services, is only partially due to greater scientific complexity, and is in a larger measure the consequence of an increase in social control. The provision of professional services means orientation on other colleagues and on specific technologies, it means 'professional dominance' instead of client-orientation, and implies inter-professional rigidities and problems of co-ordination.

A number of the criticisms levelled at the way the welfare state provides its services, and the consequences thereof, are also shared by the supporters of the welfare state.[7] The opposed standpoints arise only when drawing the conclusions from such criticism. While the supporters of the welfare state believe in its inherent capacity for reform and acknowledge the need for reforming its services, the representatives of the 'new radical conservatism' come to two different conclusions: (1) The malfunctions of welfare state services are increasing to such a degree that the consequences of this are becoming graver than the ills they were designed to remedy. The welfare state is thus held to create its own victims. (2) The only way out of this dilemma would be a radical retrenchment of welfare state institutions and of their *modus operandi* and a concomitant build-up of private safety nets on the part of the citizens.

The 'new radical conservatism' thus reaches a position which the supporters of the welfare state interpret as a radical dismantling of the institutions of social justice.

The expansion of welfare state measures which occurred after the Second World War in practically all Western industrial countries was, in the view of the proponents of the 'new radical conservatism', only possible because of profound changes in the states' economic policies, based on Keynesian concepts. According to Buchanan — a leading critic of the political economy of the welfare state — the introduction of two new functions was a prerequisite for this expansion:[8] a consistent policy of full employment and a transfer by the state of part of the national product away from the economic cycle into greater welfare consumption. The most important instrument for this was the long-term increase in state revenue, combined with a policy of deficit spending that took little account of the economy's cyclical trends. Given the institutions of parliamentary democracy, this policy — if adopted in the long term — leads to neglect of micro-economic profitability and thus to misallocation of limited resources, to a shift to mass consumption instead of necessary investment, and to inflationary pressures in combination with symptoms of stagnation. According to this critique, the political economy of the welfare state thus results in the destruction of the market economy on which liberal democracy is based, and thus also threatens the existing welfare expenditure — a state of affairs only to be redressed by governments adopting a new set of rules and returning to orthodox fiscal principles.

These thoughts lead us to the third criticism coming from the 'new radical conservatism'. Janowitz, basing himself on theoretical reflection and empirical data, has attempted to show that if the development of the welfare state gets out of hand this not only leads to instability of institutions, but also, more generally, to an undermining of the structures of social control.[9] In liberal parliamentary countries, according to him, social structures and job differentiations are shaped by income and achievement, based on work and the ownership of capital, within the framework of a market economy. The welfare state, by contrast, through transfer payments based on the principle of equality, increasingly creates an antidromous social structure. This produces an ambivalent system of social stratification which makes for vague and diffuse political preferences. This leads to the dissolution of the established system of relations between political elites and the electors they represent, and finally results in government overload to the point of its ceasing to function altogether. Beyond that, according to the criticisms of the 'new radical conservatism', it leads to serious symptoms of disintegration of the social structure. According to Peter Flora, based on Durkheim,[10] the welfare state and its measures impair intermediate social structures, the 'small safety nets' of society, and lead to anomy, selfishness, uncertainty of values and a weakening of social bonds. Increases in the suicide and divorce rates are seen as indicators of this development.

This *fin de siècle* perspective, which is gaining ground in conservative criticism of the welfare state, appears frequently in the guise of a new paradigm of the development of Western industrial countries. Yet one glance at the history of the welfare state shows that this position is merely the latest variant, empirically turned around and radicalised, of conservative criticism of social policies ever since the welfare state began. The period of reconstruction and restoration after the last war and the enormous economic growth had laid the foundation for the political consensus that allowed the expansion of the welfare state. Under increasing economic pressure, this political consensus is now threatening to crumble, and the almost classical political-economic fronts around the welfare state are beginning to re-emerge. The real basis of the interplay of social forces appears again from behind the veil of two decades of economic and political expansion. This will be briefly examined in the next section.

Alternative 'Social Configurations' and 'Social Ideas' in the Development of the Welfare State

The relatively broadly based political consensus during the phase of reconstruction, a period of hitherto rarely experienced long-term economic growth, and an undisputed enormous expansion of the welfare state in most liberal parliamentary industrial countries, particularly in Germany, created the appearance of a basically peaceable social structure, with a low incidence of conflict due to relative homogeneity, and with broad agreement on aims. The repression of the experiences of the period after the First World War and of Fascism also obscured the fact that this phase of reconstruction did not represent a final state of balance, but merely a specific phase in a longer and more profound socio-political conflict within liberal parliamentary industrial countries, and that the apparent harmony of aims would be exploded as soon as problems of economic, political and ideological structure erupted, bringing the underlying social conflict structures into the open again. The 'new radical conservatism' provided an important push in this direction, for this showed up the existence of fundamental alternatives for the development of the welfare state. The actual events were more or less echoed by the kind of scientific theories that were formulated. According to the liberal theory of modernisation, social development, and particularly the development of the welfare state, was seen as an in essence relatively homogeneous, purposeful historical process of modernisation, supported by all the most important social groupings, with relatively similar ideas about aims. More recent European experiences, however, and particularly those outside Europe, make it clear that these developments represented a precarious balance of compromise, the 'anticlinal point' of extremeley heterogeneous, and partly even antagonistic, configurations,[11] which also indicated the essential structure of the development of the welfare state. The lumping together of such — in some cases opposed — configurations can only lead to spurious generalisations, 'bad abstraction' of definition, and thence to analytical artefacts which have less and less relevance to actual problems.

These configurations were clearly distinguishable and consisted of partly antagonistic economic, political and ideological constellations of forces, interests and strategies, based on different and distinguishable, partly antagonistic classes and social strata and their alliances. Only by relinquishing scientific standards can contradictory 'social configurations' be artificially abstracted into a 'crisis of redistribution' and the 'development of the welfare state', and be summarised in a way which falsifies the problem.

The concept of the state's social policy and the change in the paradigm of social 'modernisation' can best be demonstrated by examining the development of national health care, as part of the state's welfare policy aimed at solving the crisis of redistribution.

The genesis of German compulsory health insurance since 1883 — the product of occasionally confusing strategies of economic, political and ideological alliances between classes, parties and political elites — is often regarded an an epoch-making event, signalling the beginnings of the modern welfare state. In 1890 10 per cent of the wage-earning population was covered by compulsory health insurance, its most important function being the provision of cash payments, compensation for loss of earnings in case of sicknesss, and certain other benefits in kind. Five fundamental changes have taken place since its inception: the insurance now covers more than 90 per cent of the population, thus almost reaching the point of having become a universal insurance; benefits in kind have been expanded according to specific criteria of need; the politico-economic links between health insurance and the workers' movement have been severed; the curative medical services have been expanded, in some cases measures for early diagnosis have been introduced and endeavours are made by the state and relevant groupings to build up a system of planning and information in a policy area which is gaining increasing importance both in terms of fiscal and administrative volume. Despite these changes, the basic principles of state health insurance as established in 1883 still remain intact.

The genesis, functions, structure and development of state health insurance seem at first glance to correspond to the assumptions and concepts of the political theory of modernisation; for instance in respect of specific national strategies for the solution of the crisis of redistribution, coupled with development problems arising out of the concept of equal rights to social and political participation. Empirical-theoretical examination can, however, disclose a number of serious shortcomings as well as more fundamental faults. Even such politically controversial terms as 'sickness insurance', as opposed to 'health insurance', indicate that the concepts contained in the political theory of modernisation and in still current notions about a 'universal' socio-political development problem, about mastering the physical and psychological consequences of industrialisation, serve to mask contradictory, and often hostile, 'social configurations' and 'social ideas' (Heimann) and that these are being amalgamated into a single, homogeneously defined, abstract concept. One must therefore, in an analytically somewhat pointed form, assume that before and during the inception of compulsory health insurance, as well as in large parts of its later development, more or less fundamental economic and political 'social configurations' and ideological 'social ideas' were in permanent conflict with each other. The dominant political and economic alliance between various capital groups aiming at hegemony, large parts of the traditional middle class, and the ruling political elites constituted one 'social configuration', whose social concepts contained the following essential strategic points: a narrowly defined 'negative' concept of sickness as a basic strategic principle; a rudimentary system of care based on curative benefits and compensation for loss of earnings; the severance of links between compulsory health insurance and workers' protection; control of the welfare system by state and employers, while at the same time abolishing existing or developing workers' self-help organisations; fragmentation of the compulsory health insurance's organisational structure; promotion of the traditional and newly emerging middle classes, especially the medical profession as partners in this alliance and as buffers against the workers' movement. By contrast, large and dominant factions of the workers' movement represented a 'social configuration' whose 'social ideas' aimed almost exclusively at quite opposite strategic objectives: a broadly defined, 'positively' conceived concept of health as a basic strategic principle, taking full account of the socially conditioned causes of injury to health and their unequal distribution in society; cause-oriented primary prevention as a basis for a strategy of solution; integration of compulsory health insurance and workers' protection; a unified public health service, largely self-administered by the workers; transformation of the traditional and the new middle classes into public servants, like the medical profession; changing chemist shops into public co-operative ventures. These conflicts between diametrically opposed 'social configurations' and 'social ideas' − and not endogenous, homogeneous evolutionary trends − formed the structure and the dynamism of the welfare state development. These shall be examined briefly by way of summary.

The Possibilities for the Future Development of the Welfare State

If the deliberations so far are correct, the possible future development of the welfare state in Germany, and in other comparable liberal parliamentary countries, particularly the United Kingdom, largely depends on the actual interplay of forces within society against the background of development hitherto, and on the strategies and tactics adopted by the most important groupings within these societies.

First I shall briefly outline the historical background to the present stage of the welfare state in Germany and the forces at play within it, by taking the development of compulsory health insurance as example.[12]

The history of compulsory health insurance shows very diverse characteristics of political evolution: several distinct offensive and defensive phases, as well as periods of a fragile balance between economic, political and ideological forces; four changes of strategy with very different implications during the protracted political struggles; and two clear phases of penetration and intervention by the international system in the national development of health insurance.

Against this background of a process of political evolution and its determining factors, the history of compulsory health insurance can be very roughly divided into eight phases:

(1) precursors of compulsory health insurance in the shape of workers' self-help organisations and state/communal poor relief;

(2) the beginnings of compulsory insurance and the abolition of self-help organisations through an alliance between landowners, heavy industry and feudal-conservative elites against the aims of a workers' movement on the political offensive;

(3) struggle between two 'social configurations' for the power over, and the shaping of, compulsory health insurance, against a background of precarious balance between political forces based on an alliance of both groupings during the period 1890-1914;

(4) partial strategic change, coupled with external intervention in the years 1918-20;

(5) period of fragile political balance, based on middle-class dominance, while both social configurations fight about the structure, function and further development of compulsory health insurance in the Weimar Republic;

(6) the polarisation of social groupings into expressly hostile alliances, and the strategic change to a 'Fascist counter-revolution' during the periods 1930-3 and 1933-45 respectively;

(7) external intervention by the victorious powers (in both parts of Germany), with the aim of restoring a liberal, market economy system at a time of fragile internal political, economic and ideological balance;

(8) strategic change of 1948/9 and subsequent 'balance of disparities' from 1951 onwards, bringing the restoration of the traditional system of compulsory health insurance.

The essential characteristic of the underlying class relations in the present phase of evolution of the welfare state is the clear economic, political and ideological dominance of the most important capital groups, which represent the 'block in power' and its 'ruling faction'. This permits the essential parameters of the welfare state's structure to be fixed as a scheme of compensations compatible with the system. This constellation is reinforced by a somewhat contradictory alliance with the traditional middle class and large sections of the new middle class. The main characteristic of the traditional workers' movement, certainly since Fascism, has been that large sections of the wage-earners, for all their objections, tended to accept this dominance and are to a large degree integrated into the existing apparatus of social mechanisms. Any hostile factions within the traditional labour movement, entertaining radical concepts of equality and strategies for the transformation of the welfare state, so far play a minor role, even though this may gain more force in times of crisis. In the political representation of this class structure, however, certain asymmetries can be observed. When relations between the conservative political elites and their corresponding class base ran into crisis and were disrupted as their political ineffectiveness as a ruling group became manifest in the late sixties, the offensive mounted by the social-liberal political elites, parties and groupings enabled these to establish themselves in the political arena and to become the ruling faction. During the latter's offensive phase a policy of 'internal reform' could thus be carried out, which led to a considerable expansion of the welfare state. This social policy campaign, however, soon encountered economic, political and ideological limitations which, on the level of political representation, in due course turned into a defensive, or rather into an offensive by the conservative political elites. The manifestation of this cyclical swing was the emergence of the 'new radical conservatism' described above.

Against the background of this actual constellation of forces and their offensive and defensive strategies, it is possible to outline very briefly some hypotheses regarding the future development of the welfare state in Germany.

(1) Even when the present economic crisis has been overcome, there do not, for the foreseeable future during the 1980s, appear to exist economic, political and ideological preconditions for an expansion of the welfare state comparable to that of the past 25 years. The previous period of expansive social policies thus probably constitutes an unusual phase in the welfare state's hundred-year history.

(2) In view of the constellation of forces between social classes and their political representatives, even rudimentary beginnings of a phase of transformation of social policy must be considered unlikely.

(3) Conversely, a far-reaching 'tax welfare revolt' and a consequent

roll-back (Wilensky) is equally unlikely, since the political and ideological forces the 'new radical conservatism' could muster would not be strong enough, even if there were a change of government, to counter the existing broad base of consensus that exists between social-liberal classes and elites.

(4) In view of the economic and political constellation of forces and the ideological positions taken up within the international system, extensive penetration by external power complexes into the Federal Republic which might lead to changes in strategy of one kind or another must be excluded for the foreseeable future.

(5) Since changes in strategy, whether internal through an effective offensive, or through external intervention, cannot be expected, the development of the welfare state in Germany will essentially be along the lines of a precarious balance. Disputes about social policy will range around the preservation of the substance and the levels attained so far, about their marginal extension or, more probable, their limited retrenchment.

(6) Such a weak development of controversy about the present *status quo*, however, brings its own political costs. These lie in an increasing and real danger to the human production capital, and an even greater one to the quality of life of wide sections of wage-earners, by threatening their health and thus their working capacity, their potential for attaining further qualifications and thus professional and social status, and it furthermore poses a threat to their extra-professional conditions for reproduction, through a deterioration in housing conditions and availability of space.

(7) Whether these objectively existing threats will, in the long term, produce the impetus for a further expansion of the welfare state, or indeed a transformation of social policy, or provide the occasion for an authoritarian, regressive involution of the system, will be a question of the internal erosion of the block in power and its allies, of the degree of integration within the traditional labour movement in the face of this dominance, possibly even a matter of increased external penetrations, and last but not least depend on the ability to organise and defend themselves of those forces within the workers' movement whose aim it is to achieve greater equality. Strategic changes of such dimensions, however, lie beyond the future of the welfare state as outlined here.

Notes

1. See Frieder Naschold, 'Gesamtgesellschaftliche Theorien als Grundlage für Prognosen einfacher und komplexer Systeme' in G. Bruckmann (ed.), *Langfristige Prognosen* (Würzburg-Vienna, 1977).
2. Cf, for example, Peter Flora's chapter in this volume.
3. E. Heimann, *Soziale Theorie des Kapitalismus* (Tübingen, 1929).
4. A good summary is to be found in P. Flora, *Modernisierungsforschung* (Opladen, 1974) and in G.V. Rimlinger, *Welfare Policy and Industrialization in Europe, America and Russia* (New York, 1971). Cf. also F. Naschold, 'Entwicklung des Wohlfahrtsstaates: Politische Mobilisierung und die Rolle des Staatsapparates – eine konzeptionelle und empirische Überprüfung kontroverser Theorieprogramme', IIVG Discussion Paper, Berlin, September 1978, pp. 11 ff.
5. See H. Heclo, 'Towards a New Welfare State?', manuscript, September 1978.
6. Cf. WSI Study on Economic and Social Research, no. 35, *Sozialpolitik und Selbstverwaltung*, Project headed by E. Standfest (Cologne, 1977), pp. 88 ff., also C. Altenstetter, E. Blankenburg, D. Grunow, F. Hegner, 'Probleme gesellschaftlicher Steuerung von Angebot und Inanspruchnahme öffentlicher Dienstleistungen', outline for a research programme, WZB Publikation GS-1979/1, Berlin, April 1979.
7. Cf. WSI-Studei, no. 35, as above; also M. Rein, *Social Policy* (New York, 1970).
8. Cf. J.M. Buchanan and R.E. Wagner, *Democracy in Deficit* (New York, 1977).
9. M. Janowitz, *Social Control of the Welfare State* (New York, 1976).
10. See Peter Flora's chapter in this volume.
11. Cf. Naschold, 'Entwicklung des Wohlfahrtsstaates', pp. 14 ff.
12. On analytics see N. Poulantzas, *Faschismus und Diktatur* (Munich, 1973); idem, *Klassen im Kapitalismus heute* (Berlin, 1975); also P. Mason, *Sozialpolitik im dritten Reich* (Opladen, 1977).

19 THE END OF THE WELFARE STATE?[1]

G.J. Room

Introduction

The preceding chapters have been predominantly historical in their orientation — as is demanded by the overall title of the volume. At the same time, however, the questions which the historian poses properly derive, whether explicitly or only implicitly, from the problems faced by actors in his *own* time — the present; and these questions are asked (again albeit only implicitly) in order to guide them in their choices among alternative futures.[2] It is thus entirely appropriate that at the end of a symposium such as this, the present and future problems of the welfare state should become the focus of attention. Moreover, if comparative studies need stimulating by collections such as this, so too is there a need for closer co-operation between historians and sociologists. While, therefore, the questions to be posed in the present chapter are sociological, the answers to them must be anchored in the sort of detailed historical research illustrated by the preceding contributions.

In many of these chapters the main focus has been upon policy-makers and such pressure groups as employers' organisations and trade unions. At the same time, there have been repeated references to wider social processes which provide the context of this policy-making. It is on these wider processes that we will be focusing here. Our questions will stand in direct succession to some of those posed by such sociologists as Max Weber, in the *Verein für Sozialpolitik*: for they centre on the role of social policy in securing the legitimation of the socio-political order.[3]

We shall, however, approach this via one of the other implicit themes of this work — the historical development, present state and future prospects of Social Democracy as a political movement and intellectual current. This is not to claim that the welfare states of Britain and Germany have been the creation of Social Democratic movements alone — indeed, many welfare developments have been opposed by these movements. Nor is it to ignore the differences between German and British Social Democracy — the former dominated by the thought of Marx and Lassalle, at least during the nineteenth century, the latter by that of the Fabians and, in the twentieth century, such figures as Tawney and G.D.H. Cole.[4] Nevertheless, Social Democracy has developed during the same period as the welfare state and to examine some of the dilemmas of Social Democracy in the last quarter of the twentieth century offers an insight into those of the welfare state also.

Our focus will be mainly upon Britain. As several previous chapters have recalled, for Marx Britain offered a model of the future facing less advanced nations: *'De te fabula narratur!'*[5] Today such a selection is much more problematic. More common is a focus upon the United States as providing such a model of 'post-industrial society' because, in Bell's words, there 'the processes of change are more advanced and visible.'[6] Nevertheless, it can be argued that despite its relative industrial and economic decline, Britain's current attempts to seek out a new basis of democratic social integration, appropriate to a mature industrial society in which traditional authority and economic power no longer suffice to ensure political order, hold out lessons likely to be of pressing relevance to her Western neighbours over the next half-century.[7]

We begin by looking at some of the main tenets of British Social Democracy in what is generally taken as the hey-day of the welfare state — the 1940s. We may then consider some of the principal weaknesses exposed in both Social Democracy and this welfare state over the subsequent three decades. Finally, we ask what may be the implication of this British experience for current dilemmas of Social Democracy and the welfare state in Germany.

British Social Democracy: the Hey-day

As in France and Germany, British Social Democracy attained maturity and coherence as a unified but distinct intellectual force in the first two decades of the present century — overshadowed as they were by the anticipation and experience of war. It is the Webbs and Tawney who were most influential in attempting to harness the British strands of social philosophy and analysis to a political strategy for Social Democracy. It is on them, therefore, that we concentrate.[8]

Tawney's intellectual position has certain parallels with that of Durkheim. For both of them, contemporary class conflict is an expression of the moral anarchy which a market society breeds. For neither, therefore, can such conflict be removed by economic or bureaucratic reorganisation alone. The positive role each of them prescribes for the state consists in its promotion of a principled moral order which is 'planned . . . to emphasise and strengthen . . . the common humanity which unites'[9] men and which, indeed, has a sacred character. This alone can engage the freely willed moral commitment and obligation of the mass of the population.

For Tawney, it was in the face of the wartime exigencies that the significance of this positive role was particularly and publicly evident. Full mobilisation on the military and industrial fronts required a mobilisation on the social front also — in the sense of an equality of sacrifice and a collective commitment to a more egalitarian society. This alone, in Tawney's view, could secure popular acquiescence during the war and its aftermath: an acquiescence which would go beyond either sullen or deferential compliance and would rather involve citizens as a collective force for social transformation. Out of the international conflict engendered by unprincipled capitalism would come the reordering of society as morally just and hence socially cohesive. For Tawney, then, Social Democracy involved 'a dialectic between legislation from above *and* active citizenship from below'.[10] This insistence on the necessarily democratic character of any effective programmes of social reform, with moral solidarity or fraternity both their seed and their fruit, is perhaps Tawney's principal intellectual legacy to the Social Democracy which came to political dominance only in the aftermath of another war.

Nevertheless, it was the Webbs whose ideas had the greater influence on British Social Democratic thought.[11] For them, Social Democracy as a pathway and as a goal centred in social administration and reform from above. Their confidence in the political efficacy of rational argument and their optimism as to the harmony of interests which these reforms would promote attest their indebtedness to the liberal tradition and to utilitarianism in particular.

However, when these hopes inherited by the Webbs' heirs flowered into euphoria in the 1940s, the hey-day of Social Democracy, they held dangers of intellectual myopia. First, the Webbs' social theories and political strategy encouraged a reliance on Labour governments at least to pursue policies which aimed at radical social transformation and which would heed the findings of the rational social investigator. Yet constellations of interest typically develop which link political leaders to advantaged groups in the wider society, in face of which early vision may fade and the findings of social inquiry be ineffectual.[12] Secondly, the welfare professional and administrator were seen as benignly countering the depravations of urban-industrial change.

As one Social Democrat wrote in mid-century: 'It is [the professions']
business . . . to construct a scale of human values . . . it rests with
them. . . to find for the sick and suffering democracies a peaceful
solution of their problems.'[13] Thirdly, these Social Democratic apolo-
gists, while recognising the social legislation of the 1940s as both an
expression and a catalyst of widespread commitment to shared social
purposes, tended to neglect the difficulties inherent in the political
task of mobilising such commitments in the face of self-interested
action.

Each of these hopes has been challenged by the post-war experience of the welfare state. In the present chapter, we will limit ourselves to discussion of the third. What then, more fully, did the Social
Democrats of the 1940s believe their social reforms would achieve by
way of engendering commitment to shared goals? Let us consider
their view of social integration and the possibilities of social harmony,
the role of social policy in such integration and, thirdly, the implications of social policy for individual action and group formation. Their
thought in part represents a response to the perceived failings of both
liberalism and Marxism.

For the liberal, social integration proceeds from the manifest rationality of a society organised in market or meritocratic terms: each citizen perceives that such a form of organisation identifies his own self-
interested endeavours with the common good. In contrast, Titmuss
and T.H. Marshall, whom we may take as representative of the Social
Democrats, believe that an advanced urban-industrial society cannot,
even in principle, be organised in such a way that the pursuit of self-
interest is a sufficient basis for social integration and social harmony.
A subordination of self-interest to the common interest must be
evoked. Contemporary Marxist writers see social integration under
capitalism as effected through coercion and ideological manipulation.
Appeals to the common interest run counter to the true interests
of the proletariat, whose position in but not of civil society means
that these interests cannot but be wholly in conflict with those of
other classes and, indeed, with the maintenance of class society as
such. Against this view the Social Democrats argue, first, that whatever the merits of Marx's analysis of the society of his own day, there
exists in contemporary society some potential community of interest
among members of different classes. Social integration need not, therefore, be wholly coercive, but may, in part at least, be rooted in interests
common to all. Secondly, they deny that in our advanced Western
societies coercion and ideological manipulation can suffice to secure

political stability. Rather, the latter requires some degree of freely willed acquiescence in — and commitment to — the socio-political order; and popular legitimation of the collective purpose it embodies. At the risk of over-simplification, therefore, we might summarise by saying that against the Marxist view that the social integration of contemporary Western society cannot but be coercive and the liberal view that it is basically self-interested or calculative, these Social Democratic writers echo Durkheim's thesis that social integration must be seen as essentially a *moral* phenomenon.[14]

Social policy is then seen in terms of its potential for evoking such moral commitment to the common welfare. It realises, to this extent, a novel system of social disciplines, which contrast both with the work ethic and market incentives applauded by classic liberalism and with the monopolisation of access to the means of life which, in classical Marxism, is deemed the basis of the coercive power of the capitalist. Titmuss emphasises this theme most notably, perhaps, in his first and last major works. In *Problems of Social Policy*[15] and elsewhere he examines the wartime crucible in which the post-war welfare state was forged. Universalist social policies aimed at meeting the primary needs of all citizens became an instrument for fostering moral commitment to the national war effort and sustaining public morale: this notwithstanding the additional obligations and social disciplines which this enlargement of social policy entailed.[16] Here Titmuss' debt to Tawney is especially evident. In *The Gift Relationship*[17] he is likewise concerned with the consequences of different social policies for the readiness of citizens freely to place collective needs before their own individual interests; and thereby with the uses of social policy as an instrument of *moral* discipline.

Finally, what are the implications of social policy for group formation and individual action? We have, by implication, just considered Titmuss' view of the way in which universalist social policies define as a group all those enjoying the social rights of citizenship. For T.H. Marshall, the extension of the social rights of citizenship involves the granting of a common status — in this case to all those of British nationality. Such shared honour will be subjectively perceived by the citizens concerned and will be manifested in a willingness to discharge the duties, as well as enjoying the rights, of this new status. It involves a 'direct sense of community membership based on loyalty to a civilisation which is a common possession'.[18]

As Halsey has recently argued, therefore, Social Democracy in

Britain includes a set of intellectual traditions, insights and aspirations which centre in the political ideal of fraternity,[19] albeit strongly infused with paternalism. Yet, to repeat, there has been some tendency on the part of Social Democrats to play down the political problems involved in mobilising a widespread commitment to shared purposes which will override acquisitive individualism. T.H. Marshall, admittedly, is not altogether confident that this sense of civic duty will emerge strongly and spontaneously: for 'the community is so large that . . . obligation appears remote and unreal.'[20] In contrast, Titmuss, in his last major work to which we have already referred, *The Gift Relationship*, re-affirms his belief in the possibility of engendering fraternity at this level of society as a whole, by means of universalist social policies. His study has become a contemporary classic which latter-day Social Democrats have enthusiastically embraced. By examining its argument and assumptions we may, however, identify weaknesses in Social Democracy, as an intellectual current and political movement, whose gravity the social dislocations of the 1970s further underline.

Social Democracy, Social Welfare and Social Order

Given his concern to demonstrate the contribution to social solidarity which universalist social services can make, it is not perhaps surprising that Titmuss focuses upon the National Health Service, the most prized achievement of post-war Social Democratic universalism. Titmuss explores the dependence of the sick upon their fellow citizens and the patterns of community formation and action that different modes of organising medical care may foster. The specific arena he uses to argue his case, however, is as fascinating in its selection as in the lesson he derives: the provision of blood for transfusion purposes.

Blood transfusion has assumed a continuously growing importance in medical services in recent decades. There has been a rapid growth in the demand for blood and blood products; and 'in the foreseeable future, there appears to be no predictable limit to demand.'[21] However, there are two critical characteristics of blood and of existing methods of collecting, storing and distributing it. First, it has a 21-day life when stored under refrigeration and out-dating can thus result in great wastage. Secondly, the presence of infection in donated blood — and, in particular, the problem of serum hepatitis — cannot be detected except by its effect on the recipient. These together imply that 'the attributes required of donors, if the needs of patients are to be properly met and if wastage is to be avoided, are consistency, regularity, responsibility and honesty. Dramatic, emotional and episodic responses to appeals for blood' addressed to donors whose honesty concerning their health is inadequate will foster wastage and the transmission of disease.[22]

In the NHS, blood donorship is entirely voluntary: no penalties, financial or otherwise, are involved. Moreover, such donorship cannot be portrayed as narrowly self-interested; for there are no 'tangible immediate rewards in monetary or non-monetary forms' and donors are not 'free to ... decide on the specific destination of the gifts': The latter choice is 'a moral and political decision for society as a whole' and the gift is thereby rendered anonymous. Yet such a delivery system appears to meet the criteria of effectiveness discussed above. Donors respond regularly and reliably to calls from the Health Service and this, together with the central co-ordination of a unified service, has meant that wastage has been minimal. Furthermore, the trans-mission of infection seems to have been particularly low by inter-national standards, suggesting honesty of donors in respect of their medical histories. Finally, the NHS 'has never ... been aware of a shortage or an impending shortage of potential donors'.[23] Those who already give are a broad cross-section of the society as a whole, rather than being self-selected in terms of some social or economic category; and this confirms, for Titmuss, that there is no obvious constraint upon the long-term proportion of the population who may be recruited as donors, other than considerations of donors' own health.[24]

Titmuss goes on to enquire into the meaning which donors confer on their giving. The reasons uncovered by his survey include wide-spread feelings of altruism and reciprocity, 'suggesting a high sense of social responsibility towards the needs of other members of society'. At the same time,

> no donor type can be depicted in terms of complete, disinterested, spontaneous altruism. There must be some sense of obligation, approval and interest; some feeling of 'inclusion' in society; some awareness of need and the purposes of the gift. What was seen by these donors as a good for strangers in the here-and-now could be ... a good for themselves — indeterminately one day.

That is, they held confidently to a 'belief in the willingness of other men to act altruistically in the future, and to combine together to make a gift freely available should they have a need for it'.[25]

Yet, Titmuss argues, the trust and social obligation among citizens expressed by such voluntary donation is dependent upon the NHS principle of treating according to medical need without charge to the patient. Hence, for example, what the supplier has donated the NHS may not sell: but 'must respect the donor's intentions and ... use it for the purpose for which it was intended'.[26] The intrusion of the cash nexus would render the altruism of one's fellow citizens as blood donors an insufficient condition for receipt of effective medical treatment: and would, moreover, tend to corrode that altruism, by defining medical care as the object of an individual contract rather than a community obligation. Or, equivalently, citizens' experience of the NHS mediates an image of society as a community of citizens with mutual obligations and rights, despite their anonymity; and it is in terms of this image that they orient their actions.

The NHS thus mediates a transfer of blood donations – a circulation of gifts which Titmuss likens to those documented for simple societies by Mauss.[27] Or, equivalently, its principles of treatment not only involve a collective obligation towards the sick, but also give public recognition and symbolic expression to the circulation of citizens among the roles of the healthy, the sick and the relatives of the sick. For those principles formally involve a treatment of the sick on criteria of medical need alone, and the provision of health care resources according to the abilities of the healthy to contribute. Such circulation is in turn acknowledged by citizens, who recognise their obligation to contribute when healthy, at least to the extent of freely providing blood. Mutual dependence, rather than the pursuit of independence, is the basis of mutual regard.

In contrast, Titmuss and others have argued, the provision of means-tested benefits tends to promote an image of two distinct categories of human beings: those who are independent and competent and those who 'do not share the same human feelings that move the rest of the population to behave decently'[28] and who therefore need to be controlled and disciplined for their own good, as well as that of society as a whole. Such social policies thus give symbolic expression to the supposedly minimal movement of individuals between the roles of the needy and the independent. This gulf is in turn acknowledged by citizens of the wider society; who respond in social stigmatisation of the dependent and in political support for social policies which, being focused upon the multiple pathology of that well defined category, will deny the universality of need as the basis for inclusion of the dependent in the community of full citizens.

For Titmuss, this vindicates the Social Democratic case in face of its liberal and Marxist rivals. Against the liberals, he has demonstrated that social obligation and altruism are socially necessary; but that they are logically distinct from the untrammelled pursuit of narrow self-interest, since they are by definition unconditional on personal marginal opportunity cost. Yet he has also shown that within a framework of services which give public recognition and symbolic expression to citizens' mutual dependence, they willingly affirm commitments to collective goals, even at some cost to their own interests. Against the Marxists, Titmuss has shown how universalist social policies can give public recognition to interests common to all — a recognition which evokes a response from all social classes of freely willed acquiescence in societal functioning. Despite the divisions and conflicts which may be generated within the prevailing mode of production, such social policies provide the means of establishing democratic socialism. Social Democracy thus offers not only an analysis of advanced urban-industrial society which is superior to its rivals, but also a prescription which is politically feasible.

Challenges to Fraternity: the End of Social Democracy?

We may choose to accept Titmuss' judgement that in our urban-industrial society, the promotion of moral integration is the only alternative to authoritarian repression or accelerating social conflict. Nevertheless, his study also has certain important limitations and we must therefore be circumspect in using it to generalise about the capacity of universalist social policies to evoke such integration. These limitations concern what we may, for short, term the *costs*, the *objects* and the *indivisibility* of fraternity.

The Costs of Fraternity

It may well be true that universalist services tend to engender altruism and moral obligations among citizens: that is, to promote actions oriented to collective goals, irrespective of personal marginal opportunity cost. Yet the cost of donating blood is low; the *strength* of the obligation which such services promote has therefore been tested only minimally. Yet during much of the post-war period, Social Democrats — both intellectuals and politicians — have assumed that in social programmes more generally, the costs imposed on the relatively privileged could remain limited and widespread support for such programmes thereby retained.

First, it was continuing economic growth that would enable increased standards for the social services and absolute, if not relative, improvements in the conditions of life of the underprivileged. Redistribution from the advantaged would have a secondary role only. In the event, this hope has been disappointed in the 1970s with the world recession and, in Britain at least, near-zero economic growth.

Secondly, the privileges of the few would not so much be removed, in a process of 'levelling-down', as extended to become universal rights. Sufficiently high-quality collective and universal provision would then attract support and use even by the middle and upper classes. Admittedly, this progressive translation of privileges into social rights was likely to promote escalation of statutory social budgets. Nevertheless, the appropriation and experience of social rights could also be expected to generate an increased willingness by all sectors of society to contribute to those budgets and to supplement statutory resources with voluntary effort, as a social duty of citizenship. In short, then, the political task of mobilising general commitment to the duties of citizenship could be kept within attainable limits.

Here there have been two sorts of challenge. On the one hand, the Social Democrats' optimism has waned over the sufficiency of universalist services alone to secure social rights and to change fundamentally the existing pattern of inequalities and interests. They have tended increasingly to place new hopes in additional measures of positive (or 'affirmative') discrimination towards the underprivileged.[29] Yet these do, of course, imply and appear as deliberate discrimination *against* the more privileged and more overt imposition on them of the costs of redistributive welfare.

So, too, the Social Democrats have neglected the extent to which privileges may be desired — and their extension resisted — precisely because they *are* privileges, symbolising the life-style of powerful strata and granting access to their monopolised opportunities. In education, for example, the ideology of equal opportunity has provided a widely accepted legitimation in the post-war period for the individualistic acquisition of formal qualifications within an unequal society: an acquisitiveness oriented in large measure to the preservation or improvement of credentials *relative* to those of others. The apparently unending expansion of demand for the life chances distributed by the welfare state is exposed as expressing not so much rising expectations of common standards of provision, but rather inherently unrealisable —

because universal — demands for access to positions of privilege. Here are the 'positional goods' which Hirsch has recently analysed in his *Social Limits to Growth*.[30]

In the present recession and public expenditure cuts, combined with renewed agitation across the advanced Western world over levels of personal taxation, the Social Democrats' hopes of translating privileges into universal social rights are rendered increasingly difficult. Indeed, what has for several decades been taken as perhaps the most well established universal social right — that to employment — has increasingly been translated into a privilege of the more powerful.[31] At the same time, in Britain at least, the social policy debate has tended to shift away from positive discrimination for the underprivileged and towards such issues as general educational standards and family policy. These have a more universal but also a more self-interested appeal. Together these developments seem to signify the erosion of altruism and moral solidarity in face of shared adversity.

The Objects of Fraternity

Titmuss studies a need which is likely to appear to the typical citizen as being particularly 'objective' and unproblematic in its definition. Moreover, as citizens circulate between the ranks of the sick and the healthy, they will be well aware of the potential universality of ill health and their common vulnerability. Whether or not the recipient of the blood can reciprocate the gift, therefore, he is likely to enjoy high 'moral credibility'. Titmuss may have chosen a case where the political task of mobilising society's commitment to a common object of fraternal concern is at its easiest.

More generally, however, this task is likely to be less straightforward: especially where the 'need' in question is less objective in its definition and is an adversity to which only certain sections of society tend to see themselves as vulnerable. For example, although by postwar standards rates of unemployment are now high, this tends to be concentrated in particular occupational groups and age ranges. The low moral credibility of the unemployed in the eyes of the wider society is then signified by the way in which welfare benefits are organised as much to enforce work disciplines as to enable them to subsist;[32] and, equally, by the ease with which crusaders against welfare 'scroungers' find a ready popular audience.[33]

The Indivisibility of Fraternity

In *The Gift Relationship* Titmuss focuses on personal health care: where treatment is typically provided on an individual and privatised basis and is undertaken by a profession enjoying well developed and secure claims to esoteric knowledge and public trustworthiness. In consequence, criteria for evaluating and challenging other milieux — in terms, for example, of their propensity to generate ill health — are not immediately available to the citizen who appropriates his rights to health care; but are, rather, the province of the medical professional or the epidemiologist.

Elsewhere, however, the social rights which universalist social services embody may well be as likely to promote resentment as fraternity. Indeed, as Goldthorpe has recently argued,[34] this is an aspect of T.H. Marshall's original essay on 'Citizenship and Social Class',[35] of which insufficient account has been taken by his successors. For Marshall's position differs from that of liberal pluralists such as Bendix, who see social rights of citizenship as promoting consensus and acquiescence in the stable functioning of the open — indeed, the good — society.[36] Rather, for Marshall such rights are ambivalent in their implications for social solidarity and the legitimation of the sociopolitical order. The experience of social rights may tend to engender new expectations and popular demands for further social transformation — in the occupational division of labour, for example. Here are possible lines of increased conflict rather than its abatement; with an extension rather than a reduction in the range of societal life subjected to popular political scrutiny.

In retrieving this aspect of Marshall's analysis, Goldthorpe surveys the secular implications of the growth of citizenship rights for social integration in general and the occupational order in particular. He argues that much of the industrial conflict and disruption of the 1970s must be understood as being in part the fruit of the extension of these rights. For they provide a sharp contrast with 'the unprincipled inequalities thrown up by the market';[37] at the same time, however, they facilitate the development of the instruments with which resentment at such inequalities can be given overt expression — for example, independent trade unions. In the 1970s, it has been against the inequalities in industrial rights — most notably in respect of job security and powers of decision-making — that this resentment has been most obviously directed. 'The new thrust of citizenship, in its on-going war with class, is specifically aimed against the idea ... of labour as a commodity.'[38] Goldthorpe then concludes that if these developments require that

> successive generations of a working class should have grown up alike within a stable national community, in which citizenship rights have been upheld and developed, and in which therefore workers have been able to pursue their industrial and political interests by means of their own organisations, [then the British experience] may be taken as the most developed manifestation of tendencies, or potentialities, which are in fact generally present in the societies of the advanced capitalist world.[39]

It follows that for Social Democracy to remain viable as a political movement and intellectual current, Social Democratic political leaders must abandon their confidence in the spontaneous fraternity which social reforms can both express and evoke. They will need to spell out more deliberately and consciously the costs of citizenship, the mutual obligations it involves and the wider societal reorganisation which its realisation requires.

The task of securing popular acquiescence and of overcoming the opposition of vested interests will be at best difficult. It will involve drawing on and cultivating the traditions of mutual aid which exist among both working and middle classes; advancing social policies which are openly and explicitly linked to the wider reconstruction of society as a moral order; and pointing out the costs of failure. That is, it will involve political leaders in pursuing what Weber termed the 'ethic of responsibility':[40] choosing and imperiously defining social values for their followers, having full regard to the probable consequences, rather than surrendering fateful societal decisions to the putative dictates of historical inevitability or the requirements of short-term political expediency. But to ignore these tasks is likely to promote the progressive corrosion of the gift relationships of mutual obligation and common purpose which the Social Democrats prize — that is, of fraternity itself. It is also likely to undermine the credibility and legitimacy of this political leadership itself.

Thus, as other writers have recently argued, the costs of failure are high. Hirsch contemplates our 'depleting moral legacy'. He points to the moral 'vacuum in social organisation [whereby] the market system . . . may sabotage its own foundations'.[41] So too, Fox points to the economic and industrial costs which a 'low trust' society, lacking shared moral purposes, must bear; and warns that 'once the low-trust framework exists it tends to . . . enlarge rather than minimise the area of conflict'. He searches for 'the social forces which [can] set limits to the expression of low-trust behaviours'; and argues that these can issue only from 'a radical reconstruction [of social institutions] which seeks to rally major sections of society behind shared purposes of social justice'.[42] Here, then, is a society in which the fragile legitimacy of our contemporary welfare state has been further eroded; with the political order characterised by widespread apathy or overt social conflict, together with authoritarian attempts to impose social order.[43]

Conclusion: Anglo-German Comparisons

This has been an exploration of the contemporary implications of the citizenship rights whose development and significance in Britain Marshall so profoundly and eloquently analysed. Dahrendorf has already provided the beginnings of a comparison with German developments: albeit from the standpoint of a liberal Anglophile. His discussion is rightly rooted in a historical analysis of Germany's path to modernisation. He emphasises the weakness of the liberal tradition in Germany, and the orientation of welfare provision to maintenance of established and paternalistic hierarchies rather than to the universal rights of freely associating individual citizens.[44]

It is precisely such universalism that the British Social Democrats have seen as the basis of the fraternity they seek to promote: a fraternity harking back to the mutual aid of working-class organisations and the voluntary welfare activity of the middle class, but now universalised, organised and mediated by the state. Likewise, however, it is this same universalism which also lends to social rights their critical edge: making them a catalyst to the extension of social criticism. We still await a development of Dahrendorf's account which will provide a comparative study of social welfare and Social Democracy in the two countries, drawing on the rich agenda which Marshall's analysis continues to offer. It is an agenda which, as suggested in the opening section of this chapter, will require the sort of collaboration of historians and sociologists from both countries which this book exemplifies.

Notes

1. This essay draws heavily on the author's *The Sociology of Welfare*, (London, 1979).

2. See, for example, R.G. Collingwood, *The Idea of History* (Oxford, 1961), pp. 302-34.

3. See D. Beetham, *Max Weber and the Theory of Modern Politics* (London, 1974), esp. Ch. 6 and p. 222f.

4. J.M. Winter, *Socialism and the Challenge of War* (London, 1974).

5. *Capital*, Vol. 1, Preface to the first German edition.

6. *The Coming of Post-Industrial Society* (London, 1974), p. x.

7. A.H. Halsey, *Change in British Society* (Oxford, 1978), p. 123.

8. Winter, *Socialism*. Winter takes G.D.H. Cole as representing a third strand — but goes on to argue that Cole eventually shifted into 'the Webbian centre of socialist thought' (ibid., p. 283).

9. R.H. Tawney, *Equality* (London 1969), p. 49.

10. R. Terrill, *R.H. Tawney and His Times* (London, 1974), p. 261; cf. Tawney, *Equality*, p. 219.

11. But on whether these ideas were an authentic part of the socialist and labour traditions, see E.J. Hobsbawm, *Labouring Men: Studies in the History of Labour* (London, 1964), Ch. 14.

12. Cf. Weber's discussion of those political leaders who came to live *off*, rather than *for*, politics (Beetham, *Max Weber*, pp. 228-30).

13. T.H. Marshall, *Class, Citizenship and Social Development* (New York, 1965), p. 179.

14. S.M. Lukes, *Emile Durkheim: His Life and Work* (London, 1973).

15. London, 1950. See too R.M. Titmuss, 'War and Social Policy' in *Essays on the Welfare State* (London, 1963).

16. *Problems of Social Policy*, esp. Chs. 2 and 17. See too the contribution to this volume by Dr José Harris.

17. Harmondsworth, 1973.

18. Marshall, *Class*, p. 101.

19. Ibid.

20. Ibid., p. 129.

21. Ibid., p. 47.

22. Ibid., p. 27.

23. Ibid., pp. 97, 272-3, 136.

24. Ibid., pp. 141 ff., 29-30.

25. Ibid., pp. 266, 268-9, 163.

26. A. Heath, *Rational Choice and Social Exchange* (Cambridge, 1976), p. 153.

27. M. Mauss, *The Gift* (London, 1970).

28. B. Jordan, *Poor Parents* (London, 1974), p. 183.

29. R.M. Titmuss, *Commitment to Welfare* (London, 1968), pp. 134-6. For a recent American view, see N. Glazer, *Affirmative Discrimination* (New York, 1975).

30. London, 1977.

31. A. Sinfield, 'The Social Meaning of Unemployment' in K. Jones (ed.), *The Year Book of Social Policy in Britain 1976* (London, 1977).

32. Jordan, *Poor Parents* and *Paupers* (London, 1973); D. Marsden and E. Duff, *Workless* (Harmondsworth, 1975).

33. A Sinfield, 'The Unemployed, Policy and Public Debate', mimeo, University of Essex: prepared for SSRC Workshop on Social Security, 18 March 1977.

34. J.H. Goldthorpe, 'The Current Inflation: Towards a Sociological Account' in F. Hirsch and J.H. Goldthorpe (eds.), *The Political Economy of Inflation* (London, 1978), esp. pp. 201-4.

35. Ibid., Ch. 4.

36. See D. Lockwood, 'For T.H. Marshall', *Sociology*, vol. 8, no. 3 (Sept. 1974), pp. 363-7.

37. Ibid., p. 202.

38. Ibid., p. 203.

39. Ibid., pp. 206, 197.

40. See Beetham, *Max Weber*, p. 174.

41. *Social Limits to Growth*, p. 143.

42. A. Fox, *Beyond Contract: Work Power and Trust Relations* (London, 1974), pp. 318-19, 358.

43. J.H. Goldthorpe, 'Social Inequality and Social Integration in Modern Britain' in D. Wedderburn (ed.), *Poverty, Inequality and Class Structure* (Cambridge, 1974), p. 233.

44. R. Dahrendorf, *Society and Democracy in Germany* (London, 1967), esp. Part 3.

20 FROM THE NATIONAL WELFARE STATE TO THE INTERNATIONAL WELFARE SYSTEM

K.W. Deutsch

The Rise of Welfare Policies Within a Nation: the Experiences of Western Europe

For most countries of North-western Europe the nineteenth century was characterised by six interrelated patterns of social change. The first two of these processes arose as consequences of the late stages of monetisation of the economy and of the processes which some historians have put under the heading of 'commercial revolution'. By the late eighteenth century daily life in the relatively developed West European states was permeated by monetary relationships. Individuals and companies were accumulating capital. Manufactures were spreading and the factory system and the Industrial Revolution were either beginning or about to begin.

The state machinery was becoming modern in the sense that office-holders were paid in money and were, at least in part, selected and promoted in terms of performance and bureaucratic rationality. The 'tax-collecting state', as Joseph Schumpeter called it, the bureaucratic system of administration, and a fairly well developed commercial market economy were already in place when they received the gradual or rapid impact of industrialisation, and of the political struggles of the middle class and their lower-class allies against absolute monarchy and aristocratic rule.

The nineteenth century brought mass education and nearly general literacy before the century was out. The same century brought universal conscription. Standing armies were kept at or near 1 per cent of the total population and the terms of service were relatively short, usually between two and three years. This meant, in practice, that nearly all able-bodied young men in a country, across all social strata, were taught to shoot.

Mass conscription and mass education were supplemented by the growth of mass organisations. Trade unions among factory workers, credit co-operatives and farmers' organisations among the rural population, associations of employers and manufacturers among owners of capital, and the gradual transformation of the traditional artisans' guilds into more modern interest organisations all contributed to spread the skills of social and political organisation throughout the country.

A fifth element was the rise of mass media of communication. The press, read earlier only by the educated few, now profited from the results of mass education and began to provide newspapers for the masses.

The sixth and last process to which I wish to draw attention was the change in culture and values. Disadvantaged groups increasingly learned to demand a greater share in the good things in life. Hitherto privileged groups were divided politically and psychologically between a straightforward effort to defend or even enhance their privileges with the help of whatever ideological justification came to hand (ranging from authoritarian religion to the pseudo-biology of Social Darwinism) and a less conspicuous, but very real counter-trend within their own minds and the minds of their children. This counter-trend was an increase in social sensitivity. The literature of the period is full of descriptions telling a middle-class public 'how the other half lives'.

Modern class interpretations of late nineteenth-century politics dwell on the greed of the upper classes, but they often underestimate their sense of shame. When the dockworkers' strike of 1889 in England drew attention to their poverty, many middle-class persons contributed to the support of the strikers. The theatre-going public of London's West End flocked to the plays of Bernard Shaw, such as *Widowers' Houses* and *Major Barbara*, somewhat as German theatre-goers responded to the social concern expressed in the early plays of Gerhard Hauptmann, *Die Weber* and *Rose Bernd*.

A final element in the rise of the national welfare state was that of prudent anticipation on the part of some conservative leaders such as Benjamin Disraeli, later Lord Beaconsfield, in England, and Otto, Prince Bismarck, in Germany. Disraeli had expressed his social concern as early as 1839 in his novel, *Sibyl, or The Two Nations*. In 1867 he was instrumental in bringing about the legal right to vote for the British urban working class. (The vote for the British rural workers followed in 1884.) Bismarck brought about equal voting rights for German workers for the Reichstag in 1871 (although extremely unequal voting rights remained in force for the elections to the Prussian Diet). In the two decades after 1871, Bismarck then introduced legislation that brought about national old age pensions and health insurance for workers and employees.

The details of this development are unimportant here. What counts is the interplay of the great processes of change which enhanced at one and the same time policy needs, political demands and the political and organisational capacities of large masses of the population, and on the other hand, the combination of increased social sensitivity and growing prudence and foresight among parts of the privileged strata and among some of their leaders. The result of these combined developments was the modern welfare state. Eventually this welfare state claimed to provide at least partial safeguards for wage-earners and other members of the poorer strata against old age, work-related accidents and illnesses, threats to public health, and eventually in increased measure against general risks of ill health.

The resulting type of welfare state can be described very roughly by a number of quantitative indicators. The indicators presented here will describe the modern welfare state in terms of the late 1970s as it has emerged mainly in West Europe, North America, Australia and New Zealand in the course of the last hundred years.

Among the private enterprise countries and in parts of the Communist world, as of this date in December 1978, there seems to be not a single highly developed country in the world that is not a welfare state. That is to say, every highly developed industrial country is providing the social and educational services indicated earlier.

A typical welfare state of our time has a *per capita* income of more than $5,000 at 1975 prices. Children born in it have a life expectancy of 72 years ±2. The death rate among infants is about 16 ±5 per 1,000 for the first year after birth. Literacy among people aged 15 and over is 97 per cent ±2. Income inequality among households, as measured by the Gini Index, is about 38 per cent ±7. Differently put, the top 5 per cent of income-receiving households tend to get about 19 per cent ±6 of the income, whereas the share of the bottom 20 per cent would be 6 per cent ±2. The ratio of the incomes of the top 5 per cent and bottom 20 per cent is about 4 to 1; between the top 20 per cent and the bottom 20 per cent, about 9 to 1. Inter-regional disparities, that is differences between the average *per capita* income of the richest and poorest states or provinces within a highly developed country range between 4 to 1 and 1.5 to 1. In contrast to the old empires, the modern welfare state has turned out to be an engine for the reduction of inter-regional differences.

Modern welfare states have shown a high degree of social stability, except in times of economic depression. During the 33 years from 1945 to 1978 only one government of a highly developed welfare state was overthrown by force, that of France in 1958 by the Gaullist revolution, and even that change of regime occurred with very little bloodshed. Tendencies of violence in a modern welfare state during those 33 years have remained limited to very small extremist groups with no broad popular support.

While modern welfare states show few tendencies towards violence, they show considerable trends towards change. As real incomes have risen for most people, the marginal utility of additional increments in income has declined, but the marginal utility of increments in leisure has increased. Industrial workers in many countries show a declining willingness to work overtime, and trade unions in many countries are demanding provisions for earlier retirement for workers, as well as reductions in the work week. At the same time, higher income and greater leisure have led to more frequent overloading and congestion of channels of transport and communication and of opportunities for human contact and access to desired experiences. This in turn has tended to raise the marginal utility of increments in status and power since these mean a higher priority for access to desired channels of communication. A symptom of this trend has been a partial shift in consumer spending to so-called 'status' goods and services.

Non-welfare States: the Developing Countries

The aspects which we listed as typical for the rise and function of the modern welfare state are absent in most of the developing countries. Industrialisation there is feeble. Tax-collecting systems are weak. Bureaucrats are still recruited in considerable part through patronage and family connections, rather than by any criteria of performance and pure rationality. Many public officials live only partly on their salaries, and often to a larger extent on informal payments exacted from favoured clients or from the general population. Often, though not always, there is no effective conscription, so that only small portions of the population are trained in military skills. Mass education and literacy are most often quite incomplete. Mass organisations are rare and even more rarely are they permitted an autonomous policy in defence of the interests of their members. The penetration of daily life by the mass media is incomplete. Most of such media as exist only present a viewpoint of the government or of a few privileged groups. In effect, they are not free to follow the interests of their readers in a broad and free competitive market.

The culture and values of the privileged classes in these countries are most often characterised by social insensitivity and irresponsibility. The suffering of the poor is treated as inevitable or as unimportant. Sensitivity, concern or shame about the state of affairs felt by some of the young members of the privileged strata only sometimes lead to effective reform, and more often to the political isolation of small groups and their alienation from the state.

In these countries, little or no welfare legislation exists in law and even less of it is effective in reality. On average these countries are poor and the marginal utility of additional income is quite high, even to those who already have some power in the state. Power-holders strive to get rich and the rich strive to get richer. By contrast, the value of human life is rated low and the life of the poor is worth little. The marginal utility of status and power is high, both as ends in themselves and as means to acquire wealth. But status and power are often difficult to acquire within the system, except in times of upheaval. Where the regime is stable, they are allocated by ascription. They go to those individuals who are expected to have them because of descent or family connections or membership of a political or ideological clique.

This would result in a tendency towards stagnation and immobility if the regimes were not at some time unstable. Frequent military *coups* do not change the structure of the system, but may provide a new set of incumbents for its higher offices, but larger insurrections or revolutions are not rare. Pakistan, Iran and Nicaragua might be recent examples of politics in countries of this type.

It should be noted that there are also a few poor man's welfare states in the world. These are countries with relatively low *per capita* incomes and weak or uneven industrial sectors, but with considerable welfare legislation and with some real efforts to deliver a fair degree of welfare services to a broader stratum of the population. India and Costa Rica in the private enterprise world, as well as perhaps Uruguay in the 1930s, and perhaps Cuba and China among the Communist countries might be possible examples.

Most of the world's developing countries, however, are real non-welfare states of the type sketched earlier. The *per capita* income of such a country is typically below $2,400 in 1975 prices. Life expectancy at birth is about 52 ±10 years. The infant death rate for the first year of birth is about 113 ±47 per 1,000. Literacy varies broadly around 42 per cent ±30. The Gini Index of income and inequality for households is about 52 per cent ±8. The top 5 per cent of income-receivers get about 31 ± 8 per cent of the total income and the poorest

20 per cent get about 4 per cent ±1 per cent. The ratio between the top and bottom 20 per cent is 8 to 1 and between the top 20 per cent and the bottom 20 per cent it is about 15 to 1. All these indicators of income inequality are substantially larger in a typical non-welfare state than they would be in a highly developed welfare state, in some cases by an order of magnitude. Inter-regional disparities in a non-welfare state might average 15 to 1 between the richest and poorest regions; this again is one order of magnitude larger than in the highly developed welfare states.

Whereas each welfare state has tended to develop within the hundred years or less after the Industrial Revolution, the poverty, low life expectancy and vast income inequality of the non-welfare states has existed in many cases for several centuries or more. Often it has even been made worse during the period of early monetisation and industrialisation.

Despite these differences between highly industrialised welfare states and less industrialised non-welfare ones, one should not forget that most states in both categories are countries and states that somehow have been holding together. Each of them has a fair degree of internal economic interdependence, creating something of a national market for a fair number of goods and services. Each of them is characterised by compatible institutions so as not to be torn apart by acute and uncontrollable political and economic conflict. Within each of them, in most cases, there is also a clear power gradient between the central government and the social groups and regions that support it, on the one hand, and any geographically or politically peripheral groups, on the other hand, that might prefer secession. In some societies, compatible institutions and political unity are so strong that relatively little central power has been needed and secessionist attempts were defeated by co-operative effort. Switzerland and the United States would be examples of this type. In other cases the central government has been less broadly supported but has been able to concentrate in its hands a great preponderance of power and resources. In extreme cases the armed forces under the central government's control are primarily trained and deployed for warfare, not against an external enemy, but against their own people. Even then, however, governmental instability and local uprisings in such countries are not rare.

The Present World System as a Non-welfare State

The political system of the world as presently constituted differs strikingly from the political system of its countries. There is no one preponderant centre of power. Only once, in 1946, did one country, the United States, have more than one-half of the world's income. This was an exceptional circumstance, due to the devastation of other industrial countries in the Second World War. Though American economic growth continued thereafter, the American share in world income declined as other countries recovered. Thus, the United States share in world income declined to about 33 per cent in 1965 and to about 24 per cent in 1976. The Soviet national income stood at about 15 per cent of the world total in 1965 and 14 per cent in 1978.[1]

The world shows a fair degree of economic interdependence among its market economies. There is somewhat less economic interdependence among centrally planned economies of those countries under Communist rule and still less interdependence between the capitalist and Communist countries. Even there, however, there is some interdependence, but it is limited. To give an example: there is a worldwide wheat market with interdependent prices, but 90 per cent of the world's wheat is consumed within the countries in which it is produced.

The world is poor. The average gross world product *per capita* is only about $1,833 at 1975 prices. World population is relatively fast-growing, at 1.9 per cent per year, doubling about every 37 years. World income since 1950, on the average, has been growing twice as fast, doubling every 18 years or so.

The world as a whole is manifestly ungovernable. It is divided by large divergencies of interest between highly developed and developing countries, and it is further divided between the hitherto incompatible economic institutions of market-oriented private enterprise on the one hand, and Communist central state planning on the other. Even the world's dynamic tendencies diverge. Economic interdependence in the world of 1978 is less than it was in 1878 or in 1928, but its interdependence in communication, information, science and to some extent life-styles has increased. The world at present is thus *heterotropic*; it tends to move at one and the same time in different directions in different sectors of its life.

On the whole, the world today resembles one vast underdeveloped country. Life expectancy averages about 57 ±12 years and the infant death rate is 90 ±57 per 1,000. Uniformed military forces in the world average about 0.5 per cent of its population and military expenditures are close to 6 per cent of the world income. World literacy is now 65 per cent and rising. By 1990 it is likely to reach 80 per cent and it is likely to get above 90 per cent sometime during the first decade of the next century. Mass media, such as radio, television, print and motion pictures now reach about 75 per cent of the world's adults and seem likely to reach over 90 per cent by 1990.

Economic inequality in the world is worse than in most of the world's countries, even in the badly governed ones. The Gini Index of income inequality among peoples, counting each state as a unit, was a startling 81 per cent in 1975. If one weighs each state in proportion to its population, the Gini Index of inequality still remains strikingly high at 64 per cent. The top 5 per cent of the world's population by states get 48 per cent of the world's income; the bottom 20 per cent get 0.22 per cent; the ratio between the *per capita* incomes of these two sectors is about 60 to 1.

The potential instability of this world system is manifest. A degree of peace is maintained by a balance of terror between the two alliance systems headed by the United States and the Soviet Union, respectively. The Communist government of China experienced major military tensions with the United States in the early 1950s and 1960s. In the late 1960s and in the 1970s some of its major military tensions existed in its relations with the Soviet Union; who it will consider its major adversary in the 1980s and 1990s is not easy to predict.

Minor military conflicts have persisted throughout the decades since the end of the Second World War. According to a well known speech by the then United States Secretary of Defense, Robert MacNamara, at Montreal, two-thirds of such conflicts took place between non-Communist powers or factions; only in the remaining one-third of the conflicts were Communist factions or states involved.

Among Communist powers there have been no all-out wars thus far, with the possible exception of the bloody Soviet intervention against the dissident Communist government of Hungary in 1956. The Soviet-led intervention of five countries in Czechoslovakia in 1968 involved relatively little bloodshed. There have been tensions and confrontations, however, among Communist countries, such as between the Soviet Union and China on the Ussuri River in 1969 and repeated tensions between Yugoslavia and Albania.

A remarkable fact of world politics since 1945, however, has been the absence of any warfare or even preparations for such warfare among the major capitalist countries. The evidence since 1945 thus contradicts the expectations of Lenin that wars between capitalist powers would remain inevitable.

Even so, however, the continuing warfare among minor capitalist countries, the continuing tension between capitalist and Communist alliance systems, and the proliferation of nuclear weapons to seven countries by 1978 and to perhaps an expected fifteen countries in 1990, perhaps thirty by 2010, and perhaps one hundred by 2050, makes the world an extremely endangered place. In the long run, so much poverty, so much inequality and so many weapons of mass destruction in the world arena may well prove incompatible with survival of most of the world's population.

We have seen that certain dynamic processes in the countries that became industrialised have led to the adoption of national welfare states and a decrease of instability and violence within them. Could something similar occur on the level of the political system of the world?

The Chances for an International Welfare State

The present inequality in average *per capita* income between the highly developed one-fifth of the world — counting the OECD countries together with three highly developed Communist states, the Soviet Union, the German Democratic Republic and Czechoslovakia — and the less developed countries shows that the ratio of inequality is now about 16 to 1. This follows from the highly simplified calculation that the highly developed states with one-fifth of mankind have four-fifths of the world income, whereas the less developed states with four-fifths of mankind have only one-fifth of the world income.

World income has been growing on the whole at an average of 3 per cent per year, although this growth has been divided very unevenly among states and within them. If we disregard for the moment the inequalities within the nations, we can still note that if the world's highly developed countries would consent to reduce gross average *per capita* income growth from 3 per cent to 2 per cent, they could help the less developed countries to increase the average growth of their *per capita* income from 3 per cent to 4 per cent. If this were the case, the gap between the average incomes in the rich one-fifth and the poor four-fifths of the world could be cut in half to a ratio of 8 to 1 somewhere between the years 2010 and 2020, and it could be further cut to a further 4 to 1 by the middle of the next century, to about 2 to 1 in the 2080s and to about 1 to 1 somewhere in the first 2 decades after 2100.

To increase the growth rates of the poor countries by 1 per cent per year might require a transfer to them equal to about 4 per cent of their incomes per year if we assume an incremental capital output ratio (ICOR) of 4 to 1. If we recall that armament spending now is at an annual average 6 per cent of world income, we may speculate whether the world might not succeed, with the help of modern technology, in frightening itself almost as badly for 2 per cent of its annual income as we are now frightening each other for 6 per cent. If arms control could help us reduce the percentage of armament spending to this 2 per cent level, the problem of the international welfare state could in principle be solved. In the 1950s General and later President Dwight Eisenhower suggested this approach. So did General Douglas MacArthur.

Both these leaders are now dead. What will we do while we are still living? There are perhaps three answers to this question.

(1) From a *normative* point of view, it is desirable that present extreme inequalities in world income, health, life expectancy and quality of life should be reduced, down to a more nearly tolerable level. In particular, the basic needs of all people for a minimal degree of food, health care and education could now be satisfied from the existing economic and technological resources within the world within the next two decades. According to the researches of the Bariloche group of social scientists in Argentina and the preliminary researches carried on at the International Institute for Comparative Social Research in Berlin, this could be accomplished without any catastrophic overloading of world resources and the physical and biological world environment.

(2) A second answer might be *prudential*. As now constituted as a non-welfare system, the political system of the world is extremely unstable and in serious danger of self-destruction. Making the world system more nearly welfare-oriented for the masses of its population everywhere would increase the security also of the highly industrialised countries and the chances of survival for their own populations.

(3) The third type of answer would have to be *realistic*. It may turn out, however, that there are two types of realism in social and political analysis. What may be unrealistic in the short term may turn out to be quite realistic over a long-term period. The notion that Britain would give up her rule over India was politically unrealistic in 1935 and the India Bill passed in that

year was oriented towards a perpetuation of British rule with only secondary modifications. Twelve years later, in 1947, India became independent and India and Pakistan became separate states. Similarly, short-term realistic appraisals in 1950 treated mainland China and the Soviet Union as parts of a single Communist bloc. Ten years later that appraisal was no longer realistic.

A truly realistic appraisal must include, therefore, not only the state of affairs which exists at the moment, but also the size and speed of the actually ongoing processes of change that are at work within the nation states and among them.

There is a good deal of evidence that much of what was happening in the early nineteenth and twentieth centuries within the industrialising of West Europe and North America is now happening in large parts of our entire industrialising world. Let us recall quickly the world-wide trends mentioned earlier in this chapter: the penetration of money and industrialisation into most societies; the shift of man-power out of agriculture, and the growth of cities; the spread of military conscription and the wide diffusion of miltiary capabilities; the spread of mass education at the elementary and partly at the secondary levels, as well as the world-wide growth of universities; the growth of mass organisations of many kinds; and the vast spread and penetration of mass media. Together with these plainly observable changes in many of the world's developing countries, there are some more subtle changes of culture and value patterns in the highly developed countries. There has been increased sensitivity since the 1960s in the highly developed countries to the poverty and misery of other portions of mankind. There is perhaps a slowly growing sense of shame that the rich countries are doing so little for the poorer ones. Attitude surveys suggest that there is perhaps a declining margin of utility of income and power, particularly among young people of highly developed countries, but perhaps an increasing interest in spontaneity, affection, dignity and rectitude. Most of these changes were most easily observed among the young, but the young of the 1960s are in their thirties now, and within another ten or fifteen years they will be the heads of many departments and organisations in private and public sectors.

Every large stream includes whirlpools and eddies that run counter to its main current, and people can drown in them. There have been observable instances of resistance and backlash, bitter attempts to defend entrenched habits, image and privileges – and there will be more of them. Such backlash reactions contributed to the rise of Fascist movements and regimes between the two world wars. In our own time, backlash movements were observed in the brief spells of popularity of Governor George Wallace in the United States (who in 1978 announced his retirement from public life) and the small, temporary increases in the support for such partisan movements as the neo-Fascists in Italy, the National Democratic Party in West Germany, and the Poujade movement and the OAS in France.

More drastic examples of resistance against a transition to the welfare state have occurred in many developing countries. This has happened on a basis of race discrimination in Rhodesia and South Africa, and on a combined basis of military dictatorship and economic class privilege in the regimes of such countries as Chile, Argentina, Uruguay and, to some extent, Brazil. A number of such regimes, however, have fallen, such as those in Greece and Portugal, or have gradually retreated, as those in Spain and perhaps Peru; and in all these cases their successor regimes have continued the trend towards the development of a national welfare state.

Generally, it has been a characteristic of the national welfare state that it has replaced within each country the sharp dichotomy of two classes, or as Disraeli called them, 'Two Nations', the rich and the poor, by a broader range of social gradations, with ever more people at intermediate levels within the social structure and with fewer people at the bottom level of misery.

What has happened in this respect within today's industrialised nations may now be happening also on a world scale. The analysis of the *Dependencia* theorists has mainly stressed the contrast between highly developed and poor countries; and up to this point the present chapter has done so, too. But the real development in the world is showing us an increasing number of developing countries that are moving up to an intermediate level of industrialisation, often with reduced dependence on the old metropolitan countries, and there have been even some cases of countries moving up all the way into the ranks of the highly industrialised nations of our times. Japan and the Soviet Union have more or less completed this transition. Italy has almost done so. Spain, Portugal, Greece, Yugoslavia and several countries under various types of Communist regimes, as well as Mexico and Brazil, have moved up to an intermediate stage. There are still a considerable number of countries and peoples near the bottom level of poverty, ranging from Bolivia to Bangladesh, but some of

Table 20.1: Indicators of National and International Welfare,[a] Average Values by Groups of Countries

Indicators	National[b] Welfare States n = 37	Non-welfare[c] States Excluding OPEC Countries n = 9	World n = 140
1. Wealth GNP/*capita* in US$[d]	5,270	685	1,833
2. Infant mortality[d]	16 ±5	113 ±47	90 ±57
3. Life expectancy[d]	72 ±2	52 ±10	57 ±12
4. Literacy[d]	97 ±2	42 ±30	55±34
5. Range of inter-regional disparity	≤4:1	(12.5 ± 2.5):1	122:1[g]
6. Gini Index of sectoral income inequality[f]	15% ±6	33% ±10	26% ±12
7. Gini Index of income inequality (households)[e]	38% ±7	52% ±8	81 (64)
8. Percentage of income to top 5%[e]	19 ±6	31 ±8	48%
9. Percentage of income to top 20%[e]	45 ±6	57 ±9	87%
10. Percentage of income to bottom 20%[e]	6 ±2	41 ±1	0.22%
11. Ratio of top 5% to bottom 20%	4:1	8:1	218:1
12. Ratio of top 20% to bottom 20%	9:1	15:1	397:1

Notes: a. I would like to thank Robert Grady and David A. Jodice for their research assistance. The error ranges are one standard deviation unit around the estimated means.
b. The welfare states are: Australia, Austria, Belgium, Canada, Czechoslovakia, Denmark, Finland, France, East Germany, West Germany, Greece, Iceland, Ireland, Israel, Italy, Japan, Netherlands, New Zealand, Norway, Sweden, Switzerland, USSR, United Kingdom, United States.
c. The non-welfare states are: Afghanistan, Algeria, Barbados, Benin, Bolivia, Botswana, Brazil, Burma, Burundi, Cambodia, Cameroon, Central African Republic, Chad, Colombia, Costa Rica, Cyprus, Dominican Republic, Ecuador, Egypt, El Salvador, Ethiopia, Gabon, Gambia, Ghana, Guatemala, Guyana, Haiti, Honduras, India, Indonesia, Iran, Ivory Coast, Jamaica, Jordan, Kenya, Korea (S), Laos, Lebanon, Liberia, Libya, Madagascar, Malaysia, Maldive Islands, Mali, Mauritania, Mauritius, Mexico, Morocco, Nepal, Nicaragua, Niger, Nigeria, Pakistan, Panama, Paraguay, Peru, Philippines, Rhodesia, Rwanda, Senegal, Sierra Leone, Somalia, Sri Lanka, Sudan, Syria, Tanzania, Thailand, Togo, Trinidad and Tobago, Tunisia, Uganda, Upper Volta, Venezuela, Vietnam (S), Zaire, Zambia.
d. The aggregate indicators are from Ruth Leger Sivard, *World Military and Social Expenditures, 1978* (WMSE Publications, Leesburg, Va., 1978).
e. The household level income inequality data are from Shail Jain, *Size Distribution of Income: a Compilation of Data* (World Bank, Washington, DC, 1976).
f. Charles L. Taylor and Michael C. Hudson (eds.), *World Handbook of Political and Social Indicators* (Yale University Press, New Haven, 1972).
g. Switzerland $8,630, Cambodia $71.

the largest of the world's poor countries, such as China and India, are trying to move away from this level and to ensure some welfare services to their populations already at an early stage of economic growth.

On the whole, it seems that the trends moving towards a wider spread of national welfare states and eventually towards an international welfare system are larger and stronger than the forces moving in the opposite direction.

The decision over the outcome will not be a matter of fate, but, perhaps, more largely a matter of choice and will; that is to say, of sustained political effort. But if we should choose to make this effort, we shall have vast forces on our side.

Note

1. Charles Lewis Taylor and Michael C. Hudson (eds.), *World Handbook of Political and Social Indicators*, 2nd edn Yale, New Haven, 1972), p. 306 and Ruth Leger Sivard, *World Military and Social Expenditures, 1978* (WMSE Publications, Leesburg, Va., 1978), pp. 21-3. Total Soviet income in 1976 was about 68% — and *per capita* income at about 58% — of the corresponding US figures if all are calculated in dollar prices. Communication from Prof. Abraham Bergson, Harvard University, February 1979.

NOTES ON CONTRIBUTORS

Dr Derek Fraser Reader in History, University of Bradford.

Dr Jürgen Reulecke Reader in Modern History, University of Bochum; presently University of Bielefeld.

Dr Michael E. Rose Senior Lecturer in Economic History, University of Manchester.

Dr Jürgen Tampke Lecturer in Modern History, University of New South Wales, Australia.

Prof. E. Peter Hennock Professor of Modern History, University of Liverpool.

Dr Roy Hay Reader in Modern History, School of Social Studies, Deakin University, Australia.

Dr Hans-Peter Ullmann Lecturer in Modern History, University of Giessen.

Dr Anselm Faust Lecturer in Social and Economic History University of Bochum.

Prof. Robert Skidelsky Prof. of History, Department of International Studies, University Warwick.

Dr Bernd Weisbrod Lecturer in Modern History, University of Bochum; presently at the German Historical Institute, London.

Dr Michael Wolffsohn Lecturer in Politics and History, University of Saarbrücken.

Dr José Harris Reader in Modern History, St Catherine's College, Oxford.

Dr Roger Davidson Lecturer in Economic History, University of Edinburgh.

Dr Rodney Lowe Lecturer in Economic and Social History, University of Bristol.

Dr Jürgen C. Heß Reader in Modern History, Free University of Amsterdam.

Dr Hans Günther Hockerts Reader in Modern History, University of Bonn.

Prof. Peter Flora Professor of Sociology, University of Cologne; presently at the European University Institute, Department of Political and Social Sciences, Florence.

Prof. Gaston V. Rimlinger Professor of Economics, Rice University, Houston, Texas.

Prof. Frieder Naschold Director of the International Institute for Comparative Social Research, Berlin.

Dr Graham J. Room Lecturer in Sociology, University of Bath.

Prof. Karl W. Deutsch Director of the International Institute for Comparative Social Research, Berlin, and Stanfield Professor of International Peace, Department of Government, Harvard University.

INDEX